Assessment for Effective Teaching: Using Context-Adaptive Planning

GERALD S. HANNA

Kansas State University

PEGGY A. DETTMER

Kansas State University, Emeritus

Boston ■ New York ■ San Francisco
Mexico City ■ Montreal ■ Toronto ■ London ■ Madrid ■ Munich ■ Paris
Hong Kong ■ Singapore ■ Tokyo ■ Cape Town ■ Sydney

Senior Editor: *Arnis E. Burvikovs*
Editorial Assistant: *Christine Lyons*
Production Supervisor: *Michael Granger*
Editorial-Production Service: *Modern Graphics, Inc.*
Composition Buyer: *Linda Cox*
Manufacturing Buyer: *Andrew Turso*
Cover Administrator: *Kristina Mose-Libon*
Text Composition: *Modern Graphics, Inc.*

For related titles and support materials, visit our online catalog at www.ablongman.com.

Between the time Website information is gathered and then published, it is not unusual for some sites to have closed. Also, the transcription of URLs can result in typographical errors. The publisher would appreciate notification where these errors occur so that they may be corrected in subsequent editions.

Library of Congress Cataloging-in-Publication Data

Hanna, Gerald S.
   Assessment for effective teaching : using context-adaptive planning / Gerald S. Hanna, Peggy A. Dettmer.
      p. cm.
   Includes bibliographical references and index.
   ISBN 0-205-38941-4
      1. Student evaluation—United States. 2. Classroom assessment—United States. 3. Tests and measurements—United States. 1. Dettmer, Peggy. II. Title.

LB2822.75.H36 2003
371.26—dc21

2003054938

Printed in the United States of America

10   9   8   7   6   5   4   3   2   1   09   08   07   06   05   04   03

BRIEF CONTENTS

CONTENTS

CHAPTER THREE

Instructional Contexts of Classroom Assessment   44

CHAPTER FOUR

Instructional Objectives and Kinds of Tests, Scores, and Interpretations   72

CHAPTER FIFTEEN
Derived Scores and Their Interpretation   375

PREFACE

Good student assessment practices enhance effective teaching and poor assessment practices interfere with it. Therefore, this book on assessment is framed in the broader perspective of classroom instruction. To promote intentional, purposeful, and professional use of assessment to enhance student learning, the book's themes will be used to *connect* and *integrate* a variety of topics from both the book and from readers' previous learning.

Textbooks should provide bridges to classroom applications; the practical utility of topics should not be left to readers to deduce. Students taking their first assessment course typically have had a course in educational psychology. They know something about human learning and transfer of learning from the perspectives of both behavioral and cognitive psychology. Nonetheless, most students need crosswalks that point out the important connections between learning and assessment, and that reveal the implications of these connections. Therefore, in this book the treatment of assessment is integrated; relationships among topics are highlighted, not left for readers to divine.

Some of the topics presented in the book have received either scant or no emphasis in most assessment books. Furthermore, profoundly important practical connections among the elements too often are overlooked. We believe that in preparation for the challenging profession of education, much attention should be given to *when, where,* and *why* educators should do various things, as well as *how* to do them.

Our pursuit of structure and association among topics was undertaken from the perspective of a mainstream, middle-of-the-road orientation. Our thinking over the years has benefited greatly by Norman Gronlund's important distinction between two major kinds of instructional objectives and by the writing of Lee Cronbach, Anne Anastasi, Robert L. Thorndike, and Ralph Tyler. We would point out here that many authors of other texts often treat controversial topics (e.g., criterion referencing or mastery learning) in nonevaluative and superficial ways in an apparent effort to offend none and please all. They may give pros and cons of each, yet offer little help to readers in choosing among alternative strategies. However, we profess that *professional* preparation requires help in understanding *why* a given technique should be used in some, but not all, situations; distinguishing *where* it should be used; and in knowing *how* to use it.

Throughout the book, the reader's ability to understand the content and apply it in new situations will be expanded as the material is developed in the manner of a spiral curriculum (Bruner, 1977), revisiting basic ideas at more complex and expansive levels, linking the ideas to other topics, and building on the ideas to grasp fuller and richer meaning. In this process an understanding of abstract material and the ability to transfer that understanding for use in new and novel situations will be optimized as relationships among concepts are explored and integrated.

Part I includes Chapters 1 through 4. It introduces many of the issues that will be addressed more fully in subsequent chapters. In addition, it initiates the four major themes of the book. Chapters 3 and 4 comprise the most distinctive part of the book by introducing the eight elements of our context-adaptive planning approach:

- Differing manifestations of individual differences in learning
- Kinds of subject matter

- Families of learning theories
- Types of instruction for transfer
- Instructional objectives
- Kinds of tests
- Varieties of scores
- Types of score interpretations

Part II, including Chapters 5 through 9, focuses on test construction. After Chapter 5 sets the stage for planning classroom assessments, each of the other four chapters features a type of measurement—simple objective item types, multiple-choice items and interpretive exercises, essays and other product measures and portfolios, and performance assessments and their scoring rubrics.

Part III addresses preparation, interpretation, reporting, and use of assessment information. Chapter 10 includes information on editing, producing, administering, scoring, and analyzing teacher-made tests. Chapter 11 is devoted to data management, and Chapter 12 to marking, reporting, and conferencing. In Chapter 13, we focus on assessment issues relevant to special education that the Individuals with Disabilities Education Amendments (IDEA 1997) legislation has targeted for attention by all teachers and administrators.

Part IV systematically addresses key characteristics of effective measuring instruments. These include validity, interpretability, reliability, and economy. Main topics for the final two chapters are derived scores and published measures.

Each chapter contains a number of learning aids. The Chapter Overviews and Key Terms that open each chapter orient the reader to major concepts about to be presented. Subject matter in each chapter is amplified frequently with examples from a broad range of educational settings as diverse as classroom instruction, school counseling, educational administration, and special education. Occasional sections, presented as Encapsulations, contribute comprehensive summaries or illustrations to help clarify or extend chapter content. Chapter Recaps are provided to summarize the material in each chapter.

Thinking Cap Exercises encourage further thinking about issues. Some enable readers to assess their grasp of each chapter's material by working through these exercises as they appear and by using the Thinking Cap Keys and explanations of answers. Other Thinking Cap Exercises prompt readers to extend what they have read and to make applications; these are accompanied by Thinking Cap Reflections that help readers ensure that they have grasped the extensions of the subject matter provided in the exercises.

Suggestions for Further Reading are offered to benefit readers who may wish to learn more about the material. To conserve space and to enable the references to be kept current, these are housed on our website at www.ablongman.com/hannadettmer.

The book's content is integrated across its 16 chapters by spiraling back, outward, and upward with the concepts, each time showing broader application, encouraging more depth of understanding, and seeking higher levels of transfer of the learning. Material is organized *and applied* across chapters by means of the context-adaptive planning perspective and its cap-shaped graphics. Throughout the book, attention is given both to well established principles of teaching and assessing and to recent thinking as embodied by authoritative references. We hope the result is a structured and inspiring challenge to educators to provide more effective instruction and assessment.

The book also references learning aids that are external to the chapters. Our student website at www.ablongman.com/hannadettmer offers a variety of learning aids, enrichment materials, and opportunities for practice. Two of these learning aids are standard for all chapters and are, therefore, not cited. For each chapter, the student website contains a set of expansive developmental instructional objectives that help students identify important learning. Following the objectives for each chapter are several Focusing Questions that can be used either as prequestions to have in mind while reading the chapter or as postquestions to assess—individually or in study groups—grasp of the chapter. Readers are urged to use these aids for at least the first few chapters to determine their utility.

Several of the Extensions offer substantial textual material that develops topics in greater depth and breadth than space in the book permitted. Some of these may be of interest to individual readers. Others may be assigned by instructors either as required or optional reading.

Instructor resources including a test bank and transparency masters are available electronically and are fully downloadable. Please contact your Allyn & Bacon representative for access to these resources. To find the rep in your area, please visit www.ablongman.com/replocator.

We are indebted to many people for their timely encouragement, assistance, and critical comments. To our students who have taught us so much and continue to do so. To our families and friends who put up with and support our devotion to this endeavor of promoting better classroom instruction through better assessment. To our many reviewers throughout the phases of the book's development, including the most recent, Jeffrey Oescher, University of New Orleans; Roxanne Eubank, St. Mary's University; and Kit Juniewicz, University of New England; and to colleagues and mentors, who have offered helpful critique and suggestions.

ASSESSMENT IN PERSPECTIVE

CHAPTER

1

ASSESSMENT AND EVALUATION IN TEACHING AND LEARNING

CHAPTER OVERVIEW

THE ROLE OF ASSESSMENT IN EDUCATION

STANDARDS, HIGH-STAKES TESTS, AND "NO CHILD LEFT BEHIND"

DESCRIPTIVE TERMS FOR ASSESSMENT

THEMES FOR EFFECTIVE CLASSROOM ASSESSMENT

TEACHER-MADE ASSESSMENTS AND PUBLISHED TESTS

ASSESSMENT FOR TEACHER DECISION-MAKING AND STUDENT LEARNING

A DECISION-MAKING SIEVE FOR SELECTING TYPE OF ASSESSMENT

KEY TERMS

No Child Left Behind Act (NCLB) of 2001
assessment
evaluation
measurement
test
reliability

validity
summative assessment
formative assessment
observation
standardized

Assessment and evaluation permeate all facets of our lives, and the two processes are especially relevant with regard to instruction and learning. But are educators prepared for the immense responsibility of assessing school learning and evaluating student achievement? Consider the following scenario.

SCENARIO

Jennifer, a teacher-to-be, heads off to the final session of her Principles of Assessment class reflecting on the roller coaster of thoughts and feelings this experience has produced for her these past months. She had approached the first class session with some anxiety, only to find that she was not alone in her apprehensions. As she had eased herself into one of the back-row seats that day, she could hear snippets of whispered concerns among the others:

> "I don't see why I had to sign up for this class. I'm really dreading it."
>
> "Yeah, lots of states don't require a course like this for teacher certification."
>
> "I'm terrible with math, so this is going to be an uncomfortable experience for me."
>
> "In teacher education, I've never had a class like this one and I'm scared to death."
>
> "It's probably going to be full of technical mumbo jumbo I'll never use."
>
> "And I bet this course will blow my grade point average out of the water."
>
> "I'm in the educational administration program, and I don't see how I will use anything from it when I'm a school principal."

Jennifer recalls these shared concerns and others that surfaced early on. But it turned out that the course wasn't about math or statistics after all. The focus was on development of skills that help teachers assess, evaluate, and instruct students wisely within a school climate of accountability and high-stakes testing. It also prepared educational administrators, counselors, and special educators to apply instruction and assessment principles for student achievement and school improvement.

Most importantly, the relevance of assessment to good instruction has now become crystal clear to Jennifer. She is confident that she can integrate instruction and assessments purposefully, construct assessment instruments appropriately, interpret assessment information effectively, evaluate student achievement wisely, and provide feedback helpfully to students and to their families at conference time.

Earlier in the day, she interviewed for her very first teaching position, and the interview went well. Now she looks forward to discussing that experience with her classmates and instructor and sharing several questions she was asked during the interview. "I felt well prepared," she intends to tell them. She says, "Some of my friends wondered why I thought I needed an assessment course. Well, it's paying off for me and my professional aspirations. I believe I'm going to get the position! And best of all, I'm going to be ready for it."

ASSESSMENT IN EDUCATION

Teaching, learning, assessment, and evaluation impact all of us in many ways. In schools, assessments of student learning and classroom instruction serve multiple purposes, ranging from student placements to school funding, to preparation for high-stakes tests, to alignment of curricular objectives with testing programs, and much more. Educators are under increasing pressure to match school curriculum to state tests, with important consequences resting on the outcomes (Airasian, 1996). Performances on state tests usually are publicized, and schools and districts are under immense pressure to "look good." In some areas, test scores can even have significant influence on real estate values and other commercial enterprises!

In January of 2002, the Bush administration reauthorized the Elementary and Secondary Education Act of 1965 by enacting the No Child Left Behind Act. It is perceived as an update and extension of the elder President Bush's "All Children Can Learn" mantra and six national goals for education. The new 2001[1] act set forth several goals (Dodge, Putallaz, & Malone, 2002):

[1]The act was passed by Congress in 2001 and became law with the President's signature in 2002.

- Close the achievement gap for disadvantaged students;
- Improve teacher preparation and rewards;
- Institute closely monitored accountability systems for students, teachers, and schools;
- Each state is to establish academic standards and test students annually in grades 3 through 8.

This legislation, known as "**No Child Left Behind**" (NCLB), has sweeping implications for schools and their testing programs. Moreover, it assumes that a state can fulfill the testing requirements.

When the legislation was passed, fewer than half the states came close to meeting the NCLB mandate of testing grades 3–8 every year, and now NCLB creates new demands (Lewis, 2002a). Lewis goes on to sound an alarm that in the rush to meet NCLB deadlines, states are "grabbing standardized tests off the shelf—no matter whether they meet their learning standards or not" (Lewis, 2002a, p. 179). To add to the alarm, funding for the testing requirements is inadequate or nonexistent.

Unfortunately, political demands, legislative mandates such as NCLB, and parent concerns of multiple kinds will increase pressure on educators to teach the objectives that tests assess rather than *design assessments that test the objectives of the curriculum.* Classroom teachers, school administrators, counselors, special education teachers, and related services personnel must address these realities with clear vision and wise judgment. Educators will need to be planful, knowledgeable, caring, and ethical professionals who apply sound, practical educational theory in their complex roles. The ultimate aim must be to establish excellent schools where students are prepared for success.

STANDARDS FOR ASSESSMENT OF STUDENTS

As we acknowledge the political agenda swirling around the educational scene, we should pause to reflect on existing standards for teacher competence in educational assessment. The National Council on Measurement in Education, the American Federation of Teachers, and the National Education Association have proclaimed that "student assessment is an essential part of teaching, and good teaching cannot exist without good student assessment" (Sanders, et al., 1990, p. 30). These three professional organizations sponsored a Committee on Standards for Teacher Competence in Educational Assessment of Students, which issued seven standards. The standards are:

1. Teachers should be skilled in *choosing* assessment methods appropriate for instructional decisions.
2. Teachers should be skilled in *developing* assessment methods appropriate for instructional decisions.
3. The teacher should be skilled in *administering, scoring, and interpreting* the results of both externally produced and teacher-produced assessment methods.
4. Teachers should be skilled in *using assessment results* when making decisions about individual students, planning teaching, developing curriculum, and school improvement.
5. Teachers should be skilled in *developing valid pupil grading procedures* that use pupil assessments.

6. Teachers should be skilled in *communicating assessment* results to students, parents, other lay audiences, and other educators.
7. Teachers should be skilled in *recognizing unethical, illegal, and otherwise inappropriate assessment methods* and uses of assessment information (Sanders, et al., 1990).

Each of these statements concerns teacher competencies that are believed to be helpful for teachers in making educational decisions about students and providing feedback about student achievement. They elucidate and elaborate Standard 8 of the Interstate New Teacher Assessment and Support Consortium (INTASC) and Danielson's (1996) standards for teachers that target use and understanding of formal and informal assessment techniques.

This book is designed to contribute to each of the vital skills described in the seven standards. Similarly, it aims to provide a foundation for important skills needed by school counselors as set forth in 1988 by the American School Counselor Association and the Association for Assessment in Counseling. Our central purpose is to enable educators to *use planned, balanced, and integrated assessment to enhance their instructional effectiveness.*

TERMS USED IN ASSESSMENT

At this juncture we will focus on the meaning of several important terms that recur throughout the book. The following terms are introduced here and will be illustrated further and applied throughout the book: *assessment, evaluation, measurement, test, reliability, validity, formative assessment,* and *summative assessment.*

The first term—assessment—is used in a variety of ways by educators. Perhaps the most helpful one is that **assessment** includes all of the systematic ways teachers gather information in their classrooms (Airasian, 2001; American Educational Research Association, American Psychological Association, & National Council on Measurement in Education [hereafter cited as AERA], 1999). It includes the full range of methods that teachers use to collect data for help with decision making—from scores on paper-pencil tests to assessments of products and portfolios to systematic performance assessment to formal and informal observations and interviews.

It is important to draw sharp distinction between assessment and evaluation. Testing, measurement, and assessment all refer to gathering data. As such, they do not involve judgment about acceptability or value of the thing measured or observed. For example, the assessment of a child's temperature—whether assessed by thermometer or by a hand applied to the child's forehead—tells nothing about the acceptability of the findings or about the actions that should be taken upon evaluation of the result. Neither thermometers nor hands would direct the evaluator to consider the temperature acceptable or unacceptable.

Evaluation is the application of judgment or values, or both, concerning the results of measurement or unquantified observation (Nitko, 2001). Notice the root word "value" in "evaluation." When value judgments are applied to assessment results, evaluation occurs.

In the temperature example, decision making about what to do concerning the child's temperature follows the evaluation of its acceptability. If the temperature is deemed acceptable, the decision may be to do nothing. If it is judged to be unsafe, the decision may be to give medication or consult a physician. The decision of what to do is based on the evaluation. Evaluation, therefore, is the middle step in the three-step process of assessment, evaluation, and decision making.

Making distinctions among assessment, evaluation, and decision making can be useful because the process helps us *remember where data leave off and where judgment begins.* For an example lifted from a school setting, a wood shop teacher decides that Jerri and Ian should move on to a more advanced project than the rest of the class. This decision may or may not prove to be wise. If it turns out to be unproductive, the problem could lie in the decision concerning the next project to be undertaken or it could lie in assessment error in rating their completed products of earlier projects. *Sound instructional decisions first require valid measurement or observation, or both, and then good professional judgment.*

Measurement is typically defined as the systematic assignment of numbers (or names) to attributes. This assignment may be made with a sophisticated apparatus, such as measuring the child's temperature with an electronic thermometer or measuring the woodworking product with a square and level. Or, it may be conducted with less adequate yet systematic procedures, as in a parent's hand being applied to the child's forehead to estimate the temperature or in "eyeballing" joints and finish of the wood project. Measurement can be conducted at various levels of precision; for example, the child's temperature can be reported in tenths of degrees (e.g., 103.6°F) or in crude ranges, such as normal, high, or very high. The wood project can be evaluated with a detailed and quantifiable rating scale (a rubric, which will be discussed in Part II) or by an overall assessment of good, satisfactory, or needing more work.

Some informal classroom observations lack an assignment of numbers or names. A teacher's observation that Cooper missed several similar spelling words isn't a measurement. To become one it would need to be quantified—say, that he missed seven such words out of eight. Such use of numbers would be an easy next step for the examples offered in the later section on informal observations. Even without the use of numbers, of course, such examples illustrate the broader concept of assessment.

Although the findings of many such observations can rather easily be quantified, some people balk at trying to quantify certain observational data, such as "beauty" or evidence of "love." Such qualitative observations don't fit as comfortably into a definition of measurement, yet they surely fit into our definition of assessment. It is helpful to keep in mind that the more inclusive term assessment encompasses all kinds of data gathering, including those from tests or other measurement scales and those from all kinds of observations. Hence, where either term could be used, selection is often a stylistic decision (Oosterhof, 2001).

A **test** is a formal, systematic procedure used to gather information under uniform conditions. In this book, we use the word test to refer to measures in which examinees know they are being assessed and are supposed to do their best; examples are spelling tests, sprints, glee club tryouts, and algebra examinations. Measures that are *not* tests by this definition would include rating forms of classroom behavior when pupils don't know that they are being rated, self-report interest inventories, or anonymous self-report surveys of student learning. Hence, tests are a subset of measurement devices, and measures are, in turn, a subset of assessment instruments. Figure 1.1 illustrates these relationships.

Notice that the definition of a test as a formal systematic procedure used to collect information about examinees' best performance is broad; tests are *not* limited to paper-pencil assessments. Tests also include production of various kinds of products (e.g., the wood project mentioned earlier, essays, watercolor landscapes, computer programs, model airplanes) and performance of various skills (e.g., tryout for soccer team, playing musical instruments, or simulated provision of first aid). Therefore, tests include all varieties of paper-pencil assessments, the production of all kinds of

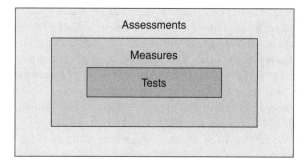

FIGURE 1.1   Relationship Among Assessments (formal and informal processes), Measures (objective, product, and performance), and Tests (teacher made and commercially published)

products, and the exhibition of all sorts of skills, *provided* that the work is done under controlled uniform conditions.

Measurements, tests, and other assessments are subject to concerns about reliability and validity.[2] **Reliability** concerns the *consistency* with which a device or procedure measures *whatever it measures*. An instrument is reliable to the extent that its scores can be replicated (Brennan, 2001). Reliability is *not* the same as truthfulness. When you encounter the word *reliability* in any discussion of assessment, "you should draw a mental equal sign between *reliability* and *consistency.*" (Popham, 2002, p. 27).

Reconsider the thermometer. Suppose it is quite reliable as a measure of temperature. How reliable is it as a measure of vocabulary? It is just as reliable for one purpose as it is for another. That is, reliability concerns *only* consistency. Of course, the scale is not at all valid as a measure of vocabulary, but its scores will be just as consistent if they are (falsely) called vocabulary scores as they will be if they are (appropriately) labeled temperature.

Validity concerns the extent to which a device or procedure assesses what it is *being used* to assess. Moreover, validity concerns the appropriateness of inferences and actions that are based on assessment results (AERA, 1999; Messick, 1989). Thus, the validity of an assessment's use is a function of the extent to which it:

- Assesses what it is supposed to assess,
- Measures all that it is supposed to measure,
- Assesses these subelements in the desired proportions,
- Taps nothing besides what it is supposed to concern,
- Has desirable consequences, and
- Is free from adverse consequences.

The construction and use of valid assessments is the central focus of this book. For example, Part II addresses the creation of classroom assessments that tap the intended subject matter, tap it

---

[2]Reliability and validity are discussed briefly in this chapter; however, their full consideration will occur in Chapter 14. For now, we might merely say that reliability means consistency. Truthfulness and usefulness probably come closest to being adequate synonyms of validity.

in the desired proportions, and are not influenced by anything else. Many chapters, including this one, address consequences of the use of various assessments.

To emphasize that validity concerns particular uses for assessments, suppose a particular clinical thermometer is a good measure of temperature. If it is used to measure body temperature, it can be said to be quite valid. That is, its scores tell the truth about people's temperature, and this truth leads to desirable consequences. On the other hand, if the device were used to measure height, its use would not be at all valid. Thus, if used to measure stature, its "scores" would be ineffective in categorizing people on that attribute.

Along the same lines, a teacher-made unit test that consists exclusively of knowledge of facts included in the unit might be a valid or truthful measure of factual knowledge. However, it would not be as valid a measure of the students' understanding of principles or of their ability to apply the facts and principles to new situations. This is an important concept to bear in mind as we develop the context-adaptive approach to integration of instruction and assessment.

Assessment that takes place after the learning is **summative assessment,** that is, for the purpose of *summing* it up. **Formative assessment** (i.e., formative assistance) assists with learning *while it is still in progress,* that is, while it is being *formed.*

Scores obtained from formative tests are *not* ordinarily used for grading. *Formative information aids ongoing instruction.* It is diagnostic in nature, designed to identify specified areas that need further study. Because pinpointing weaknesses is especially important with basic, essential subject matter, formative tests often assess mastery. Results can be used by the teacher or student, or both, to prescribe remediation of deficiencies.

An example of a summative test is when a child who has just made a paper airplane gives it a try to see how good an airplane it is. An example of a formative test is when a child who has just made a paper airplane gives it a try to see what adjustments are needed. In this case, the two tests may be identical; however, it was the intended use that made one summative and the other formative.

Sometimes when one gives a test, it isn't clear ahead of time which way it will be used. If the plane flies well, then it is finished and the test was summative. If it doesn't fly well, then the information about its flight is used to alter its design, and the test was formative. Other times, one may intend a test to be summative, but after seeing disappointing results, realizes that its greater value would lie in directing another round of improvement. At still other times, one may intend a test to be formative, but, after seeing a perfect performance, decides that further instruction isn't needed.

As we examine ways in which assessment is useful in enhancing learning, let's not fret about whether each example is summative or formative. Rather, we should use these complementary concepts to expand our understanding of the many helpful functions that assessment can provide in the service of teaching and learning.

THEMES FOR EFFECTIVE CLASSROOM ASSESSMENT

Now that we have provided a working vocabulary of terms for educational assessment, we introduce four themes that emphasize and underscore ways in which assessment and evaluation affect teaching and learning. These themes are central to, and form the basis of, the context-adaptive planning approach that we will introduce for classroom instruction and assessment. They are:

1. Teachers' instructional activities should be guided and informed by their student-assessment practices and findings.

2. Assessment practices have a powerful influence on student learning; therefore, teachers should harness that power.

3. Assessment and instructional practices should be adaptive to the *context* in which they are used.

4. A single type of assessment does not fit all instructional aims.

TEACHER-MADE TESTS

Classroom assessments are generally created and graded by teachers, are based on particular instructional aims, and are used to help teachers make short-term decisions (Spinelli, 2002). These teacher-made tests are designed with one's own students in mind and are relatively focused on the local curriculum (Johnson & Johnson, 2002). Properly used, teacher-made tests are potent educational tools that enhance instruction (Nitko, 1989).

Assessment activities consume huge amounts of teacher preparation time and class time (Stiggins & Conklin, 1992). Like published instruments, "homemade" or "custom built" tests vary greatly in quality. Some teachers develop quizzes and examinations that are indispensable features of sound instruction, whereas others create tests of such deplorable quality that their overall instructional effectiveness is seriously damaged. Many teachers realize that their assessment and evaluation procedures are important to their teaching. Yet too many lack the requisite skills for developing and using them (Gullickson, 1984; Stiggins, 1993; Stiggins, 1999; Stiggins & Bridgeford, 1985).

Teacher-made achievement tests are most widely used to assess unit achievement. Some units are small, highly sequential instructional segments that are taught for mastery. In such cases, teacher-made mastery tests are needed. As we shall see in Part II of the book, tests of this kind are relatively easy to plan and construct owing to the high degree to which their intended content coverage is explicit.

More often, however, teaching involves larger areas of content that should be taught with mindful transfer of learning as a primary goal. In these cases, teacher-made tests need to provide the desired balance of emphasis among various learning objectives. Tests that assess a variety of mental processes are more demanding to develop; therefore, their planning will be emphasized in Chapter 5. Similarly, product and performance tests that tap complex learning are relatively demanding to create and to score; the identification of the criteria by which students will be assessed is an important matter that will receive considerable attention in Chapters 8 and 9.

In assessing this latter kind of content, many teachers from primary level through graduate school use tests of very modest quality due to both an extreme emphasis on lower-level learning (Fleming & Chambers, 1983) and failure to measure achievement of their own instructional objectives (Haertel, 1986; Nitko, 1989). Alas, they often fail to focus student effort on attainment of the more important instructional objectives.

A major reason for this flawed teaching practice is that the kinds of test questions that are easiest to write—be they objective or essay—measure rote knowledge, not deep processing. It is natural to take the easy road and to "crank out" items that "flow" easily. However, if busy teachers do not engage in thoughtful preliminary planning concerning balance between recall-type questions and items that tap complex thinking, a test is likely to give more emphasis than wanted on memory and less on such things as understanding, thinking, and applying learning to other situations.

A related reason that many teacher-assembled tests are poor can be found in the quality of test items provided by publishing companies to accompany textbooks. Often contained in "teachers' manuals" or web sites, these collections of questions keyed to the texts are convenient to use. Unfortunately, publishers often give scant attention to the quality of such free accessory products. Yet some teachers, not realizing this, view the test items as meriting the same confidence that they accord the text.

Does this caution mean that one shouldn't use these test items? Not at all. The caution means that one shouldn't use the items indiscriminately. Teachers with test plans can pick and choose items to develop the parts of the tests that the questions satisfy and then develop their own items for the remainder of the test. Some inadequate items suggest ideas that can lead to relatively easy creation of good questions. Other items can be revised.

The natural "drift" is for casually produced tests to overemphasize rote learning and under-emphasize deep, meaningful learning and transfer of learning. Teachers who know this can avoid the hazard by thoughtful test planning. Knowledge is power!

Yet planning isn't enough. Student evaluation practices should be planned *at the appropriate point in time,* that is, when other aspects of instruction are being designed. Thus another factor that limits the effectiveness of much classroom testing is the lateness of its planning. Too often, consci-entious teachers who plan their tests and scoring criteria for product and performance assessments do so after much of the instruction has taken place. By then it is too late to effectively integrate eval-uation into the total instructional package. As an example, when student products or performances are to be assessed, it is important to teach students the assessment criteria so that it can help them improve what is to be assessed (Arter & McTighe, 2001).

OBSERVATIONS AND INTERVIEWS

As vital as relatively formal and standardized teacher-made tests are for good teaching, it is impor-tant to recognize that appropriate **observation** and interviewing also contribute to effective instruc-tional decision making. This is especially visible at the primary school level where prolonged teacher contact with each pupil is at a maximum. Indeed, teachers' own observations tend to be their most important sources of information for assessing their students' needs (Stiggins & Bridgeford, 1985). Some of these activities will be informal and unplanned, yet helpful in guiding decisions about curriculum, teaching methods, and testing. Others, particularly those for diagnosing special education needs of students, will be more formal and systematic.

Informal Observations and One-on-One Communication.   An example of informal observa-tion at the primary level would be the teacher observing that Bobbie frequently reverses the nu-merals "3" and "5." This observation might lead to corrective efforts. Another example would be the observation that Taylor completes the mathematics assignments with unusual speed and accu-racy, which would suggest the possibility of being accelerated in math. A third example would be the teacher's observation that Malo is usually the last child in the class to be chosen for any activ-ity in which peer choice plays a part. With information gleaned from interviews with Malo's peers, the teacher could structure situations in which this overlooked student might be perceived by class-mates as a valuable partner or team member.

An example of informal classroom observation at the upper elementary or middle school level would be a music teacher's observation that Kim has difficulty with motor coordination when playing the more technically demanding percussion instruments. For ensemble work, the teacher could assign Kim to an instrument that can be manipulated more successfully. Then there is the teacher who notes in an informal interview with José that his Spanish-language background seems to be interfering with effective oral communication in standard American English. If the teacher did not know how to help José compartmentalize the two languages appropriately, a referral could be made to a more specialized professional.

At the secondary level, an English teacher might notice Lynn's tendency to use double negatives indiscriminately in oral language but avoid them successfully in written products. The teacher could increase efforts to build on Lynn's standard usage in writing and extend it into speech behavior on relatively formal occasions. The wood shop teacher mentioned earlier might rate tie racks made by Jerri and Ian as unusually well built, suggesting that they be assigned to a more demanding and interesting task for their next project. A teacher of German might do much oral questioning that will enable her to ask each student questions that are challenging yet still likely to be answered correctly.

Informal testing and observation at the high school and college level are somewhat less common than at other levels, yet they are both prevalent and important. The trigonometry instructor notices that Toby missed several similar factoring problems in the same manner. Correction could take the form of a note in the margin of a homework paper, a reference to a section of the text, or a few words with him after the next class period. A drama coach sees Casey's self-conscious manner of movement across the stage and undertakes to help the aspiring actor achieve a more natural gait. A staff member for college student personnel notes that a freshman student has been absent from required classes on several consecutive Fridays and schedules a time to confer with the student about the portent of the missed classes. A counselor observes that Carmen will consider only those occupations that are stereotypically identified as "feminine" jobs. Awareness of this tendency could lead the counselor to help broaden Carmen's occupational horizons and enlarge the number and variety of options available to her.

Formal Observations and Interviews.   Formal observation is particularly relevant to special education teachers who are responsible for collecting data needed to make appropriate decisions regarding student placement in special education programs. Federal requirements handed down by IDEA 1997 (which we will examine in Chapter 13) are clear that teacher observations and evaluations "off the top of the head" will not suffice for determining student exceptionality and eligibility for special education services. Teachers need to gather objective information in order to document learning and behavior changes. Systematic behavior observations and interview conferences used by special education personnel employ techniques such as:

- Frequency recording (i.e., recording the number of times an event, e.g., a disruptive behavior, occurs);
- Interval recording (i.e., using observation periods marked into very short intervals);
- Time sampling (i.e., observing and recording at the end of a designated interval);
- Duration (i.e., measure of how long a behavior, e.g., staying on task, occurs);
- Checklists (i.e., evidence of attitudinal changes, adherence to procedures and rules).

Formal observation of performance when students know that they are being observed and are motivated to do their best has long been conducted by teachers of speech, physical education, science, music, and so forth. Substantial attention will be given in Chapter 9 to enhancing the value of such important observations.

PUBLISHED TESTS

Although the major portion of this book will focus on teacher-developed assessment, we will address some aspects of published instruments briefly in this section and examine them further in Chapter 16. Published, commercially marketed instruments typically provide for formal, separate, and standardized assessment. That is, the measurement is deliberate, planned, and separate from other instructional activities. It is performed under controlled or uniform conditions. A **standardized** instrument is a measurement device that is administered and scored under specified, controlled conditions.

ENCAPSULATION

From time to time in this book we include sections titled Encapsulations. Some provide a summary of preceding material from a slightly different perspective. Others present an important side issue. Still others are used as a means of amplifying an important point. Here is the first such encapsulation.

STATE ASSESSMENTS

A state assessment is a special case of published assessments that differ from commercially marketed instruments in several ways. State assessments:

- Are aligned with the state's curricular requirements,
- Typically are required of schools within the states,
- Typically have high stakes,
- Typically aren't marketed outside the state, and
- Sometimes are less expertly developed than are many commercially developed instruments.

State assessments, like other published, standardized measures, provide formal assessment that is separate from other instructional activities and is performed under controlled or uniform conditions. Even before enactment of No Child Left Behind Act (NCLB) in 2001, many states required schools to use state-developed, standardized assessments. All states now are required to have mandated, high-stakes tests in reading and mathematics by 2005–2006 and in science by 2007–2008.

Although some locally developed measures are administered and scored under specified conditions, much standardized assessment is conducted by use of commercially produced and nationally distributed instruments. For example, pupils often are given *screening tests* in order to detect major deficiencies or disabilities. Prekindergarten screening commonly includes tests of oral vocabulary, vision, hearing, and motor functions. Such standardized measures are used to identify pupils who are at risk of experiencing early difficulty in school. The purpose of identifying such children is to enable constructive action on their behalf. Without careful and responsible identification of their cognitive, affective, social, and physical needs, individuals would not receive the school services and materials necessary to develop their potential.

■ ■ ■ ■ ■

ENCAPSULATION

TO LABEL OR NOT TO LABEL STUDENTS

A key issue that arises with assessment concerning teacher decision making and student learning is labeling. Many educators and lay people voice objections to labeling students. Indeed, classifying a person can lead to a stigma; this is a danger of diagnoses and classifications. However, sensitive professional behavior can minimize such stigmas. For example, labeling students with such terms as mental retardation, hearing impairment, obesity, economical disadvantage, giftedness, or high creativity must be accompanied by constructive actions. If not, the assessment is indefensible because it invades students' privacy and subjects them to possible stigmas for no constructive purpose. Labeling without concomitant action for student welfare is unnecessary stigmatizing and a major source of reasoned "antilabeling" sentiment.

Unfortunately, some critics get so caught up in the inappropriate use of tests that they overreact and denounce all labeling. Because labels have at times been used foolishly, immoderate critics have been known to generalize their criticism to all diagnostic categories and to all standardized testing. This reaction, of course, is as ill-advised as the thing being criticized. To prevent the use of classifications (e.g., individuals who are learning disabled, diabetic, or visually impaired) that have been obtained with the best diagnostic means available (i.e., standardized tests) would deny some individuals the benefit of the constructive interventions that are available.

Returning to published tests, standardized, group-administered *tests of general academic aptitude* (sometimes referred to as intelligence tests) provide another example of formal school testing with commercially developed instruments. Such tests are routinely administered in many schools to provide information about each student's level of present measurable aptitude for regular schoolwork. This information is useful to teachers in arranging for students to be assigned tasks that are both challenging and manageable.

Specialists such as school psychologists administer standardized *individual tests of school aptitude* to students who require more intensive assessment. These tests are used widely to identify children having special needs. By knowing more about a student's present level of intellectual functioning, professionals can more wisely suggest instructional programs and interventions to suit the student's needs.

Adaptive behavior scales are used in conjunction with intellectual aptitude tests to assess the likelihood of mental retardation. Adaptive behavior ratings tap such important survival skills as dressing, grooming, shopping, and keeping quiet at appropriate times (e.g., during a flag salute). Knowledge of a person's mastery of such everyday behaviors helps educators plan appropriate instruction and structure the classroom environment to facilitate learning.

Interest inventories are another example of school use of published standardized measures. Interest scales at the secondary school level help counselors and teachers facilitate better student understanding of their budding occupational and academic interests. Based on the results, students can better choose their elective courses, plan their education, and select their future occupations.

Standardized *achievement tests* are widely used to measure the school achievement of students at all educational levels. Results help teachers judge the degree to which each examinee has achieved a command of the subject areas tested. This information can be used to plan instruction of groups or individuals and to prepare materials for individual learning needs. By and large, published achievement tests tend to encompass large bodies of content, not short units. Published achievement tests have several advantages. For example, commercially prepared instruments can be developed and reviewed by specialists; thus they can provide high technical quality and reliability. In addition, reference group data external to the individual classroom are typically available for published achievement tests.

One of the goals of this book is to help readers understand the issues involved in selecting, evaluating, administrating, and, in particular, interpreting published, standardized tests. The final part of the book will be especially relevant to this aim. However, extensive descriptions of standardized instruments and discussions of their uses for particular educational situations and student needs cannot be addressed within the intent, purposes, and length of this book.

ASSESSMENT AND EVALUATION FOR TEACHING AND LEARNING

Research has demonstrated that classroom evaluation practices have great impact upon student learning (Crooks, 1988; Marso & Pigge, 1993). Teachers should, therefore, pursue *better instruction through better assessment.* Teachers need the knowledge and dispositions that enable them to:

- Accurately assess and analyze their students' learning,
- Make appropriate adjustments to their instruction,
- Monitor their students' learning, and
- Have a positive impact on the learning of all students (National Council for Accreditation of Teachers, 2001).

This is a tall order; it is small wonder that research indicates that assessment is among the most complex aspects of teaching (Stiggins, Conklin, & Bridgeford, 1986). Classroom assessment practices that contribute to effective instruction include:

- Stressing instructional aims and targets, such as understanding, appreciation, and transfer of learning;
- Prompting study;
- Pacing students;
- Enhancing retention of material;
- Prompting review; and
- Providing useful feedback to teachers and students.

Note that we are not merely talking about the assessment *of* learning. We also are focusing on assessment *to enhance* learning, or as Stiggins (2002) has said, assessment *for* learning.

Assessment and Student Learning.   An assessment is somewhat like a ring in the nose of a bull. The beast may be relatively unresponsive to many attempts to move it. However, with a ring in its sensitive nose, it most surely is attentive to the slightest tug of persuasion on that ring. In similar fashion, many students at all levels of school are relatively unresponsive to many kinds of teacher efforts to guide their learning, but they are highly responsive to student evaluation practices. As

Erickson (1983) concluded, "*An examination is a revealing statement by a teacher about what is important*" (p. 135).

This influence of tests doesn't always work for good (Marso & Pigge, 1993). "The disturbing idea that testing can warp teaching and learning, and can in general be antagonistic to education, is not at all new" (Martinez, 1999, p. 207). At this point, one of us draws an example from his first semester as a community college student many years ago.

A required literature course was taught by a talented teacher who did much to spark students' interest in the subject. Her goals clearly focused on understanding and appreciation. During the first third of the semester, she sparked our interest in the literature. To prepare for the stimulating class discussions that involved higher-level cognitive and affective objectives, we studied the literature and we thought about it. It was a good course.

Then came the first test. It consisted largely of matching exercises—matching authors with their works, matching works with their publication dates, matching authors with their nationalities. Rather than assessing the understanding and appreciation to which the teacher's efforts had been targeted, the test measured only rote recall of facts.

What impact do you suppose this test had on our future study? It seriously undermined the instructor's otherwise excellent teaching. After we "psyched her out," we began to study for such simple memory outcomes as who wrote what when. The more complex mental processes such as understanding and appreciating the literature "were not important" because they weren't tested. If a student wanted a good grade, the thing to do was to memorize and not "waste" time on deep learning or enjoying the literary selections.

Readers could supply examples from their own experience in which poor assessment seriously weakened what was otherwise good teaching. They could also cite cases in which inappropriate student evaluation practices made poor teaching ever poorer. It is not unusual for assessment practices to divert student effort from the pursuit of instructional objectives.

As illustrated by the example, classroom assessment contributes to learning by communicating through the kind of material assessed what the students' learning targets ought to be. For example, if a teacher habitually tests nothing more than rote recall, students tend to focus their efforts on rote recall. If assessment requires them to relate their new learning to what they already knew, it fosters meaning and understanding. If teachers assess students' ability to connect various aspects of the material they are learning, then assessment causes them to mindfully seek out and attend to these meaningful connections. If assessments ordinarily emphasize use of the studied material in situations different from those in which they were taught, then students tend to set their sights on transfer of the learning to other situations.

Like many other educators, we believe that effective assessment can work in tandem with instruction to yield effective learning of a rich variety of learning outcomes. Although that potential is largely unrealized in educational settings (Martinez, 1999), a major aim of this book is to help teachers use student expectations concerning assessments to guide learning in desired ways.

Classroom assessment practices motivate students to study. If it were not for tests, many students would study much less than they do. That one may deplore this fact does not make it less true. It remains a fact of life that *most students are influenced by what they think will be assessed. Because evaluation is such a powerful force in driving student effort, it should be harnessed.*

Similarly, assessment influences *when and how* students study. If tests are administered only infrequently, many learners do not pace their study effectively; some neglect to study until the test approaches, and then they "cram." They rely on massed practice rather than the distributed practice that improves recall of information. Even at the university level, most students study most diligently when a test is imminent, which may be reflected in the growing body of research findings at the high school and college levels indicating that more frequent classroom testing is associated with enhanced student learning (Bangert-Drowns, Kulik & Kulik, 1986; Tuckman, 1998). The motivational and pacing powers of tests are resources to be recognized, respected, and harnessed.

Other important impacts of classroom testing are less obvious. One of these is known as the testing phenomenon (Glover, 1989). The mere act of taking a test—even if students have had no opportunity to study or review for it or to receive feedback from it—tends, under certain circumstances, to enhance their ability to remember the material. What are these circumstances? Basically, the testing phenomenon occurs when the testing of studied material occurs after enough time has elapsed for some forgetting to occur, yet before the material is lost. It appears that the effort of actively retrieving the "fading" material from memory enhances long-term retention.

Yet another favorable impact of assessment on student learning can come from review or cumulative appraisals. Review of previously learned material enhances permanent retention. At the secondary and college levels, there is nothing like a cumulative final examination to prompt such review.

Testing is one of a teacher's most powerful means of influencing what content students study, how much they study, how they pace their study, and what kind of learning outcomes they pursue. Therefore, *assessment is a teaching tool* having enormous power (Crooks, 1988). "If teachers test recall, students learn the facts; if teachers test more, students prepare themselves to deliver more" (Stiggins, Rubel, & Quellmalz, 1986, p. 5). This is part of the reason why assessment is an integral part of teaching. Teachers need to be keenly aware of the guiding influences that assessment practices have on student actions. A teacher's paper-pencil tests and observation scoring guides don't merely assess student learning *after* it has taken place; they also help to *shape the occurrence of the learning.* Because assessment is a tool having wide-reaching power, it behooves teachers to learn to use it expertly.

Assessment and Teacher Decision Making.   A basic tenet in education and psychology is that an assessment should be administered *only* when its results will tend to help someone make better decisions about something. To be sure, measures can serve other worthy purposes; for example, stimulating students to study. Yet it is almost always true that the proper use of measures is aimed, often among other important things, at improving decision making. Each example of school measurement or observation provided in this chapter is accompanied explicitly or implicitly with means by which the decision-making *payload* could be improved. This stress on decision making is important.

Unfortunately, one occasionally hears a teacher protest that published achievement tests are administered in her or his school, yet the results are kept locked in the principal's or counselor's filing cabinet and not used by anyone. The disgruntled teacher may go on to conclude that altogether too much testing with published instruments is being done. It is indeed a waste of time and money to test and not use the results; if results are not going to be used to improve decision making, then the test should ordinarily not be administered. To ignore test results is as foolish as to order a title search on a house one is about to purchase and then to throw away the results without considering them.

Results of tests, and of informal observations and interviews, help teachers decide what instruction to pursue for individuals and for the whole class. Such information is useful in selecting curricular content, in pacing the individual student or the class, in judging when and how much to repeat and review, and in pinpointing specific sources of student difficulties.

As teachers, we should strive always to plan and use our assessment activities in such ways as to inform the decisions that we and others make (Sanders & Vogel, 1993). We also must be able to judge the adequacy of the data used in decision making (Stiggins, 1991). The utility of a test or an observation to enhance decision making is directly related to the device's validity. For this reason, much attention will be devoted in this book to building valid teacher-made assessment instruments.

In addition to using assessment data to enhance their decision making, expert teachers also use their knowledge about assessment power—the ring in the nose of the bull—to make decisions that enhance student learning. *Good teachers exploit assessment power* by using it to cause students to attempt what the teachers want them to do. A major way they do this is by assessing the blend of subject matter and mental processes they wish students to pursue. Astute teachers ask themselves two key questions about each measure of student achievement:

1. "What does this assessment tell students about the achievement outcomes we value?"
2. "What is likely to be the effect of this assessment on students?" (Stiggins, 1991, p. 535).

Information learned within a broader framework of meaningful connections is better retained and is more apt to transfer. Also, the factual knowledge that students acquire in school may be less important than the skills that can help them continue to grow and adapt. Thus, we *need to make deep learning a central aim of education and to foster its development through student evaluation.* This aspiration leads us to emphasize understanding, transfer of learning, and other thinking skills. Moreover, it requires us to evaluate the development of these skills through tasks that demand more than recognition or recall of facts (Crooks, 1988).

This effect on learning is a major reason why we place so much emphasis on planning classroom assessments. Test content is important, of course, in order for tests to validly measure student achievement. Moreover, teachers who make constructive use of assessment ensure that their assessment activities "send the desired messages" to students concerning what is important (Nitko, 2001).

Deciding Which Type of Assessment to Use.   Teacher-developed assessments (i.e., tests, observations, or interviews) can be categorized as one of three types: objective, product, or performance. Each general type has advantages and drawbacks in terms of reliability, realism (or authenticity), and economy.

Recall now the fourth of this book's major themes—a single type of assessment does not fit all instructional aims. Just as one would not foolishly try to "peel a grape with an axe" or "cut the grass with scissors," neither should one plan an assessment that is inappropriate and inefficient to the task at hand. No single approach is suitable for assessing all kinds of learning outcomes (Danielson, 1996). For some assessment purposes, an objective test *should* be the assessment of choice. How tedious it would be for the would-be licensed driver to demonstrate recognition of all designated traffic signs during the driving portion of the exam! For such situations, an objective test (e.g., multiple choice or true-false) is appropriate. In order to determine success in omelet making, product assessment is needed. For other assessments, such as testing for appropriate pronunciation of French or Swahili, a performance test is clearly indicated. A teacher's ability to make sound decisions in selecting test types that serve assessment purposes best will be a major focus of Part II.

How should one decide among objective measures, essays and other product measures, or performance measures? Although the following rule takes into account many of the major issues that should enter into decisions concerning what kind of assessment to plan, *it is not the only consideration and should not be used in isolation.* For now, the decision rule will be previewed without benefit of its rationale. It consists of three statements:

1. Instructional objectives that can be assessed adequately with objective items ordinarily should be.
2. Of the remaining instructional objectives, those that can be well assessed with essay tests or other product measures ordinarily should be.
3. Only those instructional objectives that still remain ordinarily need to be assessed by means of performance measures.

Figure 1.2 represents this rule as the *decision-making sieve.* The instructional aims that are retained in the top level of the sieve are those that should most often be tapped by objective test questions. Of the remaining objectives, those caught in the second layer should typically be assessed by product measures. The objectives that are left in the third layer of the sieve need to be assessed by observing performance.

By the end of Chapter 9, the reader should be able to wisely and professionally select the most appropriate kind of assessment for any given assessment situation without relying on personal tradition, preference, or prejudice.

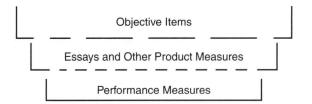

FIGURE 1.2   The Decision-Making Sieve for Selecting Assessment Method

ENCAPSULATION

Assessment and evaluation have a symbiotic relationship to the delivery aspects of instruction. On the one hand, assessment and evaluation rise out of, and are based on, instruction. On the other hand, they provide the feedback to guide teacher efforts.

Likewise, assessment and evaluation provide the feedback to guide student efforts. They communicate to students the aims of instruction. This focus of pupil efforts toward content that is assessed may have either desirable or detrimental effects on learning, depending upon how well the assessment directs pupils to desired outcomes (Marso & Pigge, 1993). In this sense, good assessment and evaluation are not merely adjuncts to effective teaching; they are vital parts of good teaching (Sadler, 1983). In addition, they provide the basis for communicating information about student achievement to parents, students, future teachers, school administrators, college admissions officers, and prospective employers.

A DEMONSTRATION TEST

Although tests should almost always be used to help make better decisions, this principle will now be violated by inclusion of a minor exception. A little test will be presented here to be used purely for instructional and preview purposes.

We ask that you take this test to provide a common experience on which to build on various topics in subsequent chapters. By entering into the spirit of learning and development, you will have some issues to contemplate as they are addressed throughout the book. This brief test will be on knowledge of state capitals—a topic that is (a) somewhat familiar to most readers; and (b) sufficiently low in importance to avoid eliciting anxiety or embarrassment.

STATE CAPITAL TEST

Please number from 1 to 10 on a piece of blank paper. Next to each numeral, write the name of the capital of the state having the same numeral as listed below. Do not consult references or people; do the best you can on your own. Your score will be the number correct.

1. Idaho
2. South Carolina
3. Illinois
4. Connecticut
5. Hawaii

6. Washington
7. New York
8. Colorado
9. Florida
10. New Mexico

After taking the test, score your own answer sheet by using the key provided on p. 20. Then consider each of the issues set forth in the Thinking Cap exercise. Finally, read the Reflections on the Thinking Cap exercise that follows pertaining to these issues.

THINKING CAP EXERCISE 1.1

1. In scoring a completion test such as this, the issue of spelling invariably arises. Should the scoring penalize for spelling errors?

2. Many readers of this book at one time or another have "mastered" the state capitals. Yet most of these same people score between 3 and 7 on the test. What, then, is "mastery"?

3. If you responded correctly to 5 of the 10 items, is it appropriate to say that you know 50 percent of the U.S. state capitals?

4. Is it more meaningful to interpret your score with respect to the fraction of the content you

answered correctly or with regard to the fraction of other examinees whose performance you excelled?

5. When individual test questions are used to infer about a person's competence, how reliable is the inference?

REFLECTION ON THINKING CAP EXERCISE 1.1

1. *Should incorrect spelling be penalized?* The answer may depend on the purpose of the test. In a geography unit on state capitals, it would be reasonable to have partial loss of credit for errors of spelling, but

THINKING CAP EXERCISE 1.1   CONTINUED

only partial. It is surely far better to misspell "Tallahassee" than to offer "Miami," "Orlando," or "Disney World" as the answer for Florida!

However, unlike a geography unit, consider the context in which the test was presented. Had the test been administered by a tutor, it might well have been given orally; the issue of spelling would then be moot. If the intent is to find the fraction of capitals known, then the artifact of test format seems less important than the knowledge. In the context in which this test was presented, we would not penalize for spelling errors when the examinee's intent is clearly correct. Yet partial penalty for spelling errors would not be inappropriate. On the other hand, "Columbus" for item 2 or "Olympus" for item 6 would be counted wrong because the errors transcend mere spelling. And, of course, there are always some borderline calls; for item 5, "Honoluuluu" might be tolerated, but what about "Honolu," "Hono," "Honulau," or "Honoluau"?

Along the same lines, a teacher of an assessment class would not want to penalize a student's misspelling of "symbiotic" on an essay describing the interrelated role of evaluation and instruction, although the teacher would mark the error to call it to the student's attention. On the other hand, this misspelling probably would be penalized if it were made in a biology class that had just studied the concept, word, and spelling of "symbiosis."

2. *What is mastery?* Although the word has a ring of definiteness and permanence to it, its meaning is really quite elusive. It is clear to most people from taking this test that "mastered" material may be forgotten unless it is used.

This question calls attention to a powerful principle. Certain kinds of learning, such as generalization, principles, and application, tend to be more permanent than rote verbal knowledge. Such kinds of meaningful and transferable learning also tend to be more useful in everyday life than nonmeaningful memorized material. Therefore, it makes excellent sense for teachers to stress the complex kinds of learning *both* in their teaching and in their testing. This duality will be a major recurring theme of this book.

3. *What is one's true score on ability to name state capitals?* If you answered 5 of the 10 items correctly, is it correct to say that you know 50 percent of the U.S. state capitals? No. Allowance must be made for sampling error. Suppose a person knows 30 of the 50 capitals. Depending on which states happened to appear on the test, the score could be expected to fall somewhere between 4 and 8; it could conceivably be anything from 0 to 10. Hence, content sampling error is a major concern to which substantial attention will be given in Chapters 5 and 15. Chapter 4 will take up another dimension of this question—what "know" means.

4. *How should one's score be interpreted?* Is it more meaningful to interpret your score in terms of content you answered correctly or in terms of how your performance compared with that of other people? It is a major contention of this book that some measures are suited only to content-referenced (often called criterion-referenced or domain-referenced) interpretations, some are suited only to people-referenced (usually called norm-referenced) interpretations, and some are well suited to both. The State Capitals Test is well suited to both kinds of interpretation. Chapters 4 and 14 will treat this issue in depth.

5. *How reliable are single test items?* The common answer, "not very," is a major understatement. Individual test questions and single informal observations are notoriously inaccurate (Nunnally, 1978). Whether an examinee answered a particular question correctly depends in part, of course, upon how much that person knows. However, it depends in larger part on luck. Did the State Capitals Test contain the state in which you now live or a state in which you attended school? If so, you had good luck. If it happened not to sample any state in which you have ever lived, you had bad luck.

A different aspect of luck involves guessing. A guess may or may not be correct. For example, "Boise" is a common guess for item 1; it happens to be correct. On the other hand, "Chicago" is a frequent guess for item 3; it is incorrect.

Short tests tend *not* to yield consistent scores. Likewise, brief, one-shot observations and single-

(*Continued*)

THINKING CAP EXERCISE 1.1   CONTINUED

performance assessments tend to produce unreliable results. If a test or subtest is expected to yield useful scores, then it must be made long enough to provide a relatively broad sample of content so that luck will have less impact on the scores. Similarly, if reliability is wanted for informal observations, then conclusions must be based on multiple observations, not on one or two brief ones. If formal performance assessment is expected to yield stable results, then it must be based on more than one performance. In this way, the random chance and luck in guessing on a test item, or having a good or bad high dive in the swim team workout, is reduced so that the information about the attribute being assessed can be more clearly detected.

The issues touched on in this section provide a preview of several of the important topics with which educational assessment and evaluation are concerned. As these and other topics are considered in later parts of the book, we shall refer back to the State Capitals Test.

KEY TO STATE CAPITALS TEST

1. Boise	6. Olympia
2. Columbia	7. Albany
3. Springfield	8. Denver
4. Hartford	9. Tallahassee
5. Honolulu	10. Santa Fe

CHAPTER RECAP

Teachers assess and evaluate continually. Some school assessment is done with published, standardized instruments. Some is done with state-prepared assessments. More is done with teacher-made tests. Much is accomplished through observations and interviews. Regardless of the data-gathering methods used, teachers measure and observe in order to gather data about student status, and then they evaluate by applying judgments to the results of the assessment. These judgments are used to plan and guide instruction. Any labeling of students must be accompanied by constructive actions to enhance learning.

Much of this book is devoted to enhancing validity of assessment; that is, we want to assess the right thing in the proper amounts and to have desirable consequences from the assessments. Moreover, we want to accomplish these ambitious aims with measures that are realistic (or authentic), consistent, and cost-effective.

Assessment is part of teaching. The fundamental purpose of classroom use of formative and summative assessment is to enhance student learning. Formative assistance provides feedback to learners and/or teachers when learning is still in progress. Summative assessment occurs after learning; it serves instruction by *helping teachers make instructional and grading decisions* and by *influencing what students study and how they pace their efforts.* Assessment is, therefore, a very powerful tool with which teachers can enhance their instructional effectiveness.

The four themes introduced in this chapter guide teachers in planning assessments that fit the context of the instruction. Instruments of measurement need to be selected appropriately from among objective, product, and performance types to fit the purpose and context of the instruction and the assessment. The decision-making sieve helps teachers in this endeavor.

SUGGESTIONS FOR FURTHER READING

Airasian, P. W. (2001). *Classroom assessment* (4th ed.). New York: McGraw-Hill.
> Chapter 1, "The Classroom As an Assessment Environment," frames a general perspective to classroom assessment and its integral relationship to instruction. Chapter 10, "Standardized Achievement Tests," stresses the impact of pressures on schools to align curricula with state curriculum objectives and national standards.

Arter, J., & McTighe, J. (2001). *Scoring rubrics in the classroom: Using performance criteria for assessing and improving student performance.* Thousand Oaks, CA: Corwin.
> This paperback volume highlights the integral relationship between classroom assessment and instruction in the context of the timely topic of scoring rubrics (a subject that will be taken up in Chapters 8 and 9).

Carr, J. F., & Harris, D. E. (2001). *Succeeding with standards: Linking curriculum, assessment, and action planning.* Alexandria, VA: Association for Supervision and Curriculum Development.
> Chapter 4, "The Comprehensive Assessment System," provides a rationale for instructional leaders to develop comprehensive assessment systems that incorporate student performance data in context to make sound decisions. Practical procedures are presented for developing comprehensive district-wide assessment plans through standards linking.

Kubiszyn, T, & Borich, G. (2003). *Educational testing and measurement: Classroom application and practice* (7th ed.). New York: Wiley.
> Chapter 1, "An Introduction to Contemporary Educational Testing and Measurement," highlights current trends in assessment, including those that go well beyond our emphasis on classroom testing.

Popham, W. J. (1999). Why standardized tests don't measure educational quality. *Educational Leadership, 56*(6), 8–15.
> The public looks to standardized tests for demonstrations of school effectiveness. Unfortunately, such tests do *not* include items on which students demonstrate much of the important learning sought by effective teachers.

Sanders, J. R., Hills, J. R., Nitko, A. J., Merwin, J. C., Trice, C., Dianda, M., & Schneider, J. (1990). Standards for teacher competence in educational assessment of students. *Educational Measurement: Issues and Practices, 9,* 30–31.
> Jointly developed by the American Federation of Teachers, the National Council on Measurement in Education, and the National Education Association, this important document elaborates on each of the seven standards listed in this chapter.

Shepherd, L. A. (2000). The role of assessment in a learning culture. *Educational Researcher, 29*(7), 4–14.
> The theme of this article is classroom assessment that supports and enhances learning. Ideas are framed in a social-constructivist conceptual framework with elaboration on ways to protect assessment practices from negative effects of high-stakes accountability testing.

Stiggins, R. J. (2002). Assessment crisis: The absence of assessment FOR learning. *Phi Delta Kappan, 83,* 758–765.
> In this chapter, the author voices concern about underemphasis of assessment that is designed to enhance learning rather than merely to assess it.

Thorndike, R. M. (1997). *Measurement and evaluation in psychology and education* (6th ed.). New York: Macmillan.
> Chapter 1, "Fundamental Issues in Measurement," provides a brief historical perspective of contemporary measurement, an excellent discussion of measurement and decision making, an overview of the measurement process, and an introduction to a few important contemporary measurement issues.

Beginning with Chapter 2, to save space in the printed book and to allow for frequent updating, current chapter-by-chapter suggestions for further reading may be found at our web site, ablongman.com/hannadettmer.

ROLE OF OBJECTIVES IN INSTRUCTION AND ASSESSMENT

CHAPTER OVERVIEW

OUR AIMS AS EDUCATORS

TAXONOMIES OF EDUCATIONAL OBJECTIVES

TWO FAMILIES OF LEARNING THEORIES
Behavioral
Cognitive

TWO TYPES OF OBJECTIVES
Mager's Behavioral Objectives
Gronlund's Developmental Objectives

MEASURES OF MAXIMUM AND TYPICAL PERFORMANCE

KEY TERMS

instructional objectives
taxonomy
cognitive domain
table of specifications
affective domain
psychomotor domain
social domain
behavioral learning theories
cognitive learning theories
behavioral objective
mastery objective

indicant
developmental objective
standard
Individual Education Plan (IEP)
annual goal (in the context of special education)
short-term objective (in the context of special education)
terminal student behaviors
maximum performance
typical performance

AS EDUCATORS, WHERE DO WE WANT TO GO?

In Lewis Carroll's delightful *Alice in Wonderland,* Alice asks the Cheshire Cat which direction is the right way to go. When the cat asks where she is going, Alice says she doesn't know. The cat then suggests that if she does not know *where* she is going, it doesn't matter which way she goes. Any road will get her there. The Cheshire Cat might have added that Alice will not even know when or *if* she has arrived! This also applies to teaching. We must determine where we want students to go in the learning process and how we will know when they succeed. Well-developed objectives are necessary for purposeful, meaningful instruction.

Educators use educational objectives as statements of destination. In this chapter, the reader will be led to anticipate the broad utility that statements of instructional intent have for classroom assessment. Three important topics that interface with our discussion of instructional objectives are learning theories, instructional objectives, and maximal and typical behaviors of students in the learning process.

AIMS OF INSTRUCTION

Instructional objectives can be defined as statements of the aims of the instruction. Although it would be more accurate to identify these aims as *objectives for student learning that we hope to help students achieve or enhance via our curriculum and our instructional activities,* telescopic language usually condenses the phrase into something like "instructional objectives" or "learning targets."

Some authors use such terms as "objectives," "goals," "outcomes," "targets," and "aims" to denote different levels of generality (e.g., broad-stroke district intents, schoolwide intents, course intents, and unit intents).[1] Other writers use the terms to indicate differences in duration (e.g., short-term aims, annual aims, very long-term aims). However, outside of special education, no single usage has achieved widespread acceptance. In this book, the terms "objective," "aim," and "target" are used interchangeably to refer to aspiration or desired learning outcomes.[2]

The topic of instructional objectives is not "owned" exclusively by any subdiscipline of education. It is common property because objectives provide the genesis for curriculum development activities. The topic sooner or later enters into most discussions of either assessment or curriculum. Our viewpoint is that it should be sooner! That is why we address the matter now in Chapter 2.

Similarly, instructional aims are the starting point in assessment activities. Discussions of instructional outcomes are germane to curriculum development and educational philosophy, as well as to educational psychology and assessment.

This chapter frames objectives in the historical perspective of their influence on American education during the past 50 years and discusses some of the major contributions that statements of educational aims have made and are expected to make in the future. The chapter will help educators anticipate the broad utility that statements of instructional intent have for classroom assessment. This background will enable readers to attend to a particular aspect of instructional objectives that receives focal emphasis in Chapter 4 without losing sight of the broader picture at that time.

---

[1]We will not use the word "goal" as a synonym of these words because the word is used in a special sense in special education, and we wish to avoid causing confusions to readers familiar with that special usage. This special usage will be addressed later in this chapter and in Chapter 13. For now, we will reserve "goal" for the discussion concerning special education. However, because of its widespread usage, we will not relegate the phrase "instructional objective" exclusively to special education's use.

[2]Another synonym used by some writers is "standard." However, because this word, in other contexts, can refer to a required level of performance, we tend to avoid it in order to avoid possible confusion.

■ ■ ■ ■ ■

ENCAPSULATION: HAZARDS OF HIGH-STAKES TESTING

Endeavors in any walk of life are best based on purposes; the same is true for teaching and learning. Unfortunately, the most lofty purposes of classroom instruction and assessment can be undermined by other political and professional agenda. In too many schools, the aims and objectives of educational curriculum have been steamrolled by standards-based teaching and high-stakes testing (Tomlinson, 2000). Such movements can impede the provision of differentiated instruction and complex learning. In addition, some assessment practices can interfere seriously with efforts to use assessment as a means of enhancing learning rather than only as a means of certifying it (Stiggins, 2002).

Thus, some aspects of contemporary assessment practices are not constructive. Awareness of such dangers helps educators to avoid them. Dangers that can't be avoided usually can be minimized when educators maximize the constructive and sound uses associated with the identification of educational purposes.

TAXONOMIES OF EDUCATIONAL OBJECTIVES

In developing better assessment techniques and instruments, it is necessary to focus on the *development of appropriate instructional objectives and assessment of student attainment of those objectives.* The need to clarify educational objectives was made clear in the Forty-Fifth Yearbook of the National Society for the Study of Education (Henry, 1946), titled *The Measurement of Understanding.* This fertile and influential volume raised educators' self-consciousness about the appalling fact that *meaningful learning or understandings were too commonly "disregarded in evaluating (and in teaching) in favor of outcomes which are more easily measured (and achieved)"* (Brownell, 1946, p. 2).

Benjamin Bloom, David Krathwohl, and several other distinguished educators had been studying the difficulties educational examiners were having in communicating about testing and evaluating the processes of teaching and learning. In 1948, they met to discuss this area of mutual interest. It became apparent to them that there was no common basis for determining or communicating what education was to be about. Their discussions led to development of the well-known Taxonomy of the Cognitive Domain (Bloom, et al., 1956).

The group had decided it would be helpful to follow the model that the great educational pioneer Ralph Tyler had developed in a related context. They agreed that articulation of the aims of instruction was integral to the task of developing tests to assess student learning. Therefore, they launched a project of formulating a system to describe assessment and to structure the components of testing. After years of discussions (before there was the convenience of e-mail!), many trials, and a pilot draft of an initial monograph, they outlined a **taxonomy,** that is, a system of classification according to natural relationships among instructional objectives.

They found that they could sort educational objectives into three main groups on the basis of the kinds of learning addressed—cognitive, affective, and psychomotor. They chose the term **cognitive domain** to address intellectual skills involving memory and thinking processes.

They acknowledged the additional need for a taxonomy of the affective domain to include objectives concerning emotional or feeling states. Such objectives would concern interests, attitudes, values, and appreciations. However, they postponed that phase of the project, recognizing the difficulty of *assessing* such outcomes.

Finally, the group pointed out the possibility of developing a third classification system for a taxonomy of the psychomotor domain to address objectives that would focus on manipulative or motor skills. However, they decided to bypass that area, too, because they found little school emphasis on psychomotor development at that time. (How different their perception might be now with the heavy emphasis on school-based classes in areas such as physical fitness, driver education, gymnastics, and keyboarding!)

The taxonomy of the cognitive domain, now nearly five decades old, is among the most widely referenced documents in educational literature, still frequently cited in curriculum materials for teaching and learning and for teaching principles and methods of instruction. Although the taxonomy is still useful, it is currently being rethought and modified by yet another group of distinguished educators to fit changing times and conditions.

Taxonomy of the Cognitive Domain

The *Taxonomy of Educational Objectives Handbook I: Cognitive Domain* (Bloom et al., 1956) classifies six categories of mental processing. The cognitive domain concerns intellectual skills; cognitive objectives involve memory and thinking processes. Most of the objectives that teachers use are cognitive. Because it is relatively easy to plan instruction and assessment for such objectives, they tend to be emphasized more than those that are affective.

The first two categories of function in this domain—knowledge (more realistically identified as recall) and comprehension—are the most basic. The remaining four—application, analysis, synthesis, and evaluation—involve complex thinking and assimilating. Functions do not necessarily occur in the order listed. For instance, evaluation may precede or replace analysis and synthesis, as demonstrated by a voter who recalls a candidate's name or photo and judges that person worthy of a vote but neglects to analyze the candidate's platform and promises.

The four more complex processes build on the two fundamental processes of knowing and understanding. Recall and comprehension are necessary for using, comparing and contrasting, judging, and making parts into the whole. Learning experiences typically progress from simpler types of remembering to more complex activities of reasoning, problem solving, and concept formation. Thus, the educational process builds on basic knowledge and comprehension to develop ability for transferring and applying learning to new situations.

The six original categories of the cognitive domain are:

1. Knowledge. This encompasses the ability to recall or recognize facts, principles, methods, and the like. Little is demanded besides bringing to mind the material as it was presented. This category has been seriously overemphasized in classroom teaching and testing (e.g., Brownell, 1946; Flemming & Chambers, 1983; Stiggins, 1997). Although knowledge is needed for all categories of the taxonomy, it alone has mere recall as its major process. The process of remembering is but one part of the more complex cognitive categories.

2. Comprehension. This category addresses the ability to grasp the meaning of messages, to paraphrase, to explain or summarize in one's own words, and to "translate" among symbols, pictures, and so forth. Comprehension, however, stops short of deep understanding. Authors of the cognitive taxonomy believed that this was the largest class of skills emphasized in schools and colleges.

3. Application. This encompasses use of ideas, rules, or principles in new situations. Most of what is learned is intended for application to problem situations in real life.[3]

4. Analysis. This includes the ability to take apart the component parts of a concept or message and show the relationship among the parts. Analysis is an aid to fuller understanding or a prelude to evaluation of material.

5. Synthesis. This category addresses the ability to put elements together into coherent wholes in ways not experienced by that individual before. Even so, this process is not truly free creative expression because it typically occurs within limits set by the problem, materials, or methodological framework.

6. Evaluation. This is the ability to assess the value of goals, ideas, methods, products, materials, and such and to make purposeful judgments about them. However, this category of the taxonomy should not be regarded always as the last step in learning. In some cases, it might be a prelude or a prompt to the acquisition of new knowledge, or new attempts to comprehend, or further applications and analyses.

The cognitive taxonomy has done much to make educators aware that a large proportion of their tests *and* their teaching practices greatly overemphasize the first two categories—memory work and translation of material—while largely neglecting application of information to new situations. Secondary teachers and elementary teachers alike often fall into such practices. As early as the 1940s, Findley and Scates proposed that too much teaching and testing focused on lower-level learning, while too little concerned abilities at higher, more complex levels (Brownell, 1946). Even today, intellectual assignments and activities having rich potential for transfer of learning (e.g., application, analysis, synthesis, and evaluation) are too often eschewed for more simple and intellectually tidy instruction, drill, practice, and regurgitation. The major purpose of Part II of this book is to help teachers overcome this problem.

THINKING CAP EXERCISE 2.1   ???

Classify the following items into one of the six categories of the original taxonomy of the cognitive domain. Some categories will be used more than once.

____ 1. How many running feet of a 6-foot-wide roll of carpet will it take to carpet my bedroom if I know the floor dimensions of the room?

A. Knowledge
B. Comprehension
C. Application
D. Analysis
E. Synthesis
F. Evaluation

____ 2. Develop a new system for sharing our school's playground equipment fairly and efficiently.

____ 3. State the components of Maslow's hierarchy of needs, beginning with the need he regarded as most basic.

____ 4. Justify your viewpoint on installing a lower speed limit for large trucks than for cars, pickups, and vans on interstate and turnpike thoroughfares.

[3]Does it seem strange that application is not at a higher level in the taxonomy? The reason for this may become evident in Chapter 3. At that time we will spiral to address this issue.

THINKING CAP EXERCISE 2.1   CONTINUED

___ 5. Give reasons why or why not acts of terrorism could increase in the next two decades.
___ 6. Describe the style of pointillism in painting.
___ 7. Compare and contrast the painting styles of cubism, pointillism, and surrealism.
___ 8. Name one well-known composer for each of three periods of music—Baroque, Classical, and Romantic.

KEY TO THINKING CAP EXERCISE 2.1

The following matches between items and categories are defensible as representative of particular categorical levels of memory and intellectual skill. However, several items could be justified as belonging in another category. For example, item 6 is best categorized as comprehension if the respondent has been taught definitions and shown examples of pointillist art styles. If, however, the concept has not been taught and learned, and the respondent is seeing the style for the first time and told it is a style called pointillism with the root word "point," the intellectual skill might represent a sophisticated level of analysis, or even evaluation.

Item 5 might be keyed as analysis or evaluation. These two categories are closely related intellectual skills, distinguished perhaps only by the personal commitment to the response, with a strong affective component. Indeed, if the reasons had been specifically taught, then the item may assess no more than knowledge or comprehension.

As initial developers of the cognitive taxonomy cautioned, we cannot make a specific assignment of taxonomic level for assessment purposes without knowing what transpired with the learner before and during instruction in relation to the instructional objective. So there may be some disagreement among users of the taxonomy regarding levels of response. However, it is important to keep in mind that disagreements and uncertainty over classification of objectives are not necessarily undesirable. The cognitive disequilibrium created by the activity can enhance transfer of learning.

1. C Application
2. E Synthesis
3. A Knowledge
4. F Evaluation
5. D Analysis, perhaps F as evaluation
6. B Comprehension, perhaps D as analysis
7. D Analysis
8. A Knowledge

Recent Changes to the Original Cognitive Taxonomy.   During the 1990s, a group of scholars led by Anderson and Krathwohl (2001) collaborated to rethink and recast the original taxonomy. Although they retained the six cognitive levels of that early work, they changed the order (a possibility that had been suggested by the originating committee) and altered the names of three levels. Their revised cognitive taxonomy now presents levels of remembering (formerly knowledge), understanding (formerly comprehension), applying, analyzing, evaluating, and creating (formerly synthesizing). The committee also added a new dimension to the taxonomy that categorizes four kinds of material processed in the cognitive levels—factual knowledge, conceptual knowledge, procedural knowledge, and metacognitive knowledge.

Examples of the kinds of knowledge in this restructuring are:

- Analyze perspectives appearing in letters to the editor of the local newspaper regarding a current topic of controversy in the community (conceptual knowledge).
- Monitor own study habits for the week prior to the semester test (metacognitive knowledge).
- Select the appropriate algorithms for solving three different kinds of math problems (procedural knowledge).

The revised taxonomy now offers educators an alternative to the original cognitive taxonomy.

Preview of Using the Cognitive Taxonomy to Plan Tests.   Before leaving the taxonomy of the cognitive domain, we will preview one way in which objectives will be used in Chapter 5 to plan classroom assessment that contributes to effective instruction. In developing *balanced* tests for most of the kinds of content that teachers teach most of the time, it is helpful to plan for two separate test-item properties: the subject matter they tap and the kind of mental process they invoke. Because these two features are relatively independent of each other, it is common practice to make a two-dimensional table.

The key verbs of the instructional objectives are used to derive the mental-process heads of the table's columns; "knows" becomes "Knowledge" and "analyzes" becomes "Analysis." The amount of weight, or number of test items, assigned to each column reflects the test-maker's judgment of that process's importance. This provides the test maker with a means of monitoring the relative emphasis given, for example, to knowledge and comprehension versus those mental processes that require deeper processing such as application, analysis, and evaluation.

Content topics are used at the left of the table to label the rows. The relative weights allocated to the rows are based on the teacher's opinion of the topic's importance.

Each cell of the resulting matrix represents the intersection of a mental process with a particular kind of content. Table 2.1 provides an example of a matrix for a middle-school test of art appreciation. Note that the numerals in this table specify the number of 1-point test questions that would be included in an assessment of the unit.

A table of specifications that uses the taxonomy does not necessarily have to include all the categories. The table provides a plan for the finished product. This plan controls the proportion of emphasis given to each content topic and to each mental process or objective. Thus, a **table of specifications** is an aid for a test maker in developing a test that provides the desired balance of coverage with respect to both objectives and content.

In Chapters 5, 8, and 9, we show that scoring rubrics, which specify the bases for assessing products and performances, can perform functions similar to those of tables of specification. Both the tables and rubrics identify the objectives of instruction and allocate the assessment emphasis that each will receive. Likewise, both provide a way by which teachers can enhance instruction by *making clear to students what the criteria for assessment will be;* this, of course, reflects our overarching theme of better instruction through better assessment.

TABLE 2.1   Art Appreciation Unit for Middle School Students

PROCESS→						
CONTENT ↓	KNOWLEDGE/ COMPREHENSION	APPLICATION	ANALYSIS	EVALUATION	TOTAL	PERCENT
Impressionism	4	3	2	1	10	33
Realism	4	3	2	2	11	37
Cubism	2	2	3	2	9	30
TOTAL	10	8	7	5	30	—
Percent (approximate)	33	27	23	17	—	100%

To veer from this focus a bit, did it worry you that the test specifications for a unit of art *appreciation* contained objectives from only the *cognitive* domain? We hope it did. Please keep that issue in mind as you read next about the taxonomy of the affective domain and as you read later in the chapter about objectives for maximum student performance versus objectives that concern typical student performance.

Taxonomy of the Affective Domain

The **affective domain** concerns emotional or feeling states. Affective objectives involve such attributes as personal-social adjustment, dispositions, aesthetic appreciations, interests, and commitments. Affective aims are vital to education. For example, teachers want pupils to like to read as well as to be able to do so, to respect as well as to know traffic laws, and to value as well as to understand the Bill of Rights. Both cognitive and affective components are, of course, typically involved in learning and doing. For example, the student who doesn't receive new information won't be able to recall it, explain it, apply it in new situations, or appreciate it. In general, neither cognitive nor affective activity exists without the other.

Unfortunately, problems surface when we attempt to assess affective activity. Affective goals are the hardest to measure because, among other reasons, their achievement can be falsified or pretended when it is desirable or advantageous to do so. Affective aims concern how students typically *do* respond rather than how they *can* respond under conditions of testing—typical performance rather than maximum performance. Because of the difficulties of gauging affective learning, its assessment is seriously neglected in most school settings.

Although they recognized the difficulty in classifying and assessing affective behaviors, a group of educators chaired by David Krathwohl in the 1960s developed a taxonomy for the affective domain corresponding to that of the cognitive domain. Their classification scheme includes five categories, again ordered from simplest to most complex (Krathwohl, Bloom, & Masia, 1964):

1. **Receiving.** Being aware of something or someone in the environment and passively attending to it (e.g., the history teacher's lecture, the volleyball coach's rules for safety and hygiene, the instruments on the car dash panel).

2. **Responding.** Reacting to the environment and responding to stimuli (e.g., explaining major issues in the Civil War, moving into position on the playing field as instructed by the coach, describing the location and function of the button that activates a car's emergency flashers).

3. **Valuing.** Demonstrating commitment by voluntarily responding and actively seeking out ways to respond (e.g., implementing the coach's game plan and applying basic skills to new game situations or following the recommended steps of the chocolate chip cookie recipe to obtain the most consistent results).

4. **Organization.** Conceptualizing and integrating knowledge and applying information to a value system (e.g., using text material, lecture, class discussion, and new understandings of the Civil War to account for its significance in the nation's history).

5. **Characterization by a value or value complex.** Organizing values into a whole and acting in accordance with newly acquired values or beliefs (e.g., voluntarily practicing learned tips for safe driving and following the tips when not being observed or graded).

Taxonomy of the Psychomotor Domain

The **psychomotor domain** concerns muscular or motor skills, manipulation of materials and objects, and acts requiring coordination. Examples are push-ups, handwriting, skateboarding, keyboarding, and driving. Of course, cognitive and affective components typically accompany psychomotor activity. For example, one must know the letters of the alphabet in order to perform the motor task of producing them, whereas copying them neatly is often as much a function of feeling toward the task as of motor skill. Pitching a baseball clearly involves not only psychomotor skills in executing the techniques, but knowledge of game rules and pitching techniques, along with interest in and commitment to the game.

Several classification schemes have been developed for the psychomotor domain. For example, the Harrow (1972) taxonomy may be particularly useful in the area of physical education. It includes reflex movements, basic fundamental movements, perceptual abilities, physical abilities, skilled movements, and nondiscursive communication.

The Simpson (1972) taxonomic structure is appropriate for motor skills in a wide range of areas. It includes the following seven categories, ordered from simplest to most complex:

1. **Perception.** Using senses to get cues that guide motor movement.
2. **Set.** Being set mentally, emotionally, and physically to take a particular action.
3. **Guided response.** Imitating and engaging in trial and error.
4. **Mechanism.** Performing movements with confidence and skill.
5. **Complex overt response.** Performing complex movements efficiently and smoothly.
6. **Adaptation.** Modifying movements to fit special situations.
7. **Origination.** Creating new movements for appropriate situations.

Assessment of psychomotor achievement typically involves assessing people's performance of a task (e.g., a set of chin-ups) or assessing products that result from a performance (e.g., a welded joint). For curricula in such areas as vehicle operation and dance performance and in the use of equipment in such classes as sewing, science, and shop, instruction and assessment of psychomotor competencies is an important part of educators' responsibilities.

Proposed Revisions for the Taxonomies

We now offer four ways in which the taxonomies might be expanded to better serve learners and teachers.

Since the Taxonomy of the Cognitive Domain was developed, interest and research in the area of creativity has expanded, with increased school emphasis on creative thinking and the development of original products. Therefore, we propose that the cognitive taxonomy be expanded with categories for imagination and creativity, while retaining the category of synthesis.

Second, because cognitive activities of imagination and creativity are accompanied by affective components, we add the categories of *wonder* (an affective state when using one's imagination) and *risk taking* (when creating a new entity) to the existing affective domain.

Third, we propose broadening the psychomotor taxonomy to become a sensorimotor taxonomy that contains not only fine and gross motor skills and muscle development, but also development of the senses—sight, sound, touch, taste, and smell, and perhaps others yet to be identified, such as balance.

Finally, we promote the addition of a social domain as an overlooked but extremely important domain of learning and doing. We now turn to that area of learning.

A Taxonomy for the Social Domain

The **social domain** pertains to sociocultural settings in and around schools. Students interact in large groups and small clusters within classrooms, on playgrounds, and in gymnasiums, labs, shops, lunchrooms, hallways, restrooms, theater stages, conference rooms, offices, and transportation vehicles. In this rich and varied social arena, students and teachers cultivate relationships and develop networks of interrelationships.

Positive social learning within the school setting takes place by engaging in successful teamwork, refining etiquette and manners, building friendships, choosing effective role models, being examples for others in socially constructive ways, leading and following others appropriately, modifying one's own preferences in order to contribute to group success, serving others for the good of all, and assisting those who are in need.

Social behavior for group survival and transmission of culture can be categorized as basic or complex. A helpful taxonomic structure for describing social behavior is organized into eight categories. The categories are (Dettmer 1995, 1997):

1. Relating. Demonstrated by behaviors such as acknowledging the presence of others, making eye contact, recognizing people, attending to them, and seeking to be with others. Learners must first relate to others before they can communicate effectively.

2. Communicating. Act of sending and/or receiving messages. Communicators speak, gesture, call, sing, signal, listen. Indeed, the most overlooked aspect of the communication process may be *listening,* for without it, there can be no meaningful auditory interaction. The same could be said of observing as a key factor in visual communication.

Communication is preceded by relating to others and accepting their presence. It can be facilitated or distorted by use or misuse of socially accepted techniques. Messages are delivered verbally and nonverbally, with the nonverbal communication system (body language) often more powerful than any spoken words.

3. Participating. Associating with others in group-focused ways, such as joining in, volunteering for, allowing oneself to be drawn in, or actively and willingly taking part in group activity. When learners relate and communicate successfully, they are ready to participate in socially constructed settings. Much of school life and later life consists of belonging to and taking part in groups, such as families of origin, domestic partnerships, business relationships, communities, organized religion, interest groups, play groups, work-related groups, friendships, and service groups.

4. Negotiating. Bargaining, bartering, arguing, considering divergent views regarding an issue, and compromising when necessary. Negotiation often takes place socially in play groups when children choose teams, explore give-and-take options, and take turns. Negotiation skills are built by relating to others in positive ways, communicating effectively, and participating successfully in various group endeavors. Mediation and arbitration are extensions of negotiation and precursors to setting aside personal preferences to accommodate and assimilate those of others.

5. Collaborating. Laboring together for success of the whole project and the group's welfare. Cooperation is a term used often to describe group work in schools. However, well-honed collaborative teamwork, with flexible leadership and followership roles, tends to be more demanding of participants and typically more productive than cooperation.

6. Adjudicating. Conciliating and settling differences with others. Conciliation is an outcome of effective negotiation and mediation efforts. Those who communicate and negotiate effectively in social settings are more able to mediate differences for the benefit of all. Through adjudication, conciliation can take place.

7. Initiating. Catalyzing interaction, even where social risks are involved, in order to activate social action and change.

8. Converting. Generating social transitions, revolutionizing social structures and convincing others to join in for new, advanced social aims.

CAPTIVATING EXTENSIONS

What is an "extension"? We have a variety of enrichment materials that, for various reasons, primarily length, were not included in the book. Yet we wish to make these available to interested readers. Therefore, some of these materials will be introduced where they naturally fit into the flow of the text. Brief introductions will be made under the heading "Captivating Extensions." Readers who wish to examine these enriching materials will be directed to parts of our web site.

Here is the first extension. If you are interested in Thinking Cap Exercises for the affective, psychomotor, or social domains, you can find one for each at ablongman.com/hannadettmer.

COMPARING SIMPLE OBJECTIVES WITH
COMPLEX OBJECTIVES

What differentiates lower-order objectives from higher-order ones? First, it is more constructive to refer to objectives as *simple* or *complex,* thus avoiding the words high and low, which may suggest inferior and superior values (Stiggins, 1997). Furthermore, the terms simple and complex are more suited to the spirit of spiraling, where simple, basic aims of grouping facts and information can evolve outward and upward into complex, abstract behaviors such as analyzing, synthesizing, and evaluating.

Airasian (2001) provided a useful set of examples to separate objectives requiring only simple recall and memory from those calling for comparing and contrasting data, applying rules to solve new problems, and synthesizing information into newly organized concepts. One example of a simple objective is "The pupil can match quotes from a short story to the characters who said them," whereas a complex objective is "The pupil contrasts motives of the protagonist and the antagonist in a short story" (Airasian, 2001, p. 87).

Simple objectives are building blocks on which more complex ones are constructed. To illustrate, in the affective domain, students must receive and respond to information before they can value it. In the psychomotor domain, using senses to perceive cues for motor activity precedes skill in motor acts involving complex movements.

Learning and doing typically involve all four domains simultaneously. Moreover, a learner who is functioning at a basic level of cognitive activity—recalling and comprehending—is also likely to be functioning at a basic level in the emotional, physical, and social domains. For example, one learner might be receiving or responding (affective) to information (cognitive) through hearing and taking notes (sensorimotor) in a class setting (social). Another might be functioning at more complex levels such as organizing thoughts and priorities (affective) to compare and contrast perspectives on a challenging topic (cognitive) by acting out (sensorimotor) aspects of the topic through participation in a simulation within the classroom (social).

All students need learning experiences at both simple, basic levels and at complex, challenging levels. Every student should have many opportunities for creative expression and production. The developmental stage of the learner, prior experiences of the learner, scope and sequence of curriculum, and the nature of the curricular content all will impact what is to be taught and when. Instructional objectives, tables of specifications, and assessment rubrics are tools that help educators structure learning environments so that students spiral through and beyond the learning experiences.

ENCAPSULATION

One of the most overlooked aspects of the domains is their potential for making students aware of how and why they are being taught and what it is that they are expected to learn and do. Students expend much effort and energy in trying to figure out what the teacher wants and what the teacher will test. Students need to be "let in on the game plan" as partners with teachers to apply the processes of thinking (cognitive), feeling (affective), doing (sensorimotor), and interrelating (social) to develop knowledge and skills.

Realizing what is expected of them enables students to set their sights on those aims. When students receive instruction and engage in practice at more abstract levels as well as basic levels, they do better on follow-up assessments (Tyler, 1931). This has important implications for such general, lifelong educational goals as preparing students to be discriminating voters, safe drivers, prudent investors, nurturant family members, or appreciators of the arts. Teachers and parents want students to continue such behaviors long after their years of formal schooling.

The taxonomies for cognitive, affective, psychomotor (or sensorimotor), and social domains are not curriculum guides. Yet they can be very helpful when used as curriculum development templates for planning, implementing, assessing, and communicating about instructional strategies and educational resources. One of the greatest contributions the taxonomies offer is an expanding vision concerning the breadth and depth of instructional and assessment practices. Our web site, ablongman.com/hannadettmer, contains a chart showing the four taxonomies and highlights parallelisms among them.

TWO FAMILIES OF LEARNING THEORIES

Objectives for learning are based on principles that emanate from theories of human learning. Before building on the link between learning theory and assessment, we will briefly review the major types of learning theories. Our purposes are best accomplished by classifying the theories into two major groups: behavioral and cognitive.

Some advocates of particular learning theories (especially the earliest advocates) have promoted their respective views as the central explanation of all human learning. This attitude, unfortunately, sets the stage for expecting teachers to choose definitively among major families of theories and to use just the one kind of theory for all of their instruction.

In contrast to that stance, our position is that each family of theories is highly appropriate in *some* teaching and assessment contexts and less suited to others. Like many contemporary scholars, e.g., Ormrod (2000), we firmly believe that both behavioral and cognitive perspectives offer very useful suggestions for educators. The challenge is to *use each* orientation or paradigm *where it works best.* The context-adaptive planning perspective that will be developed in the next two chapters is a useful tool for achieving this match.

Teachers should be situationally consistent, using each orientation where it makes sense and avoiding it where it doesn't. We draw an analogy with choice of clothing. It would be foolish to wear the same kind of apparel irrespective of weather. There can and should be consistency between *what* is worn and *when* it is worn; that is, the clothes should match the season.

Although diversity exists within each family of learning theories, it is helpful to characterize each general orientation by means of several contrasts that are pertinent to developing instructional objectives. The contrasts made are drawn mainly from Bigge and Shermis (1992), Ormrod (2000), and Woolfolk (2001).

In Chapter 3, we relate each theory to the kind of subject matter to which it seems most congenial. *We will show that the nature of the subject matter one is teaching is a useful basis for determining which orientation toward learning is most appropriate.*

Behavioral Learning Theories

What Is Learned?   **Behavioral learning theories** focus on *observable behaviors.* They use terms such as "stimulus-response association" and "reinforcement contingencies." When working in this perspective, teachers often specify educational objectives as observable behaviors. Then they organize instruction to prompt the desired behaviors and assess the outcomes based on stated conditions, behaviors, and minimum acceptable level of performance.

What Does Reinforcement Do?   Reinforcement is a central notion of contemporary behaviorism. Reinforcement develops mechanical stimulus-response associations. It causes organisms to respond to learning contingencies (i.e., what happens if . . .). Behaviorists emphasize various conditions of reinforcement that influence response rates and the likelihood that responses will reoccur.

How Are Problems Solved?   Behaviorists tend to view a problem's degree of difficulty to be a function of its similarity to other problems the learner has experienced in the past. If an attempted solution fails or if the learner has never encountered such a problem, the learner resorts to trial and error until a solution is chanced on and reinforced.

What Is the Actional Nature of Learners?   Behaviorists generally accept Locke's position that the mind begins like a blank slate. They emphasize the paramount role of environmental input via sensory experience in forming the content of the mind. The learner is viewed as a passive *receiver* of what is taught.

Perspective.   Behaviorists view learning as the *acquisition of behaviors,* not as some unobservable happening in a vague construct called "mind."

In behaviorism, learning hierarchies are seen as linear sequences of component parts, each step of which must be completed in turn in order to develop more complex learning. From this perspective, it is useful to analyze the task to be learned, to reduce it to its simplest elements, and then to organize these elements into the best instructional sequence. An important practical consequence of a behavioral model of instruction is that higher-order learning is delayed until the prerequisite skills have been mastered (Shepard, 1991).

Cognitive Learning Theories

What Is Learned?   **Cognitive learning theories** describe what is learned in terms of *mental constructs* such as understandings, appreciations, expectancies, principles, and insights. The learner seeks out and actively processes information in order to make sense of the world. Learning is an internal process that cannot be observed directly.

Teachers of this persuasion tend to identify mental as well as behavioral educational objectives and then organize their teaching to help students enlarge, clarify, and reorganize their cognitive associations. Open-ended instructional aims may be stated in terms of complex thinking operations.

What Does Reinforcement Do?   Most cognitive theorists think learning is independent of reinforcement. They view reinforcement as important mainly because it provides the person with information; this information impacts thinking or reasoning about a problem.

How Are Problems Solved?   Cognitive theorists tend to believe that students think about a problem until they gain insight into its solution. Knowledge is *constructed* by learners in their own minds rather than poured into learners' minds. Unlike behaviorism's emphasis on behavioral trial and error, cognitive theory emphasizes the person's *cognitive activity.*

What Is the Actional Nature of Learners?   Cognitive theorists think that the mind is an *active processor* of information while it reacts to and interacts with environmental events. Teachers holding this position view learners as *interacters* with what is learned. The learning process takes place within and among individuals.

Perspective.   Cognitive perspective is mental. Learning is perceived as more than the acquisition of responses; it is the integration of new content into what was previously known. Learning involves the construction or reorganization of cognitive structures. Meaning receives much attention. Cognitive-oriented teachers see learning hierarchies as complex structures like intellectual scaffolds, connecting or anchoring new material with old material. There is no one way that the scaffold must be erected or climbed. This perspective reduces (but doesn't eliminate) the importance of instructional sequences.

As suggested earlier, many specific learning theories exist. Organizing these theories into the two families discussed here provides a useful way to consider the goodness of fit of each between learning principles and principles of assessment.

TWO TYPES OF OBJECTIVES

Two influential educators, Robert Mager and Norman Gronlund, led the way in the area of instructional objectives with two very different perspectives on designing objectives for curriculum, instruction, and assessment. The differences between these types of objectives reflect basic differences in learning theory. Moreover, the differences have profound implications for instructional material, transfer of learning, and assessment practices. We are now ready to describe and contrast these two kinds of objectives *with the goal of using each in those contexts in which it works best—* a topic to be more fully developed in Chapter 4.

Mager's Behavioral Objectives

In 1962, Robert Mager's readable and enjoyable little book, *Preparing Objectives for Programmed Instruction,* ushered one kind of objective into prominence in the popular professional culture. According to Mager, an instructional objective is a description of a performance the learner should *exhibit* to demonstrate competence (Mager, 1962, 1997), for example, "When asked, recites alphabet without error." A Mager-type objective describes an intended result of instruction, or a demonstration that the student has arrived at the learning destination.

Mager thus applied the Cheshire Cat's advice to Alice in arguing that teachers first must decide where they want to go, then provide a means of getting there, and then arrange to find out whether they have arrived. Mager explained that this process entails evaluating student performance according to the selected objectives. Teachers should analyze student needs, set explicit targets, plan and instruct, and then assess and evaluate.

According to Mager, an adequate objective must have three features:

- Be an *observable student behavior* (i.e., use an active verb)
- Indicate the *conditions* (if any) under which the behavior is to be emitted
- Specify the *minimum level* up to which the behavior must come

Here are two examples of Mager-type objectives:

1. When given a written copy of a seven-digit telephone number and told to dial it, the pupil will correctly do so on a touch-tone phone within 15 seconds at least 4 out of 5 times.
2. Upon request, the student will run 100 meters on a regulation track in 14 or fewer seconds.

This approach is deeply rooted in *behavioral* psychology and provides the clarity of *behavioral* operational definitions of targets. That is, Mager-type objectives are **behavioral objectives;** they indicate *explicitly* how their attainment will be assessed. They also provide a mastery threshold (i.e., a specified minimum level of performance) by which one can judge *whether or not* they have been attained. In this sense, they are **mastery objectives.**

Assessment in this paradigm is limited to that which was explicitly specified in the behavioral objectives. Therefore, Mager-type objectives do not encourage assessment for mindful transfer of learning.

Gronlund's Developmental Objectives

Norman Gronlund (1970, 2000) provided a profoundly important insight for educators. Although Gronlund accepted the utility of Mager-type behavioral objectives in certain instructional settings, he recognized their insufficiency for many other instructional contexts. Therefore, he proposed the use of two distinct types of objectives: Mager-type (i.e., behavioral, explicit, mastery) objectives and Gronlund-type objectives.

Gronlund showed that much of the clarity of behaviorism and operational definitions can be secured without resorting to narrow, shallow, restrictive behavioral objectives. Instead, active behavioral verbs can be used as *examples,* or **indicants,** of the kinds of behaviors that a teacher would accept as evidence of student progress toward instructional objectives from any of the four domains. Each general objective is accompanied by a sufficient number and variety of behavioral indicants to convey a good sense of the extent and limits of a large, *expansive* body or domain of subject matter. An example of a cognitive Gronlund-type objective with several indicants is:

1. Understands basic terms:
   1.1 Gives an oral definition of terms in own words.
   1.2 Identifies incorrect uses of a term.
   1.3 Places terms in forms that show hierarchical relations (e.g., outlines).
   1.4 Matches terms with antonyms.
   1.5 Writes coherent comparisons and contrasts of similar terms.

This approach is rooted in cognitive psychology. Although it features the clarity of active, behavioral verbs, it does not attempt a Procrustean[4] forcing of all subject matter into behavioral objectives. Rather, it ordinarily uses cognitive or affective verbs to express the real objective. However, it does not stop with a vague cognitive or affective verb; it goes on to provide behavioral indicants (i.e., indicators) of how achievement might reasonably be assessed.

Gronlund-type objectives are **developmental.** That is, they do not conceptualize achievement as a matter of arriving at a destination; rather, they assess how far along the road the learner has traveled. The indicants provide benchmarks, or measuring sticks, of progress.

Assessment in this paradigm is *not* restricted to that which is explicitly specified in the objective or in the indicants; instead, it is defined in terms of the more *expansive, general* types of materials illustrated by the indicants. Therefore, Gronlund-type objectives encourage and prompt assessment for mindful transfer of learning.

■ ■ ■ ■ ■ ▬▬▬▬▬▬▬▬▬▬▬▬▬▬▬▬▬▬▬▬▬▬▬▬▬▬▬▬▬▬▬▬▬▬▬▬▬

ENCAPSULATION

A colleague recently proclaimed to one of us that *"Objectives are out; standards are in."* Your author responded, "I wonder if you could help me understand the difference between objectives and **standards**?" After an awkward silence, the subject was abruptly changed.

Organizations such as the National Council for Accreditation of Teacher Education (NCATE) define standards as "written expectations for meeting a specified level of performance that exist for the content that students should learn at specified age or grade levels" (2001, p. 57). How, then, does a standard differ from an instructional objective?

The best answer we have seen was provided by Popham, "The answer . . . is that there really is *no* difference between instructional objectives and content standards. Both phrases describe the educational intentions we have for our students" (2002, p. 108).

(continued)

[4]Procrustes was a notorious innkeeper in ancient Greece who cruelly stretched or lopped off the legs of all guests who failed to fit into the bed he provided.

ENCAPSULATION   CONTINUED

Then why are professional organizations parading around with standards nowadays? Because, we believe, standards are stylish. Popham summed it up with wit: "Then a small voice called out from the crowd, 'But the emperor's not wearing new standards at all; he's wearing old objectives!'" (2002, p. 107).

Now there certainly is nothing wrong with keeping up with current styles; in fact, it's often adaptive to do so. If calling aims "standards" instead of "objectives" will please the boss, then by all means do so. However, let's not confuse styles and fads with lasting progress; it is only the name that has changed.

The Role of Gronlund- and Mager-Type Objectives in Special Education IEPs

The distinction between the two kinds of objectives discussed in this section may have great utility in special education. Schools, by law, must develop for each student with special needs an **Individual Education Plan (IEP)** that includes measurable annual goals accompanied by benchmarks or short-term objectives, along with notation of the manner in which, and time by which, each objective will be assessed. In special education, the term **annual goal** often refers to the expansive, developmental aims that do not necessarily lend themselves to easy, explicit, definitive measurement (although they assuredly *are* measurable). **Short-term objectives** refer to more narrow, explicit, time-oriented, masterable short-term aims.

The suggestion will be made in Chapter 13 that it may be useful for those constructing IEPs (regular classroom teachers, special education teachers, support personnel, and students and their families) to *regard the annual goal in the IEP as an expansive Gronlund-type developmental objective.* For example, "Applies a time-management plan for completion of assignments" for the student who has trouble staying on task or "Uses research skills to investigate a problem of individual interest" for the very able student who is working ahead of the class. Progress toward goals may be more important than "goal getting." We maintain that human progress is characterized by having ongoing, challenging aspirations that anticipate success along the way, yet recognizing that learning never ends.

In IEPs, the *indicants could provide a basis for developing the legally mandated short-term objectives that are more readily measurable and lend themselves to documentation of baseline, benchmark, and performance data.* In Chapter 13, we will elaborate on these important applications to special education.

TERMINAL STUDENT BEHAVIORS

In this section, we focus on three words that are widely used to describe learning targets: **terminal, student,** and **behaviors.** Let's address these words in reverse order.

Behaviors.   We have already seen how instructional objectives are generally cast either *as* **terminal student behaviors** (after Mager) or *in terms of* terminal student behaviors (after Gronlund). The Mager-type, behavioral, mastery objectives contain the method by which their attainment will be assessed. The Gronlund-type developmental objectives provide multiple, varied means of assessment by use of several indicators (indicants) of the desired target. By being concrete, both approaches thus serve to foster clarity and measurability.

Student.   Because instructional objectives focus on what students do at the end of instruction or at some later time, they do *not* delineate ways of achieving the objectives. *Objectives focus on ends,* not means. This is an extremely important point for two distinct groups of reasons.

Students, Not Teachers.   First, it is important to note that instructional objectives are best stated in terms of terminal *student* status. Historically, many teachers' aims were to "teach" the quadratic formula, westward movement, and so on. Teacher behavior is important as a *means* of pursuing student learning, but teacher behavior is *not* the aim. Other teachers had aims such as "have students read pages 157–171 in the text" or "have a class discussion on a current civil rights issue." Here, too, the text or the discussion may be a useful mechanism for courting student learning, but reading the textbook is *not* the aim. Nor is student discussion. The objective targets *student* status.

Ends, Not Content.   Next, it is helpful to make a sharp distinction between instructional aims on the one hand and teaching methods and curricular materials on the other. By focusing on the target, teachers retain all options concerning methods of pursuing it. An analogy may be useful here. If you plan to fly to Mexico City, it is helpful to specify the destination as Mexico City and to *avoid confounding the objective with the means by which you plan to pursue it.* Thus, if pilots should go on strike, you can change your means and attain your objective.

Similarly, in teaching, it is wise to keep our objectives separate from the ways we plan to teach them. To illustrate, suppose you were a first-year primary teacher who had developed a modest unit on Eskimos to pursue such important aims as understanding and appreciating that some cultures have ways different from our own of solving major life problems, reducing ethnocentrism, understanding some of our linguistic heritage (e.g., the word "kayak" from Eskimo), and knowing some specific geographic information about Eskimo habitat and culture.

Now suppose the retiring teacher across the hall has outstanding materials for a similar unit on India and offers to give you all her materials. Would you change units? Probably. Would your important objectives have to change? Mostly not. You would still show that various cultures have alternative ways of solving life's problems. You would still try to reduce ethnocentrism. You would still show that English is enriched by words from other languages (e.g., "guru" from Hindi). You would still study maps and globes and the effects of weather on lifestyles. Although you would have to change the geographic and cultural information drastically, many of your objectives would remain unchanged. Notice that it tends to be the more important, complex objectives that would survive.

The point is this: Compared with basic cognitive objectives (i.e., knowledge and comprehension), which involve direct study of the subject matter with little attention to transfer of learning, more complex objectives provide more emphasis to transfer and more opportunities for doing so. Therefore, complex cognitive objectives (e.g., application and evaluation) *usually should be less content-specific.* To explore this important point further, please reconsider the example of a Gronlund-type objective provided on page 37. (Note, too, that it, like many cognitive objectives, does not necessarily use the key verbs in the cognitive taxonomy.)

The objective is completely *content free*! It could be used in teaching most anything. Although it typically is not practical to create developmental objectives that are content free, they can usually be rendered *content-reduced.* Notice how a content-reduced or decontextualized objective leaves teachers a rich variety of choices in selecting curriculum and methods as they pursue transfer or decontextualized learning. Thus, to the extent feasible, Gronlund-type objectives focus on students and outcomes, *not on teaching methods or curriculum.*

Terminal.   Authorities such as Mager and Gronlund agree that objectives should be stated in terms of *terminal* student status rather than in terms of *change* in student status. A common flaw in the phrasing of instructional objectives is the use of verbs that denote change. For example:

- Pupils will *learn* the first 10 Roman numerals.
- Members of 4-H will *grow* in self-concept.
- Students will *develop* greater appreciation of Bach.
- Learners will *improve* their listening comprehension.
- Runners will *increase* endurance.

There are compelling reasons to avoid verbs that denote such intended change in student status.[5] First, gain can easily be faked. Suppose grades for the 100-meter dash were to be based on gain rather than on terminal status. Some students might "fake bad" on the pretest in order to enhance their potential gain. This would reduce such a grading system to a farce!

Another consideration is that in order to measure change, teachers would have to pretest, posttest, and then compute the difference. This would not only be inconvenient, it also would introduce some very serious technical problems (e.g., see Cronbach & Furby, 1971).

Yet another difficulty with using change of status for class objectives[6] can be illustrated by the first objective in the list. What if Omar already knows the first 10 Roman numerals before the unit is taught? He does not learn them in the unit. Should he then fail the unit because the objective was not met? Of course not. Most teachers who paint themselves into this corner by use of change verbs would ignore the logical problem, walk on the wet paint, and give the student an "A." This suggests that terminal status was really the teacher's objective and that the verb "learn" did not reflect the intent. Therefore, the objective should be stated in a way that is honest and captures the intent (e.g., "Pupils will *know* the first 10 Roman numbers").

MEASURES OF MAXIMUM PERFORMANCE VERSUS MEASURES OF TYPICAL PERFORMANCE

The fourth graders are taking an end-of-unit paper-pencil test on the posture unit that they have just completed. Mike sits slumped down in his seat so that his weight is on his back rather than his rump. One leg is slung atop his desk. He thoughtfully completes the test and turns it in. It is perfect! If you were the teacher, would it distress you to have to give him an "A"?

---

[5]We will see in Chapter 13 that in special education there may be some compelling reasons to compromise on this point and to use annual goals with change verbs. However, these compulsions arise more from regulatory issues than from logic. Therefore, it may be useful, even for educators who will later have to modify this stance, to embrace its rationale at this time.

[6]This issue is not pertinent to special education IEPs, which, by definition, are individualized. Thus, the accommodation to regulations implied in Footnote 5 is made easier.

Or, we could cast the example in more real-to-life, or authentic, terms. You have just given Mike an end-of-unit performance test in which he demonstrated how he should sit at his desk, stand, and walk. His performance was perfect. However, you have noticed that his *usual* posture is atrocious. Would it distress you to have to give him an "A"?

With either version of the problem, the answer depends on your instructional objectives for the posture unit. A very useful distinction can be made between objectives and tests concerned with **maximum performance** and those that address **typical performance.** *Tests of maximum performance assess what the examinee* can *do. Measures of typical performance assess what the examinee ordinarily* does *do* (Cronbach, 1990).

To paraphrase, with tests of maximum performance, we ask examinees to do their *best* work; achievement or aptitude is assessed. In measures of typical performance, we ask examinees to reveal what they *really like* or what they *actually do,* rather than what they are capable of doing (Lyman, 1991); preferences or dispositions are also assessed.

If, on the one hand, some or all of the posture unit's objectives focused on maximum performance, then student attainment should be assessed as a measure of maximum performance, as was illustrated for Mike. Focus would be on what pupils *can do* when they know that they are being evaluated and are motivated to do their best. In such circumstances, the rules of the game are to represent oneself at one's best.

If, on the other hand, some or all of the unit's aims concerned typical behavior, then student attainment should be assessed with measures of typical performance. These measures would require rating pupils when they are *not* aware that they are being observed in order to assess their normal or typical posture. Focus would be on what pupils *ordinarily do* when they are not especially mindful of posture or motivated to be at their best. In these circumstances, we need a representative sample of what each child typically *does*—a measure that is not influenced by the fact that the behavior is being observed.

Which kind of objective is proper for a posture unit? Most of us would answer "both." If this is the case, then our objectives should address both maximum performance and typical performance. An example of a maximum performance objective might be:

1. Knows proper sitting posture at desk.
   1.1. When shown pictures of several children seated at desks, can identify the child exhibiting the best or worst posture.
   1.2. Demonstrates good sitting posture on request.
   1.3. Describes orally or in writing the proper way to sit at a desk.

This objective focuses on what children *can do* when they know they are being assessed, are expected to do their best, and want to do their best. In such maximum performance settings, faking is not an issue.

An example of a typical performance objective might be:

2. Typically exhibits good posture at desk.
   2.1. Sits appropriately when reading.
   2.2. Exhibits good desk posture during class discussions.
   2.3. Shows good posture when doing paper-pencil seat work.

This objective focuses on what children *typically do* when they do not know that they are being observed and are not motivated to be at their best.

Assessment of the second objective is much more demanding than the first. To evaluate pupil achievement of it, the teacher will have to make *several observations of each child without the child's knowledge.* The observer watches behavior *in natural settings,* records or classifies the behavior systematically and objectively as it occurs or very soon after, and converts the data into quantitative information (Sattler, 1992). To provide a good sample of behavior, observations should be distributed over several activities, over several times of day, and over several days.

Some authors, ourselves included, limit the word "test" to measures of maximum performance because the word connotes to many people a situation in which one is to do one's best. Thus, we test knowledge of posture, typing accuracy, running speed, knowledge of spelling, understanding of history, or ability to use correct grammar. We use other devices to assess characteristic posture, typical typing accuracy, typical spelling, or ordinary grammar.

One of us experienced a stark distinction between tests of maximum behavior and measures of typical behavior during the late afternoon on the last day of his first year of teaching. As the faculty sat in the lounge, student Jim ran outside the window shouting to a friend, "No, I ain't got none neither." His English teacher, Mr. Halliday, threw up his hands and cried, "Good Heavens, I've just given him a 'B'!" One can infer that Mr. Halliday's objectives included typical oral language usage; apparently his assessment devices didn't. Assessment was probably limited to tests of *maximum performance* of written language usage.

Now consider two very important issues introduced in Thinking Cap Exercise 2.2. They are designed to preview topics that will be addressed in greater depth in later chapters and to enhance reader readiness for those topics.

THINKING CAP EXERCISE 2.2   ???

Consider a social-studies citizenship unit.

- Would the more important unit objectives involve maximum behaviors or typical behaviors?
- Should the more important objectives concern student status at the immediate conclusion of instruction or at some more distant future point?

KEY TO THINKING CAP EXERCISE 2.2

Clearly, interest resides in typical behaviors at some future time. For example, we are more concerned with students' ultimate citizenship practices than with their present ability to answer factual test questions correctly.

Although the two questions presented are easy enough to answer, the ramifications are complex. It obviously wouldn't be practical to postpone awarding grades in such units until years or decades after the courses were completed. The feeble substitutes for which teachers have to settle concern such things as requisite knowledge, understanding, ability to analyze, and ability to apply. These kinds of (mainly complex mental processes) *maximal* performance are testable. Educators reason that if students lack such maximal basics, they will necessarily lack the corresponding typical behaviors. This seems like a logically sound enough case.

However, it doesn't follow that having the maximal performance will assure the desired corresponding typical behaviors. (Witness Mr. Halliday's student Jim.) Yet there is not much that teachers can do about this worrisome problem in evaluating student achievement of some very important objectives. Fortunately, *program* evaluation (in contrast to evaluation of individual students) can address this question of degree of student attainment of long-term typical behaviors.

THINKING CAP EXERCISE 2.2   CONTINUED

Follow-up surveys under conditions where former students have no motive to distort or falsify their self-reported behaviors can cast light on the effectiveness of instruction. We will revisit this topic in Chapter 9.

Now let's recall the problem raised on page 29. We asked if the exclusive use of *cognitive* objectives for a unit of art *appreciation* presented a problem. The kind of rationale invoked for citizenship can be adapted to the art appreciation unit described in Table 2.1. Our earlier considerations render the assessment specifications less problematic than they probably appeared to be at first. In addition, note the use of "evaluation" and the use of "application" and "analysis"; these may come much closer to the "stuff" of which appreciation is made than would "knowledge" or "comprehension."

CHAPTER RECAP

Instruction is best based on mindful intent or instructional objectives. We have seen that these desired outcomes provide an intersection among several subdisciplines of education, including philosophy, curriculum, psychology, and assessment.

Instructional objectives can be categorized in a rich variety of ways; different classification schemes serve different purposes. These include the traditional cognitive, affective, and psychomotor trichotomy, updated and expanded elements in all three taxonomies, the addition of a social domain, the behavioral learning theory and cognitive learning theory comparisons, the Mager–Gronlund dichotomy, and the important contrast of objectives based on maximum performance with those based on typical performance.

In considering instructional objectives and related issues, this chapter has served to introduce these issues and get readers engaged in thinking about a variety of important topics. As we spiral back and forward to various issues, we anticipate that new and richer meanings will emerge.

SUGGESTIONS FOR FURTHER READING

From this point onward throughout the chapters, to save space in the printed book and to allow for frequent updating, current chapter-by-chapter suggestions for further reading may be found at our web site, ablongman.com/hannadettmer.

INSTRUCTIONAL CONTEXTS OF CLASSROOM ASSESSMENT

CHAPTER OVERVIEW

EXPRESSION OF INDIVIDUAL DIFFERENCES
Amount of Achievement
The Time It Takes to Get There

TWO IMPORTANT ATTRIBUTES OF SUBJECT MATTER
Explicit versus Expansive
Masterable versus Developmental

LEARNING THEORIES REVISITED

TEACHING AND ASSESSING FOR TRANSFER OF LEARNING
Low-Road Transfer
High-Road Transfer

KEY TERMS

achievement dimension
time dimension
explicit subject matter
expansive subject matter
masterable subject matter
developmental subject matter
Context A

subject matter domain
Context B
Context C
transfer of learning
low-road transfer of learning
high-road transfer of learning

Chapters 1 and 2 focused on ways in which assessment and evaluation are integral to good teaching. Chapters 3 and 4 provide an integrated framework of several important educational topics and *show how they logically relate to each other and to classroom assessment and instruction.* The aim is to enhance wise professional decision making.

Some of these topics have received scant emphasis in most assessment books. Furthermore, profoundly important practical connections among the elements are too often overlooked. We profess that in preparation for the challenging profession of education, much attention should be given to *when, where,* and *why* educators should do various things, as well as *how* to do them.

Because of the inherent interrelatedness of the topics, it will be helpful to preview them at this time. The eight topics are:

1. Manifestations of individual differences
2. Kinds of subject matter
3. Families of learning theories

4. Kinds of transfer of learning
5. Types of instructional objectives
6. Kinds of assessments
7. Varieties of scores
8. Types of score interpretation

It is important for readers to realize that each topic has *extremely important practical implications for effective teaching.* By *connecting* the eight topics in a cohesive manner, we can view them as making up an arch, as pictured in Figure 3.1.

In contrast, educators who do not see the connections among the eight elements are unlikely to organize them harmoniously, and the elements may be perceived as a jumble of unrelated topics, as pictured in Figure 3.2.

If at times the topics seem to be a bit theoretical, recall that nothing is as practical as a good theory! Our goal is for readers to be able to make the kinds of sound, *practical classroom applications* that reasoning fosters.

Student assessment doesn't occur in a vacuum. It takes place in a *context of instruction.* To understand some of the extremely practical ramifications of classroom assessment, it is necessary to be familiar with the broader instructional contexts in which it occurs.

This chapter addresses those of the eight topics that concern instruction. Our treatment of these instructional topics will create the setting in which classroom assessment takes place. Although the topics are broad in scope, we will examine only those aspects that directly impact classroom assessment.

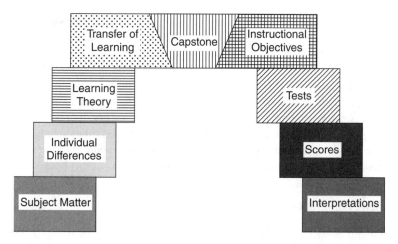

FIGURE 3.1   Elements of Instruction and Assessment Harmoniously Structured

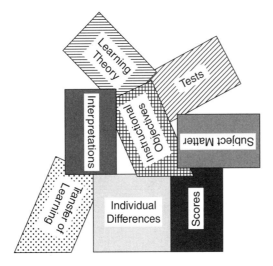

FIGURE 3.2   **Elements of Instruction and Assessment Without Structure**

DIMENSIONS OF INDIVIDUAL DIFFERENCES

Teachers have always observed (and often lamented) that students differ. The magnitude of these differences is often great. Some teachers react to the reality of diversity by ignoring it and treating all students alike, as though they *were* alike. Others react to student differences in achievement by trying to wipe them out. (The differences, not the students!) Legislators, too, seem at times to want to wipe individual differences out; the very title of the Elementary and Secondary Education Act of 2001—No Child Left Behind—seems to seek to eliminate the bottom fraction of achievement distributions. However, as Nunnally (1976) observed, the only way to make individual differences vanish is to stick one's head in the sand. For better or for worse, *variation* among students *cannot be eliminated.* On the contrary, *effective teaching tends to increase individual differences among students* (Feldt & Brennan, 1989).

When instruction is effective, *all* students learn. Those who have difficulty in learning *do* achieve, and those who learn easily achieve *more.* Before this point is amplified, it is worth previewing the idea that *teachers have a choice* as to how individual differences will be expressed. Individual differences can be channeled into an amount-of-achievement dimension, a time-it-takes-to-get-there dimension, or into a combination of the achievement and time dimensions. *This mindful choice between the **achievement dimension** and the **time dimension** is of the utmost practical importance for teachers,* and it will be a recurring topic of emphasis in this book.

The Achievement Dimension

The data shown in Table 3.1 provide an example of the results of good teaching. During the year in which these test scores were collected, the teaching of reading was, by all accounts, highly effective. Instruction both challenged the better readers and was within reach of the poorer ones.

TABLE 3.1   Growth of Reading Achievement in Three Third-Grade Classes Having Superior Teaching Procedures*

	NUMBER OF PUPILS	
READING GRADE EQUIVALENT	*Beginning of Year*	*End of Year*
8.1–9.0	0	2
7.1–8.0	0	1
6.1–7.0	1	4
5.1–6.0	2	13
4.1–5.0	7	20
3.1–4.0	37	31
2.1–3.0	38	21
1.1–2.0	8	1

*Adapted from W. W. Cook and T. Clymer, "Accelerating and retardation." In N. B. Henry (Ed.), *Individualizing instruction: The sixty-first yearbook of the National Society for the Study of Education, Part 1*. Chicago: The National Society for the Study of Education, 1962, 190–192.

At the beginning of the year, some students were reading only as well as average first graders, whereas others could read as well as typical fifth and sixth graders. Achievement ranged over six grade levels. By the end of a year of effective instruction, the bottom reader still performed at the first-grade level, whereas the best pupils were reading as well as typical seventh and eighth graders. The achievement now ranged over eight grade levels. *As a result of good teaching, the group of students became more heterogeneous.* That is, the range increased; the group became more variable.

Upon reflection, this long-recognized outcome (e.g., see Thorndike, 1924) is reasonable. Substantial evidence indicates that effective schooling expands differences among students. If students vary in capabilities and if teachers assist all to realize their potentials, then the more able will surely gain more than the less able. "Rich environments magnify differences in native ability; stultifying environments thwart them" (Mackenzie, 1983, p. 13).

Yet many people are dismayed when they encounter the principle that effective instruction increases variation among students. It seems unfair that the "rich" tend to get "richer," while the "poor" tend to get relatively "poorer." (Note the adverb "relatively.") Some teachers perceive themselves to be in a dilemma; they would like to decrease individual differences among students because these differences seem unfair (Arlin, 1984). Nevertheless, teachers are faced daily with differences in student achievement, and *these differences tend to increase with each year of schooling.*

Educators must recognize and come to grips with the principle that individual differences in achievement exist and that they tend to increase during the growing years. After making our peace with this reality, we can be *empowered to make constructive use of the principle for the benefit of all students.* Let's consider two more illustrations of the truth of the principle.

Two cars, a vintage Model A Ford and a new Corvette, have a race. Figure 3.3 shows the progress of the race. At the end of the first hour, the Model A has gone 50 miles, while the Corvette has gone 100 miles; although they started together, they are now 50 miles apart. At the end of the

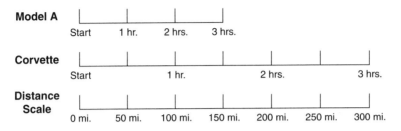

FIGURE 3.3   Car Race. The longer they race, the farther apart they are.

second hour, the respective cars have covered 100 and 200 miles; they are now 100 miles apart. At the end of the third hour, they are 150 miles apart. *The longer they race, the further apart they get.*

It is worth noting that the greater distance traveled by the faster car could be exhibited either in distance from the starting point or in travel on interesting side excursions. Similarly, the greater achievement of some students can be manifested in the *level* of achievement and/or in the *breadth* of achievement.

Now if you were the mechanic for both cars, could you change this outcome? Could you keep the range of distances from increasing over time? This could be done in one of two ways. On the one hand, you could try to make the Model A go faster. However, despite being in splendid condition, it just does not have the horsepower to go as fast as the new Corvette. On the other hand, you could try to slow the Corvette down. You might disconnect a spark plug.

A classroom analogy to the second method would be to prevent the more able readers from reading during the year. Such destructive actions could decrease variability in student achievement over time. In typical instructional situations, however, it is desirable that all students be helped to achieve their potential. When time is held constant, we know of no constructive actions that will decrease individual differences in level and breadth of achievement.

For a final example, consider the increase in individual differences in human height during the growing years. Table 3.2 reports the mean stature of males and females at several ages. The amount of individual difference is reported by the use of the standard deviation—a widely used

TABLE 3.2   Height in Inches at Selected Ages*

	MALES		FEMALES	
AGE	*Mean*	*Standard Deviation*	*Mean*	*Standard Deviation*
1	30.1	1.2	29.6	1.1
3	37.8	1.4	37.5	1.4
6	46.1	1.8	45.8	1.9
18	69.8	2.4	65.1	2.2

*Summarized from three sources: L. M. Bayer and N. Bayley, *Growth diagnosis* (2nd ed.). Chicago: University of Chicago Press, 1976; R. W. McCammon (1970). *Human growth and development.* Springfield, IL: Thomas; and Pomerance, H. H., & Krall, J. M. (1979). *Growth standards in children.* New York: Harper & Row.

measure of variability that will be explained in Chapter 11. For each gender, the general trend is for variability in height to increase during the growing years.

If you were responsible for the diet of these children, could you prevent the differences in stature from increasing with the passage of time? Indeed you could. You could see to it that tall youngsters were undernourished. Or, once people attained a height of 5 feet or so, you could starve them. Such solutions are reminiscent of Procrustes, the mythical Greek innkeeper referred to in Chapter 2 who had a compulsion that all his guests should fit his bed. Recall that to achieve this fit, he chopped the feet off some guests and stretched others on the rack to make them "fit" the bed. Dismissing such cruel and destructive procrustean options, providing the best nutrition available to every child would be the ethical choice. As a result, you would expect differences in height to expand as the years pass.

It is important to understand that we in no way suggest that teachers should be content to let low achievers stay low or be fatalistic about the status of individual students. On the contrary, ethical practice demands that we strive to maximize the achievement of *all* students. Nor is there any implication that we should necessarily treat students of varying abilities in the same manner. Remember the adage that there is nothing so unequal as the equal treatment of unequals! Or, as an ethics philosopher more recently asserted in a much broader context, "The basic principle of equality does not require equal or identical *treatment;* it requires equal consideration. Equal consideration for different beings may lead to different treatment . . ." (Singer, 2000, p. 29). Thus, dietitians should not prepare identical diets for people having different nutritional needs, mechanics shouldn't give all vehicles the same kind of fuel, and teachers shouldn't give all students the same reading materials. It is appropriate to provide different treatments to different individuals in ways to help each attain her or his maximum potential.

These diverse examples have shown that when individual differences are exhibited as achievement, they tend to increase during periods of growth. We shall now consider what happens when individual differences are directed into the time-it-takes-to-reach-a-target dimension.

The Time Dimension

If individual differences are banished from the achievement dimension, they inevitably will appear in the time dimension. This occurs when we specify a task that students should be able to perform and then have them work on it until it is achieved. For example, consider the following Mager-type objective: "When asked to, the child correctly spells 'cat.'"

Because most people eventually attain this aim, virtually no individual differences exist in level or breadth of achievement. All the readers of this book probably are equal in spelling "cat." Although little if any variability is present in student *achievement* or *performance,* it nevertheless took people varying *amounts of time* to master the task. The individual differences were channeled into the time dimension; that is, individual differences found expression as variable amounts of time people took to reach the target. If another task, such as spelling "bird," had been undertaken, the total amount of instruction required for all pupils to master both tasks would have been more variable than that needed to master only the first. In the time dimension, too, it is evident that individual differences increase as students move through an instructional sequence.

The three examples presented earlier now will be reexamined to show how individual differences can be cast in the time-it-takes-to-reach-an-objective dimension rather than the amount-of-achievement dimension. If, for the height example, we were to specify that each child is expected to attain some predetermined height, say 4 feet, 9 inches, we could note when each attained this stature and disregard the extent by which the arbitrary threshold was missed or surpassed. The first of a class-sized group might reach this height by about 8 years of age, whereas the last in the group might achieve it near age 14. Nearly all will reach the modest fixed height, but the time required to reach it will vary by several years.

In the car example, suppose each car is to be driven a fixed distance of 300 miles. At 50 miles per hour, the Model A will require 6 hours to travel this distance, while the Corvette, traveling twice as fast, will require only 3 hours. When distance, or achievement, is held constant, individual differences appear entirely in the time-it-takes-to-get-there dimension. The greater the distance, the greater the difference between the cars' traveling times.

Finally, in the reading illustration, one could specify that each pupil is to attain a grade-equivalent score of at least 3.0. Some children in a typical school may reach this arbitrary level while they are still in first grade, whereas others may be well beyond the sixth grade before attaining it. It takes people vastly different amounts of time to reach the same level.

Choosing the Dimension

Individual differences, then, are always with us. Yet teachers and other professionals must make critically important practical decisions concerning whether individual differences shall be exhibited as differences in the amount of student achievement (i.e., in the achievement dimension) or as differences in the amount of time it takes them to reach a particular level of proficiency (i.e., in the time dimension). A pivotal contention of this book is that this important professional decision should *not* be the same in all settings; it should *depend upon the instructional context.* Much more will be said about this in Chapter 4.

Figure 3.4 shows the inverse relationship between the exhibition of individual differences in (a) the level or breath of achievement and (b) the time it takes to reach a specified learning target. If the left-hand end of the seesaw goes up as far as possible, then people achieve differing amounts of success in a fixed amount of time. Inversely, if the other end goes up as far as possible, then people differ in the amount of time it takes them to achieve at a fixed level and breadth.

Of course, it is sometimes desirable to direct some of a group's variability into each dimension. For example, one could decide to have the Model A driven for 8 hours to achieve a distance of 400 miles and have the Corvette driven for 6 hours to cover 600 miles. The cars would then differ in both ways, but they wouldn't differ as much in either dimension as they would if the other dimension were held constant. In the classroom, poor spellers might spend more time studying than the best spellers, but not enough to equal their performance.

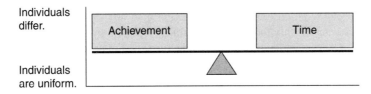

FIGURE 3.4 **Manifestation of Individual Differences**

Figure 3.4 represents the absolute necessity of individual differences surfacing in some way. It is not possible to have all students reach the same level of achievement in the same amount of time. If equal learning time and other resources are desired, as they are in many current forms of schooling, then inequalities in achievement seem inevitable. If equality of achievement is chosen, as it is in concepts such as mastery learning, then inequality of time seems necessary (Arlin, 1984). One *or* the other end of the seesaw can be depressed by circumstance or by design, but it is not possible for both ends to go down at the same time.

Some mastery learning advocates (e.g., Bloom, 1976; Guskey, 1997) have argued that mastery learning strategies offer the potential of simultaneously reducing or eliminating individual differences in both learning rates and achievement level. However, both theory (e.g., Glass & Smith, 1978) and experimental findings (e.g., Slavin, 1987b) challenge the realism of such dreams (also see Gustafsson & Undheim, 1996). If teachers pursue mastery learning in hopes that individual differences in both dimensions will simultaneously shrink, they are likely to be as disappointed as seekers of the Holy Grail or the Fountain of Youth. It is as futile to declare war on individual differences as it is maladaptive to stick one's head in the sand.

Our goals along these lines should be to *accept*—not deny—the reality of individual differences and then to have the professional insight to *direct them wisely* between the time and achievement dimensions. This combination of acceptance and choice *empowers* educators to make the best of their opportunities.

Cautions Concerning Individual Differences

We have seen that good teaching increases student differences in the achievement or in the time dimension. Thus, the absence of an increase in a group's variability suggests that good teaching has *not* taken place. However, an increase does *not* necessarily mean that all is well; individual differences can be increased by undesirable, as well as by desirable, means. For example, consider poor readers who could be deprived of suitable reading material, the Model A that could be driven on flat tires, or short children who could be underfed. Therefore, a change in a group's variability during instruction is *not* an appropriate isolated basis by which to evaluate the quality of instruction.

A note of caution should also be sounded concerning basic competency testing programs. Suppose a board of education decided to deny promotion until students reach a certain level of performance. Unless much care is taken, that established threshold may result in far more failures than anticipated.[1]

Indeed, in light of the research findings concerning adverse consequences of retention (e.g., Shepard & Smith, 1990; Paris & Cunningham, 1996), it probably would be wise to refrain from use of rigid mastery thresholds (i.e., specified minimum level of performance for mastery) for this purpose. Great care and sound professional judgment are needed for setting realistic mastery thresholds (i.e., minimum acceptable scores) for basic competency testing programs.

It is easy to blunder into one or another subtle form of the expectation that everyone will be at least average (e.g., "We expect all our students to be able to read at grade level"). Alas, we don't live in Garrison Keillor's fictional Lake Wobegon, where all children are above average. Expectations of bringing everyone up to average ignore the existence of individual differences.

---

[1]For example, suppose that a board of education, unaware of how much variability exists among sixth graders in reading, specified that students' grade-equivalent scores on a certain reading test must be at least 5.0 before promotion from sixth grade. The result would be that an appalling 30 to 40 percent of sixth graders in a typical school would be retained!

THINKING CAP EXERCISE 3.1   ???

First answer each of the following questions. Then proceed to the key to score it. For any item you missed, study the explanation.

1. The authors contend that individual differences in achievement should be
   A. ignored.
   B. denied.
   C. minimized.
   D. maximized.
   E. understood and controlled.

2. Into which dimension(s) will good teachers direct individual differences?
   A. The time dimension only.
   B. The achievement dimension only.
   C. Whichever dimension or combination of dimensions is most suitable for the subject matter.
   D. Whichever dimension appeals most to the teacher.
   E. Neither dimension, because good teaching eliminates individual differences.

3. If you were trying to teach a class of monolingual, English-speaking seventh graders to spell 20 Spanish nouns perfectly, about how long would it probably take the slowest student in the class to learn the lesson?
   A. About 10% longer than the fastest student in the class
   B. About 25% longer than the fastest student in the class
   C. About 50% longer than the fastest student in the class
   D. Several times as long as the fastest student in the class

4. If a class spent a semester studying high-school biology and all students devoted the same amount of time to the course, then achievement at the end of the semester on a comprehensive test of biology would probably be
   A. more variable than at the beginning of the semester.
   B. about as variable as at the beginning of the semester.
   C. less variable than at the beginning of the semester.

REFLECTION ON THINKING CAP 3.1

ITEM	KEY	COMMENTS
1.	E	This is a major principle. If you chose option D, see the first caution on page 51.
2.	C	See page 50. The following section also will assist in making this vital decision.
3.	D	This issue was not specifically covered, but the examples cited may enable you to guess. Only option D is in the right ballpark. Variability is usually great; it often takes slower students three to seven times as long to reach a mastery threshold as it takes faster learners (Gettinger, 1984).
4.	A	Variability increases during periods of growth. When instructional time and other resources are held constant, variability in level and breadth of achievement will increase. See pages 46–49.

Recap

We have examined individual differences from an unusual perspective, focusing on only the aspects of this broad topic that are germane to context-adaptive planning. Individual differences in achievement are universal, and they can be exhibited in either or both of two ways:

1. As differences in the level and/or breadth of *achievement*
2. As the *time* it takes to achieve at some prespecified level

KINDS OF SUBJECT MATTER

Many things are taught in schools. The various types of subject matter differ in multiple ways (e.g., knowledge vs. motor skills, spelling vs. science, basic vs. advanced, facts vs. applications, and knowledge vs. dispositions). Instructional methods that are well suited to some kinds of content are often seriously ill suited to other kinds. Indeed, it would be as naive to expect a particular set of teaching methods (e.g., discovery learning, mastery learning, or cooperative learning) to work well with all kinds of subject matter as it is to expect a particular kind of vehicle to be suitable in all terrains.

Reason suggests that the dimension—time or achievement—to which a teacher should direct individual differences for one kind of subject matter will differ from that which is appropriate for other kinds of subject matter. The kind of material to be taught should also influence the kind of learning theory upon which instruction is based, the kind of transfer of learning that should be fostered, the kind of instructional objectives that are functional, and the way in which student achievement is assessed, expressed, and interpreted. Thus, subject matter is not an isolated factor; *it has implications for much of what teachers do.* This section explores some of these implications and lays foundations for others that will be considered later.

Subject matter can be categorized in many ways. Two classifications that are helpful in matching the kind of material with appropriate expression of individual differences, instruction for transfer of learning, and student assessment are treated in this section. One distinction to be made is that between "stuff" that can readily be described or specified in its entirety versus "stuff" that cannot be laid out in full detail. We will refer to the first kind of subject matter as **explicit** and to the other as **expansive.** Another helpful distinction we will make is between subject matter that is more or less **masterable** versus material that is **developmental.**[2]

Figure 3.5 represents these two contrasts of subject matter. The contrast between explicit and expansive is depicted as a continuum of degree of explicitness, and the contrast between masterable and developmental is portrayed as a continuum of degree of masterability. For convenience, each of these continua, which can range from low to high, has been divided into only two regions. This division yields four cells (one of which will turn out to be empty). Let's consider the kinds of material that fit into the respective parts of the figure.

Explicit, Masterable Subject Matter

Some subject matter can be clearly described by fairly short statements. One way of identifying such clear-cut material is by use of Mager-type objectives, as described in Chapter 2. Four examples of such objectives for content that is both highly masterable and very specifiable (i.e., explicit) follow (cell A in Figure 3.5).

1. When presented with randomly ordered flash cards of the 26 capital letters of the English alphabet, the pupil will orally name at least 25 of the letters correctly.

---

[2]The term "developmental" is used in this book in the sense that it was used in Chapter 2 in describing Gronlund-type objectives. In contrast to mastery objectives or masterable curricular material, developmental objectives and expansive subject matter cannot be mastered; learning is open-ended and unending.

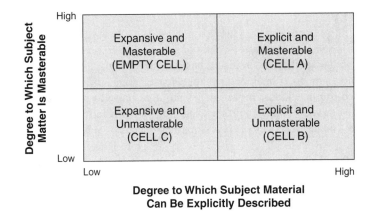

FIGURE 3.5   Dimensions for Classifying Subject Matter.

2. When approaching electric traffic signals on foot, the child will await the green light each time before crossing each of three different intersections.
3. During free play, the toddler will get to the toilet before urinating with no more than one accident per day.
4. After completing training for the assembly-line job, the worker will correctly install the five bolts on each unit with no more than one faulty installation per 100 units.

For teachers of primary-level pupils or of students who have behavioral or intellectual disabilities, this kind of objective may be rather typical of a significant part of the curriculum. It is essential for such material to be learned. It is reasonable and appropriate to demand that students *master* explicit tasks such as these. Their mastery is *essential* for minimal level functioning and/or for successful study of new material.

When it is essential that students master certain basic material, individual differences should be directed into the time dimension. The teacher will drill each child on the letters of the alphabet until they are mastered. Society cannot afford variability in how people respond to traffic lights; if it takes one child five times as long as another to learn to stop for red lights, so be it! Each child will eventually master bladder control, but the ages at which this is achieved will differ dramatically. Each industrial trainee must master the job before it is profitable to put the trainee on the assembly line. These are the conditions that characterize one set of circumstances in instruction and assessment. These conditions are called **Context A** in our approach to context-adaptive planning.

In each of these examples, the material can be mastered. One could, of course, quibble over exactly how mastery is defined. Mastery of the alphabet could just as well have been defined as 24 out of 26 letters instead of 25 out of 26, or the toddler could have been allowed only two or three accidents per week instead of one per day. Nevertheless, the idea of mastery can reasonably be applied. Teachers would have little difficulty in agreeing on which pupils had mastered the names of the capital letters or the definition of the six trigonometric functions. Likewise, therapists would be in substantial agreement concerning clients' success in overcoming bed-wetting or smoking. This kind of explicit, easily specified material can sensibly be said to be masterable. Because we would know when total command of the skill or domain was present, we can express a mastery threshold as a percentage of total mastery.

The concept of **subject matter domain** is helpful in contrasting the kind of material discussed in this section with those of later sections. In some instructional situations, the domain is very limited. Explicit subject matter can be mastered; that is, one can attain a total command of it. For example, there are only 10 Hindu-Arabic numerals. In teaching such material, we can drill on every element of the domain. We don't need to be very concerned with transfer of learning because we can teach everything in the domain. (We will qualify this statement later, but for now, let us take it as superficially true.)

Before leaving the discussion of cell A, shown in the upper-right-hand cell of Figure 3.5, it should be mentioned that *not all easily specifiable, masterable content domains merit being mastered.* For example, most readers could master the names and sequence of all English monarchs since 1066 or the name of every bone in the human body. Yet few of us need to master such material. (Just as a reminder: How *did* you fare on the state capitals test in Chapter 1?)

When it is vital for learners to master certain foundational material, individual differences should be channeled into the time-to-reach-the-mastery-threshold dimension. When it isn't particularly important for students to achieve mastery of subject matter, even if it is possible, then individual differences should be directed into the achievement dimension. We will see shortly that when the material in cell A isn't deemed important enough for us to demand its mastery, we do not assign it to Context A.

Explicit, Developmental Subject Matter

Let's open our examination of cell B of Figure 3.5 by contrasting it with cell A. One can reasonably claim to have mastered telephone dialing, the 100 addition facts, or bladder control. It isn't arrogant to claim mastery of such basic tasks. But can one reasonably proclaim oneself a master at golf, speed keyboarding, or endurance in unicycling marathons? No. There is an important distinction between the kinds of subject matter of the two lists in Table 3.3. The left-hand list consists of explicit content that, for all practical purposes, has a ceiling above which one cannot progress; that is, subject matter that can be mastered. When material of this type is taught, it is often important that each student master it.

However, when subject matter like that listed in the right-hand side of Table 3.3 is taught, there is no point beyond which we cease to value further achievement of excellence. We aren't

TABLE 3.3   Examples of Masterable and Unmasterable, Explicit Content

MASTERABLE	UNMASTERABLE
Telephone dialing	Golf
Letter names	Bowling
Multiplication facts	Multiplication speed
Bladder control	Pole vaulting
Trigonometric functions	Keyboarding speed

prepared to set a level so low that virtually everyone will eventually reach it (e.g., keyboard at least 15 words per minute) and then be uninterested in advancement beyond that modest level. Nor would we set a high-jump bar at 4 feet and remove all the pegs beyond that height. Neither sports fans nor track coaches would stand for that! We are *not content to settle for universal mediocrity.* Rather, we wish to enable each student to *develop* as much as possible within the available time.

A second important distinction between the two kinds of well-defined subject matter listed in Table 3.3 is that *masterable content is sometimes, although not always, essential for successful study of subsequent material.* Some such subject matter is inherently sequential. Children must know the letters' names before learning to spell. Trigonometry students need to know the six trigonometric functions before they can go very far in the subject. Pupils need to know the addition facts before they can efficiently study subtraction or multiplication. These examples illustrate Context A material.

On the other hand, *a certain level of proficiency of unmasterable material is usually not essential for successful study of subsequent material.* Such subject matter usually isn't inherently sequential. Students needn't reach a fixed level of skill on a particular golf course before learning tennis or before playing golf on a more difficult course. Pupils don't have to be able to multiply at some particular speed before learning to divide. Students don't have to be able to keyboard prose at some predetermined speed or accuracy before they learn how to keyboard tables.

For subject matter that is not essential for students to master, most or all of the individual differences should be directed into the achievement dimension. We would not insist that students attain some arbitrary speed in running before allowing them to move on to archery. Rather, we would sensibly hold time constant and let the individual differences be exhibited in level of achievement. Nor would we demand some particular level of achievement in basketball free throws before allowing students to practice dribbling. Here, too, individual differences should be channeled into the achievement dimension.

Cell B material, along with other material, will later be assigned to **Context B.**

Expansive, Developmental Subject Matter

Now let's look at the lower-left cell of Figure 3.5 (cell C). This cell contains the kind of subject matter that properly dominates most teachers' instruction as well as the interventions of most counselors. It dominates because most subject matter (especially that which is taught beyond the first two or three years of school and is not categorized as remedial instruction) cannot be fully laid out in detail. For example:

- Application of the Bill of Rights to current events
- Knowledge and attitudes from a third-grade unit on India
- Resolution of interpersonal conflicts harmoniously and equitably
- Appreciation of Beethoven
- Silent reading comprehension
- Use of metacognitive strategies to minimize emotional distress

Such content cannot with reasonable effort be specified in explicit detail. The instructional objectives should prominently provide for intentional transfer of learning. We should not be content that students merely can perform preidentified tasks at specified levels. They should be able to *apply* what they have learned to new situations that haven't been specifically taught.[3] Consider Thorndike's example of a unit of instruction on the Bill of Rights.

> We could test an individual's ability to identify or to recall each of the first 10 amendments to the Constitution. But if we were concerned with the meaning, the significance, and the application of these same 10 amendments in contemporary America, how could we meaningfully define and sample from that domain? In this instance the notion of "mastery" slips through our fingers (Thorndike, 1997, p. 203).

Even justices of the Supreme Court have not mastered all of the applications of the Bill of Rights. If they all had, then all relevant decisions would be unanimous!

Indeed, it isn't possible to master such subject matter. Who has achieved the ultimate in conflict resolution, appreciation of Beethoven, or insights into India? Nobody! Because we cannot define or conceptualize total mastery of such domains, *we cannot express a mastery threshold as a percentage of total mastery.*

Nor is it necessary to attain some arbitrary level of achievement in such subject matter. Why not? Because such material is not inherently sequential. The major purpose of units like these could be achieved with entirely different subject matter. Counseling or instruction concerning conflict resolution could be based on anything from domestic harmony to classroom management to industrial labor relations. A Beethoven unit could for some purposes just as well be a unit on Brahms. Most of the important objectives of a unit on India could be attained just as well by a unit on China. Moreover, if both countries were to be studied, it wouldn't matter which was studied first. Hence, teachers have great latitude in selecting subject matter to use in pursuit of this kind of important learning outcome. This is indeed one of the more stimulating and pleasurable aspects of teaching.

When subject matter (a) cannot be mastered, (b) needn't be handled at a given level of proficiency before students can move on, and (c) cannot conveniently be specified in detail, then individual differences should be directed largely or wholly into the achievement dimension. We define these conditions as **Context C** in context-adaptive planning. We cannot hope for students to "master" every possible application. Nor is there some point beyond which teachers become disinterested in the attainment of greater depth and breadth of learning. Thus, here, too, mastery thresholds (i.e., specified lowest acceptable performances) are not meaningful. Each student should be helped to achieve as much as possible within the available time. With material that is neither masterable nor highly explicit, no procrustean attempt should be made to stretch or compress everyone's learning to fit some arbitrary level of achievement.

It may be useful to digress to reemphasize the point that holding instructional time constant does *not* imply holding instructional method or curriculum constant. A rich variety of subject matter and teaching techniques could be used in a given unit according to appropriateness for the students. Thus, every attempt is made to help each learner achieve as much as possible either by using uniform content and teaching methods or, more often, by varying them.

To return to the main point, in the kinds of teaching that most teachers do most of the time, the subject matter domain is too expansive to be covered in its entirety. For example, applications for the

---

[3]An occasional reader asks for experimental evidence of statements such as these. The perspective that we build in Chapters 3 and 4 is built more on logic rather than on empirical evidence (e.g., the obvious foolishness of demanding some specified level of proficiency in running speed before allowing students to study archery). Too, much of the perspective is more philosophical and value oriented than empirical (e.g., note all the "shoulds" in this paragraph).

Bill of Rights are virtually infinite. Moreover, the boundaries of the domain are not at all precise; it is debatable whether various borderline topics (e.g., the student newspaper or "hate" speech) are part of the domain. Subject matter that cannot be specified explicitly cannot be mastered. Therefore, the examples of expansive content all fall into the lower-left-hand cell of Figure 3.5.

The upper-left-hand cell of Figure 3.5 is empty. Why? Of course! No content exists that is masterable and should be mastered but cannot be explicitly specified.

Relating the Kind of Subject Matter to the Expression of Individual Differences

Table 3.4 summarizes the connection between the manifestations of individual differences and the types of subject matter that have been discussed. At the left of the table are the letters **A, B,** and **C.** These letters provide arbitrary labels by which we shall refer to the respective kinds of subject matter. The table shows for each subject matter context the way in which individual differences can logically be exhibited.

At this point you should memorize the lettered contexts A, B, and C. In other words, we are announcing that grasp of Table 3.4 is Context A material because it will be elaborated on and used as a conceptual framework for numerous classroom assessment issues considered throughout this book. (Although knowledge of the table is Context A content, its *use* and application will be seen to be very much in Context C. An analogy may help. Memorizing the basic rules of bridge takes place in Context A because the rules are masterable and vital to those who wish to play the game. Yet applying the rules to the actual game is not masterable; the *use* of the rules to play bridge is Context C.)

Making Good Classification Decisions

When educators are charged with teaching certain subject matter, we urge them to thoughtfully classify it into Contexts A, B, or C so that their planning will be *sensitive to the context.* One reason is that the classification helps educators wisely decide how to cause individual differences to be exhibited. Other reasons are that the classification helps teachers wisely select the kinds of learning theory, transfer theory, and assessments that will serve their students best in the particular instructional context. These practical decisions are central to effective instruction and to effective student assessment.

Figure 3.6 may be helpful in making these classifications. It is organized as a flow chart in which three key questions are asked in sequence. The answers to these questions provide powerful hints about optimal context decisions.

TABLE 3.4   Relationships between Manifestation of Individual Differences and Types of Subject Matter

CONTEXT	PRINCIPAL MANIFESTATION OF INDIVIDUAL DIFFERENCES	TYPE OF SUBJECT MATTER
A	Time dimension	Explicit, vital, and masterable
B	Achievement dimension	Explicit, but cannot or need not be mastered
C	Achievement dimension	Expansive and unmasterable

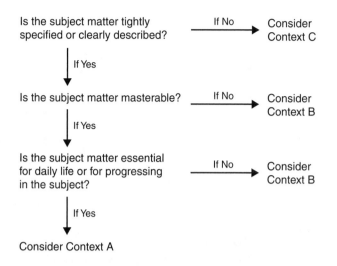

FIGURE 3.6   Flow Chart for Recognizing Instructional Contexts

THINKING CAP EXERCISE 3.2   ???

Because the classification of subject matter is so important, let's engage in some practice. Use Figure 3.6 to classify the following content domains by context.

1. A spelling lesson's emphasis on mastering the spelling of 20 specific words
2. A counseling client's intent to quit smoking cigarettes
3. A person's attempt to play darts well
4. A class's study of the meaning of the Pledge of Allegiance
5. A keyboarding class's learning of the fingers' "home positions"
6. A keyboarding class's pursuit of accurate keyboarding
7. A child with mental retardation who needs to learn basic self-care skills (Please assume the goals are realistic.)
8. The need for a pupil with a speech disorder to learn to pronounce the difference between "s" and "z" sounds in a wide variety of words
9. A library-orientation unit on how to use the library computer to find a book's call number, given its exact title

10. A library-orientation unit's instruction on using the library database to find periodical articles on subjects ranging from simple (e.g., "dogs" or "allergies") to complex (e.g., "homophobia among minority social workers" or "the contribution of lead poisoning to the downfall of the Roman Empire")
11. The attempts of an instructor of a 300-member college freshman class to learn the names of members of the class
12. Your attempts to make wise context-classification decisions

REFLECTIONS ON THINKING CAP EXERCISE 3.2

ITEM	KEY	COMMENTS
1.	Context A	The answers to the first two questions in Figure 3.6 are clearly "yes." Because the item indicated that mastery was sought, then the third question also gets a "yes" answer.
2.	Context A	All three questions in Figure 3.6 would be answered "yes."

(Continued)

THINKING CAP EXERCISE 3.2   CONTINUED

ITEM	KEY	COMMENTS
3.	Context B	The first question in Figure 3.6 gets a "yes" answer; the second question gets a "no" (as would the third, if it were asked).
4.	Context C	The first question in Figure 3.6 is answered "no"; therefore, the other questions are moot.
5.	Context A	Regarding the third question in Figure 3.6, it is worthwhile for students of keyboarding to master "home positions" even though it isn't essential for *modest* achievement. The time spent in mastering the "home positions" will be richly repaid; therefore, the teacher is wise to demand mastery.
6.	Context C	The domain is as expansive as the things that could be transcribed. The difficulty of keyboarding is not uniform.
7.	Context A	However, if it turned out that the assumption of realism of the goal proved unfounded and the child simply couldn't learn all of the specified skills, then the teacher might well "back off" and answer the second question in Figure 3.6 with a "no," thereby classifying the skills as Context B.
8.	Context A	The comments for item 7 apply here, too.
9.	Context A	The task is the same for all books if the exact title is known.
10.	Context C	Even professional reference librarians have not reached a level beyond which more excellence would not be possible and desirable.
11.	Context B	The first two questions in Figure 3.6 are answered "yes," but the third is answered "no" by most people in this situation. (If there are only a dozen students in the class, most of us would answer the third question "yes," which would prompt a Context A classification.)
12.	Context C	The domain of possible decisions is virtually infinite. The difficulty of classifying these domains differs substantially. For example, in item 11, with 300 students or 5 students, the answer may be easy; but what about 25 or 80? The third question in Figure 3.6 doesn't have to be answered given the "no" to the first question. To address it, however, we might say that the subject is *very* important, yet no specifiable level of excellence is essential for later progress. This would suggest channeling *some* of the individual differences into each dimension. In Chapter 4, we will look at other hard to call situations.

Matching Learning Theories with Subject Matter

As discussed in Chapter 2, learning theories also carry major implications for classroom assessment practices. Whereas behavioral psychology dominated American education for parts of the twentieth century, cognitive orientations are now in greater favor and "students no longer are viewed as passive recipients taking in others' knowledge" (Airasian, 2001, p. 79).

We propose that educators neither align with a particular learning theory nor swing back and forth among them with the tides of fashion. Rather, we are convinced (and we hope convincing) that the nature of the subject matter one teaches has great bearing on the utility of various orientations toward human learning. It seems fruitful to *use different conceptions of learning for different kinds of subject matter.* The three kinds of subject matter identified above will now be aligned with compatible perspectives concerning human learning.

Explicit, Masterable, Vital Subject Matter (Context A). Some material can be explicitly described in its entirety, is masterable, and is important enough to merit mastery by each student. Examples are:

1. The 10 Hindu-Arabic numerals
2. The letters of the alphabet
3. Putting the left shoe on the left foot and the right shoe on the right foot

Each of these is a crystal-clear content domain with easily identified boundaries. Each is vital for subsequent learning.

Most of this kind of material typically does not have much inherent meaning. The need is to form sets of paired associations between stimuli and responses (e.g., 4 = I I I I). There is little in such content to involve one's personal interpretation or style or with which to meaningfully interact. We do not seek creativity; rather, we need conformity—4 must equal IIII or ΔΔΔΔ or **** for all of us. No originality *please*! When learning subject matter of this kind, students can reasonably be viewed as *passive receivers* of information. Therefore, behavioral learning theories are congenial to such material.

Most of the examples provided by behaviorists on the utility of task analysis and linear learning hierarchies have used subject matter for which such approaches make good sense. Subject matter such as the alphabet or numerals is inherently sequential. When intrinsic sequence exists, learning theories that provide for careful task analysis are attractive.

Explicit Subject Matter That Can't or Needn't Be Mastered (Context B). Some material can be specified clearly, but either (a) can't be mastered *or* (b) isn't generally deemed to be important enough to justify time and effort needed for mastery. Examples, respectively, of the two types of explicit material are:

1. Pole vaulting
2. The state capitals

With regard to the mostly psychomotor skills of the first type of explicit subject matter (e.g., the pole vaulting example), one may consider two approaches. First, a behavioral orientation seems suitable for the early phases when attention is on conditioning conventional techniques; a cognitive approach may be more appropriate in the later stages when attention shifts to such outcomes as self-analysis of performance and development of personal style. Second, a learning theory that emphasizes the importance of demonstration and imitation of modeled behaviors would be attractive; such a theory (Bandura, 1977, 1986) spans the behavioral–cognitive dichotomy, with leanings toward the cognitive.

With regard to subject matter of the second type of specifiable material (e.g., the second example), a straight behavioral approach is indicated. Such material lacks inherent meaning. The task is to condition rote associations between state names and names of their capitals. Students can't meaningfully interact with meaningless material. Better to treat learners as passive receptacles of this kind of information. The only thing that separates material such as the second example from Context A is the judgment that it isn't important enough to warrant channeling individual differences into the time dimension until *all* learners master it. Hence, the learning theory choice is the same as it would be in Context A.

Expansive Subject Matter That Can't Be Mastered (Context C).   A great deal of important subject matter is low in both specifiability and masterability. For example:

1. Applications of the Bill of Rights
2. Critical thinking

Such material is rich in inherent meaning with which learners should interact. Working with it causes students to form powerful and meaningful connections—to weave it into their cognitive structures. Not much inherent sequence or linear hierarchy exists here; particular elements need not ordinarily precede others or be mastered before one can tackle the others. Instructional emphasis should be on principles, insights, connections, and understandings.

INSTRUCTION AND ASSESSMENT FOR TRANSFER

A central thesis of this book is that various kinds of subject matter are best taught and assessed in different ways. Our next step in developing context-relevant teaching and assessment returns us to the topic of transfer of learning. After two kinds of transfer are identified, general teaching methods suitable for each will be outlined; these methods arise from the learning theories on which they are based. Then the different kinds of subject matter will be aligned with the appropriate kind of transfer.

Transfer of Learning Processes

A primary goal in teaching "is to prepare students to solve problems that they have not previously encountered" (Mayer & Wittrock, 1996, p. 47). We don't teach students math so that they can continue to do assigned problems; we teach them so that they can put math to work in such ways as shopping wisely. We don't teach science to enable youth to pass science tests; we teach it to empower them with ways of seeing the world and reasoning about it. "In education, transfer is the name of the game. Without full, rich transfer of what students learn, education has not done its job" (Tishman, Perkins, & Jay, 1995, p. 156).

   Transfer of learning can be defined as the processes by which something learned has an effect on the learning or recall of something else. Transfer can be positive or negative. When the effect of transfer is beneficial to learning or recalling something, it is positive. When the effect impairs the learning of something new or the recall of something old, negative transfer has occurred.

Positive transfer of learning is fundamental to education. Mental discipline, the prevailing prescientific learning theory of the nineteenth century, was dead wrong in contending that transfer occurs automatically without the mindful effort of teachers. A century of research has demonstrated that we cannot count on transfer to occur without targeted effort; *if we want our students to be able to transfer their learning, we have to work toward this aim.*

Kinds of Transfer

Transfer of learning has been widely researched since the early days of scientific psychology. It has been studied by psychologists and educators who held a behavioral perspective regarding learning, and it has been explored by scholars of various cognitive orientations. The literature generated by these separate scholarly traditions has tended to use the word "transfer" in rather different ways.

Salomon and Perkins (1989) suggested that there are actually two separate phenomena that, unfortunately, had not previously been differentiated. To cultivate awareness of the difference, they named these two distinct kinds of events low-road transfer and high-road transfer. These two kinds of transfer have received widespread contemporary recognition (e.g., Schunk, 2000; Woolfolk, 2001) and fit nicely into a context-adaptive approach to instruction and assessment.

Low-Road Transfer.   **Low-road transfer** of training is built on *substantial* and *varied practice* to the point that *automaticity* occurs. Good instruction for low-road transfer deliberately provides practice on an ever-increasing variety of tasks. Then low-road transfer occurs by means of *automatic elicitation* of these well-learned behaviors in new situations. For example, if you are proficient in using a variety of hand calculators, you can pick up an unfamiliar model and use it quite well without much conscious effort.

To use an example from Salomon and Perkins (1989), suppose you know how to drive a variety of cars well enough so that the actions are highly automatic. Then you need to drive a four-wheel truck. You wonder whether you can. However, your concerns evaporate when you get into the cab. The setting is strange, yet familiar. For example, the windshield is there to be seen through; the steering wheel is there to be steered with. All you have to do is drive as you always have. Although it feels a bit odd, it works quite well.

Although low-road transfer occurs automatically, it is best obtained by carefully designed instruction. Suppose primary pupils are learning the names of the lowercase letters of the alphabet. The letters are posted above the chalkboard and the teacher commits much time to their acquisition by means of drill and modeling. In the end, the pupils master the letter names. So where's the transfer?

Transfer wouldn't be a concern if the teacher did not intend that pupils be able to transfer their learning, for example, to be able to name letters found in places other than above chalkboards, printed on paper of various colors and textures, and printed in different sizes, colors, and fonts. Pupils should be able to automatically name a letter when confronted with one of a new size, font, and color. *To achieve low-road transfer, the teacher would be thoughtful and intentional in providing extensive and varied practice.* In much out-of-school learning, everyday life provides sufficient variety to enable many children to achieve learning for low-road transfer on their own without formal instruction.

High-Road Transfer.   **High-road transfer** of learning occurs when the learner *mindfully abstracts* knowledge from one situation and *applies* it to a new one. Not only does the teacher intend transfer, but *the student does, too.* High-road transfer via mindful abstraction can occur quickly in a way that is qualitatively different from the gradual extension of variation with practice that characterizes low-road transfer (Salomon & Perkins, 1989). Key to this difference between the two kinds of transfer is the *intentional generalization* beyond the context of the original learning in high-road transfer.

ENCAPSULATION

Throughout this book we attempt to trigger readers' high-road transfer. For example, when we refer to an earlier discussion of a topic (e.g., "As discussed in Chapter X"), we are seeking to activate readers' past learning so that it may be transferred and extended into a discussion. Likewise, when we mention that a topic will be treated more fully at a later point in the book (e.g., "We will address this topic more fully in Chapter XX"), we are alerting readers to mentally file a current discussion in a retrievable form in the expectation that it will be useful in the future.

Note the connotative differences between the phrases "low-road transfer of training" and "high-road transfer of learning." If not overdrawn, the distinction between "training" and "learning" is useful.

The hallmark of high-road transfer is intentional, effortful decontextualization of a principle, idea, strategy, or procedure which then may transfer. The abstraction must be understood. Memorizing a statement of an abstraction (e.g., Archimedes' Law of Buoyancy) without understanding does *not* result in transfer. Similarly, rotely playing major and minor scales without understanding the physics underlying whole and half-step intervals doesn't result in transfer for musical interpretation. Nor does reading lines from Shakespeare without valuing and internalizing the meaning of the passages result in generalized appreciation of the bard's work. The abstraction must be truly comprehended, not just learned as a formula (Salomon & Perkins, 1989).

High-road transfer involves learners *perceiving generalizability.* Powerful generalization is often achieved when a learner is able to meaningfully liberate a principle from the original setting—by *decontextualizing* it. That is, an idea is generalized beyond its original context.

Matching Kinds of Transfer with Kinds of Subject Matter

Explicit, Vital, Masterable Material (Context A).   When subject matter can, more or less, be explicitly specified in its entirety, it is both limited in size and closed, as Figure 3.7 shows. The dots represent the domain's few elements. The figure is closed, or complete, to signify that the explicit subject matter is stable and fixed. The boundary is solid and heavy to represent the clear-cut nature of the domain limits.

Examples of explicit, small, closed domains include:

1. Matching names of the three primary colors with appropriate color chips
2. Making change for a dollar for items costing less than a dollar
3. Focusing a given microscope

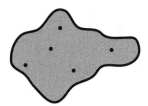

FIGURE 3.7   Limited, Closed Explicit Content Domain Suitable for Mastery Teaching

4. Naming the 26 letters in the English alphabet from printed letters
5. Naming the members of a certain class
6. Avoiding bed-wetting

"Wait a minute!" we hear a thoughtful reader exclaim. "Isn't transfer, at least low-road transfer, the name of the game in examples such as these? For example, aren't there many shades of each color? Isn't the difficulty of naming members of a class somewhat dependent upon whether they are in their seats or whether they are wearing their usual clothing and hair style? Don't we wish the child to avoid bed-wetting in a variety of beds? Is there, therefore, any such thing as a small, closed domain?"

Perhaps not. Yet relative to the much more expansive domains found in Context C, the distinction between small(er) and large(r) domains is very useful. Think of it this way: Teachers can rather easily agree which children have mastered the alphabet. Although there are many letter sizes and fonts, there are just 26 letters. Contrast that with applications of the First Amendment to the U.S. Constitution or with Archimedes' Principle! So yes, low-road transfer is the name of the game. The point is that it is *only* low-road transfer that is relevant in Context A where the domain is quite well defined and relatively small.

Drill is a technique by which many such domains are taught. The specific drill is *limited* to variations within the exact material that has been explicitly specified in the objective. At the same time, it deliberately is *systematically varied within* the narrow limits allowable. Each of the five elements shown in Figure 3.7 would be (a) explicitly identified, (b) directly taught, and (c) explicitly tested. Thus, *teaching and testing in Context A are sharply focused.* Although generalization to very similar stimuli is important, the focus in Context A is relatively sharp.

The amount of time a student spends on an essential, explicit, masterable unit should be whatever amount of time it takes to master it. In Context A, the aim of teaching and testing is mastery. Individual differences are relegated wholly or largely into the time dimension. (See Table 3.4.)

Explicit Subject Matter That Needn't or Can't Be Mastered (Context B).   When it comes to channeling individual differences, both explicit material that is not masterable and explicit masterable material that is not important enough to master can be treated in the same way. Individual differences are best channeled into the achievement dimension because there is no particular level of achievement at which it makes sense to end instruction.

Although the two kinds of content that lie in Context B of Table 3.4 are conveniently lumped together for most purposes, it will be worthwhile to separate them for the purposes of considering methods of teaching for transfer.

Explicit But Unmasterable Subject Matter.   Some material is in Context B because it isn't master-able. Most such subject matter is psychomotor. Examples of things that can be tightly or clearly specified but that can't be mastered include:

1. Weight lifting
2. Adding rapidly
3. Bowling

Such skills can be taught in the early phases in a manner quite similar to the way specifiable, masterable material is taught. Teachers guide student effort, reinforce desired behaviors, and provide for suitably distributed practice. Desired behaviors are conditioned; undesirable ones eliminated. Practice is varied to provide for low-road transfer.

After instruction is well under way, the role of the teacher may become less directive. The advanced weight lifter and the good bowler can continue to improve their performance without a teacher's continual guidance. Cognitive approaches are often more appropriate in later stages. Advanced students become able to evaluate their own performance mindfully and become relatively self-sufficient. At this point, one may pursue not only the low road to transfer via automatic elicitation of well-learned responses, but also the parallel high road to transfer via thoughtful self-evaluation. Students should be taught the performance criteria and be helped to become proficient in assessing themselves and others (Stiggins, 2001).

Explicit and Masterable But Nonessential Subject Matter.   Some material is in Context B because it is judged not to be important enough to merit mastery. Examples of specifiable and masterable subject matter that isn't important enough to be mastered are:

1. All the county seats in California
2. The value of π to 100 digits
3. Names and terms of office of all vice presidents of the United States

Such subject matter can be taught by the same methods as vital, masterable subject matter from Context A. When material lacks inherent meaning, drill is a key teaching method. The indicated route to transfer is the low road of extensive and varied practice. The only difference from Context A teaching is that because the content has been judged not to require mastery, mastery needn't be sought.

Expansive, Unmasterable Subject Matter (Context C).   When subject matter cannot be adequately laid out in its entirety, it is *broad or unlimited* in scope and/or *open*. Figure 3.8 represents an expansive content domain.

The dots in Figure 3.8 represent the multitude of elements of the domain. The figure is open, or incomplete, to represent the ever-changing subject matter of this dynamic domain. Although the boundaries of an expansive domain may be clear-cut in some places, they may be vague in others. For example, are Internet pornography, hate speech, and flag burning protected by the Bill of Rights? Because the domain contains a great number of present and future elements, it isn't feasible to specify each. This is now recognized even by some educators (e.g., Popham, 1994) who formerly advocated exhaustively detailed objectives.

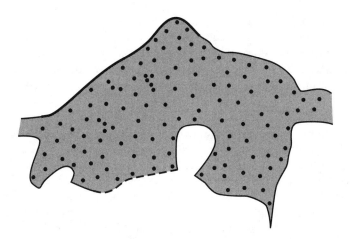

FIGURE 3.8   Broad, Open Expansive Content Domain Requiring Teaching for High-Road Transfer

This kind of expansive subject matter occupies most of the instructional time of most effective teachers. Examples of large, open domains include:

1. Current events
2. Reading comprehension
3. Classification use of the concept of "mammal"
4. Establishing and maintaining counseling rapport
5. Art appreciation
6. Automobile engine diagnosis
7. Musical composition
8. Planning and preparing nutritious meals

Cognitive theories of learning are congenial to such subject matter. Teaching methods include emphasis on understanding, intentional connection of new learning with prior knowledge, provision of different content for different students, use of problem-solving strategies, and discovery learning. Techniques such as group discussion, peer tutoring, and cooperative learning help students assimilate new information and accommodate their preexisting cognitive structures to the new material. Much exists in such subject matter with which a person can meaningfully interact.

High-road transfer receives primary attention in teaching expansive, unmasterable material and in assessing student command of it. The central role of mindful transfer will now be illustrated with a fifth-grade unit on mammals.

In selecting the specific subject matter for such a unit, perhaps only one point is vital—all mammal species provide milk for their young. The teacher could write one or more specific, explicit, masterable, Mager-type behavioral objectives about this point because that characteristic of mammals is closed. Other important characteristics of mammals, such as endothermy and the presence of a backbone, could also (although need not) be declared essential. We could develop a short set of Context A explicit masterable objectives for these elements.

What about the Context C part of the unit? The contrasting domains of *illustrative* mammals and of *sample* nonmammals are enormous. Hence, we can teach only a *sample* of the domain. We want to pick a few examples to show its breadth. Cows might be studied because they are well known as producers of milk; cats as a familiar example of carnivorous mammals; mice as an example of rodents and small mammals; bats as flying mammals; kangaroos as marsupials; seals as aquatic mammals; elephants as herbivorous and large mammals; humans as a species of special significance; and monkeys because they are especially interesting to children. Having picked these examples to show the diversity of the domain, teachers would select with equal care several noninstances of the concept in order to show the domain's limits.

The particular teaching examples are not chosen because they are necessarily more important than others that could just as well have been selected (e.g., dolphins instead of seals or hamsters instead of mice). The illustrative examples are selected purposefully because of their convenience and utility in maximizing positive high-road transfer of learning and in minimizing negative transfer.

After pupils have studied instances and noninstances of the concept by use of the original sample of animals, new examples would be selected to *provide instructional practice in transfer.* Pictures of animals not previously studied might be presented and pupils could be asked to classify the animals as mammals or nonmammals. Or, if the class had previously studied fish, amphibians, and reptiles, we could present pictures of animals not previously studied and have students classify them into these four classes, thereby integrating review and new learning. Thus, *high-road transfer is the focus of our objectives, our teaching,* and our testing.

We don't seek mastery of what is specifically sampled to be taught. Rather, we want *insight, understanding, and generalization throughout and beyond the domain.* We, therefore, cannot sensibly specify some level of achievement in the specific sample of material that happened to be taught and demand that all students come up to that threshold or level. There is no particular level of competence that a person needs to attain before proceeding to the study of birds. Indeed, birds could have been studied before mammals. Therefore, teachers can best let individual differences be exhibited as level and breadth of achievement.

As we have seen, much of a teacher's attention to high-road transfer in this unit would be aimed at transfer about mammals. Important as this transfer within the domain of mammals is, it is not enough. The high road to transfer of learning offers a much broader vision than mere transfer *within* a domain. High-road transfer should also be sought *beyond* the domain of mammals. For example, consider the matter of classification. If this important topic were new to pupils, the mammal unit would provide a wonderful opportunity to introduce the subject of classification to a class. If the topic had been studied before, the mammal unit would offer a splendid chance to spiral back upon it in order to review and enrich notions of classification. *Instruction and assessment in Context C are not narrowly targeted.*

The mammal unit reveals how four instructional topics relate to assessment. Assessment occurs in an instructional context; to be effective, it must be aligned with appropriate instructional objectives. In this example, objectives that pointed to high-road transfer were needed.

Following are several things to keep in mind in teaching for transfer of learning. They are adapted from Tishman, Perkins, and Jay's (1995) *The Thinking Classroom.*

■ **Provide models of transfer.** Show "how people, including yourself, transfer knowledge, skills, and dispositions from one situation to another. Note examples of how transfer occurs within a subject, across subject matter, and in everyday life" (Tishman, Perkins, & Jay, 1995, pp. 161).

■ **Explain the importance of transfer, highlight particular connections, and help pupils anticipate applications.** When teaching a topic, spend some time discussing *anticipated applications* and thinking about where students might use what they are learning. Ask students to "seek connections between the topic and other things it connects to, within the same subject matter, in different subject matters, or in everyday life" (Tishman, Perkins, & Jay, 1995, pp. 161–162).

■ **Interact with students and prompt them to interact with one another to encourage transfer.** Engage students in discussion and activities that encourage transfer through interaction with you and one another. Use very *diverse* "examples representing very different kinds of applications, so that students are prompted to apply the content widely" (Tishman, Perkins, & Jay, 1995, p. 162).

■ **Revisit transferred ideas.** After teaching a topic, be sure to revisit transferable ideas within the next few days and again in a few weeks to enhance transfer from the topic and to enhance retention of the more powerful ideas—that is, the transferable ones—in the topic.

■ **Assess for transfer.** Recognize students and encourage them to recognize each other when they transfer knowledge, skills, strategies, or disposition from one setting to another.

THINKING CAP EXERCISE 3.3   ???

For each item, an instructional unit is listed. Designate each unit as Context A, B, or C, paying particular attention to the kind of transfer that should be sought. Each context may be used once, more than once, or not at all. Use Table 3.5 on page 70 if you need it..

1. Conjugations of regular Spanish verbs (for students of Spanish)
2. Appreciation of Mark Antony's funeral address in a literature unit studying the play *Julius Caesar*
3. An elementary-school unit on making change
4. A fourth-grade unit on Tibet

KEY TO THINKING CAP EXERCISE 3.3

ITEM	KEY	COMMENTS
1.	A	This is essential knowledge for students of Spanish. It can be mastered, and it is important enough to merit mastery. Teaching is focused on low-road transfer.
2.	C	The content domain is not clear; that is, appreciation is expansive. Therefore, it could not be treated as Context A or B.

(If, rather than appreciation, memorization were sought, then the subject matter domain would be clear; hence it could be treated as Context A or B. Because few teachers would view it as important enough to demand mastery, its memorization fits best in Context B.)

(For the actor playing Mark Antony, memorizing the address would, of course, be Context A; its effective delivery would be Context C.)

3.	A	The content is relatively specifiable, relatively masterable, and important enough to merit mastery for low-road transfer.
4.	C	The specific content matters little; the principal aims should transcend the specifics of Tibet. Teaching is not narrowly focused. High-road transfer of learning is the major goal.

TABLE 3.5   Relationships among Subject Matter, Individual Differences, Instructional Objectives, Learning Theories, and Methods for Transfer of Learning

CONTEXT	TYPE OF SUBJECT MATTER	PRINCIPAL MANIFESTATION OF INDIVIDUAL DIFFERENCES	TYPE OF INSTRUCTIONAL OBJECTIVE	FAMILY OF LEARNING THEORIES	TYPE OF INSTRUCTION FOR TRANSFER
A	Entire content of small, closed domain readily identified in behavioral terms; content vital and masterable	Time dimension	Explicit, masterable	Behavioral	Much specific training, low-road transfer
B	Tasks readily specified in behavioral terms, but cannot be mastered or are not important enough to merit mastery	Achievement dimension	Explicit, developmental	Mixed	Varied and/or specific training in early phases
C	Content of large and/or open domain cannot be specified in detail, but can be illustrated in behavioral terms; content not masterable	Achievement dimension	Expansive, developmental	Cognitive	Mainly teaching for understanding and transfer, high-road transfer

Be sure your tests assess student ability to transfer what they have learned. Assessing for transfer will be a major topic of discussion in Part II when we focus on developing assessments of complex learning.

CHAPTER RECAP

Education should be connected (Boyer, 1987); instruction should reveal the connections among areas of study. Why? To make the learning meaningful and to render it transferable on the high road. Educated people do not keep each area of knowledge in isolated compartments. On the contrary, they understand the connectedness of topics, are aware of the rich network of relationships among fields, and seek to enlarge and enrich their grasp and appreciation of this network.

To that end, Chapter 3 has laid a broad, instruction-oriented foundation for the study of educational assessment. Why? Because classroom assessment is connected to the kind of subject matter taught, to the way in which individual differences are best handled, to the way the material is most effectively taught, and to the kind of transfer that is best sought. This chapter has "broadened the picture" enough to reveal these connections with educational psychology and methods courses, to prompt readers to activate their prior learning, and to connect it to classroom assessment.

Four features of an integrated instructional/measurement framework were presented to provide *a rational foundation upon which to base important professional decisions.* This framework, after it is expanded and illustrated with a caplike graphic in Chapter 4, will enable teachers to orchestrate assessment with instruction.

Table 3.5 summarizes the portions of a three-part structure that have been developed to this point. The order of the first two columns has been rearranged because *the cornerstone is the subject matter. Characteristics of subject matter determine what is best done with individual differences, the perspective on learning that is most relevant, and the kind of transfer that is best sought.*

When subject matter domains are explicit, masterable, and essential, individual differences should be exhibited as time needed to master. Sharply focused behavioral approaches to learning and instruction are usually best suited to such material in pursuit of low-road transfer of training.

When skill or subject matter domains are explicit but either unmasterable or nonessential, objectives should reflect a "the-more-the-better" attitude. Individual differences, therefore, should be exhibited as level of achievement.

When, as is most often the case, subject matter is not very specifiable, masterable, or essential, individual differences should be expressed in level and breadth of achievement. Cognitive approaches to learning and instruction are typically well suited to such expansive material in pursuit of high-road transfer of learning.

INSTRUCTIONAL OBJECTIVES AND KINDS OF TESTS, SCORES, AND INTERPRETATIONS

CHAPTER OVERVIEW

CERTAIN FEATURES OF INSTRUCTIONAL OBJECTIVES

ANOTHER WAY OF CLASSIFYING TESTS
Mastery Tests
Differentiating Tests

THE ISSUE OF TEACHING TO THE TEST

TWO KINDS OF TEST SCORE INTERPRETATIONS
Domain Referenced
Norm Referenced

TWO BASIC KINDS OF TEST SCORES
Raw Scores
Derived Scores

PUTTING IT ALL TOGETHER WITH CONTEXT-ADAPTIVE PLANNING

KEY TERMS

mastery threshold
explicit mastery objective
explicit developmental objective
expansive developmental objective
indicant
mastery test
differentiating measures
survey test

construct
domain-referenced interpretation
criterion-referenced interpretation
norm-referenced interpretation
raw score
derived score
CAP

Chapter 3 addressed four of the eight contextual instructional issues that have important consequences for assessment. For each kind of subject matter examined, we identified the appropriate ways for individual differences to be expressed, a suitable family of learning theories, and common teaching methods for the suitable kind of transfer. In Chapter 4, we turn our attention to four more traditional assessment topics and examine their powerful linkages with the corresponding instructional issues. Our first task is to fit functional kinds of instructional objectives into the system. Then we will round out an integrated framework by addressing the kinds of tests, scores, and interpretations that are best adapted to each teaching-learning context.

INSTRUCTIONAL OBJECTIVES

We now revisit the topic of instructional objectives in order to emphasize how they fit into context-adaptive planning, to lay a foundation for their use in Chapter 5 in test planning, and to preview how they relate to test construction and grading topics. Much of this section has been adapted and expanded from the first edition of Norman Gronlund's (2000) insightful and foresightful 1970 book *How to Write and Use Instructional Objectives*. Indeed, the entire structure laid out in Chapters 3 and 4 was inspired by Gronlund's seminal classic.

Explicit Mastery Objectives

One way to express instructional objectives—the Mager way described in Chapter 2—is to list all the specific behaviors that students should exhibit at the end of a unit of instruction. The key words in the preceding sentence are "all," "specific," and "behaviors." In teaching young children to spell their first names, one can specify the goal quite precisely by using a behavioral objective. For example:

1. When told to spell his or her first name, the pupil will do so orally without error.

Note how clear and unambiguous this aim is. Almost anyone could determine whether a child had reached it. Whereas one could debate all week as to what such free-floating aims as "understands the Bill of Rights" or "appreciates Shakespeare" mean, the meaning of this behavioral objective is easily grasped. A major advantage of such explicit mastery behavioral objectives is the ease and clarity with which one can determine *whether or not* the student has reached the target. This clarity is a major contribution of behavioral learning theories to education.

Other examples of explicit behavioral objectives that all, or nearly all, pupils could be expected to master are:

2. Given a push-button telephone, the pupil can dial at least 4 out of 5 seven-digit telephone numbers correctly on the first trial.
3. When orally presented with pairs of one-digit numbers, the student can correctly state the sum within two seconds of at least 95 of the 100 addition facts.
4. When approaching electric traffic signals, the child will stop when the light is red at least 49 times in 50.

Notice that where it is needed, the examples indicate the circumstances in which the behavior must occur; for example, it wouldn't be clear whether the addition-fact stimuli would be oral or visual, so "orally" is specified. At other times, indicating the details of the circumstances would be pointless; for example, it is understood that pupils aren't expected to pass their days dialing telephones; clearly, this behavior is to be performed only on command. Thus, conditions are specified only in reasonable detail (Mager, 1997).

Each of these objectives indicates the level of performance that is expected (e.g., "4 out of 5"). This **mastery threshold** (or minimum acceptable score) enables one to determine whether each student has *attained* the outcome, that is mastered the objective. Such Mager-type objectives are described in this book as **explicit mastery objectives.** They are also known as minimal-essential objectives.

To summarize, minimal essential, or Mager-type, objectives are explicit mastery objectives suitable for Context A subject matter. They communicate:

- the *terminal behavior* learners are expected to exhibit,
- the *circumstances* in which the behavior is to occur, and
- the *mastery threshold* that must be met.

Suitable Use of Explicit Mastery Objectives.   *Explicit mastery objectives are best used in situations where mastery of fundamental material is crucial,* no matter how much time such mastery may require. The four objectives presented earlier concern content of this kind. Content most suitable for mastery learning and the accompanying use of explicit behavioral objectives tends to be (a) essential, (b) sequential, and (c) closed (Bloom, 1971), often focusing on basic skills (Anastasi & Urbina, 1997).

Explicit mastery objectives channel individual differences entirely into the time-it-takes-to-reach-the-destination dimension. Therefore, they are suitable for small domains of subject matter that are specifiable, masterable, and vital. Such Context A domains can normally be mastered in relatively short periods of time by means of *focused training* on each element of the domain. Behavioral approaches may be best suited to such material. In pursuing mastery, teachers may provide lists of such micro-objectives when they want students to *master the specific points* covered by the objectives *and nothing else* (Cronbach, 1977). Teaching based on explicit objectives trades breadth of coverage for mastery (Slavin, 1987b).

Here is another way to indicate when such objectives are suitable. Explicit mastery objectives work *when a single definition of the objective adequately taps it.* An operational definition defines something by specifying the exact operation by which it is measured (Babbie, 2001; Fraenkel & Wallen, 2000). Note the phrase "the exact operation" in the last sentence. Thus, when there is a *single* behavior that is sufficient to demonstrate attainment of essential learning, then an explicit mastery objective will serve well.

Limitations of Explicit Mastery Objectives.   Most subject matter domains are not adequately defined by a solitary operational definition. It takes several triangulated (i.e., diverse kinds of) measures to adequately tap them. (Recall from Chapter 2 the discussion of Gronlund-type objectives in which an objective is best communicated with *several* examples of the kinds of evidence by which its achievement might be assessed, i.e., with several diverse operational definitions. That's where we are headed.)

In addition to not being very explicit, in many circumstances subject matter domains aren't masterable or aren't important enough to warrant mastery. As Cronbach (1971) noted, the concept of mastery is severely limiting—it seems to imply that one can get to the end of what it is desirable to learn.

For expansive subject matter domains, no amount of instruction can cover everything; focusing on explicit mastery objectives would chop off incidental learning of material that isn't included in the list (Cronbach, 1977). For expansive subject matter, cognitive learning perspectives are more functional, and emphasis is placed largely on high-road transfer of learning to develop competence throughout the domain. Interest is *not* restricted to the particular content that happens to be used in teaching. For example, "there is no way of describing the limits of the range of transfer of the application of a principle like Boyle's law nor of specifying the number of situations to which the student should be able to apply it" (Krathwohl & Payne, 1971, p. 23). Therefore, valid tests for such material must involve tasks that require students to transfer their learning to new, unstudied situations. Of all the possible test items or tasks that could tap such domains, the difficulties vary widely. In such contexts, it makes no sense to use objectives that attempt to specify achievement thresholds that must be met, for example, "answer 80% of Boyles' law application items correctly." If the items are easy, this specified minimum level of acceptable performance is modest; if the items are very hard, this pseudo-mastery threshold may be unreasonably demanding.

Mastery doesn't exist for such subject matter. Moreover, we wouldn't wish to specify a level beyond which we are indifferent to further achievement. We are interested in fostering each student's development as much as possible. *Our goal is maximum individual development.*

Most expansive domains aren't sequential to the extent that students must reach some particular level of achievement before being able to proceed to the next domain. Thus, good reasons exist for *not* including mastery thresholds as part of most classroom instructional objectives (Gronlund, 1970, 2000). Instruction that isn't inherently highly sequential normally best channels individual differences primarily into the achievement dimension.

What is needed, then, are instructional objectives suitable for situations in which we do not narrowly focus training on small, closed, masterable, and essential content domains. What kinds of objectives are suitable for use in Context B and Context C?

Explicit Developmental Objectives

In Context B, it doesn't make sense to set a rigid mastery level. Because the subject matter ordinarily isn't inherently sequential, there is no need to insist that all students reach some predetermined threshold. Moreover, because we wish to help students develop their potentials to the fullest extent possible, it would be counterproductive to ignore excellence beyond the point established by an arbitrary mastery threshold. The critical points are that we should neither (a) channel individual differences into the time dimension nor (b) be satisfied with universal mediocrity.

If the threshold requirement of explicit mastery objectives is dropped, they become suitable for Context B, in which case we aspire to help each student achieve *maximum development* within the time available. That is, we take a "the more the better" stance toward achievement. For want of a better name, this kind of objective is called a *developmental* objective. Examples of **explicit developmental objectives** are:

1. Types rapidly.
2. Plays golf well on a given course.
3. When given the names of all vice presidents of the United States, arranges them into the order of their terms in office.
4. Recites Mark Antony's funeral address.

Table 4.1 shows the relationship between explicit mastery objectives and explicit developmental objectives. Note that the features of explicit mastery objectives (suitable in Context A) and explicit developmental objectives (suitable for Context B) are identical except for the need to set a mastery threshold in Context A.

TABLE 4.1   **Explicit Mastery and Explicit Developmental Objectives**

EXPLICIT MASTERY OBJECTIVES (CONTEXT A)	EXPLICIT DEVELOPMENTAL OBJECTIVES (CONTEXT B)
Are terminal student behaviors.	Are terminal student behaviors.
State the conditions under which the behaviors are to occur.	State the conditions under which the behaviors are to occur.
Contain mastery thresholds that must by reached by each student.	Avoid arbitrary mastery levels; the more achievement, the better.

To Recap.   Explicit developmental objectives (a) state what terminal behaviors learners are expected to exhibit at as high a level as available study time and other resources enable and (b) indicate, where useful, the conditions under which the behavior is to be elicited. Explicit developmental objectives channel individual differences largely or wholly into the achievement dimension. They are suitable for two rather different kinds of subject matter: (a) motor skills that are clearly specifiable, but not masterable (e.g., Examples 1 and 2 on page 75), and (b) masterable cognitive material that a teacher judges not to be vital (e.g., Examples 3 and 4 on page 75).

Expansive Developmental Objectives

Until now, discussion has focused on explicit objectives; that is, explicit mastery objectives for Context A and explicit developmental objectives for Context B. Now we focus on a third kind—**expansive developmental objectives.**

Notice two important distinctions. First, contrast *explicit* and *expansive.* On the one hand, small, closed domains are explicitly specifiable. Likewise many[1] motor skills (e.g., bowling) can be made explicit. Explicit targets provide sharp focus. Explicit objectives are well suited for Contexts A and B. On the other hand, large, open, or dynamic content domains are expansive. Expansive objectives are well suited for Context C.

Second, contrast *mastery* and *developmental.* In Context A, where subject matter is explicit, has a ceiling beyond which improvement is not realistic, is highly sequential, and is vitally important, it makes sense to teach and assess for mastery. In Contexts B and C, where material has no ceiling, is less sequential, and isn't vital for daily life or progress in the subject, it is sensible to take a developmental, the-more-the-better attitude and to neither teach nor assess for mastery.

Why Explicit Mastery Objectives Malfunction in Context C.   We have seen that *expansive content domains can neither be specified in detail nor mastered.* Yet some writers (e.g., Guskey, 1997; Mager, 1962, 1997) seem to have ignored this reality, taking an extremist stance that all instruc-

[1]In Chapter 8, we will make a distinction between motor tasks performed solo under more or less standard conditions (e.g., bowling) and those that involve interactions with others (e.g., hitting a pitched baseball). The former are explicit. We will see in Chapter 8 that the latter are expansive.

tional aims must include mastery thresholds. Fortunately, other authorities (e.g., Anastasi, 1976; Cronbach, 1971, 1977; Gronlund, 1970, 2000; Krathwohl & Payne, 1971), recognizing that expansive domains are not explicit and masterable, have long cautioned against the exclusive use of explicit mastery objectives.

Let's now use an example of an expansive domain to show that explicit mastery objectives do violence to such subject matter. Recall the elementary school unit on mammals. Several explicit mastery objectives could be written, such as:

1. Writes the definition of a mammal.
2. Lists the four major characteristics of mammals.
3. When orally given the names of animals studied in the unit, states whether each is a mammal with at least 90% accuracy.
4. Lists at least seven of the eight mammals studied.

Notice how narrow, rote, and sterile the unit becomes. The aims of having pupils achieve *meaningful* verbal learning and being able to engage in high-road transfer are lost. Moreover, if this list is given to students in advance, it notifies them that they need *not* understand or be able to transfer their knowledge to new applications. The "rules" for Context A mastery learning are that teachers inform learners exactly what they must be able to do, teach them to do it, and assess it (and only it) to see if they have mastered it. Neither instruction nor assessment in Context A taps more than low-road transfer. Hence, it wouldn't be legitimate to ask students in a test to classify pictures of animals studied or verbal descriptions of animals not studied.

True, we could expand our list of behavioral objectives to include:

5. When shown pictures of animals studied in the unit, students will classify them as mammals or nonmammals with at least 95% accuracy.
6. Given written descriptions of animals not studied in class, students will label them mammal or nonmammal with at least 75% accuracy.

But now more problems surface. It still would be taboo to test with pictures of animals that weren't studied or with descriptions of ones that were. This is ridiculous! If we persisted, we could again "patch up" the list with more explicit mastery objectives. Yet teachers still could not test with orally described animals, pictures of imaginary animals, or even with real animals brought to class! We could lengthen the list indefinitely, but our efforts would never eliminate all the problems.

What Kind of Objective Is Useful in Context C?   The real objective is for students to *understand* the concept of mammal. Student behaviors such as those listed are potentially useful as *evidence* or *indicators* or alternative operational definitions of understanding, but they are *not* the actual objectives. We can accept, where appropriate, nonbehavioral verbs for instructional objectives for Context C. Yet leaving it at that would forsake the clarity that behaviorism offers because nonbehavioral verbs tend to be vague. How can we have our cake and eat it, too?

As previewed in Chapter 2, Norman Gronlund (1970; 2000) provided a breakthrough with the insight that most of the clarity of behaviorism can be secured without resorting to use of restrictive, explicit behavioral objectives. Instead, active or behavioral verbs can be used as *examples,* or **indicants,** of the kinds of behaviors that one would accept as evidence of student attainment of mental objectives. The rules of the game thus do not limit tests to the exact material used as examples;

rather, they limit tests only to the general types of material sampled by the indicants. Each general instructional aim is accompanied by enough behavioral indicants to convey a good idea of the extent and limits of the large domain. For example, two general objectives with accompanying indicants for the mammal unit might be:

1. Knows basic terms.
   1.1 Matches terms that have the same meaning.
   1.2 Selects the term that best fits a particular definition.
   1.3 Distinguishes among terms orally and in writing.
   1.4 Uses terms correctly orally and in writing.
   1.5 Describes meaning of terms with original examples.
   1.6 Arranges terms in hierarchical order, e.g., with outlines or Venn diagrams.

2. Understands the concept of mammal.
   2.1 Writes a correct definition.
   2.2 Lists several characteristics of mammals.
   2.3 When given the names of familiar animals, classifies them as mammals or nonmammals.
   2.4 Classifies pictures of familiar or unfamiliar animals as mammals or nonmammals.
   2.5 Classifies real or imaginary animals as mammals or nonmammals from oral or written descriptions.

The absence of mastery thresholds reflects the unmasterable nature of the subject matter. Open-endedness of the *sample* of behavioral *indicants* reflects the expansiveness of the subject matter domains and the need to teach and test them for depth of understanding and high-road transfer. *Neither teaching nor assessing should be narrowly targeted at the indicants.* Rather, the indicants should be viewed as alternative operational definitions of the desired learning, no one of which provides a complete picture.[2]

For another example of an expansive content domain, consider a high-school music unit. Some of the unit's general objectives would probably concern knowledge and understanding of composers and performers, their more famous works, the cultural and historical contexts in which their works developed, and so on. These cognitive objectives are similar to the kinds illustrated in the last example. But what of appreciation? How can one write behavioral indicants for the affective objective of music appreciation?

The key lies in continuing to make a sharp distinction between objectives and indicants. Indicants aren't conclusive; they only provide circumstantial evidence that objectives have, to some extent, been attained. The circumstantial evidence provided by indicants tends to be stronger in cognitive domains than in affective ones. This is mainly because feelings, attitudes, interests and so on, can often be falsified or put on.

---

[2]Use of solitary operational definitions, rather than several varied ones, can create problems in other disciplines. An amusing example was an operational definition of humankind in which making and using tools had been suggested as a *defining attribute,* that is, as *the* operational definition. When Jane Goodall first documented wild chimpanzees making and using tools (handmade sticks to fish edible termites out of holes), the great anthropologist Louis Leakey wired her, "Ah! We must now redefine man, redefine tool, or accept chimpanzees as human!" (Goodall, 1999, p. 67). The use of a single indicant of our species had been dramatically demonstrated to be inadequate!

If we were at a loss concerning affective indicants, we could ask, "How do people who clearly appreciate music differ from those who do not?" The answers to this fertile question can be phrased as indicants. For example:

3. Appreciates classical music.

    3.1 Orients ears toward source of classical music.

    3.2 Doesn't chat during concert.

    3.3 Spends own money and time attending concerts voluntarily.

    3.4 When a music recording is played, doesn't throw spit balls.

    3.5 Checks classical music recording out of library.

    3.6 Discusses content of major works and own reactions to them.

At this juncture, the dedicated teacher of music, art, or literature may explode, "But that's not what appreciation is! Appreciation is *felt,* not *behaved.*"

Precisely! That is why an affective objective is used rather than a behavioral one. That is also why behavioral *indicants,* not behavioral *objectives,* are used. Although indicants are not individually very much of the "stuff" of which appreciation is made, the point is that they provide means of evaluating learning with triangulated, operational definitions of the objective.

Table 4.2 contrasts explicit mastery objectives and expansive developmental objectives. The latter don't contain minimum acceptable scores. In addition, Context C objectives, to be suitable for the expansive material found particularly in cognitive, affective, and social subject matter domains, are usually *not behavioral.* Instead, these objectives contain behavioral examples, or indicants, to illustrate the meaning of the general objective.

To Recap.   In expansive developmental objectives, (a) nonbehavioral verbs usually express the targeted learning; (b) behavioral indicants exemplify kinds of behaviors that evidence achievement of the objective; and (c) achievement is sought at as high a level as available time and other resources permits. These expansive Context C objectives enable openness and flexibility in teaching that are not found in the narrow, shallow shaping that characterizes teaching of minimum essential objectives (Gronlund, 1985). Expansive developmental objectives channel individual differences

TABLE 4.2   Comparison of Explicit Mastery Objectives and Expansive Developmental Objectives

EXPLICIT MASTERY OBJECTIVES (CONTEXT A)	EXPANSIVE DEVELOPMENTAL OBJECTIVES (CONTEXT C)
The explicit objective states a terminal student behavior.	The expansive (usually nonbehavioral) objective is illustrated (i.e., operationally defined) with terminal student behaviors.
The explicit objective states the conditions under which the behavior is to occur.	The behavioral indicants give the conditions under which the behaviors are to occur.
The objective states a minimum level that must be reached by each student.	The objective avoids arbitrary thresholds; the greater a student's achievement, the better.

into the achievement dimension. They are suitable for large and/or open Context C domains that are neither explicit nor masterable. They prompt teaching methods that are based mainly on cognitive learning theories and that seek and *assess for high-road transfer of learning.*

It is helpful if expansive objectives are stated *in terms of* terminal student behaviors. Even though the aims are not ordinarily behavioral, they can be given relative clarity by use of behavioral examples. Although these behavioral indicants aren't, individually or collectively, the objective, they identify *some* of the ways in which the objectives may be indirectly assessed. Thus, indicants provide triangulated operational definitions of the objectives (that are often quite abstract owing to their expansiveness).

Following is a Context C objective—a Gronlund-type general statement of a terminal student learning outcome, accompanied by several behavioral indicants that would evidence its achievement:

1. Applies Bill of Rights to contemporary events.
   1.1 When given a relevant current event that has not been previously studied, identifies violations, if any, of the Bill of Rights.
   1.2 Given a fictitious scenario, identifies which, if any, of the first 10 amendments are relevant and provides a reasoned opinion concerning whether they have been violated.
   1.3 Lists governmental actions in any recently studied country that would, in the United States, be violations of the Bill of Rights.
   1.4 Given a fictitious political campaign speech, points out advocated legislation that would violate or would safeguard the Bill of Rights.

THINKING CAP EXERCISE 4.1   ???

Write the letter of the kind of objective on the right in front of each condition described in the left column.

KINDS OF OBJECTIVES

WHICH KIND OF OBJECTIVE:

A. Explicit mastery
B. Explicit developmental
C. Expansive developmental

____ 1. Establishes a mastery threshold?

____ 2. Is most consistent with a need to teach and evaluate for high-road transfer of learning?

____ 3. Uses behavioral indicants?

____ 4. Causes individual differences to be exhibited in the time dimension?

____ 5. Is best suited to subject matter that is explicit but not masterable?

____ 6. Is most appropriate for content that is explicit, masterable, and essential?

____ 7. Is most appropriate for content that is explicit and masterable but *not* essential?

____ 8. Is best suited to content that is neither explicit nor masterable?

____ 9. Would be most suitable for teachers using behavior modification to eliminate undesirable student behaviors?

____ 10. Would be most suitable for a conventional psychotherapist?

For each item below, select the single best response.

11. When expansive developmental objectives are used, should special instructional attention be devoted to the behaviors that are listed?
   A. Yes, because they are the only aims.
   B. Yes, because they are the aims on which students are likely to work the hardest.
   C. No, because they are unimportant.
   D. No, because they are only a sample of the kinds of evidence that could be listed.

THINKING CAP EXERCISE 4.1   CONTINUED

12. Why should no mastery threshold be set for certain objectives?
    A. Specification of minimum acceptable scores never makes sense.
    B. The material cannot or need not be mastered.
    C. The objectives are minimal.
    D. The objectives are behavioral.
13. Which of the following verbs is behavioral?
    A. Knows
    B. Says
    C. Values
    D. Visualizes
14. Which of the following verbs is cognitive?
    A. Comprehends
    B. Lists
    C. Runs
    D. Values
15. Which of the following verbs is affective?
    A. Counts
    B. Knows
    C. Likes
    D. Matches

KEY TO THINKING CAP EXERCISE 4.1

ITEM   KEY   COMMENTS

ITEM	KEY	COMMENTS
1.	A	See pages 73–74.
2.	C	See pages 76–80.
3.	C	See pages 77–80.
4.	A	See page 74.
5.	B	See pages 75–76.
6.	A	See pages 73–74.
7.	B	See page 76.
8.	C	See pages 76–80.
9.	A	See page 74. If teachers only sought to reduce a behavior rather than to eliminate it, then the answer would be option B.
10.	C	See pages 76–80.
11.	D	See page 78. If we did, then the indicants would *become* the students' objectives. This issue will be examined more closely in the next section and in later chapters.
12.	B	See page 78.
13.	B	"Knows" and "visualizes" are cognitive; "values" is affective.
14.	A	"Lists" and "runs" are behavioral verbs; "values" is affective.
15.	C	"Counts" and "matches" are behavioral verbs; "knows" is cognitive.

KINDS OF TESTS

Assessment instruments can be classified in many ways, for example, performance versus paper-pencil, essay versus objective, formative versus summative. For purposes of aligning various aspects of instruction and assessment, a particularly useful distinction is between mastery tests and differentiating tests.

Mastery Tests

In Context A, in which an explicit subject matter domain is masterable and vital, instruction is aimed directly at "stamping in" the specific content. Goals for surface learning of this kind of material are best communicated by means of explicit mastery (i.e., Mager-type) objectives. Such objectives for minimum essential learning dictate that individual differences will be exhibited solely as the time it takes to master the material.

In Context A, a test is used to determine *whether examinees have mastered the material.* A **mastery test** yields an all-or-nothing score, indicating that the examinee has or has not reached the preestablished threshold of acceptable performance (AERA, 1999; Anastasi & Urbina, 1997). Because the entire domain can ordinarily be tested, we need not be concerned with the representativeness of a sample of test content. Such tests are relatively easy to construct, and their scores are easy to interpret. Figure 3.7 on page 65 represents a domain that is taught and tested in its entirety.

Questions or tasks in a mastery test are easy for adequately prepared examinees. The explicit mastery objective lays out exactly what students must do. The training is then focused on the specified content, with provision for only low-road transfer of training, until the threshold is met. Therefore, students are able to answer nearly all of the questions correctly or perform nearly all of the tasks adequately. Once the domain is mastered by all students, there are no achievement differences to be revealed.

The purpose of a mastery test is to determine for each student whether more instructional time or other resources are needed. If a person's performance on a mastery test does not meet the established minimum acceptable score, then the individual should be provided with more instruction. This is the well-known teach-test-reteach cycle.

Differentiating Tests

Anastasi (e.g., 1976) long observed that *mastery testing is not appropriate beyond the basic skills.* This point cannot be overemphasized! For advanced levels of knowledge in less highly structured subjects (e.g., our mammal unit), it is neither practicable nor desirable to use highly specific objectives. Curricular coverage may proceed in various directions, depending on students' and teachers' capabilities, purposes, and interests. Under these conditions, complete mastery is neither necessary nor attainable (Anastasi & Urbina, 1997).

In Contexts B and C, individual differences are exhibited mainly or wholly as level and/or breadth of achievement. "Thus, it is appropriate and realistic to recognize and document that some people are somehow better than others at certain skills" (Cox & Dunn, 1979, p. 28). Tests of such skills should *reveal the differences that exist* among students' achievement. In other words, Context B and C tests should *differentiate* among students to reveal the individual achievement differences that exist.

Note that it is not an "evil test maker" who makes people unequal. *Individual differences exist*! Everyday life underscores this reality in providing us with music prodigies, remedial reading classes, prostheses for individuals with disabilities, sized clothing, and cafeteria food selections. At times, it is our job to assess the differences that exist with **differentiating measures.**

Differentiating Tests for Context B.   When specifiable but unmasterable skills are taught, explicit developmental objectives make sense. In this context, effort is devoted to helping each student to perform *as well as possible* within the available time. Either no arbitrary level of achievement exists beyond which further excellence is sought, or, if it does, virtually nobody consistently attains it (e.g., a bowling score of 300 or a golf score of 18). Therefore, tests suitable for Context B (e.g., keyboarding speed or long jumping) need enough "ceiling" to reveal how well the best students perform and enough "floor" to reveal how poorly the worst ones perform. That is, Context B tests need to reveal the individual differences in achievement that exist.

The purpose of Context B differentiating tests is to document the extent to which explicit developmental objectives have been achieved. In Context B, as in Context A, no sharp distinction between practice material and testing material is necessary; they are often identical. Tests may be used formatively to provide assistance as well as summatively to assess achievement. The explicit content makes test construction relatively easy.

Because Context B subject matter is explicit, students should ordinarily know ahead of time what will be tested or sampled. Therefore, when an entire domain is to be tested, test security is *not* an issue. However, if the domain is to be *sampled,* then students obviously shouldn't know ahead of time precisely which elements of the domain are to be tested.

Differentiating Survey Tests for Context C.   In Context C, in which expansive subject matter domains are neither tightly identified nor masterable, instruction is directed at broadly educating students with *some* of the domain's material so that they will be able to go beyond what is specifically studied and transfer their learning to other parts of the expansive domain. Because aims for Context C cognitive, affective, and social domains are expansive, developmental objectives channel individual differences into level and/or breadth of achievement.

The purpose of assessment in this context is to measure individual differences in the extent to which objectives have been achieved throughout expansive domains. To do this, measures must not only differentiate, they must also *survey.* A **survey test** *samples* only part of the domain's content. Because of the size and/or openness of Context C domains, it isn't possible for the test to cover all the possible content.

Along these lines it is important to understand that when the objectives involve high-road transfer, repeated retesting on exactly the same material is ill advised. If the same test were used for "second chances," then all a student would have to do would be to memorize the material that happened to be sampled on the test; the rest of the large, open domain could be ignored! If students are given "second chances," then each test should be an independent sample of the domain.

Students who request the return of their previous Context C tests to use for study should be reminded that the test items used were not necessarily more important than many others that did not happen to be sampled. This logic applies to Context C product and performance assessments as well as to paper-pencil tests. For example, suppose a student recycles a written theme after receiving feedback from the teacher. A point of view is clarified, punctuation errors are corrected, etc. The assumption might be made that the student now has the ability to independently punctuate and use written communication strategies to present various viewpoints adequately. However, the student may have only been following blindly what the teacher indicated should be done. Without a demonstration of these abilities on a new theme, unaccompanied by teacher assistance, no guarantee exists that the student now is truly capable of the tasks (Cox & Dunn, 1979).

We saw in Chapter 3 that it isn't possible to cover everything in an expansive domain. Only a sample can be taught. Effective teachers, therefore, adopt the strategy of teaching for high-road transfer of learning. *When teaching has been aimed primarily at generalization* of learning (rather than at mere surface knowledge of the exact material taught), *testing should be for high-road transfer.* The crucial indicator of students' understanding of a concept, procedure, or generalization is their ability to use it in circumstances that differ from those in which it was learned. Transferability or portability is the fundamental aspect of meaningful learning (Thorndike, 1969).

Two reasons *compel* effective teachers to assess for high-road transfer in Context C. First, because the units are taught for portability of learning, the tests will not be valid unless they assess transfer. Put differently, Context C expansive objectives and the accompanying behavioral indicants are designed to avoid extreme focus on specifics of content. They should be saturated with novel applications. Because the aims emphasize transfer, the tests cannot assess achievement of these objectives unless they also stress transfer (Gronlund, 2000).

The second compelling reason why Context C tests should assess high-road transfer is that *tests influence what students learn* (Marso & Pigge, 1993). Like it or not, most students from primary school through graduate school try to learn what they think will be tested. If this powerful force works against us, much of our teaching is doomed to failure. For example, if a history teacher consistently tests only factual knowledge (e.g., names and dates), then students work mainly to memorize this kind of low-level material. On the other hand, if the teacher consistently assesses such learning outcomes as analyses, applications, and evaluation, then students will also pursue these more complex objectives.

Evaluation exerts enormous influence on student effort. Research indicates "that the use of higher level questions in evaluation enhances learning, retention, transfer, interest, and development of learning skills" (Crooks, 1988, p. 442). Wise teachers harness this potent force. Our motto might well be "*Harness Evaluation Power.*" To do this, teachers must go to great pains to assure that they *assess what they want students to learn.*

Unfortunately, research reveals that teacher-made tests often fail to reflect the teacher's own instructional objectives and often require little more than repetition of material that was presented in the textbook or class (Fleming & Chambers, 1983). In Context C, teachers want learners to be able to apply what they have learned; therefore, they must test for *transfer,* using some novel material (Gronlund, 2000; Thorndike, 1969). Because most instruction involves Context C subject matter, testing for high-road transfer is critically important. The next several chapters of this book provide assistance in testing students' ability to use what they have learned in new situations.

Figure 4.1 shows a domain such as a mammal unit or Bill of Rights unit. The domain is large, open, and in places has unclear boundaries. Only part can be taught and only part can be assessed.

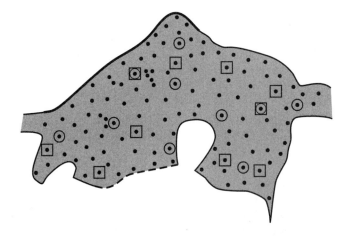

FIGURE 4.1   Broad, Open Content Domain Requiring Teaching and Testing for High-Road Transfer. (Dots in circles indicate content taught. Dots in squares indicate content tested.)

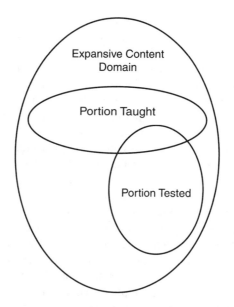

FIGURE 4.2   Expansive Content Domain Requiring Teaching and Testing for High-Road Transfer

Care is needed to avoid excessive overlap between the portions taught and the portions tested. Figure 4.2 represents this same idea in another way.

Like most educational achievement tests, most psychological tests and inventories concern vague, expansive constructs or traits. A **construct** is a trait or an abstract quality such as intelligence, prejudice, creativity, or anxiety that cannot be directly observed. Rather, we see evidence of it. Meaning is assigned to a construct by specifying activities or "operations" that will measure it (Kerlinger, 1986); that is, we refer to the measurement of a construct as its operational definition be-cause the way we measure the construct determines what our data really represent (Krathwohl, 1998).

A trait usually is regarded as an average or typical state, reflecting not only personal charac-teristics but also the conditions of the environment (Cronbach, 1990). Instruments designed to mea-sure a construct or trait such as academic aptitude, mechanical aptitude, outdoor interest, impulsivity, or extroversion must sample broadly from expansive, pliable content domains. In this respect, constructs assessed in psychological instruments share key characteristics with Context C subject matter domains. The kinds of interventions, objectives, measures, interpretations, and scores involved in Context C instruction also are used in Context C counseling and special education in-tervention.

Should Teachers Teach to the Test?   Another aspect of sampling merits special attention. This is the old debate regarding the legitimacy of "coaching" or "teaching to the test." We shall see shortly that the answer depends on the instructional targets.

It is clear to many teachers that a survey test (i.e., a Context C test) is a *sample* of student per-formance. Its purpose is to enable *generalization* beyond the sample to student achievement in the *entire* domain. It is prudent to generalize from a sample only when it is representative[3] of the domain. To enable this kind of inference, tests are carefully built to sample various parts of the domain in the desired proportions. Now if a teacher were to "peek" at the test before instruction in order to give *dis*proportional emphasis to the specific content that happens to be tested, three undesirable consequences would follow. First, the test questions would no longer constitute a balanced sample of the studied and unstudied parts of the domain; inference from the test would be biased. *Teaching the particular items sampled in a survey test renders inferences from its scores misleading.* Second, the test would no longer adequately assess high-road transfer of learning among these students; hence, its validity would be compromised. Third, because the test would not give sufficient emphasis to transfer, students in the future would strive less for transfer.

In Context C education, teaching specific content sampled by a test merely because it is on a test is counterproductive. This statement applies equally to teacher-made and to published devices, to objective tests, essay and other product assessments, and to performance tests. Likewise, it applies to instruments used to assess individual students and to those used for evaluating programs.

This line of reasoning may seem devious and nefarious to some teachers because in the paradigms of Context A and Context B training, teaching the content of a paper-pencil or performance test is entirely appropriate and professional. For content in which an assessment taps the entire domain (rather than just a sample of it), it is indeed legitimate to teach the material to be tested and nothing else. If pupils were to memorize "do, re, me, fa, so, la, ti, do," one would teach and test it in its entirety (not because it is in the test, but because it *is* the domain). Test security wouldn't be an issue because sampling isn't needed and high-road transfer isn't involved. *In Contexts A and B, the content taught and the content tested may be virtually identical.*

Some disputes regarding "teaching to the test" arise from failure to recognize the instructional implications of different kinds of subject matter and objectives. What is effective for one situation may not work for another (Sanders, et al., 1990). *Effective teachers are able to function skillfully with each kind of subject matter.* The framework for the three contexts, A, B, and C, provides a structure for using each paradigm where, and only where, it is appropriate. In Context C, use of the term "teaching to the test" is usually pejorative, referring to instructional overemphasis of the items sampled in the test. If, however, a teacher takes the phrase to mean teaching to the general domain of knowledge sampled by the test (Shepard, 1990); that, of course, is perfectly appropriate.

To Recap. In this section, appropriate kinds of tests were aligned with kinds of curricular material, individual differences, learning theories, teaching for transfer, and instructional objectives. These relationships are summarized in Table 4.3 on page 88, which expands on the material that was presented in Table 3.5 of Chapter 3. The columns are arranged in *the order in which teachers would typically consider the topics when planning instruction.* This table, in which we include the two topics that follow in this chapter, completes the introduction of the eight facets of context-adaptive planning.

---

[3]Representative samples are often sought by means of random sampling. However, because there is no way to randomly sample an infinite domain (e.g., stars in the universe or applications of the First Amendment), random sampling is often not possible in Context C assessment. Therefore, we sample *purposefully* to provide a desired blend of content and mental processes.

■ ■ ■ ■ ■

THINKING CAP EXERCISE 4.2   ???

1. Which context of Table 4.3 does *not* require a test that reveals individual differences in achievement?
   A. Context A
   B. Context B
   C. Context C
2. Content sampling is most frequent in tests designed to assess achievement of
   A. explicit mastery objectives.
   B. explicit developmental objectives.
   C. expansive developmental objectives.
3. To reveal individual differences in achievement, test questions need to be
   A. so easy that nearly everybody correctly answers each item.
   B. of medium difficulty.
   C. so hard that nearly everybody misses each item.
4. In which context is high-road transfer of learning the most important?
   A. Context A
   B. Context B
   C. Context C
5. For which context is it normally *not* legitimate to teach all of the specific subject matter that will be tested?
   A. Context A
   B. Context B
   C. Context C

6. Which context's tests are most similar to tests of psychological traits or constructs with regard to expansiveness of their domains?
   A. Context A
   B. Context B
   C. Context C

KEY TO THINKING CAP EXERCISE 4.2

ITEM	KEY	COMMENTS
1.	A	See page 81.
2.	C	See page 83.
3.	B	If everybody received nearly the same score, be it high (from very easy items in tests lacking adequate ceiling) or low (from very hard questions in tests having insufficient floor), the test wouldn't reveal individual differences in achievement. It wouldn't differentiate among people whose achievement differs. This will be treated more fully in Chapter 10.
4.	A	See page 83.
5.	C	See pages 85–86.
6.	C	See page 85.

KINDS OF SCORE INTERPRETATIONS

The previous section addressed the type of test appropriate for each context. Our attention now turns to the type(s) of interpretation that can meaningfully be given to the score of each kind of test.

If a measure is to serve any useful purpose, it is necessary for its scores to be interpretable. In this section, two major bases of score interpretation will be introduced. They will then be matched with the three contexts.

Domain-Referenced Basis for Score Interpretation

Domain-referenced interpretations (also known as **criterion-referenced,** content-referenced, and objectives-referenced statements) *tell how a person performed on certain explicitly identified material or skills.* For example:

TABLE 4.3 Relationships

CONTEXT	TYPE OF SUBJECT MATTER	PRINCIPAL MANIFESTATION OF INDIVIDUAL DIFFERENCES	TYPE OF INSTRUCTIONAL OBJECTIVE	FAMILY OF LEARNING THEORIES	TYPE OF INSTRUCTION FOR TRANSFER	KIND OF TEST	TYPE OF SCORE	TYPE OF INTERPRETATION
A	Entire content of small, closed domain readily identified in behavioral terms; content vital and masterable	Time dimension	Explicit, mastery	Behavioral	Much specific training for low-road transfer of training	Mastery—students have knowledge of the exact domain that will be tested	Raw or percent	Domain-referenced and referenced to a mastery threshold
B	Tasks readily specified in behavioral terms, but cannot be mastered or are not important enough to merit mastery	Achievement dimension	Explicit, developmental	Mixed	Varied and/or specific training in early phases	Differentiating—students have prior knowledge of exact task or domain to be tested or sampled	Raw and derived	Domain-referenced and norm-referenced
C	Content of large and/or open domain cannot be specified in detail, but can be illustrated in behavioral terms; content not masterable	Achievement dimension	Expansive, developmental	Cognitive	Mainly teaching for understanding and for high-road transfer of learning	Differentiating/survey—students have prior knowledge of general domain to be sampled, but not of exact items	Derived	Norm-referenced

- Performed CPR, using equipment provided, in the prescribed way.
- Keyboarded at the rate of 37 words per minute.
- Correctly read the time to the nearest minute from five different conventional clocks that vary in face design.
- Made 14 out of 20 basketball free throws.

To be useful, a domain-referenced interpretation must relate to an explicit subject matter or skill domain. A domain definition must be detailed and sharp enough to show very clearly what kinds of behavior are included in the domain and what facets are excluded (AERA, 1999; American Psychological Association [hereafter cited as APA], 1985). Unfortunately, some educators lose sight of this essential requisite for meaningful domain (or criterion) referencing. In pursuit of being able to describe examinee status with regard to subject matter, they attempt referencing to ill-defined, expansive domains. It *would* (note the conditional tense) be desirable to have measures that accurately describe what examinees can and cannot do. However, the problem is that this isn't possible *unless* the subject matter domains are well described (Bracey, 2000; Forsythe, 1991; Popham, 2002). Some tests referred to as criterion (or domain) referenced fail to clearly identify a domain of behavior and thus cannot form the basis for referencing test performance to the domain (Nitko, 1980). For instance, it isn't useful to know that Al correctly answered 7 out of 10 items on the test for the War of 1812, or that Jill correctly spelled 95% of the words on a test. Such statements are referenced to expansive domains; the test items could range from very easy to unreasonably difficult.

On the other hand, when a subject matter domain or skill is explicitly identified, then the interpretation can be referenced to the subject matter, that is, domain referenced. The interpretation can reveal *what the examinee can do*. The clear delineation of test content provides a measuring stick against which an examinee's performance can be compared.

This tightly specified curricular measuring stick was first dubbed a "criterion" by Glaser. In this usage, criterion is defined to mean "basis of comparison" or "continuum of knowledge acquisition, ranging from no proficiency at all to perfect performance" (Glaser, 1963, p. 529). Unfortunately, the word criterion suggests a point on the continuum and is used by many people (e.g., Mager, 1997) to mean "required level of achievement." The term criterion thus lends itself to misunderstanding and is widely misinterpreted (Jeager, 1987; Mehrens & Lehmann, 1991). "It carries surplus associations to mastery learning that are best avoided by using the more general term 'domain' instead" (Hively, 1974, p. 5). Although the term criterion is still used by some authors (e.g., Popham, 2002; Sax, 1997), it is gradually being replaced by clearer terms such as "domain" (Anastasi & Urbina, 1997). We avoid ambiguous usage of criterion in this book by using domain to refer to a body of subject matter or skills and mastery threshold to denote the minimum level of acceptable achievement specified in an explicit mastery objective.

The point was made previously that some tests alleged to be domain referenced (or criterion, content, or objectives referenced) fail to identify a clear-cut domain. Such tests are not usefully referenced to the domains. A corollary follows: Some so-called mastery tests aren't referenced to objectives that are incisive enough to make the mastery thresholds meaningful. Domain referencing is useful *only* for domains that are described clearly and incisively enough so that it is clear what performances lie within each subject matter domain and which do not (Popham, 2002; Thorndike, 1982).

Another important point about domain referencing remains to be made. Two very separate topics are confused by many educators. These *separate* and distinct issues are:

- Domain referencing score interpretation vs. norm referencing interpretation
- Mastery vs. nonmastery decisions about achievement

It is important to realize that these are quite different and independent ideas (Thorndike, 1997). This difference is crucial to the distinction between Contexts A and B.

Norm-Referenced Basis for Score Interpretation

A **norm-referenced** (or people-referenced) **interpretation** tells *how a person's performance compares with that of a group of other people.* For example:

- Obtained a grade equivalent of 4.7 from the national reference group on a reading comprehension test.
- Won the keyboarding speed contest.
- Answered more questions correctly on the World War I test than 40% of the class.
- Obtained a WISC-III IQ score of 114.

To be useful, a norm-referenced interpretation must compare a person's performance with the performance of a *well-identified* and *relevant group* of people. It would not ordinarily be useful to be told that tenth-grade Maria answered more questions correctly on an oral reading test than 74% of a national sample of third-grade students; this reference group is not likely to be relevant for a tenth-grade student. Nor would it be useful to know that Nikolai did better on an algebra test than 20% of some undescribed sample of other people; unless a reference (or norm) group is clearly described, it doesn't enable meaningful comparisons to be made. However, when a reference group of people is both adequately described and relevant to the purpose of the interpretation, then the interpretation can be *people referenced* (i.e., norm referenced). It can describe examinee status in meaningful comparison with other people.

Some published tests that are alleged to be norm referenced aren't accompanied by data for reference groups of people that are well described or relevant to the purpose of interpretation. The mere presence of normative tables in a test manual does *not* ensure the usefulness of the data. The adequacy of normative samples must be thoughtfully judged by prospective test users.

We should recognize at this point, too, as Thorndike (1997) noted, that the distinction between domain- and norm-referenced interpretations isn't quite as clear as it may superficially seem. This is true because *all* achievement tests relate to subject matter domains. The distinction between domain and norm referencing concerns how specific the domains are. A test on rules for capitalization would be restricted to a narrowly defined domain; therefore, its scores are best given domain-referenced interpretations that are related directly to that explicit domain. In contrast, a survey social studies test might cover an expansive array of topics; thus, its scores are best provided with norm-referenced interpretations that relate examinee achievement to that of others in a well-defined, relevant reference group. However, *the interpretation would not be made in a subject matter vacuum;* it would be made clear that the interpretation concerned *a survey social-studies test covering a variety of topics.* Thus, norm referencing is not void of content; it is based on the subject matter domain to the extent possible, but because that alone isn't sufficient, the interpretation is endowed with additional meaning by being referenced to the performance of other people.

Choosing Appropriate Bases for Interpretation

It may be helpful to refer back to Table 4.3 to consider the kind(s) of test-score interpretation that align(s) with each combination of type of subject matter, exhibition of individual differences, family of learning theories, type of transfer, kind of objective, and kind of test.

Context A.   Where subject matter domains are small and closed, the material is clear and masterable. If it is important for all students to master a domain, then individual differences should be directed into the time dimension by means of an explicit mastery objective in which a mastery threshold is established. Instruction often consists of specific drills on each element in the domain, and teaching methods tend to be based on behavioral learning theories designed to facilitate low-road transfer of training. Achievement is best assessed with a mastery test designed to show whether each examinee has reached this minimum level. In this context, the interpretation should be referenced (a) to the explicit content domain, and (b) to the mastery threshold. The interpretation is domain referenced to reveal what the examinee does, and it is referenced to the minimum essential level of performance to indicate whether mastery has been attained.

Examples of such domain-referenced, mastery interpretive statements are:

- Herbie successfully counted each of several groups of objects ranging in number from 2 to 20.
- When given an ordinary combination lock and its combination, Anita opened the lock within the one-minute time limit.

These statements are domain referenced because each refers to an exact domain or task (e.g., counting up to 20 objects). Each statement is also referenced to a mastery threshold because it indicates whether a given level of achievement (e.g., opened in one minute) was attained.

Context B.   Where learning tasks can be explicitly specified but can't be mastered or aren't important enough for everyone to master them, individual differences are best relegated to the achievement dimension by means of explicit developmental objectives that describe the domains but don't set "mastery" thresholds. Achievement is best assessed with tests that reveal differences among persons having various amounts of competence in the tasks. The resulting scores may be given norm-referenced and/or domain-referenced interpretations. Norm-referenced statements reveal how examinees compare with other people, whereas domain-referenced statements indicate what examinees can do. These interpretations aren't referenced to mastery thresholds.

Examples of such domain-referenced statements are:

- John Adams lived to be 90 years old.
- Max lifted a weight of 74 kilograms.

These statements are domain referenced because they refer to clear domains or tasks (i.e., staying alive and regulation weight-lifting rules). They aren't referenced to mastery thresholds. Rather, they report the *level* of achievement.

The results of these same tests can also be given norm-referenced interpretations. For example:

- John Adams long held a record for longevity among United States presidents.
- Max (aged 14) lifted a weight equal to the amount the average 14-year-old male in New Jersey can lift.

These statements are norm referenced because they compare the performance of the examinees to that of well-described reference groups of other people (i.e., United States presidents and 14-year-old New Jersey boys).

Notice that it is the *interpretations,* not the tests, that are domain or norm referenced (AERA, 1999; Feldt & Brennan, 1989; Popham, 2002). A given differentiating test having explicit content can be given both a domain-referenced *and* a norm-referenced interpretation. In Context B, both are often useful.

Context C.   Finally, where domains are large or open, the subject matter cannot be specified in detail. Individual differences are best directed to the achievement dimension by means of expansive developmental objectives. Instruction should be aimed at understanding and high-road transfer of learning. Achievement is best assessed with broad-spectrum survey tests that reveal individual differences in breadth and depth of achievement. Under these conditions, test scores must be given norm-referenced interpretations to show how examinee performance compares with that of some well-described and relevant group of people.

Examples of such norm-referenced, interpretive statements are:

- Khalaf answered more items on the mammal unit test than did eight percent of the pupils in his class.
- Angela did as well on the test in geography, culture, and religions of India as the average eighth-grade student in the United States.

These statements are norm referenced because they compare examinee performance to that of specified groups of other people. (Note, however, that they do identify the expansive domain to the extent practical.)

Results of such tests could not meaningfully be domain referenced because the content domains are open-ended and fuzzy. Referencing tests to expansive domains is like anchoring a ship to a floating platform.

To Recap.   In Context A teaching, small, closed, vital subject domains require explicit mastery objectives and mastery tests. Mastery tests reveal *whether* examines have reached a predetermined threshold of competence in tightly specified, masterable domains. Interpretations suitable for scores of such tests are referenced both to domain content and to established mastery thresholds.

Context B material is clearly defined, but either (a) is unmasterable, or (b) is not important enough to warrant mastery. Such material is best specified by explicit developmental objectives and assessed by differentiating tests that reveal *level* of achievement. Interpretations given the scores may be domain referenced to the explicit domain and/or norm-referenced to the performance of some well-described group of other people.

In Context C instruction, ill-defined and unmasterable material calls for expansive developmental objectives that usually contain cognitive, affective, or social verbs. Achievement of such objectives is assessed by differentiating tests that survey or sample subject matter domains to reveal the *breadth and/or level* of achievement. Interpretation given to such scores cannot be meaningfully referenced to the domains because they are not clearly identified. Interpretations, therefore, should be people referenced to indicate how examinee performance compares to that of relevant groups of other people.

EXTENSION

Another Thinking Cap Exercise may be found on our web site, www.ablongman.com/hannadettmer.

KINDS OF SCORES

We now need a brief consideration of the test scores used in the various kinds of teaching-testing-interpreting situations.

Raw Scores

A **raw score** is the *number of points earned.* Examples are:

1. Twenty-three letters of the alphabet correctly named.
2. Forty-nine points on a current-events test.

Closely related to raw scores are percentage scores. Examples are:

3. Eighty percent of the 100 addition facts answered correctly.
4. Seventy-three percent of the questions on the literature test answered correctly.

For interpretive purposes, raw scores and percentage scores are very similar. In Context A, where material is very clearly identified, raw and percentage scores carry inherent meaning; they convey domain-referenced information. For example, "Rick correctly named 23 letters of the alphabet" and "Yar answered 80% of the addition facts correctly" provide meaningful information about what examinees can do.

Similarly, in Context B, where tasks are explicitly identified, raw scores (but less often percentage scores) are inherently meaningful because they convey domain-referenced information. For example, "Ellen made 6 out of 20 basketball free throws" and "Jack ran 200 meters in 11.8 seconds" provide meaningful information about what these examinees can do.

Examples 1 and 3 are well suited to domain-referenced interpretation because the domains are clear-cut. Examples 2 and 4 aren't appropriate for domain-referenced interpretation because the domains are only vaguely identifiable, owing to the subject matter being expansive. These latter scores need to be converted into another kind of score in order to enable norm-referenced interpretation. So we now turn to derived scores.

Derived Scores

Neither raw nor percentage scores reveal norm-referenced status. To show how examinees' performances compare with that of a relevant and clearly described reference group of other people, raw scores are converted into **derived scores.** Many kinds of derived (i.e., converted) scores exist. In Chapters 11 and 15, we will explain their meaning, derivation, and uses.

The major categories of derived, or converted, scores can be previewed at this time. They are:

- Grade equivalents and age equivalents
- Simple ranks and percentile ranks
- Standard scores (e.g., z-scores, stanines, and deviation IQs)

The feature that all derived scores share is their *capacity to render people's performance comparable to that of other people.*

In Context C, where domains are expansive, derived scores are needed for meaningful interpretation. These interpretations must, of course, be norm referenced. For example:

- Roy's reading comprehension score equaled that of the average beginning sixth-grade pupil in the state.
- Nel's adaptive behavior rating equaled that of an average three-year-old in the country.
- Avis' United States History test score was better than those of 64 out of every 100 students in a national sample of ninth-grade students.
- Compared with others in his English class, Guy obtained a z-score of +1.7 on the vocabulary test. (The z-score is a kind of standard score that will be addressed in Chapter 11.)

Psychological constructs also lack clearly identified boundaries. Therefore, derived or converted scores are necessary to provide meaningful norm-referenced interpretations. For example, "Warrick's self-report anxiety inventory score exceeds that of 98 out of every 100 men in the country" and "Cara's IQ score on the nationally normed test was 107."

Similarly, in Context B, where the objectives are developmental and mastery either doesn't exist or isn't sought, derived scores can be given norm-referenced interpretations. For example:

- Bertha's strength of grip was greater than that of 72% of a national sample of girls in her grade.
- Ian high jumped as high as the average 11-year-old boy in his school can.

THINKING CAP EXERCISE 4.3   ???

By now, the contents of Table 4.3 should be internalized. Try to answer the following questions without reference to it, but feel free to use the table if you get stuck. For Questions 1 through 10, choose among Contexts A, B, or C.

1. For which kind of teaching should one set a level of excellence that each student must attain?
2. For which kind of material is it vital to distinguish between indicants and objectives?
3. For which kind of material does logic lead to the use of norm-referenced interpretations?

THINKING CAP EXERCISE 4.3   CONTINUED

4. For which kind of subject matter are percent scores most suitable?
5. In which context is attainment of explicit developmental objectives interpreted by means of either raw scores or derived scores?
6. For which kind of material does logic suggest interpretations that are referenced both to a content domain and to a mastery threshold?
7. In which context is achievement of explicit but unmasterable content compared with reference groups of other people, with content or skill domains, or both?
8. In which context is it *not* appropriate to "teach to the test"?
9. In which context is it *un*necessary for tests to reveal individual differences in achievement?
10. In which context does it require the most effort to assure that tests contain suitable, balanced samples of content?
11. Which applied measure would have to be norm referenced?
    A. Age
    B. Blood pressure
    C. Height
    D. Self-concept
12. Which applied measure could sensibly be domain or norm referenced?
    A. Academic aptitude
    B. Dependability
    C. Liberalism
    D. Weight

KEY TO THINKING CAP EXERCISE 4.3

ITEM	KEY	COMMENTS
1.	A	See pages 73–74.
2.	C	See pages 77–79.
3.	C	The answer could also be Contexts B and C. See pages 91–92.
4.	A	See page 93.
5.	B	See pages 93–94.
6.	A	See pages 90–91.
7.	B	See page 91.
8.	C	See pages 85–86.
9.	A	See pages 90–91.
10.	C	See pages 83–85. Chapter 5 focuses on meeting this challenge.
11.	D	Self-concept is a vague, ill-defined psychological construct. The other three domains are clear and could be either norm referenced, domain referenced, or both.
12.	D	Weight is explicit. The other three domains are ill defined. Hence, only weight can meaningfully be domain referenced. Measures of the other three domains can be interpreted meaningfully only through norm referencing.

EXCEPTIONS

To assist learning, we have emphasized differences among Contexts A, B, and C by use of relatively straightforward illustrations. However, in the process, we have oversimplified reality. Let's now briefly examine a few exceptions.

Some subject matter is best handled in one context early in training and then shifted to another context for more advanced instruction. Consider the teaching of reading. In the early primary years, much of the instructional effort devoted to reading is Context A in orientation. Such things as letter names and regular sound-symbol correspondences can be taught by use of the mastery model. However, once the average reader advances beyond second grade or so, the emphasis shifts from these mechanical features to the cognitive features of reading comprehension. Thereafter, reading instruction clearly belongs in Context C. Learning to play a musical instrument follows a similar sequence.

Occasionally, a subject matter domain cannot be assigned to a single context because it lies in borderline regions. The separation of contexts is not sharp; it is gradual. This will become more evident soon when a new graphic is introduced that displays each context as adjacent to each other context.

The addition facts present another interesting variant. Instruction should transcend a single context. The subject matter consists of two separate contexts. Initial mathematical *concepts* to be taught are within the straightforward Context C domain concerned with *understanding* addition, with heavy emphasis on meaningfulness and high-road transfer. Pupils should be able to figure out answers. Yet they shouldn't be obliged to always have to do so; they also need to memorize the addition facts. Rapid, rote recall of addition facts is clearly Context A content.

Finally, consider the legitimacy and desirability of multicontext teaching. Attention has been focused until now on the *unique* objectives or central concern of various instructional units. However, the objectives for a given unit should often include learning targets from more than one context.

Consider a unit on AIDS. Some key objectives would most emphatically be explicit, behavioral, and masterable—Context A. For example, a critical behavioral aim would be to teach avoidance of high-risk behaviors. In addition, one would seek higher-level Context C understanding and application so that students could transfer their learning to untaught, unanticipated situations, for example, needle sharing for home ear-piercing (or piercing such other body parts as may come into vogue). One would also want to develop Context C connections between current instruction and students' prior knowledge of viruses and to foster ever-higher levels of understanding of such biological material. Educators should avoid tunnel vision. We should exploit instructional units for all they are worth!

We have seen that the correspondence of kind of subject matter with the other topics that have been introduced is not always perfect. Yet the exceptions are relatively uncommon, and use of context-adaptive planning is ordinarily quite straight forward. To find a richer and fuller description of various kinds of exceptions, visit www.ablongman.com/hannadettmer.

CONTEXT-ADAPTIVE PLANNING AND GRAPHIC

Readers undoubtedly have noticed the sprinkling of little cap designs throughout the book. Some of these are side views of a baseball-type cap and others are overhead views of a cap (made rounder than an actual cap to enable formation of three congruent sectors). The significance of the cap design is introduced here at the conclusion of our consideration of the eight related topics involved in context-adaptive-planning.

The acronym CAP will be used for the remainder of the book. As some will have surmised, CAP stands for context-adaptive planning. Cap drawings and embellishing terms throughout the book guide readers' reflections on important aspects of the material. They serve as conceptual hooks on which to hold key concepts in readiness for use and application. In addition, they occasionally serve as advance organizers to help readers activate relevant past learning in order to relate it to new material.

The three sectors of the cap (like thirds of a pie graph) contain the means of making connections between instruction and assessment. They delineate Contexts A, B, and C.

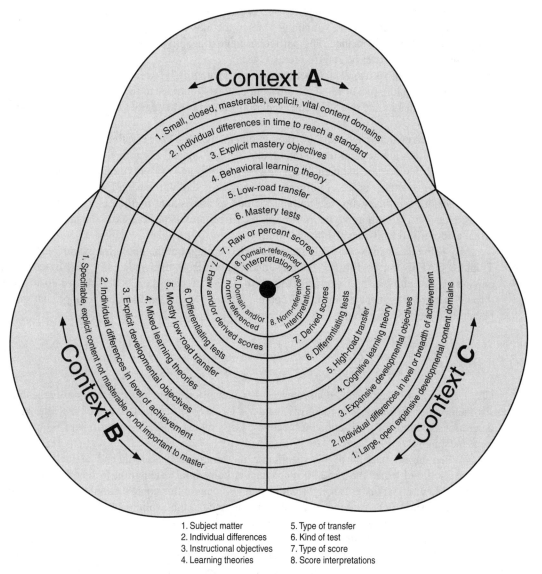

1. Subject matter
2. Individual differences
3. Instructional objectives
4. Learning theories
5. Type of transfer
6. Kind of test
7. Type of score
8. Score interpretations

FIGURE 4.3   The CAP Perspective: Context-Adaptive Planning.

The cap also is partitioned into eight concentric rings. These identify the eight topics treated in Chapters 3 and 4 and summarized in Table 4.3. Their connections for instruction and assessment can now be shown in the CAP graphic design presented in Figure 4.3.[4]

---

[4]The CAP design is a transformation of the tabular design of Table 4.3; the cap and table show exactly the same information. This is achieved (a) by "pulling" the top left-hand corner of the table around to the right in a semicircular arc and (b) by "pulling" the bottom left-hand corner of the table around to the left in a semicircular arc. This transformation contorts the three rows of the table into sectors of a circle and it distorts the eight columns of the table into concentric rings within the circle to form the CAP graphic design.

Continuing with the cap analogy, one cap (i.e., one teaching method and one assessment method) doesn't fit all learning situations. Rather, a context-sensitive outlook is needed that has a structured, yet flexible, "shape." The particular context-adaptive planning perspective that is used in this book will hereafter be referred to as **CAP.**

The cap's bill has a special function. We will rotate it to be over Context A, B, or C, or in unusual cases to straddle two of the three adjacent contexts, in order to focus on a particular context's kind of subject matter and the other corresponding elements of integrated planning, instruction, and assessment.

We all know that some caps are showy; others are more conservative. Some have more style than utility; others are more practical than faddish. Teaching and assessment can vary in these ways too. Caps can have embellishments (e.g., logos, buttons, and patterns) that tout special interests. Even the most seamless and carefully constructed cap is likely to have a few knots and loose ends on the "inside." Similarly, no instructional method or assessment method is without its kinks and ravels. Our aim is to minimize them through planful context-sensitive assessment that is carefully articulated with context-sensitive instruction.

By using these analogies and others sprinkled throughout the book, for example, sections for Thinking CAP Exercises, EnCAPsulations, and Chapter ReCAPs, we use this playful technique to emphasize and enliven the extremely *serious* business of providing better classroom instruction through better assessment by means of context-adaptive planning. Indeed, we hope that the CAP perspective will become "old hat" for educators.

CHAPTER RECAP

Chapters 3 and 4 have presented an integrated framework that enables educators to orchestrate assessment with instruction. The focus of Chapter 4 has been on characteristics of subject matter that determine the kinds of instructional objectives, tests, scores, and interpretations of scores that are most meaningful.

When subject matter is highly specifiable, masterable, and essential and instructional aims are truly explicit and behavioral, then a mechanistic, behavioral orientation to learning makes good sense, and low-road transfer is sought. Student assessment in this context should be designed to certify mastery. Mastery tests are interpreted with reference to the explicit subject matter domains and the mastery thresholds by means of raw or percent scores.

When skill or curricular domains are highly specifiable but either unmasterable or nonessential, students should be assessed with tests designed to differentiate among differing levels of achievement. These tests can be interpreted with reference to the explicit content domains by use of raw scores and with respect to the performance of other examinees by means of derived scores.

When curricular material isn't very explicit, masterable, or essential and expansive instructional aims are cognitive, affective, or social, teaching focuses on meaningful integration of new content into the learner's prior cognitive structure so that it can be appropriately anchored, retrieved, and transferred within the subject, to other subjects, and to everyday life situations. Individual differences are exhibited in level or breadth of achievement, or both. High-road transfer is central to both instruction and assessment. Assessment is designed to reveal the differences that are present in students' command of the expansive domains. Such tests are interpreted with reference to the performance of other examinees by means of derived scores.

DEVELOPING AND USING TEACHER-MADE ASSESSMENTS

CONTEXT-ADAPTIVE PLANNING OF INSTRUCTION AND ASSESSMENT

CHAPTER OVERVIEW

HOW TO CHOOSE THE MOST SUITABLE ASSESSMENT METHOD

PLANNING INSTRUCTIONALLY USEFUL CLASSROOM ASSESSMENTS FOR CONTEXT A
Special Role of Diagnostic Tests
Special Role of Pretests

PLANNING INSTRUCTIONALLY USEFUL CLASSROOM ASSESSMENTS FOR CONTEXT B

PLANNING INSTRUCTIONALLY USEFUL CLASSROOM ASSESSMENTS FOR CONTEXT C

SEEKING DESIRABLE CONSEQUENCES OF ASSESSMENT

KEY TERMS

decision-making sieve
diagnostic test
prescriptive test
pure speed test

pure power test
tables of specifications
parallel, equivalent, or alternate test forms

The various kinds of measures that teachers create are of central importance. Indeed, the assessment information that is most important for classroom use comes from classroom assessments (Brookhart, 2002). Therefore, this topic receives much attention in this book.

Creating effective classroom measures requires several attributes. First, teachers need a grounding in theory and knowledge to guide sound professional judgment concerning when and how to use various kinds of tests. Chapters 1 and 2 laid a foundation, and then context-adaptive planning (CAP) of assessment and instruction was developed in Chapters 3 and 4 to provide a foundation on which teachers can plan and implement sound assessment practices.

A second attribute for developing effective achievement measures is sufficient advanced knowledge of the subject matter to avoid stumbling on technical content issues when assessing examinee command of it. Third, teachers must be familiar with student characteristics such as reading level and ability to cope with test directions and separate answer sheets. Fourth, those who create outstanding tests need a measure of creativity! Relatively little space is devoted to the attributes listed in this paragraph because they are already present in the vast majority of teachers. Vital as they are, deficiencies in these characteristics seldom cause inadequate classroom assessment practices.

A fifth attribute for developing effective achievement measures is possession of basic techniques of test construction. Part II of this book is devoted primarily to the development of practical skills. It provides "how to" information for constructing objective tests, essays and other product assessments, and performance measures. These skills can then be used in conjunction with the perspectives provided in Part I to enable classroom assessment to be a fully integrated, highly constructive aspect of effective teaching.

A sixth quality teachers need is the ability to decide wisely when to use each of the several kinds of assessments mentioned above. This decision-making skill was previewed in Chapter 1 and will be developed throughout Part II as various item types are discussed.

Whether one is building a house, writing a research paper, organizing a meal, or preparing to assess student learning, planning is indispensable. In this chapter, we take up issues concerned with planning assessments of student achievement. As we do so, recall that school assessment exists *within the context of instruction,* and instructional contexts differ. Therefore, we will use the CAP approach to plan classroom assessment for effective assessment and for effective instruction.

For assessment to enhance learning, it must be carefully *planned at the same time that instruction is planned,* not as an afterthought. When a teacher develops a unit's subject matter and methods, the design should include aligned assessment. This includes consideration of:

- The types of assessments
- The conditions of assessment data collection
- The content of assessment as related to the content of the learning materials (Nitko, 1989)
- The timing of assessment (Terwilliger, 1989)

Let's reiterate this fundamental point. Sure, we urge early planning of classroom assessment in order to enhance assessment; that's important. More importantly, however, we urge early planning of assessment *in order to enhance student learning.* This chapter will weave in considerable discussion of *planning for constructive formative and summative* instructional *uses of classroom assessment.* This topic, which was first introduced in Chapter 1, relates to each of the three sectors of CAP.

SELECTING APPROPRIATE ASSESSMENT TECHNIQUES

Three broad categories of assessment techniques were introduced in Chapter 1. They are:

1. Objective measures (e.g., true-false, matching, completion, multiple choice, and most interpretive exercises). Such measures will be considered in Chapters 6 and 7.

2. Essays and other product measures (e.g., math proofs, shop products, computer programs, musical compositions, omelets, hemmed dish towels, works of art). Product measures and their assessment will be the focus of Chapter 8.

3. Performance measures (e.g., behind-the-wheel driving, oral tests, music contests, debates, gymnastics demonstrations, free-throw contests, lamb showing, machine operation, conflict resolutions on the playground, voluntary turn-taking in the classroom, collaborative study group activity, tryouts in music, drama, and athletics). These measures and their assessment will be addressed in Chapter 9.

An observation method or a paper-pencil item type that is well adapted for assessing some kinds of student status in certain types of subject matter may be wholly inappropriate for assessing other student attributes in other content. Teachers need skills in developing several major kinds of assessments so that each method can be used when it is most appropriate and avoided when it isn't a good match for their needs. (Caution: Don't expect a one-to-one correspondence between the three contexts of CAP and the three item types; there isn't one.)

How should one decide which item type to use? A general rule was previewed in Chapter 1. *Note that this rule isn't complete; it doesn't take account of all relevant considerations.* However, it factors in several major issues that should enter into decisions concerning what kind of assessment to plan. For now, the decision rule will be repeated without its rationale:

- Instructional objectives that can be assessed adequately with objective items ordinarily should be.
- Of the remaining instructional aims, those that can be well assessed with essay tests or other product measures ordinarily should be.
- Only the objectives that still remain need to be assessed by means of performance measures.

Figure 1.2 on page 17 depicts this rule as the **decision-making sieve.** Instructional targets that are retained in the top level of the sieve should typically be tapped by objective test questions. Of the remaining objectives, those caught in the second layer should ordinarily be assessed by essay or other product measures. The objectives that are left in the third layer of the sieve need to be assessed by observing performance.

The main limitation of the decision-making sieve is that it applies only to maximum behavior objectives that can be achieved during schooling. In Chapter 9, anonymous surveys will be suggested for objectives that don't fit these limitations. At that time, the full rationale for the decision-making process, which will be developed in Chapters 6 through 9, will be laid out. Meanwhile, the rule will serve quite well for many assessment decisions.

PLANNING TEACHER-MADE PAPER-PENCIL, PRODUCT, AND PERFORMANCE TESTS

The remainder of this chapter focuses on context-adaptive *planning* of classroom assessment. We will show how context-appropriate planning of assessment activities *promotes effective instruction,* and we will show how to use CAP in the service of *effective assessment.*

Planning in Context A

Some subject matter is clearly identified, masterable, and important enough to merit mastery. In this case, explicit mastery objectives are used to set mastery thresholds and to dictate that individual differences shall be expressed in the time dimension in order that each student shall attain minimum satisfactory performance.

Planning to Answer Instructional Questions Unique to Context A.   Context A subject matter domains contain few elements. When there are few items in a domain, it is usual to teach each and every one of them and then to test all of them. The desired low-road transfer involves only minor variations among the presentations of the elements of the material, such as the order for addition facts. Tests are used to ascertain *whether* critical achievement thresholds have been met. If they have, then instruction proceeds to the next unit. If a minimum acceptable level of performance has not been attained, then recycling is used to remediate the difficulty. Testing in Context A is **diagnostic** (to pinpoint problems) and **prescriptive** (to provide information useful in correcting these problems).

A Score for Each Context A Objective.   Reliable "mastery-nonmastery" information from summative scores is needed for *each* explicit mastery objective. This need for a one-to-one correspondence between objectives and scores is widely overlooked. Each explicit mastery objective is minimally essential. Therefore, it is necessary to verify that each has been mastered. The combining of data for several objectives would obscure this needed information.

For example, suppose a unit consists of three explicit mastery objectives and a mastery threshold of 85% has been established for each. Marge's status on the respective objectives is 100%, 75%, and 95%. Her mean percentage is 90; this is safely above the 85% threshold. However, she hasn't mastered the second objective. If it concerns truly essential knowledge or skills, then it isn't appropriate for her to be advanced to the next unit before mastering it.

Thus, in Context A assessment *it is necessary for a separate test or subtest to provide a score or subscore for each mastery objective.* Failure to separately assess achievement of each explicit mastery objective contradicts the contention that the targets were truly essential.

Special Role of Pretests.   Because Context A units are often highly sequential, learners often need certain requisite entry knowledge for successful new learning. The verification of teacher-identified essential entry skills commonly takes one of two forms. If recent instruction has been organized on a mastery model, then posttests for previous requisite units will certify each examinee's readiness for the new unit. Otherwise, the teacher may need to use one or more mastery pretests to determine whether each student is ready for the new material.

As an example of sequential material, one must be able to count before learning to add. If a teacher discovers that a student lacks vital requisite learning, then the new material isn't presented; rather, remediation is undertaken. In Context A, pretests provide vital information, and their results are used to make instructional decisions about individual learners.

Establishing the Achievement Threshold.   In planning a test for an explicit Context A domain, a teacher needs to set the level of achievement that is deemed to be essential. Unfortunately, this is often undertaken with insufficient thought and rationale. The mastery threshold is best set with a thoughtful consideration of the consequences of the two kinds of classification errors that result from use of a mastery test.

One undesirable consequence is failing a student who really does have sufficient proficiency to safely move on. The negative consequence of this error is wasting time and resources in forcing the student to spend more time on the Context A unit.

The other potential error in a mastery test is passing a pupil whose proficiency is too low to enable future progress. The negative consequence of this error is moving the student into a failing situation.

In tests for units for which the first kind of error is the greater danger, then the mastery threshold should be set relatively low so that the student may advance appropriately. In mastery tests for units in which the second kind of error is the more worrisome, the threshold should be relatively demanding so that the student is not moved on prematurely. We will spiral back to this issue in Chapter 14 when we consider consequences of test use as a validity issue.

Planning Guidance of Student Effort.   Recall the principle that assessment should guide student study in desirable directions. In Context A, this guidance is most constructive if students' knowledge of explicit test content directs them to study important elements in the domain.

However, two qualifications are needed. First, students ordinarily shouldn't have advance knowledge of item order that would enable them to memorize a test key without necessarily achieving the objective.

Second, in some unusual Context A domains where there are more items than should be chosen for any one form of a test, tests may sample the domains. For example, an objective concerning the 100 addition facts presented (a) horizontally, (b) vertically, and (c) orally might reasonably be assessed with a 50-item sample of the 300 possible items. In this case, it obviously would *not* be appropriate for pupils to have advance knowledge of which 50 addition facts were to be sampled on a particular form of the test or how each would be presented. Likewise, the particular items sampled should be varied from form to form.

Aside from these qualifications, it is generally productive for students to have advance knowledge of test content when they are expected to exhibit mastery of explicit, essential domains. The advance knowledge *prompts students to do what we want*—study the entire domain and master the low-road transfer of it.

Planning to Maintain Mastery.   The State Capitals Test in Chapter 1 demonstrated that material mastered at one time may not remain mastered forever. What then is mastery? The word implies a permanence of learning that is often unjustified.

When we declare certain material to merit mastery, we would do well to consider whether mastery is likely to be sustained over time. Mastery of some Context A subject matter is very durable, whereas other material (e.g., state capitals) quickly erodes. Central to the difference is whether the learning is used.

Much Context A material is used constantly; its unceasing utility demonstrates why it is considered to be essential. The 10 Hindu-Arabic numerals are encountered daily. Stopping at red lights and going at green ones occurs far too often for people to forget the arbitrary association. *When the subject matter of explicit mastery objectives will come into frequent use in everyday life or in future schoolwork, teachers can demand mastery and then move on to the next unit without worrying about reassessing it later.*

Other Context A subject matter is not used constantly. Examples are emergency telephone numbers and how to administer CPR. If material is essential, yet unlikely to be practiced in ordinary living, then steps should be taken to provide for permanence of mastery. A well-known way to enhance the permanence of mastery is review; this is achieved by relearning after some forgetting has had time to occur. *When the subject matter specified by explicit mastery objectives is unlikely to come into frequent use in everyday life or in future schoolwork, then it is important to ensure that mastery is permanent.* Passing a mastery test on one occasion does *not* guarantee permanent mastery.

This issue is often overlooked by advocates of mastery learning. Yet before we rush to provide excessive review of mastered material that is not likely to be needed in daily living, we might reconsider whether it was truly essential. If it concerns low-frequency emergency procedures, such as slowing one's car when a ball rolls out from behind a parked car, then it probably merits review. Otherwise, it may be some often-memorized content that really isn't essential. Examples are the state capitals, the Gettysburg Address, and the quadratic formula. It is usually a mistake to classify such content as essential. *The mastery approach to teaching and testing is best reserved for subject matter that is truly essential.* Hence the need for context-*adaptive* planning.

Planning Test Content.   To be valid, measures need to be aligned with the curricular material and objectives that they are used to assess. In the case of a Context A mastery test, validity concerns the extent to which the test measures mastery of the content or skill domain and indicates *whether* students have mastered the domain. *Explicit mastery objectives used in Context A combine both subject matter and statement of aims.* The objective contains all that is needed to show what the test should contain. This makes construction of Context A mastery tests relatively easy. Four examples follow.

Sentence Capitalization.   Miss Rainwater is teaching her primary class that the first word of a sentence is always capitalized. This generalization is vital, simple, explicit, and masterable. Notice that the domain is far from small. Therefore, Miss Rainwater is concerned with transfer of training; the point of the unit is to achieve automatic, low-road transfer to all sentences. The first draft of her explicit, behavioral, mastery objective was:

> When writing from dictation or composing, pupils capitalize the first word of each sentence at least 85% of the time.

Before continuing, let's note two problems with this objective. First, it isn't clear whether the objective concerns pupils' maximal performance when they know they are being assessed or their typical performance when they are attending to something else, such as a coherent written account of a recent field trip. The issue would be adequately addressed by simply inserting the word "can" or the phrase "typically will" before the word "capitalize."

Second, what if a pupil were to capitalize every word? In this case, Miss Rainwater wouldn't want to give credit for capitalizing the first words of sentences. To accommodate these two points, she revised the objective to read:

> When writing from dictation or composing in situations where no special emphasis is directed to the issue of capitalization, pupils typically will selectively capitalize the first words of sentences at least 85% of the time.

All that is needed is to obtain samples of work done for other reasons and determine whether the initial words of each child's sentences are capitalized at least 85% of the time and that most other words are not. The children shouldn't, of course, know ahead of time which samples of their work will be used to measure mastery of this objective.

What about the issue of permanence? Need Miss Rainwater provide time for formal review and reassessment? No; everyday schoolwork provides more review than necessary to make mastery of this objective permanent. She might best monitor written work for the rest of the school year; thus, if a pupil slips, it is caught and corrected. Subsequent teachers can also be depended on to monitor maintenance of this objective. For these same reasons, she did not set the mastery threshold as high as she otherwise might have.

This has been a rather straightforward example of a Context A unit and test. The next two examples are less clear-cut.

Name Capitalization.   Mr. Smit's class is learning to capitalize first and last names. Two things about this content make it atypical of Context A. First, the domain of names, although explicit, is neither small nor closed. Second, not all surnames are capitalized; for example, deCosta and van Meter aren't. Therefore, this content really isn't fully masterable; it is one of those exceptions discussed late in Chapter 4. Yet Mr. Smit wisely decides to stick to names that conform to the rule and treat the material as a mastery unit despite its borderline status. (He would do well to mention in passing that exceptions to the rule do exist. If such occurrences happen in his class, they would probably be learned, but their exceptionality would be noted.)

Having decided to treat the content (at least mainly) as a mastery unit, Mr. Smit writes the following explicit mastery objective:

> When composing or writing from dictation, students can, at least 90% of the time, selectively capitalize the name(s) of any person mentioned.

Needing to dictate some suitable material to the class that includes some names, he comes up with:

> Mrs. Jones drove to school to pick up Jane and her friends Mary Smith and Jim Lu. Their teacher, Miss Ann Green, had been sick that day. Mary said that the principal, Mr. Short, had taught their class.

Mr. Smit can score each test to see if the child selectively capitalizes at least 9 of the 10 names. Those who do are judged ready to move on to another objective. The others should spend more time on this mastery objective. Those who need to study more will, when they are ready, take *another form* of the test consisting of different names and different sentences. Students should *not* know ahead of time the exact content; assessing for low-road transfer is vital.

This unit exemplifies a content domain that encompasses features of both Context A and Context C. It is best taught mainly as a Context A unit because the *rule* is explicit, masterable, and very widely applicable via low-road transfer.

Roman Numerals.   Next consider a less clear-cut unit. Ms. McAlpine is teaching the first dozen Roman numerals to her fourth-grade class. Her objective for this small, closed, incisively defined, important, and masterable content is:

> When shown one of the first 12 Roman numerals, the pupil will write the corresponding Hindu-Arabic numeral with at least 95% accuracy.

FIGURE 5.1   Adequate Test of a (Too) Limited Objective.

Below are some Roman numerals. Next to each write the Hindu-Arabic numeral that has the same meaning.

VIII _____	III _____	XI _____	X _____
I _____	XII _____	VI _____	V _____
IX _____	VII _____	II _____	IV _____

Here, too, it is easy to create a mastery test based on this explicit, mastery objective. One form of her test is shown in Figure 5.1.

In this way, Ms. McAlpine develops a test that validly assesses her objective. Prior knowledge about the test and its exact contents (but not item order) serves to guide pupils to do what the teacher wants—study the Hindu-Arabic equivalents to the first 12 Roman numerals. She creates several forms of this test. One form is used as a pretest to enable some students to "test out" of the unit. This teaching practice is often overlooked as a key element in providing content and materials that best address the individual needs of students, particularly students with high ability for learning such material. She makes two forms available for self-testing to enable students to know when they are ready for a summative test. Still other forms are used as summative assessments for the first and, if necessary, subsequent attempts to pass the unit. Of course, all of these forms are interchangeable.

The use Ms. McAlpine makes of the administration of a form may be decided *after* the test, depending on how well a pupil performed on it. If a student passes the test, it is used summatively. If a student fails it, then it will be used formatively; in this case, she examines which items were missed. Very different remediation would be prescribed for the pupil who missed IX, X, XI, and XII than for the child who missed only IV and IX.

Although we shall be critical of this unit for other reasons, all the features mentioned in the two preceding paragraphs are excellent for a Context A unit.

This unit exemplifies content that has *un*wisely been *restricted artificially* to fit the format of mastery learning. Alas, some teachers would handle the unit in this way. Thinking Cap Exercise 5.1 provides an opportunity to consider how the unit might be better taught.

THINKING CAP EXERCISE 5.1   ???

1. Ms. McAlpine confined the unit to a small, closed domain. She taught the material mainly by drill and demanded only rote learning of the first 12 Roman-to-Arabic conversions.

Some teachers do just this, focusing on rote mastery of *artificially limited* domains. This makes for sterile units that do little to encourage thinking. Indeed, such units subtly indicate that school is a place to memorize, not a place to think! We weep for their students!

If the teacher were more inclined to favor a Context C approach, how might the entire approach to the unit differ? In considering your answer, also consider these leading questions:

- Is it appropriate to require translation from Roman to Hindu-Arabic numerals, but not the reverse, as Ms. McAlpine did?
- Should one arbitrarily pick exactly the first 12 numerals?

THINKING CAP EXERCISE 5.1   CONTINUED

- Are the first 12 numerals really vital? Are others *un*important?
- Is this content as devoid of meaning and high-road transfer as is common in Context A material?

2. Are the questions in item 1, Context A, Context B, or Context C questions for readers? Why?

KEY TO THINKING CAP EXERCISE 5.1

1. The answers to all the questions in item 1 are "no" or "probably not." Roman numerals don't best belong in Context A.

The domain of Roman numerals is explicit and masterable, but it is uncommonly large. Clearly, mastery isn't necessary for the entire domain, yet mastery (via rote learning) of the *symbols* I, V, and X seems vital. For these basics, individual differences would best be channeled into the time dimension. Beyond that, it isn't reasonable to demand mastery. The instructional strategy implied is to demand mastery of the first three symbols—that much *is* in Context A— and then to move on to higher-level aspects of the topic.

But the plot thickens. It is also important for pupils to master the *basic system* (e.g., the difference between IV and VI and the meaning of XVII). They will need to understand the system if they are to be able to extend it to larger Roman numerals when additional symbols (e.g., L and C) are introduced. The Roman *system* is large, but quite simple. It is moderately important and relatively masterable. The system might well be treated as Context A material to be mastered for low-road transfer.

Thereafter, instruction in Roman numerals should be in Context C, wherein high-road transfer is also important. A little work with arithmetic using Roman numerals does wonders to instill a profound appreciation of two major features of the Hindu-Arabic system—place value and zero. Without going outside the familiar system with which one has grown up, it is difficult to grasp the profound significance of these features. It would be a pity to study Roman numerals without exploiting this opportunity to build appreciation and understanding of the Hindu-Arabic system through contrast.

Another benefit to be sought is the knowledge of the monumental contribution of Hindu and Islamic cultures to Western civilization. Understanding and appreciating this heritage could be an important outcome of the unit. Yet it would be lost in Mrs. McAlpine's sterile mastery approach to the topic.

Because the first 12 numerals are important for using some clocks, should they be mastered? No; we would rely on *mastery of the first three symbols* and *mastery of the system* in order to produce *meaningful* command of the first 12—indeed the first 39—Roman numerals. By emphasizing the meaningfulness and downplaying the ability to memorize the first dozen numerals, we would try to establish the attitude that this material is to be understood and transferred, not merely memorized. *This learning disposition itself is transferable* to other units (Tishman, Perkins, & Jay, 1995).

2. The analysis undertaken in item 1 was difficult and required high-road transfer of learning. The questions definitely tapped complex Context C content and processes.

Driver Education.   Now that two not-so-obvious units have been considered, we shall consider again a clear-cut Context A situation for our final example. Mr. Keim teaches driver education and wants each student to remember where the switch is for the emergency blinkers on the car being driven. Although this knowledge is not necessary to drive, he decides to demand mastery of it because of its importance in emergencies. Accordingly, he writes the following somewhat explicit mastery objective.

On command to turn on the emergency signal, the student will, without taking eyes off the road and while driving the car, turn it on within five seconds.

As in most clear-cut Context A units, it is easy to create the performance test once the objective is well written. When a student is driving, Mr. Keim need only unexpectedly say, "turn on the emergency blinkers," and observe if the task is executed within five seconds without diverting eyes from the road. True, we could quibble about the difficulty of this task depending somewhat on traffic conditions. Yet most of us would elect to treat this as Context A content in spite of this limitation of explicitness of task difficulty. We would, of course, seek low-road transfer to various makes and models of cars and to various traffic conditions.

Planning in Context B

Some teaching material is incisively identifiable, yet mastery is either impossible or nonessential. In either case, explicit developmental objectives direct individual differences into the achievement dimension.

Planning Guidance of Student Effort.   The two kinds of Context B subject matter lead to different ways of crafting classroom assessment practices to foster beneficial study. Some skill or curricular domains are explicit yet unmasterable; most such material involves psychomotor skills, such as basketball free throws. Other Context B domains are specifiable and masterable, yet not important enough to require mastery; most such subject matter involves knowledge, such as the state capitals.

The way to maximize the study-driving consequences of Context B assessments depends on whether they will cover the entire skill or content domain or merely a sample of it. If a test is to assess a skill or an entire content domain, then test security is of no concern. An explicit developmental objective identifies the exact domain, it is taught in its entirety, and it is tested in its entirety (but without expecting mastery). Planning and developing such tests follows easily from the objectives, and there is often little difference between a practice session and a testing session.

If, however, a test is to assess only a sample of a domain, then test security is important. Although an explicit developmental objective specifies the exact domain that is taught in its entirety (albeit not to mastery), it is tested *by sampling*. The sample tested should be *representative* of the domain. If students had prior knowledge of the material to be sampled (e.g., particular states), they might learn that material better than the rest. Indeed, some students wouldn't bother to study the rest at all! The test would thereby be rendered *un*representative of the domain, and interpretations of its scores would *mis*represent student status. Thus, prior knowledge of what a test samples can both (a) compromise the test's validity in answering the instructional questions it was designed to address and (b) divert students away from the kind of study the teacher wants.

Planning the Test Content.   Explicit developmental objectives for Context B subject matter combine both subject matter and statements of instructional targets. This makes the construction of Context B differentiating assessments relatively straightforward. Examples follow.

Swimming.   Mr. Matthews coaches swimming and wants each member of the team to be able to swim a 100-meter freestyle as rapidly as possible. This explicit developmental objective concerns specific skills. Developing the assessment is easy; the performance test and the practice activity are indistinguishable. Nor would a given summative test lack formative potential; the coach may well critique a summative performance with the hope of improvement in the future.

This unit provides our first example of a pure speed test. The only thing assessed in the 100-meter freestyle was speed. With athletic skills, speed is often a central concern.

Speed of Adding One-Digit Numbers.   In cognitive skills, too, speed is sometimes a virtue even though it usually is not the central focus. This section illustrates an unusual situation in which speed is the primary issue. First, however, we need some definitions. In paper-pencil instruments, **pure speed tests** consist of very easy items that all examinees can answer correctly if given sufficient time. Such tests have time limits so short that few if any examinees can finish; hence, they measure only how fast examinees can work. In contrast, if **pure power tests** even have time limits, they are so generous that no examinee would do any better if given more time. Such tests measure only power. Speed and power exist on opposite ends of a continuum; the more speeded a measure is, the less it assesses power, and inversely.

Teachers typically are primarily interested in assessing power. Whether it is factoring algebraic expressions or reading prose, we're usually more interested in how well people perform than in speed of performance. Yet speed is a legitimate secondary concern.

Occasionally, however, a teacher needs to focus on speed. For example, Ms. Bravewolf has taught all of her third graders the *meaning* of the 100 addition facts. That is, she sought *understanding of the process* of addition. As a result, her pupils can, if given enough time to count fingers or tally marks, solve virtually any problem involving the addition of two one-digit numbers.

She more recently has been helping pupils to memorize the 100 addition facts so that they can *quickly* retrieve any sum from memory without taking the time to figure it out. The convenience of rapid addition is now her focus. To assess speed of adding, she gives a test of addition facts with a time limit so short that few, if any, pupils will complete it. This is the only way she can test *speed* of addition.[1]

Eurasian Countries and Capitals.   Mrs. Fish wants her seventh-grade geography students to be somewhat familiar with countries and their locations. This material is explicit and masterable; thus, it could be taught for mastery. However, she judges the material not to merit mastery. Therefore, she puts it in Context B. We applaud her wisdom.

Mrs. Fish has to decide whether to test all of the countries or only to sample them. If she chose to test them all, then test content wouldn't be confidential. Rather, she elects to sample the countries. Therefore, test content must be kept secure.

In selecting which countries to include on her test, Mrs. Fish divides the list into three equal groups on the basis of population. Wanting populous countries to have greater probability of being tested than less-populous ones, she decides to select countries to be tested from the respective strata on a 3:2:1 ratio. Information about the existence and degree of this "top loading" should be given to students in order to harness assessment power.

---

[1]Beware of a possible source of confusion. Mrs. Bravewolf's speed-of-addition unit, like all Context B units, channels individual differences into the *achievement* dimension. That is, instructional time is the same for all pupils; therefore, they will differ in their *achievement* of speed of addition.

TABLE 5.1   Planned Questions on a Geography Test for a Large Class

STRATA	COMPLETION ITEMS	MATCHING ITEMS	TOTAL
Top	7	6	13
Middle	4	4	8
Bottom	2	2	4
Total	13	12	25

She considers the following explicit developmental objectives:

1. Given an outline map of Eurasia, students will pronounce the names of the countries.
2. Given an outline map of Eurasia, students will write the names of the countries.
3. Given an outline map of Eurasia, students will match country numerals with names.

Because these aims are not deemed to be essential, their assessment can be combined into a single test and test score. Therefore, she must address the relative weight the objectives are to carry.

She must also consider how each objective would best be assessed. To test achievement of objectives 1 and 2, she would use an outline map with numbered countries. For objective 1, she would have students individually pronounce names of countries. For objective 2, she would have them write the names of the countries on answer sheets. Both procedures measure ability to *retrieve* names from memory and to *produce* them; they differ in the *method of production*. Testing achievement of objective 2 is economical, whereas testing achievement of objective 1 requires time-consuming individual oral testing. Mrs. Fish considers the importance of the method of production. She decides that students who can spell a country's name (or come close) can also usually name it (or come close to pronouncing its name correctly).

Before abandoning objective 1, Mrs. Fish wisely considers the consequences on student study efforts. She decides that eliminating objective 1, but retaining objective 2, would not adversely impact study effort.

To assess achievement of objective 3, she would use the outline map with countries numbered. Names of countries would be supplied for students to match with numerals. This taps student ability to *recognize* and *match* names. It saves labor of scoring handwritten materials. However, like many other teachers, Mrs. Fish values this somewhat less than their ability to produce the names. If only objective 3 were to be assessed, students might try to learn more for recognition than for retrieval. Moreover, they would neglect spelling.

Table 5.1 shows the 25-item test plan that results from all of these considerations. This example illustrates why we sometimes consider using a less-than-ideal item type to assess learning. It shows that, within limits, it is reasonable to modify assessment in order to be cost- and time-effective. It points out the need to be aware that bowing too much to expediency may cause test power to pull in the wrong direction. Finally, it illustrates the effort that knowledgeable, caring teachers expend in planning effective instruction and assessment.

THINKING CAP EXERCISE 5.2

1. Mrs. Fish's test content had to be kept secure. Why?

2. Mr. Karim uses "show and tell" for his third-grade pupils to practice making oral presentations. He develops a rating form suitable for any show-and-tell presentation with which to assess their presentations on such features as eye contact, voice volume, and posture. Should students know the contents of this rating form or should it be kept secure?

3. Suppose you were a fifth-grade teacher charged with teaching the state capitals as a part of the year's social studies work. Assume, too, that you agree with the rationale developed at the end of Chapter 1 that suggested that students need not master the 50 state capitals in order to lead full lives and be good citizens. This would lead you to assign the topic in Context B. Finally, suppose that you have decided to give the unit limited emphasis over a five-week interval and to give a 12-item quiz on five different occasions during the unit. How might you best develop a plan that would be helpful in creating all five quizzes?

KEY TO THINKING CAP EXERCISE 5.2

1. The test only sampled the domain. If students knew ahead of time which countries were to be tested, then *two* guiding principles would be violated. First, some students would study the tested countries to the exclusion of the rest, and the test would be rendered an *un*representative sample of the domain and would thus provide *misleading* information for decision making. Second, the test would fail to prompt students to do what the teacher desired—to learn as many of the countries as feasible.

2. Its content should be shared with students so that they will know what the aims are. In this way, performance assessment power is harnessed. The rating form may also be useful to students in improving their skill in self-assessment.

3. Several things should be considered. First is balance among regions of the country. This could be achieved by dividing the country into a few regions and

selecting a suitable number of states for each form of the quiz.

Second is difficulty. If raw scores are to be comparable, then states of comparable difficulty must appear in each form. Otherwise if quiz 2 happened to sample mostly easy states, whereas quiz 3 chanced to include several hard ones, then pupils would appear to know less in quiz 3 than in quiz 2; this could be demoralizing. One might use judgment concerning relative difficulty and thereby attempt to maintain at least crude equivalence among the forms.

Third is importance. Some states may be judged to be more important than others. Indeed, one might well demand mastery of the students' own state. Additionally, one might want to give more emphasis to very populous states than to others.

Table 5.2 provides one reasonable way of taking account of these factors. The teacher has (arbitrarily) specified the five states having the largest population and the home state as ones that will have more chance of being sampled in any given form of the test.

TABLE 5.2   Specifications for State Capitals Quiz

Five Big States plus Local State	4	
Region of 44 Other States	Easier	Harder
11 Northern	1	1
11 Eastern	1	1
11 Southern	1	1
11 Western	1	1

In developing the five forms of this quiz, the teacher ought to *avoid behaviors that enable students to guess which items will appear in a given form*. For example, one ought *not* to systematically rotate through the states in each region. If Oregon happens to be the western state sampled in quiz 1, then it should have no more and no less likelihood of appearing on another form of the quiz than do states such as Arizona that happened not to have been sampled previously. Students are quick to pick up on such teacher behaviors; one should be careful to *not be predictable* beyond the level specified in the test plan.

Planning in Context C

To complete our consideration of the great significance of differences in curricular context in planning instruction and assessment, we turn now to Context C. Some subject matter domains are broad in scope, not very explicit, unmasterable, and not sequentially necessary for study of subsequent topics. In this case, expansive developmental objectives are used to direct individual differences to level and breadth of achievement.

Formative tests can help students and teachers cope with such questions as "What grade would I (the student) receive on a summative test if I studied no more?" "Is there a topic in which my status is especially weak?" "Is there a particularly important part of the unit (such as the conjugation of an important irregular French verb) on which I am still weak?" and "On which I (the teacher) need to devote more class time?"

Most Context C assessment involves summative measures that help teachers answer such questions as "What grade should I assign to each student?" "How has the class as a whole achieved relative to other groups?" and "How has my new approach to a certain topic worked?"

Because the aims in Context C are developmental, it isn't necessary to separately assess achievement of each objective. Several objectives are ordinarily combined into a single score.

Planning to Guide Student Effort: Seeking Desirable Consequences of Assessment. For open-ended, unmasterable Context C material of the type that most of us teach most of the time, students definitely should *not* have prior knowledge of the exact test content. Because a differentiating Context C survey test can only sample the domain, test content is kept secure.

We can, however, easily guide student effort to emphasize some parts of a domain more than others. For example, a government teacher might tell the class that applications of the First Amendment are *much* more likely to appear on tests than applications of the Fifth. This harnesses "assessment power" by causing students to give priority to certain content.

Teachers also should direct student study effort to emphasize some *mental processes* more than others. Context C units typically contain some material that can be memorized by rote and some that requires complex mental processing. We expect students to do far more than be able to recite the facts; we want them to be able to use and transfer the information. "We want them to think" (Stiggins, Rubel, & Quellmalz, 1986, p. 5). If we want students to be able to engage in such processes as application, analysis, and synthesis, they should know this. A powerful way to get students to pursue these outcomes is to *tell them that such outcomes will be tested.*[2]

Much Context C subject matter should be taught for high-road transfer; its achievement, therefore, should be assessed for high-road transfer. The ability to generalize is assessed only if some of the material assessed is novel—that is, if the assessment exercises are significantly different from those studied (Terwilliger, 1989; Linn & Gronlund, 2000).

---

[2]Some educators may be concerned by the research showing that extrinsic rewards can decrease intrinsic motivation (e.g., Deci, Koestner, & Ryan, 2001). We think two reactions to this body of research are in order. First, for better or for worse, assessment *already* has power. We aren't trying to make it more powerful; rather, we are urging that the power be harnessed. Second, the research evidence should prompt us to do something with more rigor that we should be doing anyway—namely, to make learning interesting and intrinsically rewarding; assessments shouldn't be the only source of rewards for learning.

Planning the Test Content and Mental Processes.   Plans for Context C measures need to take into account both the (a) *mental processes* identified in the objectives and (b) *subject matter* with which the mental processes interact. This is usually accomplished by means of two-dimensional grids in which mental processes are listed at the top and subject matter topics are listed along the left-hand side. If several instructional objectives all invoke the same mental process (e.g., "understands" or "applies"), they may be combined into a single column. As previewed in Chapter 2, we call these grids **tables of specifications.** Such plans are referred to as behavior-content matrices by some authors (e.g., Woolfolk, 2001), whereas others call them "blueprints." By whatever name, tables of specification are two-dimensional plans to ensure that Context C assessments maintain *desirable balance* among the several mental processes and curricular topics that were taught.[3]

Not only is this thoughtful balance among mental processes and subject matter topics particularly important for planning Context C assessments, it is also central to the planning of instruction. By deciding before instruction begins how much emphasis to give various aspects of a unit, a teacher gains better control of both instruction and assessment and ensures that the two are consistent.

The value of developing Context C instruction/assessment plans lies in *making our wishes* concerning weight allocation *explicit* and *enabling us to monitor* tendencies to depart from intended weights. As discussed before, teacher-made tests tend to overemphasize memory while neglecting complex thinking and high-road transfer. Use of specifications can help prevent this. Planning before launching a unit is a powerful way for *teachers to seize control* of their instruction and their assessment. Thoughtfully developing assessment plans improves the adequacy with which content domains are sampled. And, as emphasized earlier, if students are "privy to the plans," assessment power can produce extremely beneficial consequences.

This section illustrates for Context C how tables of specifications "lock in" weight allocation of mental processes and topics. In the examples, notice how the numbers of mental processes and subject matter topics were kept small in order to avoid making the tables too cumbersome. Concerning topics, plans for objective tests often have from 3 to 12 rows, whereas plans for essay tests (which, of course, have fewer questions) often contain fewer rows. Concerning mental processes, specifications can be rather complex (such as using a column for each level in the original cognitive taxonomy); however, they commonly are simpler, having only three or four mental processes. Common mental process categories involve:

- Relatively rote or unprocessed knowledge or recall
- Comprehension and understanding, sometimes expanded to include analysis and synthesis
- Something involving application, problem solving, or evaluation that requires high-road transfer of knowledge and skills to situations that are new to examinees

Let's examine several diverse Context C examples of assessment planning and unit planning. As we consider these examples, we will be using implicitly the decision-making process (shown in the Figure 1.2 decision-making sieve) to select item types.

---

[3]Actually, for technical reasons, the plans only approximate intent; however, they do so adequately for classroom assessment purposes (Tinkelman, 1971).

Fifth-Grade Science.   Mrs. North is planning to have her fifth graders study vertebrate animals, the major characteristics of each class of vertebrates, and their classification into the five major groups of vertebrates. She will provide pupils with much practice in transfer by giving them new animals to classify, considering their tentative classifications, and discussing criteria for their classifications. Some of her examples will be presented with animal names and others with pictures. Still others will be presented by means of verbal descriptions. A few will be real animals at hand—the class hamster and goldfish and the pupils themselves. In addition to studying the five classes of vertebrates, the class will study the distinction between vertebrates and invertebrates.

Seeking high-road transfer of learning, Mrs. North plans to involve students actively in these activities by using small group activities, employing whole-class discussions, and providing feedback to students on their classification attempts. She hopes to seek transfer not only to other living things, such as seed plants, but to more distant areas. For example, she will ask students to identify other things that can be classified into taxonomies like living things are. After she models transfer of taxonomies to categories such as locomotives, music, and books, she will ask pupils to generate lists for cars and television programs.

Because of her teaching emphasis on high-road transfer, Mrs. North wants to give substantial test emphasis to student ability to classify *novel* examples. By making pupils aware that they will be required on the test to classify examples that they have not studied, she will guide their study efforts in this direction.

Concerning content, more class time will be devoted to mammals and birds than to amphibians. Accordingly, she wants the test to reflect these weights. After considering all of these issues, she develops the specifications shown in Table 5.3. Notice that half of the test's items are devoted to assessing high-road transfer of learning; this reflects her instructional emphases.

Mrs. North will test student recall of the characteristics specified in the first column either by use of short-answer questions or with matching exercises. For the second and third columns, she will use five-option multiple-choice items or five-option matching exercises for the top five rows to

TABLE 5.3   Specifications for a Fifth-Grade Science Test

PROCESS / TOPIC	KNOWLEDGE OF CHARACTERISTICS	CLASSIFICATION OF STUDIED EXAMPLES	CLASSIFICATION OF UNSTUDIED EXAMPLES	TOTALS
Mammals	3	2	4	9
Birds	2	2	3	7
Reptiles	2	2	2	6
Amphibians	1	1	0	2
Fish	2	1	2	5
Invertebrates	0	2	4	6
Inanimate Objects	0	0	5	5
Totals	10	10	20	40

require pupils to classify vertebrates into classes. She plans to use alternate choice items for the next row to have pupils classify animals as vertebrates or invertebrates. Finally, for the cell at the bottom of the third column, she will have students create outlines or Venn diagrams of nonanimal examples (e.g., movies and writing instruments) that were not studied in class.

This example is typical of Context C summative tests. It illustrates the principle that a test should ordinarily provide about the same relative weight to the various topics and mental processes that they receive in the unit. Thus, the specifications can ordinarily do double duty as guidelines for both instruction and assessment. This example also portrays how the plans for both test and lesson can constructively occur before a unit is launched. That is, *the time to plan the assessment of a unit test is at the same time that the unit is organized.*

Third-Grade Arithmetic Pretest.   On the first day of the year, Mr. Clark wants to assess his third graders' arithmetic skills after a summer without practice. Accordingly, in the week before school opens, he develops the test plan shown in Table 5.4 on page 116. This plan contains more detail than most teachers would have time to develop. As an example of how topics can be collapsed, Mr. Clark could have used as few as two rows, one for adding one-, two-, and three-digit numbers without regrouping and one for subtracting without regrouping. However, he chose to specify the content in more detail and thereby to control it more fully.

Mr. Clark plans two uses of the pretest results. First, he will use them to judge how much review is needed. Second, the scores will provide part of the information he will use after a week or so to tentatively divide his class into two or three instructional groups for arithmetic.

He doesn't plan to use this test to formatively diagnose specific weaknesses for individual pupils. It isn't long enough to provide dependable information such as "Mary can subtract when problems are presented in vertical but not horizontal format" or "Max can set up thought problems, but makes many careless errors in routine computations." At most, his test might provide very tentative clues along such lines. Additional testing or informal observation would be needed to substantiate or refute such hints.

This example illustrates use of a Context C test plan for a pretest. It also reinforces the principle that tests are used to improve decision making.

Eleventh-Grade United States History.   Each year, Mrs. Orr teaches several sections of eleventh-grade United States history. She retains her items in order to reuse them. Good items are hard to find and difficult to create. She has collected a rich assortment of objective and essay questions. She doesn't reuse whole tests because, in pursuit of relevance and high-road transfer, she always wants a few items to relate history to current events. She is, however, able to recycle individual questions with little danger of compromising test security. She stores her items in a password-protected computer file and finds it relatively easy to produce two or more forms of each test to discourage transmission of test information between class periods.

She uses multiple-choice and other objective questions to test knowledge of history as well as to assess some understanding, analysis, and application. She reserves the more labor-intensive essay items for those things that are not well assessed by objective items. For instance, she uses questions such as "What lessons might the history of . . . teach us about the current situation of . . . ?" "How was the President's recent decision to . . . inconsistent with President Truman's decision to . . . ?" and "What justification could a defender of both of these presidents offer to justify the inconsistency?" Use of such questions throughout the course prompts her students to look for connections as they study. Test power motivates students to seek meaning, relationships, and high-road transfer.

TABLE 5.4 Specifications for a Third-Grade Arithmetic Pretest

CONTENT \ PROCESS	ROUTINE COMPUTATION		THOUGHT PROBLEMS	TOTALS
	VERTICAL	HORIZONTAL		
Addition of two one-digit numbers	2	5	1	8
Addition of a one-digit number and a two-digit number without regrouping	2	2	1	5
Addition of two two-digit numbers without regrouping	2	1		3
Addition of a one-digit number and a three-digit number without regrouping	2	1	1	4
Addition of a two-digit number and a three-digit number without regrouping	3		1	4
Addition of two three-digit numbers without regrouping	3			3
Subtracting a one-digit number from a one-digit number	2	2	1	5
Subtracting a one-digit number from a two-digit number without regrouping	3	1	1	5
Subtracting a two-digit number from a two-digit number without regrouping	2		1	3
Subtracting a one-digit number from a three-digit number without regrouping	2		1	3
Subtracting a two-digit number from a three-digit number without regrouping	2		1	3
Subtracting a three-digit number from a three-digit number without regrouping	3		1	4
Totals	28	12	10	50

By informing them that such linking questions will be used in the final exam, Mrs. Orr encourages thoughtful course review.

For several years she has used the plan shown in Table 5.5 for a two-hour comprehensive final exam, which she counts as one-fifth of the second-semester grade. All forms of this test have 60 objective items. Each form also has two or three essay questions for a total of 40 points.

In building each form of the test, Mrs. Orr first selects or creates the essay questions and distributes the points for each among the rows and columns to which it relates. At this time she also develops her scoring guide or rubric for each item, as will be discussed in Chapter 8. She then retrieves from computer storage enough one-point objective items to complete each form of the test in conformity to her plan. To maintain the flexibility needed to accommodate the two or three big essays, she doesn't specify exact cell weights; she settles for keeping the sums of rows and the sums of columns in conformity with the plan.

Mrs. Orr recently took a graduate course in social-science curriculum development that raised her awareness of the need to give adequate teaching coverage to historical topics (e.g., military, economic, and social), as well as to historical periods. In Table 5.5, she specified her test in terms of a chronological approach to history. This has served her well in ensuring balance among periods (e.g., in avoiding overemphasis of World War I, which she personally finds fascinating). But has she maintained an appropriate balance among various topics?

To find out, she developed the alternative test plan shown in Table 5.6 to reflect her best judgment concerning weights the various topics should receive *in both the course and the tests.* She then scanned her lesson plans and found that some topics hadn't in the past received as much emphasis as she now believed them to merit. Moreover, some topics had been even more seriously underemphasized in her tests. The worst example was economic history—her own weakest suit. She believes

TABLE 5.5   Eleventh-Grade U.S. History Examination Specifications

TOPIC	KNOWLEDGE	UNDERSTANDING	APPLICATION	TOTAL %
Precontact to Revolution				10
Revolution and early national				13
Antebellum, Civil War, and reconstruction				15
Gilded Age and Progressive Era				8
World War I				5
Depression and New Deal				14
World War II				10
Cold War to Bicentennial				10
Recent and present				15
Totals	40%	35%	25%	100%

TABLE 5.6   Alternative Test Plan for Eleventh-Grade U.S. History Examination

TOPIC \\ OBJECTIVE	KNOWLEDGE	UNDERSTANDING	APPLICATION	TOTAL %
Intellectual and cultural				15
Social				15
Political				25
Economic				15
Military				20
Diplomatic				10
Totals	40%	35%	25%	100%

that it should comprise about 15% of the course and final exam. She estimated with dismay that in the past she had only given it 6% of the course emphasis and only 3% of the weight in her tests.

To remedy this, she committed herself to giving economics more attention in the course, in unit tests, and in the final exam. She wrote several economics test items to add to her file of questions. She wonders which table she should use in building next year's final exam. Ideally, she would like the features of both. This could be achieved with a three-dimensional grid, but such a complex table of specifications would be impractical. Instead she decides to use Table 5.6 next year to establish appropriate balance among topics. Then she will revert for a year to Table 5.5 to ensure that the content doesn't drift away from the desired balance among periods.

This example illustrates several things. It shows the need for looser constraints in planning essay tests than in planning objective exams. It shows that test plans are useful for final exams as well as for unit tests. It emphasizes the role of tests in stimulating mindful review. It reveals that there may be more than one sensible way to structure specifications. It also illustrates how test planning is not distinct from planning instruction; the two processes go arm in arm.

You may have noticed that some test plans (e.g., Tables 5.3 and 5.4) reflect the number of raw score points or test items, whereas others (e.g., Tables 5.5 and 5.6) show percentages of total weight. Which is best? In general, percentages may serve teachers best in initial planning of relative weight among topics and mental processes. However, number of points or test items may be more convenient as one works to develop questions for each cell of a table. It is of course possible and often useful for plans to specify both, as does Table 2.1 on page 28.

This is a good place to define the terms "alternative forms," "parallel forms," and "equivalent forms" of a test, which are used interchangeably in this book. Alternate forms of a test are forms that conform to common specifications but are not systematically more similar in content than their specifications dictate. **Parallel, equivalent,** or **alternate forms,** therefore, have the same weight allocations among topics and mental processes, but the particular test questions differ.[4]

An analogy with house plans may be helpful. If several houses are built from the same set of blueprints, the houses will be alike in only those attributes that are specified in the plans. They will,

[4]Ideally, parallel forms should also have equivalent raw scores, means, variability, distribution shapes, reliabilities, and correlations with other variables. Although these features can be approximated in published tests, even these instruments' derived scores require statistical fine-tuning to achieve interchangeability (Petersen, Kolen, & Hoover, 1989).

for example, have the same floor plans. However, they are not likely to include the same colors, styles of faucets, or carpeting.

Alternate forms are interchangeable in the sense that Mrs. Orr can use any of the several forms for testing a given class. All forms are parallel in the balance or mix of content and mental processes. Yet their raw scores should *not* be considered to be interchangeable because the forms will probably have chance differences in difficulty and variability.

Junior High School Music.   Mr. Martin teaches a required survey course in music appreciation. One of the units is "Music Around the World," in which students listen to, study, and seek to appreciate the distinctive and common features of music from four parts of the world. Mr. Martin places much teaching emphasis on such objectives as understanding, application, analysis, transfer, and appreciation. He is eager to develop a test that will go far beyond mere rote learning. Of course, he also wants to test knowledge and comprehension of features of the four music styles. He does this with multiple-choice items. The first column of Table 5.7 shows the weights he assigns to objectives that involve knowledge and comprehension.

How to assess application and analysis? One method would be to play recordings of music from various world regions and ask students to analyze, in essays, various features of the music. Another approach would be to play short excerpts from two different styles of music and ask students to compare and contrast them. The second column of Table 5.7 involves these kinds of aims. To allow flexibility for longer essay questions, Mr. Martin doesn't fill in the separate cells.

Mr. Martin also expects students to be able to recognize typical music from each of the four regions when they hear it. He assesses this with a matching exercise having the parts of the world as the options. The "questions" are auditory presentations of music selections that weren't used in class. The third column in his specifications concerns this means of testing for high-road transfer with these novel auditory stimuli.

Finally, he requires two projects—one done in class and one out of class. For each project, each student must create and perform (on any instrument or with voice) an original composition in one of the music styles studied. Each student's two projects must use different styles and instruments. These projects are local legend—the thing for which his class is famous.

The last column of his plan indicates how much weight he allocates to this means of assessing complex learning. Mr. Martin has developed a rating form, or rubric, to assess important aspects

TABLE 5.7   Music Around the World Assessment Plan

PROCESS / CONTENT	PAPER-PENCIL RESPONSES			
	KNOWLEDGE AND COMPREHENSION	APPLICATION AND ANALYSIS	AUDITORY CATEGORY RECOGNITION	ORIGINAL PRODUCTIONS
Asian	9%		5%	Use rating forms to assess two original productions played by each student
African	8%		5%	
Slavic	7%		5%	
Polynesian	6%		5%	
Totals	30%	20%	20%	30%

of these original compositions. To help students focus their project preparation on the aspects that he considers important, he shares this instrument with students early in the unit.

Mr. Martin estimates that about 40% of students' total time on the unit is spent in developing their projects. The general rule for weight allocation would specify that 40% of the assessment should be allotted to the projects. However, he has two reservations concerning the projects. First, he suspects that some students get more help in developing their out-of-class project than is desirable. Second, the reliability with which he rates the projects isn't likely to be as high as that of his unit test.

In view of these misgivings, he considers giving the projects only about 20% of the total weight. However, he knows that consequences of evaluation must also be considered. Assessment guides student effort. If the projects don't carry much weight, students will neglect them. Yet he values the projects; they get students actively engaged in the ethnic music, elicit creativity, and tap performance skills. Balancing the inclination to count the projects only 20% with the practical need to make them important in students' eyes, he compromises with a 30% weight.

This example illustrates the use of assessment specifications for a summative unit posttest of a domain that is assessed by joint use of paper-pencil and performance tests. It provides an example of planning for a rich variety of item types. It illustrates a situation in which a teacher considers departing from the typically parallel weights for a unit and its assessment. It provides for scoring criteria for performance tasks with which both to improve the assessment of the performances and to enhance instruction by communicating to students what is important in their performances. It illustrates the utility of tables of specifications in multicontext units. Finally, it reviews the fundamental principle that assessment influences what students study.

CHAPTER RECAP

Assessment is part of teaching. The fundamental purpose of classroom use of formative and summative assessment is to enhance student learning. To achieve better instruction by means of better student assessment, teachers need to assess with care and forethought. Poorly constructed classroom measures or inappropriate kinds of assessments can undermine other facets of teaching. Well-balanced, carefully crafted achievement measures enhance student learning.

The first step in developing effective classroom tests is to make sound *professional* decisions concerning the kind(s) of tests appropriate to the situation. This professional decision making is aided by use of the CAP approach.

Another step in devising sound assessments of student achievement involves careful and timely planning. By thoughtful planning, teachers can obtain desirable balance among content topics and among mental processes. An essential part of the plan for assessing products or performances is the development of the rating criteria to be used. *Planning also takes into consideration the effect that assessment practices will have on student effort.*

The next step involves using the most suitable kind of assessment. It makes sense to use the most reliable and least costly method that will do the job. The final step in developing effective teacher-made tests is to apply specific item-writing skills. These topics will be developed in the next four chapters.

CHAPTER
6

DEVELOPING COMPLETION, ALTERNATE-CHOICE, AND MATCHING ITEMS

CHAPTER OVERVIEW

WHAT DIFFERENTIATES OBJECTIVE TESTS FROM OTHER ASSESSMENTS

USES AND MISUSES OF COMPLETION AND SHORT-ANSWER QUESTIONS

DEVELOPING GOOD COMPLETION AND SHORT-ANSWER ITEMS

SHORT-ANSWER ITEMS VS. RECALL ITEMS

USES AND MISUSES OF ALTERNATE-CHOICE ITEMS

DEVELOPING USEFUL ALTERNATE-CHOICE QUESTIONS

USES AND MISUSES OF MATCHING EXERCISES

DEVELOPING EFFECTIVE MATCHING EXERCISES

KEY TERMS

objective item
short-answer item
completion item
recall-type item
supply-type item

alternate-choice item
true-false item
specific determiner
matching exercise

Chapters 3 and 4 provided information that helps educators consider the context of classroom assessment in deciding what general evaluation practices best contribute to student learning. The emphasis was on analysis of subject matter and professional decision making. Just as surgeons must first use professional judgment to decide what, if any, operation is called for, educators need professional judgment to choose appropriate student evaluation practices.

Once a surgeon decides that a given type of surgery is needed, the operation must be carefully planned. Similarly, teachers benefit from planning their classroom assessment. Chapter 5 provided assistance in planning for each CAP context. It also presented a decision-making plan for selecting item type.

Finally, specialized surgical skills are essential for the operation to be successful. Likewise, once a teacher decides on a given means of assessing students, specialized instrument-construction skills are needed to develop measures that will do the job well. Chapters 6 through 9 concern such practical assessment skills and techniques. These chapters complement the earlier, more theoretically oriented material with a body of specific "how to" information.

This chapter focuses on completion and short-answer items, alternate-choice items, and matching exercises. In general, these kinds of items are suitable for assessing examinee status on relatively simple learning outcomes. They are typically easier to construct than are multiple-choice items, interpretive exercises, essay or other product-assessment instruments, and performance assessments. The final kind of objective question, multiple-choice items, will be taken up in the next chapter.

WHAT ARE OBJECTIVE ITEMS?

Before examining various kinds of objective questions, one might ask, "What is an objective item?" **Objective items** are so named because they are *objectively scored.*

In all other respects, so-called objective items are just as subjective as other item types. When planning tests, teachers deliberate in allocating weight among content topics and mental processes specified in an assessment plan. They decide to use particular item types or blends thereof, and they decide which particular questions to ask. All of these decisions are equally subjective for all item types.

To reiterate, the only element that differs between objective tests and other kinds of tests is the objectivity with which they are scored. The scoring of objective test answer sheets can be very accurate. Once the test maker decides which option of a given question is to be keyed, then the determination of whether each examinee has selected that keyed option is entirely objective. Comparing answer sheets with the key doesn't require professional knowledge, just clerical accuracy. Marking can be relegated to conscientious paraprofessionals, competent clerks, or even machines. This also applies to some very simple performance tasks. For example, a voice-sensitive computer can score verbal answers to arithmetic questions or a clerk can objectively score a child's ability to perform simple commands, such as "Bring me the book from the table."

In contrast, judgment typically is required in assessing essays, other products, and performances. Much inaccuracy can creep into the scoring of such devices. Later chapters devote considerable attention to minimizing subjectivity of scoring.

In seeking to define "objective," emphasis is placed on what is not objective about so-called objective tests. This is an important point that helps to deprive objective tests of any inappropriate aura of infallibility. On the other hand, the feature that *is* objective—marking—is extremely important. This feature enables objective tests to be scored more reliably than is usually possible with other kinds of tests. Moreover, this consistent scoring is rapid, inexpensive, and doesn't demand professional qualifications; these are important advantages.

COMPLETION AND SHORT-ANSWER ITEMS

The first of the simple item types considered in this chapter are **short-answer items** and **completion items.** They share so many features that they are considered together. For all practical purposes, they are equivalent (Oosterhof, 2003).

Paper-pencil test items are often classified into two groups—objective and essay. Although short-answer and completion items are categorized as objective because of the objectivity with which they are scored, they differ from other objective items in one important respect. Examinees responding to completion or short-answer questions must *produce* their own answers (like examinees responding to essay questions); they must **recall** and **supply** their responses. In contrast, examinees responding to alternate-choice, matching, or multiple-choice items must *select* the correct or best options. Thus, objective completion and short-answer questions share a characteristic with essay items; they demand that examinees produce their own answers rather than recognize and select correct answers.

What Do Completion and Short-Answer Items Measure?

Figure 6.1 provides several sample short-answer and completion items. Although some item ideas are best cast as completion items, others are more easily phrased as questions to be answered. Still others can be written either way about equally well. For example, item 3 could be "What is the chemical symbol for gold? _____"

All completion and short-answer items ask examinees to produce answers. Beyond that, important differences are present. Some questions require students only to retrieve answers from memory without much processing. Others require examinees to figure out their responses.

Each item in Figure 6.1 assesses learning that can be measured with a completion or short-answer item. Some kinds of learning are best measured with such items, whereas others would better be assessed by use of other item types.

The first six questions require examinees to access information from long-term memory. Questions 2, 3, and 4 are particularly well suited for completion or short-answer format because students who don't know the answer are unlikely to have available much material from which to guess. To illustrate, consider item 4, which has only a few viable alternatives, for example, Abraham, Moses, Jesus, and Mohammed. Students raised in a predominantly Judeo-Christian culture will be less likely to know the name of the right answer—Mohammed—than the other alternatives. It may, therefore, be better to avoid a multiple-choice format that would provide them with Mohammed's name, thereby enabling guessing. This situation is reminiscent of the completion item, "South Carolina" on the State Capitals Test in Chapter 1. People who do not know the capital may miss the completion item more often than they would miss the corresponding multiple-choice item. With the multiple-choice item, they have a better chance of guessing the correct answer.

FIGURE 6.1   Sample Short-Answer and Completion Items. (See text for discussion of which items would better be cast in other formats.)

1. What was the name of the author of *Hamlet*? _____   _____
2. The set of events that brought the U.S. and the U.S.S.R. to the brink of war during the Kennedy Administration is best known as the _____.
3. The chemical symbol for gold is _____.
4. The name of the most important prophet in Islam was _____.
5. The planet having the greatest mass is _____.
6. Which political party controlled most of the South during the period of the New Deal and the Fair Deal? _____
7. $\dfrac{56}{8} =$ _____
8. A 15-kg child sits 4 m from the center of a seesaw. A 20-kg child sits on the other side so that they are in perfect balance. The second child therefore must be _____ m from the center.
9. If $x^2 - 3x - 10 = 0$, then the roots are _____ and _____.

Although items 1, 5, and 6 are also suitable for completion format, they could be cast in easier-to-score formats. Almost anyone would realize that Shakespeare was a possibility for item 1; indeed, students who are uncertain may recall his name and his alone among reasonable authors. In this case, framing the item in a format that provides other options may actually make it harder for students who don't know the answer. This is reminiscent of Idaho on the State Capitals Test; some people get it right because Boise (which happens to be the capital) is the only Idaho city they know. Formats that provide other options can cause more people who don't know the capital to miss the item.

Items 7, 8, and 9 require that students figure out and produce answers. Some teachers make a sharp distinction between the ability to *produce* an answer and the ability to *select* or *recognize* it. They contend that students who don't know how to solve a problem might know how to check alternative answers for it. For example, a pupil unable to divide 8 into 56 might know that multiplication is the inverse operation of division. Thus, each option provided in a multiple-choice item could be checked by multiplication to see if it is correct. Such a pupil could use elimination to select correct answers to such questions if they were in multiple-choice format but could not *produce* the correct answers if the problems were cast in completion format.

Although the logic of this concern is powerful, other teachers dismiss the argument with the observation that virtually any student astute enough to systematically check options in this way is also proficient enough to solve the problem in the first place.

Nonetheless, many math and physical science teachers prefer completion and short-answer items to other objective item types mainly for this reason. It is not unusual to see an entire Context C math test framed in completion and/or short-answer format. Some such tests contain questions that demand complex mental processes. Item 8 in Figure 6.1, for example, requires use of a principle. Such tests are important exceptions to the generalization that completion items rarely are adequate for entire Context C tests.

Another reason why some math and science teachers prefer completion and short-answer items is that they lend themselves to requiring students to show their work. Having students display their formulas and calculations can improve several kinds of decision making. It can provide a basis for awarding partial credit. It gives teachers an opportunity to mark papers to show students where and how they went astray. It provides teachers with feedback about what topics or processes may need review. Finally, it informs teachers of common misconceptions; this can improve future instruction.

In testing spelling, most teachers would consider their instructional objectives for spelling to be much better assessed by tasks that require pupils to *produce* correctly spelled words than by those that assess how well they can *identify* incorrectly spelled words or discriminate between correct and incorrect spellings. Furthermore, teachers may question the presentation of an assortment of *incorrectly* spelled words to be viewed and processed in the minds of impressionable learners. Thus, we see that the item type that a teacher uses to assess an objective has an influence on the validity with which that objective is assessed.

Some Rules for Constructing Completion and Short-Answer Items

Rules will be provided for each item type or assessment method considered in this book. Before considering these rules, it is important to recognize a *cardinal principle of item writing* that applies to *all* assessment tasks: *Start with an important idea.* Every test question begins as an idea in the mind of the item writer (Wesman, 1971). First, one should have in mind some *significant* element or skill to be assessed; only then is one ready to choose an item type and to draft the item or the directions for a performance task. Each of us needs to be sure to put our brain in gear before engaging our hands!

Before offering specific suggestions for constructing various item types, we want to acknowledge that, although some of the rules are based on research, the research isn't very extensive (Haladyna, 1997). Rather, the suggestions are based mainly on common sense and conventional wisdom (Millman & Green, 1989). Following are item-writing suggestions for short-answer and completion items.

1. Phrase items so that blanks fall at or near the end of statements. A completion task is more easily understood when the missing part occurs at the end of the sentence. Hence, blanks should come as near the end as possible without contorting the sentence.

Example of rule violation: _____ are animal species that provide milk for their young.

Improved version: Animal species that provide milk for their young are called _____.

2. Blanks should be of a uniform length. Variable lengths of blanks provide undesirable clues.

Example of rule violation: What was the most famous thing that Thomas Jefferson ever wrote? ___ _____ __ _____

A student about to write in "The United States Constitution" would be clued by the lengths of the blanks. Notice that the second improved version avoids indicating the number of words in the correct response.

Improved versions: What was the most famous thing that Thomas Jefferson ever wrote? _____ _____ _____ _____

What was the most famous thing that Thomas Jefferson ever wrote?_____

3. There should be only one correct way to answer an item. Some items can be correctly completed in so many correct ways that they are worthless.

Example of rule violation: The drafter of the Declaration of Independence was _____ _____.

The intended answer may have been Thomas Jefferson, but correct answers include "a man," "an American," "a Virginian," "a patriot," "a radical," and so on.

Improved version: What is the name of the person who drafted the Declaration of Independence? _____ _____

4. Use sentence structure and vocabulary that are different from that of the instructional material. One of the worst ways to create a completion item is to indiscriminately use a sentence from a text, deleting a word or two. Such items usually violate the cardinal principle of item writing by failing to measure important learning. They encourage students to memorize rather than comprehend what they read (Oosterhof, 2003). Furthermore, such items often have many correct ways by which they can be completed. The examples of poor items for rules 1 and 3 could well have been lifted verbatim from a text.

5. Avoid excessive numbers of blanks in items. When an item contains several blanks, there usually is no one correct way to fill them in. The following example illustrates the kind of mutilation sometimes found in poorly constructed completion items. Such items usually are the result of mindless lifting of material from a textbook, a violation of rule 4.

Example of rule violation: The most decisive battle in the _____ War was between
                                 General _____ and General _____ at _____.

6. Use completion and short-answer items to measure ability to *recall* significant factual information. If recognition and recall seem to be about equally appropriate indicants for an instructional objective, then it is usually easier to assess students with multiple-choice or matching exercises. On the other hand, if recall is valued more, then completion or short-answer items are indicated. In this case, of course, one should *expect recall only of important material.*

7. Decide ahead of time how to handle spelling errors and be consistent with this decision. As discussed in the State Capitals Test in Chapter 1, the situation may determine whether spelling should count. It often should, but only for partial credit. For example, a student who answers the question, "The name of the most important prophet in Islam was _____," with "Mohamed" rather than "Mohammed" surely deserves more credit than one who answers "Confucius."

8. If units of measure (e.g., dollars or miles per hour) are required, indicate that requirement. Then decide how to handle omissions and errors for each item and be consistent with this decision. Omission and errors of units in math and science often should be penalized, but (like spelling errors) usually only for partial credit. If this issue isn't important to the test maker, then it is best avoided by including the unit term in the item as was done with item 8 in Figure 6.1.

9. Avoid grammatical clues. Common grammatical clues indicate whether a missing word is singular or plural or whether the initial letter is a vowel or a consonant.

Example of rule violation: Each self-governing nation in the Commonwealth of Nations is
                                 called a _____.

Improved versions: Each self-governing nation in the Commonwealth of Nations is
                                 called a(n) _____.

                                 What is each self-governing nation in the Commonwealth of
                                 Nations called? _____

The second improved version illustrates an advantage of the direct question over the completion format: It is less likely to provide clues.

   10. Format to make scoring easy and accurate. If examinees fill in the blanks where they naturally occur, scoring is tedious. Yet this may be the best approach in lower primary grades because it is less complicated for pupils. Above the primary grades, two better solutions are available. First, a column of blanks can be provided along the right-hand side of the test booklet. The blank for each item is positioned to the immediate right of the blank embedded in the item. This enables a strip answer key to be used for rapid and accurate scoring. Second, a separate answer sheet containing item numbers and blanks for responses can enable easy scoring. In either case, the blanks are retained in the items, and examinees are instructed where to record their answers.

   11. Avoid overuse of completion and short-answer items. In general (aside from math and certain physical science tests), completion items tend to be limited to measuring recall of factual information. Some factual recall is important in most Context C units, and completion and short-answer items provide a good way by which to assess some of it. However, Context C tests typically should measure much, much more than mere recall. To tap complex mental processes, consider the techniques discussed in Chapters 7 through 9.

Directions for Completion and Short-Answer Items

The directions that precede a set of items should inform examinees of several things. They should be told where they are to write their answers. They should be reminded to write or print clearly. They should be informed whether such things as spelling and capitalization will count. In quantitative tests, examinees should be cautioned if units of measure will count. In most cases, directions should indicate that each item (in contrast to each blank) is worth one test point.

THINKING CAP EXERCISE 6.1   ???

1. At several places in this section, emphasis was placed on ways to cause students who don't know an answer to miss it. Is it appropriate for teachers to try to cause some students to miss test questions? Aren't teachers supposed to be *helping* students?
2. What two major problems arise when completion and short-answer items are overused?

KEY TO THINKING CAP EXERCISE 6.1

1. Those irritated by efforts to cause items in Context C tests to differentiate between students who know more and those who know less can be said to suffer from a "Context A hangover"; they are inappropriately applying a rationale that is suitable for Context A teaching to Context C testing.

   Tests in Contexts B and C are designed to reveal the individual differences in achievement that are present among examinees. That is, the tests are supposed to discriminate among persons on the basis of the attribute the test is supposed to assess. For example, a 100-meter race is supposed to discriminate against slow sprinters.

   In this context, a sharp distinction is necessary between one's teaching function (where one tries to enable all students to do as well as possible) and one's assessment function (where one tries to reveal how well each examinee can perform). The job of tests is to reveal examinee status. Where examinees differ in status, tests should show it so that the information revealed can then be used to enhance student learning.

   Nothing in the defense of differentiating testing is intended to endorse so-called trick questions that cause knowledgeable examinees to miss items for trivial reasons.

(continued)

THINKING CAP EXERCISE 6.1   CONTINUED

2. Serious overuse of completion and short-answer items is common. Tests consisting mainly of such questions (aside from math and some physical science tests) usually measure little beyond factual recall. Tests that overemphasize such shallow learning have two major failings. First, they are not valid measures of deep learning. Second, they communicate to students that only rote memory is important to success and that being able to understand, apply, and analyze are not important; this influences future student learning.

SELECTION-TYPE ITEMS

The key distinctions among various kinds of selection-type items are the number of options per item and how they are formatted. The **alternate-choice** item, as its name implies, offers two options. A multiple-choice item offers more options, usually three to five, and its options usually differ from one self-contained item to another. The matching exercise is formatted into a set and often provides more than five common options for all items in the set.

Alternate-Choice Items

Alternate-choice items usually have the advantage of requiring relatively little reading for students; therefore, more content often can be covered. These items have the corresponding disadvantage of limited reliability because of the 50 percent chance of correct wild guessing.

What Do Alternate-Choice Items Measure?   Alternate-choice items are appropriate whenever there are exactly two possible answers to be considered. What they assess, of course, is examinee ability to correctly choose between the two alternatives. The most common alternatives are "true" and "false." Before taking up the true-false item type, we will consider some of the other kinds of alternate-choice items.

Miscellaneous Alternate-Choice Items.   Alternate-choice questions can be used to assess student achievement of certain rather limited objectives and indicants. Context C units usually encompass a broader spectrum of learning outcomes than can be measured adequately with alternate-choice items.

However, alternate-choice questions sometimes provide the best way to assess certain kinds of learning. The miscellaneous kinds of alternate-choice items considered in this section are not at all limited to the measurement of rote recall; they often can be used to assess examinee ability to engage in deep thinking. They could be used more widely to good advantage. Following are some examples of how various alternate-choice items can be appropriately used in a wide variety of settings.

■ Kindergartners who have been building the concepts of "plant" and "animal" could be given alternate-choice items having options of "plant" and "animal." Items could be presented orally or visually and answered either orally (if administered individually) or by circling pictorial options of sets of plants and animals. Items might be statements of characteristics (e.g., "are usually able to move themselves from place to place") or names or pictures of plants and animals. Questions using the exact organisms studied in class may assess simple recall; items involving examples that weren't used for instruction could tap high-road transfer ability to apply principles of classification. The EnCAPsulation at the end of this discussion provides an elaboration of a similar idea.

■ An elementary school class that has studied the distinction between fact and opinion could be tested with alternative-choice items. Each item consists of a statement, and the directions instruct pupils to circle "F" if the statement is a fact and "O" if it is an opinion. Fact-opinion items can, of course, measure high-road transfer of learning if the stimulus statements are new to pupils.

■ If important objectives or indicants concern student ability to discriminate between correct and incorrect health practices, sewing procedures, math answers, statements of class rules, punctuations, and so on, then correct-incorrect alternate-choice items can be useful.

■ Alternate-choice items have several other uses in language arts. For example, they can be used to indicate whether words should be capitalized. A set of questions can be based on a passage in which selected words are underlined and numbered. For each selected word, students indicate whether it should be capitalized.

Certain word-choice tasks provide other language arts examples. Alternate-choice items are an excellent way to test student ability to choose correctly between "who" and "whom," "me" and "I," and so on. They also provide a good way to assess the correct choice between pairs of homophones (e.g., sum and some). Following are items for which examinees would be instructed to circle their choices.

(Us, We) students took a test today.
It is (I, me).
Please turn your application in to Mrs. Dunzeczky or to (me, myself).
Give it to (whoever, whomever) most deserves it.

Of course alternate-choice items should only be used where one choice is clearly better than the other. In this regard, what is wrong with the following item?

The faculty presented (their, its) recommendations.

A teacher preparing this item might have intended "its" to be the correct answer. However, British teachers would key "their," as might American teachers if various faculty members offered different recommendations.

True-False Items

By far the most common variety of alternate-choice questions is the **true-false item.** True-false questions provide a suitable way to examine student achievement of certain rather restricted objectives and indicants. Context C tests should rarely if ever consist exclusively of true-false questions. Although they can be constructed to measure ability to use complex thinking, they are not often so used. Testing more than rote recall with true-false items requires skillful item construction. Moreover, it is usually easier to assess deep thinking with other item types.

■ ■ ■ ■ ■

ENCAPSULATION

An interesting variation of the alternate-choice item type is the yes-no format used by some primary teachers. Contrary to the negative feelings of some older students about tests, many first and second graders enjoy the occasional challenge of "showing how much they have learned" in subjects such as science or social studies. It also gives them "bragging privileges" and learner status among older students, as in "We had a test today, too." This aspect of serious study and subsequent evaluation can guide student effort just as surely as the big chemistry exam for a high-school student.

A short test of key concepts in a unit of study can provide a teacher with helpful information for decision making, particularly if much of the unit has been explored in group work. See Figure 6.2 for an example of a brief quiz for primary students after a unit of study on insects.

Results of such a quiz can reveal pupil command of basic learning of important concepts as well as command of more complex learning involving analysis, application, and competencies in listening, observing, making inferences, and drawing conclusions. Moreover, informal observation of the children while they are taking the test provides additional information about such important affective characteristics as their confidence and their enjoyment of the activity. Such kinds of information are useful for planning curriculum and for conferencing with family members about their child's development and achievement.

Directions and quiz format for primary grade tests should be clear and concise and should be given orally, with visual demonstrations on a chart or chalkboard if necessary. The teacher might prepare a simple answer sheet and provide directions that require minimal or no reading. For example, the teacher could offer the instruction, "To show what you think is the best answer to the first item, circle the Y for Yes or the N for No in the first box of the ice cream row," while demonstrating with a sample item. To help children learn the "rules" and purposes of tests, it is good to add, "Be sure to do your own work on this test. That way I can know what you have learned."

Figure 6.3 on page 132 provides several true-false items that are formatted to be easy to score. Students would be directed to circle the "T" if the statement is true and the "F" if it is partly or wholly false. Note that these items are not all well written; some contain faults that will serve as examples in the following discussion.

Some Rules for Constructing True-False Items.   Following are some helpful guidelines for crafting true-false items that assess what they are intended to assess.

1. Use only statements that are absolutely true or false. This requirement eliminates from consideration the most important content in most fields because statements typically have exceptions. This is an important reason why true-false items are so limited with regard to the kinds of Context C material they can assess effectively. The sample true-false items in Figure 6.3 contain several violations of this basic rule.

- In item 3, it's unclear whether the question is intended to address the whole world or just the Northern Hemisphere.
- In item 4, Mohammed and Jesus have *somewhat* parallel, but not identical, places in Islam and Christianity. In Islam, Mohammed is considered to be the greatest prophet by far. In Christianity, Jesus is considered to be much more than a prophet. This item keyed "F"

FIGURE 6.2   Insects Test

Ice Cream Cone Row

1. Do a huge number of kinds of insects live on the earth?
2. Are all insects bugs?
3. Do insects have exactly six legs?
4. Do insects have three body parts?

Flower Row

5. Is every kind of insect helpful to people?
6. Do butterflies and moths look and act alike?
7. Do birds like to eat monarch butterflies?
8. Does each honey bee have a certain kind of job to do?

Happy Face Row

9. Does the queen honey bee make the honey?
10. Do people like to have termites in their houses?
11. Do grasshoppers have very long FRONT legs?
12. Do grasshoppers chew and spit tobacco?

Hat Row

13. Should people destroy bees to keep them from spreading pollen?
14. Is a praying mantis a good garden friend?
15. Should we try to get all the ladybugs out of our gardens?
16. Do people like to have cockroaches in their kitchens?

Star Row[1]

17. Does every kind of fly bite?
18. Do mosquitoes lay their eggs on water?
19. Did our class find an ant with wings?
20. Does our classroom ant farm have a queen ant in it?

---

[1]Amend Questions 19 and 20 and any others as needed to reflect experiences provided to the examinees.

might be acceptable after a thorough study of Islam, but the issue may be too technical for a basic middle-school unit. It would be wrong to key it "T" because it is not true; to so key it would deny credit to students who "knew too much." It would also be unreasonable to key it "F" because so answering requires more information than provided in the text or class.

■ In item 5, the correct time would be 12:00 *noon*. The knowledgeable examinee doesn't know whether the teacher writing the item would key it "T" or "F." If one sought to assess the technical (and widely violated) point "noon," then a multiple-choice item with options of 12:00, 12:00 A.M., 12:00 P.M., 12:00 noon, and 12:00 midnight would be preferable.

■ In item 7, the hapless examinee is left to wonder whether the teacher intends it to be false because it is not true at all altitudes (or more technically, at all atmospheric pressures) or

FIGURE 6.3   True-False Items of Variable Quality

T	F	**1.** Most insects have six legs.
T	F	**2.** All presidents of the United States must be at least 35 years of age.
T	F	**3.** There are more hours of daylight in June than in November.
T	F	**4.** Mohammed is to Islam as Jesus is to Christianity.
T	F	**5.** If it is 7:00 A.M., in five hours it will be 12:00 o'clock.
T	F	**6.** It is generally warmer in the summer than in the winter mainly because the sun is nearer during the summer.
T	F	**7.** Water boils at 100 degrees C.
T	F	**8.** Meals should not ordinarily consist entirely of fruits.

whether the teacher carelessly overlooked this important issue. If the latter, then the student who is less careless than the item writer may miss the item.

Indeed, this is the problem with all true-false items that fail to be categorically true or false. If they are keyed in a simplistic way, then the student who responds from a more sophisticated perspective will miss the question. On the other hand, if the item is keyed in a more technical way; then it may be "picky" or "tricky" for examinees who have studied the topic at a basic level.

In creating statements that are indisputably true or false, avoid words that are vague or equivocal. Words such as "recent," "short," "fast," "heavy," "cruel," "important," or "meaningful" are, in some contexts, unnecessarily ambiguous. Try to be specific, such as "less than five feet" or "one of the top three cited works."

2. True-false items should not ordinarily be lifted verbatim from textual material. A terrible way to develop true-false items is to indiscriminantly lift sentences from a text and call them test questions, for example, "Grapefruits are similar to oranges." It is equally inappropriate to insert (or delete) a negating word to make such a sentence false, as in "Grapefruits are *not* similar to oranges."

Statements that may be acceptably true in the context in which they appear in learning and teaching material are often ambiguous when presented in isolation. Moreover, such items usually fail to assess important learning. Good true-false items are ordinarily created from scratch. This item-writing rule exemplifies the cardinal principle that *one should always start with an item idea.*

3. Avoid consistent clueing with specific determiners. A **specific determiner** is a word that tends to be found much more often in true items than in false ones or vice versa.

Absolute words such as "never," "none," and "all" provide clues that a true-false item is apt to be false. This is because item writers often use such words to make an otherwise ambiguous item false. For example, a high-school physics teacher might alter item 7 in Figure 6.3 to read, "Water always boils at 100 degrees C." The item is clearly false, but it contains the clue "always." A better solution might be, "Regardless of atmospheric pressure, water boils at 100 degrees C."

The other class of specific determiners includes qualifying words such as "usually," "most," and "generally." They are more often found in true items because item writers often need to qualify statements to some extent in order to make them categorically true. For example, the author of item 1 in Figure 6.3 had to say "most" in order not to get hung up on injured insects or mutants. The word "ordinarily" is needed in item 8 to make the statement true in spite of possible exceptions.

Many students are aware of the clues provided by specific determiners and thereby consistently improve their test scores. Thus, their scores on a test reflect test wiseness as well as the attribute that the test is designed to assess. This *erodes the validity of the test as an assessment of student achievement of instructional objectives.* Consider item 1 as an example. Students who are test-wise will get the question right even if they know nothing about insects.

This caution about specific determiners does *not* dictate that they be avoided, only that they not be used in a manner that provides consistently helpful clues. Items 2 and 6 in Figure 6.3 exemplify skillful use of specific determiners in ways that will miscue, or provide misleading clues for, test-wise students who know nothing of the subject matter. Item 2 concerns an absolute constitutional requirement for eligibility. It is no less true with the "all" than without it, but the "all" causes some test-wise students who are ignorant of the constitutional provision to miss the item. Similarly, item 6's use of "generally" and "mainly" tends to make the test-wise, content-ignorant student respond "true." Because the item is false, this miscue is useful.

Some readers may be annoyed or distressed with what they interpret as our glee at causing some students to miss an item. Please note again that it is *only those who lack knowledge* of what the item is intended to assess that we wish to cause to miss the item. In these rules we take great pains *not* to trip up students who know the content well. The fundamental point is that Context C items have a function to differentiate. To put it bluntly, Context B and C tests are supposed to discriminate against people who are ignorant of the content the test is designed to assess! And *only* against the content ignorant!

Skillful use of specific determiners to provide false clues achieves two things. Obviously, it improves the quality of the items themselves. In addition, it enables one to resort to use of an occasional specific determiner in the conventional clue-providing way with impunity, such as the "ordinarily" that was needed in item 8 to make it categorically true. The important thing is for test makers to avoid careless use of specific determiners in ways that provide test-wise students with predominantly helpful clues. Their skillful use is a virtue.

4. Avoid clueing with item length. Unless efforts are made to avoid it, true items will tend to be longer than false ones because qualification is often necessary to make an item incontestably true. A remedy is to edit true statements carefully to render them as succinct as clarity allows. When this doesn't equalize the average lengths of true and false items, then "pad" a few of the false statements to make them longer.

5. Avoid double-barreled items. Each true-false item should focus on the truth or falsity of only one statement. For example, "California is a western state having more people than any other state" is a double-barreled item. Better that each important fact be measured by a separate item. Or, consider item 6 in Figure 6.3, which involves three issues—the truth of the first clause, the truth of the second clause, and the causal link between the clauses. A multiple-choice item offering several reasons why it is generally warmer in the summer would be preferable.

6. Avoid negative items. Double negatives, of course, shouldn't be used. Even single negative statements in true-false items, such as item 8 in Figure 6.3, require double-negative thinking. As another example, examinees must ask, "Is it *false* that the salt water will *not* freeze at 32°F?" This becomes logically taxing in ways unrelated to what the item is designed to assess.

If a negative item is used, then the negating word or prefix should be underlined, capitalized, printed in bold face, or italicized to ensure that it will not be overlooked. However, the most desirable means of editing such an item will usually be to rephrase it. For example, "It is ordinarily appropriate for meals to consist solely of fruit." (Notice that the use of "ordinarily" in this version will tend to mislead the content-ignorant but test-wise examinee.)

7. Maintain balance between true and false statements. Many teachers tend to develop more true items than false ones. This is undesirable because it enables content-ignorant, test-wise examinees to guess with better-than-even odds. A few teachers have the opposite quirk. Either way, some test-wise students catch on to a teacher's item-writing peculiarities, and this provides a clue. One should check sets of true-false items to assure that approximate balance is maintained.

8. Format sets of true-false questions to make scoring easy and accurate. If examinees cursively write "True" or "False," much grief may be experienced in reading their writing. Likewise, capital cursive "T" and "F" look much alike. Even the manuscript letters can be troublesome. To avoid wasting time and prompting disputes, have examines *circle* the letters "T" or "F" or the words "True" or "False."

If answers are to be recorded in the test booklet, then the true-false letters or words should be arranged in columns to the left of the item (as in Figure 6.3). Better still (for older students), a separate answer sheet, similar to those displayed in Chapter 10, can provide a column of item numbers with "T" and "F" letters to be circled. This makes for even faster scoring with no need to turn pages. The astute teacher will scan a section before scoring to catch any double markings.

9. Avoid overuse of true-false items. True-false questions have a rightful place and should occasionally be used by most teachers. In general, they are most effective for measuring recognition-type recall of factual information. Some such recall is important in most units, and true-false items provide a reasonable way to assess some of it. However, Context C tests should measure much more than mere recall of facts. Therefore, the rightful place of true-false items is limited.

THINKING CAP EXERCISE 6.2 ???

It was suggested that a separate answer sheet might be used with examinees at and above the upper elementary level. However, some students have learning, visual, or motor disabilities that make the process of transferring responses to an answer sheet frustrating and error prone. What are the teacher's responsibilities in such situations? How can such disabilities be recognized? How might accommodations be made for such students, and what should those accommodations be?

KEY TO THINKING CAP EXERCISE 6.2
The caring teacher will want to observe students carefully in order to discover perceptual, conceptual, and motor problems that *prevent them from demonstrating their competence with the material.* One might consult with special education personnel for pointers on recognizing and addressing difficulties students have with assessment procedures. For students with documented disabilities, *accommodations should be made as needed to enable students to demonstrate their competence with the subject matter the test is designed to measure.* For example, a student could be permitted to respond to items directly on the test copy rather than on the answer sheet.

For practice, the student might enter the selected responses on the answer sheet and also mark them directly on the test copy. Then the student should be encouraged to recheck both response sets if time permits. If discrepancies occur, the test copy could be used for scoring. After several such self-regulated practices, the student might become more skillful in following routine procedures, thus strengthening an important skill for life and work beyond school.

Disabilities of many varieties often have major impacts on student test performances. More attention will be given to this special education issue in Chapter 13.

Directions for True-False Items.   The directions that precede a set of true-false questions should achieve several things. They should tell examinees how and where to record their answers. The directions also should inform students that an item is to be marked true only if the statement is always true. It is to be marked false if it is always false, sometimes false, or partially false.

In most cases, beyond the primary years, the directions should inform examinees of how much each item will count. Items are usually worth one point each. It is ordinarily not worth the trouble to provide differential weights to objective test items. If the topic on which an item is based is deemed important enough to merit more credit than is assigned to other items, then the topic should be assessed by including more questions.

Finally, if the issue of guessing is not addressed in the general directions at the beginning of the test, examinees should, at the beginning of the first selection-type section, be given clear instructions concerning the circumstances under which they should or shouldn't guess if they don't know the answers to questions. Because this issue is intimately related to methods of scoring, its consideration will be postponed until Chapter 10.

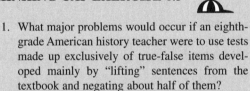

THINKING CAP EXERCISE 6.3

1. What major problems would occur if an eighth-grade American history teacher were to use tests made up exclusively of true-false items developed mainly by "lifting" sentences from the textbook and negating about half of them?
2. Can alternate-choice items measure complex levels of thinking, deep mental processing, and high-road transfer?

KEY TO THINKING CAP EXERCISE 6.3

1. The tests will tend to seriously overemphasize recognition of factual material. Unambiguous, "lifted" factual material is likely to consist mainly of trivia (e.g., the exact number of brothers that Mrs. Lincoln had fighting in the Confederacy rather than the important fact that the Civil War divided families, even the First Family). This causes two problems that relate directly to two of the major themes of this book.

The first concerns validity. The test will not be a valid measure of the broader domain of learning that the teacher probably intended. Therefore, the validity of its scores will be compromised and their utility in making good decisions will be lessened because the tests fail to capture important learning outcomes. In such cases of domain underrepresentation, "the meaning of test scores is narrower than the proposed interpretation implies" (AERA, 1999, p. 174).

The second problem concerns consequences. Tests of this kind communicate to students that the way to "succeed" is to memorize unimportant material and that it is a waste of time to try to grasp principles, notice trends, make contemporary applications, and so on.

2. Definitely! Miscellaneous alternate-choice items often measure complex learning outcomes. Even true-false items *can* assess deep thinking. (Note that items 13–16 in the primary level insects test in Figure 6.2 require more than recall, provided, of course, that the exact content hasn't been explicitly taught.) However, in practice, true-false questions usually don't tap complex learning. Tests consisting largely of true-false items often assess little beyond recognition of factual information.

Matching Exercises

A **matching exercise** is an objective item type in which a group of multiple-choice questions is formatted into a set, all having similar content and identical options.

What Matching Exercises Measure.   Matching exercises provide a good way to test recognition-type recall when it is appropriate to test several homogeneous elements. They work especially well for items calling for who, what, when, or where knowledge. Figures 6.4, 6.5, and 6.6 contain matching exercises. Notice that each exercise requires *recognition of associations,* not production of them. Notice, too, that each exercise consists of several items having very similar content.

Yet matching exercises can require analysis and synthesis of information. For example, rules could be matched with examples of the rules, principles with illustrations of the principles, and parts of an apparatus with functions of the parts. Elementary teachers sometimes use matching exercises for demonstrating knowledge of clocks and time, food groups and pictures of food, clothing for seasons, or color words with pictured objects for those colors.

However, the most frequent use of matching is to measure factual knowledge of several similar items. Examples are dates and events, inventors and inventions, and symbols and names. Figure 6.4 exemplifies how matching exercises are most often used—to measure factual knowledge about authors and their works. This can be either desirable or undesirable. If a whole unit of an advanced-placement literature course had been devoted to utopian literature, then the matching set might be a suitable way to sample knowledge of who wrote what and when. If only 20 percent of a five-week unit had focused on utopian literature, then the exercise seriously overemphasizes work-author associations. Of course, other item types should be used to assess student achievement of the more important unit objectives.

Such distortion often occurs when a teacher has in mind one or two particularly important associations (e.g., Thomas More's *Utopia* and Plato's *Republic*), and then realizes that similar (yet less important) associations could be included in a matching exercise. As a result, the test ends up

FIGURE 6.4   Matching Exercise on Utopian Literature. It probably overemphasizes (a) the topic and (b) author-works associations.

Below is a list of books and a list of authors. For each book in the left-hand column, identify its author. Record each answer by printing the capital letter that goes with the author's name in the space provided to the left of the book. Each author may match one, more than one, or none of the books.

WORKS	AUTHORS
_____ 1. *News from Nowhere*	**A.** Francis Bacon
_____ 2. *We*	**B.** Edward Bellamy
_____ 3. *Walden II*	**C.** Theodor Herzka
_____ 4. *A Modern Utopia*	**D.** Aldous Huxley
_____ 5. *Brave New World*	**E.** Jack London
_____ 6. *New Atlantis*	**F.** Thomas More
_____ 7. *A Visit to Freeland*	**G.** William Morris
_____ 8. *Looking Backward, 2000–1887*	**H.** George Orwell
_____ 9. *The Iron Heel*	**I.** Plato
_____ 10. *Nineteen Eighty-four*	**J.** B. F. Skinner
_____ 11. *Utopia*	**K.** Henry David Thoreau
_____ 12. *The Republic*	**L.** H. G. Wells
	M. Yevgeny Zamyatin

FIGURE 6.5 Matching Exercise on "Music Around the World"

Several short selections of music will now be played. Each will be identified by a number. In the blank for each selection, print the capital letter that precedes the kind of music the selection exemplifies.

   _____ Selection 1   **A.** African
   _____ Selection 2   **B.** Asian
   _____ Selection 3   **C.** Polynesian
   _____ Selection 4   **D.** Slavic
   _____ Selection 5
   _____ Selection 6
   _____ Selection 7
   _____ Selection 8

having excessive emphasis in one area, while other important facets of achievement may be seriously neglected (Wesman, 1971; Linn & Gronlund, 2000).

The best protection against overuse of matching exercises is through the use of carefully considered test plans, as discussed in Chapter 5. Thoughtful test specifications for a survey literature course might call for only a few author-works associations, probably from the better-known Utopian authors. Multiple-choice or completion items might be considered.

Figure 6.5 provides an example from Mr. Martin's "Music Around the World" unit (described on pages 119–120) of the use of matching exercises to assess Context C learning that goes well beyond rote recall of facts. These items constitute Mr. Martin's assessment of the third column of his table of specifications. Recall that he wanted to measure high-road transfer. Therefore, he must choose selections that were not used in class and that are likely to be unfamiliar to students.

Figure 6.6 provides another example of how matching exercises can measure more than simple memory. Assume that the teacher had not stressed memorization of dates of these or other events, only that students are expected to have a "ballpark" idea of when events occurred and a sense of how much of the content of a history course focuses on the recent past. Under these conditions, this matching exercise provides a good assessment of students' time perspective. It should be noted, however, that most matching exercises that contain dates involve only rote recall.

Some Rules for Constructing Matching Exercises.   The following suggestions will be helpful in developing effective matching exercises.

   1. Include only homogeneous material in each set. Matching exercises are poorly suited to topics meriting only one or two items. If they are used for such topics, one of two things is likely to result. First, dissimilar materials (e.g., some definitions, some dates, and some names of people) may be included. In this case, the dissimilarities among options would make guessing easy. Second, the topic may be expanded to provide a full matching exercise containing homogeneous content. In this case, the topic is overemphasized.

   2. Prevent examinees from guessing the answer to one of the options by means of elimination. Do not create matching exercises having the same number of elements in each column in which each option is used exactly once. One way to reduce guessing is to provide more options than items, as in Figure 6.4. Another is to provide fewer options than items, as in Figures 6.5 and 6.6; in

FIGURE 6.6   Matching Exercise on Historical Time Perspective

Below is a time line that is divided into several lettered periods. The beginning and end of each period are identified by dates. Below the timeline are significant events in world history. To the left of each event, print the capital letter of the period during which it occurred. Each letter may match one, more than one, or none of the events.

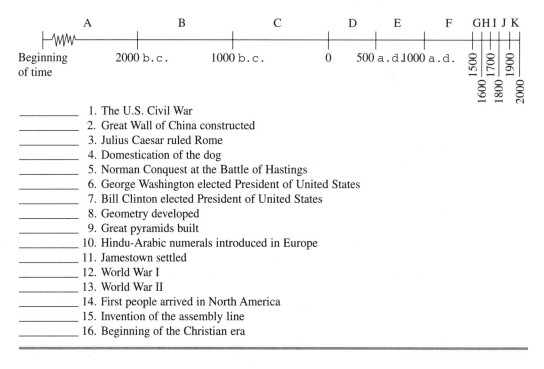

_____ 1. The U.S. Civil War
_____ 2. Great Wall of China constructed
_____ 3. Julius Caesar ruled Rome
_____ 4. Domestication of the dog
_____ 5. Norman Conquest at the Battle of Hastings
_____ 6. George Washington elected President of United States
_____ 7. Bill Clinton elected President of United States
_____ 8. Geometry developed
_____ 9. Great pyramids built
_____ 10. Hindu-Arabic numerals introduced in Europe
_____ 11. Jamestown settled
_____ 12. World War I
_____ 13. World War II
_____ 14. First people arrived in North America
_____ 15. Invention of the assembly line
_____ 16. Beginning of the Christian era

such cases, options obviously may be used more than once. Finally, directions can state that each option may be used once, more than once, or not at all.

3. Clearly indicate whether all options must be used and whether options may be reused. We prefer the directions: "Options may be used once, more than once, or not at all." However, two other ways of reducing guessing were mentioned in the preceding paragraph.

4. Specify the basis for matching stimuli and options. In some matching exercises, the ground rule for matching is self-evident, but if there can be any doubt, the issue should be addressed in the directions.

5. Thoughtfully decide which elements are to serve as items and which are to be the options. Occasionally, it is more important for students to be able to move from one set of elements to the other than vice versa. For example, in medical or automotive diagnostic work, students should be presented with symptoms and then select the appropriate response, rather than the reverse. In such cases, place the stimuli in the left-hand column and the responses in the right-hand column.

Often, however, the designation of stimuli and responses—of items and options—is arbitrary. In this case, place the shorter, simpler, easier-to-scan elements in the *right-hand* column. For example, in Figure 6.4, the columns could be reversed, but the ease and speed of test taking would suffer. Examinees shouldn't be required to reread long phrases over and over.

Matching sets are occasionally formatted by some means other than the two columns. For example, Figure 6.5 presents the options in a time line. Similarly, options can be located in a diagram, map, or other format. Occasionally, they are presented at the beginning of a matching exercise.

6. Sequence options so they are easy to locate. Examinees shouldn't be required to waste time hunting for the options. If the options are dates, put them in chronological order. If they are numbers, put them in numeric order. If they consist of such things as people, cities, or products, alphabetize them. In any way possible, sequence options in ways that render them easy to locate.

7. Keep matching exercises to reasonable lengths. Ordinarily, a matching exercise should not have more than 10 or 12 items, and there usually should be fewer. At the elementary level, the limit should be lower. Only rarely is it appropriate to devote more emphasis to a single set of similar items. Moreover, for most, it becomes tedious to work through a lengthy list of options again and again.

The matching exercise shown in Figure 6.4 is long, yet this might be tolerable in view of the capabilities of the students in an advanced-placement class. The set exhibited in Figure 6.5 could be made longer *if* it were desirable to devote more items to the objective it measures. Exceptional length could be justified because the number of options would remain very small. Because the time-line options in Figure 6.6 are very easy to scan, the unusual length would be acceptable *if* the test specifications called for so many items on this kind of content.

8. Be sure each matching item has one clearly best option. It is very easy to create matching exercises in which some items can be defensibly answered by two or more options. Care is necessary to avoid this. Potential problems that might occur further reinforce the recommendation that matching items work best when constructed with homogeneous material.

9. Keep each set of matching items on a single page. Annoyance is caused, time is wasted, and clerical errors are increased by requiring examinees to flip back and forth between pages. Items should be rearranged to enable each matching exercise to fit on a single page. If necessary, part of a page should be left empty in order to start an exercise on a new page so that it will fit.

10. Use numerals to designate the item stimuli and letters for the options. Figures 6.4 and 6.5 illustrate typical layout, numbering, and lettering of items and options.

11. Avoid overuse of matching exercises. Although matching exercises *can* be used to assess deep learning, they rarely are. The typical matching exercise distorts test emphasis with respect both to mental processes (overemphasizing recognition of recall) and content (overemphasizing the kinds of materials conducive to being included in matching exercises). Therefore, this item type should be used sparingly and thoughtfully.

12. Think ahead to the scoring process. Number the stimulus items on the left and include space for writing the response. Use capital letters for the response options on the right. Elementary teachers should ordinarily resist the temptation of designating connecting lines to indicate the matched pairs; horrendous scrambles of lines can result.

THINKING CAP EXERCISE 6.4 ???

Identify the major faults with the following matching exercise. There are many!

Instructions: Draw a line to connect each person in the left-hand column with the corresponding entry in the right-hand column.

1. Theodore Roosevelt
2. Lyndon Johnson
3. George Washington
4. John Philip Sousa
5. Leonard Bernstein
6. Francis Scott Key
7. *Uncle Tom's Cabin*
8. *Tom Sawyer*
9. Henry Ford
10. Dwight D. Eisenhower
11. Richard M. Nixon
12. Jimmy Carter
13. Bill Clinton

A. Republican
B. Democrat
C. Assembly line
D. Election of 1904
E. Steamboat
F. Mark Twain
G. Harriet Beecher Stowe
H. "Stars and Stripes Forever"
I. Election of 1788
J. "The Star-Spangled Banner"
K. Election of 1964
L. *West Side Story*

KEY TO THINKING CAP EXERCISE 6.4

This matching exercise is a disaster. First, the content is not at all homogeneous; inventions, elections, musical compositions, political parties, and books are all mixed indiscriminately into one exercise. Because there are not enough items of any one of these subsets to make up a good exercise, other item types would be preferable.

If one were (undesirably) going to mix such diverse content, one would want to move the two authors into the same column as the other persons. One would also want to place the three elections together and put them in chronological order. At least two items lack a clearly preferable option. Item 1 can be answered defensibly with option A or with option D, whereas options B and K are each correct for item 2.

The basis for matching isn't specified. This makes the mental processing of all items more difficult than necessary, and it creates the problem noted in the previous paragraph for items 1 and 2.

The method of drawing lines to show responses might be acceptable to use with young children for very short exercises; however, with long exercises like this one, the lines would result in a tangled visual nightmare.

Finally, this matching exercise, like most poor ones, taps only rote knowledge. Although nothing is wrong with measuring knowledge of any of the facts covered in this exercise, one certainly hopes that there would be more to a unit and its assessment than this kind of surface learning.

CHAPTER RECAP

This chapter provided some "do's" and "don'ts" to help teachers create effective completion, short-answer, alternate-choice, and matching items. In general, these item types are most effective for assessing recognition or recall of factual information.

In assessing student retention of factual knowledge, teachers should remember the importance of emphasizing *important* information, thereby prompting students to try to be discriminating in focusing their study on *important* facts. Although these item types (among others) are often used to measure trivia, at their best they are used to assess important information that students should know. In addition, each of these kinds of questions can, at times, be used effectively to assess facility in the use of complex kinds of thinking.

Because of the inherent limitations of each of these item types, they are not sufficient for most paper-pencil tests. Although such simple kinds of test questions make a valuable contribution to many excellent examinations, they usually are best used in combination with multiple-choice items and/or essay questions.

DEVELOPING MULTIPLE-CHOICE ITEMS AND INTERPRETIVE EXERCISES

CHAPTER OVERVIEW

DEVELOPING INSTRUCTIONALLY HELPFUL MULTIPLE-CHOICE ITEMS
Constructing Appropriate Stems and Useful Options
Polishing Multiple Choice Items
Preparing Appropriate Directions

WHAT INTERPRETIVE EXERCISES CAN MEASURE

DEVISING EFFECTIVE INTERPRETIVE EXERCISES
How to Avoid Making Flawed Items

KEY TERMS

multiple-choice item
stem
option
keyed response
distractor
decoy
foil

complete-question item
incomplete-sentence item
right-answer items
best-answer items
interpretive exercise
context dependence

Short-answer, alternate-choice, and matching items are now behind us. More complex kinds of questions, such as multiple-choice and essay items, are generally better suited for assessing deep learning such as making applications, analyzing logical arguments, estimating quantities, or recognizing the origins of unfamiliar works. Still more similar to real life—more authentic—are interpretive exercises in which novel material is presented and questions are asked about it. In this chapter, we take up the multiple-choice item and the interpretive exercise.

MULTIPLE-CHOICE ITEMS

The multiple-choice question is by far the most widely used type of objective item. This popularity is a result of its remarkable versatility. Multiple-choice items are appropriate for measuring an exceptional array of mental processes and an amazing variety of subject matter. Moreover, their scoring is easy, fast, and objective. For these and other reasons, multiple-choice items are preferred for virtually all paper-pencil cognitive tests, including elementary, secondary, and college achievement and aptitude tests, college and graduate-school admissions tests, and professional certification, licensing, competency, and proficiency examinations (Haladyna & Downing, 1989a).

Some Vocabulary

The Parts of the Multiple-Choice Item.   A **multiple-choice item** is a self-contained question that consists of a stem and three or more choices. The **stem** is the first part; it asks a question or sets a task. Following the stem are the **options** among which examinees must choose. Options are also commonly referred to as the choices or alternatives. One of these, the **keyed response,** is the right answer or best answer. If selected by the examinee, it yields credit.

The other options are called **distractors, decoys,** or **foils.** These names describe the function they serve. For students who don't know the material on which the item is based, the purpose of the wrong options is to distract examinees away from the keyed response. That is, the wrong choices are designed to decoy or to foil examinees who are ignorant of the content.

Please note again that *educators do not try to foil examinees who have a command of what the item measures, but seek to foil those who don't.* In measuring achievement in Contexts B and C, teachers *aim to differentiate.* (Actually, it could be said that *all* tests are designed to differentiate. In Context A, the need is to distinguish students who have mastered an explicit mastery objective from those who haven't. *If* the instruction has been successful in bringing all students up to mastery, then the mastery test's scores won't differentiate *among those taking the test.* Yet Context A tests should be designed to differentiate between masters and nonmasters.) In Contexts B and C, the need is to differentiate among students who have achieved various amounts of competence on expansive developmental objectives. Educators always want students who know what an item measures to get it right, and teachers always want those who do *not* know what the item assesses to miss it. In this way, items yield information about examinee achievement that will aid decision making.

Two Major Formats of Multiple-Choice Items.   Some multiple-choice items are phrased as questions. In Figure 7.1, items 1 and 2 both have stems that are complete questions, and they end with question marks. The options can either be punctuated as complete sentences, as shown in the left-hand column, or left unpunctuated, as styled in the right-hand column.

Other multiple-choice items are phrased as incomplete sentences. Items 3 and 4 have incomplete-sentence stems. Because each option provides a way to complete the sentence, the options *per se* aren't capitalized, and each ends with a period. Some item writers end incomplete-sentence stems with a colon, as shown in the right-hand column version of item 3. Others end them with a dash. Most avoid superfluous marks because they just create more work.

Some item ideas are more easily developed into **complete-question items,** whereas others are better given expression as **incomplete-sentence items.** There is little reason to try to force items into one format or the other. Nor do sets of multiple-choice items need to be consistent; the two item formats can be mixed.

However, many item ideas are equally suited to either phrasing. This is certainly true of the two item ideas shown in Figure 7.1. In this case, it may be better to opt for the complete-question format because it has fewer potential pitfalls, including those of grammatical consistency between the stem and the options and among the options. An example is item 4 in which the articles "a" and "an" could easily have been botched in a way that would provide a grammatical clue. This hazard

FIGURE 7.1   Complete-Question and Incomplete-Sentence Multiple-Choice Items.

SAMPLE ITEMS	ALTERNATIVE STYLES
1. Who was the third President of the United States?	1. Who was the third President of the United States?

A. John Adams.
   B. John Quincy Adams.
   C. Andrew Jackson.
   D. Thomas Jefferson.
   E. James Madison.
	(1). John Adams
	   (2). John Quincy Adams
	   (3). Andrew Jackson
	   (4). Thomas Jefferson
	   (5). James Madison

2. Which of the following foods provides the best combination of nutrients?	2. Which of the following foods provides the best combination of nutrients?

A. Applesauce cake.
   B. Banana split.
   C. Pineapple milkshake.
   D. Pumpkin pie.
	1 applesauce cake
	   2 banana split
	   3 pineapple milkshake
	   4 pumpkin pie

3. The third President of the United States was	3. The third President of the United States was:

A John Adams.
   B John Quincy Adams.
   C Andrew Jackson.
   D Thomas Jefferson.
   E James Madison.
	a. John Adams.
	   b. John Quincy Adams.
	   c. Andrew Jackson.
	   d. Thomas Jefferson.
	   e. James Madison.

4. Of the following foods, the one that provides the best combination of nutrients is a(n)	4. Of the following foods, the one that provides the best combination of nutrients is

A. applesauce cake.
   B. banana split.
   C. pineapple milkshake.
   D. pumpkin pie.
	(a) an applesauce cake.
	   (b) a banana split.
	   (c) a pineapple milkshake.
	   (d) a pumpkin pie.

was avoided in the complete-question format shown in item 2. The limited research available (Haladyna & Downing, 1989b) is consistent with this rationale.

Figure 7.1 also demonstrates the various ways by which the options can be designated—by numerals, capital letters, or lowercase letters, each of which may or may not be enclosed within parentheses. The item numerals and the option-designation symbols may or may not be followed by periods. The test maker is free to go with whatever style he or she prefers. Of course, items within a test should be styled consistently. In general, our preference is to avoid unnecessary punctuation.

Two Major Kinds of Multiple-Choice Content.   In some items, the keyed response is clearly the only right answer possible. For example, in items 1 and 3 of Figure 7.1, option D is categorically right and the other options are decisively wrong. In such cases, the keyed response may also be called the *right answer*. In other items, the keyed response is not categorically right and the other options aren't absolutely wrong; rather, the keyed response is only the *best answer* available. Items 2 and 4 illustrate best-answer items.

Right-answer multiple-choice questions are suitable for purely factual information and for computation problems in which one option is clearly right and the rest are absolutely wrong. The directions for **right-answer items** instruct examinees to select the *one right answer* for each item. In this situation, it is permissible to offer options such as "All of the above," "More than one of the above," or "None of the above."

However, most subject matter domains consist mainly of material for which some options are better than others, but for which none is absolutely right. Hence, most test content is not appropriate for right-answer directions. Items 2 and 4 in Figure 7.1 are a case in point. Option D is clearly the best option because pumpkin pie contains food from the vegetable, grain, dairy, and meat/egg groups, but it is far from an ideal way to balance a meal! The directions that accompany sets of **best-answer items** instruct examinees to select the *one best answer* to each question.

Fortunately, it's not necessary to segregate these two kinds of items into separate test sections or to provide separate directions for each. They can be mixed if they are preceded with best-answer directions, not right-answer directions.

What Do Multiple-Choice Items Measure?

Figure 7.2 illustrates the breadth of content and mental processes that multiple-choice items can assess. In every case, examinees must *recognize* and *select* (in contrast to produce) the best option from those presented. Yet the level of mental processing varies greatly among the questions. In the first item, the task is mainly that of retrieving information from long-term memory. If the learning has been mentally encoded in exactly the same words used in the question, then item 1 will tap only rote surface learning. On the other hand, if the wording of instruction and the item differ, then the learning outcome measured will not be as shallow.

Items 2–9 involve more complex thought processes, *provided that instruction did not use the same words or examples.* In examining these items, assume that wording, examples, or cases are new to examinees. Item 2 requires examinees to relate egg-cooking methods to calories. Item 3 requires the identification of an example of "smallest." Although it should be relatively easy for young children who have learned the concept of "smallest," the question clearly requires mental processing that evidences understanding and ability to apply the concept.

Item 4 involves the classification of a novel example. It taps a slightly deeper kind of meaningful verbal learning. No amount of mindless memorization would enable pupils to answer this item correctly unless they understand the meaning of the options. Such understanding, of course, comes in degrees. Some novel examples that could be used for test questions would be easy to classify, whereas others would be more demanding.

Item 5 also requires more than rote recall. In addition to recognizing an example of a category (copyright), the examinee must address the relationship between copyrights and patents. Similarly, item 6 requires consideration of a relationship (between hair and scales). This goes beyond mere knowledge that fish have scales, gills, and fins.

When items require more than rote knowledge, requisite knowledge may be needed. In item 5 students must know the categories of things that are patentable and those that can be copyrighted. Similarly, for items 2 and 4, examinees need to know the meaning of the terms used in the options. To deal with the relationship in item 6, the child must know what scales are. Therefore, such items

FIGURE 7.2   Illustrative Breadth of Content and Mental Processes That Multiple-Choice Can Tap.

1. The Marshall Plan was announced shortly after the end of the
   A. Revolutionary War.
   B. Civil War.
   C. First World War.
   D. Second World War.
   E. Korean Conflict.

2. You are going to eat two eggs. Which method of preparation will produce the *fewest* calories?
   A. Fried
   B. Omelet
   C. Poached
   D. Scrambled

3. Draw a circle around the *smallest* box.

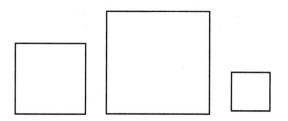

4. An explorer found an animal species that has not been classified before. It has warm blood. It takes good care of its young and provides milk for them. It can fly very well, can swim a little, but cannot get around well on land. What kind of animal is it?
   A. An amphibian
   B. A bird
   C. A fish
   D. A mammal
   E. A reptile

5. A patent is to a new kind of mousetrap as a copyright is to a new
   A. kind of copy machine.
   B. medical drug.
   C. musical composition.
   D. surgical procedure.
   E. variety of rose.

6. A mammal's hair is most like a fish's
   A. bones.
   B. fins.
   C. gills.
   D. scales.

(continued)

FIGURE 7.2   Continued

7. People who believe in capital punishment offer several reasons to support it. Some of these reasons reflect values. Others are based on testable facts. Which of the following reasons could best be tested?

   A. Capital punishment reduces crime.
   B. Society should be protected from criminals.
   C. Victims of crimes should be compensated.
   D. Wrongdoers deserve to be punished for their crimes.

8. What was the public reaction to the choice of Jimmy Carter as president?

   A. Disagreement by a large minority with the system by which the choice was made
   B. Disagreement by the majority with the choice
   C. Overwhelming agreement with the choice
   D. Overwhelming support of the system by which the choice was made

9. Some people support the use of lie detectors in hiring government workers. They admit that the use of lie detectors invades the privacy of job applicants, but they believe that national security justifies this invasion of privacy. What is the *unstated assumption* in their rationale?

   A. National security is *not* improved by use of the devices.
   B. The devices are *not* valid.
   C. The devices do *not* invade privacy.
   D. The devices are valid.
   E. The devices invade privacy.

10. Which of these body parts is a *joint*?

   A. Your head
   B. Your knee
   C. Your nose
   D. Your thumb nail
   E. Your tongue

still measure knowledge. Their virtue is that rote knowledge alone doesn't suffice; examinees must be able to *process* what they know.

Item 7 taps one dimension of the distinction between statements of value and statements of fact. It might be a good item in a context where instruction had focused on helping students recognize which kinds of statements are philosophical and which are empirical. Item 8 requires examinees to make sharp distinctions between the process of decision making in a democracy and satisfaction with the decision. Assuming this particular application was not used in class, it measures student ability to transfer learning. This item also requires basic factual background before the higher levels of reasoning can come into play.

Item 9 involves examinee ability to recognize unstated assumptions. If the example is not one previously encountered, such items measure relatively high levels of reasoning. Of course, domain-specific knowledge is usually needed as well. Item 9 presupposes familiarity with polygraphs and with the concepts of invasion of privacy, national security, and validity.

These examples illustrate some of the many kinds of thinking that multiple-choice items can validly assess. At times, this versatile item type may be appropriate for entire tests.

However, it obviously cannot tap most psychomotor skills, affective attributes or dispositions, or social skills. Indeed, multiple-choice items are even unable to assess some important cognitive attributes. They don't measure how well examinees can produce, generate, or create. They don't assess how well students can express their ideas in their own words. They don't show how well learners can operate a car or how well teachers can control a class. For that matter, they are not well suited to measuring how well teachers can write multiple-choice items! Later chapters will address other assessment methods that get at some of these important kinds of learning outcomes.

Some Rules for Composing Multiple-Choice Items

Following are rules for developing multiple-choice items. Before examining them, we might again acknowledge that although the rules reflect conventional wisdom, expert opinion, and common sense (Millman & Green, 1989), they aren't based on a solid foundation of research. Few of the rules have received adequate study (Haladyna & Downing, 1989b).

Although rules furnish helpful guidelines for developing test items, you may find cases where an exception to a rule may improve an item (Linn & Gronlund, 1995). We should be responsible to our students for preparing good items; if this requires a *thoughtful* violation of a rule, then break it (Haladyna, 1997). Rule 15 concerning parallel construction among options will be a case in point. In rare cases, forcing parallelism would be awkward. If the results would be contorted, it is better to tolerate minor nonparallelism among the options.

1. **Measure significant student learning.** This rule derives directly from two key themes of Chapter 5. The first concerns making tests valid: *Measure what you have been trying to teach.* The other principle concerns the power that tests have in influencing student effort. Because students tend to study the kinds of things that are tested, *assess what is important in order to constructively guide their study.*

Multiple-choice tests, like those using other item types, often fail to capture the richness of the subject matter domains they are designed to assess. Yet it is more fruitful to examine the variety of cognitive demands *within* item types than it is to compare the cognitive demands of item types *per se* (Martinez, 1999).

Sadly, many teacher-made tests measure little beyond rote learning (Fleming & Chambers, 1983) and even fail to match their own aims (Nitko, 1989). We all need to be on guard against the temptation to "crank out" items that easily "flow" rather than crafting ones that assess important learning.

For example, suppose a history textbook explained that President John Tyler, the first vice president to succeed to the office, established that the successor shall exercise all the duties of the office, rather than merely head a caretaker government. Suppose the test also happened to mention that Tyler had 14 children—a presidential record. Both of these testable features are facts, but one concerns an important historical precedent, whereas the other is trivial. The items in Figure 7.3 demonstrate how either fact can be developed into a technically sound multiple-choice question. The second item, however, is far more valid because it *measures something important and it signals students to focus on important facts* rather than on inconsequential ones.

2. **Formulate the issue in the stem.** By the time examinees finish examining an item stem, the nature of the required task should be clear. Examinees shouldn't have to wade through several options before being able to divine what is expected.

FIGURE 7.3   Technically Sound Items That Measure a Trivial Fact and Significant Fact.

ITEM MEASURING TRIVIAL FACT	ITEM MEASURING SIGNIFICANT FACT

1. Which U.S. president had the most children?
 	
  A. Cleveland
  B. Hayes
  C. Madison
  D. Tyler
  E. Washington
	1. Which U.S. president established that a vice president who succeeds to the office shall exercise the full powers of the office?
	
	  A. Chester Arthur
	  B. Andrew Jackson
	  C. Andrew Johnson
	  D. Lyndon Johnson
	  E. John Tyler

Stems that fail to formulate tasks are often written before their authors come up with good item ideas. The flawed version of item 1 in Figure 7.4 illustrates a stem that fails miserably to formulate an issue. The author probably lacked an item concept other than the wish to "have a questions on cows." Once such a vague stem is created, the item writer often merely completes the question with several unrelated true or false statements. One shouldn't start composing an item until a clear focus on what is to be measured has been achieved.

Because item 1 isn't based on a coherent item idea, there is no one right way to fix it. Improved version 1a focuses on the number of births, whereas 1b concerns varieties of mammals. Other ideas that could be addressed are that cattle are mammals or the structure of bovine feet or digestive systems.

Item 2 in Figure 7.4 provides another example. The item writer had an idea of wanting to test something about pine wood, yet lacked a vision of what to test. The improved version focuses on one particular attribute of pine.

This rule provides another example of a rule that should, on rare occasions, be broken if doing so results in a question that is, overall, easier to read.

3. Express ideas clearly, unambiguously, and briefly at the lowest reading level feasible. A useful technique for improving the clarity of stems is to present them as questions (Oosterhof, 2003). Question-formatted stems may also be more efficient in word count. For example, if an item about bees is going to have options of drone, queen, or worker, then "Which honeybee makes the honey?" is clearer and shorter than, "The honeybee that makes the honey is the."

The reading difficulty of an item should not cause some students to miss it. Questions may, of course, rightly contain difficult words and expressions that are part of the content to be tested; otherwise, the reading should be no harder than necessary. If some pupils taking an arithmetic test fail to solve "story" problems because they can't read them, then the test is (invalidly) measuring reading as well as (validly) assessing mathematics applications. If several history students can't understand what the test questions are asking, the test is contaminated to that extent.

Most objective items must be able to stand on their own without clarifying context. This isolation creates hazards of ambiguity and misunderstanding. Avoid use of words or phrases that can reasonably be interpreted in more than one way. Write items so that all students will interpret them in the same way.

FIGURE 7.4   Stems That Fail to Formulate the Issue and Improved Versions of the Stems.

FLAWED ITEMS	IMPROVED VERSIONS

1. Cows
 	
  A. are marsupial mammals.
  B. are rodents.
  C. are used for their milk.
  D. have single, undivided hooves.
  E. usually give birth to two or three calves at a time.
	1a. How many young do cows most often give birth to at a time?
	
	  A. 1
	  B. 2
	  C. 3
	  D. 4 or 5
	  E. 6 to 10
	
	1b. To which major group of mammals do cows belong?
	
	  A. Monotreme
	  B. Marsupial
	  C. Placental

2. Which of the following is true of pine wood?
 	
  A. It is quite hard.
  B. It is quite soft.
  C. It comes from trees that grow mainly in the tropics.
  D. It is quite dark.
	2. How is pine classified in terms of hardness?
	
	  A. Hardwood
	  B. Medium wood
	  C. Softwood

Item 1 in Figure 7.5 on page 150 illustrates ambiguity. What does "about the same" mean? Within a few months? Within a decade? The improved version eliminates this ambiguity. It also achieves greater brevity in the stem.

Item 2 demonstrates other sources of ambiguity. Strictly speaking, of course, the sun doesn't set; the earth rotates. Students who understand this have to guess the sophistication of the item writer. If the item is naively conceived in everyday language, option D is keyed; but if it hinges on the earth's rotation, then option E is keyed. Assuming that the teacher intends the first meaning, then the ambiguity is removed by eliminating the "none of these" option. Sophisticated examinees still may grumble at the naivete of the item, but they won't miss it.

There is another compelling reason to eliminate the "none of these" option. In most places at most times of the year, the sun does not "set" exactly in the west. In the northern hemisphere, it tends to "set" in the southwest. Therefore, "none of these" may be the best option.

Even after purging the "none of the above" option, a problem still remains. In some places, such as parts of Alaska in the winter, the direction is more south than west; hence, south, option C, would be the best answer in some places and times of year. What to do? The stem could be modified to read, "In most places, the sun sets in the" or "In our state, the sun sets in the."

4. Consider a variety of novel stimuli to enhance realism. Items of any type that tap understanding need to include something unfamiliar. In addition to verbal stems, items can employ novel stimulus media such as sketches, tables, pictured apparatus, pictured tools, and political cartoons. Items based on such material tend to be more relevant to ways in which the subject matter is used

FIGURE 7.5   Ambiguous Items and Their Improved Versions.

FLAWED ITEMS	IMPROVED VERSIONS

1. Compared with the average life span of American females, the average life span of American males is
  A. shorter.
  B. about the same.
  C. longer.
	1. Compared with American females, the average life span of American males is
	  A. shorter.
	  B. within a year of being the same.
	  C. longer.

2. The sun sets in
  A. the east.
  B. the north.
  C. the south.
  D. the west.
  E. none of these.
	2. The sun sets in the
	  A. east.
	  B. north.
	  C. south.
	  D. west.

in everyday life—more authentic. Because the discussion of interpretive exercises will be devoted to use of such material with *sets* of items, no more will be said at this time about this means of assessing high-road transfer of learning.

Although any kind of item that assesses deep mental processing needs to include something fresh, it shouldn't be too exotic. Assessing high-road transfer requires careful choice of situations. Excessive novelty, especially if coupled with logical complexity, creates items that assess the ability to reason *independent* of subject matter; achievement tests, in contrast, should assess high-road transfer *of* the subject matter. Thus, problems must be new to students, but not too unlike those used in class. Excessive novelty can usually be avoided by drawing on situations from students' everyday life experiences and/or by including any factual information that would be needed to solve a problem within the item stem (Findley & Scates, 1946; Linn & Gronlund, 2000).

5. Ensure that each item has one option that is clearly best. Experts in the subject should be able to agree on the best option. Ambiguity is one source of problems. Another difficulty concerns differences of expert opinion. If an item's keying hinges on an issue on which experts lack consensus, the item violates this rule.

It should be noted that this rule does *not* prohibit the use of opinion items. One common way is to transform these into knowledge items with wording along the lines of "In the opinion of the author, ..." In addition, it is legitimate to focus items on opinion *when experts' consensus is present.* Thus, it might be permissible to ask which of four presidents was the best if the options are Grant, Harding, Washington, and Pierce; but it would be unreasonable to ask the same question for Cleveland, Monroe, Polk, and Van Buren. Similarly, it would be acceptable to ask which of four novel works of art was the best as long as experts would be able to agree.

One occasionally encounters a type of multiple-choice item for which examinees are instructed to mark each option that is true. This item type is quite useful in *questionnaires* (e.g., "Place a check next to the name of each of the following kinds of pets you currently own.").

However, multiple-response items are generally *not* recommended for use in *tests* because they suffer from several problems:

- They can only be used with right-answer items, never with best-answer ones.
- No uniquely defensible way exists to score the many possible combinations of incorrectly marked decoys and unmarked keyed responses.
- Such questions are usually more effective if recast into true-false items.

6. Avoid clueing with position or length of keyed responses. Most test makers have item-writing quirks. Many of these tendencies are fairly common. Test-wise students who know these common habits are able to score systematically higher than their achievement merits (Cronbach, 1990). We should do everything we can to prevent this unfair, content-irrelevant advantage. The remedy is for the item *writer* to be test wise, and to use this knowledge to ensure that examinee test wiseness doesn't provide a systematic advantage.

One such feature is location of the keyed response. Many teachers tend to "bury" the keyed response among the middle options. Such a teacher making a 40-item, four-option, multiple-choice test might end up with only about 5 questions keyed "A," about 15 keyed "B," about 15 keyed "C," and about 5 keyed "D." This teacher's students could benefit much by adhering to the rule: "If I think I know an answer, choose it; otherwise, select a middle option."

Another feature is option length. Inexperienced, careless, or rushed item writers tend to produce keyed responses that are, on average, longer than the decoys. This arises from the need to qualify the keyed response in order to make it the best option. Test-wise students can gain a consistent, unearned advantage by following this rule: "If I think I know an answer, choose it; otherwise, select the longest option." Some examinees will even have operational rules that incorporate both of these features; for example, "If I think I know an answer, choose it; otherwise, pick the longest of the middle options."

Such clueing can be avoided in several ways. A method applicable to a wide variety of subject matter is to put the options in alphabetical order. Another is to use a random process, such as rolling a die, to assign response positions (e.g., A, B, C, D) to keyed responses. When options are numerals, they should be put in numerical order unless doing so would provide a clue (as in the item, "Choose the smallest of the following numbers"). Such methods help item writers avoid getting into unconscious patterns that provide clues. It will be instructive for the reader to reexamine Figures 7.1 through 7.5 to consider how this issue of option ordering was handled in each.

Even after using these processes, an option in a given test may happen to be seriously underused or overused. As a last step, it is wise to tally the frequency with which each option is keyed. If the frequency turns out to be very uneven, then a few options can be changed to enhance balance. Easy changes to make in selected items are changing ascending numeric order to descending order and reversing alphabetization. This last check is also useful in avoiding having a "long run" of consecutive items that have the same keyed responses.

7. Avoid clueing with familiarity of keyed options. Many teachers produce keyed responses that contain the exact phrases that were drilled in class (Wesman, 1971). When this occurs, students who have learned the pat phrases by rote can get items correct without necessarily understanding them. William James made this point with a story of a class visitor who noticed that the geography book discussed the heat of Earth's interior. The visitor asked the class, "Suppose I dug a hole into the ground many hundreds of miles deep. At the bottom of the hole, compared with the top, would it be cooler, warmer, or the same?" None of the class knew. Then the teacher said, "I'm sure they know if we ask the question right. In what condition is the interior of the globe?" Half of the class immediately parroted, "In a state of igneous fusion" (James, 1899, p. 150).

Here's another example. Suppose science students have studied the law of buoyancy and have learned Archimedes' Principle: "Any object floating or submerged in a fluid is buoyed up by a force equal to the weight of the displaced fluid." The teacher intends, of course, that students understand its meaning. Item 1 in Figure 7.6 fails to assess understanding; rote memorization of the statement would suffice to answer the question correctly.

This item has multiple flaws. It violates rule 6 as well as rule 7. Even if a content-ignorant student is not test wise enough to choose the longest option when it is in a middle position, the student is likely to answer the item correctly because option C "sounds familiar."

Clever item construction can turn "sounding familiar" into an advantage for using the test to differentiate productively. Effective foils can be created by use of familiar phrases where they don't belong. Option D in item 2 is a case in point; it uses the familiar-sounding words "buoyed" and "displaced fluid." The keyed option A conveys the correct idea without using the familiar wording.

A teacher who has carefully planned the test is less likely to create an item like item 1 in Figure 7.6. Planning and considering mental processes would probably sensitize one enough to recognize that item 1 doesn't delve beneath the surface. The test plan may call for an item dealing with *a* correct statement (in contrast to *the* correct statement) of the law of buoyancy. If so, item 2 might be used to require students to distinguish between correct and incorrect paraphrases, thereby assessing comprehension or understanding. In spite of its appalling length, item 2 is better than item 1 in demanding more than rote recall and in having a keyed response that doesn't contain the most familiar sounding wording, isn't the longest option, and isn't in a middle position.

A thoughtful test plan would probably call for some questions that assess mental processes beyond either rote knowledge or paraphrase. Item 3 measures ability to use the principle to predict an outcome. This would be a good item if this particular application is novel and if examinees have the requisite knowledge that pure water is heavier than the other options.

Items 4 and 5 of Figure 7.6 require less requisite knowledge. In addition to ability to apply the principle, item 4 requires examinees to sort out relevant from irrelevant information. Item 5 gets at application in a way that requires simple computation.

Items 2–5 are consistent with each of the previous rules. Persons who mindlessly commit material to memory without processing it will not know how to attack the problems and will rightfully get most of the items wrong. Yet most of these items should be relatively easy for students who understand the principle.

8. Use only plausible distractors. Item 6 in Figure 7.2 on page 145 illustrates this rule. Each distractor is a fish part. Any distractor that was not a part of fish anatomy (e.g., wings or antlers) wouldn't be plausible.

For another illustration of adherence to this rule, examine item 4 in Figure 7.6. Each foil is designed to be attractive to students who don't understand the generalization. Option B states an obvious, yet irrelevant, fact. Option C states a less obvious fact, but one whose impact would contribute (negligibly) to buoyancy, not to sinking. Option D, concerning the respiration of the passengers, may seem plausible to examinees who lose sight of the key issue because people in a closed car would indeed consume oxygen.

FIGURE 7.6   Avoiding Rote Associations. See text for discussion of flaws in items 1 and 5.

1. Which of the following is a correct statement of the law of buoyancy?
   A. Any object that has sunk in liquid will weigh the same amount as the displaced liquid.
   B. Any object that is floating in a gas will weigh the same amount as the displaced gas.
   C. Any object floating or submerged in a fluid is buoyed up by a force equal to the weight of the displaced fluid.
   D. The weight of an object is not affected by whether it is in a fluid.

2. Which of the following is a correct statement of the law of buoyancy?
   A. When an object is put into a gas or liquid, it replaces some of the gas or liquid. This is true whether the object sinks or floats. This replaced gas or liquid has some weight. The object is pushed up by the same amount of force as the weight of the replaced gas or liquid.
   B. When an object is put into a gas or liquid, it replaces some of the gas or liquid. This is true whether the object sinks or floats. This replaced gas or liquid has some weight. The weight of the object will be increased by an amount equal to the weight of the replaced gas or liquid.
   C. When an object is put into a gas or liquid, it replaces some of the gas or liquid if it sinks but not if it floats. This replaced gas or liquid has some weight. The weight of the object will be increased by an amount equal to the weight of the replaced gas or liquid.
   D. When an object is put into a fluid, it displaces some of the fluid if it sinks, but not if it floats. This displaced fluid has some weight. The object will be buoyed up by a force equal to the weight of the displaced fluid.

3. A balloon is filled with salt water. It is then submerged in several fluids. In which fluid would it weigh the *least*?
   A. Carbon dioxide
   B. Helium
   C. Pure water
   D. Vegetable oil

4. A car had a full tank of gas, three people in it, and its windows closed. It went off a bridge into a deep, cold river. At first it floated, then it sank. Why did it finally sink?
   A. Because the air in the car leaked out and was replaced by water.
   B. Because the engine was cooled by the river water.
   C. Because the gasoline in the tank was lighter than the river water.
   D. Because the people in the car had used up most of the oxygen trapped in the car.

5. A wood block has a volume of 5 cubic centimeters and weighs 4 grams. Five cubic centimeters of a certain liquid weighs 3 grams. If the block is placed in this liquid, how much will it weigh?
   A. 1 gram
   B. 2 grams
   C. 3 grams
   D. 4 grams
   E. 5 grams

Now consider item 5 on page 153. Each of its foils could also well be chosen by students who don't understand the principle. Option A, of course, is the keyed response (4 g minus 3 g). Option B can be obtained by subtracting 3 g from 5 cc, option C by simply using the 3 g, option D by using the 4 g, and option E by using the 5 cc.

Notice that items 4 and 5 don't have the same number of options. Some item writers feel compelled to develop the same number of options for each multiple-choice item in a test. This seems unwise; the issue isn't the number of distractors but their quality (Haladyna & Downing, 1989b). For some items, only three or four plausible options can be generated. In the case of item 4, we were out of good ideas after four. Creating additional ones that will fail to attract any content-ignorant examinees is pointless. If you can generate only three good options, stop there. At other times it is possible to generate five or more effective options. If so, it may be desirable to do so because a larger number of options reduces the chances of examinees selecting the keyed response by guessing.

How should you devise plausible distractors? Some experts recommend that multiple-choice stems first be administered as completion items in order to learn what wrong answers students actually produce. These wrong answers are subsequently used as distractors in multiple-choice items. Research, however, doesn't support this advice (e.g., Johnson, 1976; Loree, 1948); teachers can do about as well with much less work by thinking up the distractors themselves.

Recall three attributes of good item writers:

1. Effective item writers know the subject matter in considerably more depth than the test assesses. This helps one to know what is important and how to avoid content pitfalls. It also helps one to know content that can and cannot be used as foils. Recall the item concerning the direction of the sunset. To avoid these pitfalls, the teacher must know much more about geography and astronomy than the item seems superficially to measure.
2. Good item writers know the techniques of crafting items. Such knowledge helps one avoid the numerous pitfalls covered in these (too numerous) rules.
3. Excellent item writers know students and the kinds of errors they make. This enables test makers to judge which distractors will be attractive to students who lack the knowledge assessed by the item, and in doing so, learn which students understand the concept (or were lucky in their selection!).

Consider first-year algebra as an example. Suppose students have just learned to multiply literal numbers that are raised to powers, such as $(x^5)(x^2)$. Algebra teachers know how common it is for students to multiply the exponents and answer x^{10}. (Recall that the correct way is to add the exponents; thus, the correct answer is x^7.) Multiplying the exponents is a high-frequency conceptual error in first-year algebra. Thereafter, it is more likely to be a careless error, but it remains common. Knowledge of frequent student errors will enable the algebra teacher to include x^{10} as a distractor.

9. Avoid items in which incorrect reasoning yields the keyed response. A frequent cause of good item ideas "going sour" lies in a keyed response that can be obtained by an incorrect process. This applies to all item types, not just multiple-choice questions. Four examples follow. Notice in each how the problem is best avoided by the item writer knowing the kinds of errors that students commonly make.

■ In algebra, the test maker would want to avoid the item stem $(y^2)(y^2) =$. This item will malfunction in either completion or multiple-choice format because students who do the wrong thing and multiply the exponents will get the right answer. Thus, the item won't differentiate between those who can perform the multiplication and those who cannot, and the teacher won't have the information needed to guide instruction.

■ Item 5 of Figure 7.6 on page 153 provides a second example. Students can get the right answer by the wrong process. Recall that the proper way to obtain the answer was to subtract 3 g from 4 g. Unfortunately, the student who subtracts 4 from 5 (doing violence to nonequivalent units) will also get the right numeric answer.

■ Map work at the elementary level furnishes another example. A common misconception is that all rivers flow south. In some parts of the country, this results from overgeneralizing from local rivers. The misconception can also result from the reasoning that "north is up on a map; south is down. Water flows downhill. Therefore, water flows south."

Suppose a teacher in Texas is making an imaginary map to test map skills. A test item is to ask the directions of a certain river and the four options are to be the four primary compass directions. The teacher would be well advised to avoid a river that flows south because some pupils would get the item right via their *mis*conception.

■ For a final example, consider the flawed item 1 and its improved version in Figure 7.7 on page 156. Why is the second item better? The issue here is that some pupils have the misconception that a pronoun's antecedent is the noun immediately preceding it. Therefore, one should be careful not to create items in which this mistaken belief yields correct answers. In the flawed version, the error happens to produce the right answer for the wrong reason; this will limit the extent to which the item can differentiate between those who can correctly identify the antecedent of a pronoun and those who cannot. The improved version is free from this fault.

The improved version of item 1 also moves the word "the" to the stem. In general, when a word or phrase appears at the beginning of each option, it should be moved to the end of the stem to reduce reading time.

Both versions of item 1 illustrate a sensible ordering of options. By putting them in the order in which they occurred in the stem, students should have less trouble finding a particular option than they would with any other order.

10. Avoid grammatical clues. Clues of number or gender help examinees eliminate some foils. Likewise, the articles "a" and "an" enable students to reject decoys that start with vowels or consonants, respectively. The flawed version of item 2 in Figure 7.7 shows how a teacher's failure to attend to this detail enables examinees to eliminate option C. The improved version of item 2 shows one way by which this clue can be avoided. The two versions of item 4 in Figure 7.1 on page 143 illustrate other ways.

11. Avoid options that include other options. Item 3 of Figure 7.7 demonstrates this problem. In the flawed question, the student could reason that neither "chairman" nor "chairwoman" could be uniquely correct because if it were, then "chairperson" would be, too. Hence, the person not knowing the item would have only three options among which to choose.

FIGURE 7.7 Item Flaws and Their Corrections.

FLAWED ITEMS	IMPROVED VERSIONS
1. "After rushing through the gate into the yard, the dog dug up the bone and settled down to enjoy it." The "it" in the last sentence stands for A. the gate. B. the yard. C. the dog. D. the bone.	1. "The dog rushed through the gate and hid the bone in the yard where no other dog would find it." The "it" in the last sentence stands for the A. dog. B. gate. C. bone. D. yard. E. other dog.
2. A polygon with six sides is called a A. hexagon. B. pentagon. C. octagon. D. quadrilateral. E. triangle.	2. A polygon with six sides is called a/an A. hexagon. B. pentagon. C. octagon. D. quadrilateral. E. triangle.
3. The presiding officer of the United States House of Representatives is the A. chairman. B. chairperson. C. chairwoman. D. president. E. speaker.	3. The title of the presiding officer of the United States House of Representatives is A. chair. B. president. C. president pro tem. D. speaker.
4. A moa was a giant A. bird. B. dog. C. mammal. D. reptile. E. turtle.	4. A moa was a giant A. amphibian. B. bird. C. fish. D. mammal. E. reptile.
5. At the end of the story, Ray Short was A. dead. B. married. C. poor. D. rich. E. sad.	5. At the end of the story, Ray Short was A. dead. B. insane. C. married. D. poor. E. sad.

Item 4 also illustrates the problem with the options that include other options. Even students who have no idea of what a moa is would have better-than-chance odds of guessing the right answer. Test-wise students could reason that it couldn't be a turtle because if it were, the item would have to be double keyed for reptile. Likewise, it couldn't be a dog because that would also make mammal correct. Therefore, it must be either a bird, mammal, or reptile. (It was an enormous, now-extinct New Zealand bird.)

12. Avoid unskilled use of options that are opposites. Inexperienced item writers are prone to have one of the pair of opposite options as the keyed response more than its share of the time. Item 5 in Figure 7.7 illustrates this. Opposite options C and D are the best guesses, especially because they are among the middle options. Similarly, the flawed version of item 2 in Figure 7.4 on page 149 provided this clue.

Of course, opposites can be used skillfully to miscue those who don't know what an item is designed to measure. It is sometimes useful to employ a pair of opposite options, provided that both are wrong.

Another way of using opposite options without providing clues is shown in item 8 of Figure 7.2 on page 146. Options A and D are opposite; so are options B and C. Thus, there is no clue. Similarly, item 9 in Figure 7.2 used two sets of opposites.

13. Avoid negative items where possible. Where they are used, call attention to the feature that makes them negative. In general, test questions should focus on what is right, not on what is wrong. Item 1 in Figure 7.8 illustrates the typical use of negative stems. If a history class has studied the achievements of Franklin Roosevelt's first two terms, it is easier for the teacher to place several accomplishments and one nonaccomplishment in a list and ask examinees to identify the latter. The improved version represents the more desirable approach of focusing on what is true rather than on what is false. The improved version also illustrates how a key word or phrase can be made conspicuous.

Yet at times it *is* appropriate to use negative stems. When teaching has emphasized what *not* to do, then negative stems are called for. For example, "If you find an unconscious person who has fallen from a ladder, you should *not* . . . ." Or, "Which behavior tends to make others *dis*like a person?"

FIGURE 7.8 More Item Flaws and Their Corrections.

FLAWED ITEMS	IMPROVED VERSIONS
1. Which of the following events did not occur during Franklin Roosevelt's first two terms? **A.** Attack of Pearl Harbor **B.** Bank Moratorium **C.** Creation of the SEC **D.** Creation of the WPA	1. Which of the following events occurred during Franklin Roosevelt's *first two* terms? **A.** Attack of Pearl Harbor **B.** Bank Moratorium **C.** Election of Harry Truman as Vice President **D.** Roosevelt stricken by polio
2. Liability insurance for a given car in a certain city will likely cost least if the only driver of the car is a **A.** 17-year-old female with good grades. **B.** 17-year-old female with poor grades. **C.** 17-year-old male with good grades. **D.** 17-year-old male with poor grades.	2. Liability insurance for a given car in a certain city will likely cost LEAST if the only driver of the car is a **A.** 17-year-old female with good grades. **B.** 17-year-old female with poor grades. **C.** 17-year-old male with good grades. **D.** 17-year-old male with poor grades.

When a negative stem is used, a safeguard is needed to prevent examinees from overlooking the one minor word or prefix that reverses the stem's meaning. Attention should be called to the negative element; it can be italicized, bolded, capitalized, or underlined. Some of these options were used in the previous paragraph's examples.

It is also good practice to highlight other words that may reverse examinees' mental sets. For example, "Which of the following is *smallest*?" Item 2 in Figure 7.8 on the previous page shows another way of making such unexpected words conspicuous.

Double negatives should always be avoided. If a negative stem is used, no negative options should follow.

14. Avoid inappropriate use of such options as "none of the above," "all of the above," and "A and C above." Recall that such alternatives have no place in the *best-answer* items that populate most tests. This kind of option violates logic and grammar by asking examinees to select the *best* option and then offering such choices as "none of the above" and "all of these" as the "best."

Such choices are so frequently misused that they have a bad reputation even where they are legitimate. Indeed, most authorities advise against any use of these options (Haladyna & Downing, 1989a; Oosterhof, 2003). Note that our recommendation is to avoid only *inappropriate* use of the options. When testing content that is categorically right or wrong under right-answer directions, they may be used with care.

Unskilled item writers who use such options tend to employ them as the keyed response either too much or too little. Many who use "all of the above" in multiple-choice items have it as the keyed response in at least half of the questions in which it appears. Others use such choices as "fillers" when they are out of ideas and rarely have them serve as the keyed response. Either way, it provides yet another basis for a teacher's test-wise examinees to guess answers without knowing content.

15. Write options that are grammatically parallel to each other. A "nicety" of item writing is parallel construction among the options, particularly in the incomplete-sentence variety of multiple-choice items. Item 1 in Figure 7.9 illustrates an awkward item that is improved by developing parallel construction of the options.

In addition to having options that aren't grammatically consistent, both versions of item 1 violate rule 2; the issue isn't provided in the stem. When all the options are similar (e.g., names of cities), this issue is of little consequence, but since the options of the flawed version "go off in different directions," this violation of rule 2 is worrisome.

16. Beware of humor. Item 2 of Figure 7.9 illustrates an attempt at humor. Such attempts often lead to trouble. In this case, "Short Beach" (whether or not it's humorous) won't be very plausible to children in Long Beach, California (which was founded by a Mr. Fillmore) because its beach isn't short. The more blatant attempt at humor, "Holdless," will also be chosen by few, if any, of the pupils who don't know the right answer.

Another problem with humor is that it often backfires. Persons who, under the stress of being tested, fail to recognize the teacher's attempt to be cute, may feel aggrieved when they later realize that they lost credit because of the teacher's playfulness; to them, it is *not* funny. Yet another problem with humor is that an examinee may lose focus when others react audibly to humor during a test.

17. Avoid clueing with similar phrasing in the stem and the keyed response. If important words or phrases in the keyed response also appear in the stem, students who lack knowledge and

FIGURE 7.9   Additional Examples of Item Flaws and Their Corrections.

FLAWED ITEMS	IMPROVED VERSIONS
1. Our city was first named	1. Our city was first named

A. before anyone lived in it.
  B. by its first resident.
  C. Fillmore City.
  D. in honor of its first minister.
  E. to attract settlers.
	A. Baytown.
	  B. Fillmore City.
	  C. Long Beach.
	  D. Oceanville.
	  E. Winter Resort.

2. What was the first name given our city?	2. What was the first name given our city?

A. Fillmore City
  B. Holdless City
  C. Long Beach
  D. Short Beach
	A. Baytown
	  B. Fillmore City
	  C. Long Beach
	  D. Oceanville
	  E. Winterburg

3. The Cuban Missile Crisis took place when the U.S.S.R. shipped missiles to	3. A major international crisis took place when the U.S.S.R. shipped missiles to

A. Cuba.
  B. India.
  C. Mexico.
  D. Yugoslavia.
	A. Cuba.
	  B. India.
	  C. Mexico.
	  D. Yugoslavia.

4. To *inaugurate* is to	4. To *inaugurate* is to

A. elect.
  B. install.
  C. lock up.
  D. remove.
	A. elect.
	  B. incarcerate.
	  C. put in place.
	  D. vindicate.

are grasping for clues will be attracted to the options that look more similar to the stem. The flawed version of item 3 in Figure 7.9 illustrates this.

Like several other hazards, this one can be turned to our advantage. Item 5 of Figure 7.2 on page 145 shows how a key word can be used to miscue. The use of *copy* machine in option A provides an irrelevant association with *copy*right in the stem and may appropriately render this foil more attractive to those lacking the targeted knowledge.

Prefixes also present a particular hazard. The flawed version of item 4 in Figure 7.9 would be guessed by many people lacking knowledge because of the prefix "in-." In the improved version, this clue has been eliminated. Moreover, two false clues have been incorporated into distractors. The prefix "in-" is now associated with a distractor, and the ending "-ate" is associated with two decoys.

18. Do not let one item clue other items. As one focuses on developing each item, it is natural to fail to remember all the other questions in the test. This creates the *likelihood* that the content of some questions will give away answers to others. Interitem clueing, of course, is a problem not only with multiple-choice items, but for other item types as well. Teachers tend to violate this rule most frequently as item types change.

For example, suppose a true-false item concerns whether the United States joined the League of Nations, and the student doesn't know the answer. Later, a multiple-choice question asks the identity of the most influential person in preventing the United States from joining the League of Nations. Upon reading the multiple-choice question, the examinee realizes that it provides the answer to the earlier item.

One remedy for this problem is to draft tests early enough so that they can be put aside for a few days before a final reading. Another way to minimize the possibility of item clueing and many other flaws is to ask a colleague to proofread the test. This professional service can, of course, be reciprocated. In the process, both teachers are likely to get some good ideas for later use.

THINKING CAP EXERCISE 7.1 ???

Think of your own experience in *taking* multiple-choice exams. You have probably often been able to deduce an answer, or at least to improve your guessing odds, when you didn't know the answer.

- Which two or three rule violations have helped you the most in your own test taking?
- Can you think of any additional methods you have used that aren't treated in the rules? In other words, what additional item-writing rules might the list well have included?

- Which rules have you learned enough about that will enable you, as a test taker, to exploit your instructors' violations of the rules?

KEY TO THINKING CAP EXERCISE 7.1
Although the multiple-choice rules were designed to cover most of the important issues, they are not exhaustive. (Yes, they may have been exhaust*ing*!) Your thoughts about the rules may enhance your item-writing skills.

Developing and Polishing Items

In the discussion that accompanied Figures 7.1 through 7.9, mention was made of the various features of items that serve to make them effective. A few illustrative items will now be examined for some "tricks of the trade" that will help you to polish your test questions. Good item writing is obviously a career-long, *developmental* Context C endeavor!

Example 1. The second version of the item in Figure 7.3 on page 148 illustrates a process by which foils can be thoughtfully created. Of all the potential distractors, which would work best to discriminate between examinees who know and those who don't know this fact? Other vice presidents who succeeded to the presidency would be the initial obvious set. This gives us Millard Fillmore, Andrew Johnson, Chester Arthur, Theodore Roosevelt, Calvin Coolidge, Harry Truman, Lyndon Johnson, and Gerald Ford. Which should we select?

Andrew Johnson comes to mind because of the difficulties he had with a hostile Congress over his attempt to follow the precedent. By good fortune, the list of possible decoys contains two Johnsons. The double occurrence of that name will make it more attractive and distract those students who lack the crucial knowledge away from Tyler. The list now contains Andrew Johnson, Lyndon Johnson, and John Tyler.

At this point, Andrew Jackson comes to mind even though he did not attain office by succession. His name serves to provide two Andrews as well as two Johnsons. Some test-wise students who do not know the material look for recurring features among the options. One might reason, "There are two Andrews. The test maker is trying to tempt us with the wrong Andrew; therefore, the right answer is probably one of them. Likewise for two Johnsons. One option has both Andrew and Johnson; it's the best one to guess." Such reasoning would often lead to the keyed response.

Because options are both plentiful and brief, one might well add a fifth option to make lucky guessing less likely. Theodore Roosevelt might be used because his name would be among the most familiar on the list and might therefore "draw" some of the students who lack the knowledge. Or, because his name is relatively obscure, Chester Arthur might be attractive to some students who are acutely aware that they won't recognize the right name.

Example 2.   For another example, consider a math item having the stem $3 + 5 \times 4 - 2 \times 6 =$. (The correct answer is found by first doing the multiplications, then doing the addition and subtraction.) To obtain desirable foils, we would work the problem in the most likely incorrect ways. The most likely error may be 180, which is obtained by working from left to right without regard for order-of-operation rules. Another error would be 20, obtained by wrongly adding 3 and 5 first and then proceeding correctly. Another is 126, obtained by correctly adding the products of 5×4 to 3, and then wrongly subtracting 2 and multiplying the difference by 6. Another would be 96, obtained by reversing the proper order of operation.

Figuring out these options was a bother. Even after going to the trouble, we are left to worry that some students will make still different errors. Because the questions could be given right-answer directions, "none of the above" could be considered as a catch-all. These considerations help us to understand why many math teachers prefer to use this stem in a completion item rather than in a multiple-choice question.

Example 3.   Now consider the evolution of an item idea. Sometimes the idea for an item that assesses complex mental processes springs directly to mind. At other times, it gradually develops as a question is revised several times. In Figure 7.6 on page 153, item 2 could have been evoked by a recognition of the shallowness of the learning tapped by item 1. Likewise, item 3 might have evolved out of dissatisfaction with the low level of thinking required in item 1 and the shocking length of item 2.

Example 4.   For a final example, consider an elementary-level reading passage that described how Mennonites migrated to Kansas from Russia. They brought a variety of wheat called Turkey Red. Turkey Red started Kansans in growing hard winter wheat—the variety that soon made Kansas the "Breadbasket of the Nation."

One of the items drafted for this reading passage concerned the country from which the Mennonites came to Kansas. No country was mentioned in the passage besides Russia and the United States. What options would you use?

Russia, of course, would be the keyed response. At first, foils of England, Germany, and Spain were drafted. Then the item writer recalled that Mennonites had previously migrated to Russia from Germany; hence, Germany had to be replaced. This illustrates the need for test makers to know their subject matter well beyond the level at which it is being tested.

On further review, Turkey came to the item writer's mind because of the name of the wheat variety. Still later, the author had the creative idea of Mennon; although there is no such country, it certainly sounds plausible that Mennonites would come from Mennon. Thus, the final item, after much evolution, contained the distractors Turkey and Mennon. These two distractors proved to be extraordinarily effective in differentiating between better readers and less capable ones.

Directions for Multiple-Choice Items

The instructions that introduce multiple-choice or other objective items should inform examinees of several important things. They should indicate the relative credit of the items. Objective items should ordinarily be equally weighted because usually the number of items on each topic directly reflects the importance of the topics.

Multiple-choice directions should forcefully indicate that *only one* answer may be selected for each item. (Any item with more than one option marked should be scored as wrong.) For best-answer items, examinees should be told to select the *one best* answer; for correct-answer items, they should be told to select the *one correct* answer.

Examinees should be told how to mark their answers, for example, by circling, underlining, or by filling in circles (sometimes called bubbles). When tests are administered by computer, examinees respond by pressing a keyboard key or by using a mouse.

Finally, the topic of guessing should be fully addressed. Chapter 10 will discuss this important issue. For now, suffice it to say that the directions concerning guessing should honestly inform examinees whether it is in their best interest to guess when they don't know an answer.

ENCAPSULATION

Recall the example featuring Turkey Red wheat. Its last sentence stated: "These two distractors proved to be extraordinarily effective in differentiating between better readers and less capable ones." Reflect once again on your thoughts and feelings toward this validity issue.

Is this laudable educational psychology—developing assessment items that so directly separate good readers from poor ones? Is it fair to the less-able reader? Some educators are uncomfortable with explicit efforts to differentiate between excellent and mediocre academic performance, believing that professionals who spend their careers helping young people learn should balk at efforts to sort students in such ways.

The reply must be, "No, we shouldn't balk at using differentiating items." It is important to recall two major purposes of assessment—to direct students in their study efforts and to guide teachers in their decision making for instruction. Educators aim to increase the capabilities of all students across wide domains of content and thinking processes. To do this most efficiently, it is necessary to *determine where students are in their learning and then to provide the ways and means they need to progress.*

INTERPRETIVE EXERCISES

The item types considered so far are sometimes criticized as being artificial or unlike real-life tasks. This analysis is obviously sound for *some* instructional aims. Objective items wouldn't serve well in assessing the skill of riding a bicycle. Nor would free-standing objective questions that lack graphics tap student ability to evaluate works of art or skill in interpreting maps and graphs.

For other instructional aims, the criticism that objective items lack authenticity is ill founded. Recall that the first step in determining what kind of assessment method to use is to realize that instructional targets that can be assessed with objective items ordinarily should be. Thus, if a class has been working on recognizing causes of events, multiple-choice items offer an efficient and reasonably realistic way to assess this cognitive achievement. In this same vein, when pupils are learning to distinguish between fact and opinion, alternate-choice questions provide a direct, relevant, economical, and reliable way to assess their learning.

Let's return to examples for which the criticism that objective items aren't authentic makes sense, for example, bicycling, composing coherent paragraphs, evaluating works of art, and interpreting maps and graphs. The pursuit of authentic assessment of bicycling will require performance assessment, which will be addressed in Chapter 9. Authentic assessment of composition will obviously require written tasks that are addressed in Chapter 8. The other two examples will be considered in the next part of this chapter. If students are learning to evaluate works of art by use of accepted criteria, the quest for authenticity suggests having them react to novel works of art. If pupils are learning how to interpret maps or graphs, realism is achieved by asking pupils to interpret unfamiliar maps or graphs. These needs for realism can be accommodated with objective items accompanied by stimulus materials, such as novel maps, tables, or works of art, upon which the items are based.

An **interpretive exercise** is a set of test items accompanied by material upon which they are based. The purpose is to determine how well examinees can *extract meaning from or interpret the unfamiliar;* this, of course, typically is Context C subject matter. Most readers have taken tests containing interpretive exercises. For example, in typical reading comprehension tests, examinees are presented with a reading passage that they haven't previously seen, and it is followed by several multiple-choice questions *based on the passage.* The purpose is to determine how well students can obtain meaning from the passage.

Map skills also are traditionally assessed with interpretive exercises. The stimulus is an unfamiliar map followed by a set of items. Each question should be based on the stimulus so that it cannot be answered without reference to it. Hence, the items assess student ability to secure information from the map.

Interpretive exercises are particularly useful when we aren't sure that all students have the same background in content and when we want them to *apply* content but deem it unnecessary that they first memorize it (Stiggins, 2001). Material for the stimulus, be it a poem, map, musical passage, or diagram, serves to provide all examinees with the same material in a more cost-effective manner than other authentic procedures typically enable. The test questions that follow the stimulus are usually objectively scorable—a virtue from the perspective of both economy and reliability.

When examinees haven't previously studied the stimuli, interpretive exercises *measure examinee ability to process new material;* that is, they *assess high-road transfer* of learning. The tasks can, among other things, require that pupils read, infer, interpret, draw conclusions, predict, measure, calculate, estimate, or use maps, graphs, tables, indices, or tables of content. Interpretive exercises can thus measure many important kinds of complex learning (Airasian, 2001) in a wide variety of subject matter and grades. Their classroom use sends the important message to students that school learning should enable them to obtain meaning from realistic, novel material. That is, by assessing high-road transfer, interpretive exercises communicate that *transfer of learning is an important instructional aim* (Linn & Gronlund, 2000).

What Can Interpretive Exercises Measure?

Interpretive exercises are as diverse as the ingenuity of their creators. The introductory material can vary widely. Most exercises use multiple-choice items; however, other kinds of items, such as alternate choice and essay, can be referenced to the stimuli. Following are descriptions of some kinds of interpretive exercises. To illustrate the breadth of this assessment method, the examples will range from the commonplace to the exotic.

Interpreting Tables.   The ability to "read" the kinds of data summarized in science, social studies, and math tables can be measured authentically with interpretive exercises such as that shown in Figure 7.10. The information contained in this figure would probably not be very well known to students; hence, it might be acceptable. Greater assurance of unfamiliarity could be secured by using fictitious data; for example, lengths of reigns of monarchs of an imaginary country.

    Novelty of the stimulus material is fundamental to validity. That is, if an interpretive exercise is to reach its potential in assessing high-road transfer, it *must* assess something that wasn't previously studied. Student ability to answer items correctly should demand *application of* prior learning, not mere recall of it. The general term for this linkage to the stimulus is **context dependence.** An example will follow shortly.

Reading Comprehension.   The ability to extract meaning from written prose or verse is central to literacy both in native tongues and other languages. This ability is usually measured by presenting some material to be read followed by multiple-choice questions about the material. Length may range from a sentence to long passages. Like other interpretive exercises, a critical attribute of a reading comprehension test is that the information necessary to answer questions be *un*familiar to examinees. If they already knew the answers, we wouldn't know whether correct answers were based on the prior knowledge or on the ability to derive meaning from the passage.

    For example, a passage in a middle-school reading test about Cleopatra and her brother might be accompanied by a question asking the name of their country. The problem is that many students have a prior association of Cleopatra and Egypt without reading the passage; hence, the ability to answer the item is probably not very context dependent, or, as it is known in the special case of reading tests, it would not be very passage dependent. On the other hand, an item asking the name of Cleopatra's brother would be more acceptable because few students would possess that prior information. The way to build passage dependence into a test is to base reading tests on selections that don't contain material that examinees already know.

    Most authors of interpretive exercises prefer to create their own stimulus passages, tables, maps, etc., because they can be developed and altered to serve the assessment purposes.

Listening Comprehension.   The ability to obtain meaning from the spoken word is critically important. Although some features of listening comprehension might be better assessed with oral, "conversational" tests, many aspects of the ability to decode the meaning of oral language can be assessed with interpretive exercises that don't require the cost in time or reliability that is associated with individual oral testing. The passages are read "live" or played on audio or video

FIGURE 7.10   Interpretive Exercise Based on Table.

ITEMS 1–3 ARE BASED ON THE TABLE BELOW.

Tudor Monarchs

Henry VII	1485–1509
Henry VIII	1509–1547
Edward VI	1547–1553
Mary I	1553–1558
Elizabeth I	1558–1603

1. How long did the Tudors reign?
   A. 24 years
   B. 45 years
   C. 118 years
   D. 128 years
   E. 218 years

2. Which Tudor had the longest reign?
   A. Henry VII
   B. Henry VIII
   C. Edward VI
   D. Mary I
   E. Elizabeth I

3. Elizabeth I was 25 years old when she became queen.
   About how old was she when she died?
   A. 30
   B. 31
   C. 49
   D. 63
   E. 70

equipment. Paper-pencil, multiple-choice items are usually used to assess student grasp of what they hear.

Listening comprehension is vital both to daily life and to success in school. Even at the university level, learning from oral presentations such as lectures, discussions, and reports from group work remains essential for success.

Signing Comprehension.   Closely paralleling reading and listening comprehension of written and spoken language is signing comprehension of visually signed language either as a native or as a second language. Here, of course, the stimulus would be visual, either "live" or, for much better standardization, videotaped. Students could then be tested via written multiple-choice questions. Or, if examinees were not literate in a written language, they could be tested via individually administered signed conversation. The former would be an interpretive exercise, whereas the latter would be a performance assessment, which will be discussed in Chapter 9.

Study Skills.   Interpretive exercises are particularly well suited to measuring student ability to use resources such as dictionaries, thesauri, library catalogs and databases, tables of contents, indices, and Internet search menus. Figure 7.11 contains a set of matching items for elementary children concerning use of encyclopedias. Such an exercise may not be as realistic as a trip to the library for one-on-one performance testing on encyclopedia use, yet the advantages of the interpretive exercise are compelling because it:

- provides a relatively high degree of *realism* or *authenticity;*
- offers each child a chance to engage in *the same* task without concern about word-of-mouth contamination of task novelty for youngsters who are tested later than others;
- yields more *reliable* findings; and
- provides a *cost-effective* and *labor-effective* assessment in a group setting.

Interpretive exercises thus provide an excellent method of assessing students' high-road application of their study skills.

Map Interpretation.   Map skills are commonly assessed with interpretive exercises because they provide a very realistic simulation of real-life map usage. To be sure, a paper-pencil map skills test won't be as authentic as a car trip to an unfamiliar locale for a real-world test of roadmap usage, yet the advantages of the relatively realistic, standardized, economical, convenient, reliable paper-pencil measure are convincing.

FIGURE 7.11   Interpretive Exercise on Encyclopedia Use.

Directions: Below is a picture of the volumes of an encyclopedia. Each volume has information about subjects that begin with the letters shown. Questions 1–4 below are based on this picture. To the left of each question, write the number of the volume that answers the question. Each volume may be used once, more than once, or not at all.

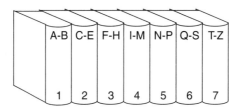

_____ **1.** Which volume would be the best to find whether Catherine the Great ruled Austria, France, or Russia?

_____ **2.** Which volume would contain information about grasshoppers, crickets, and butterflies?

_____ **3.** Which volume would give you the most information about Bertrand Russell, a famous English mathematician?

_____ **4.** Which volume would be most likely to have pictures of a poodle, a Saint Bernard, and a German shepherd?

Suppose a test maker wants to know if pupils can use the key to determine distance. A multiple-choice question can ask how far it is from one city to another. Here again, if transfer is to be assessed, it is important to ensure that students do not have prior knowledge. For example, one wouldn't want to ask how far New York City is from Chicago because some students already know this without the map. Better to use a map of an obscure place; better still to create a map of an imaginary place, thus ensuring that no one has prior knowledge. *The latter technique has the added advantage of enabling the map to be altered to fit the testing needs.*

Although interpretive exercises based on maps usually rely exclusively on multiple-choice items, a broader variety of item types can be considered. For example, alternate-choice items could focus on which of two countries was better suited for growing various crops or developing specific industries. Or, an essay item could ask students to compare and contrast the pros and cons of two potential sites for a steel mill or meat-processing plant.

Such questions raise the issue of whether stimulus materials must be sufficient to enable examinees to answer questions without additional background knowledge. No, they need not be sufficient provided that the requisite knowledge is either (a) universally known to examinees or (b) course relevant. An example of needed knowledge that might not be fair concerns a ski resort. If all the pupils in the class know that skiing is done in high, cold places, all is well. But if some students haven't had the opportunity to learn this and if it has not been part of the course, then it would be unfair to presume it.

An example of necessary knowledge that could be course relevant is found in a map item asking which city would be the best location for a steel mill. This question cannot be answered solely on the basis of information contained in the map. Examinees also have to know that steel production requires coal and iron, that transportation is needed for raw resources and finished products, and that a labor force is necessary. If this information has been part of the social studies course, then it is fair and valid to create interpretive exercise items that require both the ability (a) to decode raw resource, population, and transportation indicators on a map, and (b) to integrate this information with the requisite knowledge. Indeed, it is the *synthesis* of such skills that renders the interpretive exercise a superb means of assessing high-road transfer of learning.

A similar issue attends items 2 and 4 in Figure 7.11. Is it fair to assume that pupils know that grasshoppers, crickets, and butterflies are insects? Assuming the science curriculum has covered this, then it's *desirable* to tap pupils' ability to use superordinate categories on a test because *this simulates use of the encyclopedia in real life.*

History and Current Events.   Unfamiliar political cartoons provide a splendid way to measure student grasp of issues in the social sciences. For example, an uncaptioned cartoon can be accompanied by a multiple-choice item asking "What is the point of this cartoon?" Or a cartoon can be accompanied by an item asking the name of the historic person or group to which it is sympathetic or hostile. A single cartoon often will give rise to two or three items.

Application of Terminology.   Figure 7.12 illustrates the use of a very short passage to assess introductory psychology students' ability to apply their knowledge of terminology. Note how this exercise assesses much deeper learning than would a matching exercise calling for matching terms and definitions.

Analysis of Art Objects.   An art appreciation course or unit might well use interpretive exercises summatively to assess important learning outcomes. Each stimulus could be either an art object

FIGURE 7.12   Interpretive Exercise Based on Matching Exercise.

Directions: In items 1–5, match each example that follows with its technical name. Each response may be used once, more than once, or not at all. Print your responses to the left of the item numbers.

In times past, an organ grinder and his monkey could be found at fairs and carnivals. Whenever the music was playing, the monkey would beg for pennies and would tip its hat whenever given one. Every few minutes the monkey would deliver the pennies collected to the organ grinder and receive a bit of food in exchange.

_____ **1.** Begging penny   **A.** Discriminative stimulus
_____ **2.** Organ music   **B.** Operant
_____ **3.** Penny   **C.** Primary reinforcing stimulus
_____ **4.** Person to beg from   **D.** Secondary reinforcing stimulus
_____ **5.** Bit of food

such as a sculpture, painting, or mobile *or a picture of it.* Test questions could be created to assess such things as ability to identify, analyze, and/or evaluate such features as period, theme, style, technique, balance, movement, color, and texture.

When such exercises are used to *assist* students in learning, class discussion of questions after students have taken a test can be a very helpful instructional technique. Such *formative* use of interpretive exercises helps students know what the expected learning outcomes are and how to achieve them.

Interpretation of Scientific Experiments.   Student ability to interpret results from scientific experiments is effectively measured by interpretive exercises. Experiments can be pictured, described in words, or shown during the test with a slide, PowerPoint, or videotape presentation.

Interpretation of Charts and Graphs.   A common use of context-dependent exercises involves the interpretation of charts and graphs in math, science, or social studies.

Music Reading.   Another example of interpretive exercises would be an excerpt of printed music followed by test questions. A few bars can suggest numerous items that tap such varied skills as ability to decode symbols indicating clef, time, and key, names of lines and spaces on the staff, and note values.

Music Appreciation.   If a music appreciation class were studying musical analysis or evaluation, a useful way to assess transfer of these complex cognitive processes would be to play a tape of an unfamiliar passage of music. The accompanying questions could be printed as multiple-choice items. To assess understanding and appreciation of music tone and mood, examinees could listen to one novel composition in minor mode and one in major mode, and then, in essay form, describe characteristics and uses of each mode.

Vocational Education.   In vocational education, an electrical-circuit diagram or plumbing blueprint could serve as the stimulus to a set of multiple-choice items concerning the meaning of, or directions contained in, the stimulus. This taps the cognitive tasks. In agriculture education, interpretive exercises can facilitate both teaching and assessing as an intermediary between the textbook and expensive, time-consuming field trips. A teacher can use pictures or slides to assess student proficiency in making correct interpretations about such attributes in farm animals as breed character, muscle, size by age, balance, and health. Exercises can also effectively assess multicontext units, for example, an interdisciplinary unit involving aspects of agricultural economics along with animal or plant attributes, ecological considerations, and weather and climate conditions that impact productivity.

Students also could be asked to critique videotaped performances, such as wiring an electrical circuit or making a neat, durable weld, or grading a beef carcass. Items might address the adequacy of the performance for safety, speed, durability, and neatness.

In the last paragraph and several other examples, it is important to note that the interpretive exercise provides a measure of examinees' ability to evaluate the work of others, not their ability to do the work themselves. The latter would require a performance measure. However, the more objective and economical interpretive exercise can be used to help students learn and use the criteria by which work is judged. It is important for students to acquire proficiency in self-assessment (Ormrod, 2000).

Social Studies.   Students could study examples of television or Internet advertisements to identify the types of propaganda techniques implicit in each (e.g., bandwagon, glittering generality, and name-calling). The advertisements could even be familiar ones provided that they had not been used for class analysis during the unit of study.

Archeology and Paleontology.   Archeology students might be presented with pictures of pottery specimens they have not previously examined to analyze for style, period, culture, and function. Or, students of paleontology might be shown pictures of unfamiliar animals' jaw bones for analysis and deduction concerning the creatures' habits, diets, and habitats. Multiple-choice questions would serve well in either situation.

Suggestions for Developing Interpretive Exercises

The previous discussion demonstrates that possibilities for developing useful interpretive exercises range as far and wide as the subjects provided in the curriculum. They are limited only by teacher time, creativity, and resourcefulness in finding or creating stimulus material. Seven recommendations are provided for composing interpretive exercises.

   1.   Find or create relevant stimulus materials. When the subject matter is expansive, Context C teaching and testing should concern high-road transfer of learning. We want students to be able to *apply* their learning to situations that are somewhat similar, yet not identical, to those studied. Assessing their ability to use learning in *new* circumstances both (a) enhances the realism and validity of the test and (b) signals students that ability to apply their learning is important.

If, for example, pupils have been studying how to use pie graphs, the best way to test their skills is to have them interpret *different* or *new* pie graphs. If the teacher has 12 graphs with which to teach and test the unit, then a couple of them might be set aside for use in testing. The novelty of those to be used in the test shouldn't be compromised by "teaching to the test," either intentionally or inadvertently. No special teaching emphasis should be devoted to the features found in the test graphs. Whatever the subject matter, one always needs to obtain new stimuli for use in assessment. Where to get them?

Good stimulus materials should be collected or created and saved for use and reuse. They can be found in all sorts of places, including supplementary textbooks and newspapers. The best ones are often created specially for testing.

Few of us can sustain creative marathons; ideas for good exercises usually occur one at a time. It is useful to jot down creative thoughts when they occur. If a notion for a good interpretive exercise occurs while reading the evening paper or driving to work, it should be cut out or jotted down at the first opportunity. It is foresightful to keep a file of testing ideas for each unit.

2. Ensure context dependence. When creating interpretive exercises, it's very easy to slip and produce some items that are answerable *without* reference to their stimuli. The purpose of context-dependent exercises is to assess examinee ability to obtain information from stimuli and to process that information. Hence, the ability to answer each item must *depend* on correctly decoding or processing its stimulus.[1] Careful editing, at a time subsequent to the original writing, helps to identify items that lack context dependence.

3. Modify the stimulus materials to suit assessment purposes. As one drafts test items, one often thinks of ways in which the stimulus could be altered to advantage. A stimulus might be edited slightly to eliminate ambiguity in a test item. Or, it could be changed to make an opportunity to add an item or two. A stimulus change can sometimes even render the test item capable of assessing valued learning outcomes beyond those originally envisioned. Successive refinements of items will lead to revision of the stimulus, and conversely. The test maker should move back and forth, fine tuning until the stimulus and its items are well aligned.

4. Seek sufficient numbers of items per stimulus. It wouldn't do to have students study a two-page reading passage that is followed by only one or two multiple-choice items. Nor would it be efficient to have examinees view an entire motion picture if only two or three questions are based on it. In selecting and developing stimulus materials, test makers should use only those that can support enough test questions to justify the time it takes to examine the material. A very short stimulus, such as a cartoon, may be acceptable if it only yields an item or two. However, a long stimulus would have to give rise to several items in order to be cost-effective with regard to examinee time.

5. Avoid letting blocks of items depart from the specified weight. It is possible to get so carried away in producing items for a given stimulus that sight is lost of the desired number of questions for a cell in a test's plan. Test makers should remain mindful of their specifications and resist temptation to depart from them (unless, of course, they have new insights that lead them to thoughtful revision of the test plan).

Would 10 items on the Figure 7.10 exercise about Tudor monarchs be too many? Yes. Even if specifications called for that many, it would be better to have two shorter sets based on somewhat different stimuli. Shorter sets would enhance content sampling and would make it easier to avoid interitem clues. However, there is certainly no fault in generating many items for a stimulus that will support them, such as a few bars of printed music.

---

[1]In rare cases, one may decide, for convenience of grouping, to mix into interpretive exercises some items that measure mere knowledge. (A few published tests do this, and it is illustrated in the Extension cited later in this chapter.) There really is no harm in this practice provided that one *realizes that the knowledge items don't assess transfer* and, therefore, don't satisfy test specifications that call for application.

6. Adhere to accepted item-writing rules. One should observe the rules, such as avoiding careless use of specific determiners, preventing items from clueing each other, seeking brevity, and avoiding ambiguity.

For tests designed to measure any kind of achievement *other than* reading, it is important to keep the reading demands of stimuli low. If students miss items on a health test because they can't read the stimulus materials, then the test is measuring the irrelevant construct of reading achievement in addition to the relevant construct of health achievement. In this situation, the measurement of reading is *in*valid; it contaminates the exercise as a measure of health achievement (AERA, 1999).

As mentioned in Chapter 6, a matching exercise shouldn't be split between two pages; nor should free-standing items such as multiple-choice questions. Although the temptation is often greatest for interpretive exercises, which tend to be longer, they too, if possible, should be contained on single pages or facing pages. Examinees shouldn't have to turn pages back and forth between a stimulus and its items.

7. Provide clear, appropriate directions for each exercise. Ordinarily, each interpretive exercise should open with a statement identifying the items that accompany a stimulus and signaling their dependence on the stimulus. For example, "Items 7–12 are based on the map shown below. Use it to answer the questions." Or, "Carefully read the following newspaper ad, and then answer the three questions that follow it." Or, "Below is part of the Table of Contents from a book. Questions 1–6 are based on it. After you read each question, refer to the Table of Contents to decide which page would contain the *beginning* of the section you wish to find."

ENCAPSULATION: COLLABORATION

Generating excellent interpretive exercises is not only time intensive, it's also a demanding task. It is a good idea to form reciprocal test-critiquing groups of two or three people. A "fresh eye" can detect many an item flaw or other problem.

From another angle, several of the examples in this chapter imply collaborating or teaming with educators in other curricular areas. Such efforts may be fruitful in helping students develop linkages among subjects. Collaborating teachers may pursue transfer to other subjects both in their teaching and in their testing.

THINKING CAP EXERCISE 7.2   ???

Below is a reading passage followed by a set of test questions. You are asked to critique the items. The exercise contains several item types, thereby providing an opportunity to apply the material in Chapter 6 as well as that of this chapter.

The set as a whole has problems in the directions to examinees and in the order of item types. You need not address these topics; they will be taken up in Chapter 10.

Your task is limited to identifying what is wrong with each test item in the interpretive exercise. Many of the questions suffer from multiple faults. Simply note what is wrong with each; you need not try to revise it. Indeed, many of the items in this exercise are so fundamentally flawed that they should be discarded rather than revised.

(Continued)

THINKING CAP EXERCISE 7.2   CONTINUED

Passage

As Lewis ate his "ham on rye" sandwich, he wondered what "rye" was. Later that afternoon at the library, he looked it up in the encyclopedia and learned the following:

Rye cereal grass grows to be about five-feet tall and produces an edible grain. This grain is used to make flour for bread, for animal feed, as a pasture plant, and for making alcoholic beverages. The plant's strong straw is used for animal bedding and roof thatching as well as for making cardboard, hats, and other products.

Rye is a relative of wheat that was long considered to be a weed because it invaded prehistoric wheat patches. But, as people migrated northward, the cold-resistant rye could survive where the wheat could not. It thus became a valued grain crop rather than an unwelcome invader. It probably originated in Asia Minor and gradually spread throughout Asia and Europe where it is now cultivated extensively.

Rye is sometimes called the "grain of poverty" because it grows in poor soils that will not support wheat. Although not quite as rich in protein as wheat, rye flour usually is made from the whole grain and therefore is richer in protein than white wheat flour.

Test Questions
1. What would be the best title for this passage?
   A. Useful Weed   C. Wheat's Poor Cousin
   B. The Grain of Poverty D. Ham on Rye

2. The author of the passage is
   A. feeling sorry for rye because of its bad reputation.
   B. concerned with rye's nutritional features.
   C. interested in the history of rye.
   D. trying to proselytize the use of rye.

3. "It" in line 2 refers to
   A. ham sandwich.
   B. afternoons.
   C. libraries.
   D. rye.

4. Rye is not as rich in protein as wheat because
   A. it will not grow where   B. it provides variety
      wheat grows.   to diet.
   C. it has more uses.   D. it is easy to grow.

5. Rye
   A. originated in Africa.
   B. stalk is used for thatching roofs.
   C. used for making pumpernickel bread.
   D. has a bad reputation.

6. The word "cultivated" means
   A. refined.
   B. nurtured as a desired domestic crop.

(Continued)

THINKING CAP EXERCISE 7.2   CONTINUED

    C. plowed.
    D. grown.

7. T F Wheat is always more nutritious than rye.

8. T F Because it is more susceptible to cold, wheat is not as desirable as rye.

9. Rye is sometimes called _____.

10. Lewis looked "rye" up in the _____ in the _____ in the _____.

KEY TO THINKING CAP 7.2

Item Flaws. These items have many, many flaws. You are not expected to catch all of them. The problems for each item are roughly ordered from the most serious to the least worrisome.

1. No clear *best* answer exists. Too, the basis by which "best" is to be judged is not specified. Finally, some measurement specialists share our preference for a vertical arrangement of options. Others are open to horizontal arrangement of an item's options provided that they all appear on the same page and are arranged consistently among items.

2. First, there is no best answer. Calling for an inference is permissible *if* there is a good basis for making the inference. Next, the vocabulary level of "proselytize" is quite high. (Even in a reading test, the difficulty is intended to lie in the passage.) Third, the issue isn't formulated in the stem. (Are we seeking the author's nationality, gender, age, motive, or what?) Finally, the options aren't grammatically parallel.

3. First, "it" is singular, but some of the options are plural; this provides a powerful clue. Second, finding the "it" in the passage should be made easy by numbering lines, bold facing the word, etc. Third, each option should end with a period.

4. There is no best answer; indeed, the options do not address the reason for rye having less protein than wheat. Too, the negative "not" in the stem should be highlighted in some way. Next, the negative in option A creates a double negative with the stem—a taboo. Also, the options are not only arranged in a nonvertical format, but in one differing from that of item 1. Finally,

the word "it" should be moved to the stem to avoid repetition in each option.

5. No best answer exists among options B, C, and D. The correctness of option C is problematic because this correct fact is not presented in the passage; it requires specialized external knowledge. The issue is not formulated in the stem. Option C lacks a verb. The options aren't parallel.

6. There is no one best answer; if this item were intended to refer to the meaning of "cultivated" *in the passage's context,* then that should be so stated. Assuming that option B is the keyed response, it is conspicuous by virtue of its length. In addition, an item should *never* be split between two pages (or even between two columns); it is too easy for examinees to overlook the options on the next page. The options aren't parallel. "Cultivated" should be highlighted in the passage to make it easy to locate.

7. The "always" clues false, which the item is.

8. Triple-barreled item! (1. Is wheat more susceptible to cold? 2. Is wheat less desirable than rye? 3. If "yes" to both of the above, then is susceptibility to cold the reason for the lesser desirability?) The item is ambiguous (by virtue of point 3). It is also ambiguous with respect to the geographic location where it would be desirable.

9. No one best response. ("A Cereal Grass," "A Weed," "The Grain of Poverty"?)

10. No one best response. (That is, the exact verbiage of the passage is not essential to its meaning.) Unreasonable number of blanks! Inconsistent length of blanks.

CAPTIVATING EXTENSION EXAMPLE TO RECAP PARTS OF CHAPTERS 5, 6, AND 7: AN INTEGRATED MIDDLE-SCHOOL UNIT ON AUSTRALIA

We have prepared a detailed example of integrated teaching across geography, multicultural values, language arts, life science, earth science, music, computer use, logic, and math to illustrate:

- How tests and unit planning interface
- How tests can assess complex learning outcomes as well as simple ones
- How the entire teaching-assessment enterprise is integrated
- How a unit can emphasize high-road transfer of learning yet hold students accountable for important factual information
- How multicontext teaching can be advantageous
- How integration across traditional disciplines can be productive

You may access this unit on our web site, ablongman.com/hannadettmer.

CHAPTER RECAP

Multiple-choice items are the most widely used objective item type. They are efficient in providing much information per unit of testing time. They are appropriate for a wide variety of subject matter and mental processes with examinees ranging in age from early primary and older. Multiple-choice items clearly merit their great popularity. However, as will be stressed in Chapters 8 and 9, some very important outcomes of school learning aren't adequately assessed by multiple-choice questions.

Constructing multiple-choice items requires considerable skill in item writing, knowledge of examinees, and grasp of subject matter. Much time, effort, and attention to detail is required to do justice to students' study and effort. Meritorious items grow out of:

- Careful preliminary planning of the unit of instruction
- Detailed planning focus on the table of specifications for the total assessment
- Insightful and/or creative forethought in generating good item ideas
- Thoughtful, skillful, and creative revision of items

Interpretive exercises enable teachers to measure some (yet definitely not all) complex mental processes in more effective ways than individual questions allow. Interpretive exercises are often the best for assessing deep thinking and high-road transfer. Their greatest virtue is the *realism* with which they represent or simulate *application*. When based on objective items—as they commonly are—interpretive items also have the great advantage of being reliably and easily scored.

However, interpretive exercises require more time, effort, and resourcefulness to prepare—and more examinee time to take—than do other objective item types; these are very real disadvantages. The question to ask is: "Are interpretive exercises the *best* format for my *instructional and assessment* purposes?" When their superb capacity to *assess high-road transfer of learning* and *to signal its importance* leads to an affirmative answer to that question, they are well worth the effort.

None of us will ever fully master the challenging literary forms discussed in this chapter. Creating and collecting good multiple-choice questions and interpretive exercises that *contribute to our teaching effectiveness* is a career-long, *developmental* endeavor.

DEVELOPING AND SCORING ESSAYS, OTHER PRODUCTS, AND PORTFOLIOS

CHAPTER OVERVIEW

USES AND MISUSES OF ESSAY EXAMS

COMPOSING EFFECTIVE RESTRICTED-RESPONSE AND EXTENDED-RESPONSE ESSAYS

USING RUBRICS TO SCORE ESSAYS EFFECTIVELY

DEVELOPING AND MARKING OTHER PRODUCT MEASURES

USING PORTFOLIOS

KEY TERMS

essay question
restricted-response essay
extended-response essay
analytic marking
holistic marking

product measure
realistic assessment
authentic assessment
portfolio
scoring rubric

Product assessment predates history. Long before the advent of written language, products such as handmade tools were surely evaluated both formatively and summatively. You yourself have been evaluating products since early childhood (e.g., drawings, paper airplanes, braids, and products assembled from Legos, Tinkertoys, or Lincoln logs). You have done so both to improve products while they were still under construction and to evaluate them after they were completed.

This chapter concerns the more systematic assessment of various kinds of products. As with other methods of assessment, our aim is to enhance student learning.

ESSAYS

This chapter places special emphasis on essays, which are a special kind of product. Essays are the oldest form of paper-pencil assessment. Indeed, essay and short-answer tests dominated paper-pencil testing until a century ago when objective items came into use. Essays now coexist as a complement to objective item types. The sieve, first presented in Chapter 1 and reappearing in various chapters throughout the book, provides guidance for deciding when each is best used. Readers may wish to review the sieve at this time.

The Nature of Essay Items

Why are essays, a kind of product, featured so prominently? Other kinds of product measures tend to be subject specific; art teachers assess art products, math teachers evaluate math proofs, and so on. Essays, in contrast, are used by teachers of virtually all subjects.

Like completion and short-answer items, examinees must *compose* essays. Unlike completion and short-answer items, no one response to an essay has *exclusive* claim to correctness (Ahmann & Glock, 1981). Since no single answer to an essay question is uniquely correct, the quality of responses must be judged subjectively *by a person knowledgeable in the subject* (Stalnaker, 1951).

The popularity of objective item types in the past century attests to several serious limitations of the older essay item type. Essays take more time to administer, require more time to mark, can sample less subject matter per unit of testing time, and tend to provide less reliable results than objective items. They also offer more opportunity for bluffing or rambling by students who have only marginal command of the material.

Yet objective item types haven't eclipsed essays. They remain useful because they are superior to objective items in measuring such important educational outcomes as student ability to produce, design, explain, defend, criticize, organize, and integrate. Students also can demonstrate individual writing styles, vocabularies, and divergent thinking in essay exams.

Two features that all **essay questions** share are their requirements that examinees *retrieve* material from memory (rather than merely recognize it) and that they *compose* answers in their own words (rather than select the words from fixed choices). In other important ways, essay questions differ widely. They may require only that information be retrieved from memory or they may necessitate additional deep processing. They may provide structure concerning how the answer is to be formulated or they may let examinees decide. They may pinpoint what topics are to be included in the answer or they may leave this to the examinees' discretion. Some of these differences highlight a useful distinction between restricted-response and extended-response essays.

Restricted-response essays *provide structure*—structure for the examinee *and* structure for the person evaluating examinee performance. Examinees have less freedom of response. They are informed of what content is to be included, and they are typically provided with information about the relative weight of topics. They may be told how their response is to be organized, and they may be instructed as to the essay's expected length.

Linn and Gronlund (2000) provided instructive contrasts among objective interpretive exercises, restricted-response essays, and extended-response essays. Figure 8.1 illustrates the kinds of learning that can be assessed with each. For now, focus on the first two columns, and note the tight parallelism between learning outcomes tapped by the two item types; the difference hinges on the distinction between (a) recognizing or selecting the answer versus (b) retrieving, formulating, presenting, or explaining the answer in one's own words.

Figure 8.2 on page 178 provides examples of essays calling for relatively restricted responses. The advantages of the structure illustrated in Figure 8.2 are:

- Students are informed about what is expected of them; thus, if they can do it, they will.
- Ambiguity of questions is reduced.

FIGURE 8.1   Types of Complex Learning Outcomes Assessed by Interpretive-Exercise Objective Items, by Restrictive-Response Essay Items, and by Extended-Response Essays. (Adapted from Linn & Gronlund, 2000, p. 240.)

OBJECTIVE INTERPRETIVE EXERCISES assess student ability to *select* the answer, such as:	RESTRICTIVE-RESPONSE ESSAYS assess student ability to *supply* the answer, such as:	EXTENDED-RESPONSE ESSAYS assess student ability to *create* and/or *organize* an answer, such as:
■ Recognize a novel example of a concept	■ Describe a novel example of a concept	■ Generate, organize, and express ideas
■ Select a novel use of a rule	■ Describe a novel use of a rule	■ Integrate learning from various fields
■ Identify causal relationships	■ Describe causal relationships	■ Recognize applications of principles
■ Select plausible hypotheses	■ Develop plausible hypotheses	■ Evaluate the worth of ideas
■ Choose feasible ways to test hypotheses	■ Devise feasible ways to test hypotheses	
■ Identify credible conclusions	■ Formulate credible conclusions	
■ Recognize unstated assumptions	■ Supply unstated assumptions	
■ Identify faulty assumptions	■ Avoid faulty assumptions	
■ Rate the adequacy of procedures	■ Critique the adequacy of procedures	
■ Rate analogies for relevance	■ Present relevant analogies	

■ Testing time is saved by enabling examinees to focus on what "counts" rather than to provide "shotgun" coverage of everything that could conceivably be included.

■ Scoring is easier, faster, and more reliable because all examinees have attempted the same task in the same way.

Item 4 in Figure 8.2 is less restricted than the others. This illustrates the existence of a continuum among essay questions concerning degree of restriction.

Extended-response essays provide examinees greater freedom to choose information they think is relevant when formulating their answers. The right-hand column of Figure 8.1 illustrates the kinds of learning outcomes that are assessed with extended-response essays.

Figure 8.3 on page 179 provides examples of questions. Items 1, 2, and 3 parallel the first three restricted-response examples presented in Figure 8.2. The restricted-response versions are superior for assessing students' command of subject matter.

An item like item 4 might be suitable in an advanced placement or college class. Because it taps student discretion concerning what to include in the answer, it would be appropriate only if the instructor were open to different approaches to answering the question. Item 4 may lie on the extended-response side not too far from the middle of the restricted-extended continuum.

Item 5 of Figure 8.3 illustrates the most common of the appropriate uses of extended-response essays—to measure how well students can compose. It does not require unique content knowledge and no structure is specified. This item lies very near the extended-response end of the continuum.

FIGURE 8.2   **Sample Restricted-Response Essay Questions.**

1. Describe the peanut and its importance using about one paragraph each for (a) its nutritional value, (b) its effect on soil, and (c) its uses and their origins.
2. Compare and contrast the music of two well-known American composers, Aaron Copland and George Gershwin. In two or three paragraphs, describe (1) the major styles and musical structures in which each one composed, (2) some of each composer's most popular works, and (3) the impact of the two composers' artistry on the music world.
3. In what ways does wealth contribute to, or fail to contribute to, happiness and satisfaction in life? In answering, consider these equally important issues:
   ■ Whether money is satisfying as an end in itself
   ■ The role of money in providing security or freedom from anxiety
   ■ Whether the accumulation of money retards spiritual development
4. In a paragraph or two indicate what Thomas Jefferson probably would have thought of a proposed constitutional amendment to allow group prayer in public schools. Be sure to include the basis for your belief.

The advantages of reduced structure are that questions can assess examinee ability to (a) judge what content to use, (b) organize that content, and (c) coherently structure it. Yet the lack of tight constraints, which requires students to demonstrate higher-order skills, renders extended-response essays much less efficient for assessing more focused learning. This is because various students can "go off in different directions." Moreover, the lack of structure introduces serious scoring difficulties (Linn & Gronlund, 2000). These are formidable disadvantages that need to be factored into decisions concerning which kind of essay to use. Payne (1992) offered extremely useful criteria that can be stated as three helpful questions for considering which kind of essay item to use:

1. Has the teacher taught higher-order expressive skills, and are these learning outcomes included in the table of specifications? If so, assessing the skills has obvious merit. If not, it isn't appropriate to base grading on them.
2. Will the essays test for higher-order organizational skills? If not, the extended-response essay has little advantage. For example, the first three restricted-response essays in Figure 8.2 would be more useful for assessing subject matter content than their extended-response counterparts in Figure 8.3.
3. Will part of the grade—preferably a separate part from that reflecting content achievement—be based on these composition skills? If not, it isn't wise to forego the advantages of the restricted-response essay.

When to Use Essay Items

Different kinds of achievement require different assessment methods. Teachers should use the most reliable and efficient options *that assess the objectives* (Stiggins, 2001). It makes good sense first to ask which of our instructional objectives can be validly assessed with objective items. As we stressed in Chapter 1, aims that can adequately be examined with the easier-to-use and more reliable objective item types ordinarily should be. However, aims that cannot validly be tapped by ob-

FIGURE 8.3 Sample Extended-Response Essay Questions.

1. Describe the peanut and its uses.
2. Compare the music of George Gershwin with that of Leonard Bernstein.
3. In what ways does wealth contribute to or fail to contribute to happiness and satisfaction in life?
4. Michael Gorbachev is widely respected for allowing a union of countries to dissolve without bloodshed. Abraham Lincoln is revered for preventing a union of similar age from dissolving at enormous cost in bloodshed. Reconcile.
5. Select one of the following topics and spend the next 90 minutes writing an essay on it.
    5a. Describe your favorite state and explain why it is your favorite.
    5b. Discuss the teacher whom you liked the most (no names please!) in your whole school career and explain why this person was your *most* favorite teacher.
    5c. Describe the attributes of the person who would be your ideal mate/spouse/domestic partner and explain why you value these characteristics.

Note: The first three items would better be cast as restricted-response questions.

jective items need to be assessed with more valid measures such as product or performance assessments. *A measure's relevance to intended learning is more important than great economy or maximum reliability.* Thus, essays are most useful for assessing learning that cannot adequately be measured with objective items, yet can be tapped by essay questions.

An obvious example would be the ability to *compose* well-developed, purposeful paragraphs. If we want to know how well a person can write, there is one clearly superior way to find out—have the person write and then assess the results as accurately as possible. Although objective items suffice for measuring mechanics of expression, when the intent is to assess how well people actually *compose* paragraphs, examinees must prepare the paragraphs.

The first item in Figure 8.2 provides another example. If the teacher were satisfied that students could *identify* or *select* the peanut's nutritional values, *recognize* or *choose* from options the effect it has on soil, and *select* from options a correct description of its uses and their origins, then objective items would work. If, however, the teacher wants to assess students' ability to *recall* and *express* in their own words the peanut's nutritional value, its effect on soil, and its uses and origins, then the essay is indicated.

Recall that the first step in the decision-making rule is to use objective items to assess most instructional objectives that lend themselves to this method. Although this is generally sound practice, the rule requires some equivocation. To illustrate, remember Mrs. Orr's detailed plans in Chapter 5 for her history final. Admirably, she used multiple-choice items to assess knowledge of history as well as some understanding, analysis, and application. She reserved essay questions for learning targets that aren't well assessed by objective items.

She may well have had additional reason for using some essay items. Some students typically do better on objective tests, others on essay tests. It seems fairer for tests to contain both item types in order *not* to give a systematic advantage to either group of students. This issue of balance is one reason why the decision-making rule shouldn't be used in isolation. When should the principle of balance be invoked? Balance is certainly *not* a virtue when there is only one sensible way to assess instructional targets (e.g., ability to compose letters or operate a car). Balance can be considered only when one's general, Context C objectives can be assessed in a reasonably valid way by more than one method.

Consider the following expansive developmental objective and its indicants.

1. Understands terminology.
    1.1 Matches terms with correct, but novel, definitions.
    1.2 Given a novel situation, selects from several options the term that best describes the situation.
    1.3 Provides original examples of a given term's applications.
    1.4 Uses terms correctly in writing.

The first two indicants point to objective items; the last two indicate essay items. Which to use? The first step in the decision-making rule leads to objective items. The criterion of balance suggests a mixed objective and essay test. Still other considerations such as anticipated impact on student study effort, teacher preference, and class size may pull one way or the other. The point is that the *decision-making rule doesn't suffice.* Other things such as assessment balance and logistics should also be considered.

Developing Restricted-Response Questions

Developing effective essays requires both skill and effort. This section provides suggestions for devising restricted-response questions that (a) validly assess instructional aims and (b) have desirable consequences upon student efforts.

1. Use essays mainly to measure complex mental processes. Although essays can be used to measure factual recall, they don't provide a reliable, cost-effective means of doing so. To illustrate, suppose a science teacher wants to assess student knowledge of the names of the three main kinds of blood vessels and understanding of their respective functions. The knowledge goal would best be tapped with a select- or supply-type of objective question. The understanding goal could well be assessed either with multiple-choice or essay items.

Items 1 and 2 in Figure 8.4 exemplify essays that tap complex mental processes. In focusing on the complementarity of arteries and veins (in wording different from that used in instruction), item 1 penetrates beneath surface knowledge. Novelty plays a larger role in item 2; yet students who understand circulation should find it relatively easy to analyze the case presented in item 2 and detect why it isn't possible.

For another example, suppose an upper elementary class has been studying a particular work of fiction with a focus on the concept that everyone has problems. Class discussion focused on each character's problems with consideration that some were obvious to other people whereas others weren't. Items 3 and 4 in Figure 8.4 illustrate essay items that measure mental processing beyond mere statement of the principle that "everybody has problems." It is assumed, of course, that class discussion hasn't focused on the exact applications referenced in these items; some item novelty is essential in assessing complex thinking.

2. Phrase items so that examinees know what is expected. Students should know what the charge is; the basis on which answers will be evaluated should be clear. If the teacher has definite

FIGURE 8.4   Sample Restricted-Response Essay Items That Measure Complex Mental Processes.

1. Briefly explain how arteries and veins complement each other. That is, tell how they work together to make up an effective system of circulation. Focus your discussion on arteries and veins, but mention briefly how the capillaries fit into the system.

2. Suppose a certain animal's circulation system consisted of arteries and capillaries, but no veins. What key problem would this create? In other words, why would this circulation system **not** work?

3. Remember when we read "Jim and the Oak Tree." Jim's sister Cynthia was usually unpleasant to Jim and his friends Mick and Joe. The boys thought Cynthia was "just plain mean." Think of two problems that could have caused Cynthia to act the way she did to the boys. List these two possible problems in at least a complete sentence each.

4. Think of someone you have known whom you never thought of as having any problems, or at least not big ones. Now use what we have learned about everybody having problems to identify two problems that this person probably had. Explain why you think each problem was likely.

expectations concerning what the answers should cover, then the item should make this clear. On the other hand, if the teacher is open to a variety of approaches, less structure is acceptable.

Figure 8.5 provides examples of vague items that have been revised to provide clearer instruction. When ambiguity is removed, some ways of interpreting an item are eliminated. The purpose of the restriction is to eliminate those that the teacher doesn't desire and focus students on those issues that the teacher intends. Other improved versions would, of course, be possible.

In item 1, ambiguity is caused by the fact that three Kennedy brothers (not to mention the likelihood of others having that surname) each served in the U.S. Senate. Another source of ambiguity is the issue of which senate—national, state, or foreign. Even if students realize that the item is intended to refer to John F. Kennedy, a third difficulty lies in the fact that he was twice elected to the U.S. Senate.

Item 2 refers to a long period of history prior to the 1960s when Roman Catholics abstained from eating meat on Fridays for religious reasons. Here's the ambiguity: Because many markets carried fish on Thursdays and Fridays to accommodate Catholic customers, the best selection of fish—for fish lovers and for Catholics—was available for Fridays. The revised version of item 2 eliminates this reason why many people ate fish on Fridays.

FIGURE 8.5   Ambiguous Essay Items and Their Improved (But Still Poor) Revisions.

AMBIGUOUS ITEMS	IMPROVED VERSIONS
1. Describe the election of Mr. Kennedy to the Senate.	1. Describe the election of John F. Kennedy to his first term in the United States Senate.
2. Why did many people used to eat fish on Fridays?	2. What was the religious reason why many people used to eat fish on Fridays?
3. What causes the price of an item to go up?	3. In general, if more people want to buy an item, what happens to its price? In a well-written paragraph, explain why.

For an elementary class that has studied the effect of demand on price, item 3 is ambiguous for students who know more than this one relationship. Other factors (e.g., supply) affect price. The revised version focuses on the relationship between supply and price. These items have been improved by clear thinking and careful wording.

Even though ambiguity has been eliminated from the items in Figure 8.5, their quality is still very modest. Although the content is meaningful, the three improved items require nothing more than retrieval of static material from memory. Therefore, they tend to violate rule 1 of the decision-making sieve.

   3. Focus topics appropriately. First drafts of items are often absurdly open-ended, giving little or no hint concerning what examinees are expected to address. Figure 8.6 provides examples of inadequately focused questions and some improved versions. To emphasize the point that there are often many possible ways to focus an item, the first two examples have each been restricted in alternative ways; such focus obviously limits and alters the learning that is assessed.

   How well do the improved items in Figure 8.6 conform to rule 1 and involve complex mental processes? If the class's study hasn't focused on family or business in its study of modern communication, then improved items 1a and 1b call for some original thinking beyond mere recall. The adequacy of improved items 2a and 2b also depends on how closely they parallel instruction. If some novelty characterizes the items, they may tap deep learning. Improved item 3 seems likely to require original (yet fairly easy) thinking.

FIGURE 8.6   Inadequately Focused Items and Their Improved Versions.

INADEQUATELY FOCUSED ITEMS	IMPROVED VERSIONS
1. Discuss modern communication in the United States.	1a. Describe how modern communication in the United States helps business.
	1b. How has family life in the United States been influenced by the invention of the airplane and the telephone?
2. Describe the growth of the American Labor Movement from the Industrial Revolution to the present.	2a. Public and government attitudes toward organized labor have changed in the United States from the Industrial Revolution until the present. Contrast the early public attitudes with current ones.
	2b. Describe two major problems faced by early American labor organizers that are no longer big problems. How was each of the problems overcome?
3. How has Spanish culture influenced life in the United States?	3. Imagine that Columbus had been financed by Henry VII of England and that Spain never became a major New World power. Describe some likely ways in which our Standard American English language in the United States would be different from what it now is.

4. Provide appropriate structure. The amount of organizational guidance desired depends on the maturity of the examinees and the learning outcomes to be assessed. If one wants students to respond along relatively uniform lines, then it is generally desirable to provide the components of the answer. However, if one wants to tap ability to choose the elements, then, of course, the elements shouldn't be provided.

Item 1 in Figure 8.7 provides two levels of structure for an elementary-school science item. The structure of the improved version achieves several things. Student discussion is focused on what the teacher has in mind; thus the item is a more valid measure of what it is intended to assess. The consistency of marking is enhanced because all pupils attempt to respond to the same elements; thus comparability is increased. Finally, pupil ability to bluff is impeded; those who lack the desired knowledge are hampered in attempts to "talk around the topic."

Items 2 and 3 in Figure 8.7 provide other examples of desirable structure. By providing guidance, the teacher ensures that the intended topics will be addressed by those students who are able to do so.

How well do the items in Figure 8.7 require thinking beyond mere recall? Improved item 1 seems to, provided that pupils haven't been instructed to memorize the comparison and contrast. Improved item 2 seems mainly to require recall. Such learning should ordinarily be assessed with objective items. Improved item 3 clearly requires important high-road transfer of learning to everyday life.

5. Phrase questions to elicit the desired responses. Wording is important. It can make the difference between questions that elicit verbatim retrieval of meaningless information and ones that require mindful processing of richly meaningful information. Between these extremes are many items that require recall of important meaningful material, such as improved item 2 in Figure 8.7.

FIGURE 8.7   Additional Inadequately Structured Essay Items and Their Improved Versions.

INADEQUATELY STRUCTURED ITEMS	IMPROVED VERSIONS
1. Compare caterpillars to true worms.	1. Compare and contrast caterpillars and true worms. Explain how they are alike and different in: (a) the major group of animals to which each belongs, (b) their methods of locomotion, and (c) their life stages.
2. Describe life insurance.	2. Describe life insurance with about a paragraph each explaining (a) its purpose, (b) how it works, and (c) what kinds of people most need it.*
3. How has Spanish culture influenced life in the United States?	3. Spanish culture has influenced life in the United States, even for those who have no Spanish or Mexican ancestry. Give one example each of its influence on our (1) food, (2) language, (3) place names, and (4) recreation. Your examples must be ones that were **NOT** used in class.

*Although improved from the perspective of structure, this item still seems to fail to assess more than mere knowledge.

Phrasing, then, is the means of following the first suggestion to use essay questions for the assessment of complex mental processes. To provide assistance in following this suggestion, Figure 8.8 contains two lists of common essay item phrases that are worth contemplation. The phrases in the second list are apt, in many situations, to demand deeper thinking.

Another important angle concerns prompting the desired study activities. Because students tend to study in ways that reflect the kind of learning their teachers assess, it is important to phrase a suitable fraction of test items—be they objective or essay—in ways that elicit complex mental activities. This guides students to more deeply process what they try to learn in the future rather than merely to commit it to memory.

6. Indicate the relative weight of essays. The value of each question in a test should be indicated. This can be accomplished in several ways. If all the questions carry the same weight, the directions can so indicate. If items have unequal importance, then this information should accompany individual items, often with an indication of the number of points possible in parentheses at the end of each question. Relative importance can also be communicated by suggesting the number of minutes to be allocated for each item.

7. Sample learning as fully as feasible. Because essay questions take longer to answer than do objective questions, essay tests contain fewer items. These larger sampling "chunks" often lead to serious imbalance of content, with tested topics being overemphasized and unsampled ones neglected. Although this limitation is inherent, it should be controlled.

FIGURE 8.8   Essay Phrases Likely to Prompt Recall Versus Higher Levels of Thinking.

PHRASING LIKELY TO REQUIRE ONLY RECALL	PHRASING LIKELY TO CALL FOR HIGHER LEVELS OF THINKING
What were the three major causes of the Civil War?	In what important ways does a . . . differ from a . . . ?
Define an "out" in softball.	Compare and contrast. . . .
Describe the battle of New Orleans.	Analyze the reasoning behind the recommendations to. . . .
Explain how to convert inches into centimeters.	
How does photosynthesis work?	If . . . , what would be the likely effect on . . . ?
Outline the fall of Rome.	What would happen if . . . ?
Explain "balance of nature."	Judge the importance of. . . . In explaining, focus on. . . .
Identify the major exploits of Alexander the Great.	
List the key events in the Watergate scandal.	A new kind of . . . has these features: . . . . Evaluate its likely value.
Quote FDR's two most famous lines.	
Describe the nutritional value of sugar.	Why is it difficult to achieve both . . . and . . . at the same time?
Reproduce Mark Antony's funeral address.	
Who was Hamlet?	Identify the major assumptions underlying the case for. . . .
What is relativity?	
	What values are likely to motivate people to . . . ?
	How would . . . likely have responded to the proposal to . . . ?

One way to maintain content balance in essay tests is to devise questions that span more content. For example, if a class has studied the presidential elections of the twentieth century, a question could span two elections by asking students to "evaluate the relative importance of the 'Catholic issue' in the elections of 1920 and 1960. Make a case either that the differences do or do not represent a trend in voters' religious tolerance."

Another way to enhance content balance is to use brief-response rather than long-response questions. A larger number of more focused items enables broader content sampling. This solution tends to be quite attractive in content areas in which emphasis is in assessing student command of some area *other than* ability to compose. By providing more structure and focus, teachers of social studies, literature, science, and so on, can specify relatively focused responses that require less time. However, if a language arts teacher is interested in testing students' ability to *organize* and *structure* content, restrictive essay questions won't do the job. In this case, extended-response essays would be indicated. We turn now to the topic of their development.

Developing Extended-Response Questions

The utility of extended-response items is concentrated in assessing how well students can exercise judgment in making and executing content, structure, and organization decisions; that is, how well they can compose. Its greatest use is found in language arts.

Why is this so? Recall the three questions (from Payne, 1992) that should all have affirmative answers before extended-response essay items are used.

1. Have I tried to develop students' higher-order expressive skills, and are these learning goals included in the test specifications?
2. Am I going to assess the essays for the higher-order organizational skills?
3. Am I going to base part or all of the grade on these composition skills?

Such questions can be answered "yes" much more often by teachers of language arts than by teachers of other subjects.

How well do the rules presented for restricted-response essays apply to extended-response questions? Thinking CAP 8.1 is designed to prompt active thinking about this question.

THINKING CAP 8.1 ???

Directions: Following are the seven suggestions for developing restricted-response essay questions. Your task is to *assess the relevance of each rule for extended-response essay items.* In a few words, focus your ideas on how each rule applies to situations in which extended-response essay questions are suitable. Then compare your ideas with those presented in the key.

1. Use essays mainly to measure higher mental processes.
2. Phrase items so that examinees know what is expected.
3. Focus topics appropriately.
4. Provide appropriate structure.
5. Phrase questions to elicit the desired responses.
6. Indicate the relative weight of essay questions.
7. Sample learning as fully as feasible.

(Continued)

THINKING CAP 8.1 CONTINUED

KEY TO THINKING CAP 8.1

1. This is even more applicable for extended-response items than for restricted-response ones.

2. Although applicable, the rule may be less important in extended-response situations where teacher expectations are not focused on any one way of fulfilling expectations.

3. Although *much* less focus is appropriate, the rule is applicable.

4. This suggestion is not very applicable for items at the extended-response end of the extended-restrictive continuum. A central purpose of such essays is to assess how well *students* can provide appropriate structure.

However, for extended-response items that concern subject matter content nearer the middle of the continuum, some structure is needed. This will be discussed shortly.

Concerning structure, Stiggins (2001) offers interesting advice to writers of effective essay items. They "must invest thoughtful preparation time in writing exercises that challenge respondents by describing a single complete and novel task. Sound exercises do three things" (Stiggins, 2001, p. 169):

- Specify the knowledge that examinees are expected to have and use.
- Indicate the mental process(es) that students are to engage in.
- Provide appropriate structure.

Item 4 of Figure 8.3 on page 179 has been expanded with Stiggins' three criteria in mind. Notice how the revision greatly improves the item by the inclusion of more structure for this semi-extended-response history question.

> In our study of the dissolution of the U.S.S.R., you learned that Gorbachev is widely **respected** in the United States for having *allowed* **a union of countries to dissolve without bloodshed.** When you studied the U.S. Civil War last year, you learned that Lincoln is **revered** in the United States for having *prevented* **a union of similar age from dissolving— at enormous cost in human life.**
>
> Compare and contrast the circumstances of these two situations, focusing on a *reasoned analysis and evaluation* of whether each leader did the right thing for the circumstances he faced. Then *draw a conclusion* (a) that is *logically consistent* with your evaluation of the two situations and (b) that in some way *reconciles* the apparent paradox that each leader is respected by the same Americans.

5. Although applicable, the rule is less important in extended-response situations where teacher expectations aren't sharply focused on any one approach to responding.

6. This is fully applicable if there is more than one question in the test.

7. This is applicable, yet the use of extended-response essays to a considerable degree entails a "write-off" of a very full content sampling. However, individual items often draw from a broad array of content. From another angle, the intended learning to be sampled is largely composition, and the extended-response essay taps it nicely.

ENCAPSULATION

Additional questions can be raised about constructing test items that concern controversial subject matter, for example, in the area of biological ethics or significance of historical events on the present and future. What are the key points examinees will be expected to include in their responses? What instructional opportunities can essay exams provide that are not found in objective tests?

By thinking through questions such as these, and discussing them with colleagues, you may develop greater respect for the strength and versatility of essays. And you will be forearmed with appropriate practices. For example, one way to treat controversial topics is to make it clear to students that they are to present a particular position and provide supporting material for it (regardless of whether they or the teacher agree with it).

Some Instructional Issues

A major instructional attribute of essays is the opportunity for the teacher to comment on strong and weak points and make suggestions for improvement. We turn now to less obvious instructional issues. A major theme of this book calls attention to the fact that the means by which people are assessed tends to influence the direction their efforts will take. This section examines the probable instructional impact of two sets of practices that are commonly used with essay tests.

Whether to Offer a Choice of Questions.   Many teachers provide students with more essay questions than they are required to answer. The popularity of this practice resides mainly in two causes. First, the practice is popular with students. They think that they are being given something. This, of course, is illusory. Interpretation of Context C scores must be norm referenced; the important issue about people's performance is their status relative to that of other people. Therefore, providing a choice of tasks doesn't give the individual examinee any comparative edge. Second, essay tests, having relatively few items, tend to provide less complete sampling. This limitation may prompt teachers to fret that their essay tests lack comprehensive coverage.

These two conditions set the stage for the following scenario: A unit consists of six topics, and the test plan calls for an item on each. The teacher dutifully develops the six essays and then is dismayed to realize that answering all six would require much more time than is available. What to do? Ah! Do the popular thing and give examinees a choice of four of the six questions. The students are happy in the illusion that they have been given something, and the teacher is happy in the illusion that content balance has been preserved. Actually, of course, it hasn't. The four questions that each examinee selects provide just as imbalanced a coverage of the total unit as would have resulted from the teacher's choice of four items.

The common reasons that most often lead to offering a choice of questions are, therefore, unsound. What else is to be said for and against the practice?

The conventional wisdom expressed in measurement books is that choice of tasks shouldn't be offered. Here's the thinking: When various people perform different tasks, the basis of comparability is reduced. To illustrate with an extreme example, at a track meet Hank competes only in the pole vault and Joe only in the 100-meter dash. The two events have no common contestants. Each places second in his event. Who performed better?

Who knows? To make comparative (i.e., norm-referenced) statements about people (as we need to in Context C), we must have a basis by which to compare each examinee's performance with that of a relevant group of other people. To the extent that students perform different tasks, the basis of comparison—the basis of norm referencing—is eroded.

The reasoning that leads to the taboo on choice of questions is sound. No doubt about it; offering a choice of questions reduces reliability. Yet we believe that reliability should *not* be the only consideration.

Another vital issue concerns consequences of assessment practices on student effort. To consider this impact, let's return to the scenario in which the teacher offered students a choice of four out of six questions. Suppose some astute youngsters have the teacher "psyched out" and correctly anticipate an item on each of the six topics and then a choice of questions. They reason that they can safely neglect one or two of the topics from their study and reallocate the time saved to the other topics. Would this appall you? *That* seems to us to be the key question.

In many settings, it would indeed be undesirable. If each of the six topics is important or if the topics are somewhat sequential (as might be the case in geometry or Spanish), then you would be dismayed that an evaluation practice was leading students to an undesirable study practice. In that case you obviously should *not* offer a choice of questions. Even if you were neutral concerning prompting uneven study of topics, you shouldn't offer a choice because doing so reduces reliability.

In other cases, however, it wouldn't distress you that some students opt out of one or two of the topics with immunity. For example, in a unit on short stories, a teacher might not mind if a student studied four of the stories more intensively. There is nothing vital about any one of them, and uniform knowledge of the stories is no particular virtue.

If you like the idea of giving a choice of study emphasis, then go ahead and offer a choice of questions, but let all students know ahead of time how they will be tested. There should be no special benefit to those who "psych you out." Also, remember that offering the choice does have a cost in reliability.

Whether to Provide Questions in Advance.   Another common practice is to hand out exact essay questions ahead of time so that students can prepare for them. Is this advisable?

The answer to this question, like that of many others, depends on the nature of the subject matter. If it consists of an explicit, vital, Context A domain, then each student must master it in its entirety. In that situation, test content is no secret. It is unlikely, however, that one should be using essay questions with such material. Objective items are more efficient in assessing most kinds of simple knowledge.

On the other hand, if the subject matter is an expansive, unmasterable, Context C domain, as is ordinarily the case when essays are suitable, then *the essence of good testing is unbiased content sampling.* In this case, test content must be kept secure if the test is to provide a basis for *valid inference about examinee status on the total domain.* It is *not* appropriate to "teach to the test" by providing questions ahead of time (or by other means). Doing so only renders the test results *mis*leading.

THINKING CAP 8.2   ???

Following are test information dissemination practices of four teachers. Each is teaching a Context C biology unit on food chains. Suppose the test of each is (wisely or unwisely) going to consist of six short essay questions. Judge the appropriateness of each practice from the perspective of its *impact on student study.*

1. Teacher 1 gives the six questions to students ahead of time so that they can learn what they are expected to know and can do well on the test without having to "psych out" the teacher.

2. Teacher 2 provides students with the parallel forms of the test that were used for the past two years. This year's form will be parallel to the previous two forms.

3. Teacher 3 provides students with a list of 20 questions from which the six to be tested will be selected.

4. Teacher 4 hands out a list of five particularly important questions with the information that two of them will appear on the test.

THINKING CAP 8.2   CONTINUED

KEY TO THINKING CAP 8.2

1. In Context C, teacher 1's practice in effect reduces the original rich and diverse content domain into a mere six elements. That will tend to be all that is "important" to the students. The message conveyed by the testing practice is that high-road transfer of learning isn't valued. That is deplorable!

2. Teacher 2's practice provides students with useful guidance concerning item types, test coverage, and mental processes assessed, and it avoids providing them with a means of focusing on the particular information that will be sampled in the test any more than on other equally important information that happens not to be sampled. By providing parallel forms of more than one previous year, the teacher may better enable students to realize that exact items are not repeated.

3. Teacher 3's practice is similar to that of teacher 1, but is less outrageous because it has reduced the content domain to 20 items rather than to only six.

However, the practice is still unfortunate because it prompts memorization rather than learning with an aim of high-road transfer.

4. The practice will achieve its aim of focusing student study on the five questions handed out. It also has the virtue of informing students of just how much of the test (two of six questions) will be drawn from this important subsample of content. Yet students are apt to memorize the answers to these five distributed items rather than to try to understand them and be able to apply the underlying concepts.

Teacher 4's intent would be better served if students were told that *the topics addressed* by two of these five distributed items will appear in the test, but that the wording and other details will be altered to ensure that they *understand the underlying concepts*. If this idea is new to students, one might provide examples of how content can be altered; for example, one could offer several questions based on one of the highlighted topics.

Scoring Essay Tests

Stories about the unreliability with which some essay tests are scored are legend. The problem was publicized long ago when Starch and Elliot (1912) showed that a student's English essay test might receive an assessment anywhere from failing to outstanding depending on which English teacher marked it. They also published studies in which math teachers independently marked a geometry exam and history teachers graded an essay history test. The unreliability of the marks was found to be as shocking in one subject as in another.

Recognizing the chaotic status then common in marking essay exams, Starch and Elliot asked what could be done to secure greater objectivity of marking. This section presents the rules that have evolved over the ensuing decades. The recommended procedures differ for restricted-response and extended-response essays, so they will be considered separately.

Analytic Scoring of Restricted-Response Essay Tests.   Recall that restricted-response essays are designed to be unambiguous concerning what is expected. They are used to assess student command of subject matter in relatively focused topics. This focus—or restriction of response—enables one to prepare relatively detailed criteria for marking that can be applied **analytically** to award designated numbers of points for coverage of specified material. This approach, as embodied in the following rules, enhances reliability of marking by rendering it as objective as the nature of the task allows.

1. **Maintain examinee anonymity during scoring.** A marker of essays should ideally not know whose work is being marked until after the assessment is completed. This can be achieved by having students place their names on an inconspicuous part of their tests (e.g., the back of the last page). This protects the process from the contaminating influence of the teacher's prior expectations, which can be substantial (Chase, 1968, 1979; Hughes, Keeling, & Tuck 1980).

To illustrate why this protection is needed, suppose a teacher comes upon an ambiguous paragraph in an essay. If the teacher knows the student to be very capable, then meaning may be projected into the ambiguous paragraph. However, if the teacher believes the student to be inept, then the ambiguous part is apt to be interpreted as nonsense. Anonymity thus protects against prejudicial marking of individual students who are known to the teacher. It simultaneously provides a safeguard against prejudicial assessment on the basis of gender, ethnicity, or other factors.

2. **Develop marking criteria.** At the time each essay question is created, develop scoring criteria that can be applied systematically to all papers. Marking bases—also known as assessment *rubrics*—can be more fully detailed when items are highly structured. (We will illustrate scoring rubrics more fully with other kinds of product assessments.) Figure 8.9 shows an item that is highly structured; hence, it is highly amenable to analytic scoring. This enhances reliability of marking.

Developing marking criteria focuses one's attention on the need to establish the *relative importance of an item's elements*. Without this thought, one will probably be inconsistent from student to student in the relative weight given to the component parts. For example, the elementary teacher scoring the item in Figure 8.9 might be so impressed with a pupil's enumeration of over a dozen uses of peanut products that the teacher overlooks the fact that the answer did not address the effect on soil.

Another benefit of scoring rubrics is the help they provide in focusing marking on the *content* of the answers rather than on excellence of expression. Answer outlines provide immunity from being "snowed" by an eloquently written essay that says little.

Yet another reason for developing explicit bases for assessment concerns *drifting expectations*. Leniency (or severity) of ratings may change as a rater becomes more referenced to a group's performance; to the extent this happens, an assessment can turn into a lottery (Congdon & McQueen, 2000).

FIGURE 8.9   Sample Scoring Key for Highly Structured Essay.

Item 1: Describe the peanut and its uses, using about one paragraph each for (a) its nutritional value, (b) its effect on soil, and (c) its uses and their origins. (20 points)

Scoring Key: (*a*) Good source of protein (3 points, or if peanut protein is distinguished from animal or complete protein, 4 points), carbohydrate (2 points), and fat or oil (3 points). Maximum: 7 points.

(*b*) Roots produce nitrogen products (2 points) that fertilize or revitalize soil (3 points), making it very useful in crop rotation (2 points). (A good discussion of either revitalization or rotation could adequately imply the other.) Maximum: 6 points.

(*c*) The peanut is used to make peanut butter (2 points), edible peanuts (1 point), animal food (1 point), peanut oil (2 points), and other (specified) use(s) (1 point), and the plants make hay for animals (2 points). Many of the uses were invented to create a need for the plant because of its benefit to soil (2 points). Maximum: 7 points.

Bases for marking should be established *at the time questions are devised* because of the (a) relative ease of doing it then rather than later and (b) the impact the process can have on the item. Thinking about how an item will be scored may prompt clearer phrasing or specification in the item as to how much weight will be given to the various parts of the answer. For instance, for the item in Figure 8.9, it was during development of the scoring rubric that the idea occurred to the item writer to assess knowledge that many peanut uses were developed to create a market in order to prompt crop rotation. This idea led to the addition of the last three words of the item.

This item illustrates a practice that some teachers find useful. Maximum credit in each part of the answer can be secured in somewhat varied ways. In part (c), for instance, the sum of the possible points is 11, yet it would be unrealistic to expect pupils to cover all of these subtopics in a brief paragraph. Therefore, earning any 7 of the 11 points secures maximum credit. Doing more in part (c) would not compensate for deficits in either of the other parts.

3. Examine several students' answers on each question before marking any. This process serves two purposes. First, it lessens the tendency for expectations to drift after assessment begins. Second, examining a few (ideally all) papers can reveal inadequacies in the scoring criteria before the marking is launched.

4. Mark one question at a time. In marking a set of exams, mark each student's question 1 before proceeding to anyone's question 2. Then the next item should be assessed for each student before going on to the third item, and so on. One reason for evaluating one item at a time is economy of time and effort. It is easier to retain in mind the scoring criteria for one item than for a whole test.

Another reason is to prevent the *halo effect,* which is the influence of the assessment of a person's performance on one item on the assessment of the person's performance on other items. Each question should ordinarily provide *independent* data. The halo effect can be a serious source of contamination of independence. Imagine that a student's fourth essay has some unusual flaw that renders it incorrect, yet worthy of partial credit. A teacher who knows that a student's first three items were superior is likely to deem the error in the fourth item to be minor. Inversely, a teacher who remembers the first three items as inferior is more prone to judge the error in the fourth item more severely.

5. Systematically vary the order in which papers are assessed. In marking one item at a time, the set of papers should *not* be examined in the same order in each cycle. By varying the order, we prevent the influence of drifting expectations from accruing to the consistent advantage of some students at the expense of others.

Moreover, if the same order were maintained, then the evaluation would well be influenced by an *order effect.* If one has just read a brilliant essay, then the next paper will suffer from comparison. On the other hand, if one has just examined several disastrous efforts, the next one, even if only fair, is likely to seem superior (Hales & Tokar, 1975; Hughes, Keeling, & Tuck, 1980).

Fortunately, we can largely prevent contamination from halo effect, order effect, and drifting expectations with simple procedures. After marking the first question, work through the set of papers in reverse order; this tends to equalize the influence of drifting expectations. Then shuffle the set to minimize order effect. After working through a third time, reverse for the fourth pass. Then shuffle again, and so on.

6. Do not ordinarily penalize for poor handwriting or mechanics of expression. Such variables as handwriting, grammar, and skill in composition can influence scoring of essays (e.g.,

Chase, 1968, 1983; Marshall & Powers, 1969). This contamination can occur even when readers are directed to score on content alone (Marshall, 1967).

This rule is perhaps the most controversial one offered in this section. Three issues are relevant. First, important exceptions exist. Second, the rule has a sound rationale. Third, if you decide not to follow it, these factors must be included in the scoring criteria.

First, the exceptions. Language arts teachers would, by and large, be better advised to count mechanics of expression than would other teachers. When it is part of the subject matter of English courses, such material obviously merits testing. Although one wouldn't be inclined to dispute this line of reasoning, it might also be pointed out that essays do *not* provide a particularly good way to assess such material. For example, students can avoid hard-to-spell words by paraphrasing; if some students avoid difficult words whereas others don't, the spelling component of the test may be as much a measure of test-wiseness as of spelling. If a teacher wants to test spelling, dictated items with written responses provide a superior way to do so.

The other major class of exceptions to this rule involves subject-specific words. For example the biology class that has been studying human circulation would probably be responsible for spelling "veins," "arteries," and "capillaries"; thus, a penalty for misspelling these words would be appropriate. If spelling errors of subject-specific words are to be counted, then a decision must be made as to how much.

Aside from such exceptions, the rationale for the rule is this: A history test should assess command of history; a driver education test should measure knowledge, understanding, and skills relevant to driving. To count handwriting or spelling in such tests is to introduce contaminants. Yes, educationally significant "contaminants," but they aren't what the test is designed to assess. Therefore, by and large, mechanics of expression, spelling of words that are not content specific, and handwriting (providing it can be read!) shouldn't count in the content scores of essay tests. It is, however, helpful and appropriate to point out the errors.

Teachers who decide they cannot agree with this rule should make conscious decisions concerning the penalty for poor handwriting, mechanics of expression, and spelling. Rule 2 applies here: If they are counted, then the scoring criteria should specify their weight and this should generally be known by students before the test.

7. If the results are especially important, use multiple markers. This practice isn't ordinarily practical for classroom teachers. However, when a major decision, such as college admission or licensure is based largely on an essay examination, having several markers independently assess each essay enables the final decisions to be based on their pooled judgment. As the old saying goes, "several heads are better than one."

Holistic Scoring for Extended-Response Essay Tests. The minimal amount of structure and content in extended-response essay questions renders full-blown analytic scoring inapplicable. Consequently, the reliability of marking tends to suffer. Yet reliability is vitally important. How, then, can we render the marking process as objective as possible without doing violence to the nature of the task?

The first line of attack is preventative—using extended-response essays only when more restricted-response ones would fail to tap what we need to assess. That is why the first three items in Figure 8.3 on page 179 are better cast as restricted-response items, as shown in Figure 8.2. Recall Payne's (1992) three questions on page 178 that require affirmative answers before extended-response items are justified. Even if they are justified, because restrictiveness of response exists on a continuum, it is prudent to provide as much focus for essays as one can, staying within the limits of assessing the targeted student behaviors.

Yet English and advanced foreign language teachers occasionally need to test how well students can express themselves in situations largely lacking restrictions. An example of such an item was presented as item 5 in Figure 8.3. Other examples are "Explain how you spent last summer" and "Write a persuasive essay taking a forceful position on any one of the 20 topics supplied on the attached list."[1]

On rare occasions, a teacher of another subject could answer "yes" to Payne's penetrating questions and decide to ask an extended-response question.

In order to assess how well examinees can express themselves, the question must concern some topic with which each student is very familiar. For example, the advanced placement teacher considering item 4 of Figure 8.3 should carefully consider the justification of assuming that all students would (or at least should) be familiar with the underlying facts of the U.S. Civil War and the dissolution of the U.S.S.R. Often the best way to ensure this background familiarity is to allow a choice of topics. Each student did different things last summer, hence each is writing on different things. Each will select a familiar topic for the persuasive essay. Under these conditions, scoring criteria obviously cannot be analytic with respect to content.

Similar individuality is found in certain assignments that are (a) designed to relate to the interests and needs of individual students or (b) designed to be realistic. For example, a high-school term paper might be written on any approved topic of the student's choice. Or, a journalism assignment may be for each student to cover a different story. Or, a university class in classroom assessment may have a project of developing a teacher-made assessment suitable for the grade level and subject matter that the student is preparing to teach. In such cases, the choice of tasks is indispensable to the realism and utility of the assessment.

Clearly a loss of comparability occurs when such essays, papers, or projects are used for student assessment. However, the gain in authenticity of assessment and the gain in relevance to the interests and needs of students may far outweigh the loss of reliability. Therefore, the teacher must assess the products as reliably as possible in spite of the diversity of topics. Fortunately, some degree of analytic marking is possible for most such assignments. For example, regardless of the topic of the story, the journalism teacher can assess how well each story addresses the "who," "what," "when," "why," "where," and "how" topics. Similarly, regardless of the topic of an extended-response essay, the teacher can separately assess such broad topics as adequacy of ideas, organization, word choice, and adherence to conventions (Arter & McTighe, 2001).

In most extended-response essays, especially those used by language arts teachers, the assessment requires holistic or global marking. In **holistic** (meaning wholistic) **marking**, the teacher forms an overall impression of each essay and marks it accordingly. Such global assessment is at one extreme of a continuum; it contrasts sharply with highly analytic assessment having detailed and relatively objective scoring rubrics. Most essays should be designed to lie in the analytic range of the continuum, although the degree to which they lend themselves to explicit marking criteria differs. Other essays, however, such as those considered in this section, lie nearer the global or holistic end of the continuum.

Yet we are still well advised to seek as much structure as the subject matter allows. In the case of the journalism project's topics of "who," "what," "why," and so on, or the English essay's rubric

---

[1]It should be understood, of course, that teachers of language also test command of subject matter such as literature in much the same way that teachers of science or history test their subject matter. In such cases, all of the rules for developing and scoring restricted-response essays apply.

specifying such topics as organization and word choice, the *separate topics can be scored holistically.*

Even when measures must be scored almost entirely holistically, steps should be taken to enhance accuracy of marking so that grades aren't awarded capriciously. Objectivity of marking extended-response essays is maximized by use, to the varying degrees they are applicable, of the marking suggestions provided for restricted-response essays. Let us now consider these rules one by one.

- Protecting examinee anonymity is just as feasible in global marking as it is for analytic marking, and the need for the rule is greater because of the reduced objectivity of scoring.

- Establishing clear and detailed bases or rubrics for marking is relevant, albeit less feasible. With holistic marking, it's not possible to develop detailed marking criteria along the lines illustrated for the peanut item. Yet it is almost always possible to formulate *some* criteria. For example, even in the most creative writing exercise requiring the greatest degree of evaluative reaction to the whole, one can still address such issues as the extent, if any, to which poor handwriting and spelling and punctuation errors will be penalized.

- Examining several essays before marking any of them is especially important in holistic marking. To the extent that one's marking criteria in global assessment are less firmly anchored, one is especially vulnerable to drift of expectations.

- When there is only one extended-response essay in a test, it is not possible to mark one item at a time or to vary the order in which questions are examined. However, if there are two or more items, these rules apply.

- The case against penalizing for poor, yet legible, handwriting is the same in creative writing essays as in content-specific essays.

- Although in most classroom settings it is impractical, use of multiple markers should be given more consideration for holistic marking because of its greater subjectivity.

Directions for Essay Tests

If all items in an essay test are to be given equal weight, then it should be indicated in the directions. If the questions are to be given markedly unequal weights, then the directions might well alert examinees to the need to note item weights as they read individual items.

Directions should make explicit any rules concerning allowable resources. No doubt should exist about whether dictionaries or thesauri may be used. Should they be? In answering this question, the teacher should consider the learning outcomes the test is designed to assess and the impact that assessment practices may have upon student study.

Directions should provide necessary logistic information. They should tell students where to write their names. If a teacher insists that essays be written in ink or that term papers be computer printed, then directions should so specify. (Of course, if class rules concerning these issues have been well publicized and have become habitual, then they needn't be repeated on each assignment or test. However, if any possible doubt exists, information is best repeated.)

PRODUCT MEASURES

In product assessment, the examinee is directed to create a specific product (e.g., essay, fired pot, research paper, math proof, charcoal sketch, or tuned-up engine). The product is assessed after it is completed. Some products are created under tightly controlled conditions, whereas others are produced in the variable settings of everyday life. The assessment of products can be analytic, objective, and detailed or it can be impressionistic and global.

The Nature of Product Measures

Variety.   Assessment of educational achievement is enriched by a wide variety of product measures. Some examples will illustrate the breadth of practices that come under this heading.

■ A primary class has been studying manuscript writing. Each child copies a sentence from the chalkboard and creates a written product that can be evaluated for quality of handwriting. In this case, the products are developed under uniform conditions.

■ A keyboarding teacher is interested in how accurately and rapidly each student can keyboard. Each student is provided a copy of a given passage and directed to keyboard as much of it as the time limit allows under timed, highly controlled (e.g., monitor off) conditions. The resulting copy is a product that the teacher can examine to determine how accurately and rapidly each student performed.

■ Students in a woodworking class have spent several weeks making sturdy, four-legged, step stools to conform to specified drawings. The instructor grades the project by examining each finished stool and rating it on each important feature.

■ An art teacher who has been instructing pupils in certain techniques gives an assignment that involves use of these methods. The resulting products are then examined to judge how skillfully pupils use the techniques.

If the assignment is completed in class, the conditions under which it is completed may be quite controlled; in this case, a relatively strong basis exists for assessment. If the work is assigned as homework, then the circumstances under which students undertake the tasks may vary widely; in this case, the less uniform conditions render the assessment less than ideal for judging skills.

■ High school or college students are given a demanding assignment to produce a research paper. When completed, these products are graded.

As in homework, out-of-class projects, and major compositions, this is a case in which conditions are not well controlled. Thoughtful teachers are acutely aware that the amount of assistance (legitimate and questionable) that students receive differs greatly. Yet it isn't practical for students to complete long, complex projects under well-controlled conditions. Thus, a judgment is often made that the loss of uniform conditions is an acceptable trade-off for the realism of the work conditions under which a project is completed outside of class.

■ A cooking teacher is interested in how well students can follow a new recipe. This ability to transfer prior learning is tested by giving each student a copy of the recipe and sufficient ingredients, equipment, and time to make it. The finished products are then assessed.

Product vs. Objective vs. Performance Measures.   These above examples illustrate the rich diversity of products. They can range from ones for which there is only one right form the results can take (e.g., assembly of a rifle's parts) to ones having enormous latitude (e.g., an art mobile). The defining feature of **product measures** is their focus on assessment of the final *product* of examinee labor, *not* on the production *process* or on test questions *about* the work.

To sharpen this distinction, reconsider the keyboarding test. On the one hand, the teacher could have given an objective test about how to keyboard. This would provide a useful method of assessing *knowledge* of such things as proper margin size. Objective items could also validly assess *understanding* of why certain things are or are not recommended, *analysis* of the likely impact of doing various things, *evaluation* of pages, and so on. An objective test, however, couldn't provide an assessment of students' actual *skill* in keyboarding. Educators have long recognized (e.g., Findley & Scates, 1946) that valid measures must assess the targeted attributes. The things that objective items could tap may be important, but they are not the central skill of keyboarding. Thus, they don't provide **realistic** or **authentic assessment** of the real-world, everyday-life skill.

On the other hand, the teacher could observe students as they keyboard. This would be a useful and authentic means of assessing certain aspects of performance, such as posture, hand positioning, and eye activity. However, it would be much more time-consuming to observe each individual while the entire page is produced than to test all students at the same time and then only inspect the finished products.

Portfolios.   Let's turn to the "hot topic" of portfolio assessment. A **portfolio** is a systematic and purposeful collection of a student's work. Artists and models use large cardboard folders to carry work samples that demonstrate their skills and versatility. Even teachers are now called on to create portfolios of their own work. Some school districts ask teachers to assemble their teaching artifacts such as tests, letters to parents, work sheets, lesson plans, and study guides into notebook portfolios for the purpose of teacher evaluation. Some applicants for teaching positions now appear for interviews with disk-stored, notebook, or Internet-accessible electronic portfolios of completed lesson plans, tests, and other informative products.

Elementary teachers have long collected samples of pupils' work in manila or accordion-file folders to show parents during conferences and to provide a focus for discussion. However, in the past, many teachers didn't fully harness "portfolio power." That is, they didn't use portfolios in ways that involve students in forging links between instruction and assessment. Examples of overlooked potentials for portfolios include:

- Securing student ownership in the learning process
- Contrasting best work and typical work
- Involving students in assessment of achievement
- Creating a record of continuous improvement
- Fostering an inclination to engage in reflection and self-assessment
- Facilitating active family involvement in conferences
- Providing electronic records in a wide range of performances
- Crossing subject-matter boundaries to facilitate multicontext integration

It must be acknowledged that portfolio assessment is demanding. Issues arise such as where to store them and when to assess the elements of a portfolio. In most classroom situations, of course, it is appropriate to assess and return each product as it is completed. Then the critical question is,

"Is there good reason to assemble these assessed products into a collection?" Sometimes it makes excellent sense to develop a collection of completed works *after* students have received feedback on them.

By retaining these works in a portfolio, we can demonstrate not only the terminal level of student achievement, but also what it took to get there (Kubiszyn & Borich 2003). For example, portfolios of seventh graders' research papers might include the original outline, a revised outline, the first draft, the second draft, and the final product, each accompanied by teacher feedback. Or, a university assessment class might construct portfolios of student-produced tests on units of their choice. Each student's final product might be preceded in a portfolio by a list of instructional objectives, a revised list of objectives if needed, a list of content topics, a table of specifications, a revised test plan if needed, a draft test, another draft if needed, and the final test. Each of these steps could be given constructive feedback by the instructor. Thus, portfolios can reveal something about students' "persistence, effort, willingness to change, skill in monitoring their own learning, and ability to be self-reflective"[2] (Kubiszyn & Borich, 2003, p. 175).

Portfolios are widely used both for *assessment* of student work and for *instruction*. Whichever the purpose, the sample of work that is included must be a thoughtfully selected sample that "tells the story" the portfolio is designed to relate. The fundamental criterion for portfolio content selection is the purpose of the portfolio (Ward & Murray-Ward, 1999).

Examples of *assessment* portfolios might include a teacher's collection of student work in math to show parents both what processes the student can perform and how neatly the work is organized. In this case, the teacher might want examples both of maximum performance and of typical performance. Or, a teacher might assemble an art portfolio to reveal the student's best work and the variety of things the student can do. Or, an English teacher might include several drafts of a student's theme to reveal how well the individual benefits from feedback. In such cases, the teacher might or might not share decision making with students concerning what to include.

Assessment uses of portfolios can thus exhibit aspects of achievement such as students' typical work, their maximum work, and the benefit they obtain from formative assessment as a project evolves. In addition, assessment portfolios can show student *growth* over time (Rolheiser, Bower, & Stevahn, 2000). For example, dated samples of best work during a school year in math or art can vividly demonstrate student progress.

Instructional uses of portfolios often give students ownership by allowing them to decide what to include. Portfolios can be a very useful means of developing student skills in evaluating their own work. Self-evaluation—a critical skill in developing independent learning ability—can be emphasized by asking students to include some form of self-evaluation and thoughtful reflection on each entry in their portfolios (Linn & Gronlund, 2000). This enhancement of students' self-evaluation capabilities is considered by many to be the most important benefit of portfolio use (Popham, 2000).

The instructional use of portfolios is often accompanied by their use as a focus for topics addressed in parent-teacher conferences. They also can provide a medium for active student participation or leadership in parent-student-teacher conferences.

Although portfolios are attractive both as aids for instruction and as assessment devices, they are not without limitations. Their assembly may be quite time-consuming. The student time spent in assembling portfolios may be well spent; however, teachers need to ensure that portfo-

---

[2]By the way, a research paper that is assessed in such steps would enjoy a large measure of immunity from cybercheating.

lio demands don't foster busy work that contributes neither to greater student learning nor to better assessment (Linn & Gronlund, 2000). As one might expect, portfolios have been warmly embraced by "educators who regard traditional assessment with less than enthusiasm" (Popham, 2000, p. 299). However, if they are overused for assessment, significant problems occur in reliability of assessment and in economy of instructional and learning time. Fortunately, their moderate use, accompanied by professional knowledge, effort, and time, can produce—at reasonable costs of reliability and time—information about a learner that no other tool can match (Kubiszyn & Borich, 2003).

The New, the Old, the Good, the Bad, the Fad. Portfolio assessment has become more popular in recent years as teachers in many disciplines collect samples of student products in accordion folders, on disks, and in boxes, laundry baskets, and even wheelbarrows! Similarly, the well established field of performance assessment has recently come into vogue. And the long-recognized need for realism of assessments has, of late, been trumpeted under the banner of "authentic assessment" as though it were some sort of revolutionary new insight. In much popular and professional literature, multiple-choice testing is "out," and product and performance assessment is "in" (Madaus & O'Dwyer, 1999).

The fanfare in the past two decades attending portfolio assessment, authentic assessment, alternative assessment, and performance and product assessment could lead educators who lack a sense of history to conclude that these are exciting, important, new discoveries in education. *They are certainly important,* but they are *not* by any stretch of imagination new (Madaus & O'Dwyer, 1999; also see Findley & Scates, 1946). As Darling-Hammond observed:

> American education has been down this path before. The criticisms of current education reformers—that our schools provide most children with an education that is too rigid, too passive, and too rote-oriented to produce learners who can think critically, synthesize and transform, experiment and create—are virtually identical to those of the Progressives at the turn of the [last] century, in the 1930s, and again in the 1960s. Many reforms were pursued in each of these eras; the interdisciplinary curriculum; team teaching; cooperative learning; the use of projects, portfolios, and other "alternative assessments"; and a thinking curriculum aimed at developing higher-order performances and cognitive skills. (1993, p. 754).

Unfortunately, when new terms, such as "authentic assessment," are coined, some educators think the *concepts* they represent are, therefore, new. Not necessarily! Performance and product assessment have been around for a very long time. For example, the Bible's Book of Judges contains accounts of an oral test concerning pronunciation of the word "shibboleth" and of a performance test given by Gideon concerning shields and swords. Likewise, the ancient Olympics obviously involved competitive performance tests. More recently, published typing tests have been available in this country since the 1920s. By 1971, when Fitzpatrick and Morrison's splendid discussion on performance and product evaluation was published, the discipline had a very solid scholarly foundation. Research based on performance assessment has been enlarged in recent decades by such scholars as Richard Stiggins.

As Robert Slavin warned, "Educational innovation is famous for its cycle of early enthusiasm, widespread dissemination, subsequent disappointment, and eventual decline—the classic swing of the pendulum" (Slavin, 1989, p. 3). And as Linda Darling-Hammond (1993) observed, the cycle for product and performance assessment has been running for a century.

We aspire to *help educators avoid the overuse of performance, portfolio, and product assessment in situations where other methods would serve better.* This danger exists when performance assessment, also known as alternative assessment and authentic assessment, is "in style," as it is at this writing. We are equally eager to *help educators avoid the underuse of performance and product assessment in situations where they are appropriate.* This danger is greatest when they are "out of style," as they may well be before most readers retire from their profession. As emphasized before, we need different assessment methods for different assessment purposes; hence, *professionals should use each method, or a combination of methods, where it best fits.*

When to Use Product Measures

We again spiral back to the three-step decision rule that applies to most classroom assessment situations:

1. Those instructional objectives that can, with reasonable realism, be assessed with objective items typically should be.
2. Of the remaining instructional targets, those that can be assessed authentically with essay or other product measures ordinarily should be.
3. Only the remaining aims should be assessed by means of performance measures.

(Recall that this rule shouldn't be used in isolation and that other criteria should be considered. By way of further qualification, we shall see in the next chapter that the rule applies best to short-term instructional aims that concern maximum performance.)

The rationale of the rule can be developed a little more at this time. Three examples will be used to illustrate use of this three-step rule.

Interpreting and Constructing Graphs.   Suppose a class has studied the *interpretation* and *construction* of charts, tables, and graphs. What method(s) should the teacher use to assess student achievement?

As noted in Chapter 7, context-dependent items provide an excellent way to assess learning outcomes concerning ability to *decode* and *interpret* the stimuli (Terwilliger, 1989). To estimate this kind of achievement, we needn't move beyond the first step of the decision-making sieve. Because of the novelty of the material presented for interpretation, it is possible to test complex mental processes and high-road transfer with objective items. One might also consider essay questions about stimuli to assess ability to *produce* coherent interpretations.

The most authentic way to assess ability to *construct* charts, tables and graphs is obviously to have students do it. Although it provides less breadth of coverage and requires more testing and marking time, we must measure the right "stuff" in a realistic context.

A teacher might provide prose or tabular data and direct students to construct pie or bar graphs to represent it. In some situations, the test directions might permit—or require—use of computer-graphics software. The student products would then be evaluated. The assessment of each examinee's graph will take more time than would marking several objective times, but it is well worth the effort. It's not possible to measure student ability to *construct* or *produce* graphs with objective items. Thus, this instructional aim *demands* a move to the second step of the three-step decision-making rule.

Composing Coherent Directions.   A second example of the decision-making rule is the ability to compose easily comprehended directions. If a teacher, a prospective employer, or a committee conducting an outcomes assessment needs to know how well people can write directions, then there is one best, most authentic way to find out—have them write directions and then *carefully* assess the results.

Driving a Car.   A driver education instructor might consider the decision-making sieve for assessing students' driving. Before doing so, let's discriminate between *knowledge of* driving laws, traffic signals, and safety rules that can be assessed well with objective items and actual *skill in* driving. Both are important. Indeed, students must exhibit both in order to be licensed.

Concerning driving skills, the first two steps of the decision-making rule don't end the quest for an appropriate assessment method; neither objective items nor products can adequately reveal how well a person can operate a car. Therefore, the instructor must move on to the final step. This leads to performance assessment—observing the student as the car is driven and rating various features of the performance. Unfortunately, this method is even more time-consuming (and unnerving) than rating products, yet it is the only authentic way to estimate driving skills in real-world situations. The next chapter will be devoted to performance assessment.

Developing Product Measures

The following rules for devising effective product measures parallel those for developing essays.

1. Use product measures to assess achievement that isn't more easily or more reliably assessed by other authentic means. That is, follow the decision-making rule. Although measuring the target attributes is our central aim, we should assess them *by the most reliable and most economical methods available* (provided that doing so doesn't have adverse consequences on student effort). We should pursue authenticity with a *primacy* of purpose, but never with a *singleness* of purpose. The following three examples illustrate the difference.

Consider the ability to *produce* proofs in high-school geometry. It isn't possible to test this ability with objective items. Teachers who are keenly interested in students' ability to *develop their own proofs* may seem to have no alternative to proof products. However, before embarking on the extra difficulties inherent in product assessment, it is prudent to ask if *some* of the goals could be approached with objective items *about* proofs. If so, product measures could be reserved to supplement objective items. For example, the geometry teacher might consider using multiple-choice items to determine if students can identify from verbal statements what is given and what is to be proved. This option is quite attractive; it would increase breadth of subject matter sampling and be more economical of student and teacher time. Thus, more time would be available for using proofs to assess the learning that only they can tap.

Or, consider the metal shop teacher interested in student ability to *drill* holes. The instructor could consider showing pictures of people drilling and ask objective questions to see if examinees can recognize what is right or wrong about the procedures picture. This option is unattractive; the test would be hard to prepare and, more importantly, it wouldn't tap important motor skills. The shop teacher would probably elect to assess a product with student-produced holes in it.

Finally, suppose a third-grade teacher wants to know if pupils can *mix* primary colors to obtain desired shades. The most straightforward—obviously authentic—way to measure this objective might be to provide sample shades and the three primary pigments and ask each pupil to match the shades. Is there a better way to authentically tap the instructional outcome? We think so. The teacher could, for example, show a picture of a particular color (e.g., yellow-green) and a picture of a target color (e.g., a mid-green). Students could be asked which primary color needs to be added to the first picture to produce the second. Because *knowledge,* rather than the motor skills used in mixing pigments, is what differentiates pupils on this learning, this option seems attractive. It would save a great deal of set-up trouble and mess, not to mention cost of material, and would enable more items and greater breadth of sampling.

These examples show that an unthinking rush to an obvious "authentic" assessment is unwise. It is efficient to use product measures when objective items, for one reason or another, will *not* do the job. Moreover, it is sensible to resort to product measures mainly for the parts of the job for which the objective items are not suited. Yet, when objective items don't suffice, it is vital that product measures be used in spite of the attendant logistical difficulties.

2. Focus and structure tasks clearly so that examinees know what is expected. Suppose a sewing class has studied techniques for making buttonholes. To obtain a summative measure of student skill in crafting a neat, functional buttonhole, product assessment would be in order. Students would each be given cloth, thread, and either needles or access to the sewing machine, depending on the instructional objective. Directions for the task should clearly specify what aspects of the product are going to be evaluated (e.g., neatness, evenness of stitching, appropriate placement and size, and straightness of the opening). Indeed, the directions for the task might contain a copy of the preplanned criteria to be used for scoring.

3. Identify and assign appropriate relative weight to aspects of tasks. Suppose a wood shop class is given the stool assignment described earlier. This task has several facets, and the relative weight of features such as joint strength, adequacy of sanding, and smoothness of varnish should be clearly indicated *in advance.* In addition to being an issue of fairness, the advance information about relative importance of aspects of the project guides student effort.

Or, consider an art test in which students are asked to create five simple products. The relative weight of the products should be known to students so that they can budget their time appropriately.

4. Sample learning as fully as feasible. A more complete sample of the breadth of student skill can often be obtained from several varied, short tasks rather than from one long task. For example, in the art test described in the preceding paragraph, several simple or partial tasks may provide a fuller picture of each student's skills than would one complete product. Or, a sewing teacher having taught five different stitches might have students produce a line of half a dozen stitches of each; this yields a more comprehensive assessment of skills in use of these five stitches than would a complete garment that only used two or three of them.

On the other hand, sometimes it is more realistic to have students fully complete an *integrated* product. Where this is the case, be it the development of a work of art, a math proof, or a meal with everything ready to serve at the right time, it's important for the teacher to choose the product with great care. The product *should encompass as many of the component skills as possible.*

Assessing Products

The rules for marking products other than essays are highly similar to those for marking essays. Moreover, they have the same purpose—to make the scoring as reliable as feasible. To illustrate the product-assessment rules, it will be useful to refer to three varied examples:

- The wood shop stool project
- A homework assignment consisting of planning a balanced meal
- An art project of creating an original collage

1. Maintain examinee anonymity during scoring. This rule applies equally to other kinds of products just as it does to essays. It is especially important when assessment must be relatively global (e.g., the art collage) rather than analytic (e.g., the stool).

2. Develop marking criteria. Here, too, is a rule that applies equally to essay and other kinds of products. Figure 8.10 illustrates a scoring aid in which a teacher (a) identified and (b) thoughtfully established weight among aspects of the product. Like a scoring rubric for an essay (e.g., Figure 8.9 on page 190), developing the rating form for this wood-shop product requires professional judgment. A teacher should deliberate on the relative importance and the amount of instructional time devoted to the various aspects of the task. Those considerations are then used to assign a weight to each aspect.

Handwriting provides another example in which the development of clear marking criteria enhances both the reliability of the marking and the formative assistance that the assessment provides students. There is a reasonable agreement among experts in the analytic assessment of handwriting that the criteria by which writing readability should be judged include size, slant, spacing, and shape (Rosenblum, Weiss, & Parush, 2003).

To review points stressed earlier, the scoring criteria or rubrics:

- Should be developed at the time the assignment is crafted
- Enable the marker to give each element its due and only its due
- Help prevent drift of expectations
- Facilitate student learning

Let's amplify the final point. Is publication of the marking criteria an effective way to harness assessment power? Of course it is! It would be foolish for the wood shop teacher to keep secret the criteria by which the stools will be graded. Far, far better that the bases for scoring be given to students when the project is assigned, enabling effort to be focused on the kinds of learning that the

FIGURE 8.10   Sample Scoring Key for Product Measures.

Wood shop, four-legged, square, stepping stool project from directions that include drawings and model. (50 points)

Scoring Key: Correct dimensions—5 points
Fit of joints including invisible pins—7 points
Glueing of joints—5 points
Smoothing of top and legs from
    Planing—4 points
    Sanding—9 points
Decorative grooving—3 points
Staining—5 points
Varnishing—5 points
Waxing—7 points

teacher deems important. This also prompts and enables students to engage in self-assessment (Ormrod, 2000; Popham, 2000).

3. Establish sample products to serve as benchmarks. A good way to keep one's expectations from drifting is to root them in examples, perhaps ones saved from previous years, to help keep in mind the ratings appropriate for various levels of proficiency. For example, suppose a 7-point rating scale were being used to assess a geometric proof. Two or three examples each of 7-point proofs, 4-point products, and 1-point proofs would be helpful benchmarks to maintain a "fix" on one's benchmarks and prevent them from drifting.

This method has long been used (e.g., Thorndike, 1910) in the global assessment of handwriting. A test manual contains specimens of handwriting ordered from very poor to excellent. The rater then compares a particular child's handwriting sample with the benchmarks in the manual in order to identify the one with which it is most similar.

4. Assess one feature of the project at a time. Marking one item at a time is clearly appropriate for essay exams or mathematics problems where awarding partial credit may involve judgment. But what of integrated products such as the assignment of planning a balanced meal, the art collage, or the wood-shop stool?

In cases such as the balanced-meal assignment or some art projects, the adequacy of each element is not wholly independent of the other elements; each must be considered in relation to the others. For example, a dessert of pumpkin pie would fit better into a meal of roast beef, potatoes, and green beans than a meal that includes eggs, milk, and a yellow vegetable in earlier courses. Similarly, each element in a collage must be evaluated in terms of how well it contributes to unity of theme and how it influences other aspects of line, balance, and color. These are exceptions to the rule calling for separate analytic scoring of each feature or item. In such cases, each student's product should be considered in its entirety.

However, where such holistic assessment is indicated, it is still important to maintain as much objectivity of marking as possible by use of a scoring aid that calls attention to aspects that should enter into the global assessment of the gestalt. Thus, an art collage marking aid might focus attention on such elements as theme, color, line, balance, and neatness; yet the assessment would be holistic after each element had been considered. Likewise, a rating form for meal planning might address balance of nutrients, harmony and balance of color and texture, seasonal or regional availability of produce, and cost of the meal before calling for the global rating of the meal as a whole.

The wood-stool project illustrates a product that cannot physically be divided up like essay or math items can, yet it lends itself to marking one element at a time. If there were a whole set of stools to be marked, then the teacher could set them out in a row on work benches with a marking form next to each. The instructor could then move down the row marking the first element—correct dimensions—for each stool. Then the teacher would work back up the row marking the second element—fit of joints. Then the stools would be rearranged to prevent order effect, and the process would be repeated for the third and fourth elements, and so on.

However, if the stools are handed in one at a time as each is completed, then delaying feedback to students until a whole set of stools has accumulated would be too high a price to pay for the enhanced objectivity due to anonymity and avoidance of halo effects. In this case, the use of a rating form would be especially helpful in anchoring the teacher's marking criteria.

Although the topic of rating forms will be considered more fully in the next chapter, a few comments will be helpful here. Rubrics can be used for either domain-referenced or norm-referenced interpretations. When the subject matter to be rated lies in Context A, interpretations need to be referenced to the domain and to the mastery threshold. When Context C material is assessed, interpretations need to be norm referenced. Context B subject matter can be meaningfully interpreted either way.

Woodworking involves much Context B content; hence, one would have a choice of how to devise rating forms. Figure 8.11 illustrates a rating form for the first element of the wooden stools. The ratings are domain referenced because they are made with respect to explicit material—the dimensions.

Although this approach can be used with Context B material, it tends to introduce problems because it is extremely difficult to fully specify all of one's implicit criteria. Suppose a student had two measurements that were off just slightly more than $1/4$ inch whereas the others were virtually perfect. Would one really want to rigidly assign a zero? Probably not. Yet if we persisted in trying to specify fully all of the possible scoring situations, excessive time and effort would be devoted to developing the rating form. Moreover, the resulting rubric would be so detailed that it would be cumbersome to use.

Scoring criteria that are operationalized in this style provide one kind of **scoring rubric.** The highly specific delineation of partial credit is attractive to some because it seems to reduce the need for rater judgment. Such examples are ill-considered attempts to use rubrics in very analytic ways for performances that would better be assessed globally (see Mabry, 1999).

Another example of a "criterion-referenced" rubric having similar flaws is provided in Figure 8.12. It was designed for a portfolio consisting of five news stories involving Context C subject matter for a journalism class. Because one cannot fully specify Context C material, the objectivity of these rubrics is more illusory than real. The five levels don't cover all the possibilities. Rater judgment is still needed. Following are questions that illustrate some of the problems with simplistic rubrics of this kind:

- How should one rate a portfolio having only three stories that are done exceptionally well? Surely three stories done exceptionally well merit more than a Level 1 rating that specifies three stories done only tolerably well? The rubric doesn't allow a higher rating.
- How should one rate a portfolio having all five stories that only satisfy Level 1 conditions? Surely five fair stories are better than three. Yet the rubric doesn't recognize this.
- Why should a rater be prevented from awarding, say, 44 points in a borderline case?
- How would one rate a portfolio that had only two superbly done stories?

It is often better to avoid such excessive precision and "objectivity" and its attendant disallowance of judgment. *Evaluation requires judgment.*

FIGURE 8.11   Sample of a Flawed Domain-Referenced Rating Form.

Correct dimensions. Circle the numeral that best describes the stool's measurement.

5	All within $1/16''$
4	Most within $1/16''$ and none off by more than $1/8''$
3	All within $1/8''$
2	Most within $1/8''$ and none off by more than $1/4''$
1	One off by more than $1/4''$
0	More than one deviation over $1/4''$

FIGURE 8.12   Sample of Flawed Scoring Rubrics for a Journalism Portfolio.

LEVEL	NO. OF STORIES	ADEQUACY OF STORIES
I (10 points)	3	Less than adequate attention to three or more of the key story elements (i.e., Who, What, Where, Why, When, and How) in one or more of the stories.
II (20 points)	4	Less than adequate attention to one or two of the key story elements in one or two stories.
III (30 points)	4	Adequate attention to all of the key elements. Treatment may either vary from poor to excellent or may hover at adequate for all elements.
IV (40 points)	5	Adequate attention to all of the key elements. Treatment may either vary from poor to excellent or may hover at adequate for all elements.
V (50 points)	5	Superior treatment of all of the key elements in all of the stories.

The journalism teacher might better consider rating each of the five stories when it is prepared, thereby providing students with timely feedback. Each paper could be awarded, say, from 0 to 10 points on the basis of its adequacy. Then, if a portfolio is desired, it could be built by the student as each story is returned after assessment. These common-sense provisions solve the problems raised by the questions we presented.

Returning to the wood-stool assignment, Figure 8.13 on page 206 illustrates one way the stools could be judgmentally rated with reasonable economy and reliability. Although the norm-referenced form doesn't indicate what the reference group is, it would probably be the students in all of the teacher's classes in this and recent years. Had domain-referenced ratings been preferred, the directions wouldn't mention or encourage comparison with other people (yet raters would be hard pressed not to do so).

Notice how the design of this marking matrix allows the instructor to use general rating categories of poor, fair, good, and excellent (with shades of pluses and minuses for each) and then to drop straight down and circle the numeral nearest to the desired *location* without having to retain in mind the number of points allocated for each element. This enables differential weighting of elements without increased mental demands on the rater. Notice too that such a rating form enhances objectivity of ratings; it minimizes halo effect and renders the assessment of each element independent from the assessment of the other elements.

5. Systematically vary the order in which projects are evaluated. As with essays, the systematic bias introduced by order effect is eliminated by making each "pass" or "run" through the projects in a different order. This rule and the previous one take on special significance for portfolios.

Suppose a teacher of art or sewing has assembled several products for each student into a portfolio. Let's assume that the *same* several projects are included in each student's collection. If

FIGURE 8.13   Sample Rating Form for a Wood Stool.

STUDENT NAME: _____   TOTAL SCORE: _____

For each aspect of the stool, circle the numeral that best represents the student's work in comparison with other students who have taken this course. To obtain the total score, add the nine circled numbers.

	Poor		Fair		Good		Outstanding		
Dimensions	0	1	2	3	4	5			
Joints	0	1	2	3	4	5	6	7	
Glueing	0	1	2	3	4	5			
Planing	0		1	2	3	4			
Sanding	0	1	2	3	4	5	6	7	8	9
Grooving	0		1	2	3				
Staining	0	1	2	3	4	5			
Varnishing	0	1	2	3	4	5			
Waxing	0	1	2	3	4	5	6	7	

the teacher were to work through the stack, completing the assessment of each portfolio before going on to the next, there would be great danger of both halo effect and of order effect. This is easily prevented by marking one project at a time and also varying the order from "pass" to "pass" through the entire group of students' collections.

6. If the results are especially important, use multiple markers. This practice isn't ordinarily practical for classroom teachers; however, it may well be practical in important contests and the like. Too, if a major decision were to be based on a product, such as the decision to adopt a textbook for districtwide use, reliable assessment is vital. In such cases, having several raters independently assess each text being considered would enable the final decisions to be based on their collective judgment.

If multiple-markers are used, it is important to control for possible differences among them in central tendency and in variability. *Errors of central tendency* concern the systematic tendency for some judges to rate more generously or severely than others. *Errors of variability* result when the ratings of some judges are spread out more than those of other judges. Both of these sources of error introduce the serious problem that an examinee's score depends, in part, on who rates the work rather than on the work's quality. Training of raters can reduce these problems. There is also a need to statistically ensure equal weighting of all raters. This topic will be taken up in Chapter 11.

Directions for Product Measures

Directions for product measures should inform examinees how they will be evaluated. This not only helps to give all examinees an equal start, but it directs study efforts. For example, in a meal-planning assignment, students need to know whether consulting resources about nutritional attributes of various foods is acceptable. Or, in preparing a theme, students should know whether using spell-check software is considered academically honest.

Should either of these be acceptable? If an assignment is to be done out of class, the teacher cannot control use of resources; it seems fairer to explicitly allow them so that all students will operate on the same rules. If the work is to be done in class, the teacher should consider the project's purpose and the impact on student preparation.

Instructions should also provide routine "house-keeping" information. For example, instructions for the wood-stool project should specify when and how the finished product is to be turned in and how ownership should be identified.

Finally, directions for each assignment, theme, report, or project should make the due date absolutely clear. Will late projects be accepted? If so, what penalty will be assessed for unexcused delinquency? (Of course, if class rules have already made this absolutely clear, then directions for each assignment need not necessarily repeat them.) Veteran teachers can attest that much conflict is avoided by having these kinds of rules *in writing*. "Paving a paper trail" (i.e., protecting oneself with documentary evidence of some course of action—in this case providing timely notice of deadlines and penalties) serves several very useful purposes. First, written rules are fair; they prevent most potential misunderstandings, problems, and conflicts from occurring. Second, written explanations of requirements are appreciated by parents and students. Finally, they usually give the teacher the "winning hand" on the rare occasions when conflicts or appeals do occur.

CHAPTER RECAP

Product measures can tap many extremely important educational outcomes that cannot be adequately assessed by objective item types. The kinds of learning best assessed with products share two attributes. First, the focus is on student ability to *produce* or *develop* something; in the case of essays, this involves the examinees *formulating* and *composing* answers *in their own words*. Second, adequate evaluation can be based on examination of finished products.

Product assessment tends to be less reliable and less economical than objective tests. Because of this, instructional objectives that can be adequately assessed with objective items ordinarily should be. However, when learning is more realistically assessed with essay or other product measures, then they should be used—and used as reliably as possible. Along these lines, extended-response essay items tend to be less reliable than restricted-response items. Therefore, for objectives that can be assessed with either, restricted-response questions are preferred.

Product measures are less reliable than objective tests because products come in larger "chunks" and because assessing them is inherently less objective owing to the need for rater judgment. To maximize reliability of products, one should (a) carefully develop the production tasks to *assess* as *broadly* and unambiguously as feasible within the content or skill domain and (b) *mark* as *objectively* as possible.

The kinds of assessment a teacher uses will communicate to students what is important for them to learn. For example, if essays demand only recall of facts, the test power focuses student effort on that kind of learning. If questions require more mental processing, then the evaluation practices direct student effort toward learning that tends to be more permanent, more meaningful, more interesting, and more practical. The same, of course, can be said of objective questions. Item type and format (e.g., essay vs. objective) seem to have less impact on students' efforts and achievement than do their expectations of the mental processes and content to be assessed (Crooks, 1988).

CHAPTER 9

DEVELOPING AND SCORING PERFORMANCE MEASURES

CHAPTER OVERVIEW

WHEN TO USE PERFORMANCE ASSESSMENTS

FORMATIVE AND SUMMATIVE USES OF PERFORMANCE MEASURES

BALANCING RELIABILITY, ECONOMY, AND AUTHENTICITY

ASSESSING INTERACTIVE VS. NONINTERACTIVE PERFORMANCE

ASSESSING MAXIMUM AND TYPICAL PERFORMANCE

USING RUBRICS IN PLANNING INSTRUCTION, GUIDING STUDENT EFFORT, AND ASSESSING PERFORMANCE

A BRIEF CONSIDERATION OF PROGRAM EVALUATION

KEY TERMS

performance assessment
oral test
simulation
interactive performance measure
rubric
checklist

rating scale
program evaluation
outcomes assessment
short-term objective
long-term objective

Performance assessment involves observing and assessing behavior *while* it is under way. It requires students to actually demonstrate proficiency rather than to answer questions *about* proficiency (Kane, Crooks, & Cohen, 1999). Some observations can be preplanned to assess tightly specified performances and conditions. Other opportunities to judge proficiency may arise spontaneously (Stiggins & Bridgeford, 1986). Assessment of student performance can be detailed, analytic, and objective, or it can be holistic and impressionistic.

Performance assessment plays a major role in day-to-day classroom evaluation. This chapter will address the nature of this important means of assessment, offer suggestions for developing effective measures, provide methods of enhancing the reliability and validity of scoring this type of measure, and discuss implications for better teaching via better use of teacher-conducted performance assessment.

THE NATURE OF PERFORMANCE ASSESSMENT

Performance assessment is indispensable to the assessment of a rich variety of achievement, ranging from preschool to graduate school and from recreational pursuits to the workplace. Examples such as archery contests and foot races have been around for a *very* long time.

The **oral test,** a form of performance assessment, dates to antiquity and preceded the essay exam. In spite of their shortcomings, oral exams continue to be used because they are superior to other item types in assessing *certain* kinds of learning. They can permit flexibility that written exams lack. They can allow for expansion, probing, correction of question misinterpretation, and clarification of response.

Yet, oral or other kinds of performance assessments aren't typically our method of choice—if we have a choice. As emphasized before, teachers should ordinarily resort to performance measures only when other methods won't do the job. In such cases, teachers should assess performance with an eye both to formative and to summative decision making.

Formative Use of Performance Assessment.   In formative assistance, teachers want to see what is right or wrong with specific aspects of students' performance in order to *provide helpful diagnostic feedback* for improvement. Performance measures are used when it is necessary to witness the performance, not just inspect a final product, in order to pinpoint problems. Here are several examples of *formative* uses of performance assessment:

1. The band director listens to each trombone player's performance in order to offer *suggestions for improvement.*
2. The cooking teacher observes the mixing of a cookie recipe, *making suggestions* regarding such things as accuracy of measures and whether the baking soda is first mixed with the flour before being added to the wet mix.
3. The cooking teacher observes the preparation of a cookie recipe, *making suggestions* concerning sanitation in food preparation and safety in using an electric mixer.
4. The physical education instructor watches each child kick the kickball and *offers suggestions for improvement.*
5. The metal shop teacher observes students using the metal drill to *ensure that each student uses safety goggles.*
6. The keyboarding teacher moves around the room as students keyboard, observing their posture and *making suggestions* that will reduce fatigue of hands, wrists, arms, back, and eyes.
7. The primary teacher watches children as they copy a written exercise from the chalkboard. *Specific suggestions are provided* to individuals concerning posture, positioning of paper on the desk (distinguishing in particular between left-handers and right-handers), and grasp of the pencil.

In each example, the purpose of the observation is improvement. In pursuit of this enhancement of performance, feedback is ongoing. There is, however, another way in which the examples differ. In cases such as examples 1, 3, 4, 5, and 6, performance assessment is virtually the only way by which one could assess student performance. In other cases, such as examples 2 and 7, product assessment is also feasible. Here performance assessment is used mainly to provide formative assistance; helpful suggestions for improvement can be made and bad habits can be nipped in the bud.

Summative Use of Performance Assessment.   Teachers also use performance measures to evaluate the status of student achievement. At times, most or all of a unit's achievement can be measured only by means of performance measures. At other times, at least some summative assessment can use more economical and reliable methods; yet some aspects can't adequately be evaluated by objective or product measures. In this case, performance assessment should be used to fill in the gaps left by the other methods.

Several examples follow that parallel those provided for formative assessment. The difference is that the *summative* decisions concern level of student performance.

1. The band director listens to each trombone player's performance *in order to assign chairs* for the next nine weeks.
2. The cooking teacher observes the mixing of the cookie recipe, *grading* such things as correct proportions of ingredients and whether the baking soda is first mixed with the flour before being added to the wet mix.
3. The cooking teacher observes the preparation of a cookie recipe, *grading* the sanitation of the food preparation and safety in using an electric mixer.
4. The physical education instructor watches each child kick the kickball in order to *rate the adequacy* of the kicks.
5. The metal shop teacher observes students using the metal drill to *pass or fail* each on use of safety goggles.
6. The keyboarding teacher moves around the room as students keyboard, *rating* their posture.
7. The primary teacher watches children as they copy a written exercise from the chalkboard. *Ratings are made* for use in report cards of specific performance features such as posture, positioning of paper on desks, and grasp of the pencils.

Here, examples 1, 3, 4, 5, and 6 require performance assessment as the key way to assess performance objectives. In examples 2 and 7, however, product assessment would be more cost-efficient; performance assessment would be justified in summative assessment only as a way to tap aspects of performance not captured in the product.

In practice, the distinction between formative and summative evaluation is often somewhat blurred. When grading, teachers commendably often "keep their teaching hat on" and give feedback aimed at enhancing future student performance.

THINKING CAP 9.1   **???**

Following are four problems in classroom assessment. For each, apply the decision rule to decide among objective tests, essays and other product measures, and performance measures. Also consider whether each teacher would be concerned mainly with formative evaluation, summative evaluation, or about equally with both.

1. The director of the school play must for each major part select the student to be cast in it.

2. Once casting is completed, the director of the play holds rehearsals.

3. Consider Mr. Martin's unit on "Music Around the World" described on pages 118–120.

4. A teacher of Spanish is developing a final examination to assess student achievement in (a) reading comprehension, (b) writing, (c) listening comprehension, and (d) speaking.

THINKING CAP 9.1   CONTINUED

KEY TO THINKING CAP 9.1

1. Because objective tests and product measures are ill suited for casting, the director will have to endure the problems associated with performance assessment. (These problems, as well as how to cut losses from each problem, will be addressed in detail later in this chapter.)

This could be taken to be a straightforward case of summative evaluation for selecting the one or two best actors for each role. Germane to casting, however, is another issue—the matter of *matching* of persons to roles. Thus students' summative evaluation is not their achievement in the abstract, but their achievement *in relation to* the role being cast.

Another issue could enter into casting—student "coachability." That is, the teacher might want to estimate how quickly students can modify their performance to adapt to instruction. Performance could be assessed with several critiques and reperformances per student. *During* the process it is formative, but *after* the last round of critique and performance, the director would make the summative decision concerning who gets the part.

2. The way to provide ongoing diagnostic feedback concerning students' performance of their roles obviously is to have them perform and then critique their efforts. Other levels of the sieve have nothing to offer to this formative endeavor.

3. Mr. Martin used objective paper-pencil items to assess all that could be assessed with such devices—knowledge/comprehension and auditory category recognition. The application and analysis objectives were less amenable to objective items, so he used essays for them. He used performance measures only to fill in the gaps. Because the creative productions had to be performed in order to be judged, he relied on performance assessment for this part of his unit.

The focus of Mr. Martin's end-of-unit assessment is, of course, *summative,* yet the application/analysis section and the original production section would probably also have some formative flavor (e.g., mention of strengths and weaknesses).

4. By virtue of its being a final exam, all four skills would be assessed summatively. Reading comprehension is well suited to interpretive exercises with multiple-choice items. Written product assessment is necessary for evaluating student ability to compose and transcribe. Listening comprehension is highly amenable to interpretive exercises having multiple-choice items based on auditory stimuli.

The only way to measure people's ability to speak Spanish is to have them talk! This leads to serious problems in logistics, cost, and reliability, yet there can be no compromise. Much of this chapter is devoted to coping with these difficulties of performance assessment.

DEVELOPING PERFORMANCE ASSESSMENTS

Some performance measures are so straightforward that their assessment requires little comment. This is true of Context A performance tasks, such as reciting the alphabet. Similarly, some Context B tasks are easy to assess. For example, the keyboarding teacher's need to assess posture is accommodated without special arrangements; students' posture is there to be observed most any time. Or, the kindergarten teacher's need to screen children for behavior disorders might be achieved without much special arrangement beyond the need for the teacher to be sensitive to potential behavior disorders.

Other instances of performance assessment occur in more contrived situations. The director casts students for parts in the play by auditions, the swim coach must bring the camcorder to the pool to record dives, and the Spanish teacher needs to organize class time to enable individual oral testing. In such cases, there is some artificiality in the performance. Thus, students trying out for the play may be more (or less) self-conscious and anxious than they would be during most performances, divers' performance may be altered by the distraction of being recorded, and conversations during the Spanish test may be rather artificial in content and style.

Two issues inherent in performance assessment merit our attention:

1. The *realism* or *authenticity* of both the (a) content and (b) the milieu in which the performance is exhibited and the various costs associated with its pursuit.
2. The presence or absence of *interaction* with others during the performance.

Authenticity and Related Attributes

The artificiality of both the content and setting of some assessment is an undesirable invalidating feature. To phrase it positively in traditional scholarly prose, we seek *realism* in the circumstances in which performance is exhibited (Fitzpatrick & Morrison, 1971). To assert the same point in contemporary popular prose, we seek *authenticity* in the content and circumstances of performance.

However, authenticity doesn't exist in a vacuum, and we need to know that lack of realism isn't the only hazard to a test. Just as the sailor must steer clear of all reefs, not just one, so, too, must we. As we navigate our way through the Strait of Validity, three reefs endanger our journey:

1. Poor realism/authenticity
2. Poor reliability
3. Poor economy

Those who recklessly fail to heed the danger of any one of these perils place their ship, their cargo, and themselves at risk.

The Costs of Authenticity.   The adjective *authentic* "is usually intended to suggest that the performances being assessed are important in the real world and that they are highly contextualized" (Kane, Crooks, & Kohen, 1999, p. 7). Authentic assessment occurs in the students' natural environment, such as cooperative learning groups, large group discussions, social interchanges in cafeterias, creative settings such as art or music classes, and recreational settings on playgrounds (Spinelli, 2002). Unfortunately, authenticity has formidable costs; when the context for performance assessment is highly authentic, it often is *not* uniform and/or is *not* economical to assess. Different students perform in different situations, and great trouble and expense may be incurred in observing them in these different times and places. Moreover, comparability is sacrificed, and this erodes reliability.

For example, if one observed real-life Spanish conversations of students of the language, the different demands of the various "authentic" conversations would render assessment very difficult in two ways. First, adjustments would have to be estimated for the unequal difficulties of the dissimilar conversations. The lack of task uniformity would reduce the accuracy with which the test revealed differences in achievement. Second, the costs of making such naturalistic observations would be prohibitive. Indeed, many students of Spanish don't have casual Spanish conversations with anyone!

FIGURE 9.1a   Costs of Maximizing Authenticity.

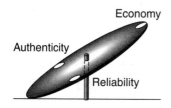

FIGURE 9.1b   Costs of Maximizing Economy.

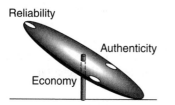

FIGURE 9.1c   Costs of Maximizing Reliability.

Figure 9.1a illustrates this cost of maximizing authenticity. We see that if realism/authenticity is elevated as much as possible, the other two important attributes—reliability and economy—are critically depressed.

The Costs of Economy.   Unfortunately, the other virtues have costs too. Suppose that the Spanish teacher decided to pursue economy with an absurd singleness of purpose; the result was a short objective test of conversational proficiency. The authenticity would be wiped out. Moreover, the brevity of the test would make it relatively unreliable as well. Figure 9.1b shows the costs of maximizing economy. If economy is raised as high as possible, then the other two attributes are depressed unacceptably.

The Costs of Reliability.   Let's stay with the same example to consider the third possibility—that of maximizing reliability. A long objective test would result. Results would be impressively consistent, but its length would make it costly and its use of objective items would destroy any authenticity. Figure 9.1c illustrates the costs of maximizing reliability. We see that if reliability is enhanced too much, the other two important characteristics suffer.

Figure 9.1 has an important moral: Because realism, reliability, and economy are all important, teachers should carefully consider the trade-offs among them and seek to *enhance each only to the extent that it doesn't cost too much of the others.* Because narrow-sighted efforts to enhance one often gravely compromise the other two, the best strategy is to seek a tolerably high level for each, rather than to maximize any one.

A common compromise is to use a task that is only somewhat authentic in order to achieve greater economy and reliability via uniformity. For example, a performance task of conversing with the Spanish teacher may provide more nearly uniform conditions and difficulty. However, a teenager's performance in conversing with the teacher may differ markedly from an unthreatening chat with a peer or shopkeeper. Although the more uniform, contrived exchange with the teacher would suffer some loss of realism; the resulting gains in reliability and economy would make the trade-off attractive.

Rationale for the Decision-Making Sieve.   We have now developed the basis with which to present the central reasoning behind the oft-mentioned, three-step, decision-making sieve presented in Figure 1.2 of Chapter 1. The trade-offs summarized in Figure 9.1 are the pivotal issue. The rationale is as follows: Authenticity of assessment is essential for validity and must never be forsaken. Yet reliability is also vital for validity, and it, too, must never be disregarded. Finally, economy is an important consideration that cannot be ignored. Hence, we give primary consideration to realism, but pursue it with an eye on reliability and economy. We typically *choose the most reliable and most economical assessment method that will provide reasonably realistic assessment of attainment of the intended educational outcomes.*

Let's emphasize this fundamental statement by reorganizing the decision-making sieve into a different schematic. Figure 9.2 depicts the decision-making rule as a flow chart that provides guidelines for selecting the method of assessment.

FIGURE 9.2   Decision-Making Flow Chart.

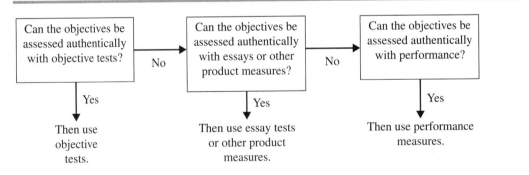

Caution 1. This flow chart is only applicable to the assessment of short-term objectives of maximum performance. It does not address objectives concerning typical performance or long-term objectives.

Caution 2. The issues leading to this flow chart are not the only issues that merit consideration. For example, the consequences of evaluation methods on student effort, balanced assessment, and logistic issues also merit consideration.

This flow chart, like the sieve, is incomplete. A vital issue not reflected in the body of Figure 9.2 is the impact that assessment practices have on student effort. This *always merits serious consideration.*

Also recall that we have qualified the rule in several places to legitimize sacrificing some economy and some reliability in order (a) to use diverse assessments methods that aren't all vulnerable to the same kinds of distortion (i.e., to triangulate data-collection methods) and (b) to accommodate the mixed preferences of students concerning item types.

Finally, the flow chart also fails to address an important possibility: What if the answer to the last question depicted in the chart is "no"? In that very important case, the educational outcome probably doesn't lend itself well to assessment *for student grading purposes.* However, such objectives can still be assessed very adequately in program evaluation.

Simulation and Authenticity. When a green traffic light turns yellow, a driver must judge whether there is time to move completely across the intersection before it turns red. A driving examiner needs to assess how good a student is in judging whether to decisively drive through or to stop. Would this skill best be measured in a natural context or in a contrived one?

In natural settings, the examiner has the examinee drive and hopes that a light turns yellow when the student is in the "decision zone." This provides maximum authenticity, yet one might have to drive for some time before an opportunity presents itself to assess this important skill. The costs of authenticity would be both lack of economy and low reliability (owing to the small sample of student behavior on nonuniform tasks).

In a contrived context, the examiner might use a simulation. A **simulation** is an artificial representation of the real thing. Suppose the school owns a simulator or trainer that has a speedometer, realistic controls, and a screen display of traffic and signal conditions. With electronic apparatus less sophisticated than that of many computer games, *excellent controlled and uniform simulation can be achieved along with highly reliable computerized scoring of multiple performances.*

(Not to be overlooked are trade-offs among several kinds of economy. With the simulator, the cost of purchase would be great. With the real-world drive around town in hopes of encountering a yellow light or two at the right time, the cost in time and car expenses would be enormous. Economic considerations thus include examiner and examinee time, money to purchase tests or simulators, money or time to score tests, money to maintain equipment, and risks and hazards involved in assessment.)

Simulation may provide a superior means both of *teaching* and *testing* the skill. In this case, the loss of authenticity may be small compared with the enormous gain in controlled uniformity, reliability, and economy. Yet, no matter how realistic performance-based simulation may be, it is still imitation; thus, examinees don't necessarily behave in the same way they would in real life (Swanson, Norman, & Linn, 1995).

Conversing with the Spanish teacher was another example of a simulation of everyday conversation in Spanish both for teaching and for assessment purposes.

Let's now examine the three-way trade-off among authenticity, reliability, and economy by use of a final example. Consider a test on the first-aid topic of stopping severe bleeding. Our decision-making rules eliminate objective and essay tests about first aid because we want to see how students actually *perform* first aid.

If it is uneconomical to drive around looking for "stale" yellow lights, think how uneconomical it would be to go looking for an accident! Having pupils perform on real accident victims is not only well nigh impossible, it would also be unethical because of physical dangers for victims and emotional hazards to pupils. Moreover, each examinee would be confronted with a different set of needs; comparability would be nil with the result that reliability would plummet. Thus, extreme authenticity is to be avoided; simulation is clearly preferable.

We could, for example, direct pupils to show how to stop bleeding from an imaginary deep gash in Mike's forearm. Such play-acting has only feeble resemblance to a real accident, yet in view of all the problems with more realistic teaching or assessment, our humble simulation seems quite tolerable. Hence, we must endure a worrisome cost in realism to secure tolerable reliability, adequate economy of time, and acceptable ethical practice.

To ReCAP.   Authenticity (i.e., realism), economy (i.e., practicality), and reliability (i.e., consistency) are difficult to pursue concurrently; they vie for our favor. As we grapple with teaching and assessment issues, wisdom dictates that trade-offs must be thoughtfully made. The decision-making rule provides a way to simultaneously address authenticity, reliability, and economy. We must never lose sight of any of these attributes. Because things done to enhance one tend to weaken the others, we must reconcile ourselves to the need for balance among them. Simulation often provides a desirable compromise for both formative assistance and summative assessment.

Performance assessment has achieved faddish popularity in recent years. As mentioned before, so-called alternative assessment came into style about every three decades in the twentieth century. When its down sides (i.e., its costs in reliability and economy) became widely recognized, it fell into disuse (Darling-Hammond, 1993).

To put performance assessment into the perspective of a scholar and researcher who has devoted a distinguished career to its advancement, we paraphrase and abridge the balanced stance of Richard Stiggins.

> Advocates contend that performance assessments provide "high-fidelity" representations of complex kinds of achievement that are relevant to life beyond school (Wiggins, 1993). Others urge great caution in embracing this movement because performance assessment brings with it significant technical problems. They correctly note that it is a very difficult assessment method to develop and use well (Dunbar, Koretz, & Hoover, 1991). Virtually all serious research done in education and business leads to the conclusion that performance assessment is a complex way to assess.
>
> Educators need to keep performance assessment in perspective. It is not the best of all assessment methods in all contexts. Nor is it so difficult to use that it is beyond the reach of typical teachers. It is one of many tools capable of providing effective assessment of our objectives. In that sense, it indeed is a valuable tool.
>
> Be forewarned that use of performance assessment *professionally* is not easy. Do not take its methods lightly; they are not "assessment by guess." There is no place in the professional use of performance assessment for ethereal "intuition." Credible evidence is needed. Attaining an appropriate level of assessment rigor requires careful thought, thorough preparation, and meticulous attention to detail. Educators who are unwilling to invest the time, energy, and technical knowledge needed to do performance assessment well place their students' academic success directly in jeopardy. (Stiggins, 2001, p. 186)

Interactive Versus Noninteractive Performance Measures

From the perspective of CAP, performance assessment takes place in all three contexts. Some examples now will be considered along with the extent to which the performance measures in each context require examinees to interact with other people, events, or circumstances.

Context A—Explicit Mastery Objectives. Context A subject matter is explicit, tightly specified, and vital. Its explicit masterability implies that it is uniform; only low-road transfer is needed. Therefore, the subject matter is *not* interactive. For example, unlocking a combination hall locker is a task that middle-school students can and should master. Pronouncing the name of each letter of the alphabet is also vital and masterable. Rating forms and checklists designed to assess such specifiable and masterable performance tasks should, of course, be domain referenced.

Context B—Explicit Developmental Objectives. Context B subject matter is wholly specifiable, but not vital. Examples are free throws in basketball, knowledge of all Eurasian capitals, track events, and keyboarding speed tests.

Tasks in Context B also tend to be noninteractive. Thus, assessment is quite easy. The performance tests are relatively simple to create, easy to score, and uncomplicated by demands of realism that they be *interactive* with the behavior of other people, weather conditions, and so on. Reasonably high authenticity can be achieved along with relatively high reliability; there is little need to trade off one against the other.

True, some Context A and B situational factors exist (e.g., noise and distractions in the school hall when the locker is being unlocked or the audience behavior at a track event). Removing the performance from the natural context would somewhat enhance control of uniformity and reliability at the expense of realism. However, the issue is often not a very big one in Contexts A and B because (a) the natural situation doesn't cost much in uniformity, and (b) if simulation is elected, it can be quite realistic.

Context C—Expansive Developmental Objectives. Context C subject matter isn't highly specifiable and can't be mastered. High-road transfer is necessary for Context C learning to be useful. The low specifiability is *caused by the inherently interactive nature of many Context C tasks.*

Interactive, high-road transfer features make it impossible to specify fully either the difficulty or the situation in which tasks are performed. Illustrative **interactive performance measures** are playing football, participating in a class discussion, and riding on horseback. The actions of other people or animals influence the difficulty of the performance. Similarly, flying an airplane involves interacting with weather and machine, and maintaining appropriate classroom discipline involves interacting with the circumstances.

In Context C performance, the uncontrolled features—often resulting from the role of other persons, animals, weather, or circumstances—require that meaningful interpretation be norm referenced.

The unspecifiable, interactive features of Context C tasks make economy and reliability hard to attain. The trade-off between realism and reliability can be painful; the more realistic a task is, the less reliable it tends to be (Fitzpatrick & Morrison, 1971), and conversely. Likewise, the trade-off between realism and economy is often painful; the more realistic a task is, the less economical its assessment tends to be, and conversely.

Let's consider again the Spanish teacher's oral test in conversation. Practical constraints led to simulation rather than assessment in "real" situations. Hence, the realism was significantly eroded by the artificiality of the simulation. Thus, a price in realism was paid.

Too, the way the teacher responds to the conversational efforts of various students will reflect and follow from what they say. This necessary interaction clearly limits the uniformity of tasks from person to person and thereby limits the equality of task difficulty. Thus, reliability is eroded.

In addition, test security may be compromised due to previously tested students passing information to yet-to-be-tested students. To prevent this, the teacher might vary the conversation from student to student more than would otherwise be necessary. This lack of uniform content would further compromise comparability and reliability.

Thus, in Context C performance assessment, the teacher often faces multiple problems. The need to examine one student at a time can consume much time. The need to interact reduces task uniformity, comparability, and reliability. The need to protect test security further limits comparability and reliability. The logistics of what to do with students while they are not being tested can be troublesome. Finally, the realism of the performance tasks often is only modest. In devising Context C performance measures, one should thoughtfully consider all the problems and use sound, professional judgment concerning the best balance among the considerations.

With all of these disadvantages, why do teachers use Context C performance measures at all? Because that is the only valid way to assess student attainment of some important instructional objectives. Yet awareness of the multiple problems highlights the rationale of the decision-making rule: Performance measures should ordinarily be used *only* when other measures will not do the job.

THINKING CAP 9.2 ???

Following are four applied assessment problems. For each, use the sieve or flow chart to decide on the best way to assess the instructional objective.

1. In teaching primary children the Pledge of Allegiance, the teacher wants each child to be able to recite it.
2. An elementary school has been studying principles and procedures to be used in case of a school fire.
3. A scout leader wants scouts to know the proper way to fold the flag.
4. A driver education teacher wants students to recognize *by their shapes* and properly respond to various traffic signs.

KEY TO THINKING CAP 9.2

1. The way to find out if a student can recite the Pledge of Allegiance is obviously to have the child recite it. Clearly, a performance measure is in order for this Context A task. (See also the second and third paragraph of discussion for item 3.)

2. Consider first the simple, *normal* route of exit a class is supposed to use. One could test this with paper and pencil (e.g., draw the route of exit on the sketch of the building) or with a performance test of actually exiting the building. Such simple Context A tasks are masterable, but, lacking interaction with circumstances, have deplorable authenticity. To see why, consider a real-life fire scene in which some people are highly excited and in which the normal route or exit is blocked. The Context C task of exiting the school is interactive with circumstances and people.

How could we achieve decent realism? Clearly we can't set the school on fire for assessment purposes! Nor is it practical to test each child separately while a whole school full of accomplices realistically simulates school-on-fire behavior. Alas, we are unable to achieve good authenticity; therefore the Context A tasks described in the preceding paragraph are about as good as we can do.

3. The leader would surely dismiss paper-pencil testing *about* flag folding because of poor authenticity and artificial task complexity. Could the product of the

THINKING CAP 9.2   CONTINUED

properly folded flag be assessed? Yes, but the finished product would not reveal if procedures were satisfactory (e.g., if the flag was kept off the ground).

The leader would surely opt to have each scout tested separately by a performance test. Test security is not an issue with Context A content. Each person's test can provide vicarious practice to others.

It is not known ahead of time whether each scout's test will be formative or summative. If there are problems, they will be corrected formatively. If the task is done correctly, the student will be summatively passed.

4. Although performance is the instructional aim, the *real problem is cognitive* knowledge of sign meanings, not executing the performance that results from

that knowledge. Use of the decision rule leads to the use of objective items to assess achievement of this (underlying cognitive) objective. There's no need to endure the various costs of a performance measure. A matching exercise might be best. In the first column would be the shapes of various traffic signs; in the other column would be the words telling what they say, for example, "stop" and "yield."

One might be concerned by the issue that the objective items would test maximum performance, whereas the goal involves typical responses. This is a good thing to be concerned about. Yet this concern doesn't lead to use of a performance test because a behind-the-wheel performance would also yield maximum performance.

SCORING PERFORMANCE MEASURES

In Chapter 8, we addressed problems associated with the reliability of scoring products where the products "stand still" to be evaluated. Greater problems are associated with the reliability of scoring performance when the performances "fly by." Fortunately, however, "the relatively low reliability of performance tests is not an entirely universal or necessary characteristic" (Fitzpatrick & Morrison, 1971, p. 268).

The greater difficulty of achieving sound assessment of performance measures makes it necessary for teachers to be better prepared to make the crucial observation while the performance is under way. That is, we must know exactly what we are looking for *before* we start assessing. Just as we need to develop key points to outline a model answer for essay questions, so must we determine clear criteria for assessing performance tasks.

Developing Clear Criteria

The overarching rule for providing fair and reliable scoring of performance is to *develop clear evaluation criteria.* Similarly, the key way to harness evaluation power is to make people (be they students, teachers, corporate CEOs, or bus drivers) aware of the criteria by which they will be evaluated.

In developing criteria for scoring, the elements of the performance should be thoughtfully analyzed *before instruction commences* (Mehrens, Popham, & Ryan, 1998). This is important because, among other reasons, we wish to enable, encourage, and prompt self-appraisal (Arter & McTighe, 2001; Findley & Scates, 1946; Ormrod, 2000).

An early decision should be made regarding whether assessment will be analytic or global. Some performance tasks are well suited to analytic marking in which various elements of the task are identified and each is rated and given the desired weight. Tasks suitable for analytic marking would be sending an e-mail message and repairing a flat bicycle tire.

Other performance tasks seem to defy analytical assessment. Yet even the most difficult tasks can, to some degree, be broken down into components. *Scoring is improved by analytic assessment to as great an extent as the task being evaluated lends itself.* Several examples will illustrate the use of the principle of using clear evaluation criteria as analytically as the nature of the task allows. Our aim is to ensure "that the performance ratings reflect the examinee's true capabilities and are *not* a function of the perceptions and biases of the person evaluating the performance" (Stiggins, 1987, p. 33). Thus, the nature of the task helps educators opt for more or less assessment detail. Another factor is the use that is to be made of the assessments. If they are to be used to make global judgments about student status, the criteria "only need to be detailed enough to ensure consistent ratings. If, however, the assessment is to be used to diagnose student strengths and learning needs," then "all essential aspects of performance must be present." Moreover, descriptive detail is needed to communicate the bases of assessment to students. "What is left out of the criteria will be left out of the performance or product" (Arter, 1999, p. 37).

Rubrics in Planning Instruction and in Assessing Performance.   As we saw in Chapter 8, assessment criteria can be formatted as **rubrics**[1] that provide the criteria that describe performance proficiency. Rubrics can be structured either for analytic or holistic assessment.

Now let's make more explicit a fundamentally important point about planning instruction. *Rubrics are useful in planning instruction* as well as in assessing performance. Like tables of specification, *rubrics should be developed before instruction begins.* This maximizes their potential to

- sharpen teacher thinking about instructional aims,
- ensure that assessment flows from instructional objectives,
- focus teacher planning of content and skills to be taught,
- align assessment with instructional content,
- let students know which features a performance should (and shouldn't) exhibit, and
- enable students to engage in more effective self-assessment.

Thus, assessment criteria should, in addition to defining the criteria used to assess performance, be communicated to students early on (Mehrens, Popham, & Ryan, 1998; Whittaker, Salend, & Duhaney, 2001). Making the content of rubrics known to students (whether or not the teacher uses the actual rubric as the vehicle of communication) helps them learn to assess their own performance (Arter & McTighe, 2001) and it harnesses evaluation power.

Of course poorly constructed rubrics can cause evaluation to work against desired kinds of learning. Features that are overlooked in rubrics tend also to be overlooked in instruction and in learning (Arter & McTighe, 2001). Thus, as emphasized in Chapter 5, before a unit is launched, careful planning is needed jointly for assessment and for other aspects of effective instruction.

Rubrics can be laid out as **checklists,** which usually require all-or-none or present-absent assessment of each rated component. Checklists are often quite narrow and concrete, being used primarily for assessing processes (Herman, Aschbacher, & Winters, 1992). Alternatively, rubrics can be designed as **rating scales,** which have numbers or points assigned along a continuum of performance levels. This enables assessment of level of proficiency of each identified aspect.

[1]"Rubric" is a two-dollar synonym for "criteria" or "rating form." Compared with the traditional meaning of rubric, which meant "heading," the newer assessment meaning is rather strange. As Popham (2000) suggested, one might surmise that those who adopted this usage preferred an esoteric term to a more comprehensible descriptor such as "scoring guide." However, the word has achieved considerable popularity, so we bow to convention and use it.

Developing effective rubrics is exacting work. Trial and error may be required. One way to expedite the development of valid criteria is to address the many possibilities during staff development activities that have been designed to encourage cooperative efforts among teachers. During such activities, groups of teachers can construct, critique, try out, revise, and share a variety of rubrics. The ripple effects can have significant impact on both assessment and instruction.

Examples.   Following are several diverse examples of rubrics.

Oral Book Report.   Consider an upper-elementary level oral book report. It is a Context C task because there are as many book reports as there are books and because there's no one best way to report on any one book. Figure 9.3 displays a form that might be used for this performance.

FIGURE 9.3   Summative Rating Form for Oral Book Report.

Student: _____

For each step, record the numeral that best represents the pupil's performance.

CONTENT	PRESENTATION
Title Provided	Speed
_____ (0) No	_____ (4) Slow
_____ (1–3) Partial	_____ (5) Good
_____ (4) Yes	_____ (2–4) Rather Fast
	_____ (0–1) Very Fast
Author Provided	
_____ (0) No	Articulation
_____ (2) Yes	_____ (0) Poor
	_____ (1) Fair
Description of Book	_____ (2–3) Good
_____ (0) None	_____ (4) Excellent
_____ (1–2) Scant	
_____ (3–5) Good	Volume
_____ (2–3) Excessive	_____ (0–1) Inaudible
	_____ (3) Hard to Hear
Illustrative Anecdotes	_____ (4) Good
_____ (0) None	_____ (3) Too Loud
_____ (1–2) Scant	
_____ (3–5) Good	Language Usage (Word Choice, Sentence Structure, and Grammar)
_____ (1–3) Excessive	_____ (1) Poor
	_____ (2) Fair
Summary Evaluation	_____ (3) Good
_____ (0) None	_____ (4) Excellent
_____ (1–2) Scant	
_____ (3–4) Good	Posture and Gestures
_____ (2–3) Excessive	_____ (0) Poor
	_____ (1) Fair
	_____ (2) Good
	_____ (3) Excellent
CONTENT TOTAL: _____	PRESENTATION TOTAL: _____

This performance task consists of two separate features that should *not* be mingled. The content of the report is something quite apart from the style of the report's delivery. Actually, the content could better be assessed with a product assessment—a written report. However, because the teacher wanted to give pupils experience in speaking in front of the class, the book report was chosen as the content to be presented. The teacher has decided to sum the items within each major part of the rating form.

The rating rubric serves several purposes. First, by being analytic, greater reliability and validity are apt to be achieved. Next, the form provides each pupil with useful information that can be used for improvement; thus, this summative rating also has excellent formative utility. Third, students are informed as to how they will be rated by being given advance copies of the forms, so the teacher can communicate priorities. For example, anticipating that talking too rapidly will be a major problem, the teacher explains that pace will count more than any other element. It can also be explained that it is much more serious and more common to talk too rapidly than it is to speak too slowly, and that the resulting point ratings reflect this. The same point can be made about the problem of speaking inaudibly. Thus, students' prior knowledge of how they will be rated enables the assessment to enhance learning and encourages student self-direction.

An attribute shown in Figure 9.3 involves linear versus curvilinear scales. Some items, such as language usage, are inherently linear. That is, more of an attribute is better than less of it, and even more is better still; hence, scores range from low to high. Other items, such as use of illustrative anecdotes, are inherently curvilinear. That is, more of an attribute is better than less of it, but even more is *not* better still; hence, scores range from low to high to low again. Speaking volume is another attribute on which we would want to grade on a curvilinear scale; thus, there is an optimum level, and points are lost if volume is *either* softer or louder than the optimum.

Public Speaking.   Our next example is more sophisticated and more interactive. Figure 9.4 shows a rubric that might be used by a college public speaking instructor to assess a student's speech.

Several things about this rubric merit mention. At the top, a global rating is provided in letter grades augmented by verbal descriptors. The instructor made this summative assessment holistic because the instructor believes that a speech is more than the sum of its parts; the adequacy of a speech is a function of the *relationships among its parts and the interaction between the speech and the audience.* If any one feature is bad enough, the entire performance may be seriously marred. Therefore, the summative assessment is a global judgment that is made *after—and is informed by—* the analytic assessment. The latter provides a safeguard against the instructor overlooking features that ought to be factored into the holistic rating. (The elementary teacher in the previous example might well have taken this perspective, too.)

The analytic ratings thus serve two purposes. First, they guide the instructor's attention to relevant matters on which to base the global evaluation. Second, the ratings are designed to offer specific feedback to students to assist them in the preparation of subsequent speeches. These ratings are more detailed than might be appropriate at the secondary level.

Each item has a "Not Applicable" (NA) rating option. It is wise to provide for the possibility that a criterion may not be germane to a given situation. For example, eye contact is not relevant to radio speech. Similarly, some rating forms have a "No Opportunity to Observe" column to provide a means of avoiding rating people on aspects of performance that the rater hasn't witnessed.

Notice the curvilinear nature of some of the rubric's criteria, for example, "previews main points." The amount of preview can be either insufficient or oversufficient; the rubric reflects this.

FIGURE 9.4   Public Speaking Performance Rubric.[1]

PUBLIC SPEAKING PERFORMANCE RUBRIC

NAME: _____   DATE: _____

GLOBAL RATING	A+	A	A–	B+	B	B–	C+	C	C–	D+	D	D–	F
	SUPERB			GOOD			FAIR		POOR			INADEQUATE	

Audience Analysis	*Overdone*			*Excellent*		*Adequate*		*Poor*	*NA*
Targeted to audience				4	3	2	1	0	___
Originality of approach		2		3	2		1	0	___
Maintains audience attention				6	5	4	3	2	1	0	___
Stimulates intended reaction (e.g., interest, appreciation, concern)				6	5	4	3	2	1	0	___

Message	*Overdone*			*Excellent*		*Adequate*		*Poor*	*NA*
Opens in attention-getting manner				6 5 4	3 2	1	0	___
Articulates theme clearly				6 5 4	3 2	1	0	___
Previews main points	1	2		3	2	1	0	___
Information is new and interesting				3	2	1	0	___
Cites various supporting materials (e.g., examples, stories, statistics, quotations)	3 4	5		6 5 4	3 2	1	0	___
Originality of topic				4	3	2	1	0	___
Effective use of language				3	2	1	0	___
Sufficient length	0 1 2 3	4 5		6 5 4	3 2	1	0	___
Conclusions focus on main points	3	4		5	4	3	2	1	0	___

Delivery	*Overdone*			*Excellent*		*Adequate*		*Poor*	*NA*
Appears confident		2		3	2	1	0	___
Uses voice effectively				5	4	3	2	1	0	___
Uses gestures expressively	2	3		4	3	2	1	0	___
Avoids distracting mannerisms				4	3	2	1	0	___
Maintains and varies eye contact				6	5	4	3	2	1	0	___

Comments:

[1]This rubric was inspired by a rating form copyrighted by Nancy R. Goulden. Its topics were adapted slightly from hers, and are used with permission. The differentiated, curvilinear weighting and the graphic formatting were devised by us.

In contrast, other criteria are linear; for example, it would be hard to imagine too much maintenance of audience attention.

Notice, too, how the instructor's estimate of the relative importance of the criteria is reflected in the number of maximum points available for each. In other words, if the summative rating were to be analytic, it would be the sum of the individual ratings. This information helps students to know where to put their preparation priorities. Although this assignment of weights is more subjective than we might wish, the allocation of relative points should be informed by the instructor's subject matter expertise and thoughtful deliberation.

The layout of the form makes it unnecessary for the rater to remember the differing number of possible points for each criterion. If a rater judged the performance on an item to be a bit on the poor side of adequate, the rater need only drop down to the appropriate row a bit to the right of the "Adequate" heading and find the nearest numeral to circle.

The rating form concludes with a section for open-ended comments. This provides for qualitative feedback that can touch on elements not in the regular criteria. It also provides a place for a teacher to make encouraging, upbeat comments.

This example is a good place to note that peer assessment and self-assessment should be considered as ways to help students to understand what constitutes excellent work (Mehrens, Popham, & Ryan, 1998). Instructors could have students rate each other on this rubric as a means of helping students *learn the criteria of good performance.* Teachers might also use videotaped speeches as an interpretive class activity to give students practice in using the scoring rubric; class discussion would follow. Another thing teachers might do to help students learn the bases by which speeches are judged would be to ask them to rate themselves on the rubric, perhaps from a videotape. Their self-ratings could then be compared with the instructor's ratings as a means of helping students gain skill in self-assessment. Whatever methods are used, instructors should teach self-assessment (Popham, 2000).

Finally, note that some educators (e.g., Mabry, 1999) fret that rubrics may constrain creativity. This is a realistic concern if a simplistic rubric does violence to the nature of a complex task. This is most apt to occur when someone unwisely attempts to eliminate judgment from the evaluation of an interactive Context C performance. Along these lines, educators should try to identify other important criteria that are missing from their scoring rubrics. Is their absence worrisome in that the rubrics will direct student effort away from the unmentioned criteria? If so, one would want to revise the rating forms.

Rubrics should be revised when inadequacies come to light. Revision doesn't necessarily mean greater length; it also can be achieved by use of broader categories. And of course, revision of rubrics implies aligned revision of instruction.

Band Tryout for Chairs.   Miss Snider is the band director in a large high school and occasionally has tryouts for each instrument for chair assignment. Always eager to harness assessment power as much as possible, she announces dates in advance and indicates that scores will be based on four components.

1. Her global rating of each player's overall skill. This is to *avoid having a single performance test be too important.* She makes these holistic ratings a day or two before the tryout in order to prevent them from being influenced by the tryout performance.

2. Her global rating of each player's dependability (e.g., punctuality and deportment). This is to *motivate good behavior* and to *communicate that citizenship is often as important as skill in performance.* She often augments this holistic rating with comments indicating features of dependability that led to the ratings. These ratings also are made before the tryout.

3. Her global rating of each student's performance on a selection of his or her own choice. This is to give students a chance to show their best work, both in terms of the *demands of the selection chosen* and *skill with which it is played.* She will provide comments that indicate how the global rating is a function of *both* of these features.

4. Her global rating of each student's sight-reading performance on an unfamiliar selection that she keeps secure until the private (to prevent vicarious practice for the later-tested students) tryout begins. This is to provide a *consistent element to the assessment.* She will offer comments aimed at formative assistance.

Figure 9.5 provides a form containing all four of these holistic ratings on 8-point scales with benchmarks of Poor, Fair, Good, and Superb. Notice how Miss Snider used enough intervals to enable reasonably fine discriminations without having to generate another four adjectives.

A disadvantage of this form's convenient inclusion of all four ratings is the danger that a halo effect may cause the teacher's ratings of past skill and dependability to color her ratings of their present performance. This is a real danger, yet it seems questionable that she could "erase" her memory any better by having the ratings on separate sheets of paper.

How should Miss Snider weight the four components to arrive at the total rating shown in Figure 9.5? At first, she considered weighting the components equally. Then she convinced herself that a musician's contribution to a band is more than a simple sum of components; if any one aspect is bad enough, the person may be worthless to the group. Thus, a case could be made for as-

FIGURE 9.5   Global Ratings of Aspects of Band Performance.

Student's Name _____

GLOBAL RATING BY INSTRUCTOR	POOR		FAIR		GOOD			SUPERB
Overall skill	1	2	3	4	5	6	7	8
Dependability[1]	1	2	3	4	5	6	7	8
Performance on selection of the student's choice[2]	1	2	3	4	5	6	7	8
Sight-reading performance on an unfamiliar selection[3]	1	2	3	4	5	6	7	8

Total =

[1]Comment:

[2]Comment:

[3]Comment:

signing chairs on the basis of each student's one lowest area. After considering impact on student effort and morale and clarifying her desire to prompt extra effort in each person's weakest area without making the other factors unimportant, she decided to allocate double weight to each student's lowest area and equal weight to the remaining three components.

Miss Snider was aware of the subjectivity involved in assigning weights, but she was satisfied that she had given the decision her best professional judgment. Finally, she decided to provide students with advance notice of her system to ensure that everybody would know the rules and to harness assessment power.

Drama.   Mr. McDowell teaches high-school drama. One of his goals for the year was to develop a rubric for assessing student skills in acting. He wanted to use the scale for several important purposes:

- To assess students for formative assistance
- To assess students for summative grading
- To teach students conventional criteria by which performance is assessed
- To encourage students to engage in self-assessment for improvement

He identified seven categories that his rubric should include. To these preidentified topics, he added "other" to enable coverage of unforeseen or unusual aspects of performance.

Mr. McDowell pondered whether the scale should be additive or global; that is, whether the whole was merely the sum (or average) of the parts or if it was more. With the inclusion of the final category of "other," he decided that the sum could *typically* be considered to be the sum of the parts; yet, he believed that any one aspect, particularly if it were extremely poor, could eclipse the others and spoil the total. Therefore, he decided to make the final rating global. However, he charged himself with explaining his rationale to any student whose holistic rating wasn't the same as the average of the seven parts.

Mr. McDowell then constructed a 9-point rating scale for each of the categories. Figure 9.6 shows his rating scale.

To achieve the several above-mentioned aims, he decided that each actor would be rated by the teacher, by peer cast members, and by her- or himself. He pondered the purposes to which he should put the *peer* ratings:

- For instructional use to the raters in learning about the criteria of performance? Yes, definitely!
- For the formative assistance use of the ratees? Yes.
- For grading? No. However, he decided to inform the class that if the peer ratings of an actor systematically differed from his ratings, he would seriously rethink his own assessment.

Next, he contemplated the purposes to which he should put the *self*-ratings:

- For the instructional use to the students in learning about the bases by which acting is judged? Yes, most definitely!
- For the formative use of the ratees? Yes, most definitely!

FIGURE 9.6   Rubric for Rating Acting.

CRITERIA	DEFICIENT		ONLY FAIR		ADEQUATE		GOOD		OUTSTANDING	NA
Voice	1	2	3	4	5	6	7	8	9	—
Diction	1	2	3	4	5	6	7	8	9	—
Movement	1	2	3	4	5	6	7	8	9	—
Characterization	1	2	3	4	5	6	7	8	9	—
Memorization of lines/cues	1	2	3	4	5	6	7	8	9	—
Concentration (in character)	1	2	3	4	5	6	7	8	9	—
Dramatic effectiveness	1	2	3	4	5	6	7	8	9	—
Other (specify)	1	2	3	4	5	6	7	8	9	—

Overall Rating = _____

Comments:

- For grading? No, and students should know ahead of time that it won't be used for grading, because it has the potential to lead to counterproductive gaming behavior. Mr. McDowell decided that when a student's self-ratings differed very much from his and peer ratings, he would meet with the student to try to help the student (a) learn the criteria, (b) improve, and (c) develop realism of self-assessment.

The assessment process for the Context C performance tasks required organization. Mr. McDowell knew that he shouldn't depend on memory to rate students; retention is selective and easily distorted. Rather, he should systematically rate each student, say, once a week, and sum the results.

To maximize reliability, he would need to arrange for all actors to have equally demanding roles. Since that isn't possible, he sensibly decided to rate each actor on how well she or he performed the role that was assigned. He would use his "comments" section to note if the roles were unusually easy or demanding. Ratings would influence both grades and assignment to more or less challenging roles in future plays.

He found that the rubric substantially reduced subjectivity in his assessments. With the detailed assessment rubric, students were able to view their achievement in terms of clear objectives. This removed much of the "mystery" and anxiety in students' minds about how their performance was assessed. It also reduced ill feeling and disputes that resulted from low ratings. Students also became more aware of their impact on co-actors in dramatic production whom they supported, and were supported by. Finally, they had the responsibility of evaluating their own achievement.

Group Participation.   As one aim of cooperative learning activities during sixth-grade social studies, Ms. Hu sought to have students develop social, affective, and cognitive skills by working together effectively to complete assigned tasks. Early on, she engaged the students in developing a rubric for participation in the group and contribution to the task. She had several objectives in mind, so she began with an explanation of those objectives before soliciting others from the class. Her objectives included: bringing ideas and resources to the group; leading out when appropriate; deferring appropriately to group decisions; following others constructively when called for; encouraging peers to contribute their best efforts; reinforcing peers for their work; and helping to resolve differences equitably.

Ms. Hu realized that she wouldn't be able to assess each student reliably on each of these components for the same task. Overcoming the temptation to dispense with formal assessment plans and "wing it," she thought of several ways to fulfill her need. She could select just two or three behaviors to observe during the upcoming activity and save the rest for other occasions. She could engage the services of a colleague who shared her philosophy and practices of both cooperative learning and the importance of observational assessment. Being in an inclusionary school, where special education teachers frequently co-taught in the classroom with general education teachers and collaborative groups of students, she might divide the task among two or more of these teachers. Special education personnel typically have extensive training in observational techniques and could assist her in both rubric development and the actual observations.

Consideration of these possibilities brought other problems to Ms. Hu's attention. There were issues of reliability—effects of task difficulty, time frame, composition of groups, and certainly the question of interrater consistency of ratings. Scheduling difficulties removed the option of trading responsibilities with a colleague to gain a second opinion. Special education teachers did indeed conduct much observation, but usually to watch individual students in one or only a very few behaviors. There would need to be discussion and consensus about the interactive and somewhat holistic nature of this observation of social and affective behaviors for Context C objectives. Perhaps the most troublesome area was the question of validity—whether the assessment would indeed target those behaviors she believed were most important for developing interpersonal skills.

Because of these concerns, and in spite of the obstacles, Ms. Hu decided to prepare for the cooperative learning unit very carefully. The initial scoring rubric would include only a few of her aims for cooperative learning activity outcomes. Yet anticipating that things left out of the rubric will be left out of the performance, she promised herself that other criteria would be addressed during subsequent social studies lessons. She thus planned for a unit-to-unit evolution of the rubric.

Figure 9.7 shows her completed rubric. She determined that the rating form should be structured in a norm-referenced manner, reflecting the performance of these students and others she has had in recent years. Yet she appropriately sought as much domain clarity as possible by structuring the content dimensions as clearly as she could. By doing this and by using her district's outcomes-based standards of communicating effectively and working together productively, she narrowed her rating scales content to the areas shown in Figure 9.7.

Each student was given a copy of the rubric to use as a guide for self-assessment. Both the self-assessment and Ms. Hu's assessment became a part of each student's portfolio for student-guided parent-teacher conferences at mid-semester. Ms. Hu's plan was to have students critique the rubric after conclusion of the activity. The critiques and her own observations would probably lead to modifications to improve the rubric for use at another time.

FIGURE 9.7   Rating Form for a Cooperative Learning Activity.

Directions: For each aspect of student participation, circle the numeral that best represents the student's behavior in comparison with other students who have engaged in these kinds of cooperative learning activities. To obtain the total score, add the five circled numbers.

Behavior:	Poor		Fair		Good		Outstanding	
Leadership of Group	0	1	2		3		4	5
Followership Within Group	0	1	2	3	4		5	6
Contribution of Ideas	0	1	2	3	4	5	6	7
Encouragement of Others' Efforts	0	1		2		3	4	5
Resolution of Differences	0		1		2		3	4

Total =

Comments:

Two Potentially Useful Suggestions

Much attention has been given to the one major rule for evaluating performance—identify the criteria and be ready to observe them while the performance is under way. Two other suggestions can be offered for occasional use. One is to electronically record the performance. If a summative assessment is particularly important, then being able to view the performance, or parts of it, more than once may enable the teacher to make better judgments. If the assessment is serving a formative purpose, then viewing the recording can often help the student to improve. This formative use of recorded performances has enormous potential in subject areas such as athletics, speech, music, and theater.

The other suggestion is to use multiple raters of performance when the decision is especially important. Actually, this is commonplace in many kinds of contests. Multiple judges in the final rounds of debate tournaments, 4-H events, and swim meets are more the rule than the exception. However, in school settings, it is often impractical. It might be noted that if performances are electronically recorded, the problem of securing multiple raters is often lessened because each can work on scoring when it is convenient.

An additional situation in which multiple raters are practical (even when the decision to be made concerning the measurement is not unusually important) is the previously noted instructional value of peer ratings. It is common practice in speech, debate, and driver education class, for example, to have students critique each other's performance. The purpose is not only to provide constructive feedback to the performer, it is also to sensitize student raters to the important features of the task.

MAXIMUM VERSUS TYPICAL PERFORMANCE

It is time to spiral back to the distinction between what a student *can do* under conditions that produce maximum effort and what the person ordinarily *does do* under typical conditions. In performance assessment, the distinction may be very important because people don't consistently perform at their best. Several issues enter into considerations of whether to address students' maximum performance or their typical performance. Let's examine some examples that highlight some of the issues. We will then relate the topic to CAP.

Examples.   Consider first an omelet-making performance test. The teacher might reason that students who decide to make omelets in everyday situations will be motivated to do a good job. Who, after all, enjoys eating a bad omelet? Hence, it isn't necessary to distinguish between students' maximum efforts and their typical efforts; the two will not differ sharply. The teacher needn't worry about assessing omelet making under typical conditions.

Consider next the proper use of safety goggles in a shop class. The teacher would reason that students who use power equipment in everyday situations will often be tempted to take shortcuts that can have dire consequences. Therefore, the distinction between students' maximum efforts and their typical performance is important, and the two may differ greatly. The teacher would want to assess students' typical use of the safety goggles under work conditions as commonplace as can be arranged. Fortunately, as long as students are in the class, the instructor can observe their typical behavior; therefore, assessment of this typical performance is practical.

Finally, consider the teacher of music appreciation whose expansive developmental objective was:

1. Appreciates music.
   1.1 Orients ears toward source of music.
   1.2 Does not chat during concert.
   1.3 Spends own money and time attending concerts voluntarily.
   1.4 Checks tapes out of library.
   1.5 Discusses content of major works and own reactions to them.

Achievement of this objective, like most affective and social ones, is easily faked. The teacher might reason that some students will not develop much appreciation, but will go through the motions to satisfy the course requirements. However, because it would be impractical to assess typical performance and because no catastrophic consequences would result if a student failed to appreciate music, the teacher might well decide not to target typical performance for grading purposes.

Another reason a teacher may wisely decide to neglect assessment of this important aim for grading reflects the potential for assessment to become perverted. For example, if students discover that they are being graded on the number of tapes they check out of the library, many will start checking out large numbers without listening to them. Librarians will be burdened, patrons who want the tapes will be unable to secure them, and the grading practice will be invalid. This scenario illustrates the issue behind the admonition: *Do not let indicants become the students' objectives.* Checking out items is a useful indicant of appreciation *only* if it is measured under typical conditions. The moment it is measured under maximum conditions—as it would be if it were to be used for grading—it ceases to be a credible indicant.

Yet for *program evaluation,* one might be interested in using several such indicants. If the school is evaluating the music education *program* rather than individual students, then students probably wouldn't be motived to fake. In this context, anonymous survey items (e.g., "Did this course give you a greater appreciation of music?") would probably be even more useful than the performance indicants.

Where Does CAP Fit In?   It is useful to consider the assessment of typical performance from the perspective of CAP. Context A material is vitally important. This is the kind of typical behavior that teachers should feel *compelled* to access when it is possible to do so, even if doing so is awkward.

In Context B subject matter, teachers can best take a "the more the better" stance. Where one can assess student achievement of typical performance objectives, one should; where it is impractical to do so well, one needn't be compulsive. This flexibility results from the fact that Context B explicit developmental objectives aren't essential.

Similarly, Context C material isn't vital; hence, one needn't feel compelled to assess every aspect of its typical performance. Moreover, as just illustrated for music appreciation, the very act of assessing certain indicants of expansive developmental objectives can lead to undesirable consequences. In such cases, it seems a lesser evil to neglect (for grading purposes) the assessment of such objectives.

DIRECTIONS AND PROCEDURES FOR ASSESSING PERFORMANCE

Instructions should inform examinees of the things that would enable an expert in the task who is not familiar with the teaching and testing conditions to achieve an excellent rating. More specifically, directions ordinarily are designed to inform examinees of the following:

- The conditions under which they are to work, such as time limits, and allowable aids (e.g., tools, instruments, and references)
- The criteria that will be used to assess the performance
- The relative weight of various aspects of a performance task or the relative weight of various performance tasks

Beyond that, the directions that accompany performance measures should depend on the nature of the task. Measures of maximum effort in noninteractive tasks ordinarily present no special problems. As is true of most tests, the instructions should, in addition to these bulleted items, inform examinees as to when they will be assessed.

We now turn to instructions for the more challenging kinds of performance assessment, measures of typical performance and assessment of interactive performances.

Measures of Typical Performance

Assessments of typical performance present special problems. If examinees are to be assessed when they are performing as they most typically function, then they must *not know when their performance is being observed.* If, for example, an instructor were to inform physical education students (even unintentionally by an instructor's action such as carrying a clipboard) when they will be rated on being good sports, then the performance assessed wouldn't be one of typical behavior; it would shift to one of maximum behavior.

It often is best to inform students *how* typical performance will be assessed but *not when* it will be assessed. An example of formal appraisal of typical performance would be an elementary teacher's statement that each pupil will be rated on six different occasions for seat posture *when students aren't necessarily expecting them.* The teacher might then make a point of systematically rating children's posture at their desks on three different days at diverse times of day while the class is engaged in dissimilar kinds of desk work. Additional systematic observation might be planned during a film, as the class takes a test, and during a class discussion. This would provide a formal assessment of typical sitting posture that is good in both realism and content sampling. A single observation, no matter how authentic, couldn't provide a reliable assessment.

Another example is observation of a student's typical interpersonal behavior (as distinct from best-manners performance) in class discussions. A teacher might systematically rate each pupil several times. Students would be kept ignorant of when they were to be observed.

These examples accentuate an important point. In both cases, the teacher rates each student *several times in diverse settings.* In the second (and harder) case, the teacher might resolve to rate each participant's first contribution on a certain day. This protects against the tendency for raters to choose to rate those occasions in which a student's behavior conforms to the rater's preconceptions. Being *systematic* guards against such biased, unnecessarily opportunistic observations.

Another example of formal and systematic observation of typical behavior concerns a shop teacher who wisely makes a point of always glancing up when a power tool is switched on to see if the user is using appropriate safety equipment. The instructor's motives are fourfold. First is accident prevention; when a violation of the safety rule occurs, it is promptly halted. Next, offending students will know that the errant behavior was observed and may learn from the resulting censure. Third, the teacher probably would use the results for grading. Finally, the instructor would expect the immediate corrections or reprimands of errant students to foster vicarious observational learning in other class members.

These examples of posture, interpersonal behavior, and use of safety equipment illustrate systematic and formal observation of typical performance. In each of these cases, students should know ahead of time how they are going to be assessed.

In other circumstances, observation cannot be fully anticipated or planned; that is, it has to be opportunistic. For instance, pupils' sneezing and mouth-covering behavior can only be observed when the child sneezes. For a fortunate few, it may never be observable by the teacher; for others, numerous observation opportunities occur.

Another example of opportunistic observation concerns driver education and the cautious reactions appropriate when a Frisbee lands in the street ahead of the car the student is driving. What directions should be given concerning such observation? Students can know that they will be observed, rated, and graded if and when opportunity to observe cautionary actions occurs. Moreover, transfer of learning is expected. Instructions might have touched on balls rolling out from behind parked cars and on animals often being pursued by children, but it probably would not have addressed other items. Needless to say, the lack of student-to-student comparability will limit the reliability of such measures. (However, remember simulation; that would be an excellent way to assess targeted behaviors such as this more systematically and less opportunistically.)

When a behavior can only be observed opportunistically, we don't condemn the use of opportunistic observations. Protection against systematic bias in selection of episodes can be provided by resolving to observe and record *every* episode of relevant behavior that opportunity presents.

Interactive Performance Measures

Performances that interact with the examiner present valuable opportunities to probe and delve into selected aspects of achievement in a manner *tailored to the particular examinee.* For example, a major advantage of oral tests over essays is the examiner's ability to pose follow-up questions. That is, oral tests typically are interactive and branching. A teacher conducting one in conversational Spanish might upon hearing a student use a wrong verb act surprised and exclaim in Spanish, "Really! He did *what*? Remarkable!"

Such follow-up questions or clues reveal whether the student can adeptly correct the error with minimal damage or, with more directed probing and hints, correct the error with somewhat more damage to the student's ratings. Successive "customized" questions or tasks also enable the examiner to verify whether a student really has a serious misconception or merely misspoke.

Yet another variety of follow-up task is illustrated by a first-aid test one of us witnessed. The task was to stop severe bleeding of a deep wound on the upper arm. The rubric contained the desired behaviors of (a) applying direct pressure on the wound, (b) elevating the wounded limb, and (c) applying pressure on an "up limb" pressure point. The examinee carefully, slowly, and neatly bandaged the wound loosely without doing any of the desired things. At this point, the examiner wondered if the student had misunderstood the directions. So a follow-up situation was created on the spot in which the victim had a severed foot; this situation was described graphically in very simple language. Again the examinee slowly provided a neat, loose covering to the "truncated" lower leg. The individualized follow-up task greatly enhanced the examiner's confidence in failing the examinee!

The directions for these kinds of interactive performance measures should reassure examinees that follow-up questioning or tasks are sometimes used only to check their confidence in a correct answer. They should also explain that subsequent questions or tasks provide an opportunity to recover partial credit from mistakes.

PROGRAM EVALUATION

We have briefly touched upon the topic of program evaluation in several places of the book so far. We now shall take a slightly closer look at the topic.

As we know, student evaluation concerns using data to judge the status of individual pupils. In contrast, **program evaluation,** which is also known as **outcomes assessment,** involves the use of data to judge the adequacy of courses, programs, and curricula for students *in-general.* Although this book's focus is directly on student assessment, it will be useful to put it in perspective by briefly contrasting it with program assessment. As we do this, it will be helpful to review the contrast between long- and short-term objectives and the contrast between objectives addressing maximum behavior and those concerning typical behavior.

In student assessment, we have seen that assessment of individuals' maximum behavior is relatively easy, whereas assessing their typical behavior (e.g., in driving safety or ethics in interpersonal relationships) for grading purposes is much more challenging. Unless we are very careful, some of these highly important typical-behavior objectives may go unassessed. Although we often can't adequately grade individual students on their safe driving practices, some such instructional targets are of *fundamental* importance. Schools, therefore, need to assess *curricular* effectiveness in helping students *collectively* achieve typical-performance learning through *program evaluation.* Before delving into this more fully, let's identify a similar challenge.

Virtually all of our attention to student assessment has involved **short-term objectives;** that is, objectives that can be achieved and assessed while the student is still in the class (or at least in the school). **Long-term objectives,** by contrast, aren't attained while students are in a class or a school. Examples of long-term objectives involve aspects of parenting, citizenship, avoidance of alcohol misuse, management of a family budget, and lifelong appreciation and support of the arts. Although assessment of such long-term objectives for grading purposes is impossible because they aren't achieved or exhibited until after grades are awarded, these include some *very* important topics that we should not neglect! Here, too, program evaluation offers a remedy.

The simultaneous consideration of short-term vs. long-term aims and of maximum performance vs. typical performance yields four kinds of instructional objectives relevant to student evaluation and four corresponding aims germane to program evaluation. These are shown in Figure 9.8.

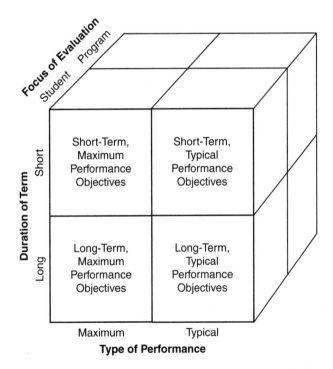

FIGURE 9.8   Four Kinds of Instructional Objectives in Student and Program Evaluation.

The appropriate kind of assessment technique depends in part on which of these eight kinds of evaluation is being conducted.

In student assessment, we have found that the three-step decision-making rule is extremely helpful in selecting assessment methods for classroom situations involving achievement of *short-term, maximum-behavior objectives*. Major techniques for assessing achievement of many objectives for *programs* also can be grouped into the three sieve categories of objective tests, essay and other product assessment, and performance assessment.

Additional techniques that can be used to gather credible information about *program* effectiveness via *survey* research include:

- Anonymous self-reports by students about their typical behaviors
- Reports by others (e.g., parents) about students' typical behaviors
- Anonymous alumni self-reports about their maximal skills and competencies and about their typical behaviors

In *anonymous* self-report surveys designed to assess programs, students aren't motivated to falsify. For example, we noted for music appreciation that for program evaluation anonymous self-report survey items (e.g., "Did this course give you a greater appreciation of music?") could be very useful as indicants of typical status. Likewise, in anonymous surveys of alumni, people have no motive to fake. Under such conditions, self-report (e.g., "Have you attended a concert during the past six months?") can be persuasive. Although survey research is beyond the scope of this book, it is important for educators to realize that it offers valuable tools for assessing student attainment of typical-behavior objectives and long-term objectives.

In program evaluation, we need not forsake assessment of *any* important group of objectives; such neglect tends to distort evaluation results and to have adverse consequences on programs. *Long-term and typical-behavior educational outcomes shouldn't be ignored just because they may not be practical to assess for grading purposes.* Their attainment *can* be assessed for programs, and it should be.

CHAPTER RECAP

Performance assessment is based on observation and judgment (Arter, 1999). It enables teachers to assess many important outcomes that are not adequately measured by other means. Being able to execute a performance differs from being able to plan it or to evaluate how well someone else performs it. If we want to know if a person can play a given selection of music, pitch a baseball, or speak French, the only way to find out is to have the person do it. It may be inconvenient, but it is the only suitable way to assess achievement of such objectives.

Performance tests are best for assessing attainment of objectives that require witnessing the performance rather than by inferring it by examining its results. For example, if we want to know how well a person can fly-cast, we learn much more by watching several casts than by counting the day's catch (which is influenced by other factors). Yet performance assessment isn't the panacea that some enthusiasts seem to think it is. An assessment system that was predominantly performance oriented would have enormous practical, technical, and financial obstacles (Madaus & O'Dwyer, 1999).

Performance measures tend to be much less reliable and much less economical than objective tests. For this reason, they ordinarily should be used only when they clearly provide a superior way of assessing objectives. Because the reliability of performance measures is limited, its enhancement is important. Establishing clear marking criteria helps greatly. Multiple measures of a repeatable, uniform performance, such as a (Context A) task of counting up to five objects aloud or a (Context B) gymnastics feat, improves reliability. For less explicitly controlled tasks, ratings from multiple settings and varied circumstances are necessary to adequately sample the Context C domains. Finally, use of multiple raters also enhances reliability.

Skillful use of performance measures involves two related components. The directions and the performance tasks have to be devised so as to elicit a realistic sample of the behavior of interest. This is achieved with thoughtful and careful crafting of the task to be tested and the situations in which it will be observed. Then the performance needs to be assessed in a way that can produce reliable ratings. The appropriate use of performance measures to supplement paper-pencil and product assessment not only provides for balanced student evaluation but also enhances instruction by communicating to students the relative importance of various educational objectives.

Program evaluation, or outcomes assessment, is employed to determine adequacy of courses, programs, and curricula in general. Student attainment of long-term objectives and typical-performance objectives can be assessed with a number of techniques, including survey research.

SECURING, MANAGING, USING, AND REPORTING ASSESSMENT INFORMATION

EDITING, PRODUCING, ADMINISTERING, SCORING, ANALYZING, AND STORING TEACHER-MADE TESTS

CHAPTER OVERVIEW

FROM TEST ITEMS TO A FINISHED TEST

ADMINISTERING TESTS

DEALING WITH GUESSING

MAKING SCORING EASY AND ACCURATE

TEASING INFORMATION OUT OF ITEM-BY-ITEM DATA

STORING AND RETRIEVING TEST QUESTIONS

KEY TERMS

"mark every item" directions
item analysis
differentiation index
proportion passing (*p*-value)

Earlier chapters have focused on planning assessment methods and developing valid tasks to assess student achievement of instructional aims. We shall now address issues of assembling, editing, producing, administering, scoring, analyzing, and storing teacher-made tests. Some of the topics apply equally well to paper-pencil tests and to product and performance assessments, whereas others are relevant to only some kinds of assessment tasks.

ASSEMBLING CLASSROOM TESTS

After a teacher creates or compiles the items or performance tasks necessary to satisfy his or her table of specifications, the questions or tasks have to be sequenced into a well-designed test that includes appropriate directions. These final touches contribute significantly to the overall quality of the measure and are well worth the time and effort they require.

Organizing the Mixed Test.   Tests that foster and assess student learning across a broad spectrum of mental processes often consist of more than one item type. There is no virtue, however, in systematically using each major item type in a test; just as a surgeon or carpenter should not feel compelled to use every available tool for any one operation or job, the teacher should use only those item types that are most appropriate. Most tests also contain questions that vary in difficulty. This section concerns the organization of tests that contain items of mixed types, difficulty, or subject matter.

Organizing by Item Type.   Ordinarily, the main organizational feature is item type. Thus, all of the questions of a given kind are grouped together and accompanied by appropriate directions (Millman & Greene, 1989). The simpler item types are located early in the test to ensure that examinees have time to attempt all items that they would probably have the least need to ponder. These criteria give rise to the following rules.

- If completion, short answer, and/or alternate-choice items are used, their separate section(s) should precede the rest of the test, in any order.
- If multiple-choice and/or matching items are used, their separate section(s) should come next, in either order.
- If interpretive exercises are used, they usually should be next, regardless of item type. However, short interpretive exercises consisting entirely of only a few multiple-choice items may be embedded within multiple-choice sections.
- If essays and/or other products are used, they should appear in the last section.

Organizing by Difficulty.   In organizing tests, item difficulty is subordinate to item type. If the items within each item type differ in difficulty, the rule is to arrange them from easiest to hardest (Millman & Greene, 1989). However, a teacher usually doesn't know the exact item difficulty, so the rule is applied by estimating item difficulties. Although it is not vital that item order closely parallel item difficulty, it is nice for the first few items within each section to be relatively easy so that examinees can get off to a secure start. It is also desirable for any items that are clearly the most difficult to come at the end of their respective sections in order to minimize the possible impact of discouragement on student effort.

Most educators want most tests to measure power more than speed. (Yet, as we'll see later, some degree of speed is needed for logistical reasons.) Therefore, test makers often seek to minimize impact of speed. If a test is at all speeded (i.e., if any examinees lack sufficient time to attempt all items), then placement of the hardest items at the end of the test minimizes the impact of speed. This, of course, is most possible when the test consists of only one item type. Examinees who lack the time to attempt the last few questions are penalized the least if unattempted items are the ones they would have had the poorest chance of answering correctly.

Organizing by Content or Objectives.   It is rarely useful to organize tests by content or instructional aims. Individual matching exercises, however, should be homogeneous in subject matter.

Providing Appropriate General Directions.   Tests should open with general instructions. These directions should tell how much total working time is available. They should also indicate how and where students are to mark their answers or perform their tasks. If separate answer sheets are used, examinees should be reminded to put their names on them. They need to be cautioned to take particular care in recording their responses on the answer sheet. They also should be reminded to look over their papers when finished to locate any items that they may have intended to mark but overlooked. Finally, general instructions often should instruct examinees who have questions to remain at their desks and let the teacher come to them.

The general directions should bring to the examinees' attention any peculiar features of the test. Any unusual provisions (e.g., allowing students to use their notes) should be explained in the directions and made known to students at the beginning of the unit to enable them to prepare appropriately. Directions should indicate which, if any, resource materials (e.g., dictionaries) and tools (e.g., hand calculators) may be used; this, too, should be known by students in advance. This kind of prior knowledge not only reduces anxiety, but also serves to guide student effort.

As an example, suppose a science teacher who does not value formula memorization decides to write all the needed ones (and perhaps some additional formulas that will *not* be needed to ensure that students can identify the relevant ones) on the board. If the teacher kept this intent secret, then some students would devote study time to memorizing formulas rather than to practicing their use. Assessment power is better harnessed by telling students ahead of time what they do and do not need to memorize.

Finally, the directions should address the issue of guessing. Students should be informed that it is wise to guess when they can do so "intelligently," that is, with partial knowledge. They also should be told whether it is in their best interest to guess on items about which they know nothing. This topic will be addressed later in the chapter.

The general directions discussed here apply to the entire test. Additional directions are necessary whenever there is a change of item type. Chapters 6 through 9 provided information about appropriate directions for each major item type.

EDITING THE FINAL TEST

After the questions have been ordered, the entire test should be subjected to a final round of editing. The main purpose of editing at this point is to identify items that provide answers or clues to other items. Previous editing was focused at the item level; the probability is great that some questions will clue others. Therefore, editing is needed to eliminate interitem clueing.

The final round of editing should also attend to issues of balance. Whereas item writing and selection are focused on adequacy of individual items, when a group of items of high individual quality are assembled, various kinds of imbalance can result. Although adherence to a test plan will have prevented much imbalance of subject matter, few plans are detailed enough to prevent all of it. For example, a mechanics of expression quiz may specify three items on comma usage but not specify *which* comma uses. This might result in a quiz having all three items on commas in series but none on other uses. The teacher who notices this in the final editing would probably replace two items with others.

Another kind of balance concerns stereotyping people by such traits as gender, ethnic group, or age. For example, an arithmetic application test might have a number of story problems. Are the boys usually cast with jobs such as newspaper delivery and grocery store sacking, while the girls baby-sit? Or, has the teacher leaned over backward to avoid this to the point of creating reverse stereotyping? A tally of traditional versus nontraditional portrayals will help achieve balance. At the same time, this final check provides a last chance to ensure that one has not overused Anglo names or slipped into use of outdated gender-limiting occupational titles such as "policeman" or "stewardess."

Yet another kind of balance concerns the frequency and order of response options. The key to objective items should be developed *at this time* in order to tally the frequency with which various responses are used. For example, in a true-false section, the number of true and false answers should be about equal; if serious imbalance is found, a few items can be altered or replaced.

Recall that each multiple-choice option should be keyed roughly the same number of times. Suppose a tally of 30 four-option, multiple-choice questions showed 4 A, 9 B, 11 C, and 6 D answers. This imbalance is great enough to be a concern, especially since test-wise examinees will, when in doubt, gravitate toward the middle options. The teacher should seek ways to alter some of the items keyed B and C into items keyed A and D. After modifying several, suppose the resulting tally is 6 A, 8 B, 7 C, and 9 D answers. This is close enough to equal use of options. In addition to balance of options, the sequence of keyed response options should vary randomly.

Some textbooks suggest asking a colleague to critique one's tests *without* providing the key. The process of having to examine each question carefully enough to determine the answer will elicit more careful scrutiny and helpful feedback than if the key were available for "peeking." Most teachers do not find it practical to impose on a colleague to check their tests; nor are they eager to incur the obligation of reciprocating. However, those who do typically find that many potential problems can be corrected or avoided before the test is put to use; moreover, the teachers offering the service often get some ideas for their own use.

REPRODUCING CLASSROOM TESTS

Written tests should almost always be reproduced on paper (unless they are to be administered by computer). Writing a test on the chalkboard is rarely adequate. Likewise, dictating objective tests is not acceptable, even for brief true-false, completion, or short-answer questions. (Spelling tests are an exception; dictation is often the best way to present items.)

Once questions have been arranged into the desired order, they need to be laid out page by page. When doing so, items should never be split between two pages nor should any set of items in a matching or interpretive exercise be divided.

One should use a consistent style. Figure 7.1 on page 143, for example, illustrated some acceptable ways of formatting multiple-choice items. Although one method may be about as good as another, students should not be subjected to shifts in style.

A decision must be made as to whether test copies are to be handwritten, typed, or computer printed. When might each be best? The master copy of short quizzes or tests—such as those that will fit nicely on one side of one sheet of paper—can be handwritten (although they need not be).

This is especially attractive at the elementary school level, where quizzes tend to be quite short and where teachers often have extremely legible handwriting. Longer objective tests should almost always be keyboarded.

If the teacher maintains a computerized item file, the creation of a test is greatly simplified and does not have to be rekeyboarded. Page layout and formatting are also much easier with word processing. Moreover, the final round(s) of editing also can serve as proofreading. As more teachers use personal computers for word processing and item banking, these methods are becoming the dominant ways by which master copies of teacher-made tests are prepared. More discussion on this topic will be included later in the chapter.

The master copy should be neat, uncrowded, and legible. Ease of reading also can be enhanced by propitious use of spacing (Dillman, 2000). Let's identify for multiple-choice items some of the things that ease the burden of reading. (These will be illustrated explicitly in Figure 13.2 on page 342.)

- If stems are underhung, the items are better set off one from another.
- A second-level underhang for options helps to separate options from each other.
- Continuous single-spacing between the stem and options and among options shows that the parts of the multiple-choice item go together.
- A blank line between successive items helps to identify the separateness of each item.
- Double-column formatting makes reading easier (and saves paper).

Examinees have enough to contend with in test-taking without having to decipher nearly illegible or poorly spaced material. They should be free to focus their attention on the test content. Even if the master copy is neat and legible, problems can occur in its reproduction. For example, copy-machine operators need to ensure that the glass cover is clean and adjust the machine as needed. Regardless of the method of reproduction, an inexpert or careless operator can turn a neat, clean original into an unattractive, illegible copy.

As a precaution, teachers should double check their master copy of the test before printing and check the reproduced copies before distributing them. Instances have occurred where the keyed copy was duplicated inadvertently and handed out to examinees! (Alas, to his great embarrassment, it happened recently to one of your authors.)

ADMINISTERING TESTS

Proper administration of either a teacher-made or a published test requires more than a casual observer might notice. One should attend to several important considerations even before examinees arrive. Perhaps the most obvious is providing an adequate, comfortable working space. Examinees need room to lay out the tests and answer sheets. Desks or tables are preferable, but armchairs can suffice when necessary. Seating for examinees should be sufficiently spaced so that it would be difficult and noticeable—not easy and tempting—to look at another's answer sheet.

Other needs to which one should attend before the test include provision for reasonable climate control, adequate lighting, freedom from glaring light, the condition of the work surface, and insulation from interruption or excessive noise. Hence, one should set the thermostat (if the room has one) well ahead of time. The shades should be checked to ensure that sunlight doesn't shine in students' eyes or on their desks. If regulations permit, the teacher might turn off intercommunication with the office or send a note asking that interruptions during the test be minimized. A notice on the classroom door announcing the test helps to minimize interruptions. Such a notice might read, "TESTING IN PROGRESS: Please come back later."

By way of advance preparation of students for testing, teachers can do several things to prevent problems of unauthorized help. The first and best step may be the one most overlooked. In earlier discussions about transfer of learning, complex thinking, and best effort, we stressed the importance of letting students in on what we expect of them. Testing is an area in which teachers need to *educate students about academic honesty.* It is good to create opportunities *before test time* to instruct students about honesty in taking tests, doing individual assignments, and so on. One can explain to students *why tests are important, how test information is used* to facilitate their development, and that testing is an *individual* endeavor. Depending on the age and sophistication of the group, teachers might elaborate on negative long-term effects of test dishonesty and students' own positive use of information from their tests.

Advanced preparation of students for testing should also address such things as necessary supplies, the test date, the test duration, and the test-taking strategy. Instruction in test-taking skills will, of course, be intended to be applicable to a wide variety of classroom and published tests. It may address such issues as reduction of test anxiety, test wiseness concerning features such as those addressed in Chapters 6 and 7, careful reading of test directions, preparation, pacing, and answer-changing. If test-taking strategies that are unrelated to the content domain being assessed either enhance or hamper "test performance, these strategies and the implications should be explained to all test takers before the test is administered" (AERA, 1999, p. 116).

THINKING CAP EXERCISE 10.1   ???

After you finish reading the directions to a published or teacher-made test and ask, "Are there any questions?" a student asks, "If I change my mind about the answer to a multiple-choice question, should I change my answer?" How would you answer?

KEY TO THINKING CAP EXERCISE 10.1
Most teachers would answer something like, "No. It is usually better to stick with your first impression." *This answer is wrong*!

Much research over seven decades has demonstrated the benefits of mindfully changing answers to objective items. A changed answer is about twice as likely to gain a point as to lose one (Mueller & Wasser, 1977). This has also been found true of computerized tests (Vispoel, 2000). Yet the myth is robust, perhaps because of selective recall of anecdotal evidence (Hanna, 1989). Examinees may be more apt to remember bad changes and forget good ones.

Once students are assembled, necessary supplies (e.g., scratch paper, pencils, and resources such as dictionaries and tools such as rulers) may need to be distributed. Such activities should be completed before distribution of test questions and answer sheets. If adequate preparations and announcements have been made beforehand regarding what to bring and what may be used, much less confusion and delay are likely to occur at the time of the test.

As students are about to start the test, they should be helped to feel relaxed, yet serious. Care should be taken to avoid making the experience any more threatening than necessary. At the same time, a serious tone should be sounded, encouraging students to work hard and to do their best.

Teachers should refrain from delivering announcements, assigning homework, or making comments unrelated to the test. This includes interjections of attempted humor or witticism, even if they are meant to lighten the atmosphere. Such humor may disrupt some examinees' focus and increase their anxiety.

A major job of the examiner is to ensure that each student does his or her own work—that no cheating occurs. This task has multiple prongs:

- Education before testing
- Test security
- Watchfulness during testing
- Appropriately reacting to academic dishonesty if it is detected

Concerning education, cheating needs to be defined as an unethical form of falsification or lying. Students need to understand that it is unacceptable and will be censured. Students, especially younger ones, need help in *clarifying the concept with a variety of examples* of cheating and noncheating behaviors. The detail, of course, should increase with age. At the primary level, looking at another's paper or whispering answers may be key illustrations. By high school, the concept should be enlarged to include such forms of academic dishonesty as purchase of ready-made reports, failing to give proper credit to sources, and failure to use quotation marks where they are appropriate.

Tests and their keys should be kept under lock and key. As more teachers store their tests on hard drives, CDs, or disks, corresponding theft-prevention security measures are needed. Electronic protection of computer files is also necessary.

Concerning attentiveness, several procedures are useful in preventing cheating:

- Being alert during the test
- Adequately spacing desks or chairs
- Requiring desks to be cleared of items not used in the test
- Having standing, posted classroom rules that prohibit all forms of communication (e.g., looking; talking; passing messages by use of paper, infrared beams, radio signals, hand or vocal signals, etc.) during tests

When supervising a test, one should not continuously wander unnecessarily around the room or stand by an examinee's desk looking at her or his paper. At best, this distracts students; at worst, it creates anxiety, causing examinees to think the teacher suspects them of cheating. The idea is to be attentive yet unobtrusive.

The most important thing teachers can do to prevent cheating *during* a test is to be *alert*. The teacher should sit or stand in a place where each student's head is visible; if this is not possible, frequent movement helps in monitoring the entire class. It is tempting to use testing time to do other things such as mark assignments or clean the closet. Some such activities distract examinees, and they all distract the teacher from the *primary duty of supervision.*

At a minimum, the teacher should glance up very frequently to scan the class. When an examinee is considering looking at another's paper, he or she usually first assesses the risk. When such a person glances up and sees an alert, attentive teacher in the front of the room, the examinee usually decides not to cheat.

If a teacher suspects a student of looking at another's paper, the best approach is usually to intensify surveillance of that individual. Most such examinees will glance up from time to time to see if the teacher is watching. When this happens, the teacher should *be looking directly at the examinee.* This may recur several times. If their eyes meet each time, the problem will usually be nipped in the bud, and no disciplinary problem will arise that requires overt confrontation or action.

In spite of reasonable precautions, a rare student will still cheat. In such cases, it is best *not* to disrupt the class with an emotionally charged scene in which the offender is humiliated and the teacher is perceived by other students as a hostile aggressor. Rather, the situation should ordinarily be handled later in private. It is extremely important for the examiner to be level-headed, clear, firm, and consistent in cases of cheating or suspected cheating. It can be helpful to generate a list of consequences from which an appropriate action may be selected for each individual situation.

Each statement made so far in this section applies to the administration of published instruments as much as to teacher-made ones. An observation that is especially relevant to published tests concerns unusual occurrences that may impact scores that would otherwise become a matter of record. For instance, a grand mal epileptic seizure during an aptitude test would invalidate the test for *all* persons present. Similarly, an earthquake almost severe enough to prompt evacuation during an achievement test would invalidate the subtest in progress at the time. The examiner should ensure that notation of serious irregularity is made on any scores from such tests.

Another consideration that differs between published and classroom tests concerns the ability of the teacher to make announcements and corrections *related to the test.* This, of course, is taboo for published instruments because alteration of the controlled, uniform procedures would render the norm-referenced scores uninterpretable, hence, useless.

Regrettably, teacher-made tests sometimes have flaws, so some provision is needed for examinees to ask questions. Standing classroom practice should be established concerning what students are to do if they have questions during a *teacher-made* test. They should *not* speak up with their questions; such behavior not only causes interruptions but often clues other students. Nor should they be allowed to come to the teacher's desk; this creates traffic noise, obstructs the teacher's view of the class, wastes time standing in line, and might enable and tempt them to look at other students' answers. Students should remain in their seats and raise their hands.

Once the teacher comes to an examinee, the student should *whisper* the question. The teacher must decide whether the item is seriously flawed. If the student's question arises from "knowing too much" or spotting a flaw in the item, it should be answered. If the question reveals a typographic error of consequence, it should be corrected. If the question points out an ambiguity, it should be clarified. When the teacher decides to answer or clarify a question, the answer should be given to all students; a general announcement is preferable to having to double key or void items when they are later discussed in class. In such cases, the teacher should make a note to correct the flaw before reusing the item.

When the teacher decides that an answer to a student's question is not needed, the teacher might best whisper something to the effect of "I cannot answer that" or "The question is correct" and *nothing else.* By whispering this rather loudly, other students will observe that the student did not benefit from questioning. As a consequence, they will be less likely to ask inappropriate questions.

Many of the topics considered in this section concern various aspects of control of uniformity of testing conditions. Attention should be given to providing all students equal amounts of working time, equal *lack* of advance access to test content, and so on. In order to interpret students' test performances meaningfully, in either a domain- or norm-referenced manner, the tests must be *administered* and *scored* under *established conditions.*

SCORING TEACHER-MADE TESTS

Chapters 8 and 9 addressed issues and made recommendations for scoring essays, other kinds of products, and performances. This section addresses issues relevant to scoring objective tests.

Separate Answer Sheets.   Separate answer sheets can significantly reduce the labor of scoring objective tests. When older examinees take longer tests, much scoring time can be saved if the scorer does not have to flip through each student's test booklet to find answers. Of course, their use has no practical advantage unless a test or quiz exceeds one page in length. Figure 10.1 illustrates an answer sheet that was customized for a particular teacher-made test. Figure 10.2 provides an example of a more generic answer sheet that might be used for various multiple-choice tests consisting of 50 or fewer items having five or fewer options.

FIGURE 10.1   Sample Customized Answer Sheet.

Name: _____

Directions: Circle the T or the F for each true-false item.

1. T F	**5.** T F	**9.** T F
2. T F	**6.** T F	**10.** T F
3. T F	**7.** T F	**11.** T F
4. T F	**8.** T F	**12.** T F

Directions: Neatly write or print the word that best goes in each blank.

13. _____
14. _____
15. _____
16. _____
17. _____
18. _____

Directions: Circle the letter of the one best answer for each multiple-choice item.

19. A	B	C	D	E		**28.** A	B	C	D	
20. A	B	C				**29.** A	B	C		
21. A	B	C	D			**30.** A	B	C		
22. A	B	C	D	E		**31.** A	B	C	D	E
23. A	B	C	D			**32.** A	B	C	D	E
24. A	B	C	D			**33.** A	B	C	D	
25. A	B	C	D	E		**34.** A	B	C		
26. A	B	C	D	E		**35.** A	B	C	D	E
27. A	B	C	D	E						

FIGURE 10.2   Sample Generic Multiple-Choice Answer Sheet.

Name: _____

Instructions: Indicate your answer for each multiple-choice question by filling in the circle under the letter of the one best answer.

	A B C D E		A B C D E		A B C D E
1.	○ ○ ○ ○ ○	18.	○ ○ ○ ○ ○	34.	○ ○ ○ ○ ○
2.	○ ○ ○ ○ ○	19.	○ ○ ○ ○ ○	35.	○ ○ ○ ○ ○
3.	○ ○ ○ ○ ○	20.	○ ○ ○ ○ ○	36.	○ ○ ○ ○ ○
4.	○ ○ ○ ○ ○	21.	○ ○ ○ ○ ○	37.	○ ○ ○ ○ ○
5.	○ ○ ○ ○ ○	22.	○ ○ ○ ○ ○	38.	○ ○ ○ ○ ○
6.	○ ○ ○ ○ ○	23.	○ ○ ○ ○ ○	39.	○ ○ ○ ○ ○
7.	○ ○ ○ ○ ○	24.	○ ○ ○ ○ ○	40.	○ ○ ○ ○ ○
8.	○ ○ ○ ○ ○	25.	○ ○ ○ ○ ○	41.	○ ○ ○ ○ ○
9.	○ ○ ○ ○ ○	26.	○ ○ ○ ○ ○	42.	○ ○ ○ ○ ○
10.	○ ○ ○ ○ ○	27.	○ ○ ○ ○ ○	43.	○ ○ ○ ○ ○
11.	○ ○ ○ ○ ○	28.	○ ○ ○ ○ ○	44.	○ ○ ○ ○ ○
12.	○ ○ ○ ○ ○	29.	○ ○ ○ ○ ○	45.	○ ○ ○ ○ ○
13.	○ ○ ○ ○ ○	30.	○ ○ ○ ○ ○	46.	○ ○ ○ ○ ○
14.	○ ○ ○ ○ ○	31.	○ ○ ○ ○ ○	47.	○ ○ ○ ○ ○
15.	○ ○ ○ ○ ○	32.	○ ○ ○ ○ ○	48.	○ ○ ○ ○ ○
16.	○ ○ ○ ○ ○	33.	○ ○ ○ ○ ○	49.	○ ○ ○ ○ ○
17.	○ ○ ○ ○ ○			50.	○ ○ ○ ○ ○

Unfortunately, separate answer sheets increase the complexity of the examinee's task. Young children should not be expected to cope with them. A general rule might be that answer sheets should not be used below third grade; they should be used in third grade only with average or higher classes that have been well instructed and supervised in their use; they can ordinarily be used in fourth grade and above with appropriate instruction and supervision.

Accuracy of Scoring, Converting, and Recording. Recall that the defining characteristic of the objective item is the reliability with which it can be scored. Once a key has been made, a set of answer sheets can be scored with little or no need for subjective judgment. This is a major advantage of so-called objective questions. Yet the fact that they *can be* scored accurately does not ensure that they *will be.* The possibility of scoring error always exists.

The job of the teacher, clerk, or aide in scoring an objective test is to ensure complete accuracy of scoring. This job is made easier if the layout of the test or answer sheet is done with scoring in mind. For example, completion items are much easier to mark if the answers are written in a single column of blanks provided along the right-hand side of the test booklet or on a separate answer sheet, such as those shown in Figure 10.1, than if they are embedded in the questions. Another thing that makes scoring easier and more accurate is to avoid having students write or print letters. (Deciding among letters such as a, c, d, and e is a scorer's nightmare and encourages student quibbling over the results.) Rather, direct them to circle T or F or letters of multiple-choice options. Figures 10.1 and 10.2 demonstrate ways to render students' responses in order to score them rapidly and objectively.

Even if a test or answer sheet has been designed to make scoring easy and accurate, effort is still necessary to ensure accuracy. Some people make many clerical errors in counting the number of items marked correctly, and even careful scorers occasionally err. A place where errors can creep into scoring of published tests is in the conversion of raw scores into derived scores or percentage scores. Arithmetic mistakes can lead to serious errors.

A final place where errors can occur is in recording scores in a grade book. Entry of data in the wrong row and numeral transposition are especially common. It is worth noting that the use of computerized record keeping does *not,* in itself, provide assurance against these kinds of errors in data entry.

Teachers in some schools have access to optical scanners that can rapidly and (if properly used) accurately score special answer sheets (which usually are as generic as the one shown in Figure 10.2). When such answer media are used, students should be well instructed and supervised in properly and neatly using them. If coupled to computers, such technology can also generate the needed conversions and record the scores in grade rosters.

Confidentiality. Students have a right to privacy. If scoring of tests, assignments, projects, or other assessments is to be performed by clerks, teacher aides, or volunteers, it is ethically and legally important for the papers not to be identifiable. This can be accomplished by using code numbers.

Even more important, having students exchange identifiable test papers for grading or calling out identifiable scores for the teacher to record is highly questionable. In addition to the important ethical and legal aspects of such practices, they are also highly questionable on grounds of scoring accuracy and of use of student time.

DIRECTIONS REGARDING GUESSING

Test-taking strategies, such as guessing, self-pacing, changing answers, and checking one's work, can consistently impact scores. Because the use of such strategies is irrelevant to what a test is designed to assess, they undermine score validity. This section addresses the problem created by guessing. As you read about guessing, expect, seek, and pursue high-road transfer of learning to other test-taking practices.

The Problem.   Suppose Mary and Joan are taking an 80-item, four-option, multiple-choice test. Assume, too, that each confidently knows the answers to 44 of the questions and is wholly ignorant of the answers to the remaining 36. Further suppose (also a bit simplistically) that when they guess, average luck yields right answers exactly one-fourth of the time (because each item has four options). Clearly, Joan and Mary have the same knowledge and deserve the same final score.

Mary is timid and always leaves blank those questions for which she does not know the answer. In contrast, Joan is bold and never leaves an item unanswered; if she doesn't know it, she guesses. Because each knows 44 of the answers and is totally ignorant of the remaining 36, Mary will get 44 right and omit the remaining 36. Hence, her status is:

MARY:	NUMBER RIGHT	NUMBER WRONG	NUMBER OMITTED
	44	0	36

Joan will get correct the 44 items she knows and will guess on the remaining 36. With average luck, she will get one-quarter of these 36 right (i.e., another 9 items) and three-quarters wrong (i.e., 27). Thus, her number right will be 44 + 9, or 53:

JOAN:	NUMBER RIGHT	NUMBER WRONG	NUMBER OMITTED
	53	27	0

Mary and Joan deserve the same score because they know the same amount. However, if nothing is done to make their test-taking behavior more similar, they will receive different number-right scores. Moreover, Joan's advantage won't be limited to this test; it will be consistent over time and across different subject areas. The problem, then, is that student differences in personality or test-taking sophistication, which are not relevant to the subject matter domain the test is being used to measure, give some a systematic advantage over others of equal knowledge. This is a *major affront to fairness and to validity.*

Two Ways to Level the Playing Field.   Before considering workable solutions, let's dispense with a method that does *not* work. Some test makers try to get all students to act like Mary and to avoid guessing. To accomplish this, they instruct students *not* to guess. The directions can be strong (e.g., "Do not guess") or moderate (e.g., "Guess intelligently, but not wildly"). The fundamental problem with such directions is that some students violate them. The directive is not enforceable because students who miss an item may claim (often truthfully) that they really thought they knew the answer. Thus, such directions by themselves cannot solve the problem.

Fortunately, two approaches to obtaining justice are serviceable. They are to (a) provide directions that cause all students to adopt the same guessing strategy or (b) adjust the final scores in an effort to remove the benefit some examinees gain from guessing.

Solution via "Mark Every Item" Directions.   Directing all students to **mark every item**, guessing if necessary, is effective because it is to their advantage to conform. At the high-school level, such directions can read as follows:

> Your score will be the number correct; therefore, be sure to *mark every item.*

For younger examinees, the idea may require more explication. For example:

> Answer every question. If you know the answer to a question, mark it. If you do not know the answer, make the best guess you can. Your score will be the number of items that you answer right, so be sure to *mark every question.*

When students omit an item, the teacher can point out to them that they have penalized themselves. Thus, teacher and student are on the same side in trying to get students to follow the directions in the future, and pupils quickly learn to comply. People like Mary are thereby caused to adopt the more test-wise practice of people like Joan, and the injustice is righted.

This solution works well. Most educators perceive guessing as a behavior that is appropriate in some situations. They see tests as places where guessing is permissible and adaptive, and they see no significant risk of the transfer of guessing behaviors to situations in which it is inappropriate. They like the simplicity of number-right scoring. This method is the preferred solution of most authorities and of most classroom teachers.

Solution via Scoring Formula.   For the few teachers who have serious reservations about directing students to guess wildly, there is another solution, widely known as formula scoring. Few teachers find it attractive because it is relatively complex and time-consuming to use. Because few would be interested in learning more about it, we refer any who are to sources such as Hopkins (1998), Sax (1997), or Thorndike (1971). We will not address it further except to say that educators responsible for preparing high-school students for the PSAT and SAT need to learn about formula scoring in these tests' preparatory materials. Also, those few teachers who use highly speeded, selection-type tests need to learn about formula scoring.

Honesty of Test Directions.   Test directions should tell examinees honestly what to do to maximize their scores (Thorndike, 1971; AERA, 1999). The best strategy for maximizing scores obviously depends on how the test will be scored. Authors of both classroom and published tests sometimes fail to realize that their directions regarding guessing *must be compatible with their method of scoring.*

If scoring is to be done the easy and common way—for number correct—then the instructions must tell examinees to mark every item. In this case, it is unethical to urge avoidance of guessing because those who follow such directions will tend to answer fewer items correctly than they otherwise would. Educators should not reward violations of rules.

The goal of directions should be to provide all examinees with an equal opportunity to perform optimally (APA, 1985). A mismatch of directions and scoring procedures can give a systematic advantage to people like Joan and a consistent disadvantage to those like Mary. Yet many published tests instruct examinees to guess intelligently but not indiscriminately and then score for number right. This is unethical in teacher-made tests and in published ones alike.

ITEM FILES

As often emphasized, classroom assessments not only measure student achievement, they also shape it (Crooks, 1988). Therefore, creating sound classroom assessments is part of effective teaching (Sadler, 1983). To capitalize on the powerful tendency of students to learn what they believe will be assessed, teachers need to give primary emphasis to the learning outcomes they most value. These often concern complex mental processes and high-road transfer.

Developing Context C items that effectively measure deep learning requires effort, time, creativity, test-making skills, competence in the subject matter, and knowledge of learner characteristics. Even then, many of the questions we create prove to be flawed in one way or another. Because good items are so hard to come by, it behooves us to retain those that work well.

Retention of good items is best accomplished by use of a file of items for each unit. Then when it is time to build a new test, one can retrieve from the folder, card file, or computer file those items that have been used in the past. New questions need only be composed to fill in the cells of the table of specifications that are inadequately represented, or to make alternative items for purposes of test security, or to insert items that represent updated subject matter presented during instruction.

Retention and reuse of test items is very helpful. However, habitual reuse of whole tests is often ill advised, especially at the secondary level. For one thing, unit content often does and should change from year to year. For another, students can pass old tests along to younger students, enabling them to "study to the test." This risk would be greatest if teachers allowed students to keep their old tests. For Context C tests, test security is important.

Allowing students to keep their old tests is usually ill advised, even when tests are substantially revised from one year to the next (Terwilliger, 1989). There is little reason to let students retain their tests. After returning students' tests to go over the results and discuss various questions, the tests usually should be recollected at the end of that session.

Yet some students are eager to keep their tests for what they consider to be the best of reasons. What are their good-faith reasons? First, they may expect individual questions to be reused later in the course, such as on a final examination. Items in Context C tests should *not* be reused the same term. Each test is a mere sample of the subject matter domain; hence, we should do nothing (such as retesting with the same items) that encourages students to focus their study emphasis on what *happened* to be sampled in the past to the neglect of that which happened not to have been sampled.

Second, some students wish to restudy their errors, item-by-item, to correct their misconceptions. Yet in Context C, individual items are not essential and need not be remediated. Other material that happened not to have been sampled in the test could be studied just as advantageously. Moreover, test items are not designed to be study aids, and, being isolated and atomistic, they are not as effective in this respect as materials such as study guides that are developed with this aim in mind.

Third, some pupils may wish (or be expected) to bring tests home to report to their parents. This is not necessary; parental monitoring of Context C work can be done with scores and grades without full tests. Parents might better be encouraged to keep informed about their children's studies by receiving and examining curricular material. Parents will benefit from having these aspects of measurement explained via classroom newsletter, school handbook, or parent conferences, and they should, of course, feel welcome to inspect their children's tests at school and to ask questions during the parent-teacher conference.

As test items are used, a record of their effectiveness should be kept. Good items can be retained and poor ones should be discarded or revised. How does one assess item effectiveness? The next topic addresses one important dimension of this question.

ITEM ANALYSIS

It is possible to collect various kinds of data regarding the functioning of objective items, product items, and performance items. Some information concerns reliability (i.e., consistency), whereas other information concerns validity. Although later we will consider these topics from the perspective of total scores, let's direct attention now to data regarding individual items.

Some kinds of data analysis are based on advanced theoretical concepts and complex statistics. For example, item response theory has made significant contributions to assessment and opened up exciting new possibilities such as individualized, adaptive testing (Anastasi & Urbina, 1997). Important as such developments are to commercial test production, they have limited utility for classroom teachers.

Some kinds of data are reasonably collected for teacher-made tests; however, most are not. This section addresses only information that is easily secured for classroom tests. This restriction focuses attention on traditional item analysis applied to Context C assessment (and to those Context B measures that sample explicit domains not deemed important enough to master).

The Nature and Limitation of Item Analyses.   Traditional **item analysis** concerns the extent to which information for each item agrees with information obtained from the total measure to which it belongs. In other words, the kinds of item analysis considered in this chapter address the contribution of each question, product, or performance task to the total score's ability to measure differences in examinee status, that is, to differentiate among students in their achievement.

Recall that in Contexts C and B material, individual differences should be channeled into the achievement dimension. Thus, students ordinarily differ markedly in achievement, and tests are supposed to reveal differences among those having varying levels of achievement. The main point of traditional item analysis is to determine *how much each assessment task contributes to the differentiating power of the score.* Hence, the topic is pertinent *only* to tests that are designed to differentiate; traditional item analyses are *not* useful with Context A mastery tests.

The concern, then, is with how well the score of each item of a test agrees with the score of the whole test (or subtest). That is, how consistent is the score of each objective item, product, or performance with the total score? It is important to note that this question concerns reliability, not validity. Traditional item analysis data don't directly address the issue of whether items—or even whole tests—measure what they are intended to measure. For this reason, item analysis data should always take a back seat to *judgment about relevance to the intended purpose.*

What item analysis data *can* do is to *focus attention* on assessment tasks that function peculiarly. The resulting scrutiny often draws attention to validity issues that might otherwise escape notice.

A **differentiation index** is a measure of an item's agreement with the total score. This section introduces a kind of differentiation index that is useful to teachers and easy to calculate by hand. Its possible values range from −1.00 to +1.00; most of the actual items that teachers use have *p*-values that range from about 0.0 to about +0.5.

Conducting an Item Analysis by Hand.   At present, most teachers who want to use the information provided by item analysis will find it easiest to obtain it by hand. An added benefit from hand analysis is the opportunity to become more insightful about the data and its significance as information is analyzed and synthesized.

Following is a relatively simple way to *estimate* the correlation between each item's score and the total score. The steps will be more meaningful if the reader traces them through the examples that follow. Indeed, walking through the procedure may well prove instructive even for those who do have computer capability because the insights gained can enhance item-writing skills. We will first outline how item analyses are conducted with multiple-choice items; examples will then bridge the small gaps to other kinds of measures.

1. After scoring all the tests or answer sheets (using either number right or formula scoring), arrange them in order of scores from high to low.

2. Take out the highest 27% of the answer sheets (this fraction yields the most stable results). Round, if desired, to make the whole number more convenient for computing decimal fractions. For a typical classroom size, this rounded number might conveniently be 10. Take out exactly the same number of the lowest answer sheets. In the event of tied scores at the bottom score of the high group or the top score of the low group, *randomly* select from those tied scores the number of answer sheets needed.

3. For each item, tally the number of persons in the high group who responded to *each option.* Do the same for the low group.

4. Convert these tally marks for the respective groups into numerals. Then convert the numerals into decimal fractions by dividing each of these numbers by the number of persons in the high or low group.

5. Estimate an item's differentiation index by subtracting the decimal fraction of the low group that responded correctly from the decimal fraction of the high group that answered correctly. Do the same for each option of that item.

6. Estimate the **proportion passing (*p*-value)** expressed as a decimal fraction by computing the mean of the fraction of the two groups that answered correctly (i.e., add the two fractions and divide by 2).

To show how item analysis can be used with completion and alternate-choice items, we will first illustrate item analysis with some data from the State Capitals Test

FIGURE 10.3   Item Analysis for State Capitals Test.

	TALLY HIGH	TALLY LOW	FRACTION HIGH	FRACTION LOW	DIFFERENTIATION INDEX	P-VALUE
ID	8	5	.8	.5	.3	.65
SC	3	1	.3	.1	.2	.20
IL	8	4	.8	.4	.4	.60
CT	7	5	.7	.5	.2	.60
HI	10	10	1.0	1.0	.0	1.00
WA	6	4	.6	.4	.2	.50
NY	9	4	.9	.4	.5	.65
CO	10	9	1.0	.9	.1	.95
FL	7	4	.7	.4	.3	.55
NM	9	1	.9	.1	.8	.50

presented in Chapter 1. In reading the next section and studying Figure 10.3, please refer often to the six steps.

Assume that a class of 36 took the State Capitals Test. First, 27% of the 36 examinees is computed. The product, 9.72, is rounded to 10 for convenient calculation. Thus, the top 10 and the bottom 10 answer sheets are to be used. The number in each group answering each item correctly is tallied and converted into a decimal fraction. This is shown in Figure 10.3. (Recall that this was a completion test; therefore, there are no multiple options to compute as shown in step 3.)

For Idaho, 8 of the 10 high scorers got the item right, whereas 5 of the bottom 10 answered it correctly. Thus, 8 out of 10 converts into the decimal fraction .8; similarly, 5 out of 10 equals .5. The differences between these fractions (i.e., .3) is the *differentiation index* of the item for this particular class. The mean of the .8 and the .5 provides an estimate of the fraction of the *total* group that answered the item correctly $\frac{(.8 + .5)}{2} = .65$, as in step 6.

Notice that very easy items don't differentiate well. If everyone answers an item correctly, it does not differentiate at all between those who know more and those who know less. In this test, the least satisfactory items *from the perspective of revealing differences among examinees' achievement* were Hawaii with $p = 1.00$ and Colorado with $p = .95$. Likewise, if an item were missed by everyone in the high and low groups alike, it couldn't differentiate.

A perfect positively differentiating item would be answered correctly by everyone in the high group and by none in the low group. Thus, the fraction of the high group answering correctly would be 1.00 and the fraction of the low group would be 0.00; the differentiating index would thus be maximized at 1.00. The proportion passing, designated as p, would be .50. The closest any item came to this was New Mexico, which produced an impressive differentiation index of .8, with a proportion passing, or p, of .50.[1]

We will next illustrate item analysis with a Context C, 50-item, multiple-choice test administered to several classes totaling 77 students. Twenty-seven percent of 77 is 20.8. This might best be "rounded" down to 20 in order to simplify computation. Recall that this number of papers is to be

---

[1]Some writers refer to p as *difficulty index*. We avoid this term because it breeds confusion.

FIGURE 10.4   Item-Analysis Data for a Satisfactory-Appearing, Four-Optioned, Multiple-Choice Item. Asterisk indicates letter of keyed response.

	OPTION A	OPTION B*	OPTION C	OPTION D
High	.10	.85	.00	.05
Low	.15	<u>.35</u>	.25	.25
Differentiation Index		.50		
Proportion Passing		.60		

taken from high-scoring papers and an equal number is to be taken from low-scoring papers. Data for three items of this test are displayed in Figures 10.4, 10.5, and 10.6. Keyed responses are marked with asterisks. Each item is shown separately with all its options; in addition, its differentiation index and proportion passing (*p*-value) are reported.

First, consider the item data reported in Figure 10.4. Option B is the keyed response. Of the 20 examinees in the high group, 2 marked "A," 17 correctly chose "B," 0 chose "C," and 1 chose "D." Of the low 20, 3 marked "A," 7 correctly selected "B," 5 selected "C," and 5 chose "D." Each of these numbers was divided by 20 to obtain the decimal fractions displayed in Figure 10.4. The item differentiation index of .50 was computed by subtracting the fraction of the low group answering the item correctly from the fraction of the high group answering it correctly (.85 for the high group minus .35 for the low group = .50). The proportion passing, that is, the fraction of the combined groups answering correctly, .60, was obtained by computing the mean of the fractions of the high and low groups (.85 for the high group +.35 for the low group = 1.20. 1.20 ÷ 2, for *p* = .60). The data for this item look highly satisfactory.

Next, consider the data for a five-option item displayed in Figure 10.5. Here we introduce the computation of a differentiation index for each distractor as well as for the total item. Overall, the item functioned very well; its differentiation index was .60 and the *p*-value was .45. Yet option B contributed nothing to the question's differentiating power because as many high students as low students chose it. This fact should direct the teacher's attention to option B. Studying it may reveal a flaw that can be corrected. If not, the item might well be left as it is.

FIGURE 10.5   Item-Analysis Data for a Good-Differentiating, Five-Optioned, Multiple-Choice Item Having One Suspect Option. Asterisk indicates keyed response.

	OPTION A	OPTION B	OPTION C	OPTION D*	OPTION E
High	.00	.15	.05	.75	.05
Low	<u>.25</u>	<u>.15</u>	<u>.20</u>	<u>.15</u>	<u>.25</u>
Differentiation Index	−.25	.00	−.15	.60	−.20
Proportion Passing				.45	

FIGURE 10.6   Item-Analysis Data for a Poor-Differentiating, Four-Optioned, Multiple-Choice Item Having Omissions. Asterisk indicates keyed response.

	OPTION A*	OPTION B	OPTION C	OPTION D	OMIT
High	.70	.05	.00	.25	.00
Low	.60	.10	.00	.15	.15
Differentiation Index	.10	−.05	.00	.10	−.15
Proportion Passing	.65				

Finally, consider the data shown in Figure 10.6. This figure introduces a mechanism for dealing with omissions; they are tallied in a column included at the right of the figure. The item differentiation index is a modest .10. In looking for a reason, attention is drawn to option D, which was chosen by more *high* scoring students than low scoring ones. It should be examined to discover what makes it more attractive to good students than to poor ones. Or, because option C also failed to help the question differentiate between high and low achievers, the item might well be discarded altogether.

In these ways, item-analysis data can *direct attention* to questions or options that may be flawed. Once attention is drawn to an item, *content decisions should be made mainly from the perspective of validity.* Does the item assess what it is intended to assess and nothing else? Items should never be deleted, edited, or accepted on the basis of item-analysis data alone.

Caution should also be sounded concerning the limited stability of data obtained from single classes. Differentiation indices will vary somewhat from class to class owing to instability of data from small samples. Also, slight class-to-class variation in instruction and in the paths that class discussions may take can influence student performance on individual items. It is important, therefore, to avoid over-interpreting information gathered from single classes. The best practice is often to record the data along with the item in the file and await the accumulation of more data from other classes before taking them very seriously.

Along the same lines, historical events can change item data. For example, the Florida data displayed in Figure 10.3 on page 253 were gathered before the extraordinary presidential election of 2000, which focused intense national news coverage on Florida and its capital for over a month. The item would surely be easier now than it was in 1999.

A Closer Look at Proportion Passing.   Although the differentiation index is, for many purposes, the most important single outcome of an item analysis, the proportion passing also provides useful information both in its own right and because of its impact on differentiating power.

Test Purpose Should Impact Distribution Shape and p-Values.   If a test is to be used to flag only the lowest achievers, say, 5% of a group, then, other things being equal, the test will be more effective if its items are relatively easy. The items in it might be targeted to be answered correctly by, say, 90% to 99% of the group. Indeed, that is the kind of top-heavy (which statisticians call negatively skewed) distribution that a Context A mastery test typically yields. Easy tests of this kind are good at differentiating between very low and poor performance, but they are not at all effective in separating persons in the upper levels of achievement.

On the other hand, if a multiple-choice test is designed to identify only the top, say, 10% of the examinees, as might be the case in awarding scholarships or prizes, then the test will be more efficient, other things being equal, if its items are quite hard. Such hard tests yield bottom-heavy (i.e., positively skewed) distributions and tend to be good at differentiating between very high and moderately good performance. However, they are ineffective in differentiating among persons in the lower levels of achievement.

Most of the time teachers design tests to reliably differentiate among examinees at all levels of achievement. For those situations, the following section is important.

What Difficulty Level Enables Good Differentiation?   As noted, an item that is correctly answered by everyone cannot differentiate among students whose achievement differs. Nor can one that is missed by everyone. Nor can any other item that is answered correctly by the *same fraction* (whatever it might be) of high- and low-scorers. The ideal item—from the rather narrow perspective of differentiation power among the total group—is one that would be answered correctly by all the high examinees and missed by all the low ones. However, this is virtually impossible because, among other things, students who do not know the answer often guess it correctly. Thus, the ideal fraction passing, or *p*-value, is more than 50% (except on those completion items on which guessing is not a factor).

Experts don't fully agree on what the ideal *p*-value should be in order to maximize potential differentiation power. Many adhere to the convention that it should be midway between the chance-level score and a perfect score. Others accept the more sophisticated technical rationale of Lord (1952), which leads to somewhat higher recommended *p*-values. Figure 10.7 shows the fraction passing that is recommended by each system.

Of the two sets of *target p*-values, we prefer Lord's values. For one thing, his values yield tests having very slightly greater reliability (if other things are equal). For another, student morale is higher if mean raw scores are higher. Finally, students who are accustomed to percentage grading tend to panic when the mean score is lower than their expectation of what the average performance should be. Although one can explain that the norm-referenced meaning rather than the percentage score is the important thing, this takes time and the concept often proves to be quite elusive for students in environments where most other teachers use percentage grading (pseudo) standards. (More will be said about this topic in Chapter 12.)

FIGURE 10.7   Recommended Ideal Fraction Passing (Lord's Target) Objective Items.

ITEM TYPE	(TRADITIONAL TARGET) FRACTION PASSING	(LORD'S TARGET) FRACTION PASSING
Completion or Short-Answer Items	.50	.50
Alternate-Choice Items	.75	.85
Three-Option Items	.67	.77
Four-Option Items	.63	.74
Five-Option Items	.60	.69

Item Analyses for Product and Performance Measures.   Let's now extend these procedures to other methods of assessment. Suppose a math teacher has administered to classes having a total of 91 examinees a test consisting of 26 short-answer items, a 4-point essay, and a 5-point formal proof. Partial credit is possible for the essay and proof. Figure 10.8 displays the item-analysis data for the two product measures.

Twenty-seven percent of 91 equals 24.57; this is rounded to 25. For the high and low groups separately, the teacher computed the mean score on each product measure. These means are then divided by the number of possible points to obtain the *fraction of possible points.* Next, the differentiation index is found by subtracting the fraction of possible points for the low group from that of the high group. Finally, the mean of these fractions in the high and low groups yields an estimate of the fraction of possible points for the total group—a *p*-value.

We see that the essay item functioned very well; it was undertaken successfully much more often by the better students (as measured by the total test) than by the poorer ones, and it had a good differentiation index of .53. The formal proof did not differentiate as sharply between high and low groups; its index was .176. This may have resulted from the item being too easy to enable stronger differentiation.

In similar fashion, one can perform an item analysis on *each element* of an analytic scoring rubric for a performance measure; in this case, the total score on the rubric would be used to identify the high and low groups. Alternatively, one could conduct an item analysis on *each separate rubric* (be it analytic or holistic) for product or performance measures by use of the total scores of several separate measures to identify high and low groups. Thus, the rationale of item analysis is applicable to every kind of achievement measure treated in Part II.

FIGURE 10.8   Item Analysis Data for Product Measures.

ESSAY ITEM (4 POINTS POSSIBLE)

	Mean Score	Fraction of Possible Score
High	3.60	.90
Low	1.48	.37
Differentiation Index		.53
p-Value		.635

FORMAL PROOF (5 POINTS POSSIBLE)

	Mean Score	Fraction of Possible Score
High	4.92	.984
Low	4.04	.808
Differentiation Index		.176
p-Value		.896

Using Item-Analysis Data to Improve Teacher-Made Tests.   Miss Tamblyn teaches a fifth-grade unit on vertebrates. Her unit test contains (among other things) a matching exercise in which pupils are shown pictures of *un*studied vertebrates to be classified. (Bravo! She is testing for high-road transfer.) Because she didn't happen to revise the unit and the test had no obvious flaws, Miss Tamblyn used this test for three consecutive years and then pooled the three sets of answer sheets for an item analysis before revising and refining it. Figure 10.9 presents the results for selected items.

The first of the pictures was a frontal view of an armadillo. The data in Figure 10.9 show that the item did not differentiate well between high- and low-scoring pupils. *The value of the item analysis in this case is the attention it attracts to the item.* What's wrong with it?

Reflection brings to mind a validity issue. It is surely appropriate to expect pupils to recognize nursing as a clue, but what would be the corresponding clue from a front view of an armadillo? None is obvious enough to render the item valid for fifth graders. Pupils could eliminate fish, bird, and amphibian from consideration, but the distinction between reptile and mammal was unreasonably hard. What to do? The item might well be discarded. Or, a picture of a mother armadillo nuzzling her young could be provided.

This item illustrates how item-analysis data can direct attention to malfunctioning items. Once such items are inspected, reasons for their disappointing functioning often becomes apparent. When the reason doesn't come to mind, a colleague can sometimes be coopted to help identify the problem. Or, high-scoring students who missed the item can be asked why they chose their responses. The point is that an item should never be revised solely on the basis of its item-analysis data; rather, negative data should attract scrutiny, and this thoughtful consideration is usually sufficient to identify flaws.

The second item for which Figure 10.9 reports data is a picture of an unfamiliar mammal nursing her litter. The differentiation index for this item (.10) is also disappointing. The problem is that the item is too easy; the nursing litter seems to be too obvious a clue for fifth graders. Too obvious, that is, from the narrow perspective of differentiation.

But is it a *valid* item? Provided that some students did not know this distinction *before* the unit, and provided it was an instructional objective, then it certainly seems to be a content-relevant idea to test. This validity consideration supersedes the issue of differentiation; Miss Tamblyn might decide to leave the item intact.

On the other hand, she might reason that this huge Context C domain has more potential items than she can ever use; therefore, she might seek a replacement item that is both valid and better at differentiating. The third item addressed in Figure 10.9 meets these two criteria. The nursing clue is very much present, yet not so blatant. As a result, the item is just as valid as the preceding one and it is also much more differentiating.

Let's consider another example of using item-analysis data to improve tests. Mr. Fong taught his 28 elementary pupils to make rough visual estimates of linear measures. He tested this skill with multiple-choice items. Twenty-seven percent of 28 students rounds to 8, so he tallied the responses of the top eight and bottom eight answer sheets. With such small numbers, he was very careful not to over-interpret the results.

FIGURE 10.9   Item-Analysis Data for Several Five-Optioned Matching Items. Asterisk indicates keyed response.

FRONT VIEW OF ARMADILLO

	OPTION A* (MAMMAL)	OPTION B (BIRD)	OPTION C (REPTILE)	OPTION D (AMPHIBIAN)	OPTION E (FISH)
High	.45	.00	.55	.00	.00
Low	.40	.00	.55	.05	.00
Differentiation Index	.05	.00	.00	−.05	.00
p-Value	.425				

UNFAMILIAR MAMMAL NURSING HER YOUNG

	OPTION A* (MAMMAL)	OPTION B (BIRD)	OPTION C (REPTILE)	OPTION D (AMPHIBIAN)	OPTION E (FISH)
High	1.00	.00	.00	.00	.00
Low	.90	.00	.05	.05	.00
Differentiation Index	.10	.00	−.05	−.05	.00
p-Value	.95				

UNFAMILIAR MAMMAL WITH UDDER VISIBLE

	OPTION A* (MAMMAL)	OPTION B (BIRD)	OPTION C (REPTILE)	OPTION D (AMPHIBIAN)	OPTION E (FISH)
High	1.00	.00	.00	.00	.00
Low	.65	.05	.20	.10	.00
Differentiation Index	.35	−.05	−.20	−.10	.00
p-Value	.825				

Figure 10.10 shows one of his items and its data. The item had a modest differentiation index because it was very hard for the high and low groups alike. Reasoning that a somewhat easier version of the item would be just as valid and would also probably be more differentiating, Mr. Fong pursued both validity and differentiation power by modifying the distractors. He used the revised item the following year with a class of 30. Figure 10.10 shows that it functioned much more adequately.

Are Hand-Analyzed Item Analyses Worth the Trouble?   Many readers have probably been wondering how a busy teacher could possibly find time to analyze every item of every test and to thoughtfully use the results. It would probably divert too much effort away from other aspects of instruction. Therefore, we don't propose that teachers analyze items for *every* test they give. Rather, we urge them to conduct occasional analyses on at least *some* items and to reflect on the findings.

FIGURE 10.10   Item-Analysis Data for Item *Before* and *After* Revision. Asterisk indicates keyed response.

Original Item: The approximate height of the teacher's desk is:
A. 2 feet.
B. $2^{1}/_{2}$ feet.
C. 3 feet.
D. $3^{1}/_{2}$ feet.

	OPTION A	OPTION B*	OPTION C	OPTION D
High	.25	.375	.25	.125
Low	.25	.25	.25	.25
Differentiation Index	.00	.125	.00	−.125
p-Value		.313		

Revised Item: The approximate height of the teacher's desk is:
A. $1^{1}/_{2}$ feet.
B. $2^{1}/_{2}$ feet.
C. $3^{1}/_{2}$ feet.
D. $4^{1}/_{2}$ feet.

	OPTION A	OPTION B*	OPTION C	OPTION D
High	.00	.875	.125	.00
Low	.125	.375	.375	.125
Differentiation Index	−.125	.500	−.250	−.125
p-Value		.625		

Thoughtful consideration of item-analysis data serves two purposes. First, item analysis improves the quality of particular tests upon which it is performed. It helps teachers to make more informed decisions concerning which items to retain intact in their item files, which to attempt to improve by editing, and which to discard outright.

Second, item analysis helps teachers gain insights concerning such things as students' option-selection processes, characteristics of effective questions, and item-writing errors. Studying the results of an item analysis on one's test provides instruction in test making. Thus, contemplating the findings of an occasional item analysis with other teachers can be a professional development activity having positive multiplier effects that extend well beyond that test. This faculty-development use can be amplified by collaborating with a colleague or two as in jointly contemplating item-analysis data for an occasional test.

THINKING CAP EXERCISE 10.2 ???

Suppose the following four questions were administered to 88 students in several sections of a high school English or biology class. Twenty-seven percent of 88 is 23.76; to facilitate computation by hand, the teacher "rounded" this to 25. Examine the item-analysis data for each item. Where the data are worrisome, examine the content of the item to determine what should be done. (The asterisk indicates the keyed response.)

1. Return your application either to Rev. Stith or to
   A. I.
   B. me.
   C. myself.
   D. we.

	Option A	Option B*	Option C	Option D
High	.00	.92	.08	.00
Low	.04	.60	.32	.04
Diff. Index	−.04	.32	−.24	−.04
Prop. Passing		.76		

2. "The monkey scampered up the rope, leaped to the swing, grasped the other beast by the collar, and ripped *it* off." The *it* stands for
   A. monkey.
   B. rope.
   C. swing.
   D. other beast.
   E. collar.

	Option A	Option B	Option C	Option D	Option E*
High	.00	.00	.00	.00	1.00
Low	.04	.00	.00	.00	.96
Diff. Index	−.04	.00	.00	.00	.04
Prop. Passing					.98

(continued)

THINKING CAP EXERCISE 10.2   CONTINUED

3. The correct spelling of the possessive of Gladys is:
   A. Gladyss.
   B. Gladyes.
   C. Glady's.
   D. Gladys's.
   E. Gladyss'

	Option A	Option B	Option C*	Option D	Option E
High	.00	.00	.12	.88	.00
Low	.08	.04	.44	.40	.04
Diff. Index	−.08	−.04	−.32	.48	−.04
Prop. Passing			.28		

4. Which of these species of animals has the biggest brain size in relation to its body size?
   A. A particular kind of fish
   B. A particular kind of snake
   C. A quarter horse
   D. An African elephant
   E. A human

	Option A	Option B	Option C	Option D	Option E*
High	.20	.00	.00	.00	.80
Low	.00	.00	.10	.10	.80
Diff. Index	.20	.00	−.10	−.10	.00
Prop. Passing					.80

KEY TO THINKING CAP EXERCISE 10.2

1. The differentiation index of .32 is very adequate. Although options A and D contributed little to the item's differentiating power, no better distractors come to mind. The item might well be retained without revision. Or, if the test contains an alternate-choice section, the item could be converted into, "Return your application either to the Rev. Stith or to (myself, me)."

2. The question differentiated very poorly because it was too easy to be capable of revealing individual differences among these examinees. Scrutiny of the item suggests two hypotheses.

First, students at this level may have a good command of identifying antecedents of pronouns.

Second is an item flaw. The noun that immediately precedes the pronoun is the keyed response; therefore, students who have the misconception that a pronoun's antecedent is always the noun that comes right before it will get the item right for the wrong reason. This consideration suggests use of a revised stem such as "The monkey scampered up the rope, leaped to the swing, grasped the other beast by the collar, and bit *it* on the head."

If you failed to notice this item flaw, it may well be because you focused on the data without keeping the item content in mind. This oversight would be more probable if the item and its data were on different pages. One should *store items and their item-analysis data next to each other.*

THINKING CAP EXERCISE 10.2 CONTINUED

3. This item appears to be terrible; it differentiates in the wrong direction! When this happens, the first thing to do is to check the key. In this case, the only thing wrong is that the teacher miskeyed the item. When the key is changed to option D, the differentiation is seen to be a very respectable .48. The fraction passing is now .64. When an incorrect key isn't the explanation for negative differentiation in a good-sized sample, inspection usually reveals one or more other item flaw(s).

Notice that the teacher didn't include Gladys' as an option. This is because some teachers consider it to be a correct alternative.

4. This item didn't differentiate at all. At casual glance, it appears to tell the teacher nothing helpful. But wait; why would five of the high students mark option A? It turns out that these five students are close friends, are all talented in science, and are voracious readers of a variety of material, although somewhat casual readers of text assignments! Also, one has a parent whose profession is ichthyology. Could they have assimilated information from reading, TV, or family dinner table discussions that is more current than the text or the teacher's knowledge? Yes, they could. (Mormyrids, or elephant-nose fishes, are recognized by ichthyologists as having relative brain sizes that rival or exceed that of humans.)

This example illustrates one of the benefits that post-test discussions can have on further learning as students talk about a subject and share their varied experiences and discoveries. It also gives the teacher a fine opportunity to model an attitude of lifelong learning and to demonstrate pleasure in learning with and from the students and other sources.

What to do about the item? For the present class, double key it. For the future, one might best eliminate option A or replace it with something like "A particular kind of bird," or "Birds that can learn to talk."

COMPUTER STORAGE AND RETRIEVAL OF ASSESSMENT DATA

Technology can increase our productivity in numerous ways. Although some of the more dramatic technology programs for schools may garner the publicity, classroom teachers are quietly discovering numerous workaday ways in which a personal computer and some well-designed software can assist them with their myriad responsibilities. Here are some of the primary areas that have demonstrated, or show promise of providing, significant contributions to teaching and learning.

■ **Organization and revision of instructional objectives.** Word processing enables objectives to be easily modified. This minimizes clerical work and maximizes time available for instruction and measurement tasks (Kubiszyn & Borich, 2003).

■ **Personal computer test-bank files.** These were described earlier in the chapter. Test items—either teacher-created or commercially prepared—can be grouped and coded by instructional objective, subject matter, type of cognitive function, grade level, and subject field (Stiggins, 1997).

■ **Test preparation and editing.** Payne (1997) targeted word processing as a great boon for teachers in test preparation. Test templates ease the development and revision of tests. Some programs will generate alternate item orders of tests and print out teachers' keys. Moreover, parallel forms of tests can be compiled to reflect similar content and difficulty level.

- **Optical scanning.** Computerized scoring machines read examinee responses and compute scores. They also can perform item analyses. Some will link objectives, assessments, and student records, at a relatively reasonable cost (Stiggins, 1997).

- **Data analysis software.** Programs can provide differentiation indices and *p*-values for items and options within items. They also may provide statistical information such as frequency distributions, measures of central tendency, measures of variability, standard scores, standard errors of measurement, and confidence intervals. (These topics will be addressed in later chapters.)

- **Grade books.** Computerized grade books can provide attendance forms, eligibility lists, honor rolls, seating charts, customized report forms, and flexible grading options for multiple grade levels. They also may compute averages and apply weighting formulas. (These topics, too, will surface in subsequent chapters.) Although computerized grade books may simplify record keeping, they don't make the process any more fair, objective, or valid. A teacher still must decide what information to include, what weight to attach to each item used, and what method to use to summarize the information (Guskey, 2002).

- **Individual Education Plans (IEPs).** More will be said about this in Chapter 13.

- **Online services.** Teachers increasingly search for resource persons and materials to help with their measurement and evaluation issues and concerns.

- **Records management.** Computer-aided records management can include organization of records for students, groups, classes, and entire schools to facilitate planning, instruction, assessment, and program evaluation.

- **Computer-based testing.** Tests can be administered, scored, and interpreted using a computer and appropriate software. Note, however, that online testing requires significant amounts of student access time. Also, some teachers have questions about possible misuses of this technique. Areas targeted as most problematic include unfair test administration by untrained examiners, lack of computer skills by examinees, and equivalence of computer scores with conventional test scores (Venn, 1994).

- **Computer-assisted instruction (CAI).** Students can go to the computer lab to complete activities at their level and bring back item-by-item records of their performance. Some programs include audio capability, which can provoke meaningful interaction between student and material. This process has built-in formative assessment. However, it is very time-intensive, with a single student engaged at the computer for some time.

- **Electronic portfolios.** A technique that has promise in performance areas such as science labs, vocational courses, athletics, or cooking classes is videotaping the lab work and storing the tape in an electronic portfolio to be critiqued with a rubric and commentary at a later time. The lesson objectives and rubric form would be shared with students beforehand, and perhaps even co-developed with them. Then the individual student's performance could be discussed in a student conference and a parent conference. (Note that issues of confidentiality apply to videotaped performances as much as they do to test papers.)

■ **Computer essay grading.** There is considerable interest in computerized marking of essays as a *complement* to essay grading by a teacher. Some studies during the last 30 years reveal that computers can grade essays as satisfactorily as a single teacher ordinarily does.[2] (Whether this is a highlight for technology or a low mark for the current state of essay assessment by teachers is debatable!)

To summarize this brief overview of computer technology contributions to assessment, the main benefits seem to be time savings, computational accuracy, easier analysis of data, records of actual performances for careful review, and efficiency in producing assessment materials.

On the other hand, computer technology creates the need for caution and prudence so as to avoid compromising student and family privacy or security of test materials. As an example, test results and other assessment data should not ordinarily be communicated by e-mail. One of the author's rules of practice for electronic communication is to send only what she would be willing to post on her office door. As another example, computer disks with assessment information should be housed in locked places. For further protection, it is good practice to make back-up disks and retain those off-site in secure places. Teachers who prepare tests on school computers should file their work in locked computer files. As a cautionary note, they must be sure to master the Context A task of how to unlock those files when they need them!

School districts that aim to use computer technology successfully must plan for that success. Sufficient funds must be budgeted not only for good hardware and software, but for keeping everything up and running. Technical support must be budgeted from the start. Additional funds will be required to upgrade programs as they become outdated. Finally, intensive staff development is vital in order to equip all personnel with skills and confidence to use the technology productively.

CHAPTER RECAP

Effective teacher-made tests don't just happen. They are thoughtfully designed to be contributing components of integrated instructional efforts to enhance student learning. Examinations are skillfully crafted item by item. Appropriate directions to accompany the questions are created. Tests then are carefully assembled, edited, and formatted. Finally, they are reproduced in ways that render them legible and attractive.

Concern for fairness dictates that all examinees operate on the same footing with regard to test-taking strategies. Prior instruction, test directions, and scoring procedures should assure that no one has a systematic advantage because of individual differences in content-irrelevant attributes, such as tendency to guess when in doubt.

---

[2]The general method is for the computer to be programmed to identify *many* specific indicants of good writing (e.g., generous use of adverbs). Persons seriously exploring this topic are strongly urged to consider well the adage that one should not let indicants to developmental objectives become the objectives. If one does, assessment power is very likely to corrupt instruction!

Effective use of either published or teacher-made tests also requires careful attention to test administration. The work environment must be conducive to maximum performance, and testing conditions must be uniform from student to student. Therefore, every effort must be made to ensure that all have a fair chance to do their best and that none has an unfair advantage over others. Concern for fairness obviously requires the prevention of cheating, which is best achieved via the dual avenues of prior education concerning academic honesty and keen surveillance during testing. Concern for fairness also directs attention to the need to eliminate disabling test anxiety. A calm, serious, and relaxed atmosphere is sought.

After a test has been administered, scoring requires close attention to accuracy. Likewise, the recording of scores in grade books or computer files must be done with care to ensure accuracy.

A teacher can gain considerable insight into instruction and assessment by conducting test-item analyses and studying the results. Investing time and thought to analyzing students' performance can help target student misconceptions, flag poor test items, spot ways in which items can be edited and improved, and identify good items that should be saved for reuse.

When time and effort are conserved by competent use of computer technology, school personnel have more time and energy to plan curriculum, assist students with their interests and needs, and make wise instructional decisions. The rapidly developing fields of technology will continue to provide practical assistance to teachers who are willing to learn about it and then to use it.

MANAGEMENT OF MEASUREMENT AND EVALUATION DATA

CHAPTER OVERVIEW

FREQUENCY DISTRIBUTIONS AND
  PERCENTILE RANKS

KINDS OF AVERAGES

MEASURES OF VARIABILITY

STANDARD SCORES

CORRELATION

COMBINING DATA FOR GRADES

KEY TERMS

measurement
statistics
frequency distribution
percentile rank (*PR*)
measure of central tendency
average
mean (*M*)
median (*Md*)

mode (*Mo*)
measures of variability
range
standard deviation (*SD*)
standard scores
z-scores
correlation

This book concerns the use of classroom assessment in pursuit of effective teaching. Among the things needed to pursue this central goal are quantitative capabilities in the following topics:

- Comprehending descriptions of reference groups
- Understanding and being able to correctly use various kinds of derived scores
- Knowing how an instrument's reliability and validity are investigated and reported
- Understanding and evaluating what test manuals and research articles report about tests' reference groups, reliability, and validity
- Analyzing data for purposes of reporting student achievement

To help achieve these aims, we will present some statistical concepts in this chapter. Statistics are tools we shall use to pursue our assessment goals; the study of statistics *per se* is *not* our aim. This focused purpose allows the selection of only those topics that provide keys to educational measurement.

Measurement and statistics are sometimes confused. **Measurement** typically concerns *assessing* the size, degree, or amount of things by use of numbers. In contrast, **statistics** involves the *analysis of data by use of mathematics.* For example, the height of each person in a class can be measured. Determining the class's average height requires statistics. Statistics provide the mathematical tools by which the results of measurement are analyzed.

Before plunging into selected statistics topics, some reassurance may be helpful. Mathematics and statistics strike terror into the hearts of many education students. If you are such a person, be reassured! First, computation is only a minor topic in this book. Second, we don't assume that readers are skilled in mathematics; all that is assumed is that you took a semester or so of high school algebra *and have forgotten most of it.* Third, the arithmetic will be kept very simple. We want you to understand the concepts. To keep examples easy, very small numbers of cases will be used, usually between 4 and 10; this provides less likelihood of arithmetic mistakes that may distract one from the topic being studied. To keep the calculations simple, examples have also been "rigged" so that all means will turn out to be whole numbers and all numbers for which square roots are needed will be perfect squares.[1] You will not be asked to "master" (yet again!) the little-used algorithm for extracting square roots. Knowing that an answer will be a whole number, you can obtain it with a minimum of trial and error.

A few somewhat technical words of explanation at this point are in order, especially for those readers who have taken a statistics course. First, descriptive statistics (rather than the more difficult inferential statistics) are the focus of this chapter; therefore, N, rather than $N - 1$, will be used in formulas. This emphasis also renders unsuitable for present purposes the standard deviation formulas programmed for many calculators and computers. (Don't worry; the calculations are so simple that a calculator is often more nuisance than help.) Second, ungrouped data will be used because they better enable a clear view of what formulas do. Third, our discussion avoids various technical issues (e.g., interpolating medians among tied scores) not central to our measurement purposes. Our focus is on the *meaning* of statistics as *applied to educational assessment;* this emphasis is likely to provide some new or enhanced insights even for readers who have a background in statistics.

FREQUENCY DISTRIBUTIONS AND PERCENTILE RANKS

When several people have taken a test, the resulting scores must be organized. Suppose that a group of 50 people took our State Capitals Test. The first step taken to make scores more manageable is to arrange them vertically in numeric order. Thus, scores could be tallied in a **frequency distribution,** shown in Table 11.1.

Although the derived scores and their interpretation will be explored more fully in Chapter 15, it will be helpful to introduce percentile ranks and standard scores in this chapter. Recall from Chapter 4 that derived scores are used in making norm-referenced interpretations. **Percentile ranks (*PRs*)** are a kind of derived score that is particularly well suited for norm-referenced interpretations of performance on published instruments.

---

[1]We are indebted to John T. Roscoe for many of the frequency distributions used in this chapter.

TABLE 11.1   Frequency Distribution

RAW SCORE	FREQUENCY TALLY
10	I
9	III
8	II
7	II
6	IIII IIII
5	IIII IIII II
4	IIII IIII
3	IIII
2	IIII
1	
0	I

We will define *PR*s as the percent of a reference group that an examinee excelled or equaled.[2] Thus, if Simone obtains a *PR* of 38, she performed as well as or better than 38 out of every 100 students in a particular reference group.

Table 11.2 shows the next step in developing *PR*s. Although this isn't something that a classroom teacher typically needs to do, understanding the basis of *PR*s can help you use them meaningfully in interpreting scores of published tests. The first two columns of the table are headed with the conventional symbols. Uppercase "*X*" (or another letter near the end of the alphabet) stands for

TABLE 11.2   Percentage Frequency Distribution

X	*f*	PERCENTAGE
10	1	2
9	3	6
8	2	4
7	2	4
6	10	20
5	12	24
4	10	20
3	5	10
2	4	8
1	0	0
0	1	2
	50	

[2]These are technically known as top-of-interval *PR*s. The definition of bottom-of-interval *PR*s doesn't include the phrase "or equaled." Mid-interval *PR*s are defined as the percent of the reference group excelled plus one-half the percent tied. Mid- and top-of-interval *PR*s are the more common kinds. In longer instruments, the distinction among the varieties of *PR*s is not very important.

the raw score and "*f*" represents the frequency. The tally marks from Table 11.1 have been converted into numerals and entered in the *f* column. The last column of Table 11.2 indicates the percentage of the total group that obtained each raw score. Each entry is found by dividing its frequency by the number of people in the group (50 in this example) and multiplying the resulting decimal fraction by 100 (to obtain a whole number). Thus, 1 divided by 50 yields the first entry of 2%, 3 divided by 50 is 6%, and so on.

Table 11.3 on page 271 provides the next step. For the cumulative percentage column, we add the percentage of persons who received each raw score to the percentage who received all lower scores. This step simply involves adding the percentage entry in each row to the entries in all rows below it and entering this sum in the right-hand column.

Cumulative percentages are very similar to *PR*s; only one thing remains to be done. By convention, *PR*s of 0 and 100 are avoided. All other numbers are rounded to the nearest whole percent. The bottom of the range is defined as 1 (or 1−, .1, .01, etc.), and the top is set at 99 (or 99+, 99.9, etc.). The right-hand column of Table 11.3 contains this feature.

Although other features of *PR*s will be addressed when we return to them in Chapter 15, this introduction provides a sense of what they are. From this point forward, we will be able to use this kind of derived score to illustrate various issues.

THINKING CAP EXERCISE 11.1   ???

1. Ten students have taken the State Capitals Test and obtained the following scores. Make a table showing the percentile rank associated with each possible raw score.

STUDENT	RAW SCORE
Alma	6
Bert	5
Chuck	10
Dennis	3
Frank	1
Ramona	5
Henry	8
Irma	2
Jennifer	4
Kelly	7

X	f	PERCENTAGES	CUMULATIVE PERCENTAGE FREQUENCY DISTRIBUTION	PRs
10	1	10	100	99+
9	0	0	90	90
8	1	10	90	90
7	1	10	80	80
6	1	10	70	70
5	2	20	60	60
4	1	10	40	40
3	1	10	30	30
2	1	10	20	20
1	1	10	10	10
0	0	0	0	1−

2. Describe in words what Ramona's *PR* means.

KEY TO THINKING CAP EXERCISE 11.1

1. The major steps for producing *PR*s are shown below.

2. Ramona, whose raw score was 5, performed on this sample of questions as well as or better than 6 out of every 10 (or 60 out of every 100, or 60%) of the students who took the test.

TABLE 11.3   **Cumulative Percentage Distribution and Percentile Ranks**

X	PERCENTAGE	CUMULATIVE PERCENTAGE	PERCENTILE RANK
10	2	100	99+
9	6	98	98
8	4	92	92
7	4	88	88
6	20	84	84
5	24	64	64
4	20	40	40
3	10	20	20
2	8	10	10
1	0	2	2
0	2	2	2

MEASURES OF CENTRAL TENDENCY

Suppose four classes test and we wish to compare their scores. Rather than trying to compare full distributions, *summary statistics,* which condense distributions into single numbers, are compared. This section and the next describe measures by which distributions are summarized.

A **measure of central tendency,** or **average,** condenses an entire frequency distribution into a single number that represents the size of the entries in the distribution. Many people think of an average as being something like, "You get the average of several numbers when you add them up and then divide by the number of them there are." Actually, this is a description of only one kind of average—the arithmetic mean. In statistics, the word "average" is a nonspecific term that stands for numerous measures of central tendency. In this book, the word "average" will be used only in this generic sense; in order to sharpen our concepts, thinking, and communication, several specific terms—mean, median, or mode—will be used to refer to particular kinds of averages.

Assume that the State Capitals Test has been given to each of four classes. To make the calculations easy, the illustrative classes are artificially small. The distributions are listed in the following table. Because the classes are so small, it will be more convenient to relist ties (such as the two 6s in Class A) than to provide separate X and f columns.

CLASS A	CLASS B	CLASS C	CLASS D
10	7	9	10
9	7	4	10
7	5	4	9
6	5	4	5
6		4	5
4			4
			3
			2

Means.   The most widely known measure of central tendency is the **mean.** It is computed by use of the formula.

$$M = \frac{\Sigma X}{N} \text{, where}$$

M stands for the mean

Σ is the operation symbol meaning "the sum of" or "add up what follows"

X denotes raw score

N is the number of cases (e.g., examinees)

For Class A, the mean is computed by adding the six scores and dividing this sum (42) by the number of examinees (which is 6). Thus, in Class A, $M = 7$; in Class B, $M = 6$; in Class C, $M = 5$; and in Class D, $M = 6$.

Means, like other kinds of averages, enable us to compare the overall performance of groups. The four class means reveal that Class A evidenced the most knowledge of state capitals and that Class C showed the least.

Medians.   The **median,** symbolized Md, is the point in a distribution that divides it into two equal parts. For example, if seven people wish to find their median height, they could arrange themselves in order by stature; the height of the middle person would be the median. To find the median of any distribution of scores, simply arrange the scores into order and then take the middle score(s). In distributions having an odd number of scores, the middle score is the median. In those having an even number of cases, the median is the midpoint between the two middle-most scores.

For Class A, the median is midway between the two middle most scores, 6 and 7; hence, $Md = 6.5$. For Class B, the median is halfway between 5 and 7; thus, it is 6. Class C contains an odd number of students; therefore, its median is the middle score, which happens to be one of the 4s. For Class D, the median is midway between the two scores nearest the middle—5.

Modes.   A third common measure of central tendency is the **mode.** The mode (Mo) is the most frequently occurring score. In Class A, the mode is 6 because more people obtained that score than any other. In Class B, there is a tie between 5 and 7; thus, the modes are 5 and 7. In Class C, the mode is 4, whereas Class D, like Class B, is bimodal, with modes of 5 and 10.

Here are the central tendency statistics for the four classes.

CLASS A	CLASS B	CLASS C	CLASS D
10	7	9	10
9	7	4	10
7	5	4	9
6	5	4	5
6		4	5
4			4
			3
			2
$M = 7$	$M = 6$	$M = 5$	$M = 6$
$Md = 6.5$	$Md = 6$	$Md = 4$	$Md = 5$
$Mo = 6$	$Mo = 5$ and 7	$Mo = 4$	$Mo = 5$ and 10

Notice that in some distributions, two or more of the averages may be identical, whereas in other distributions, all three values may differ.

Other Measures of Central Tendency.   We have examined the three kinds of average that are most often used in educational statistics. There are additional common kinds of averages that need not be addressed. Examples are rolling means (e.g., one's mean weight over the past three days), weighted means (e.g., counting a big test more than a small one), geometric means (i.e., the square root of the product of two numbers), and truncated means (i.e., the mean of what is left after the top and bottom score are discarded).

Evaluation of Measures of Central Tendency.   Reflection on the distribution for Class A permits one to intuit the relative power or adequacy of the three kinds of average. The mode is inherently unstable because it is based on few cases. In Class A, the mode was determined by only two persons. The mode ignores most of the cases, yet is supersensitive to a minority of cases. For instance, if the person receiving a 4 had instead attained 8 points, Class A's mode would not have changed at all. Yet if one of the people who received a 6 had instead scored 7, the mode of the entire class would have been altered.

The median is more consistent because it uses all the data (albeit not with maximum efficiency). In Class A, if the person receiving 4 points had instead obtained 7 or 10 points, the distribution's median would have been altered. However, if the person's score had changed from 4 to 0 or 5, the median would have been unaffected. The median is sensitive only to which half of the distribution contains each score; it is indifferent to where within that half each lies.

Finally, the mean is the most dependable of the three summary statistics because it efficiently uses all cases in a distribution. The impact of a change in *any* score on the mean is exactly proportional to the amount by which the score changes.

Let's express these ideas another way. Suppose you're interested in the average age of the junior class in a large high school. In order to generalize to this population, you might use a sample. Suppose you have randomly drawn 20 separate samples of 25 juniors each and have computed the means, medians, and modes of the ages of the people in each. Because each mode was based on very few cases, you can expect your 20 modes to be quite inconsistent from sample to sample; hence, the mode is a poor statistic from which to generalize from the sample to the population from which it was drawn. The medians, being more efficient in their use of data, will wobble less from sample to sample; hence, the median is a better statistic from which to infer from a sample to a population. The means, however, being based on efficient use of all 25 people in each sample, will be the most consistent measure of central tendency from sample to sample; it is the most powerful statistic of the three.

When to Use Each Kind of Average.   Because the mean possesses superior statistical properties over the other measures of central tendency, why are the others ever used? There are two general reasons.

Purpose.   First, there are occasions when the median or the mode better serves one's purpose. Consider a distribution of ages at which youths drop out of secondary school. Which kind of average is best? It depends on one's purpose. For an administrator computing the cost of educating students for the years they remain in school, the mean might be indicated. For a sociologist concerned with the *typical* dropout's unreadiness to cope with the adult world, the median would be preferable. For an educator seeking to target a timely intervention shortly before the age at which the greatest number terminate, the mode might be best. We should use the kind of average that best suits our purpose. When it is legitimate, the mean serves most, but not all, purposes best.

Scale Properties.   The second reason why the median and the mode are sometimes needed arises in situations in which the mean cannot be computed. Because the mean is sensitive to the exact size of each score, its proper use requires measures that have *equal units* or intervals. Fortunately, most common measures have equal units. For example, money comes in equal units; thus, the difference in value between $1 and $2 is exactly the same as that between $1,566 and $1,567. Because money is measured with a scale that has equal intervals, we can compute means of amounts of money, such as the mean daily balance in a bank account. Similarly, temperature is measured with equal units. The difference between 100°C and 99°C equals the difference between −10°C and −11°C. Thus, the mean of several temperatures can be found. Likewise, time, distance, and weight are measured with equal-interval scales. Finally, raw test scores are generally considered to have equal units.[3]

When measures have markedly *un*equal units, however, the mean may *not* legitimately be used. What, then, should one do? Where the cases can be arranged into order, the median can be employed. Thus, if 15 people are running a race, the eighth to finish is at the median. Medians are often used in situations where scores can be rank ordered but lack equal units (as in the race where the distance between consecutive people is probably *not* equal). In such cases, the median is attractive because it is the more powerful of the suitable kinds of average.

Several kinds of derived scores lack equal units of measurement. Grade equivalents and age equivalents, which are taken up in Chapter 15, are common examples. This is dramatically illustrated by visiting four classes in a school district when oral reading is taking place. The difference between the median first grader's reading and that of the median second grader is great enough to be readily apparent. Much less difference exists, however, between typical ninth graders and typical tenth graders. A basic developmental trend is that growth slows down during the growing years and stops when maturity is reached. The absence of equal intervals of grade-to-grade growth renders the mean inappropriate for summarizing a class's distribution of grade-equivalent scores. It is also inappropriate for averaging an individual's grade-equivalent scores from several subjects. This is something to keep in mind during parent-teacher conferences.

Percentile ranks are another kind of derived score that lacks equal units. That *PR*s lack equal units is evident from examining a frequency distribution such as that shown in Table 11.3 on page 271. In the final distribution, one raw score point equates to very few *PR* units in the extremes of the distribution but to many *PR* units in the center of the distribution. To illustrate, suppose your score on the State Capitals Test was 9; this equates to a *PR* of 98. Had you earned one more point, your raw score of 10 would convert to a *PR* of 99+, thus 1 point or raw score amounted to only about 1 *PR* unit. Now suppose your original raw score had been 5; this yields a *PR* of 64. Had you received one more point, your raw score of 6 would equate to a *PR* of 84. This 1 point of raw score amounted to 20 *PR* units. Because *PR*s lack equal units, neither the mean nor any statistic based on it may be used to summarize distributions of *PR*s.

In addition to being used by default when the mean is inappropriate, medians sometimes are

---

[3]Statistical purists may point out that raw scores do not have perfectly equal units. However, most workers in applied educational measurement contend that raw scores come close enough to having equal intervals to justify the use of means and statistics based on the mean.

used for two other reasons even where means could be computed. First, recall that the median is the best kind of average to show the status of the most typical individual in a group. Second, the median is sometimes used as a convenient, rough measure of central tendency.

Alas, in some situations the scores cannot even be ordered. When the data being summarized cannot be put into order, neither the mean nor the median can be computed; only the mode can be used legitimately. For example, what is the average state of birth of the members of a class? We cannot add states and divide to get a mean. Nor can we arrange them in numeric order. The only meaningful way to address the issue of the average state of birth in a group is to use the mode.

THINKING CAP EXERCISE 11.2   ???

For items 1–8, which measure of central tendency would best serve for each purpose?

1. A principal reporting a school's average daily attendance.
2. A teacher reporting the number of addition facts known by the *typical* member of the class.
3. A teacher wanting a quick, rough average of a group's performance on a spelling test.
4. A teacher reporting the' average of several percentile ranks of a student on a published test.
5. A psychologist reporting the average mental age of a group of children.
6. A teacher discussing the average ethnicity of the children in a class.
7. A report of your class's average raw score on this exercise.
8. Find the mean, median, and mode of the following distribution.

   10
   10
   9
   8
   4
   4
   4

KEY TO THINKING CAP EXERCISE 11.2

1. Mean. Because children come in equal intervals, the mean is legitimate. For most purposes, the mean would best capture the intent of averaging, but for a few, the median might be preferred.

2. Median. Although the scores are considered to have equal units of measure and the mean could properly be computed, the teacher's interest was on the skill possessed by the typical child in the class.

3. Median. Although the mean is appropriate and preferable, the median provides the desired crude estimate.

4. Median. The mean is not legitimate because *PR*s lack equal units of measure.

5. Median. Mental ages and other age and grade equivalent scores lack equal units of measure; therefore, the mean is not appropriate. The median is the best by default.

6. Mode. Ethnic groups are not orderable, hence, only the mode can be used. (This, of course, is a case in which we probably would elect not to use a summary statistic; rather, we would provide the entire distribution. Inclusionary thinking would also dictate allowing each person to report more than one ethnic heritage if appropriate.)

7. Mean. Raw test scores are generally considered to have approximately equal measurement intervals. Hence, one would opt for the most sensitive summary statistic available for the class.

8. $M = 7$, $Md = 8$, $Mo = 4$

MEASURES OF VARIABILITY

As useful as measures of central tendency are, they don't capture or summarize all the important kinds of information contained in frequency distributions. This point is illustrated by the story of the individual who lay with head in the oven and feet in the freezer while commenting that the mean temperature was quite satisfactory! For an assessment example, consider again the data for two classes.

CLASS B	CLASS D
7	10
7	10
5	9
5	5
	5
	4
	3
	2
$M = 6$	$M = 6$

Each class has a mean of 6. However, measures of central tendency reveal nothing of the conspicuous difference between the classes in another dimension. Class D is obviously more variable than Class B. The much greater heterogeneity of Class D would require more effort by its teacher to provide for individual differences.

It is a serious oversight to attend only to central tendency and to ignore differences in diversity within distributions. For another example, consider the story of the statistician who drowned while trying to ford a river with a mean depth of only 6 inches!

Measures of variability (i.e., measures of dispersion, heterogeneity, individual differences, etc.) enable us to condense into single numbers this second aspect of distributions that concerns *the extent to which scores vary from one another.* Two measures that summarize dispersion will be considered for distributions based on equal-interval scales: range and standard deviation.

Range.   The **range** describes the number of intervals over which the scores of a distribution vary. The method of finding the range that will be used in this book is simple. Subtract the smallest score from the largest score. Thus, the range of scores for Class B is $7 - 5 = 2$. Class D's range is 8. This confirms what can be noticed at a glance concerning relative variability in these very small distributions; in larger distributions, the differences are less likely to be evident from inspection.

The range, as a statistic that summarizes distributions' dispersion or variability, has the advantages of being widely known, easily understood, and quickly computed. Unfortunately, it is a very crude measure because it *is based on only two cases*—the largest and the smallest. It thus ignores most of the data. Because the range is based on so few cases, it is a poor statistic. For an illustration, compare Classes E and F (page 277).

Class E consists entirely of persons who deviate greatly from its mean, whereas Class F contains few examinees whose scores differed markedly from its mean. Yet the classes have identical ranges of 10. This is because the range is not sensitive to most of the available data.

CLASS E	CLASS F
10	10
10	9
10	5
10	5
0	4
0	4
0	3
0	0
$M = 5$	$M = 5$

In spite of its limitations, the range is useful for some rough-and-ready purposes in which precision can be sacrificed. For example, we will make good use of the range later in the section on combining data for grading purposes. Such uses are most defensible when one notes anomalies such as the excessive contribution to the range made by an extreme score.

Another disadvantage of the range is that it leads to a statistical dead end; it doesn't provide a stepping stone to other statistics. We clearly need a more powerful measure of variability. This need gives rise to the widely used standard deviation.

Standard Deviation.   As a statistic that describes a distribution's variability or scatter, the standard deviation is free from the problems that plague the range. However, its computation is more involved. Class B will be used to illustrate its computation. First, compute the mean of the raw scores; this is shown in the Computation Box 11.1. (For now, don't worry about the formula at the bottom of the box; it will be explained later.)

Next, find the amount by which each raw score (X) deviates from the mean. This second column is headed with the lowercase of the same letter (x) to stand for the deviation score of variable X. Enter the amount and direction of each raw score's deviation from the mean of 6. The first score, 7, is 1 more than the mean, so enter a +1. Likewise for the second raw score. The two scores of 5 are each 1 point below the mean of 6, so enter −1 for each.

Except for one problem, the mean of these deviation scores could be computed and would be a good measure of variability expressed in raw-score units. The problem is that means of distributions of deviation scores are always zero! Hence, the simple mean of the algebraic values of distributions of x-scores wouldn't differentiate among distributions of differing variability. What to do?

One could treat all of its values as positive numbers and compute their mean. Although this statistic, the mean deviation, is a fine method of quantifying variability, it doesn't provide a good foundation for more complex statistics such as measures of relationship.

A better way to get rid of the negative signs is to square each x-score. In Computation Box 11.1, the third column contains the squared deviation scores and is headed x^2. The mean of these squared deviations is another good descriptor of variation. Moreover, it paves the road to more advanced statistics. This mean of x^2 scores is known as the variance. Useful as it is, this statistic won't be used in this book because its values are not interpretable in terms of raw score units. Instead, its positive square root will be used. This square root of the mean squared deviations is known as the **standard deviation (SD).**

COMPUTATION BOX 11.1   Standard Deviation of Class B

X	x	x^2
7	+1	1
7	+1	1
5	−1	1
5	−1	1

$$M = \frac{\Sigma X}{N} = \frac{24}{4} = 6$$

$$SD = \sqrt{\frac{\Sigma x^2}{N}} = \sqrt{\frac{4}{4}} = \sqrt{1} = 1$$

The widely used standard deviation reports a distribution's variability in raw score units. Aside from being a bother to compute if one has to do it by hand, the *SD* has no significant disadvantages. After one grows accustomed to it, the *SD* is easily understood and easily interpreted. A formula for the standard deviation is:

$$SD = \sqrt{\frac{\Sigma x^2}{N}}$$

In Computation Box 11.1, the third column of data consists of the squared *x*-scores. Each of the first two entries is the square of +1; this is +1. Each of the last two entries is the square of −1; this too is +1. The sum of these squared deviation scores is 4. The *SD* is found by dividing the sum of the squared deviation scores (4) by the number of cases (4); we then take the positive square root of the quotient to obtain the *SD*.

Computation Box 11.2 demonstrates the calculation of the standard deviation for another distribution. In this distribution of Class D, the mean is 6. Therefore, each entry in the *x*-score column is the amount by which the corresponding raw score differs from this mean, and the algebraic sign of each *x*-score indicates the direction by which its raw score differs from the mean. For example, 10 is 4 more than the mean of 6; therefore a +4 is entered in the *x*-score column. When all of the *x* entries have been made, one can check the work by summing the *x*-score column. It should always equal zero, within the tolerance of rounding error. If it doesn't, one or more errors have been made.

The next column consists of the squares of these *x*-scores. Because the squares of all positive real numbers are positive and the squares of all negative real numbers are also positive, no entries in x^2 columns will ever be negative. When this column is completed, its sum is found.

The *SD* is computed by dividing this sum of the x^2 column (72) by the number of cases (8) and extracting the positive square root of the quotient. This yields the *SD* of 3.

COMPUTATION BOX 11.2   Standard Deviation of Class D

X	x	x^2
10	+4	16
10	+4	16
9	+3	9
5	−1	1
5	−1	1
4	−2	4
3	−3	9
2	−4	16
$\overline{M = 6}$		72

$$SD = \sqrt{\frac{\Sigma x^2}{N}} = \sqrt{\frac{72}{8}} = \sqrt{9} = 3$$

Readers who may still feel insecure about their ability to compute SDs are urged to return to p. 277 and compute the SD of Class E. Its SD is 5. Those who don't get this answer can go to our web site at ablongman.com/hannadettmer to see its calculation. The same process may be repeated for Class F if desired; its SD is 3.

Some readers are surely wondering, "Why bother with computation in this electronic age? We don't compute SDs by hand anymore." True, we don't. The computations *with simplified data* offered in this book are designed to *reveal the meaning behind* the calculations *so they will not be shrouded in mystery.*

THINKING CAP EXERCISE 11.3   ???

1. Compute the mean and standard deviation for Class A.

   CLASS A
   10
   9
   7
   6
   6
   4

2. Find the range and SD for Class C.

   CLASS C
   9
   4
   4
   4
   4

THINKING CAP EXERCISE 11.3   CONTINUED

3. A friend remarks that the air pressures of his car's front tires are supposed to be about 30 psi. He just measured them; one was 12 psi and the other was 48 psi. How might you best respond to his comment, "Oh well, they average out about right"?
   A. What kind of average do you mean? Mean, median, or mode?
   B. Good.
   C. The variability is OK.
   D. The variability is dangerously high!

4. Someone new to Topeka, Kansas, might be told that the mean annual temperature is a comfortable 65°F. What more might the newcomer want to know?

KEY TO THINKING CAP EXERCISE 11.3

1. M = 7; SD = 2.

2. Range = 5; *SD* = 2.

3. D. Your friend is, of course, a menace to himself and others. *Each* tire must approximate the designated air pressure. The average (of whatever variety) is beside the point.

4. What the variation is. If the range were from −20°F to +110°F, then it would *not* be comfortable!

So What?   "OK," some disgruntled reader is thinking, "I understand how the standard deviation is computed and what it means, but so what? Who wants a standard deviation anyway? What is it for?" The aims presented in the first paragraph of this chapter may merit review.

The *SD,* like other statistics introduced in this chapter, is used for such purposes as describing samples used in estimating test reliability and validity and deriving some kinds of scores. Such statistics can provide derived scores that are useful tools for using assessment to improve teaching. The next section concerns a kind of derived score.

Before leaving the standard deviation, it might also be pointed out that it is widely used in fields other than educational assessment. For example, it is used in medicine in ways like that shown in Table 3.2 on page 48 to show dispersion of height. In addition, it is a common measure of companies' stock volatility or price fluctuation (Bogle, 1999).

STANDARD SCORES

A few derived scores have already been encountered. Percentile ranks and grade equivalents exemplify two of the three general kinds of converted scores that were outlined in Chapter 4. Standard scores are the third general group of derived scores.

As their name suggests, **standard scores** are closely associated with, and arise from, standard deviations. Hence, this is a good place to introduce the concept of standard scores and their computation. They can then be referred to as the need arises in subsequent chapters. However, the full development and explanation of their uses will be left for Chapter 15.

Standard scores are a group of derived scores that are particularly useful when computations need to be performed. The prototype of the standard-score group is the *z*-score; **z-scores** *are derived* *scores expressed in terms of distance from the mean in* SD *units.* An efficient formula[4] for the z-score is:

$$z = \frac{x}{SD}$$

Computation Box 11.3 shows the calculation of a set of z-scores for one of the classes used earlier. First, the mean must be computed. Next, the *SD* is computed by use of the now familiar formula. Finally, the new step is performed; the z-score corresponding to each raw score is calculated by dividing its x-score by the *SD* of the distribution. (Caution: It is the *x,* not the x^2 that is divided by the *SD.*) The top raw score of 10 is 3 raw score units greater than the mean of 7; thus, its deviation score is +3. This +3 is divided by the *SD,* which is 2, to obtain the z-score of +1.5. The next case is 2 raw score units above the mean. When this +2 is divided by the *SD* (2), the z-score is found to be +1. The third score is equal to the mean; thus, 0 divided by 2 equals 0. The next two cases have raw scores that are 1 point *below* the mean; when −1 is divided by the *SD,* the quotient is found to be −.5. Finally, the last score is 3 raw score units below the mean. When −3 is divided by the *SD,* −1.5 results. A final check on one's work can be made by algebraically adding the z-score column; its sum should (within the limits of rounding error) be zero.

We mentioned earlier that deviation scores, that is, x-scores, express norm-referenced status in terms of distance from the reference group's mean *in raw score units.* By contrast, z-scores express normative status in terms of distance from the mean *in standard deviation units.*

The advantages of expressing deviation scores in terms of standard deviation units is one of *comparability.* Suppose, for example, that a seven-year-old girl is found to be 5 pounds lighter than the national mean for her age and gender; that is, her x-score for weight is −5 *pounds.* Suppose also that she is 2 inches shorter than the mean of this reference group. Thus, her x-score for stature is

COMPUTATION BOX 11.3   z-Scores of Class A

X	x	x^2	z
10	+3	9	+1.5
9	+2	4	+1.0
7	0	0	0.0
6	−1	1	−0.5
6	−1	1	−0.5
4	−3	9	−1.5
$M = 7$		24	

$$SD = \sqrt{\frac{\Sigma x^2}{N}} = \sqrt{\frac{24}{6}} = \sqrt{4} = 2$$

$$z = \frac{x}{SD}$$

[4]Statistics books often use formulas for *SD* and *z* (often with different symbols as well) that are computationally more convenient. We use the algebraically equivalent forms that better reveal the underlying meaning of the respective statistics.

−2 *inches*. These metrics of pounds vis-à-vis inches are useless for comparing her relative status on weight and height. We are tied to the artifacts of the metrics with which she was measured. Now, suppose we knew for this reference group the *SD*s of weight in pounds to be 4 and its *SD* of height in inches to be 3, then we could convert each of the *x*-scores into a *z*-score as follows:

<table>
<tr><td align="center">**WEIGHT**</td><td align="center">**STATURE**</td></tr>
<tr>
<td align="center">$z = \dfrac{x}{SD} = \dfrac{-5 \text{ lb}}{4 \text{ lb}} = -1.25$</td>
<td align="center">$z = \dfrac{x}{SD} = \dfrac{-2 \text{ in.}}{3 \text{ in.}} = -.67$</td>
</tr>
</table>

This shows her relative status in weight and height with respect to the reference group. Notice in the calculation how the *units of measure cancel out*. By dividing the deviation score (which is expressed in the whatever unit of measure happens to be used) by the *SD* (which is expressed in the same metric), the unit of measure cancels out. We are thereby liberated from the artifact of the original metric (pounds and inches in this case).

One final point from this example merits mention. Two domain-referenced scores that are referenced to different domains cannot be directly compared. The only meaningful way by which to achieve comparability is by the use of a common reference group (or highly similar groups) of people that bridge the incommensurate domains. Pounds couldn't be compared with inches even though each measure was well suited to domain referencing. *Comparability was achieved by norm referencing both measures to the same reference group* of people. This is an important use of norm referencing; we will spiral back to it when test batteries are discussed in Chapter 16.

Some readers may feel a need to think their way through Computation Box 11.4, which is another example of the calculation of *z*-scores.

COMPUTATION BOX 11.4   Another Computation of z-Scores

X	x	x^2	z
16	+8	64	+1.33
16	8	64	+1.33
14	6	36	+1.00
6	−2	4	−0.33
6	−2	4	−0.33
4	−4	16	−0.67
2	−6	36	−1.00
0	−8	64	−1.33
$M = 8$		288	

$$SD = \sqrt{\frac{\Sigma x^2}{N}} = \sqrt{\frac{288}{8}} = \sqrt{36} = 6$$

$$z = \frac{x}{SD}$$

■ ■ ■ ■ ■ ▨▨

EXTENSION

It happens that effect size, a measure that is widely used in summaries of quantitative research studies, is *very* closely related to z-scores. With very little extra effort, you can visit our web site, ablongman.com/hannadettmer, to extend your assessment literacy concerning z-scores to a facet of research literacy involving effect size.

CORRELATION

One statistic remains to be mentioned. It is a measure of relationship—of correlation—between two variables. The study of correlation follows nicely from the topic of standard scores. A correlation between two variables would, if we took the time to develop the topic, turn out to be nothing more complicated than the mean of the products of corresponding z-scores.

Correlation (or co-relation) concerns relationships. It is an expression of the degree of "in commonness" or "going togetherness" between two measures. When a quantitative statement of the degree of "going togetherness" or "correlation" between two variables is needed, a correlation coefficient is calculated. The most common measure of correlation is the Pearson product-moment coefficient of correlation (*r*).

The possible range of values of Pearson *r* is from +1 to −1. A coefficient of +1.00 represents a perfect positive relationship (or perfect direct variation between the variables); if one knew a person's status on one of the variables, one would know the person's exact status on the other variable with total certainty. High scores would go with high scores, and low scores would go with correspondingly low scores.

At the other extreme, a coefficient of −1.00 depicts a perfect *negative* (or perfect inverse) relationship; if one knew a person's status on one of the variables, one would be certain of the individual's status on the other variable. However, in this case, high scores on one variable would go with low scores on the other.

Midway between these two extremes, a correlation of 0.00 signifies the total absence of relationship. Knowing an individual's status on one of the variables provides no hint about her or his status on the other variable.

Here are a few ballpark examples of the size of *r*s between pairs of familiar variables.

- The correlations between alternate forms of class-period-length published tests hover around .9.
- The *r* between individual items in classroom or published tests is often less than .2.
- The *r* between academic aptitude scores of siblings is about .5.
- Among adults, arm length and leg length correlate about .7.
- Scores on a modern language aptitude test and grades received in a foreign language a year later correlate about .5.

EXTENSION

This discussion of correlation will suffice for understanding the contents of this book. However, a fuller explanation would be necessary background for understanding validity and reliability beyond the level addressed in this text. We offer a much more comprehensive treatment of this important topic at ablongman.com/hannadettmer.

EXTENSION

THE REGRESSION EFFECT

Will the sons of NBA players turn out to be as tall as their fathers? The children of extraordinary parents tend to be closer to the mean than their parents. The "r" in Pearson r stands for the word "regression" or "pull" toward the mean. The phenomenon, known as the "regression effect," is profoundly important in a wide variety of fields ranging from educational research (e.g., Dooley, 2001) to investments (e.g., Bogle, 1999) to biology, economics, and agriculture. For an introduction to this fascinating far-reaching, and practical topic, visit ablongman.com/hannadettmer.

COMBINING DATA FOR GRADES

People in many walks of life have occasion to combine several component elements of data into summary composites. An application of major relevance to teachers involves figuring term grades by combining Context C and Context B scores for paper-pencil tests, daily work, homework, book reports, other products, performances, and other criteria. *The mechanics of such a task are not as simple as most people assume.* Often, due to lack of understanding of principles of weighting grades, teachers use procedures that *do not accomplish their own intent* (Stiggins, Frisbie, & Griswold, 1989).

Before focusing on how to properly combine data, let's note that some situations exist in which components should not be combined at all. When assessing achievement in Context A, one shouldn't combine measures of the respective objectives. This follows from the explicit mastery objectives used; each Context A objective is deemed to be vital. Therefore, one should not add or average students' achievement across several objectives; we have seen that doing so would allow superiority in some domains to compensate for deficiencies in others. Permitting compensation is sensible in most situations, but not in those where mastery of each objective is judged to be essential.

When combining parts into totals or averages does make sense, two major steps are involved. First, a judgment is made as to how much weight each part merits. Second, that decision must be competently implemented.

Establishing Intent

A teacher responsible for combining several data sources into one summary score must first address the issue of how much each component should contribute to the composite. In some schools, this is entirely the teacher's choice. In others, policy dictates some of the weights; for example, a school might have a rule that homework will count one-third of the grade in seventh-grade math.

The composite measure may be either a mean or a total; the relative weights of the contributing parts are the same. Because it is easier to compute totals than means, our discussion and illustrations will use totals.

The issue of appropriate relative weight has no quantitative solution; *it involves judgment.* It is to be expected that reasonable people may differ somewhat, just as they would in establishing the relative weights to the parts of a scoring rubric. How much should a final examination in ninth-grade English contribute to the semester grade? Although there is no one right answer to such a validity question, people who know the circumstances are likely to have similar opinions. Thus, English teachers familiar with the course and a particular school's 50-minute final exam period would probably find a 10% weight to be skimpy or a 40% weight to be too much. However, perfect consensus is unlikely.

We shall now consider examples from two teachers' classrooms.

Ms. Lenelli's Intent.   Ms. Lenelli needs to assign term science grades to her fourth graders. For the last nine weeks, the class has conducted experiments, completed five worksheets, and taken a summative test on the term's work. How much should each of these elements count?

Ms. Lenelli considers the relative amounts of time spent on the various worksheets and judges it reasonable to count each the same amount. She similarly decides to assign equal weights to the two experiment reports. After brief yet thoughtful consideration, she decides that the relative allocation of credit among the parts will be:

Two experiment reports at 15% each	30%
Five worksheets at 6% each	30%
Test	40%

Before taking our next example, let's identify the criteria that should be used to make this kind of judgment.

Bases for Establishing Relative Weights of Parts.   Several things merit consideration in allocating weight.

■ **Time devoted to each facet.** This includes homework as well as class time. If other things are equal, it makes sense to count components in proportion to the time allotted them.

■ **The relative importance of the objectives assessed by each part.** Other things being equal, components that tap major objectives should receive more weight than those assessing less-important aims. For example, in a driver-education course, the portion of the behind-the-wheel performance test that concerns response to various emergencies might be weighted *far* more than instructional time or testing time might imply.

■ **Component uniqueness.** When important objectives are assessed by only one element, such as a single oral test in a foreign-language course, the element may merit more weight than it otherwise would. (Alternatively, of course, the teacher may wisely consider assessing the important goal by additional methods, enhancing validity in the process of using triangulated indicants.) On the other hand, when several measures tap the same objective, then each should be assigned less weight than it would receive if it were unique.

■ **Reliability and validity of the constituent parts.** Other things being equal, it makes sense to give more weight to measures judged to be more valid and reliable than to those thought to be less valid or less reliable.

Mr. Wendt's Intent. For a second example of establishing relative weights among components, we consider a high school English class. Mr. Wendt's nine-week term grades are to be based on (a) an oral report, (b) a written book report, (c) 20 daily class or homework assignments, (d) three quizzes, and (e) a major examination. How much should each count?

On the basis of time spent, Mr. Wendt *tentatively* assigns weights as follows:

Oral report	5%
Written book report	11%
20 daily assignments (at 2% each)	40%
Three quizzes (at 8% each)	24%
Major exam	20%

However, when he contemplates the criteria of importance and uniqueness of the components, he decides to allocate a great deal more credit to the oral component and somewhat less to the daily work.

When he considers component validity, he recalls his frequent suspicion that an occasional book report was plagiarized and that some homework reflected more than optimum help from others. Accordingly, he decides to weight them a little less. Finally, the criterion of reliability of marking prompts him to acknowledge that the grading of the oral report is probably less consistent than that of other components. This consideration moderates his earlier inclination to greatly increase its weight; he decides to increase it only moderately. After taking all of these issues into account, his judgment yields the following weights.

Oral report	10%
Written book report	10%
20 daily assignments (at 1.5% each)	30%
Three quizzes (at 10% each)	30%
Major exam	20%

These two examples illustrate how teachers should thoughtfully decide how much emphasis they want to give each thing that contributes to a grade.

■ ■ ■ ■ ■

ENCAPSULATION

Students should be given advance notice regarding how important each element is (Terwilliger, 1989). This information reduces the number of complaints and increases the ease of defending those grades that may be disputed. More important, *advance knowledge of relative weight of tasks guides student effort.* Grading practices influence most students. This impact should be thoughtfully used by teachers to enhance student learning. Just as test power can be harnessed by informing students what will be tested, grade power should also be harnessed.

The Mechanical Problem

Before we address how to achieve the desired weights for the above two examples, it will be fruitful to focus for a time on the problem and the common misconceptions.

A teacher has given four Context C tests. The possible points, means, and standard deviations for the tests are reported as follows. Answer this question before proceeding: If the teacher simply added each student's four scores, which test(s) counted the most?

INFORMATION	TEST 1	TEST 2	TEST 3	TEST 4
Points	100	90	60	50
M	50	70	58	30
SDs	10	6	1	12

If you think Test 1 is the most influential in determining the total grade, you probably are responding to the fact that it has the most points. Most educators think or assume that the weights that elements carry are proportional to their possible points. Although this answer is common, it is wrong!

It is wrong, that is, in the context of grading on the basis of *relative* standing (Hopkins, 1998). In Context C, meaningful marks must be norm referenced. Thus, grading on the basis of total raw or percentage scores is *not* appropriate.

To illustrate why your answer is wrong for norm-referenced grading, consider two students' performances on Tests 1 and 4. Each performed quite erratically, 1 *SD* above the mean on one test and 1 *SD* below the mean on the other.

STUDENT	TEST 1	TEST 4	TOTAL
Allister	60	18	78
Beatrice	40	42	82

If Test 1 carried more weight than any other test (as you thought it did), then it would follow that Allister, who did well on Test 1, should have a larger total than Beatrice, who did well on Test 4. But he doesn't; Beatrice has the larger total. Therefore, the test on which she did well (Test 4) counted a bit more than the one on which she performed poorly.

If you chose Test I, go back and select another answer, this time *from a norm-referenced perspective.* Reconsider the question, then find the answer in the following text that corresponds to your new answer and read it.

If you think Test 2 counts the most in determining the total grade, you probably are responding to the fact that it has the largest mean score. This is a common misconception; many teachers think the weights that elements contribute to a total are proportional to their means.

If you think Test 3 is the most important influence on the total grade, you may be attending to the irrelevant fact that its mean score yielded the largest percentage correct.

If you think Test 4 is the most influential, you are right! Why does Test 4 weigh the most? The answer relates to the variability of its scores compared with the variability of scores of the other components. In general, the element with the most variable scores will contribute the most (Nitko, 2001; Payne, 1997).

Solutions to the Mechanical Problem

The method that seems intuitively appropriate to most people for weighting the parts cannot be depended on to achieve the intent. How, then, can teachers achieve desired relative weight? Here is the general rule: When several scores are combined, *the relative weight of the components is proportional to their standard deviations*[5] (Hopkins, 1998; Nitko, 2001).

Because the elements of composite scores contribute in proportion to their *SD*s, the way to control the contribution of each part is to manage the size of its *SD*. Fortunately, *SD* size is easily managed. If each score in a distribution is multiplied (or divided) by any number, the *SD* is multiplied (or divided) by that number.

Now we can answer the important question, "How can a teacher make each of several sets of scores contribute the same amount to a total (or average) score?" Suppose the teacher whose test data were reported on page 287 wanted to have Tests 2 and 4 count the same amount. How can this be accomplished? We have seen that number of points and means of the tests are *not* relevant to the issue. What *is* germane is the *relative variability* of scores in the distributions.

The *SD* for Test 2 is 6; the *SD* for Test 4 is 12. The easiest way to cause the *SD*s to become equal is to multiply each student's Test 2 score by 2. Where did the 2 come from? We saw that the *SD*s were 6 and 12, respectively. Wanting them to be equal (because the teacher wished the tests to count the same), we ask, "By what number must the 6 be multiplied to change it to 12?" To change 6 to 12, multiply by 2. Therefore, the easiest way to achieve equality between the tests is to multiply *each student's* Test 2 *score* by 2.

Practical-minded readers may doubt that it is realistic to expect a busy teacher to know the *SD* of each distribution in a grade book. For the increasing number of teachers whose scores are kept on computers, it is indeed realistic to have the computer calculate the *SD*s. However, for those of us who still figure grades with hand calculators, the range is usually quite serviceable, especially if one verifies that a very extreme score does not radically impact a class's range.

To illustrate, suppose the ranges for two tests are 48–81 and 45–55. The range for the first (i.e., 81 − 48 = 33) is about three times that of the second (whose range is 10). If one wanted the

---

[5]Actually, weights are influenced by both the variability of the respective components and the intercorrelations among them. Because a serviceable approximation is provided by the *SD*s alone, it is customary to ignore the intercorrelations.

tests to contribute the same to the total score, approximate equality would most easily be achieved by multiplying *each student's score* on the second test by 3.

With this rough solution to the mechanical problem, we can now return to our two examples.

Ms. Lenelli's Science Grades.   Recall Ms. Lenelli's thoughtful intent of weighting the components as follows:

Each of two experiment reports	15%
Each of five worksheets	6%
Test	40%

We have seen that distributions of scores can be adjusted *after* the data are in. This is sometimes necessary, but advance planning can obviate the need for most after-the-fact data manipulations. Much time and effort can be saved with foresight.

A simple rule can provide the light necessary to foresee and prevent the need for most such after-the-fact adjustments. The rule is that (assuming that one uses longer tests for more important components) variables of the same kind are likely to have SDs and ranges that roughly correspond to their intended weight. However, components of different kinds may chance to have SDs and ranges that differ greatly from the intended weights. The opportunity to avoid labor concerns the word "chance" in the previous sentence; with foresight, components of different kinds can be adjusted so that their SDs and ranges will be roughly what is desired. If this is achieved, later alterations are unnecessary.

Ms. Lenelli wants the two experiment reports to count the same. She presumably will have pupils do them with similar formats and will assess them with comparable rubrics. To make them count approximately the same, all she probably needs to do is assign them equal possible points. Suppose her rubrics allocate 10 points on each experiment report, and she expects a range from about 3 to 10 for each. If nothing unusual happens, she can reasonably assume that their SDs and ranges are about equal and that they, therefore, count approximately the same amount.

Similarly, if the worksheets are similar in content and format, then allowing the same number of possible points for each will probably cause them to have roughly equal SDs and ranges. How many points for each should be possible? To achieve equity among the worksheets, it doesn't matter. With foresight, however, Ms. Lenelli can probably approximate the desired balance *between* worksheets and experiment reports at the same time. Suppose she considers a 5-point scale for each worksheet and expects the ranges to hover around 3 (e.g., the scores to range from 2 to 5). This range is a little less than one-half that of the 7 anticipated for each experiment report; therefore, she would expect each worksheet to count a bit less than half as much as each report. So it appears that the contemplated 5-point scale for the worksheets would serve nicely to approximate the intended 15% to 6% ratio.

Finally, she can determine the range that is desired for the test. The test is to count nearly three times as much as either experiment report (i.e., 40% is 2.67 × 15%). The anticipated range for each report is 7, thus the desired range for the test would be estimated from this source to be about 19 (i.e., 2.67 × 7). For the worksheets-test comparison, the test is intended to count nearly 7 times as much as any one worksheet (i.e., 40% is 6.67 × 6%). The range for each worksheet is 3; thus the desired range for the test would be estimated from this source to be about 20 (i.e., 6.67 × 3). Taking both or either of these two rough estimates, 19 and 20, Ms. Lenelli knows how to aim the range of her final distribution of test points.

Suppose she used a very similar test last year. It had 25 objective items, and the scores ranged from 14 to 24. This is a range of 10. A simple and adequate thing to do would be to give 2 points per item; this would have yielded a range of 28 to 48, which equals 20.

With this kind of planning, Ms. Lenelli can achieve a very adequate approximation to her intended weights with very little actual work. On the other hand, if she waits until the end of the term to address the issue, she will probably have to alter the variability of at least one component in order to achieve the desired balance among them.

Was it wise for Ms. Lenelli to base this year's scaling of components on data from previous years? Might not one class be more or less variable than past groups? Yes, it might; however the *relative* size of the *SD*s or ranges of the respective elements doesn't ordinarily vary greatly from group to group. Admittedly, it would be preferable to ensure exact proportionality among the *SD*s, but unless calculations are being done by computer, it probably isn't worth the effort.

If, however, Ms. Lenelli's grades at Utopia Elementary School were kept on a computer and she had software with which to easily specify the *SD* of any set of scores entered, then it would be sensible and adaptive for her to be more perfectionistic. For example, she could specify that whatever scale is entered for the worksheets be converted into derived scores with the *SD* of 6, that whatever scale is entered for the experiment reports be transformed into derived scores having the *SD* of 15, and that whatever set of scores is entered for the test be converted into scores with the *SD* of 40. Then, thanks to technology, her competence in using it, and her knowledge of this topic, she would nicely approximate her intent without doing much work at all.

A beginning teacher, of course, wouldn't have the benefit of previous years' data. Thus, adjustments (whether or not the computer is doing the work) would very possibly be needed after all the data have been collected.

■ ■ ■ ■ ■

ENCAPSULATION

Anyone worried by the fact that Ms. Lenelli will have only a possible 50 points for her test rather than the more usual 100 is suffering from a percentage-grading hangover! Recall that the grading of this unit takes place in Context C, in which norm referencing is necessary. In Context C, component scores need not be changed into percentages. The domains are fuzzily defined and content difficulty is not fixed; therefore, a percent begs the question "Percentage of what?" (Nitko, 2001, p. 363); thus, meaningful domain-referenced interpretation via raw scores or percent scores isn't possible. Reporting Context C elements as percent scores creates unnecessary work and opportunity for computational errors. Converting each element into a percent doesn't assure equilibrium among them; the component-to-component *SD*s of percent scores are just as variable as the component-to-component *SD*s of raw scores.

Mr. Wendt's English Grades.   After a few minutes' deliberation, Mr. Wendt has decided on the desired weights for the parts of his high school English term grades. If he can anticipate the original ranges or *SD*s of the elements and transform them into ones that have the desired relative values, he can save himself the trouble of manipulating scores during the end-of-term rush. Listed here are his desired weights for each part and the range of scores he has commonly obtained for each in the past (before he resolved to save labor via foresight).

COMPONENT	DESIRED WEIGHT	TYPICAL OLD RANGE
Oral report	10%	2–10
Written book report	10%	5–20
Each of 20 daily assignments	1.5%	0–3
Each of 3 quizzes	10%	6–15
Major exam	20%	29–70

Mr. Wendt can start with any convenient range and alter the others into the desired proportionality with it. He decides to start with the daily work and to retain the 0–3 scale he has always used. Knowing from experience that the scores are usually distributed over the whole range, he knows that his 0–3 scale will yield a range of about 3 for each assignment.

He considers the other components in turn. For the oral report, he wants the range to be 6 or 7 times as great as the one for each daily assignment (because 10% is 6.67 × 1.5%). He asks himself, "What do I have to do to the present range of 8 (i.e., 10 − 2) to make it 6 or 7 times 3, or about 20?" "Multiply it by about 2.5," he calculates. Hence, he alters his former 10-point rating scale into a 25-point scale. Assuming he uses about the same fraction of the scale as he did before, the resulting range should be about 5–25. This is the intended range of about 20 points.

For the book report, he again needs a range that is 6 to 7 times that of each homework assignment. His old 20-point scale produced a range of 15 (i.e., 20 − 5). He decides to go to a new 25-point scale. Its range will probably be about 6–25. This 19-point range is about the desired size.

Before reading on, put yourself in Mr. Wendt's place and decide what he might most easily do for the quizzes and the exam. Then proceed.

For each quiz, he needs the range to be about 6 or 7 times 3 (again because the desired 10% weight for each quiz is 6.67 × the desired 1.5% weight for each homework assignment). The old range of 9 (i.e., 15 − 6) was only about 3 times that of each homework assignment. If he doubles it by counting twice as many points for each question, its range will become 12–30. This 18-point range is the desired 6 or 7 times the 3-point one for homework.

Finally, he wants the range for the exam to be somewhere around 40 (because the 20% weight for the exam is 13.33 × the 1.5% weight for each homework assignment which has a range of 3; thus, 3 × 13.33 = 40). Its old range is 41. That is close enough; he decides to leave it alone.

■ ■ ■ ■ ■

ENCAPSULATION

Let's digress here to consider a public relations issue along with the statistical one. Suppose that in the past, Mr. Wendt has experienced some ill will when he awarded only 5 or 10 points out of a possible 20 for the book report. Could he sweeten the taste without changing the normative meaning? Sure. Instead of using the 25-point scale that he decided upon, with its expected typical range of 6–25, he could employ a 50-point scale for which a typical class's range would be 31–50, or a 100-point scale for which most classes would have a range from about 81 to about 100. In each case, the range is 19. In norm-referenced assessment, the differences are purely cosmetic. Which would be best? In view of the fact that many students are oriented toward a percentage grading system, a range that resembles their expectation might be desirable, perhaps 31–50.

EXTENSION

The problems of weighting components for grading are very similar to the problems of weighting parts in other kinds of totals. You may want to visit ablongman.com/hannadettmer for some out-of-classroom examples (e.g., "Selecting the playground champion" and "Filling the vacant pulpit"), some of which are rather amusing (or so *we* think).

CHAPTER RECAP

Raw data are often condensed by use of summary statistics. Two features of distributions—central tendency and variability—are usually summarized. Three widely used measures of central tendency are the mean (M), median (Md), and mode (Mo). Most uses are best served with the more powerful mean where it is permissible (i.e., when it is based on a measure that provides equal units), but occasionally the median or even the mode is the more meaningful.

Variability, or individual differences, are often summarized by the use of the rough-and-ready range or the much more adequate standard deviation (SD). Most of the more advanced statistics that educators encounter are based on the mean and the standard deviation.

Of the several kinds of derived scores used for norm-referenced interpretation, two were introduced in this chapter. Percentile ranks (PRs) provide easily understood statements concerning the percent of a reference group examinees excelled or equaled. For most interpretive purposes, PRs are the derived score of preference.

The prototypic kind of standard score—the z-score—provides a measure of an examinee's deviation from a group mean; this deviation is measured in standard deviation units. For most computational or research purposes, standard scores are the derived score of preference.

Many educators assume the weight of each graded element is determined by its possible points. This is untrue of norm-referenced assessment. Parts contribute to a composite score approximately in proportion to their SDs or roughly in proportion to their ranges. If a computer is doing the work, one can afford to be precise in controlling the weights of parts of grades. When teachers do the calculations by hand, rough approximations are sensible.

MARKING, REPORTING, AND CONFERENCING

CHAPTER OVERVIEW

REASONS FOR GRADES

THINGS THAT CLOUD THE MEANING OF
GRADES

HOW TO MAKE GRADES MEANINGFUL

HOW TO CONDUCT PARENT-TEACHER AND
PARENT-STUDENT-TEACHER CONFERENCES

KEY TERMS

multiple-marking system
percentage grading
class-curve grading

anchor measure
family conference
parent partnerships

SCENARIO

Let's listen in on the end of a conversation about grading practices among several teachers in the faculty lounge at Kennedy Middle School.

Mr. A declares, "I require 93% or higher on my tests for grades of A."

"I only require 90% on tests for an A," Mrs. B comments a bit sheepishly.

"Guess I'm at the 'happy medium' with the requirement of 91%," coos Ms. C.

"How about you?" someone asks Mr. D, who has remained uncharacteristically silent.

"I only require 85% for an A," he admits defensively.

Mrs. B looks relieved at no longer being an outlier.

Meanwhile, Mr. A thinks, "Oh, ye of low expectations!" and says, "Oh! I favor maintaining high expectations of excellence. I think it prompts better student learning."

Questioning eyes now fall upon Miss E who has not commented. Finally, she says, "Please help me to understand what you are talking about. What do your thresholds of 93%, 90%, 91%, and 85% mean when we do not know the difficulty of your tests; *93% of what*?"

Silence falls upon the room, for none can answer.

Our discussion of marking begins with the functions that grades serve. Some sources of ambiguity in grades will then be examined; identifying things that cloud meaning will help us avoid pitfalls. Next, the topic of marking will be related to the CAP perspective in order to formulate criteria of effective grading systems. These criteria lead to rational and constructive marking practices. The chapter will conclude with a discussion of effective communication with parents and students through conferencing.

Teachers are required to provide periodic reports of student achievement. This communication usually uses one or more of letter grades, conferences, letters, and checklists (Oosterhof, 2001). The primary function of these activities is to communicate the level and breadth of student achievement. Key recipients of this information are students and parents[1] who have both a need and a right to achievement information in terms they can understand (Payne, 1997; Thorndike, 1997).

Wanting to be fair in grading their students, teachers spend much time recording, combining, agonizing over, explaining, and defending their evaluations. Hence, they need to be skilled in developing valid marking procedures that are solidly based in student assessment (Sanders et al., 1990). The assessments should be directly linked to instructional objectives that reflect both subject matter content and the complexity of the learning outcomes (Terwilliger, 1989). Because skilled planning includes preparation to communicate *meaningful* information, the functions of evaluation are best served when marking practices are harmonious with the elements of CAP.

As stressed in Chapter 5, evaluation should be planned at the same time instruction is planned. An evaluation plan should be developed early in the instructional sequence to provide timely information for students and parents concerning the basis of grading. Terwilliger (1989) identified the following essential elements about which a classroom evaluation plan should be explicit:

- The timing of data collection (e.g., dates for tests, due dates for assignments and projects)
- Conditions under which data will be collected (e.g., kinds of tests, availability of reference materials and computational aids during tests, whether late homework and projects will be accepted and the penalties for lateness)
- Methods by which the data will be used to arrive at summative grades (i.e., the relative weights of the items of data)

Regrettably, professional consensus has not emerged concerning the purposes of grades, what they should represent, and how they should be determined. Student achievement of a given amount and kind can yield a C from one teacher and an A from another. The differences reside in various sources of confusion about grades (Hills, 1981), in teachers' differing standards, and in conflicting definitions of what constitutes grades. In addition, a number of out-and-out mistakes sometimes occur when teachers compute student grades (Stiggins, Frisbie, & Griswold, 1989), ranging from transposing numerals to use of incorrect methods of weighting the elements that are to be summed. Marking is an aspect of professional practice in which many teachers' competence is less than adequate (Hills, 1991). We hope this chapter helps to rectify that situation.

PURPOSES AND FUNCTIONS OF GRADES

Many significant needs are met in whole or part by school marks. The varied purposes of communicating student achievement can be sorted into three categories. Communicating student achievement can:

---

[1]For convenience, we say "parents" rather then "parent(s) or guardian(s)." Too, if custody has been legally denied one or both parents, the term "parents" means "custodial parent or guardian(s)." Alternatively, the matter is sometimes resolved by using the all-inclusive term "families." In this regard, families are defined as "people who live together and care for each other."

1. Directly benefit individual students and their parents
2. Facilitate the work of teachers and schools
3. Meet societal needs

These purposes are all based on the supposition that grades *reflect the extent to which students have achieved the instructional aims.*

Helping Students and Parents.   Marks provide feedback to students and parents concerning student achievement. This important reporting function helps parents monitor student effort, provide encouragement, offer assistance, and remain informed. "If students are to improve, they need to know where improvement is needed" (Thorndike, 1997, p. 208).

Feedback also enables young people to gain self-knowledge. Grades provide achievement information by which students learn more about their intraindividual relative strengths and weaknesses and about their capabilities and limitations in comparison with others. This information facilitates important decisions concerning course selection, future education, and career choice. Developing a realistic self-concept is an important part of growing up.

Some educators resist providing informative feedback for fear it will damage self-concept. In this connection, a sharp distinction between self-concept and self-esteem is very helpful.

Positive self-esteem is desirable. When it comes to self-concept, however, we seek *realism*. If Joe is an inept speller or driver, he should know this. He is best served by honest feedback about his skills so that he can make realistic provisions for overcoming them or for learning to live with them. Grades should enhance realism of self-concept concerning achievement. This feedback should be provided in such a way that it does not imply an evaluation of the person's worth (Thorndike, 1997). Even when grades are low, high self-esteem is possible and desirable. Molly may be inept at spelling, sports, or music and still believe herself to be a very worthwhile person. Positive self-esteem is something that educators should value and work for; however, it does not happen to be a purpose of grading.

Helping Teachers and Schools.   Grades help teachers monitor student progress. This institutional function has several constructive purposes. At the level of the individual pupil, it enables teachers to individualize instruction. At both the individual and group levels, information about student achievement helps teachers develop instructional strategies. Too, recent grades help teachers to estimate the level of instruction that will best meet the needs of each student; effective teaching is aimed at a level appropriate to the learner (Slavin, 1987a).

Some elementary teachers group their pupils within classes into less heterogeneous subgroups for reading and mathematics instruction. This so-called homogeneous grouping enables teachers to instruct subgroups in which student capabilities are more similar so that the level and pace of instruction can better be targeted to the capabilities of the respective subgroups (Woolfolk, 2001).

Schools also use marks as entry requirements for certain courses at the secondary and college levels where many courses have prerequisites. For example, a high school might not allow students to enroll in a physics course unless they have at least a C in algebra. Schools also use marks to determine eligibility for various activities such as athletics and student government.

Grades at all educational levels are sometimes used for grouping students in the same course or grade. For example, a middle school might offer three levels of seventh-grade mathematics designed to meet the needs of students having differing levels of achievement in the subject.

Meeting Needs of the Larger Community.   Although school marks are confidential and can generally be released only with written permission of parents (of minors) or students (if they are adults), grades are used by institutions outside the school for important functions. For example, when a person applies for admission to college, a transcript of secondary school records is usually required. In some instances, grades serve as a basis for reaching selection decisions regarding whether to admit students. In other cases, marks help colleges make placement decisions, such as which math course would be most appropriate. And, of course, grades are a basis by which scholarship and award recipients are chosen.

Business, industry, and government also have frequent occasion to ask job applicants to supply transcripts. The marks students receive in high school and college provide prospective employers with much valuable information.

Another use of marks involves licensing for practice or certification of competence. Before people are legally allowed to practice a variety of occupations (e.g., electrician, teacher, or physician), governmental regulatory agencies assess qualifications. Grades from occupational preparation institutions help to certify competence, thereby protecting the public from deficient practitioners.

SOURCES OF AMBIGUITY IN GRADES

When the meaning of grades is unclear, the purposes of grading are not well met. Yet teachers in a school may differ sharply in their operational definitions of the meaning of grades (Stiggins, Frisbie, & Griswold, 1989). Although achievement measures such as tests are the major factor in grades, ability and effort are also often considered (Brookhart, 2002). This section addresses some of the issues that cause marks to be ambiguous. (We will delay until later in this chapter the discussion of whether grades should be domain referenced or norm referenced.)

Effort Versus Achievement.   Fran, a fourth grader, works very hard in math, but has great difficulty with the subject. She tries harder and spends more time on math than any other pupil in the class. She gets much good help at home; therefore, her homework is exemplary. However, on tests, her performance hovers in the next-to-bottom tenth of her rather typical class. What letter grade should she receive in math? (For purposes of discussing this and later examples, the common A, B, C, D, and F grades will be used.)

Some teachers would assign Fran about a D on the grounds that her achievement was higher than only 10 to 20% of typical fourth graders. A few might award her an A because her effort was superb. Many would assign her a B or a C in the belief that both her achievement and effort are relevant. Thus, one year Fran may receive a C or D, whereas the next year she might be awarded an A or B even though she performs consistently. How well do these grades serve their *primary purpose of communicating*? Alas, not nearly as well as they would if teachers could agree on the basis for grading.

Next consider tenth-grader Hank who has verbal aptitude scores in the top 1% of students his age. He works very little in social studies, yet he has no difficulty with the subject. In class, he often "clowns" and causes mild disturbances and distractions. He rarely turns in assignments or homework. However, on tests, his performance is at the very top of his rather typical class. What letter should he receive?

Some teachers would award Hank an A on the basis of his very high test scores. Many others would argue that his homework should count as part of his achievement measure and that it, averaged in some way with his high tests, would lower his grade to a B or even a C. A few would suggest that he should receive a very low grade—D or F—because he is not using his ability. A few others would favor awarding a D or an F to reflect (or punish) his unsatisfactory behavior. Many teachers would take more than one of these criteria into consideration, compromising among them (McMillan, 2001; Truog & Friedman, 1996), even if doing so was contrary to their own beliefs concerning ideal practice (Cross & Frary, 1999).

If the Frans and the Hanks can both bring home the same C grade, one must question what a C means. Parents certainly will! Clarification is needed concerning the attribute(s) that marks are supposed to communicate. It is apparent that a single letter grade cannot adequately represent both achievement and effort without suffering from grave ambiguity.

It is obviously undesirable for a student's grade to depend on who taught a course or which other people were enrolled in it. Assessment authorities (e.g., Linn & Gronlund, 2000; Marzano, 2000; Ward & Murray-Ward, 1999) generally agree that a grade is needed that is a *pure measure of achievement* uncontaminated by such issues as student effort, student aptitude, teacher-to-teacher variations of thresholds, and achievement of classmates.

Need for Multiple Marks. On the one hand, achievement is far too important to have its report obscured by mixing it with anything else (Kubiszyn & Borich, 2003). On the other hand, such attributes as effort and behavior are also very important and should be reported; information about them should not be clouded by being mixed with anything else. Thus, single letter grades do not suffice. A **multiple-marking system** is needed to do justice to the multiple dimensions; each important dimension merits a separate, unambiguous mark (Guskey, 2002; Linn & Gronlund, 2000).

This clarity of reporting is best achieved by defining a main grade—which in grades 1 through 12 typically is a letter grade (Robinson & Craver, 1989), most often A, B, C, D, and F—to be a *pure measure of achievement* (Airasian, 2001; Kubiszyn & Borich, 2003; Terwilliger, 1989). Such a definition prevents its meaning from being confounded with information about aptitude, motivation, behavior, and so on.

If this definition is applied to Fran and if homework did not count, she would most likely receive a D to reflect her low achievement. Hank would receive an A to report his high attainment. Yet situations are complicated by legitimate differences among teachers concerning whether they count the (often formative) homework as part of the summative grade. Recall that Chapter 5 presented the pros and cons of doing so. If the homework counted some modest amount, then Fran would probably get a C and Hank would probably receive a B.[2]

The need for more information than one grade can provide can be satisfied in many ways. Many have a second category, such as effort or citizenship, with which to report on a second important realm. To avoid confusion between systems, some schools use a different set of symbols for the citizenship or effort mark, for example, E (excellent), S (satisfactory), and U (unsatisfactory).

---

[2]Hank's situation would be further complicated if the homework he was assigned were the same as other students. He might soundly argue that the purpose of (formative) homework is to enable him to learn; his learning is assessed on the (summative) tests. Because he performed extremely well on the tests, the homework was obviously unnecessary. One wouldn't want to have to dispute this point.

However, if his homework was individualized to the extent of being something from which he would benefit, his argument would not refute the legitimacy of counting homework as an achievement measure and lowering his grade if he did not do it.

By providing for separate reports of at least two dimensions of student activity, a multiple-marking system provides much clearer information. For example, Hank's academic grade of B coupled with an effort grade of U tells us much more about his performance than a single system could. It helps explain why his achievement was not higher.

Written messages offer another common way to communicate more information on a report card than a single symbol can encode. In generations past, these notes were hand written. Modern technology now enables teachers to keyboard *individualized* notes that are computer-printed on report cards (after using spell check and grammar checks, of course).

THINKING CAP EXERCISE 12.1   ???

A suggestion often made for reporting achievement of students like Fran is to note the level at which they have been working and the success they have achieved *at that level*. Thus, Fran's report card might indicate that even though she is in the fourth grade, she has been working on second-grade arithmetic and has achieved about average compared with second graders who are working on second-grade math. Evaluate this suggestion.

KEY TO THINKING CAP EXERCISE 12.1
This method, which is used in some report cards that are designed to enable it, may have more merit for highly sequential content such as math than it does for less linear subject matter such as social studies. The approach certainly has the attraction of offering the struggling student the opportunity to make good grades (on easier work).

The major problem is that this approach uses a reference group to which the student does *not* belong. For many purposes, people would not much care how fourth-grade Fran compares with second graders; they would have much more use for norm-referenced statements concerning her status among fourth graders.

Marking, reporting, and conferencing with parents of children with disabilities present many complex issues for teachers. We will cycle back to this topic in the next chapter in the context of special education.

Extra Credit.   Students and their parents sometimes ask if additional work may be submitted in order to raise an academic grade.

Should we give credit for the extra work? Assuming a system with two grades, one for achievement and one for effort, then it seems sensible to recognize extra work in the effort assessment. But should it *directly* enhance the achievement grade? If the extra work results in *demonstrably* improved achievement, then of course it should. Otherwise, the extra effort should not ordinarily be allowed to distort the report of achievement.

The following analogy may highlight the logic behind this hard-nosed stance. Suppose Jason asks his physical education teacher if he will take one second off his best recorded time in running a mile for every 50 push-ups he does. Or for every extra mile he runs? Should the teacher agree? Of course not! These activities may be laudable and may well be reflected in reports of Jason's effort, but they should *not* be used as a rationalization to falsify his speed in running a mile.

This example was for a performance task for which *level* of achievement (i.e., speed) was the only issue; that is, breadth of achievement was *not* relevant. What about subject matter for which breadth of achievement is also germane?

Suppose a biology class has certain required experiments and tests. Mike, who has a B+ average on these, wants to branch out and do *relevant and enriching* additional experiments in order to try to raise his course grade to an A. Should we give credit for the extra work? Again, assuming a multiple-marking system, it certainly seems sensible to recognize extra work in reporting effort. But should it directly enhance the *achievement* grade? If the extra work results in improved *level* of achievement, then it clearly should. However, if the extra work enhances only *breadth* of achievement, then the answer isn't so clear-cut.

Recognizing the greater breadth of achievement argues strongly for allowing the extra credit. However, one should also consider carefully whether the impact of such an evaluation practice will prompt students to seek quantity rather than quality of work. If one decided to award academic credit for the extra breadth of achievement, then this feature should be built into the fabric of the unit and announced at the beginning to let all students know—up front—the rules. However, the downside of this would be the danger that some students may be lax early on in the belief that extra credit later, if necessary, could salvage their grade.

Terminal Level of Achievement Versus Progress.   Sixth-grader Stella finds spelling difficult. At the end of fifth grade, her spelling was about average for beginning third graders. Late this year, it had improved to the point of being about average for beginning fifth graders. What letter grade should she receive in spelling?

Many teachers would award Stella a D or C because her achievement is still somewhat low for her grade. Others would assign an A to reflect the excellent gain she made in a single year. Still others would find merit in both of these ideas and settle for a middle-ground B or C.

The issue here is whether Stella's achievement mark should represent her terminal level of achievement or her progress. Recall the discussion in Chapter 2 concerning instructional objectives. They are best phrased in terms of *terminal* student behaviors. Marking and reporting should, of course, reflect the extent to which students have achieved objectives (Terwilliger, 1989). Therefore, consistency demands that grades also be conceived in terms of terminal student status. Why should grades and objectives both be based on terminal level of achievement rather than progress?

First, progress is obviously fakable (Hopkins, 1998). For example, if a physical education teacher announces that grades will be based on improvement during the term, some students may deliberately perform poorly on the pretests in order to be able to "improve" during the term.

Second, because grades communicate to students and parents, help the schools, and inform external agencies, all are better served if marks clearly report student terminal status. Thus, Stella should receive a D or a C. An A for her spelling progress would report nothing about her present status.

Third, determination of progress, improvement, or gain requires comparison of pre- and posttest scores. Difference scores (e.g., posttest score minus pretest score) are always less reliable than either the pretest scores or the posttest scores. Thus, any system of marking based on difference scores (e.g., progress or comparison of aptitude measures with achievement measures) will be less consistent than either of the measures on which they are based (Nitko, 2001; Popham, 2000). Moreover, use of difference scores causes some very serious technical statistical problems.

Finally, few teachers who use the rhetoric of gains really mean it. For example, suppose a keyboarding teacher has an objective that each student will *learn* the home position of the eight fingers, but Sarah enters the class already *knowing* them. Because she does not *learn* them in the class, should she be penalized? Of course not. This demonstrates that the real objective was not that she learn the home positions so much as that she know them.

Why does grading based on mixtures of terminal level of achievement, effort, and improvement persist? Cross and Frary (1999) concluded that the deplorable practice was perpetuated not only by lack of teacher understanding of the underlying issues but also by poor advice appearing in certain widely read journals. We also cannot ignore public pressure upon teachers emanating both from misinformation and emotion in this sensitive area.

Distribution Shape.   Everybody knows that it is easier to earn a given grade from some teachers than from others; a major defect of grades is the lack of clear understanding of what they mean concerning level of achievement. Take Mr. Moore and Mr. Duncan who both teach senior English in the same school. They are equally competent teachers, and their students, on average, are equally capable. In typical sections, however, their respective grade distributions might be:

	MR. MOORE	MR. DUNCAN
A	5%	40%
B	15%	45%
C	40%	12%
D	30%	3%
F	10%	0%

Joe is a rather poor student in English, typically achieving better than only about one-fifth of his peers. What grade should he receive?

The answer, of course, is a matter of definition. The way Mr. Moore defines grades, Joe merits a D. By Mr. Duncan's definition, Joe should receive a B. What are Joe's parents or a prospective employer later examining his transcript not knowing the peculiarities of particular teachers to make of his grade of D or B?

Not only do teacher differences impede communication, they also cause another problem. The differences, as counselors and administrators can attest, create a wave of attempted transfers from Mr. Moore's classes to Mr. Duncan's.

The remedy to these problems lies in the attainment of greater similarity of definitions. Unfortunately, this is easier said than done. Teachers often exhibit great ego involvement in their grading practices. For example, Mr. Moore may pride himself on his high expectations and high demands and be extremely resistant to "cheapening" the value of grades. Mr. Duncan, on the other hand, may take pride in his high grades, thinking they evidence successful teaching and learning. In reality, of course, their grade distributions reflect only the artifact of their respective definitions or conceptions of the "proper" meaning of grades.

Both teachers will agree that there is a problem. Any progress they can make toward converging their differences would help better communicate the meaning of grades to their several audiences. Although it may not be feasible to get Mr. Moore and Mr. Duncan to agree to the same shape of grade distribution, it would probably be possible to get each to compromise a little. Staff development programs can help teachers understand that no "cosmic" right distribution of marks exists; rather, distributions are matters of social convention.

Recognition that the definition of marks, like other definitions, is simply a convention, leads to a suggestion for teachers who are new to a school. Grade distributions in a given school depend in part on the local culture; therefore, new teachers are well advised to explore the local meaning of grades and to stay within tolerated limits (Thorndike, Cunningham, Thorndike, & Hagen, 1991).

Avoiding unacceptable deviations from the convention helps achieve better communication (not to mention greater job security!).

Thus, if we were new teachers in a school where most of the faculty grade much like Mr. Moore (who gives much lower grades than we would prefer), we would tend to maintain the local meaning of grades by largely conforming. On the other hand, if we were to teach in a school where most teachers award grades like Mr. Duncan (who awards higher grades than we would prefer), we again would seek to preserve the meaning of the grades by largely conforming. As we gained more experience, we might expect to exert more influence on the school's expectations concerning distribution shape as well the underlying rationale of grading.

TOWARD A RATIONAL SYSTEM OF GRADING

Like other features of a culture, marking practices are often accepted with little thoughtful analysis of their rationale and functions. In examining marking practices, one's perspective might best be similar to that of a cultural anthropologist who examines a set of behaviors and tries to understand their functions and the way in which they fit into the total culture. Grading practices should thus be examined with dispassionate objectivity (Thorndike, Cunningham, Thorndike, & Hagen, 1991).

The most fundamental decision that an institution or teacher must make may be the choice between an absolute or a relative grading method. If an absolute method is chosen, the methods of evaluation should be designed to yield meaningful domain-referenced interpretation. If a relative method is selected, then the system should be fashioned to provide meaningful norm-referenced interpretation. As discussed in Chapter 4, one cannot wisely choose between these major approaches without considering the kind of subject matter. *The nature of the subject matter dictates the kind of referencing (and other aspects of CAP) that is appropriate.*

When grades report achievement in explicit, masterable, vital (Context A) domains, domain-referenced grading should be used *for each minimum essential objective separately.* Report cards can state each minimum essential objective and provide places to check mastery or nonmastery (and perhaps borderline) status. At the lower elementary level, portions of report cards sometimes consist of such domain-referenced checklists for reporting attainment of specific objectives. Figure 12.1 shows a section of a report card designed to report the mastery status on each of several explicit mastery objectives.

When grades report achievement in explicit, nonessential, or unmasterable (Context B) domains, it isn't necessary to report achievement for each objective separately. The logic of CAP dictates that achievement of this kind of subject matter can be interpreted either by means of domain referencing or norm referencing. If domain referencing is chosen, report cards should be designed to be referenced clearly to each domain separately with a report of achievement for each. Figure 12.2 illustrates such a section.

Although the approach illustrated in Figure 12.2 can work, it is not the choice of most teachers or schools. Because Context B objectives are not essential, there is little reason to go to the trouble of domain-referencing summative reports of achievement for each separate aim. Rather, it is common practice to combine achievement across several objectives and to report each student's composite status by means of norm referencing. (In this case, one would need to know how to combine the raw scores of the separate activities to make each count the desired amount.)

When grades are used to report student achievement of developmental objectives for large, open-ended, unmasterable, nonessential (Context C) domains, *meaningful reporting demands norm*

FIGURE 12.1   Portion of Report Card Suitable for Context A Content.

MATHEMATICS—GRADE TWO, THIRD QUARTER

Skill	Status		
	Not Mastered	*Partial Mastery*	*Mastered*
Uses commutative property of addition (e.g., if 6 + 3 = 9, then 3 + 6 must = 9)	_____	_____	_____
Explains place value (e.g., 52 = 5 tens + 2 ones)	_____	_____	_____
Supplies missing addends under 10 (e.g., 3 + ? = 8)	_____	_____	_____
Adds three 1-digit numbers	_____	_____	_____
Adds two 2-digit numbers without regrouping	_____	_____	_____
Adds two 2-digit numbers with regrouping	_____	_____	_____
Supplies missing subtrahends under 10 (e.g., 6 − ? = 2)	_____	_____	_____
Supplies missing minuends under 10 (e.g., ? − 3 = 8)	_____	_____	_____
Subtracts 1-digit numbers from 2-digit numbers without regrouping	_____	_____	_____
Subtracts 2-digit numbers from 2-digit numbers without regrouping	_____	_____	_____
Reads conventional clocks at quarter hours	_____	_____	_____
Determines value of combinations of coins up to a dollar	_____	_____	_____
Constructs simple pie graph	_____	_____	_____
Reads simple pie graph	_____	_____	_____

Source: Adapted from Millman, J. (1970). Reporting student progress: A case for a criterion-referenced marking system. *Phi Delta Kappan, 52,* pp. 226–230.

referencing. Adequate referencing to expansive content domains is not viable. Much confusion would be avoided if this important fact were more widely recognized.

Because Context C aims are not essential, there is no need to report student achievement separately for each learning target. Here, too, it is common practice to combine achievement across several objectives.

What if the content taught during a reporting period is drawn from two or three contexts? In this case, it may make the most sense to separate the report of Context A material from the rest. The Context A material can be organized into a checklist indicating the mastery or nonmastery of each explicit mastery objective. Alternatively, in those cases in which almost all students have mastered

FIGURE 12.2   Portion of Report Card Suitable for Domain-Referencing Context B Content. This method is not the method of choice of most teachers.

PHYSICAL EDUCATION—EIGHTH-GRADE BOYS' TRACK	
Event	*Status on Best of Three Attempts*
100-meter dash	_____ Seconds
400-meter race	_____ Seconds
1600-meter race	_____ Seconds
High jump	_____ Meters
Long jump	_____ Meters
100-meter low hurdles	_____ Seconds
100-meter high hurdles	_____ Seconds

all the Context A objectives, it may be easier to gloss over minimum essential objectives with a mere comment that all *except those listed* have been met.

Another option would be to fail any student who does not master each and every explicit mastery objective. This decision could be seen as a logical consequence of the contention that such aims are truly vital. However, a major difficulty with this approach is the arbitrary periodicity of school reporting cycles. Mastery learning is designed to bring nearly everyone to mastery *eventually*. When individual differences are directed into the time-it-takes-to-reach-the-mastery-threshold dimension, it is hard to justify a demand of mastery at some arbitrary point such as the end of a reporting cycle.

Once the Context A content of a course or subject has been handled, it is customary and sensible to *combine achievement of all Context B and C objectives into one composite grade.* The rest of this section is devoted to the issue of how this total grade—which usually reflects achievement of several developmental objectives—is best determined.

We will now consider the two most common methods of assigning such grades to students. From an analysis of the virtues and vices of each method, a set of considerations for rational and effective marking systems will be derived. The concept of anchor measures will then be developed. Meaningful norm-referenced grading in Context C by use of anchor measures will then be derived.

Two Prototypic Grading Systems[3]

Two widely used groups of methods are used to determine grades.[4] **Percentage grading** is the most common variety of a group of methods that attempts to orient grades to "absolute standards" or universal expectations (without regard to task difficulty). **Class-curve grading** is the most common of those methods based on relative, norm-referenced orientations. These two common systems will be the focus of this section. Although each system has numerous variants, most teachers fall quite neatly into one camp or the other.

[3]Much of the remainder of this section on developing a rational grading system was adapted from Hanna and Cashin (1988). Used with permission.

[4]Other methods are used by relatively few teachers; McKeachie (1986) and Terwilliger (1971) discussed several of these less-common grading methods (e.g., contract grading) and their problems.

Percentage Grading Systems.   Percentage grading systems are the most widely used basis for assigning (either letter or percentage) grades. In such systems, teachers use "absolute standards" in the form of the percentage of possible points required for each grade. Advocates believe this provides advance notice to students of what they have to do in order to earn various grades.

But does an announcement that "students will need to average at least 90% to earn an A" really communicate anything useful? Does it clearly specify the content? No! Does it communicate the difficulty of the tests on which this "standard" or expectation must be maintained? No!

Such an announcement doesn't answer—or even address—the crucial question: "Ninety percent *of what*?" It doesn't answer the question because most courses or subjects include broad, variable ranges of Context C subject matter. The difficulty of the material and its exact composition appropriately varies from teacher to teacher and from year to year. The objectives of most elementary and secondary school subjects are—and should be—expansive and developmental. They can be pursued by various content routes; thus, *the exact content is not tightly specified.*

Such large, open, vaguely described Context C domains do not give rise to meaningful interpretation of student achievement in terms of either raw or percentage scores. Recall that domain-referenced statements must relate to a domain of material that is *very clearly specified.* The domain definition should be sufficiently detailed and explicit to show clearly what facets of behavior are included in and what facets are excluded from the domain (AERA, 1999).

An important consequence of the size and lack of incisive description that characterizes Context C material is *uncontrolled item difficulty.* A teacher can (intentionally or inadvertently) develop a test on which no student is likely to obtain even 70% of the possible points. Likewise, one can create a test on which most students easily attain over 90%. Raw scores and percentage scores are as dependent on test characteristics as on student characteristics (Mehrens & Lehmann, 1991); that is, raw scores are *artifacts of test difficulty.* For this reason, announcements of "absolute standards" such as, "You must average at least 84% to earn a B," create only an *illusion* of informative clarity; they really tell nothing because they don't answer the question "Eighty-four percent of what?"

Such statements tell nothing, that is, unless an implicit understanding exists concerning test difficulty. Difficulty, of course, is inherently norm referenced. Thus, for a percentage marking system to convey information, it must *violate its intrinsic domain-referenced nature and be rendered covertly norm referenced.*

As testimony to the truth of this bold claim, consider what happens when a test turns out to be too hard. Suppose a teacher uses percentage grading in a class that has always exhibited normal competence. Now, on a certain newly constructed 40-item objective test, the top score is only 80%. Does the teacher assign unusually low grades? Often not. Most teachers who find themselves in this predicament do one or another form of *violence to the meaning of percentage grading.* After they paint themselves into a corner, they walk on the wet paint. How?

A few void the test. Some go ahead and count it, but rig the next one to be very easy in order to compensate. Others let students correct their errors for partial credit on (only) this hard test. Still others are more generous than they would otherwise be in awarding partial credit. Many teachers engage in strange arithmetic practice such as counting each of the test's 40 items at 3% rather than 2.5% or giving everybody a 10% or 25% bonus.

Another common adjustment is to scale the "percentage" grades to the top person in the class (80% in this example). Thus, a score of 60% would be elevated to 75% (60/80). This, of course, *is norm referencing,* and one cannot do worse than to select a single individual for the reference "group"!

Such adjustments are not compatible to the rationale of absolute-standard (i.e., universal expectations), domain-referenced, percentage grading. These methods don't represent true percentage grading; such pseudo-percentage systems are ways people fix the messes that they get into by use of a fundamentally flawed system. It would be preferable to adopt a grading system that avoids both the predicaments and the deceptions.

In subjects having expansive subject matter, the material is variable in difficulty; for example, one could test knowledge or application of given facts or principles with easy questions or with difficult ones. *Expansive content domains do not tie down test item difficulty.* Thus, interpreting student performance in terms of either raw or percent scores (i.e., domain referencing) cannot be meaningfully achieved. There are no statistical, educational, or psychological bases for linking arbitrary percentages of ill-defined domains to grades (Mehrens & Lehmann, 1991; Nitko, 2001).

THINKING CAP EXERCISE 12.2

Several common methods of adjusting (pseudo) percentage grading have been sketched. Let's apply the theme that "evaluation has impact" and consider some unintended consequences of various practices. Identify any undesirable effect on students of each of the following ways teachers "walk on the wet paint."

1. Voiding the test that turns out to be too difficult
2. Rigging the next test to be much easier
3. Awarding partial credit unusually generously
4. Performing "eccentric" arithmetic
5. Scaling to the top student.

KEY TO THINKING CAP EXERCISE 12.2

1. Students who have not prepared for the test are rewarded, whereas those who have conscientiously studied are punished. This may impact undesirably on their future study behavior. Voiding also reduces the validity of the grades as balanced measures of achievement.

2. A given level of performance would result in unrealistically adverse feedback on the first occasion and unrealistically favorable feedback on the second. Such misleading feedback tends to hinder students' development of self-monitoring and realistic self-appraisal.

3. This alone usually would not suffice to solve the problem. It also might distort students' understanding of the seriousness of their mistakes.

4. Awarding 6% for each of 20 items teaches that 100% of something may not be all of it. What kind of arithmetic modeling is this?!

5. Scaling everyone's grade to the performance of the top student sets this individual up for group censure. Such a student may learn that it is unwise to perform at one's best because peers disapprove of "curve busters." Moreover, it provides an extremely unstable basis for grading because it is based on data from only one student.

Class-Curve Grading Systems.   Like other teachers, those who grade on class curves value giving advance notice to students regarding what is required to receive various grades. They seek this by issuing such statements as, "To earn an A, you must be among the top 20% of the people in this class in total end-of-term points." Does such information really communicate how hard students must work in order to receive a given grade? No.

At the elementary level, the children assigned to a given teacher may be more or less capable than those assigned last year. Similarly, at higher levels, some sections of a course often contain better students than others. Persons in classes having many poor students can more easily rise to the top than can those in better classes. Thus, a student in the A stratum in the poor section might well receive only a B or even a C in a high section. This section-to-section fluctuation typically *makes a one-grade difference for several students per section.*

We have an apparent paradox. On the one hand, norm referencing is the only logical foundation upon which to base grades for Context C content. On the other hand, the only method of achieving norm referencing of which most teachers are aware—grading on a class curve—is ordinarily unsatisfactory because it introduces instability arising from small class sizes. Don't despair; there *is* a way out. First, however, let's identify the other major problems associated with class-curve grading.

Grading on a class curve forces students to compete for grades. Yet learning is not inherently competitive.[5] One person's success in learning does not predispose others to less success. Class-curve grading, however, creates a *predetermination* of a section's grade distribution *regardless of student learning.* Such a situation causes students to feel helpless and to lack a sense of efficacy.

Perhaps the greatest evil of class-curve grading is its impact on interpersonal relations. Suppose there can be only four A grades in a certain class, and Sue ranks fifth. The only way she can earn an A is by bumping someone else. The bumped person need learn no less, but in class-curve grading someone must receive a lower grade in order for Sue to receive a higher one. In such a system, a grade not only reflects a student's achievement, it is also a function of the achievement of others in the class.

Having to bump others or being bumped fosters ill will. Marking on a class curve doesn't encourage group study or cooperative learning; instead, it promotes isolation and exclusion. Class-curve grading doesn't motivate students to help one another to learn; on the contrary, self-interest is best served by interfering with the learning of one's fellow students.

THINKING CAP EXERCISE 12.3 ???

1. If there were no way out of the apparent paradox and you had to choose a pseudo-percentage marking system or a class-curve system, which would be the lesser evil?

2. Ms. Jenkins uses domain referencing for setting a passing pseudo-threshold (e.g., 60%) and class-curve grading for differentiating among the other grades. Mr. Khalaf uses pseudo-domain referencing to establish the standard necessary for an A (e.g., 90%) and a class-curve system for distinguishing among the other grades. How do the problems of these systems compare in seriousness with those of sole use of percentage grading or class-curve methods?

KEY TO THINKING CAP EXERCISE 12.3

1. Following is our personal response. So-called percentage grading has serious logical and assessment problems. Class-curve grading not only has logical and assessment problems, it has grave social evils. We abhor its impact on interpersonal relations. If forced to choose between the two bad systems, we would choose one or another of the adulterations of percentage grading.

---

[5]We have no universal objection to competition. When there can be only one first-chair clarinetist in the band, competition is inherent. Similarly, only one person can be elected class president. Learning, however, is *not* inherently competitive; one person's success in learning needn't and shouldn't doom another to learn less.

One common adjustment that we would assuredly *not* use is to scale the percentages to the performance of the top student. This covert norm referencing to a sample of one person represents the worst of both systems. It sets the top student up to be disliked (if not persecuted) by peers.

2. Such schemes have the advantages and limitations of one system in one part of the distribution of grades and the benefits and problems of the other system in other parts of the distribution. These mixes of two inadequate systems do not produce hybrid vigor! Rather, they produce a more confusing set of problems than does either system used by itself.

Characteristics of Sound Grading Systems in Context C

In seeking a better system of Context C grading, we should strive to avoid the pitfalls identified for percentage and class-curve grading practices. At the same time, we should seek to tap the full, undiluted values of each approach. Our pursuit of this dual aim will be assisted by identifying desired attributes of grading systems.

Obtain Relevant Norm Referencing.   The subject matter domains of most courses are large and flexible.[6] Instruction is typically aimed at high-road transfer of learning. It isn't possible to describe the domains with enough precision to render domain referencing meaningful. Hence, the only viable means of interpreting performance is by means of norm referencing.[7]

A sound system of Context C grading must be referenced to a *relevant* group of people. The pursuit of relevance usually dictates that the reference group consist of other (past or present) students in the grade or course.

Avoid Instability of Small Samples.   Sound grading must also be referenced to *stable* groups. This requires groups large enough to avoid marked group-to-group fluctuation. The need for stability dictates that reference groups *not* consist of individual classes. The grades awarded to students in a given section should be free to reflect the group's achievement if it turns out to be unusually high or low. Similarly, grades should reflect section-to-section peculiarities in variability.

Avoid Psychological and Social Evils of Fixed-Sum Systems.   A *fixed-sum game* is a situation in which there is a preestablished amount of reward that must be shared among the participants; for one person to receive more means that another or others must get less. Tennis and poker are fixed-sum games. Merit badges in a scout troop and sales from the sales representatives of a company are not fixed; everyone can do well and the total can be increased.

The total amount that students in a class can achieve is not predetermined. Grading systems should reflect this reality. Cooperation should not be thwarted by systems of reporting achievement. Counterproductive competition among peers should never be fostered. These considerations dictate

[6]Recall that earlier in this chapter separate approaches were described (and illustrated in Figure 12.1) for grading Context A material.

[7]Note that norm referencing per se does *not* require that the individual class serve as the reference group. Nor does it dictate the shape of the distribution of grades or suggest that the bell-shaped normal curve requires some specific fraction of students to fail (Mehrens & Lehmann, 1991).

that the reference group be (at least largely) external to the section being graded (unless the section is enormous, as in some college courses).

Provide a Sense of Efficacy.   A closely related criterion is that students should have a sense of control over their learning and over the grades that report it. They should know that if the achievement is unusually high or low in their class, then the grade distribution will faithfully reflect this reality.

Be Defined and Interpretable.   A marking and reporting system should be highly interpretable (Thorndike & Hagen, 1977) and communicable (Stiggins, 2001). It is also desirable that the definition of grades be consistent from section to section and from teacher to teacher. This consistency is achieved by norm-referenced definition of grades' meaning by comparison to a stable, relevant reference group of other students.

Anchorage to a Larger, More Inclusive Reference Group

Analysis of the two common grading systems may seem to produce a quandary. Norm referencing is the best foundation on which to base grades in courses having Context C subject matter. Yet the best known means of achieving norm referencing—class-curve grading—is wholly unsatisfactory, if not unethical. *Anchor measures provide an escape from the apparent dilemma by permitting referencing to a larger, external reference group.* Instead of section-by-section referencing, a more inclusive reference group is sought upon which to base norm referencing. This group best consists of either (a) all students in various sections of the same course for whom common data are available or (b) all students who have taken a particular course from the same teacher for several years for whom common data are available (Terwilliger, 1989).

An **anchor measure** is the link to those data. It is a device with which one can judge or "take the bearings" of a whole class's status. Suppose all the sections of the same high school biology course (i.e., sections taught from the same syllabus and text) took the same final exam. This test could be used to reveal if and how the groups differed in mean scores. The grade distributions in the several sections could reflect the differences. Such an exam would be said to be an anchor test. Or, suppose prior mean grade point averages (GPAs) were available for the students in each section. If some sections were found to have higher mean GPAs than others, then the section-to-section distributions of biology grades could thereby be adjusted.

To provide anchorage, a variable need have only one attribute: It must correlate with performance in the course being graded. The greater the relationship the better. Thus, common tests across sections would provide stronger anchorage than would prior grades.

Notice that some anchor measures (e.g., common tests or projects) should contribute to the evaluation of each student. Others (e.g., aptitude test scores, grades in prerequisite courses, or GPAs) clearly should *not* be used to evaluate student course work. The former are preferable anchors because they tend to be correlated more strongly with course achievement and because they enable a realistic sense of efficacy.

Anchor measures can help to meet each characteristic of sound grading systems. When a course achievement variable is used to anchor achievement of students in one section of a course to a large number of other students who have taken or are taking the same course, the anchor provides the needed link to satisfy all of the criteria that have been identified. The group of relevant other people who have had the same course provides meaningful, interpretable, and appropriate norm referencing; this satisfies the criteria of providing relevant norm referencing and of being interpretable.

The large size of the reference group meets the criterion of stability. The ability of each section's grades to rise or fall with student achievement liberates students from needing to compete with peers; this satisfies the criterion of not pitting students against each other in a fixed-sum system. This capacity of a class's grades to reflect its achievement also provides its members with a realistic sense of control over their destiny; this satisfies the criterion of providing efficacy.

The processes by which anchor measures are used can be relatively simple and intuitive. This is the approach used in the following examples that illustrate their use.

Example 1: Teacher's Use of Unit Test as an Anchor Measure.   Mrs. Frank teaches in a small elementary school. Each year she teaches her well-polished "Life in the Kalahari" unit to her fourth-grade students. The test for this unit provides a measure that links classes across the years. Because this test is revised only every several years, Mrs. Frank uses it to anchor each section to all of her past sections in recent years.

Suppose that Mrs. Frank thinks that the distribution of grades for *typical* classes should be about 20% A, 30% B, 30% C, 19% D, and 1% F. Comparison is *not* within each small class, but with several previous years' classes. If a class's achievement is unusually high or low, its grades will reflect this; thus, *grading is* not *on a class curve.*

This year Mrs. Frank had only 12 pupils. Table 12.1 on page 310 shows the cumulative distribution of test scores on the unit for a few previous years' classes and the distribution for this section. The percentage of previous pupils receiving each grade on the test approximates the announced distribution of grades for typical classes. Table 12.1 also shows that her present class performed considerably better than average. Her goal, therefore, is to award grades to her present class that reflect its greater-than-typical merit.

The left-hand column of Table 12.2 on page 311 provides Mrs. Frank's distribution of *total* points accrued in the Kalahari unit (by whatever system she uses to combine components). These totals include pupil performance not only on the anchoring unit test, but also on tests for other social studies units, assignments, reports, and so on. (This total need not be made up of the same components each year.) The question is, "Where should Mrs. Frank draw the lines separating the A, B, C, D, and F grades for this class?"

The general aim is to draw the lines in places where the resulting distribution of grades will most closely coincide with the shape of the class's distribution on the anchor measure. In addition, it is conventional wisdom that one should draw the lines that separate adjacent grades in parts of the distribution where there are relatively large gaps.[8]

Mrs. Frank's class this year is clearly superior. Note that 5 out of 12 received grades of A on the anchor test. Therefore, she would want to award more than the typical 20% (i.e., two or three) A grades. Given the reasonable break in the distribution of total points shown in Table 12.2 between the fifth and sixth pupils, she awarded five A grades; this, fortunately, coincides with the number of pupils who received A marks on the anchor measure.

---

[8]This seems sensible to teachers and students alike. It also has an important public-relations advantage. Larger breaks between grades reduce the tendency of persons who fall at the top of a grade interval to argue, trying to salvage the point or two that would put them into the next higher grade interval. It is good to avoid unproductive bickering over grades. From a statistical point of view, however, the large gaps in a distribution of a single class usually reflect nothing more than the instability of small samples. From this perspective, it can be soundly argued that gap size should be ignored (except for ties of course). We find the statistical argument persuasive, yet the public-relations issue is very important. We take the expedient course and yield to the conventional practice, that is, generally using any large gaps to separate grades.

TABLE 12.1   Example of Teacher Use of Test as an Anchor Measure

DISTRIBUTION OF SCORES FOR SIX PREVIOUS CLASSES			SCORES OF PRESENT CLASS
X	f	Grade	f
40	1		
39	0		1
38	3		1
37	3	A (20%)	
36	4		1
35	3		2
34	4		
33	4		
32	5		1
31	3	B (29%)	
30	7		1
29	7		2
28	5		
27	6		1
26	5		1
25	4	C (31%)	
24	3		
23	5		1
22	3		
21	2		
20	4		
19	2		
18	1		
17	2	D (19%)	
16	1		
15	1		
14	0		
13	0		
12	1		
11	0		
10	0		
9	1	F (1%)	

TABLE 12.2   Points Earned by This Year's Class

DISTRIBUTION OF TOTAL POINTS	GRADE
349	
337	
330	A
317	
311	
299	
287	
276	B
268	
255	
230	C
202	D

In deciding how many Bs to assign, Mrs. Frank noted that four pupils earned this grade on the anchor test, and in the distribution of total points a reasonable break occurred with four Bs. Because there was not a great deal of difference between the Bs and Cs in the anchor scores, she would have felt free to deviate from the exact number of four had the break in the distribution been a bit higher or lower.

For C grades, this occurred. Although the bottom three pupils received Cs on the anchor test, one was a low C. The relatively large break in the distribution of totals between the bottom two people prompted Mrs. Frank to draw the line between them, giving only two Cs and one D. This illustrates the common situation in which the distribution of grades on the anchor measure does not perfectly coincide with the distribution of final grades.

It is important to understand that the five pupils who received A grades for the course are not necessarily the exact ones who received A grades on the unit test. Anchor measures are used to get a navigational-type fix on classes. They are not, of course, the sole means of assigning course grades to individuals.

All the criteria of sound grading systems on pages 307–308 were satisfied. The grades were rendered interpretable by being norm referenced to the larger, more stable, highly relevant group of previous youngsters who had studied the unit and taken the test. At the same time, the psychological and social evils of putting children in a fixed-sum pit to fight it out were avoided. Finally, pupils were provided with a realistic sense of efficacy.

Example 2: Sections Taught by Several Teachers.   Suppose a large secondary school has nine sections of second-year algebra taught by four different teachers. With so many teachers who may have differing orientations toward grading, a common norm-referenced meaning of grades needs to be defined. Consistent definitions of grades' meaning will make the grades more able to serve their primary purpose—communication. Moreover, some students attempt to transfer from "stingy" teachers to "generous" ones. This can be avoided by adhering to common norm-referenced grading practices.

Consider the (unlikely) worst-case scenario in which the nine sections all use different text, symbols, or terminology. Even here, anchorage can be achieved. One attractive approach would be for each teacher to anchor this year's classes to his or her own prior students, as Mrs. Frank did.

Another approach would be to find some limited common test content (e.g., story problems and factoring) that could be used for the nine current sections. If an occasional common quiz is used or if some portions of selected tests are common across the several sections, the basis for linkage enables estimation of the sections' relative achievement, helping each teacher to know how to scale letter grades for assignments and tests throughout the term.

Even in this worst-case scenario, two ways have been shown to use anchor measures to satisfy all the criteria of good grading systems. In the more likely cases in which the teachers use the same text and terminology, occasional common texts could more easily anchor all nine sections to each other and/or to previous groups; this, too, could satisfy all the criteria.

THINKING CAP EXERCISE 12.4   ???

1. Suppose you are a first-year teacher in a small elementary school and you teach the only section of third grade. You have informed yourself of the local customs concerning grade distributions, but you don't know how typical your 19 third graders are. What are some of the ways by which you could "get a fix on" your class?

2. The four sixth-grade teachers in a school have decided to anchor their English grades to the sum of the four classes. For an anchor measure, they are considering use of (a) an objective mechanics of expression test that they all use and believe to be valid, (b) an out-of-class assignment that they all use that involves an oral report on a book, or (c) an essay test that they all use with each teacher scoring her or his own class's papers.

Assume that all three measures correlate about the same with overall achievement in sixth-grade English and that all three could count equally in contributing to English grades as defined by each teacher. Which measure would be the best anchor?

3. In using anchor measures, should one seek to have distributions of grades reflect differences among classes in variability as well as differences in central tendency?

KEY TO THINKING CAP EXERCISE 12.4

1. Prior data (e.g., the opinion of the experienced second-grade teacher who taught most of the children last year or last year's published achievement test scores) could serve to estimate the level of your class's achievement. However, it would not provide a realistic sense of efficacy or avoid the evils of fixed-sum systems. Use of published achievement test scores from late in the current school year would be preferable. Although scores of published tests are seldom appropriate for use in assigning grades to *individual* pupils, they can be useful in assessing a class's status in comparison to a national reference group.

2. In scoring the oral reports and essays, some teachers will probably be systematically more generous than others. This ruins their utility as anchor measures. For this reason, products and performances are not nearly as satisfactory as objective measures for anchoring.

3. Yes. Although group-to-group fluctuation is not as great in variability as it is in central tendency, it is certainly a purpose of anchoring to account for this issue.

Anchorage in the Context of Ability Grouping. Some schools engage in systematic homogeneous ability grouping of students. For example 22 sections of sophomore English could consist of 5 enriched sections, 12 regular sections, and 5 basic ones. We obviously do *not* expect similar distributions of grades in sections that have systematically been created to be dissimilar. Any reasonable anchor measure would suffice. The techniques of anchoring are fully applicable and especially important where ability grouping is practiced.

An Alternative Approach

The method of anchoring a class's norm-referenced grades that was just presented is, in our opinion, the preferred approach, and we hope you will be permitted to and disposed to use it. Yet many conscientious teachers reject it. Nonetheless, understanding the system will, at the very least, provide you with a rational basis either to accept or reject it.

Among those who reject the use of anchor measures, several reasons dominate. They follow with our comments in parentheses.

- The method prevents immediate and clear feedback to students about status. (True, use of anchor measures doesn't *enable* such feedback at all times. But neither does percentage grading, which often provides a less than honest *illusion* of meaningful feedback [Thorndike, Cunningham, Thorndike, & Hagen, 1991]. Therefore, this is not a sound reason to reject use of anchored norm-referenced grading.)
- Use of anchor measures prevents teachers from being able to summarize a student's overall standing at any point in time. (Before the anchor data are available, this is a problem.)
- It is too complex and takes too much time from other things that teachers should be doing. (It must be conceded that the method is relatively complicated.)
- Use of anchor measures upsets students and parents because it is not what they are accustomed to. (It indeed can, especially if it is not explained simply and meaningfully.)
- School policy dictates percentage grading. (In some schools, this is, unfortunately, true. That is part of the reason for this section.)
- It may be professionally hazardous to deviate very much from conventional percentage grading. (We are sympathetic to this reason. It is the other thing that prompted us to develop this section.)

So what advice might be given to those who make an informed decision not to use anchor measures to achieve meaningful norm-referenced grading? Recent Thinking CAP Exercises have laid some foundation.

We first mention two things that we most emphatically implore you *not* to do.

- Do *not* link class grading to the performance of the top student. This yields wildly unstable grades and has grave social consequences.
- Do *not* use class-curve grading. This, too, yields relatively unstable data and has deplorable social and psychological side effects.

What then to do? The problems of pseudo-percentage systems seem far preferable to the problems and evils of class-curve systems. If a user of pseudo-percentages understands their logical shortcomings and grasps the *need for covert norm referencing,* the system can be improved, surreptitiously if necessary. That is, the expansiveness of the Context C domains severely limits the meaningfulness of raw or percentage scores. By recognizing percentage standards or thresholds in Context C to be illusory, one is liberated from rigid, superstitious, literal adherence to them. One becomes free to adjust the data to serve socially constructive ends.

As one example, scoring of essays, other products, and performances can be fashioned to yield numbers that conform to pseudo-percentage expectations. This solution was provided on page 291 for Mr. Wendt's book reports. Indeed, if we think of the scores on a 100-point scale as a *point* scale rather than as percentages, much difficulty is avoided. If the common 10-point interval for grades is used, then 89–87 could be thought of as meaning B+, 86–83 as B, and 82–80 as B−. In other words, a numeric scale can be used as a more refined way of expressing status than letter grades; the notion of "percentage" can be avoided, and one can thus avoid the issue of "Percent of what?"

For another example, suppose an essay test's scoring rubric had a possible range of 0–10 and an actual range of 2–10 in a class for which informal anchor data implied typical achievement. If the teacher wanted to convert the resulting scores into so-called percentages, each entry in the rubric could be multiplied by 10; this would yield an actual range of 20–100. *Bad idea*! This would produce a huge percentage of failing students, which would be inappropriate in a class having typical achievement. A better adaptation would be to multiply each entry in the rubric by, say, 5 and then to add 50 pseudo-percentage points to each. This would yield a range of 60–100. (The 60 is 5 times the previous floor of 2 plus 50; the 100 is 5 times the previous ceiling of 10 plus 50.)

Unfortunately, a fully satisfactory remedy is not as simple for objective tests.[9] A widely used informal approach is for the teacher to try to create a test at a difficulty level that yields a distribution of percentage scores that conforms with his or her judgment of what students in the class merit. Where do the teacher's expectations about the class come from? From off-the-record norm referencing.

When prior knowledge enables good aim of test difficulty, no adjustments are needed. However, if the test turns out to be too hard (or too easy), the teacher adds (or subtracts) some constant number of percentage points to each score. Of course, students will be much more understanding of the propriety of awarding extra points to their scores on a hard test than to subtracting them from their scores on an easy one.

This method yields results that are similar to the method of "eccentric" arithmetic (e.g., awarding 3% or 3 points for each of 35 items) without modeling bad math. A simple additive adjustment can be an open and honest recognition of the need to adjust scores because the teacher's aim (with respect to difficulty) was off target. One can say something like, "I unintentionally made the test a little too hard, and I don't want to penalize you because of it."

---

[9]Experienced teachers could, with much trouble, select from their test files items that had known percentages of examinees passing. Similarly, teachers having access to large, computerized item banks could also know something about item difficulty before a test is administered. If most of a test's items are thus chosen to yield a desired shape of distribution, the result will usually turn out to be reasonably close to the intended shape. Such *indirect norm referencing* can be quite sound and still provide the illusion of being criterion referenced in settings where such a fiction is required. For example, such rigging is needed for civil service exams for which there is a preset passing score such as 70. However, this method is not practical in classroom settings.

The adjustment is usually based informally on the teacher's best guess. *This guess should be understood to be a norm-referenced estimate of the status of the particular class in comparison to a relevant, larger, external reference group.* Although this estimate is best based on systematically collected anchor data, it more often is based on the teacher's less formal, yet informed, perception of the class's status.

By using informal, rough-and-ready estimates for those adjustments that are needed, teachers can achieve some of the benefit of anchoring by means of their estimate of the status of a particular class. At the same time, they can, if necessary, conform to the illusion of percentage grading with absolute standards. In ways such as these, those who feel compelled to use a bad system can make it much less unacceptable.

A Special Problem.   Another statistical hazard lurks in the weighting of daily work and homework. Although it is a special case of the last chapter's topic of weighting, the rationale provided in this chapter sets the stage for intellectually acceptable solutions to this problem.

Intended weights of daily work or homework often do not come out as desired. Suppose a teacher wants all daily homework assignments to contribute equally to the final grade. If each is recorded as a percentage, a teacher might conclude that the intended equality of weights would be achieved. Alas, this is not necessarily so.

To illustrate, suppose a teacher has the following range.

A = 90–100
B = 80–89
C = 70–79
D = 60–69
F = 0–59

In a given week, Brian's three homework grades are 92%, 79%, and 0% (the zero was because he did not turn it in). His mean for the week is 57%. Does it seem fair that his grades of A, C, and F should average F? No, to most of us it would seem more appropriate for him to receive a C. Thus, *a zero can be deadly* (Nitko, 2001).

The problem arises because the percentage range of F grades is much greater than that of any other grade. Hence, the adverse impact of a missing grade is far greater than the beneficial impact of a perfect grade. In seeking to avoid this problem, it is helpful to make a sharp distinction between an F (which Brian may deserve for the missing assignment) and a zero (which may carry too severe a penalty).

Of several methods of avoiding an excessive impact of very low F grades, two seem preferable to us on grounds of simplicity and avoidance of public-relations "waves." One method is simply to alter the F range of what one records in the grade book to be F = 50–59. Under this system, Brian's 92%, 79%, and 0% would be recorded as 92%, 79%, and 50%. The mean of these is about 74%. This yields the C that most of us thought was fair.

The other method is to record 4, 3, 2, 1, 0 instead of A, B, C, D, and F, respectively. (Strong precedent exists for this method in that it is used by most schools and colleges to compute GPAs.) Then compute the mean of the recorded numbers and convert the result back into a letter grade.

■ ■ ■ ■ ■

EXTENSION

ANCHORING AND DRAWING LINES

If you would like to work through a detailed example that involves both use of an anchor measure and drawing the lines that separate grades, you can find it at ablongman.com/hannadettmer.

COMMUNICATION THROUGH CONFERENCING

A teacher's responsibility for evaluating student work does not end with marking and recording the grades. Results of evaluations must be communicated to students and their parents. Many teachers regard this as one of the most demanding aspects of their role. Formal communication to discuss a student's progress in learning and behavior typically is conducted in a **family conference.**

Preservice teachers and new teachers in particular are apprehensive about meeting with family members to discuss a student's progress in learning and behavior. The demands of conveying sensitive information to dedicated parents about their most precious "possession" can cause butterflies in the stomachs of even experienced, veteran teachers. However, teachers should regard the parent-teacher conference as not only an obligation, but an opportunity (Payne, 1997).

Challenges Inherent in Conferencing with Parents

Teachers are not the only ones who may have butterflies before conferences. Many parents have their own apprehensions. Some reluctant parents have a sense of foreboding when they enter a school, perhaps recalling days long ago when their own schooling was painful and confidence-eroding. Others may have performed well in school, but now are mystified and troubled by their own child's problems there. Some of the families a teacher might meet may have lifestyles and life circumstances that are largely unfamiliar to the teacher, for example, same-sex parents or migrant workers. Other families with whom the teacher will confer may include the child of the superintendent, school board member, or employer of one's domestic partner! A variety of dynamics will shape the scenario of any parent-teacher interaction. So how can educators ensure that their conferences cultivate (a) an appreciative understanding of school programs, policies, and practices, (b) cooperation between home and school, and (c) assurance that their child's needs will be met?

As educators, we can be assured of one thing. No parents begin the day wishing the worst for their child. No family members enter a conference hoping that their child will do poorly in school, be miserable, or fail. Having accepted this surety, teachers can more easily assume responsibility for the success of their interactions with parents. Attending to a number of details before, during, and after the conference event will help achieve that success.

The foundation for effective conferences is built well ahead of conference time. The first interaction between teacher and family should be a positive one. Therefore, teachers will want to open the lines of communication in positive ways. It is desirable that teachers' first contacts with parents be upbeat and informational in nature.

One vehicle for doing this is a newsletter listing classroom rules and procedures, along with grading methods and criteria. It is particularly effective to preface such information with enthusiastic descriptions of major curriculum areas, specific topics of instruction, and key concepts that will be addressed. Major instructional objectives for these areas can be given, which then lead into providing information on marking and grading. Just as teachers strive to instill in their students a spirit of curiosity and excitement toward the learning along with their assertive and firm expectations concerning rules and procedures, so, too, can they use such tactics to convey their classroom expectations to the parents. Newsletters may also include invitations for parents to visit the classroom, to inquire about class happenings, to seek conferences if they have concerns, and, if they wish, to volunteer for various services. In any event, a newsletter, fact sheet, or other vehicle distributed to busy families should be brief, interesting, well written, and personalized.

That personal touch might be accomplished in a space for individualized, handwritten comments of a warm and friendly nature about the child and his or her important place in the classroom. Perhaps the space could be signed by the teacher and the child. A personalized touch such as this also helps ensure that the material will arrive home in timely fashion.

What Parents Should Expect from Teachers.   Parents bring to conferences a variety of expectations concerning student assessment, and educators should be prepared to fulfill reasonable expectations. To meet this challenge, the teacher's knowledge and skills must extend far beyond mere ability to provide information in the form of scores. Teachers need to have clear understanding of such topics as norm referencing, criterion referencing, various kinds of derived scores, confidence bands (Woolfolk, 2001), "authentic" assessment, and district-wide testing. These understandings must be presented in lay language that is neither more nor less informative than parents need and desire and is neither patronizing nor pontificating in tone. These are tall orders for a busy, overworked, and perhaps inexperienced teacher! The remaining chapters provide several Thinking CAP Exercises and a number of examples to provide educators with more confidence in communicating information to parents.

Parents expect teachers to interpret their child's test results clearly in terms that lay people can understand. Chapter 15 will address this important topic. They also expect that the information will be communicated efficiently and caringly. Parents expect educators to understand the strengths and needs of their child and to be able to problem-solve effectively for their child's welfare.

Teachers should apply concepts gleaned from sound developmental theory to assess and accommodate each student's abilities and achievement levels. A quick review of Chapter 1 will help readers recall various types of formal and informal assessments with which student needs can be investigated. Observations, interviews, products, performances, self-report inventories, and paper-pencil classroom and published tests all are potentially useful in determining how best to enhance student development.

When conferencing with families, teachers should demonstrate excellent skills of communication and problem-solving as members of a home-and-school team. Another valuable skill is problem-*finding*. The greatest hurdle in constructing appropriate interventions for children with special needs is initial identification of the learning and/or behavioral problem(s). Communication and conferencing with parents of children with special needs will be addressed in more detail in Chapter 13.

What Teachers Can Learn from Parents.   A hallmark of successful work with parents is eagerness to learn more about families in order to understand their situations and to meet their needs. Family members are students' first and most influential teachers (Dettmer, Thurston, & Dyck, 2002). Professional educators must recognize the family's impact on student achievement. For example, a teacher who aspires to meet the needs of children of migrant agricultural laborers needs to become familiar with the linguistic, cultural, religious, family, and housing conditions in which such children live.

Teachers have much to learn by collaborating with families in **parent partnerships.** Parents have the most comprehensive knowledge and deep understanding of their children. They are *the* experts in regard to their child. However, it is very hard to be objective about one's own children. Teachers are the experts on instructional goals and objectives, methods for achieving them, accountability for achievement, and techniques of assessing achievement. However, they may not be very knowledgeable about families' histories, lifestyles, and aspirations.

Certain kinds of information are *not* to be solicited from parents. Examples are political affiliation; mental and psychological problems potentially embarrassing to the student and family; sexual behavior and attitudes; illegal, antisocial, self-incriminating, and demeaning behavior; and income (other than that required by law to determine eligibility for reduced school fees or lunches).

Skills Needed for Effective Conferencing.   Communication includes three elements: a sender, a message, and the receiver(s). Productive coordination of these elements for a successful parent-teacher conference requires several basic steps:

1. Preparing materials and information for the conference
2. Arranging the facilities and schedule
3. Establishing rapport with parents and demonstrating respect for diversity
4. Listening attentively and responsively to family members and the student
5. Presenting information professionally and caringly
6. Identifying problems and concerns
7. Problem-solving as a team member
8. Conveying sincere commitment to the student's welfare and development
9. Following up and following through on conference outcomes
10. Evaluating the conference for improvement of future interactions

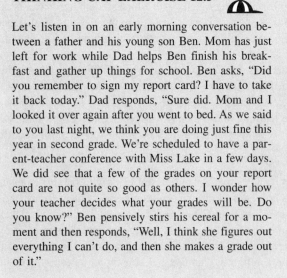

THINKING CAP EXERCISE 12.5   ???

Let's listen in on an early morning conversation between a father and his young son Ben. Mom has just left for work while Dad helps Ben finish his breakfast and gather up things for school. Ben asks, "Did you remember to sign my report card? I have to take it back today." Dad responds, "Sure did. Mom and I looked it over again after you went to bed. As we said to you last night, we think you are doing just fine this year in second grade. We're scheduled to have a parent-teacher conference with Miss Lake in a few days. We did see that a few of the grades on your report card are not quite so good as others. I wonder how your teacher decides what your grades will be. Do you know?" Ben pensively stirs his cereal for a moment and then responds, "Well, I think she figures out everything I can't do, and then she makes a grade out of it."

An important event in Ben's school life is about to occur. His teacher and his family will meet to discuss Ben's progress toward instructional aims. It will be both an obligation of Ben's teacher to convey those objectives and an opportunity to describe his progress and explain the significance of his report-card marks.

1. When Ben's family arrives at school for the parent-teacher conference, what will they expect to learn from Ben's teacher?
2. What can Ben's teacher learn from the parents?
3. What preparations should the teacher make for this very important home–school interaction?
4. Describe a scenario in which Ben's teacher and family will communicate effectively, plan productively, and learn, confident that Ben's welfare is a priority in school and home.

THINKING CAP EXERCISE 12.5   CONTINUED

KEY TO THINKING CAP EXERCISE 12.5

1. Ben's mom and dad can expect his teacher to describe the instructional aims of the unit(s) for which Ben received his grades. They may want to learn a bit about the curriculum used to pursue the objectives. They would want the teacher to explain the basis on which grades are determined and how those grades will affect future plans for Ben's schoolwork.

2. The teacher can expect to learn more than she knows at this point about Ben's interests, his feelings toward school, and his confidence in having the ability to do what is expected there. She also wants to know how his parents regard his progress to date and what

expectations they have for Ben.

3. The teacher can use steps 1–10 to prepare for, plan, conduct, and evaluate the conference. Later sections of this chapter will provide details for implementing the steps.

4. An astute teacher might want to enjoy a chuckle or two with the parents over their seven-year-old's innocence and candor in describing his grades to his father, but she should be very sure that his parents leave the conference with the perception that grades reflect what Ben *can* do, and the assurance that she will continue to build his academic self-esteem in every way she can.

A Closer Look at the Steps

Let's return to and examine in more detail the 10 steps presented earlier for creating successful parent-teacher conferences.

Steps 1 and 2: Preparing for the Conference.   When a conference is initiated by the teacher, parents should be informed about the purpose and content of the meeting. If the conference is parent initiated, the teacher should ascertain the intended purpose and be prepared with materials that address that purpose.

Teachers will want to gather samples of the student's work, both good and not so good, for parent viewing and discussion. If appropriate, the portfolios should contain both norm-based and domain-based assessment interpretations. To increase reliability of the interpretations, samples should include multiple observations on which the student's marks were based, and to improve validity, the assessments should not be influenced by extraneous or irrelevant characteristics of student behavior (Sax, 1997). Teachers will want to learn any previous history of the child and the family that is relevant in conducting an effective conference, but they should take special care to prevent their perspectives from being biased by such information.

In some cases, written communication about the materials to be discussed might be provided to parents before the conference to allow more time for perusal; however, such communications would need to be prepared with utmost care in wordsmithing and mechanics of expression (Sax, 1997). Information delivered in careless form can be misunderstood and misinterpreted in ways damaging to subsequent interaction.

If adhering to the more typical practice of waiting until the conference for perusal of material, sufficient time must be built in for parents to look it over carefully. Conversation should be avoided while they are doing this. It is helpful for all to have notepads on which to jot down questions and comments they may have when discussion resumes. When teachers take notes during conferences, it is a good idea to share those notes with parents, thereby assuaging any apprehension about the content and also allowing them to clarify points or to remind the teacher of key points that may have been omitted.

An important part of conference planning is scheduling the time and place. Schedules should vary among days and times of day so parents can find a time that best fits their work schedules. Conferences shouldn't be planned for times when teachers are rushed or their energy has been exhausted by an intensive day in the classroom. Indeed, scheduling can be quite vexing. School administrators should assume responsibility for providing conference times that accommodate all. This may require hiring substitutes or orchestrating team teaching for parent conference days. Conferences must not be too closely spaced. Families do not want to be rushed when discussing the well-being of their child.

In today's hectic world, it is tempting to suggest telephone conferences or e-mail exchanges. On occasion this may be appropriate. However, problems can surface with these methods. There is no eye contact or important reading of body language. Too, phone calls may not come at convenient times, and, even if prearranged, are easily interrupted. A severe limitation is the absence of student work and classroom products to view and discuss. There is also the potential for compromised confidentiality. It is all too easy to send a message to a wrong party. Furthermore, informal exchanges conveyed by e-mail can become a permanent record if printed out and stored; then, in the event of subsequent retraction or correction, they may not be retrieved as amended.

For a face-to-face conference, families can be invited to bring other adults who are involved with the child and who can help with identification of needs and development of plans. This is particularly helpful for parents whose fluency in English is limited and who may communicate best with another family member acting as supplemental interpreter.

The conference room should allow privacy with no interruptions in order to secure confidentiality. Having other parents waiting within hearing range is disconcerting to parents who may already be having negative feelings about the situation. A useful tactic is to post on the closed door a tactful sign that announces "Conference in Session" or "In Conference Now—Please Come Back Later."

Considerate teachers will provide directions for getting to the classroom along with a map and instructions for parking. They also will arrange secure storage areas for coats and bags and adult-size chairs for sitting around a table in an L-configuration where all can interact with equal status. The teacher will want to be in a position to note the clock unobtrusively, so as to manage the agenda and conclude the conference on time. Finally, teachers must be punctual for conferences, arriving early and greeting the family at the conference room door.

These points are basic, minimal tips for the organization of adults' limited time and the respect and courtesy that should be afforded to all. A caution is in order here. First-time teachers sometimes *over*-prepare for parent conference day(s), laboring over details such as elaborate collections of student work, fancy cookies for refreshment, or memorized verbal messages with which to impress parents. But such activity may do more harm than good by inflating parental anxiety and drawing valuable time away from identification of needs and solution-finding for those needs. Better to conserve one's energy for the communication and problem-solving aspects of the process.

Occasionally an impromptu conference evolves from a chance meeting that has not been organized as a parent-teacher session. This can create problems; the interaction may not occur in an area that allows privacy, needed information may not be accessible, and the teacher may be unprepared. Therefore, impromptu conferences are best avoided. If such an interaction starts, it may be wise for the teacher in a politely assertive way to arrange a specific conference time and place in the very near future.

Steps 3 Through 8: Conducting the Conference.   Two key rules for a successful interaction with parents are to *begin on a positive note* and make sure to *end on time*! A positive way to start is to emphasize what the child has accomplished and the progress that has been made (Payne, 1997).

Oral communication is a two-way street. Talking is only one side of the street, listening is the other, and the more important side in most cases. The teacher should listen to the parent(s) and student with respect, and listen, and then listen some more. For how long, one might ask? Experts in communication stress that we should listen until we grasp the other person's viewpoint. In some cases, that may be quite a long time and quite a challenge! When parents have expressed what they want to say and have asked their questions, the teacher should then share information and initiate the problem-solving process.

It is most helpful to be honest and objective, particularly when poor grades are involved. Teachers must control their emotions and refrain from being defensive. Parents, of course, don't know all the pressures that teachers have in their school roles (Payne, 1997). In that same vein, teachers don't know all the stresses affecting their students' families. The most helpful part of the communication is responsive listening (Dettmer, Thurston, and Dyck, 2002) in which teachers encourage parents to express feelings about their child to the teacher as a nonjudgmental, caring listener who is actively engaged but refrains from offering unsolicited advice or premature solutions.

The astute teacher takes great care not to talk about other teachers, students, or parents. Nor should the achievement or behavior of siblings ordinarily be a part of the conversation. It is important to eliminate all educational jargon (i.e., "alphabet soup") when conversing with parents and students. Terms to be avoided by teachers wherever possible are negative and pejorative phrases such as "falling farther and farther behind," "just does not apply himself," "is lazy," "is failing in most subjects," or perhaps the most disheartening phrase of all for parents to hear, "I just do not know what to do with this child any more."

Teachers will want to explain what is taught and what is assessed. They should discuss the pros, cons, and uncertainties about assessment to arrive at the most workable, promising options. "Here is a description of the lesson. This is the assessment of your child's learning based on performance. Let's plan what we can do *together* to help your child achieve to the fullest extent possible." Parents who volunteer ideas and take active part in developing plans for learning are much more supportive partners in seeing that the plans are carried out. If at any point during a conference teachers do not know something asked by parents, they should say so, promise to find out and report back, and then do so.

In the very rare event that a parent should become angry and verbally aggressive, the teacher will need to remain calm, speak more softly as other voices rise, and stay with concrete evidence to make necessary points. It doesn't help to argue with parents, particularly in matters of grades. Feeding an argument with contradiction fuels resistance because it is perceived as criticism of the family, home, and parenting. A conference that degenerates into an argument may best be concluded as soon and smoothly as possible, with an invitation to continue at a later time when tempers have abated.

Step 9: Following Up and Following Through.   One of the most important yet neglected phases of interaction with parents is the aftermath of the parent-teacher conference. As the conference draws to a close, the teacher should see that specific, concrete plans are made for next steps. Who will be responsible for what? When? Where? How will results of this follow-up phase be made known to all concerned? It is up to teachers to be accessible and to keep in regular contact with the family (Rich, 1998).

Step 10: Evaluating the Conference.   It is appropriate here to emphasize evaluation of conference outcomes. Teachers probably do this informally by asking themselves, "Was this a good experience?" "Did everyone leave with positive feelings about the conference?" "Did each person leave knowing more helpful information about the child's strengths, interests, and needs?" "Does everyone who participated know the next steps and persons responsible for each of them?" "Were arrangements made for next interactions with this student and the family?"

Even though teachers may run through such questions and reflect on them briefly, they should look for more reliable and valid measures to evaluate the outcomes of such demanding and important professional responsibilities. Figure 12.3 presents one set of criteria for evaluating the outcomes of parent-teacher conferences. Why bother with such a rubric? Because, like most rubrics, it directs attention to criteria that might otherwise be overlooked. Just as we seek to help our students gain skill in self-assessment, so should we ourselves.

After the conference, the teacher should reflect on the event and rate the interaction using a checklist that includes criteria and values such as these. Items rated low would be targeted for improvement in subsequent conferences. The checklist should be modified to fit each school's context and each teacher's preferences for form of feedback. Items may be altered, and others might be added. Any modification of the instrument should, as this one does, allow space for free-response comments after completion of the specific items. Such comments can be rich sources of data. Permission is hereby granted for readers wishing to reproduce the instrument in its present form to do so.

A corresponding rating form for the parent or other family member also can be crafted. Our web site contains material for a starter that can be customized for obtaining parent perspectives concerning parent-teacher conferences.

Parent ratings should be done anonymously in order to provide raters the security to be candid. The family member(s) might be given the form at the completion of the conference with a request that it be filled out in, say, the library, and be put into a box designated to retain them. After completing the round of conferences, the teacher could use the parent ratings to assess overall effectiveness of the conferences. (Recall the discussion in Chapter 9 of parent ratings for program evaluation; this is an instance of it.)

Student-Guided Family Conferences

Conferences in which students are actively involved and teachers take a back seat for the event are appealing to many teachers and parents. Stiggins (2001) offers specific steps for successful implementation of the student-led conference. For teachers who don't wish to commit to the activity at that level, a student–parent–teacher conference guided by the student, with the teacher assisting from the sideline or behind the scene, is an attractive option.

Student-guided conferences can provide several benefits for students, families, and teachers. They highlight the importance of collaboration between school and home educators to help students achieve learning goals. They provide opportunity for active involvement of students in setting their own learning goals and assessing their progress. Students will take more ownership in the learning process and demonstrate more self-direction toward learning when they have a voice in what, when, where, why, and how they will learn.

Student age need not be a factor in determining who should participate in the conferences. First or second grade is not too early for students to begin attending conferences that are about and

FIGURE 12.3   Teacher Rating Scale for Teacher-Family Conference.

CONFERENCE ASSESSMENT BY TEACHER/CONVENER

Directions: Check one option for each item to indicate the amount of your agreement or disagreement with that statement. If your rating for an item is "somewhat disagree" or "strongly disagree," or you wish to make any further comment on that item, please explain in the box for that item.

1. Preparations (e.g., agenda, portfolios, facilities) for the conference were excellent.
__Strongly Agree
__Somewhat Agree
__Somewhat Disagree
__Strongly Disagree

2. The event began and ended on time.
__Strongly Agree
__Somewhat Agree
__Somewhat Disagree
__Strongly Disagree

3. The meeting started on a positive note by discussing student strengths.
__Strongly Agree
__Somewhat Agree
__Somewhat Disagree
__Strongly Disagree

4. The purpose of the conference and each person's role in it were well understood by all.
__Strongly Agree
__Somewhat Agree
__Somewhat Disagree
__Strongly Disagree

5. Student work samples were well-chosen and helpful in fulfilling the session's purposes.
__Strongly Agree
__Somewhat Agree
__Somewhat Disagree
__Strongly Disagree
__Not Applicable

6. Teacher(s) exhibited respect for diversity and for all participants and their values.
__Strongly Agree
__Somewhat Agree
__Somewhat Disagree
__Strongly Disagree

7. All participants felt free to express their views.
__Strongly Agree
__Somewhat Agree
__Somewhat Disagree
__Strongly Disagree

8. Idea-generation and problem-solving were effectively used.
__Strongly Agree
__Somewhat Agree
__Somewhat Disagree
__Strongly Disagree
__Not Applicable

9. A promising plan of action was developed.
__Strongly Agree
__Somewhat Agree
__Somewhat Disagree
__Strongly Disagree
__Not Applicable

10. Plans for follow-up and follow-through were made cooperatively.
__Strongly Agree
__Somewhat Agree
__Somewhat Disagree
__Strongly Disagree

Other Reflections: _____
_____
_____

for them. This topic will be addressed further in Chapter 13 when development of the IEP for students with special needs is discussed.

Wolf and Stephens (1989) pointed out some important considerations to take into account when including students in conferences. At the outset, school staff should clearly define the purpose of including students and be prepared to convince skeptics that such participation is important. They should gain support of parents and maintain open communication lines, offering the procedure as an option. Students should be well informed about the process so that they are enthusiastic and ready for the event. Careful preparations must precede the conference, and upon conclusion it should be assessed by each participant. The assessment becomes a tool for improving the process.

Steps in Student-Guided Conferences.   As in the parent-teacher conference, adherence to basic steps will ensure a successful experience. Together, the student and teacher can discuss these 10 steps and be prepared to:

1. Determine the purpose(s) of the conference.
2. Formulate goals for the conference and prepare the invitation to family members. In the invitation, family members should be clued as to what to expect and ways to contribute.
3. Develop an agenda and determine location, seating plan, introductions format, and possible opening and closing remarks.
4. Select samples of work and pertinent information that focus on accomplishments, interests, and any major concerns. The student typically selects material to be displayed and discussed during the conference and prepares descriptions of activities that were involved in the learning experiences. Student responses also can be prepared in anticipation of questions or concerns that parents might bring up.
5. Rehearse a simulated conference.
6. At conference time, explore ideas for further learning and achievement.
7. Set reasonable goals.
8. Adhere to the time schedule, summarize, and close on a positive note.
9. Determine follow-up and follow-through procedures for attaining the planned goals.
10. Evaluate the event with rubrics.

Some of these steps involve only short elements of time. However, as with the parent-teacher conference, the student-guided conference must not be hurried. A 30-minute segment of time might be reasonable. Busy teachers, particularly those at the secondary level with dozens of students, will require strong administrator support and innovative scheduling ideas to achieve successful student-guided conferences. Some will be more successful than others. However, by talking through the process with students and by demonstrating and modeling conferencing techniques during the rehearsal, teachers can help students contribute to successful home–school partnerships in very positive ways.

Student-guided parent conferences provide numerous benefits for students, their families, and their teachers. These experiences, to an even greater extent than the student-involved parent conference, promote student ownership in their own learning. Encouraging the student to complete a rating form similar to teacher and parent rating forms as an evaluation of the event will provide rich opportunity for self-assessment and enhancement of learning. A starter for a student rating form may be found on our web site.

CHAPTER RECAP

Providing meaningful reports of student achievement is a time-consuming part of teachers' work. Yet this time is well spent because of the several important functions that grades serve. Like one's assessment practices, one's grading system should be planned carefully at the time instruction is designed. This thoughtfully established student-evaluation system should be communicated to students early on, and it should be used mindfully to enhance learning.

The meaning of grades is optimized if each kind of mark represents distinct and important information. Thus, it is desirable for one mark to represent a pure measure of terminal student achievement. In addition, one or more other marks are needed to report on such other important things as apparent effort or citizenship. The meaning of marks is also enhanced when a school's faculty shares similar perspectives concerning appropriate distributions in typical classes.

To achieve their purposes, grades need to be rooted in a rationale that is consistent with the subject matter and other aspects of CAP. Grading also needs to be structured to avoid adverse impact on interpersonal relationships and mental health. Marks also need to be meaningful and interpretable. These multiple aims are best achieved in Context C, with grades that reflect student achievement reported by means of norm referencing to stable, well-described, relevant groups of other students. This is often best achieved by use of anchor measures.

Parent-teacher conferences are an integral component of teachers' grading and reporting responsibilities. These interactions can invoke feelings of apprehension and anxiety in all participants. However, careful planning by teachers before the conference, which includes providing information to parents, giving close attention to effective practices for managing group interaction, diligently following up and following through with the conference, and evaluating conference outcomes, can make this event one of the most productive and gratifying components of the home–school partnership for serving student learning needs.

Student-guided conferences are a way of involving students in the planning and evaluation of their work. Careful preparation, rehearsal of a simulated conference, and evaluation of the event will strengthen student skills for this promising experience.

ASSESSMENT ISSUES FOR STUDENTS WITH SPECIAL NEEDS

CHAPTER OVERVIEW

KEY TERMS

entitlement
Education for All Handicapped Children Act (P.L. 94-142)
free and appropriate public education (FAPE)
least restrictive environment
individual education plan (IEP)
Individuals with Disabilities Education Acts (IDEA and IDEA 1997)

annual goals
short-term objectives
benchmarks
adaptations
accommodations
modifications

What is special about assessment of students receiving service in special education programs? Legal, ethical, and practical considerations guide our planning and decision making for the instruction and assessment of students identified as exceptional and eligible for special services.

The advent of special education programming in U.S. schools can be traced to Rhode Island's pioneering adoption of a compulsory school attendance law; by 1916, all states had one. No longer would children with disabilities be ignored. As classrooms became more heterogeneous in ability and increasingly culturally diverse, the practice of "teaching to the middle" tended to exclude many students from a suitable education. Thus, the concept of special education, or instruction designed for students with special learning needs, was formed. It became a visible example of society's willingness to recognize individual needs of school-age children and to respond to the limitations of regular school programs for serving those needs (Ysseldyke & Algozinne, 1990). When all are to attend public schools, those schools must be prepared to instruct in ways that serve each student's individual learning needs.

STUDENT ENTITLEMENT VERSUS STUDENT NEED

Recall from Chapter 3 the observations—and sometimes lamentations—by teachers that *students differ.* Over the years, differences within schools have increased, first with special education, then with mainstreaming, and now with inclusionary classrooms. In 1975, P.L. 94-142[1] promised teachers help from special education personnel to deal with those differences. However, due to the increasing numbers of students placed in special education, the burgeoning cultural and linguistic diversity among students, and escalating demands brought on schools by educational reforms, standards, and demands for accountability, teachers have had to energetically row upstream just to stay in place. Complex issues swirl around the planning, instruction, and assessment of student learning for *all* students in this turbulent educational and social climate.

Some students need support in the form of remedial programs, instruction in English as a second language, or special education. Some have documented disabilities. Students who have *both* documented disabilities *and* need are entitled to special education. An **entitlement** is a legislative mandate for service (Howell & Nolet, 2000). Special entitlements exist for two types of students: those with documented disabilities (of the kinds recognized for eligibility) and those deemed at risk due to cultural, linguistic, or socioeconomic situations that lower their probability of school success. The largest entitlement program in the United States is special education.

To amplify, students having needs, but not having a documented disability, risk, or giftedness, are not entitled to special education programming. Similarly, students having documented disabilities without having special learning or behavioral needs are not entitled to special education services. An example would be students with correctable, defective vision. Both documented exceptionality and need must be present to be eligible for (entitled to) special education.

As stressed throughout the book, assessment and evaluation are tools to enhance student learning and to guide decision making. Assessments that inform teachers about student needs have "inside" purposes of monitoring each student's acquisition of skills and competencies. These assessments are frequent and they focus on individual students. They tell what and how to teach and are used for making instructional decisions.

Educational assessments conducted for purposes of legal monitoring and evaluation of entitlement programs have purposes that originate "outside" the classroom. Data from such assessments are reported as *group* results for classes and schools and are used in allocating resources and initiating reforms, but not necessarily in making instructional decisions (Howell & Nolet, 2000). Both "inside" and "outside" purposes factor into the IDEA 1997 legislation requiring participation of students with disabilities in state- and local-level assessments of student achievement. It is to that topic that we now turn.

SPECIAL EDUCATION LEGISLATION

When the **Education for All Handicapped Children Act (P.L. 94-142)** was signed by President Ford in 1975, it became the first federal compulsory special education law. It guaranteed a **free and appropriate public education (FAPE)** for students with disabilities. Furthermore, this education

---

[1]Federal laws are identified as follows: P.L. means Public Law (in contrast to less common Private Laws). The first numeral (94 in this case) indicates that it was passed by the 94th Congress. The numeral after the hyphen (142 in this case) is the numerical order of the law among those originating from that congress.

was to be provided in environments like those provided for those who do not have disabilities. A legal term for this mainstreaming provision is **least restrictive environment.** Some states included gifted students and a few included gifted and talented students in the category of exceptional students. It is generally recognized that about 10 percent of the nation's school-age children are now considered eligible to receive special education services; in states where gifted children are included, the percentage approaches 15 percent.

A special education program of instruction and assessment must be based on a formal document, the **individual education plan (IEP),** which serves as a tool for determining the student's present levels of functioning and lists annual goals and short-term objectives. It describes services to be provided and the extent to which the student will participate in regular education. It names a starting date and expected duration of special education services and specifies the evaluation plan to be used annually and periodically, typically coinciding with evaluation of students in regular education.

In 1990, President Bush signed amendments to the Education for All Handicapped Children Act, thereby creating the **Individuals with Disabilities Education Act (IDEA).** At this time the language of the law was changed from handicaps and "*the* handicapped" to disabilities and "*students with* disabilities" thereby promoting a people-first language format. People-first language *prompts us to think inclusively and to plan* appropriate paths of instruction for the student. Inclusive thinking raises consciousness that we are addressing only one attribute of a person, *not* the defining attribute of the person's existence. When people are addressed first, the phrases become:

- "People who have developmental disabilities," rather than "the developmentally disabled"
- "The student who was absent Friday," not "the absentee"
- "That pupil who hasn't yet mastered the multiplication facts," not "that slow math pupil"
- "The child who just moved to our community," rather than "the new kid on the block"
- "The kindergartner who is reading *National Geographic,*" instead of "the smart child"
- "The student who is Muslim," not "the Muslim"
- "Persons who are gay or lesbian," instead of "gays and lesbians"
- "People who are dying," rather than "the dying"

Other parts of IDEA focus on parent partnerships in children's learning programs and include the requirement of transition plans (preschool-to-school and school-to-work) within IEPs. In 1997, President Clinton signed further refinements to IDEA through P.L. 105-17, or **IDEA 1997.** For our purposes here, the most relevant element of IDEA 1997 concerns the assessment of students with disabilities.

Each state is required to ensure that children with disabilities are included in general state- and districtwide assessment programs, with appropriate accommodations where necessary (Council for Exceptional Children, 1998). The child's IEP must include a statement of any individual accommodations in administration of state or district assessments of student achievement that are deemed necessary for the child to participate in the assessment. If the IEP team determines that the child will not participate in part or all of a particular assessment, the IEP must include a statement of why that decision was made and then a description of how the assessment will be done. State or local education agencies must have guidelines for participation in alternate assessments by the small percentage of students who cannot participate in regular programs. States must report numbers and performance of children participating in alternate assessments. States must also address the performance of all students with disabilities, including those participating in alternate assessment, in the State Improvement Plan performance goals and indicators (Kleinert, Haig, Kearns, & Kennedy, 2000).

A section of the IEP denoting participation in state and district assessments is to provide answers to questions such as the following (Yell, 1998):

- Will the student participate in state- or districtwide assessments? Yes __ or No __.
- If the student will not participate in these assessments, the methods by which the student will be assessed are _____.
- Rationale for excluding the student from participation is _____.
- Will modifications be required for the student to participate in assessments? Yes __ or No __.
- Modifications are _____.
- Rationale for modifications is _____.

Another key aspect of IDEA 1997 was that the IEP must include a description of how the student's progress toward *annual goals, short-term objectives,* and *benchmarks* will be measured, along with how often, and in what manner parents will be informed. The term "benchmark" has been linked with objectives to create the phrase "benchmarks or short-term objectives" as a way of emphasizing the importance of using frequent measures to assess a student's progress toward the annual goals (Yell, 1998).

These requirements are tall orders for busy classroom teachers and special education personnel! It might be mentioned that one other part of the IDEA legislation stated that the emphasis is to be on best educational practices for children rather than on paperwork for paperwork's sake. The overworked teacher does not know whether to laugh, cry, or write this stipulation off as an oxymoron!

We should also note two other laws that help students receive the FAPE to which they are entitled. These are Title V of the Rehabilitation Act (Section 504), and the Americans with Disabilities Act (ADA). Educators need to understand these laws in order to fulfill their intent of providing students the services to which they are entitled (and to avoid litigation).

Schools face an additional challenge in the accurate assessment of disabilities in those students who are culturally and linguistically diverse. IDEA mandates that a student cannot be determined to have a disability when the basic problem is inadequate familiarity with the language used for assessments. Obviously, we need to test people in a language they understand.

However, comparable tests do not exist in most languages. Moreover, cultures and subcultures that are different have differing activities, tasks, toys, puzzles, problem-solving techniques, concepts, values, and vocabularies; therefore, it is common for neither test items nor responses to lend themselves to accurate translation. For example:

- Suppose a British test item in 1960 asked, "If I can buy 4 lollies for sixpence, how many can I buy for a shilling?" Suffice it to say, that a comparable item for the United States, which has neither coin mentioned, would be of questionable equivalence in difficulty.
- A math item about train schedules translated into Samoan will have little meaning to a student of a culture that has no trains whatsoever (and few schedules that are taken seriously)!
- The American English word "hotdog," could, if translated literally into Spanish, be "bitch in heat"! This would be likely to cause more confusion than help to a child with limited English proficiency.

As educators grapple with these complex assessment issues, two concerns frequently surface. First, how do we deal with very low-incidence kinds of cases (e.g., students who speak only a very obscure language)? Second, how do high-incidence kinds of disabilities (e.g., learning disabilities) interface with school reforms that link achievement to graduation?

THINKING CAP EXERCISE 13.1

Suppose you are teaching in a state whose policymakers have just adopted a merit-pay system that awards raises to individual teachers for increases in student test scores on an annual battery of published tests. At this point in the book, with its emphasis on better teaching through better assessment, what concerns come to mind?

Jot down your concerns and then prioritize them from greatest to least. If the raise-for-score-increase idea appeals to you, jot down your thoughts about that, too.

KEY TO THINKING CAP EXERCISE 13.1

Perhaps your reaction was to get out the atlas and plan your move to another state! If that isn't an option, you may have pondered any or all of these issues, and perhaps more:

1. This practice would probably result in "teaching to the test."
2. Are these tests linked to the curriculum we use and the teaching methods I prefer?
3. This practice runs a great risk of prompting a reduced emphasis on instructional objectives that are not assessed by the published test.
4. Some students will improve more than others. Will teachers who are assigned students with disadvantages be penalized?
5. How does IDEA 1997 with its requirement for including students with disabilities in the tests affect this situation?
6. Will the previous point increase collaborative efforts among general and special education staff?
7. Not all students can participate, even with accommodations. When these decisions become high stakes for teachers' own welfare, who will decide which students shall participate and what accommodations shall be made?
8. Who will monitor and evaluate the success of this approach? Will the unforeseen adverse consequences (as well as those that are foreseeable) be addressed in evaluating the success of the program?

APPLYING THE LOGIC OF CAP TO IEPs

We now focus on the instructional aspect of teaching and assessing students with special needs. CAP is well shaped for attending to individual differences of learning and behavior needs. So when the CAP "fits," we will wear it comfortably and efficiently. For example, it is our conviction that a Context C perspective is not only appropriate, but *essential* to engender the deep learning that all students can and must achieve, regardless of disability or cultural/linguistic diversity.

However, special education teachers will need to make some minor alterations in CAP to fit the body of regulations imposed by PL 94-142, IDEA, and IDEA 1997. Such regulations include requirements for construction of the IEP for students with disabilities. In a considerable number of states, this also includes students identified as gifted.

With a little patience and bit of snipping and stitching here and there, the CAP will not only fit the needs of special education teachers and their students, it also will enhance the serviceability of the IEP. To ensure a good fit, however, we need to apply some carefully selected patches and neat seam work.

The therapist Albert Ellis suggested that being rational in an irrational world is a major challenge to which we should aspire. We say, "Hear, hear!" One arena in which we have struggled to achieve as much rationality as real-world constraints allow concerns the mandated development of IEPs for students with special needs. We strongly support the *intent* of legislation designed to provide a FAPE for all children. Our recommendations for doing so include emphasizing the *right of all students to achieve at both mastery and developmental levels* and a framework for providing ultimate objectives (such as being a responsible adult citizen), annual goals (a term used in IEP development), and short-term objectives (as the term is used in IEPs).

Legal Demands

After screening, identification, and placement in special education, the student is to have an individual plan that provides annual goals and short-term objectives based on the data that justified placement in special education. Both school personnel and family members are required to participate in the development of this document. The IEP statement of performance levels, goals, and objectives, along with methods, implementation and duration dates, person(s) responsible for implementation, and assessment criteria for completion, *are to be developed collaboratively during the IEP conference* by home and school IEP team members. Family members are *not* simply to be asked to sign a plan that was fully formed prior to the meeting.

Special education teachers put much time and energy into the development of IEPs for students with special needs. IEP conferences may be held before, during, or after school; finding a time when all persons (which often best includes the student) can attend the meeting with the least inconvenience and hassle is a formidable task. Thoughts and feelings, and sometimes patience and endurance, are at a premium for this very important event.

Therefore, to increase the efficiency and atmosphere of the meeting, some school administrators and supervisors have begun to encourage development of sample IEP goals and objectives, often stored as computer banks, to enable shopping among ideas and alternatives. The IEP is developed on the spot, but the preprinted materials have been perused beforehand and are available at the conference for scanning, discussing, selecting as fits the student's needs, or modifying for particular needs and circumstances. The student's family typically welcomes the availability of possibilities and appreciates the attention afforded their child before the conference. However, to reiterate, under no circumstances should the family feel that the goals and objectives have been selected prior to their meeting, much less finalized.

P.L. 94-142 and IDEA 1997 stipulate that:

■ **Annual goals** (by that exact name in special education regulations) must be developed for each classified student in a meeting of the interdisciplinary team that includes the *participation* of parent(s) or guardian(s) *and* general education teacher(s) in constructing the IEP. These goals must be based on data that justified the student's placement in special education.

■ In special education language, **short-term objectives** are **benchmarks** or objectives in the student's progress toward the annual goals and are to be achieved in the time framework that is specified. They are to be measurable, of course, with student progress assessed at least as frequently as that of student progress in general education, for example, at end points of grading periods. Any objectives that are not met are to be continued, revised, or replaced.

In our opinion, an annual goal may be from Context A, B, or C. Moreover, we believe that across the gamut of special education *objectives of each type have a contribution to make.* For example, we contend strongly that pupils with mental retardation, behavioral disorders, or learning disabilities should pursue some goals that aspire to achievement beyond mere (Context A) mastery of minimum essentials. Developmental objectives (Contexts B and C) also are highly relevant to students classified for special education. However, when putting these objectives into special education language as required for IEPs, we will refer to them as *annual goals.*

Under the IDEA 1997 amendments, the annual goals are to be measurable. The student's achievements toward IEP goals are to be evaluated at least annually. Suppose an annual goal were "The student will, by May 10, practice responsible social behaviors." Wow! That is about as nonmasterable, expansive, and developmental as an aim can be. Who among us has achieved the ultimate? However, we have no problem so far because we believe that expansive developmental statements are permissible for annual goals.

Another example of an annual goal might be "The student will be able to solve real-life and 'story' problems that involve multiplying two numbers together, one of which is expressed in terms of money." Still no problem. For the young pupil or the special needs student, this would be an expansive developmental objective (or, in special education terms, an annual goal). (For the typical adult with no disabilities, the same objective might be viewed as a hybrid between Contexts A and C.)

The Regular Education CAP Solution

In CAP, no particular time duration, such as "annual," is attached to developmental objectives. In special education, annual goals must, obviously, be annual. They can, of course, be retained or revised as appropriate from year to year. Or, they can be replaced by more pressing annual goals in periods shorter than a year. Therefore, we see no problem, for the purpose of developing IEPs, in calling Context C objectives annual goals. (However, we urge educators not to take the word "annual" too seriously.)

In CAP, one develops several indicants for each annual goal (i.e., expansive, developmental objective). Recall that indicants do *not* have mastery thresholds attached to them. Indeed, we have presented a compelling case that indicants are only *examples* of the kind of behavior that would evidence status on the goal and that the *indicants themselves are not objectives.*

Here, then, is an example of an annual goal and corollary indicants:

1. The student will practice responsible social behaviors.
    1.1 Responds appropriately to personal obligations in school settings (e.g., attendance, punctuality, compliance with school rules).
    1.2 Identifies instances of appropriate and inappropriate student behavior in an instructional setting.

1.3 Respects the rights of others.

1.4 In authentic settings, distinguishes between authority figures and nonauthority figures.

1.5 Responds appropriately to authority figures.

1.6 Responds appropriately to community needs.

The Problem

The problem in special education with the Context C expansive developmental objective just shown is that the indicants do not set mastery thresholds; that is, the examples are not cast as mastery objectives. Therefore, what we consider to be sound, rational practice will not meet legal requirements for IEPs. We contend, of course, that the problem is with the requirements, not with the CAP perspective! But we all know who has the bigger stick. Similarly, we all know the "golden rule," which is, "Them that has the gold makes the rules." Thus, in order for school districts to comply with the regulations in order to receive special education funding, it is the CAP perspective—not the regulations—that will have to be bent. Thus, we see the relevance of Albert Ellis's challenge to be rational in an irrational world and, in the process, to stay out of trouble.

Our Attempt to Be as Rational as the Constraints Allow

What to do? Let's fulfill the need to get the "gold" to operate the program while doing as little damage in the process as possible.

The best solution that we see is to play the game of treating the indicants as objectives in a way that makes them as realistic as possible for the *individual* student. Think of it this way: In special education, when we set a threshold of mastery for a Context B or C pseudo-mastery "objective," we can individualize for the particular person; thus we can set it to aspire realistically to a level attainable within a grading period. Then, when we assess the person's mastery or nonmastery of each short-term "objective" (in the simplistic, "either-or" methods demanded), we can (subversively) keep our brains engaged and notice the actual *level of achievement,* as well as the attainment or nonattainment of the threshold.

Suppose a student did not reach the threshold set during a given grading period. If achievement fell far short of the mastery threshold, the short-term objective might be revised so as to change the threshold downward. If the student nearly reached it, the objective might simply be retained. Or, suppose a pupil did reach the threshold set. If the level of achievement barely reached the threshold, then the threshold might be raised very little for the next grading period. However, if the pupil far exceeded the threshold, then it might be raised quite a bit during the next grading period. Or, the pseudo objective might be replaced with a new one more appropriate to the pupil's new level of functioning.

Example 1: Transformation of a Context C Objective.   Table 13.1 provides an example of how a Context C objective and its indicants can undergo transformation into a serviceable IEP annual goal with short-term objectives.

Notice how the transformation of indicants into short-term objectives required that the indicants lose much of their generality; thus, "personal obligations in school settings (e.g., attendance, punctuality, compliance with school rules)" was restricted to a particular obligation (e.g., arriving on time). Therefore, IEPs should rotate the illustrations used in short-term objectives from one

TABLE 13.1   Conversion of an Expansive Developmental Context C Objective and Its Indicants into an IEP Annual Goal with Sample Short-Term Objectives

CONTEXT C EXPANSIVE DEVELOPMENTAL OBJECTIVES AND INDICANTS	IEP ANNUAL GOAL AND SHORT-TERM MASTERABLE "OBJECTIVES"	COMMENT ABOUT THE ADAPTATION
1. The student will practice responsible social behaviors.	1. By [date] the student will exhibit responsible social behaviors in common school settings.	The annual goal (i.e., the expansive, developmental objective) was adapted by inserting a duration and focusing on school settings.
1.1 Responds appropriately to personal obligations in school settings (e.g., attendance, punctuality, compliance with school rules)	1.1 Arrives to class on time at least X% of the time by [date].	The standard would be set with the individual child's past performance in mind. Likewise, it would be adjusted in revision to suit the individual.
1.2 Identifies instances of appropriate and inappropriate student behavior in an instructional setting.	1.2 By [date] on at least X out of 5 occasions, when asked, "who should be called upon," names a class member whose hand is up.	This is an indicant that, once "mastered," might well be replaced by another, e.g., "From a picture identifies pupil who is talking in class X% of the time."
1.3 Respects the rights of others.	1.3 By [date] when joining a line, does not crowd in at least X% of the time.	Once mastered, could be changed to another relevant topic, e.g., interrupting others.
1.4 In authentic settings, can distinguish between authority figures and non-authority figures.	1.4 By [date], can identify X out of three obvious people in a story who should be obeyed and Y out of three obvious people who should not necessarily be obeyed.	Difficulty, of course, varies with the story, and the word "obvious" does not tie it down. However, once "attained," a new adjective could replace "obvious," e.g., "semi-obvious" or "subtle."
1.5 Responds appropriately to authority figures.	1.5 By [date] follows teacher's directions at least X% of the time.	Once attained, "teacher" could be changed, e.g., to "police officer," or "class monitor," and/or percentage can be changed.
1.6 Responds appropriately to community needs.	1.6 When asked by teacher, willingly makes posters for a Red Cross or March of Dimes drive.	Once attained, situations could be made more motivationally challenging.

TABLE 13.2   Treatment of Expansive Developmental Context C Objective as a Life Goal and Conversion of Some of Its Indicants into IEP Annual Goals with Sample Short-Term Objectives

EXPANSIVE DEVELOPMENTAL LIFE GOALS WITH SELECTED INDICANTS	SELECTED SUBORDINATE EXPANSIVE DEVELOPMENTAL IEP ANNUAL GOALS	SELECTED SHORT-TERM MASTERABLE OBJECTIVES
The student will practice responsible social behaviors.		
1. Responds appropriately to personal obligations in school settings (e.g., attendance, punctuality, compliance with school rules)	1. By [date] responds appropriately to personal obligations in school settings (e.g., attendance, punctuality, compliance with school rules).	1.1 Arrives to class on time at least X% of the time by [date].
		1.2 By [date] walks, rather than runs, in hallway X or more % of the time.
		1.3 By [date] accepts assignments (e.g., passing out paper) X or more % of the time.
		1.4 When an assignment (e.g., taking a note to the office) has been accepted, by [date] conscientiously executes it at least X% of the time.
3. Respects the rights of others.	3. Respects the rights of others more frequently in more settings by [date].	3.1 When joining a line, joins at the end at least X% of the time by [date].
		3.2 Waits to speak until another has finished at least X% of the time observed by [date].
		3.3 By [date], no longer borrows items without explicit permission with no more than 1 observed relapse per week.
5. Responds appropriately to authority figures.	5. Responds more appropriately to authority figures a larger fraction of the time by [date].	5.1 Follows teacher's directions at least X% of the time.
		5.2 By [date] abides by directions of school crossing guard X or more % of the time.
		5.3 Follows suitable directions of student monitors at least X% of the time by [date].

grading period to the next. Also, one will often want to use more than one particular illustration (e.g., multiple short-term objectives could address punctuality in more than one place, attendance, and compliance with each of several school rules).

An alternative method is to convert a Context C objective into *several* IEP annual goals. If the original developmental objective is extremely expansive, it might better be treated as a *life* goal rather than an annual goal. Then some or all of the indicants that apply to the student's present life can be phrased as less expansive (yet still quite expansive) developmental Context C objectives and converted into corresponding IEP annual goals. Then, of course, short-term objectives or benchmarks flow from the annual goals.

Table 13.2 on page 335 illustrates this approach with the same material as was used in Table 13.1. As shown in Table 13.2, the life goal was judged to be too broad for an annual goal. Therefore, some of its indicants (i.e., numbers 1, 3, 5) were transformed into more constrained, yet still expansive, developmental annual goals, each of which contains (typically annual) duration.

These expansive developmental annual goals contain change verbs. Although this ordinarily is not advisable, in special education it seems less undesirable than creating a ceiling above which progress is not sought.

Most of the subordinate short-term objectives could be increased greatly in number by altering the verbs (e.g., in 1.1 it could be "returns cafeteria tray" or "treats books with care" rather than "arrives to class on time"). The mastery thresholds of the short-term masterable objectives should be set with the individual child's past performance in mind. Likewise, they would be adjusted in term-to-term revisions to suit the individual's improvement.

Which is the better of the methods shown in Tables 13.1 and 13.2? In general, we prefer the approach shown in Table 13.2, unless the original Context C developmental objective is unusually constrained for an expansive objective.

Example 2: Evolution of Annual Goal and "Short-term Objectives" for Critical Thinking.[2] Suppose Ms. Ash, a regular classroom teacher, wants to infuse selected aspects of critical thinking into her instruction of various subjects. This would be an example of multilevel teaching. (Never mind what she teaches or the level she teaches; the expansive developmental objective is sufficiently content free to make it very broadly applicable.) Ms. Ash has been much impressed and influenced by *The Thinking Classroom* (Tishman, Perkins, & Jay 1995) and *How to Write and Use Instructional Objectives* (Gronlund, 2000). After some contemplation, she comes up with this Context C objective:

  2. Uses critical thinking skills.
    2.1 Distinguishes between facts and opinions.
    2.2 Defines terms that are involved in the language of thinking.
    2.3 Formulates valid conclusions from written material.
    2.4 Identifies bias in written or oral statements.

---

[2]This example draws illustrative material from Gronlund (2000) and Tishman, Perkins, & Jay (1995). Original to us is the alteration of an expansive developmental Context C objective and indicants into an annual goal and short-term objectives suitable for special education.

2.5 Contrasts terms that in the language of thinking have similar meaning (e.g., think vs. feel; assume vs. surmise vs. speculate).

2.6 Distinguishes among supportive statements, irrelevant statements, and countersupportive statements.

2.7 Distinguishes between facts and inferences.

2.8 Identifies cause-effect relationships.

2.9 Identifies errors in reasoning.

2.10 Can identify where peers correctly and incorrectly use terms in the language of thinking (e.g., hope vs. expect; feel vs. believe; argue vs. suggest vs. allege).

2.11 Evaluates the credibility of sources cited in an argument.

2.12 Identifies unstated assumptions in arguments.

2.13 Distinguishes between relevant and irrelevant arguments.

2.14 Formulates questions that are relevant to a problem.

2.15 Uses similar "thinking terms" correctly in writing and orally (e.g., guess vs. speculate vs. conclude; think vs. feel; suggest vs. assert vs. claim vs. insist vs. argue).

2.16 Distinguishes between warranted and unwarranted generalizations.

2.17 Specifies assumptions that would be needed to make a conclusion true.

Before you conclude that Ms. Ash is a compulsive eccentric who doesn't know when to stop writing indicants, please consider how extremely helpful these varied indicants would be in generating IEP annual goals and short-term objectives along the lines that were illustrated in Table 13.2. Savor the rich breadth of critical thinking that is suggested by Ms. Ash's indicants (and by countless others that could be generated); this objective is a gem!

ReCAP.   The education of most students with special needs, like the education of others, should include subject matter from Contexts A, B, *and C.* For most kinds of exceptionality (with the notable exception of giftedness), more Context A instruction may be appropriate than would be true for regular students. *More, yes; all, no!* As noted earlier, we contend that most special education students are capable of benefiting greatly from significant amounts of Context C education.

Furthermore, some basic objectives may be appropriate for all students, but the indicants can be individualized for children by skills, interests, needs, and abilities. Stainback, Stainback, and Stafanich (1996) illustrate this point by suggesting that an objective of communicating effectively might include one student's objective for learning to write letters to friends, another's for dictating a letter into a tape recorder, and yet another for expanding picture-board vocabulary options for communicating with friends. Again, one size, or mastery threshold, doesn't fit all!

This section has outlined procedures with which educators can *better meet the intent* of legislation for special education without tripping over regulatory details of implementation that can result in denying such students their *right to as expansive and developmental an education as possible.* Objectives always must be interpreted as minimal statements of expectations and not the outer limits of the learning. We hope that the procedures presented in this section will help educators break out of a narrowly behavioral "training" mode that forsakes high-road transfer of learning. Rather, educators ought, insofar as their students are capable, to function in an expansive, developmental, "educational" mode that fosters high-road transfer.

ASSESSMENT ADAPTATIONS FOR STUDENTS WITH
SPECIAL NEEDS

Some educators use the terms adaptation, accommodation, or modification interchangeably. We will not do so. For our purposes, **adaptation** is the overarching term that includes accommodations and modifications as types of adaptation. Any adaptations used with a student are to be described in the IEP.

Accommodations are changes and supports in regular test conditions made to remove sources of measurement error created by disabilities. Accommodations are designed *to achieve valid,* not optimal, *scores* (Fuchs, Fuchs, Eaton, Hamlett, Binkley, & Crouch, 2000). The constructs being measured are not altered; accommodations involve changes in the ways tests are administered (Tindel, 2002).

Examples of accommodations include reading a history test to the student, writing answers dictated by the student, putting text into Braille, or providing sound amplification. Other accommodations are changing the setting or extending the time of *power* tests. Notice that accommodations, which are designed to remove the impact of a disability, would not benefit students without disabilities; letting a person with normal vision take a test in Braille would not help that person.

In elementary schools particularly, most accommodations are regarded as temporary, to be faded and eventually removed when the student no longer needs them. However, some disabilities—for example, blindness or hearing impairment—necessitate lifelong use of accommodations.

In Chapter 7, we mentioned the need to make sure that interpretive exercises or other item types did not impose demands that were irrelevant to the thing being assessed. For example, a science test should not be so hard to read that some students cannot input the science questions. In this case, we were advocating the avoidance of the need to accommodate. If it happens that in spite of keeping the readability low, a pupil with a grave reading disability still cannot manage the test, then the sensible accommodation would be to have the test read to the student. The purpose *is to cause the test to be valid as a measure of science,* the *same* science that other students have studied and are tested upon.

In order to comply with the need to include students with disabilities in state testing programs, most states have developed guidelines for test accommodations. Some have stringent guidelines, whereas others are more flexible (Johnson, Kimball, Brown, & Anderson, 2001).

Modifications are techniques that alter the task or test in way(s) that make it different from those being performed by others in the same class or activity. They change the work or amount of work to allow for more accurate evaluation of student performance (Bryant, Dean, Elrod, & Blackbourn, 1999). These changes in curriculum and test mean that the student is being tested on something *different* or more restricted than are others.

Examples of modifications involve changing the goals, activities, or outcomes for students (e.g., reducing the number of spelling words for a student to master) (Dettmer, Thurston, and Dyck, 2002). Another example of modifications would be extending the time limits of tests designed to assess *speed.* Using tests designed for, and normed on, individuals with disabilities is sometimes recommended; however, few such tests are available.

Assessment results obtained under irregular conditions *need to be reported as alternate scores.* One potentially useful approach is to administer tests under normal conditions before attempting modification. This allows study of both conventional and altered conditions (McGloughlin & Lewis, 1994).

Occasionally general education students challenge accommodations that are denied to them but could assist them in meeting graduation requirements or in achieving a higher class rank, thereby having more opportunity or scholarships. Some may regard accommodations and modifications for just a few students as unfair. A problematic question will be, "Shouldn't a student who is low-achieving be allowed to benefit from adaptations just as readily as students with disabilities?"

The short answer is: Accommodations, yes; modifications, no. Concerning accommodations, Elliott, Ysseldyke, Thurlow, & Erickson (1998) offered this scenario:

> You are a person who needs to wear corrective lenses to read and write. You enroll in a graduate class and attend all classes wearing your glasses during lectures, class activities, and completion of assignments in class and at home. The night of the final exam arrives, and . . . the instructor announces you will have three hours to complete the exam and requires all students wearing corrective lenses to remove them. The instructor notes that there will be no unfair advantages given to those students who wear glasses. (p. 23)

This instructor's results will demonstrate how well eyeglass wearers perform on the final *without* their corrective lenses. But who cares? Correction of vision, like other accommodations, does not confer an advantage; it is designed to *remove a deficit that is irrelevant to the thing being assessed.* Accommodations thus serve to *enhance the validity of a test* in measuring what it is being used to measure; that is good for all students. Enough said.

Modifications, however, are designed to measure something different for the person being tested than for most students. This seems appropriate only for students entitled to a modified curriculum. Recall that in the case of modification, the record should disclose the fact that modified or alternative assessment was used; therefore, there is no advantage to the student needing modification, fair or otherwise. The justification for modification centers on validity. If the aims or instruction and the curriculum are altered for a student with special needs, then an achievement test, to be valid, must reflect the modifications.

The topics of accommodation and modifications are complex, having important educational, measurement, legal, and social-policy ramifications (Pitoniak & Royer, 2001). Figure 13.1 lists ideas for accommodation and modification that can sometimes be made for students with special needs. Some change the manner of presentation, whereas others change the manner of response or alter processes used to obtain the responses. As to whether each is an accommodation or a modification, the instructional objectives and the student characteristics would often need to be known in order to say. Likewise, whether each is appropriate is also answerable only in light of the test purpose and student characteristics.

Reader-Friendly Tests

If one were to survey the accommodations that students with special needs most frequently need, the list would include several topics already addressed in this book from the perspective of making tests measure what we want them to assess without tapping things that the tests aren't supposed to assess. In other words, many things suggested in this book as being examinee friendly would, from

FIGURE 13.1   Assessment Adaptations for Students with Disabilities (not classified as to accommodation versus modification).

Fold or line the paper to help the student who has a spatial problem.

Use graph paper or lined paper turned vertically.

Make the schedule flexible, administering the test in several brief settings.

Alter the time of day when the test is given.

Allow for frequent breaks during testing.

Use alternatives for recording, such as marking in test book, typing answers, telling answers to the proctor for later transcription.

Provide large-print copies or Braille tests. (Large print slows reading rate, so use only when necessary.)

Have narrators or tape recorders and magnifying glasses for those with vision problems.

Provide a box or line to the left of each direction or step so student can check them off as they are completed.

Avoid fluorescent or glossy paper, fonts with characters having tails and curlicues, dittos, and handwritten materials, especially if in cursive.

Highlight or underline verbs in the test directions.

Use space to separate each step in the procedures and number each step.

Provide adequate white space to separate lines of text.

Highlight or color-code items on tests.

Decrease the number of test items.

Seat examinees away from noises and confusion.

Paraphrase instructions into simpler language.

Provide a demonstration of how test tasks are to be done.

Offer positive reinforcement for test-taking effort.

Teach test-taking skills such as clue words, time management, and careful reading.

Allow use of special equipment or materials.

Check adequacy of furniture, wheelchair accessibility, lighting, restroom accessibility.

Use study carrels, cubicles, or areas with movable partitions.

Allow tests to be taken in the resource room.

Provide review opportunities before the test.

Refrain from grading down for spelling errors.

Co-opt special education personnel for assistance with test administration.

Reduce the amount of material on a page.

Use a word processor for writing and editing.

Provide a calculator or computer to check work.

Read written directions or assignments aloud.

Allow a taped or written report instead of an oral report.

Increase the size of answer bubbles on test answer sheets.

Provide masks or markers to keep the place on the page.

Provide a tape recorder, typewriter, word processor, abacus, calculator, or communication device.

Allow an oral report instead of a written report.

Allow students to have sample tests to practice.

Supply recognition items and not just total recall items.

Ask questions requiring short answers.

a special education perspective, also be suitable accommodations for various students with high-frequency special needs. The list would include:

- Provide power tests with generous amounts of working time in order to avoid assessing speed in addition to power.
- Keep readability and vocabulary (other than subject-specific words) relatively low in order to avoid assessing reading in addition to what you intended to assess.
- Arrange options vertically.
- Emphasize key words such as *not* and *least* that are at risk of being overlooked.
- Avoid contorted logic such as having negative multiple-choice item stems in combination with negative options.
- Never split a question between two pages or two columns.
- Avoid splitting a matching exercise or an interpretive exercise between two pages.
- Avoid use of separate answer sheets with younger pupils.

To this set of user friendly features we should add:

- Use an easily read type font.
- Use type that is large enough to be easily read.
- Keep line lengths relatively short. For example, multiple-choice items set in two-column format are easier to read than are ones with long lines that may make finding the next line more challenging.
- Use spacing to clue readers about content. For example, leave a blank line between successive true-false questions. User-friendly, pacing of multiple-choice items has been modeled throughout the book except in some thinking cap exercises.

Figure 13.2 illustrates how spacing of multiple-choice items can be used to advantage. To show that formatting can aid comprehension, the figure contains two items that readers may find somewhat challenging. In the improved version, the underhang of the stems enables a free-standing item number to provide conspicuous demarcation of the beginning of each item. The second-level underhang for options (e.g., option A in item 1) serves to separate the options one from another. Finally, the spacing makes clear that each stem's options go with it, and not with another stem.

Teachers who use these varied means to render tests examinee-friendly obviously will better accommodate the needs of students having identified special needs. In addition, these same practices help the test scores of all examinees to more accurately reflect the intended learning targets without being distorted by irrelevant things. They enable the difficulty of test questions to reside in the subject matter and not in the communication.

PORTFOLIOS AND SPECIAL EDUCATION STUDENTS

Portfolios have special appeal for teaching and assessing of students served in special education programs. For the special education teacher, who uses many types of informal data to make instructional decisions, portfolio assessment can be the glue that structures the varied data into a meaningful picture (Wesson & King, 1996).

FIGURE 13.2   Formatting Impacts Comprehensibility.

POOR USE OF SPACING	IMPROVED USE OF SPACING
1. Common aims of teaching include such performances as "observes safety rules in the home" and "expresses difference of agreement amicably." Such aims can be cast in terms of typical performance or in terms of maximal performance. Which should receive more emphasis in the *objectives* (in contrast to the assessment)? **A.** They should receive about equal emphasis in the objectives. **B.** Maximal performance. **C.** Typical performance.	**1.** Common aims of teaching include such performances as "observes safety rules in the home" and "expresses difference of agreement amicably." Such aims can be cast in terms of typical performance or in terms of maximal performance. Which should receive more emphasis in the *objectives* (in contrast to the assessment)? **A.** They should receive about equal emphasis in the objectives. **B.** Maximal performance. **C.** Typical performance.
2. Each of the following objectives is likely to be assessed mainly as maximum performance. For which is this limitation of assessment the most worrisome? (A) Administers CPR correctly. (B) Avoids driving too close to the car ahead. (C) Cooks pancakes to the desired degree of doneness. (D) Serves well in tennis.	**2.** Each of the following objectives is likely to be assessed mainly as maximum performance. For which is this limitation of assessment the most worrisome? **A.** Administers CPR correctly. **B.** Avoids driving too close to the car ahead. **C.** Cooks pancakes to the desired degree of doneness. **D.** Serves well in tennis.

Portfolios promote student involvement in their own learning through shared planning with the teacher, self-assessment, and reflection on achievement toward annual goals and short-term objectives. Because emphasis in portfolios is placed on what students *can* do rather than what they *cannot* do, a portfolio embodies the spirit of the individual student's IEP (Wesson & King, 1996). Collections of best work, as evaluated by student and teacher, are ideal vehicles for integrating assessment with instruction (Kleinert & Thurlow, 2001). Kleinert, Green, Hurte, Clayton, and Oetinger (2002) found that by including students in construction, monitoring, and evaluation of their own portfolio work, the alternate assessment process facilitated learning of new skills. These researchers determined that students' active involvement in constructing their own assessments more strongly predicts alternate assessment scores than does teacher time, and thus reduces the burdens of overworked special education teachers.

GRADING AND REPORTING ISSUES FOR STUDENTS WITH SPECIAL NEEDS

Butler (1997) recognized the public tip of a very large educational iceberg with these candid comments:

> Educators disagree about grading practices for students with disabilities. The inclusion movement has made grading students with disabilities even more controversial as increasing numbers of students with special needs receive a significant proportion of their instruction in general education classes just when educators are being asked to raise academic standards. (p. 14)

Butler then asked who should decide on requirements to be used for students with special needs and how stringent grading practices should be for all students. She also pondered the responsibility of assigning grades to students in special education that are based on IEP objectives, which differ significantly from general education objectives in various courses. Then there is the troubling issue of denying a student who has documented disabilities a regular diploma, thereby reducing postschool opportunities and potentially violating the student's civil rights. In addition, identifying courses as "special education" on permanent records may jeopardize students' future opportunities.

In an extensive study of some aspects of these problems, a national survey was conducted of report card grading and classroom practices of adaptation. Teachers at all grade levels found letter and number grades more helpful for students without disabilities and pass-fail and checklist grades more helpful for those with disabilities. Yet more than 80% of school district policies mandate letter grades. Teachers indicated willingness to modify grading criteria for students with disabilities, basing grades on improvement or IEP objectives, giving separate grades for effort, and adjusting grades and grading weights according to ability. One grade was not perceived as useful for communicating multiple messages about student performance (Bursuck, Polloway, Plante, Epstein, Jayanthi, & McConeghy, 1996).

The survey also revealed that general educators had complete responsibility for grading about half the time, and they worked collaboratively with special educators about 40% of the time. About 40% reported that they found portfolios helpful for students with disabilities, who often are poor test-takers. On the issue of fairness, most teachers thought grading adaptations were unfair, but only if adaptations were made solely for students with disabilities. They thought that adaptations should be considered for all students (Bursuck, Polloway, Plante, Epstein, Jayanthi, & McConeghy, 1996), and, as indicated in a later report, that students learn in different ways and should be treated as individuals (Munk & Bursuck, 1998).

Stiggins (2001) asked rhetorically how we should grade various students in inclusionary classrooms who are pursuing fundamentally different objectives. He then provided these words:

> In my opinion, this single issue renders simple letter grades out of date and insufficient as a means of communicating about student achievement. The only solution I can find for this problem is to add more information to the reporting system, by identifying the targets covered by the grade reported. Without that detail, we cannot communicate about individual differences in the grades assigned within the same classroom. (p. 441)

Adaptations recommended by the aforementioned group of researchers and others include:

- Varying grading weights for different products or assignments
- Using contracts and modified course requirements
- Grading on improvement through assignment of extra points
- Adding on information about effort and achievement gained from portfolios

- Adding written comments, such as explaining performance on IEP objectives
- Using pass-fail grades
- Using checklists to show percentage of objectives met

Each approach has pros and cons, most of which have been addressed in previous chapters. It should be recognized, however, that the "answers" provided in Chapter 12 and elsewhere are much less adequate for students with special needs. Therefore, suggestions such as those just listed deserve to be rethought for special education as professionals seek solutions that contain the fewest and least serious ethical and assessment problems.

Grading student work is one issue, recording the grades and credits is yet another. The search for inclusive and fair diploma options and graduation policies has led to different "answers" in different jurisdictions. Significant differences exist among states in regard to the exit documents presented to students with disabilities. Sometimes similar requirements earn different types of exit documents in different states (Thurlow, Ysseldyke, & Reid, 1997). Thurlow and Thompson (2000) suggested giving names to diploma options that correspond to knowledge and skills demonstrated by the student and clarifying the implications that different diploma options have for continued special education services.

The all-encompassing purpose of grade reporting is to communicate information. When grades and earned credits are recorded, the information speaks for the student. The teachers are not on hand to explain that information and any adaptations that were made. If the information is to be used for decision making about the student's future, it must be forthright and in a readily understandable form.

Students and their families who participate in special education programs become quite sophisticated in matters of rights and responsibilities. As for staffing and conferences, they have "been there and done that" many times. Their collective voice advocates and supports attending to the special needs of children. These students, their parents, and their subsequent teachers, counselors, and administrators will benefit from the conveyance of clear and comprehensive information to those who need to know.

Educators, too, can benefit from having accountability demonstrated by careful and caring recording of useful information for those who need to know. All in all, legislative agenda and mandates that emphasize accountability, school reform, system quality, and "No Child Left Behind" will require strong will and dedicated resources to ensure that children served by IDEA will not be left behind (Lewis, 2002b).

CHAPTER RECAP

Legislation in the last quarter of the twentieth century created entitlements and mandates that have occupied much of the educational spotlight. Our challenge is to provide the best free and appropriate public education in the least restrictive environment from which students will benefit.

"Assessment is the focal point in the special education classification, placement, and programming process" (Spinelli, 2002, p. 3). We have examined some ways in which the CAP orientation can be adapted to meet the intent of legislative mandates, to meet legal and regulatory requirements for continued funding of programs, and to provide as rich an education as possible for students with special needs.

We also have examined two basic approaches to assessment procedures that both pursue validity (a topic of the next chapter). On the one hand, when students with special needs have pursued instructional objectives and curricula that are the same as other students pursue, accommodations of assessment procedures are, at times, needed in order to eliminate irrelevant sources of individual differences in the assessment results. Such accommodations help assessments to better assess the targeted material. On the other hand, when students with special needs have pursued instructional objectives and curricula that differ substantially from that of other students, then modification in assessment is needed in order to cause the assessment to parallel modifications that were made in the instruction. Such modifications help to align assessments to the targeted material.

Finally, some of the complex issues surrounding grading and reporting achievement of students with disabilities have been examined.

CHOOSING AND USING PUBLISHED INSTRUMENTS

CHAPTER
14

FEATURES OF EFFECTIVE ASSESSMENTS

CHAPTER OVERVIEW

ECONOMY AND PRACTICALITY

INTERPRETABILITY REVISITED

A CLOSER LOOK AT VALIDITY

TWO WAYS TO CONSIDER RELIABILITY

KEY TERMS

interpretability
validity
content-based validation
criterion-related validation
predictive validation
construct validation
construct irrelevance
construct underrepresentation

predictive bias
reliability
content-sampling error
occasion-sampling error
examiner error
scorer error
reliability coefficient

This chapter provides a transition from teacher-made assessments to published tests and their use. Each of its four topics is germane both to the consideration, development, and use of all manner of classroom assessments and to the selection, use, and interpretation of all kinds of published instruments.

All effective measures have several widely recognized characteristics. These characteristics of useful measures can be categorized in a variety of ways. In this book, we organize them under four headings:

1. Economy and practicality
2. Interpretability
3. Validity
4. Reliability

These four characteristics are relevant to assessment instruments in all fields. In studying this section, keep in mind that each feature applies not only to educational assessments, but also to assessment of distance, pitch, time, hearing, eyewitness testimony, temperature, earthquake intensity, and stock-market performance. *Let this serve as an advance organizer for high-road transfer of learning.* Thus, you should "think big" when studying these characteristics. In addition to applying the topics broadly to fields outside of education, you should seek to apply them to the full spectrum of educational measures: to teacher-made tests and to published tests; to measures of maximum performance and to measures of typical performance; to paper-pencil tests and to performance assessments; to instruments and procedures that tap cognitive attributes and to those that assess affect, motor skills, or social skills and dispositions; to power tests and to speed tests; to summative measures and to formative ones; to mastery tests and to tests designed to differentiate. The characteristics of good measuring instruments have very broad application.

ECONOMY AND PRACTICALITY

In this section, we first bring together under one topic various practical features of measures. Most of these considerations are economic in nature and were important in developing the rationale for the sieve.

Before starting, let's activate some of your relevant knowledge. Among the practical considerations are economy of time, money, and scoring; these have been considered in numerous places and the trade-offs among economy, reliability, and authenticity have been emphasized, especially in Chapter 9. This potpourri of features that affect the extent to which the use of an instrument or procedure is practical is variously referred to as economy, practical features, or logistic considerations. Some of the features are relevant to teacher-developed and published tests alike, whereas others apply only to published instruments.

Cost. The value of student time devoted to taking a test and the value of professional time spent in administering and interpreting it are usually far greater than any money spent in producing or purchasing the test and its answer sheet. Hence, educators should give only limited weight to the cost of production or purchase. One aspect of cost is the reusability of testing materials. Some instruments can be used only once, whereas others are designed for repeated reuse. The production or purchase of durable, reusable test booklets, performance equipment, diskettes, or CDs can involve significant up-front investment, but the per-student cost may well be less when the investment is figured over the expected life of the booklets or equipment. Recall the merits of separate answer sheets, discussed in Chapter 10. Typically, separate answer media can be scored with relative ease and accuracy and enable costly test booklets to be reused.

For published tests, a final aspect of cost is that of scoring. Published tests are scored locally by hand or electronically either locally or by the publisher. Publishers typically offer a variety of scoring services from which users may select those desired. This expense, like the purchase of answer sheets, is a recurring one.

Time. When teachers develop their own tests, they make their length convenient. When schools purchase published tests, however, the length is set. Publishers of longer tests often organize subtests into lengths that fit conveniently into class periods. In addition to the actual working time, allowance must be made for distributing materials, reading directions, answering questions, and collecting materials after the test. These activities usually require from 5 to 15 minutes, depending on test complexity, examiner efficiency, and examinee characteristics.

Although test brevity is an obvious virtue, recall the inherent trade-off between length and reliability. Short tests tend to be unreliable; longer ones tend to be more reliable. The most effective way to make a test more reliable is usually to lengthen it. Therefore, persons selecting published tests must not pursue brevity with singleness of purpose. Nor should they expect to find tests that are both short and reliable.

Ease of Administration.   Classroom tests vary in the ease with which they can be administered. Other things being equal, ease is always preferable. Published instruments also differ; some require substantial preparation time and tedious attention to detail in order to follow regular procedures. For example, one of us once used a group-administered geometry aptitude test that had 17 separately timed subunits in 40 minutes of working time! With this many opportunities to err in timing subparts, errors are likely. (Alas, he forgot to start the stopwatch for one of the sections.)

Some published tests, such as individually administered aptitude tests such as the Wechsler Scales, demand specialized skill and experience of examiners/scorers. For this reason, such devices should be used only by those who have had coursework devoted to their use. Even among the kinds of instruments that regular classroom teachers are qualified to administer, score, and interpret, there is considerable variation in demands. Therefore, the ease with which a test can be used merits attention when developing or selecting tests.

Ease, Speed, and Accuracy of Scoring.   Recall from Chapter 4 that once a raw score is obtained, it must, if interpretations are to be norm referenced, be converted into some sort of derived score. Some published tests' manuals or computer software make this task easy and relatively error free, whereas others require users to enter a sequence of tables to make successive conversions. Moreover, the ease of using tables is impacted by print size, spacing, and use of guide lines, shading, and color. When errors creep into scoring, the problem is more than one of mere convenience and time; *scoring errors reduce reliability and validity.*

If potential users of published tests wish to hand score answer sheets for quick results, then availability of appropriate answer media and scoring devices, such as overlay stencils, are important. If one wishes to have electronic scoring and conversion of raw scores into derived scores, then the availability of necessary answer media and scoring services merits consideration. Cost, accuracy, and turnaround time are also important issues.

Availability of Desired Derived Scores for Published Tests.   As will be seen in Chapter 16, manuals of published tests and scoring services commonly provide several kinds of derived scores. Percentile ranks and percentile bands are the derived scores of choice for most interpretive purposes whereas standard scores are needed for most research or computational uses. Before purchasing a test, users should verify that the kind(s) of scores needed are available.

Availability of Interpretive Aids for Published Tests.   After tests are administered and scored, results often need to be interpreted and explained to students and parents. Some published tests are accompanied by clarifying devices to help interpret scores to lay people. Such interpretive aids are usually designed to simultaneously highlight both (a) what is revealed by the test score and (b) the limits of what is known from the scores.

Several tests have interpretive aids that provide vivid graphic displays of confidence bands of percentile ranks. We will emphasize in later chapters that such percentile bands help students and parents understand that one must allow for a margin of error in test scores.

Some publishers provide computer-generated printouts of prose interpretations as an option that can be purchased along with scoring. In general, these interpretive aids explain to parents and students what the scores mean. It is important to realize that the quality of such interpretive aids can be no better than the sophistication of the programs that generate them. "Test users should not rely on computer-generated interpretations of test results unless they have the expertise to consider the appropriateness of these interpretations in individual cases" (AERA, 1999, p. 118).

Face Appeal.   An important issue is the impressions of examinees and others concerning how "valid" a test *seems* to be.[1] If a test strikes lay people as appropriate, better rapport and public relations result. If its content appears irrelevant, significantly outdated, or simply silly, poorer cooperation results, "regardless of the actual validity of the test" (Anastasi & Urbina, 1997, p. 116). For example, a test of basic arithmetic for use in adult basic education programs should not have application questions that would be appropriate for children (e.g., Mother gave Mary $20 to buy a necklace costing $13.95 with tax. How much change should she receive?) It is important to consider the credibility of a test to examinees.

INTERPRETABILITY

Because any educational measure must be interpretable via either domain referencing and/or norm referencing, another feature of good measuring instruments is **interpretability.**[2] To help integrate the material in this section with previous learning, let's activate more of your relevant knowledge. In Chapter 4, we first examined the need for a basis of interpreting classroom assessments. The alternative bases of norm referencing and domain referencing have entered into discussion of many topics. Any useful educational measure—be it teacher made or published—*must* be accompanied by at least one of these means of meaningful interpretation.[3]

Yet some assessments deplorably lack *both* bases of interpretation. Some tests that are alleged to be criterion or domain referenced don't define a domain clearly enough to provide a basis for an informed referencing of the interpretation to an explicit domain (Forsyth, 1991; Nitko, 1980; see also Nitko, 2001). Likewise, some tests said to be norm referenced don't describe reference groups in enough detail to enable users to judge their relevance to their interpretive purpose.

---

[1]This important attribute is often called "face validity"; however, that term is a misnomer.

[2]A sound basis exists for treating interpretability as an aspect of validity, and some authors do, for example, AERA (1999); Nitko (2001). We address it separately for convenience of presentation.

[3]Some educators add a third basis for interpretation—improvement. But that begs the question: Improvement as measured by what kind of referencing? In addition, the discussion later in this chapter concerning difference scores (e.g., comparison of pretest scores with posttest scores) indicates problems with this approach.

Domain Referencing in Contexts A and B

Recall that domain-referenced interpretations relate to what the examinee can do with subject matter or skill domains. Such a domain must be described in enough detail to indicate very clearly what it includes and what it excludes (AERA, 1999). When a test's content or skill domain is explicit, interpretation can be meaningfully referenced to its content (i.e., domain referenced). When subject matter is not clearly and tightly specified, that is, when the domain is expansive, interpretation cannot meaningfully be domain referenced.

Contexts A and B domains are explicit; hence, performance can be referenced to them. Would it also make sense to reference performance to that of other people?

In a Context A unit, most students achieved mastery of the essential content by the conclusion of successful instruction. Where everybody is virtually perfect, everybody is average, and little is gained from so describing them.

In Context B, significant amounts of individual differences exist in achievement after effective instruction. Because people differ, reporting relative status conveys information.

Norm Referencing in Contexts B and C[4]

Recall that norm-referenced interpretations relate examinee performance to the performance of other people. A reference group must be described in enough detail to enable test users to know its nature. When a reference group is adequately described and relevant to the interpretive purpose, interpretation can be meaningfully people referenced (i.e., norm referenced). However, interpretation cannot meaningfully be norm referenced if there is no reference group, if a reference group is not adequately described, or if it is not relevant to the purpose of interpretation.

Individual differences in achievement clearly exist in Contexts B and C. Hence, performance can meaningfully be norm referenced. Would it also make sense to reference performance to subject matter or skill domains?

In Context B, there can be good reason to reference performance to content. Because the content is explicit, it is possible and meaningful to reference performance to it.

In Context C, it is not possible to reference interpretation very fully to the expansive, fuzzily defined content domains.[5] An *illusion* of domain referencing can be created by such statements as "Jay has achieved a 75% mastery of current events." However, such utterances are meaningless because the content domain is not sufficiently laid out to identify *what* he has achieved 75% of. Nor do we know the difficulty of the items used to assess his achievement.

Let's now identify some groups to which examinee performance might be referenced.

---

[4]Other books commonly refer to comparison groups of other people as norm groups, and they typically refer to kinds of converted scores used for norm-referenced interpretation as norms. Thus, the word "norm" is often used to refer to entirely different topics—reference groups of people and scores. To make matters worse, the word also has meanings in Standard American English that differ from assessment language. To avoid confusion, we use the term "reference group" to refer to comparison groups of other people and the term "derived scores" to refer to scores used in norm-referenced interpretations.

[5]That is, in Context C domain referencing does not *suffice*. Yet it is obviously necessary to have *some* sense of test content. The statement that "Anna scores higher than 35% of a national sample of seventh graders" obviously needs to be accompanied by a description of test content (e.g., spelling vs. running vs. math). That was the point in Chapter 5 of careful planning and description of the subject matter of Context C tests. Their domains should be described *as clearly as is practical*; the point here is that this is not clear enough to enable domain referencing to suffice.

Norm Referencing to the Class.   Chapter 12 showed that when norm referencing is needed to interpret teacher-made tests, they are sometimes referenced to the teacher's own class. For grading purposes, this is extremely undesirable. For some other functions, such as dividing a fourth-grade class into three groups for reading instruction, the class at hand is the most appropriate reference group to use.

When interpretations of published tests are to be norm referenced, they, too, could be referenced to single classes. This, however, is uncommon because much larger, more stable groups are ordinarily available.

Norm Referencing to Larger External Groups.   Chapter 12 showed how interpretations of teacher-made tests can, by use of anchor measures, be indirectly norm referenced to larger external reference groups. It was seen that this is often highly desirable.

For published tests, it isn't necessary for teachers to go to this trouble because national reference-group data are ordinarily supplied. Moreover, the scoring services available for many published instruments also provide optional, additional reference-group data for such groups as the user's own class, school, and school district.

Bases for Assessing National Norms.   By far, the most common comparative data accompanying published instruments are national reference groups that enable an examinee's performance to be compared with that of a *representative sample* of other examinees of a *given description*. This section mentions the issue of the *representativeness* of the sample. The next section addresses the *relevance* of the reference group to one's interpretive purpose.

Although practitioners don't conduct national norming studies, it is desirable for them to be able to judge the adequacy of published normative data. Reputable test publishers usually attempt to gather reference-group data from random samples. For example, the publisher of a sixth-grade math test might seek data that are based on a random sample of sixth-grade students. The sampling is ordinarily national in scope for commercially distributed tests and statewide in scope for state-produced assessments. The topic of evaluating the adequacy or representativeness of the reference group is beyond the scope of this book. Interested readers are urged to read our discussion of this important topic at ablongman.com/hannadettmer.

Assessing the Relevance of Normative Samples.   We have seen that national reference groups are desirable when educators wish to compare a student's performance with a national cross-section of students in the same grade or subject. The broader issue is that norm-referenced comparisons should be made with respect to a *relevant* group of other examinees. No matter how extensive, representative, and recent a sample may be, the resulting reference-group data will be helpful only if the population sampled is one with which the user wishes to compare examinee performance. Users of published tests must, therefore, always be acutely aware of what reference group was used to obtain derived scores.

To illustrate, suppose you have just taken a reading test and are told that you performed at the 90th percentile. Should you be elated? Not until you know what the reference group is. If it is one of reading-disabled seventh graders, you probably would not be thrilled to learn that you outperformed most of them. However, if it were a reference group of Ph.D. candidates, you might have cause for elation.

Or suppose one of us has just taken a personality inventory and is told that her profile is *very* strange, being two or three *SD*s from the mean on several subscores. Should we be alarmed about her mental health? Not until we inquire about the reference group. If it were a carefully selected sample of Midwestern female professors (which she is), then we would have cause for concern. But if it turns out to be a sample of outback Australian aboriginals, then we wouldn't be concerned that her profile differed markedly from that of an irrelevant reference group.

However, suppose that she were planning to spend three years in field research among outback aboriginals. Now the reference group would be relevant in judging how she would fit into that culture. That she has no aboriginal ancestry is immaterial. The principle can be put this way: If we want to know how a fish will get along in a particular pond, compare it with the fish in that pond. If we want to know how it will fare in another pond, then compare it with the fish in the other pond.

This principle prompts some test users to compare students' performance with that of samples that are *not* representative of all students in the country. For example, the principal of a Bureau of Indian Affairs reservation school might want to compare local pupils with other Native American reservation youth. That is, the administrator would wish the publisher to separate (i.e., disaggregate) the data for this category of youth from the national normative data.

This comparison may not be feasible if there are not enough Native American reservation pupils in the national reference group to provide stable data or to be representative of reservation-dwelling Native American students. There are, however, certain groups for whom data are sometimes available.

Inner-City School Norms.   Like the reservation principal, educators who work with inner-city students may contend that it is unfair to compare their students with a national cross section of other students, most of whom have far greater advantages. From one point of view, they obviously are right. No question about it, our society does not distribute opportunity equally to all its young. However, that isn't the issue.

The question of which reference group is preferable depends largely on the intent of the norm-referenced interpretations. On the one hand, if the purpose is to judge how each person stands in comparison with grade-mates across the country, then national norms make the most sense. On the other hand, if the goal is to judge how each student has progressed *in the disadvantaged context of the inner city and its school,* then inner-city or local norms would indeed make good sense (Ricks, 1971). However, one wouldn't want to rely *exclusively* on inner-city norms. An inner-city school could be average in comparison with other such schools, and this could obscure the very real educational, economic, and social problems. Solving these problems demands that we be aware of them.

Fortunately, inner-city educators need not decide between inner-city norms and national norms. Both can be used simultaneously, and this often makes the best sense.

Ethnic Norms.   Along the same lines, spokespersons for various minorities sometimes suggest that it would be more fair to compare children from a given group with others from the same group than to compare them with a national cross section. For example, suppose one were interpreting aptitude or achievement test scores for a group of rural Hispanic students. For the purpose of judging how well they can function in their present situation, local norms or rural Hispanic norms would be suitable. But for predicting how well they might *at first* function if they should enter the mainstream, national reference-group data would be preferable (Ricks, 1971).

Occupational and Gender-Specific Norms.   Sometimes there is merit in comparing an individual with persons who work in a particular occupation. Suppose a person took a spatial aptitude test for the purpose of considering dentistry. It would be useful to compare this person's score with those of people who work in this field. One might also wish to use general norms, but the occupational norms would be especially useful.

In this culture at this time, gender differences exist in some kinds of achievement and aptitude tests, some favoring males and some favoring females (Cronbach, 1990). Gender differences also exist in some kinds of interest inventories. It is, therefore, common for interest and aptitude measures to provide separate reference-group data for males and females. Although interpretation is usually based on same-gender data, it is occasionally productive to employ cross-gender and total-group reference-group data as well.

Course-Based, Grade-Based, and Age-Based Reference Group Data.   National reference group data are commonly based on people who are enrolled in a given course, are in a given grade, or are of a given age. Which makes the best sense?

At the secondary and college level, many elective courses are not taken by all students. For example, only some high school students elect chemistry. If a teacher administers a published chemistry achievement test, the reference group providing the most meaningful interpretations would be one consisting of other students in high school chemistry, not 16-year-olds or high school juniors (many of whom haven't studied chemistry).

For courses studied by all students, normative data can be based on others of either the same age or the same grade. In this country, achievement tests are accompanied by reference-group data based on others of the same *grade*. However, aptitude tests typically have reference-group data based on others of the same chronological *age*. (In addition, some achievement and aptitude tests provide both age-based and grade-based reference-group data.)

VALIDITY

Chapters 5 through 10 concerned the topic of building validity into classroom assessments. We will now broaden our notion of the kinds of information that can evidence validity, and we will amplify the book's theme that evaluation has impact.

Validity is often described as the extent to which a device assesses what it is being used to assess and nothing else. Along these lines, validity can be characterized as how well a test "fulfills the function for which it is being used" (Hopkins, 1998, p. 72). Validity is "the most fundamental consideration in developing and evaluating tests" (AERA, 1999, p. 9).

Note well that it is not a test itself that is valid to some extent; rather, it is the various *uses* to which it may be put. An instrument may be highly valid for some purposes, fair for other uses, and worthless for still others. To illustrate, suppose a person buys a bathroom scale. If it were used to rank order a group of third graders by weight, the device might be highly valid. If it were used to order them by height, it would function only poorly for this use. If it were used to measure their achievement in spelling, it would be worthless for this job. Thus, it isn't the scale itself that is valid or invalid; it is the uses that might be made of it that are valid to various extents.

Recall the important idea that tests are ordinarily useful only to the extent that they *improve decision making.* The concept of validity is relevant to each potential use of a measure and to its resulting decision(s). Recall also the theme that assessment has impact and that educators should be mindful of its consequences. Validity of a measure or procedure is judged by the consequences of its use. Although it is a theoretical topic, *validity focuses on the extremely practical and important issues of test utility and impact.*

Validity evidence comes in a rich variety of forms. Various kinds of data have traditionally been grouped into categories called content-related, criterion-related, and construct-related validity evidence. However, authorities now conceptualize validity as a unitary concept (AERA, 1999; Messick, 1989).

Although validation often should include several kinds of evidence because no one method of validation is sufficient for each specific use of an assessment (AERA, 1999), the one(s) of primary concern relate to the anticipated interpretation(s), inference(s), and decision(s) to be made from the scores. For example, if a test is used to predict next year's college grades of high school seniors, then the evidence of primary—not exclusive, just primary—interest concerns how well the test forecasts next year's college grades. However, if a test is used to measure pupil knowledge of this week's spelling lesson, then the kind of evidence that is of most interest focuses on how well the test matches the objectives and content of the spelling lesson.

First, the three traditional kinds of validity evidence will be discussed. Then we will address the important issues of the relationship between validity and educational decision making. Finally, the validity of an assessment's use will be considered in light of the probable consequences of that use.

Content-Focused Evidence

In this section, we focus on achievement tests. Whether achievement measures are commercially developed or are created by individual teachers, they should be evaluated by considering, among other things, how well they tap the targeted kinds of achievement. This applies equally to objective tests, to essay and other product assessments, and to performance measures; to mastery tests and to tests that differentiate; to pretests and posttests; and to formative tests and summative tests.

When a test is used to measure achievement, most interest should focus on the degree to which the sample of test tasks is representative of the content domain of interest. **Content-based validation** relies on considered, data-based judgments regarding the relationship between the test and the content domain.

Does this topic sound familiar? It should! Chapters 5 through 9 were focused on planning and constructing tests that would *authentically* assess the "right stuff." Assessing the targeted "stuff" in a realistic manner is what content-based validity is all about.

Building Validity into Teacher-Made Achievement Tests.   Validity is built into achievement measures. *The most persuasive evidence that an achievement measure is valid is usually a consideration of how thoughtfully it was planned and developed.*

So how does a teacher build valid tests? By attending carefully to its development. Chapter 5 focused on planning tests so that they will reflect the intended subject matter and mental processes. Chapters 6 through 9 addressed methods of preparing items and tasks that authentically assess the domain on which instruction focused and nothing else (e.g., test-wiseness, test anxiety, or visual impairment). Chapters 8 and 9 also offered suggestions for scoring measures so as to avoid score contamination by extraneous factors. Chapter 10 addressed a variety of issues, such as directions concerning guessing, that influence what tests actually measure.

A major purpose of this book is to enable teachers to build validity into their classroom tests. The topic needs little space here because Chapters 5 through 10 have already considered it at length.

Assessing Validity of Published Achievement Tests.   When a teacher, school district, or state selects an achievement test or battery of tests, validity should be a central consideration. The kind of validity evidence of greatest relevance to this task concerns how well the test content matches the instructional aims. The professional task is to judge how well validity (from the local perspective) was built into the test.

A key step of the search for content evidence of a published test's validity is to study the test. Each question should be scrutinized. This inspection provides a sense of how expertly the items were crafted and reviewed, of content balance, and of the relative weight allotted to various mental processes.

Another step in securing content-based evidence is to study the test manual's description of the developmental procedures. How adequately was the content domain described in advance? As we saw in Chapter 5, advanced planning provides protection against content imbalance. A well-constructed achievement measure "should cover the objectives of instruction, not just its subject matter. Content must, therefore be broadly defined to include major objectives, such as the application of principles and the interpretation of data, as well as factual knowledge" (Anastasi & Urbina, 1997, p. 115). Knowing how the content domain was identified and how it described precisely what the test plans specified, and how items were developed, edited, field-tested, and revised, helps one to answer the question, "Was validity (for my intended use) built into this test?"

Another dimension to the question concerns the indicants that are actually measured (in contrast to the instructional objectives). For example, commercially distributed achievement tests rely mainly on objective items; in some—but not all—cases this compromises authenticity. If, for example, major instructional objectives concern students' ability to express themselves orally or to develop logical arguments, then selection-type items don't assess the entire achievement domain. In such cases, no amount of care in developing excellent test items that adhere to test specifications can rectify a systematic underrepresentation in the specifications of the targeted achievement domain. One should be careful not to overgeneralize from the indicants sampled; rather, *one should consider how well the indicants sampled represent the domain in real-to-life ways.*

These important facets of validity involve judgment about the alignment of test content with instructional objectives. Thus, content-focused validity evidence is judgmental, not quantitative.

Validity Depends on the Situation.   A test that is highly valid for assessing achievement in some settings may be seriously deficient in other situations. For example, suppose a published test in high school French focuses exclusively on the written language. Miss Foix's French course heavily emphasizes the written language. She may (if other things are satisfactory) find the test to be highly valid for measuring how well her students have achieved her instructional objectives. Mr. Dubois's course gives equal attention to the oral language, to the written language, and to French culture. Therefore, he will find the test to be relatively invalid for assessing his students' achievement of major course objectives. Even if it is exemplary in other respects; the test underrepresents his curriculum.

The point is that test validity cannot be judged in the abstract. What is properly judged is the *match* of a test with some particular use to which it is to be put in a particular situation. Thus, *validity is not an attribute of a test;* it is an attribute of *the interaction of a test with a situation in which the test is used to make decisions.*

Content Considerations Are Necessary but Not Sufficient.   Subject matter deliberations are indispensable to understanding what curricula material and mental processes achievement tests measure and which they may neglect. However, content considerations may not reveal some of the subtle excess things that may inappropriately influence scores. For example, the impact of examinee test wiseness, the effect of test reading level, the influence of prior familiarity with stimulus material in interpretative exercises, and the consequences of gender or cultural bias will not necessarily come to light from the judgmental processes described earlier. For that reason, additional sources of validity evidence are appropriate for achievement tests; we will take up such topics later in the chapter.

THINKING CAP EXERCISE 14.1   ???

1. Two elementary schools have very different emphases in their math curriculum. School A focuses heavily on computational skills and gives less attention to math applications. School B emphasizes application of math to real-life situations and gives less emphasis to computation. Now suppose each school is looking for a published math test that matches its curriculum. Test X emphasizes computational skills, giving less attention to application. Test Y emphasizes application and provides less coverage to computation. Test Z provides a balanced assessment of computation and applications. If other things are equal, which test is the most valid *in each school*?

2. Mrs. Fox teaches tenth-grade biology in a school where all of her students are at least average in reading. Her tests are masterpieces of assessing a combination of knowledge of important facts and principles and applying this learning to novel situations. She relies heavily on interpretive exercises to assess high-road transfer.

    Her friend, Mr. Pine, teaches the same course from the same course of study in a school in which several of his students are quite poor in reading. He has not had a course in classroom assessment and has rather poor tests. He wonders if he should accept a collegial offer from Mrs. Fox to use her tests. Should he?

3. One of Mrs. Fox's students has a serious motor disability and cannot record his responses.

What accommodations, if any, should she make for him?

KEY TO THINKING CAP EXERCISE 14.1

1. Test X is best suited to School A and Test Y best meets the needs of School B. Tests X, Y, and Z are not valid or invalid in any absolute sense. That you or we might prefer Test Z is irrelevant. What must be judged is the relationship of test content with the proposed test use.

2. Because her students are adequate readers, Mrs. Fox's interpretive exercises were probably written without much attention to controlling the reading difficulty. However, because many of Mr. Pine's students are poor readers, he should ensure that the test doesn't measure reading because reading is *irrelevant to biology*. He might be able to borrow item ideas for rewriting and he may be able to modify the readability of the stimuli and items, but he should at least screen them and be prepared to modify them before adopting them.

3. As we saw in Chapter 13, she definitely should provide assistance in recording answers. The test is supposed to assess competence in biology—not motor control. Therefore, the accommodation to eliminate the *irrelevant* factor of motor control renders the test a more valid measure *of biology*.

THINKING CAP EXERCISE 14.2   ???

1. In which CAP context is it most difficult to build validity into an achievement test? Why?
2. For each of the following classroom achievement measures, assess the importance of content-based validity evidence.
   A. A primary teacher's Context A unit test on knowledge of the fire exit route.
   B. A physical education teacher's Context B test of shooting accuracy in archery.
   C. A teacher's observations of pupils' typical behavior in interpersonal relations.
   D. Your final examination in a course.
   E. Debaters' performance in a tournament.

KEY TO THINKING CAP EXERCISE 14.2

1. Context A and B domains are clearly specified; thus, it is fairly easy to develop test content that matches the explicit instructional domain. Moreover, sampling is often unnecessary because an entire domain or skill can often be included in the test.

However, in Context C, content domain boundaries aren't as clear. Hence, it is harder to develop tests that mirror the expansive instructional domain. Hence, sampling is necessary because Context C domains are too large to be tested in their entirety.

For these reasons, two-way tables of specifications are drawn up for Context C tests. They provide control over the sampling of curricula topics and over the sampling of mental processes. In addition, when scoring is not entirely objective, rubrics provide control over what content actually counts.

2. All five cases involve measuring achievement. Validity of all achievement tests concerns the extent to which a measure assesses student performance on instructional objectives and nothing else. This is a vital concern regardless of CAP context.

Criterion-Based Validity Evidence

Criterion-related validation typically concerns the correlation of an instrument's (or procedure's) scores with those of some accepted measure of the thing the instrument is used to measure or predict. All criterion-related studies are similar in design; the main difference among them concerns when the criterion data are gathered.

At times, a test is used to predict some future event; in such cases the future event serves as the obvious basis—the criterion—for assessing the test. **Predictive validation** is investigated by following up and comparing the original predictive scores (e.g., forecasts of the next day's rain) with scores of one or more criterion measures (e.g., the rainfall on the day following each prediction). When predictions are made, their validity should be investigated. Many educational decisions are based on forecasts. Following are examples of questions that call for predictions.

- What grade in first-year French is Miriam most likely to receive if she takes the course?
- Would Amanda benefit more from regular instruction in math than from acceleration?
- Should John be classified as having a learning disability? (i.e., Would he benefit more from LD interventions than from regular instruction?)

Useful prophecies improve decisions. This assistance is maximized when forecasts are valid.

At other times, use of an instrument is considered for reasons of economy or safety as a substitute for a recognized measure; in such cases, the recognized measure serves as the criterion for assessing the substitute test. Concurrent validation is investigated by comparing scores of the substitute measure with those of the more credible or better established measure. For example, a paper-pencil test about cooking might be used as an economical surrogate for a more authentic performance test. A skin-patch test may be used in tuberculosis screening as a cost-effective and safer substitute for a chest X-ray. A short paper-pencil personal adjustment survey could be used as a substitute for a lengthy interview by a skilled clinician. When substitute measures are used, their validity should be checked.

Construct-Related Validity Evidence

Some instruments are designed to assess abstract characteristics such as verbal reasoning, introversion, art appreciation, trigonometry applications, and leadership. Such attributes are called constructs because they are theoretical constructions about the underlying nature of observable behavior. Of course, *tests can measure only observable behavior;* therefore, indicants are used to estimate people's status on constructs.

All kinds of validation concern the extent to which tests assess the targeted domains without being contaminated by anything else. When the domains are abstract constructs, the term construct validation is sometimes used to represent the process of building knowledge about the extent to which tests capture the targeted constructs and nothing else. The term was traditionally used to signify kinds of validity evidence other than content-based and criterion-related evidence (Kane, 2001).

Construct validation *consists of building strong logical cases based on circumstantial evidence that tests assess the intended constructs and nothing else.* It explains the meaning of test scores and reveals *networks of their relationships with other variables.* Like other scientific exploration, it involves interactions among curiosity, speculation, data collection, and critical review of possible interpretations of the evidence (Cronbach, 1990).

Two major factors that erode construct validity can be presented at this time. As you consider them, you will realize that *the ideas have received major emphasis in Chapters 5 through 10 and 13,* as well as earlier in this chapter.

First, **construct irrelevance** is the impact on test scores of factors that are not relevant to the construct the test is supposed to tap. Examples are test wiseness and enabling characteristics of learners (e.g., ability of students to *read* math application problems). Such unrelated elements distort the meaning of scores (AERA, 1999).

Second, **construct underrepresentation** concerns the extent to which a test systematically fails to tap crucial features of the construct it is supposed to assess. Examples are the failure of many classroom tests to provide appropriate weight to deep learning and high-road transfer and the sacrifice of authenticity (usually to enhance reliability or economy). *Construct underrepresentation causes test scores to have narrower meaning than intended* (AERA, 1999).

It is worth emphasizing that, although classroom uses of product and performance assessment have appropriately been enthusiastically espoused for their directness, they are subject to the same validity criteria as other forms of assessment (Congdom & McQueen, 2000). Like paper-pencil tests, product and performance measures yield distorted results to the extent that they underrepresent the construct of interest or tap construct-irrelevant attributes. Because of time constraints, *performance tests are especially vulnerable to construct underrepresentation.*

Construct-related validation is central to the study of measures intended to assess abstract constructs such as academic aptitude or anxiety. In addition, construct-related validation is used to supplement the content-focused validation of achievement tests and the criterion-based validation of tests used for prediction or as substitutes for preferable tests.

Example of Construct Validation of a Test of Silent-Reading Comprehension.   Many kinds of logical evidence are useful in validation, and most are far beyond the scope of this book. For a much fuller introduction to the topic, visit our web site at <u>ablongman.com/hannadettmer</u>. Following is an example that will (a) illustrate a few of the educationally important kinds of validity evidence, (b) show the breadth of the kinds of evidence used, and (c) provide the flavor of the process of simultaneously building a logical circumstantial case that both a construct and the device used to assess it are valid.

Of course, the kind of validity evidence of primary interest for an achievement test concerns content; suppose that careful examination of a published multiple-choice test of silent reading suggests that it is a good measure of our notion of what reading comprehension is. However, before adopting the test, we check some research studies of this test reported in scholarly journals in order to supplement the content-based evidence.

■ In one study, examinees were given the reading test and were independently assessed for test wiseness. These two measures were unrelated. This builds confidence that the test's scores aren't influenced by individual differences in the construct-irrelevant attribute of test wiseness.

■ Another study describes a process in which individual examinees were asked to think aloud as they worked on the test items. Analysis of the results provided researchers with insights concerning the mental processes that the test assessed and the differences among examinees in what the items assessed. These findings enable one to better judge the extent to which items were measuring what one wants to assess.

■ The manual describes how representatives of various minority groups reviewed the test for bias. This, too, fosters the belief that the test's scores are not impacted by construct-irrelevant differences in ethnic background. (Although appropriate, this qualitative evidence, in itself, doesn't guarantee the absence of some of the kinds of bias that will be discussed later in this chapter.)

■ The manual reports that the reading scores correlated moderately with scores of a critical-thinking test, with scores of a literature test, and with a test of science. The constructs of critical thinking, literature, and science would be thought to be related—but only moderately—with reading achievement. Because the findings conform to expectations, they add circumstantial evidence that the reading test is valid.

■ The manual reports that 75% of the reference-group sample attempted the last item. Therefore, at least 25% of examinee scores appear to be influenced by speed. For educators whose definition of reading comprehension focuses largely on power, this amount of speededness may be a problem. However, for those whose construct includes ability to comprehend at a reasonable pace, this degree of speededness might be viewed as tolerable or even desirable.

■ We find a well-designed study of passage dependence. A large number of pupils were randomly assigned to two groups. One group took the test under regular conditions. The other took it with the passages removed in order to show how well the items could be answered without the materials upon which they are based. The chance-level score for this 40-item, four-option, multiple-choice test is 10. Therefore, the mean score of the group that took the test without the passages shouldn't be much more than 10. Suppose, however, that their mean score was 20, whereas that of the group taking the test under regular conditions was 30.

The mean of 30 is greater than 20, so we infer that the test does measures some reading comprehension. However, it is supposed to measure reading comprehension *and nothing else.* The mean of 20 is so much more than the chance-level score of 10 that we must conclude that the test measures something that is construct irrelevant—and a lot of it! Such findings undermine validity claims.

(Recall from Chapter 7 the recommendation to ensure context dependence of interpretive exercises by using novel stimuli and being sure items are based on these stimuli. Teachers who do this for their classroom tests are attending to this important aspect of validity.)

This example showed how construct validation is appropriate for achievement tests (which are primarily validated on the basis of content considerations). The important point is that it is not sufficient to rely on only one category of evidence of the validity of a particular test use (Messick, 1989).

Validity and Decision Making

Repeated emphasis has been directed to the principle that tests should be used to facilitate better decision making. A physician should not order a blood test for anemia unless she or he intends to receive the results and use them. Nor should a teacher administer a test unless the results are intended to result in better decisions.

This principle doesn't, of course, argue that tests serve only decision-making functions. Repeated emphasis has also been given to the important roles that tests play in promoting, guiding, and pacing student study. Yet our present focus is on the use of tests as instruments that inform decisions. Two examples will highlight the idea that *validity of a data source concerns the extent to which its use enlightens decision making.*

Passing Thresholds of Mastery Tests.   In teaching Context A material that is essential in its own right or is essential for later work in the subject, mastery testing in indicated. Formative use of mastery tests is valid to the extent that it helps teachers better know what additional assistance is needed for each pupil. Summative use is valid to the extent that it enables teachers to make wiser decisions regarding whether to advance individual pupils to the next topic.

One should consider carefully which kind of error is the more serious, recycling a pupil who could succeed if advanced or advancing one who will later falter. *This should be the basic issue in setting passing thresholds for mastery tests.* In some cases (e.g., the need to know how to use a car's brakes before driving it), consequences of premature advancement are disastrous. In other situations (e.g., a unit on capitalization of proper nouns), consequences of premature advancement are minor; the pupil would be quickly recognized and given additional instruction.

In Contexts B and C, advancement may have few adverse consequences. That is why mastery tests aren't useful—that is, aren't valid—in Contexts B and C.

Teacher Referral of Pupils for Assessment.   In this example of the validity of decision making, the concept of validity is applied to procedures and processes rather than to test usage. Consider the teacher's role in referring students who may need various kinds of special services, ranging from free school lunches to programs for persons with mental retardation to speech therapy. The ideas associated with validity are applicable to such decisions of whether to refer for further assessment.

Classroom teachers cannot be expected to be familiar with the exact criteria for free lunches, hearing deficit, giftedness, clinical depression, and so on. Various specialists are needed to help make such decisions. *The teacher's job is to refer the pupil to a specialist.* This referral, of course, requires awareness of possible problems that students may have and a commitment to notice enough to alert specialists when they are needed.

Screening procedures should result in referral of more people than actually turn out to be diagnosed to have the problem. To see why, consider the two kinds of errors that a screening process can make in, say, identifying primary pupils who may have undiagnosed vision defects. First, it (mis)identifies some children who have adequate vision as having a problem. Second, it fails to identify some children who have a defect. Which kind of error is more serious in human *consequences?* Flagging a child who ultimately turns out not to have a problem causes no serious harm because the comprehensive assessment that follows will reveal and correct the error. However, failing to identify one who really suffers from a deficit can be very damaging because no subsequent attention is given the case. Thus, good *ultimate* decision making is facilitated by screening and referral processes that overidentify more than they overlook. A good rule is: *When in doubt, refer.*

Consequential Bases of Judging Validity[6]

It was suggested that it is better to go to the expense of providing a complete vision test for a child who turns out not to have a defect than to overlook one who has a problem. That contention, of course, reflects our values. Because this value is widely shared, its subjective nature may not attract attention. Yet it is good to recognize that *values drive interpretations of validity.* Indeed, the words "valid" and "value" are derived from the same Latin root. Validation processes should address the value implications of score interpretations (Messick, 1989).

For example, a faculty might accept as valid a screening process that picks up all the youngsters who have hearing defects as well as twice that number of others. However, it might reject as invalid a process that identifies three quarters of the children who have problems and no others. This reflects its values.

All consequences of test use should be considered, including unanticipated side effects. Following are examples of appropriate consideration of consequences of test use. The first three examples review selected applications of a central theme of this book—harness assessment power.

Frequent Testing. In addition to improving decision making, recall that classroom assessment serves as the ring in the nose of the bull. It has power over students. Hence, an important way to evaluate validity concerns the desirability of the impact(s) of test use. Frequency of testing influences student learning. In a typical high school class, giving a test every week or two is superior to giving only one a month (Bangert-Drowns, Kulik, & Kulik, 1986), probably owing to its tendency to prompt and pace study. The impact of test frequency on learning should be a major factor in deciding how often to test. This consequence of test use is no mere side effect. It is central to the teacher's purpose.

---

[6]Although some scholars prefer to treat the consequences of test use as separate from validity, the topic is often subsumed under validity by others (Kane, 2001).

Offering a Choice of Tasks.   Many teachers offer students a choice of essay questions on which to write or tasks to be carried out in a performance test. This practice may enable foresightful students to exempt themselves from studying some of a unit's content. In some situations this will be desirable; in others, not. Either way, wise teachers anticipate consequences, judge their desirability, and design assessment practices that foster desirable student outcomes and inhibit undesirable ones.

Assessing Complex Mental Processes.   The third example of validity "side effects" emphasizes that teaching is enhanced by harnessing assessment power to influence student effort in desired ways. If teachers' assessments consistently tap deep learning, then students will be more likely to pursue it. Less expert teachers, however, are prone to overemphasize surface learning in their tests. This emphasis tends to direct student effort toward the acquisition of less important material that is likely to be quickly forgotten. Such unfortunate direction of effort is obviously an unintended side effect.

Expert teachers anticipate the consequences of their assessment practices so that their actions will produce desired effects. They seek this impact as an integrated aspect of their instruction. This consequential basis for evaluating the utility of assessment has been a focus of this book since Chapter 1.

The danger of underrepresenting complex learning applies to state assessments as well as to teacher-made measures. One analysis of tests that were developed to support instruction based on states' own standards found that many underrepresented the more advanced content and skills (Gandal & McGiffert, 2003). Putting high stakes on such tests—as NCLB requires—raises grave concern about the adverse consequences of such tests.

Concerns about the No Child Left Behind Act.   The No Child Left Behind Act of 2001 requires that states, among other things, annually test students in grades 3 through 8 in math and reading. It imposes severe penalties on schools that fail to demonstrate "adequate yearly progress" on these high-stakes accountability tests. Space permits us to anticipate only two consequences of this Act.

Probable Impact on the Curriculum.   After a state launches use of high-stakes tests, it is reasonable to anticipate that instruction will be narrowed and focused on what the tests measure. The tests aren't likely to tap all of the important learning sought by effective teachers (Popham, 1999). An expected result would be a decreased emphasis on important aspects of the curriculum that aren't assessed by the state assessments (e.g., music, creative writing, and physical education). Moreover even for subjects that are tested, schools may eliminate topics that aren't on the tests (Amrein & Berliner, 2003). Such narrowing of the curriculum would tend to enhance scores on each state's *own* assessment to which the narrower curriculum is tightly aligned. However, it *wouldn't be expected to enhance learning.* Nor would it be likely to improve performance on broader measures, for example, scores on the National Assessment of Educational Progress.[7]

---

[7]To assess this logic, Amrein and Berliner (2003) examined past data on each of the 18 states that previously had their own high-stakes assessment. They compared performance of students on four separate measures before and after each state instituted its high-stakes test policy. On average, the broader-based achievement measures did *not* increase.

Possible Political Impact.   A consequence of high-stakes accountability testing without commensurate funding to improve school facilities, to enhance teachers' salaries, and to minimize the enormous problems associated with poverty—even before children start school—is likely to be continuing publicity of many poorly funded schools' "failures" to show "adequate yearly progress." As Lewis observed, "Perhaps the paranoid sentiment of many critics of the federal policies may turn out to be correct. That is, perhaps this is all a plot to discredit public education to the point where privatization and choice are seen as the only answers" (Lewis, 2002a, p. 180). Along these lines, Bracey (2002) suggested the term "Trojan horse" could be used to describe the Act.

Whether such consequences would be desirable or not is, of course, a matter of values.

Test Bias.   Bias is an aspect of validity that has generated substantial discussion, emotional heat, and research. The term "test bias" has so many meanings (Flaugher, 1978; Kaplan & Saccuzzo, 2001) that its unqualified use often results in confused quarreling rather than informed discourse.

One way the term is used relates closely to the notion of differentiation. Contexts B and C tests are designed to reveal individual differences that are relevant to intended uses of the tests. In this sense, a spelling test is supposed to identify poor spellers. Thus, in one meaning of the word, the test is biased against poor spellers. This is *not* the way the term is usually used in measurement discussions. The word "fairness" may better capture our meaning.

Bias in Content.   Another way that test bias is used concerns aspects of test content. In this sense, a science test that contains traditional gender-role stereotyping in all its application problems might be said to be biased. If this impacts the relative scores of males and females, then the stereotyping creates an obvious problem. Even if it doesn't impact scores, there is the consequential concern that the stereotyping may restrict subsequent inclusive thinking of test takers.

Content bias also concerns cultural and geographic differences. For example, a multiple-choice aptitude item asking whether we play baseball in the fall, spring, snow, or water puts pupils who live in regions that have perpetual snow cover at a disadvantage. For them, snow is the best answer.

Differences in Groups' Status.   Another meaning of test bias concerns mean differences among groups. If Euro-Americans obtain higher mean scores than African-Americans on a test, some would say it is biased. Whether this has anything to do with test validity depends on *why* a difference exists. Suppose instead that the "test" was longevity data. On average, in the United States, whites live longer than blacks. That is a fact, and it is not sensible to condemn demographers who collect or publish the data. On the contrary, knowledge of such facts promotes awareness of health problems among minority populations.

Now suppose an academic aptitude test shows a minority-nonminority difference. On average, nonminority persons receive higher scores than minority persons. That is a fact, and it doesn't seem sensible to condemn the test for the reality. On the contrary, knowledge of the fact promotes the realization that a problem exists (for those of us whose values lead us to consider the inequity to be undesirable). Yet it seems reasonable for some minority spokespersons to fear that some people will conclude that there is an inherent superiority of nonminority over minority involving aptitude. That *use* of the test data, without consideration of economic, cultural, language, educational, and social differences would, of course, be invalid.

Bias in Scoring.   Whenever test scoring procedures are not completely objective, possible bias in scoring should be considered (Cole & Moss, 1989) and, where possible, prevented. It was recommended in Chapter 8 that teachers scoring essays or other projects should not know whose work is being read. Similarly, rubrics were urged for making the assessment of products and performances as objective as feasible. In addition to preventing individual bias, anonymity and objectivity also provide protection against ethnic bias, gender bias, and other forms of group bias.

Predictive Bias.   An important kind of potential test bias concerns systematic under- or overprediction for groups. An analogy illustrates the predictive aspects of this issue.

Suppose a meteorologist makes daily forecasts of the next day's maximum temperature for Phoenix, Arizona, and for Fairbanks, Alaska. For most days, the predicted temperature for Phoenix is greater than that for Fairbanks. Does this reveal prejudice? Of course not. The job is to predict. The validity of the enterprise resides in the degree to which the prophecies come true. If the temperatures of the two cities really differ, the job of the forecaster is to predict the differences correctly.

If, however, the forecaster consistently predicts that one city is going to be cooler than it turns out to be, then there is consistent underprediction for that city. This is the essence of **predictive bias.** The temperature example is a rather simple illustration because the validity of the criterion measure was virtually unassailable. Alas, this is rarely the case in education.

Here is another example (adapted from Cole & Moss, 1989). Suppose the Hispanic students in a school score, on average, lower on an academic aptitude test than the Anglo students. Suppose also that the groups differ in the same direction and amount on GPA the following year. The conclusions people draw from these findings will depend on their prior assumptions. To some, the grade difference demonstrates a lack of test bias. To others, the test score and grade differentials indicate bias in *both* the test and the school grades.

The topic of bias arising from over- or underprediction is complex and takes one far beyond consideration of a particular test. It also calls attention to issues of fairness in the *criterion* measures. Much of the research on this topic has focused on college admission tests. It can be summarized in the following sentence *if* one is willing to accept the validity of the criterion of college GPA. Empirical investigations of actual test use have typically found either *no significant bias* of this kind or *a very slight tendency* for the future status of members of minority groups to be *over*predicted (Anastasi & Urbina, 1997; Kaplan & Saccuzzo, 2001).

RELIABILITY

Discussion now turns to reliability—the final characteristic of all effective measures. The topic has popped up in many places throughout the book. In this chapter, reliability will be treated systematically so that in Chapter 16 we will be able to put it to use in the practical task of interpreting results of published tests to parents and students.

The Basic Concept

Whenever we measure anything, our result contains some chance error. This *un*systematic error makes all measures in all fields less than perfectly consistent. The **reliability** of scores is *the extent to which scores are consistent* or replicable (Brennan, 2001). *Unreliability* concerns the extent to which measures are inconsistent.

Part II of this book examined ways to make classroom tests and their marking as reliable as we reasonably can. Recall that reliability is just as important for, say, portfolio or performance assessments as it is for paper-pencil tests (AERA, 1999); in pursuit of reliability of marking, we use rubrics.

Brennan (1998) offered this helpful aphorism: "A person with one watch knows what time it is; a person with two watches is never quite sure" (p. 6). The point, of course, is that when we have only one measure, such as a performance or a product, we should *not* deceive ourselves into thinking that we know a person's true status; error of measurement *is* present even if we do not know how great that error is.

Like teacher-crafted assessments, published tests should be made as reliable as feasible. Moreover, their *manuals should include information about their reliability in enough detail to enable test users to judge whether scores are consistent enough to support the intended use of the test.* The word "scores" in the previous paragraph includes the total score, each subscore, and each reported cluster of item scores (AERA, 1999). If a manual supplies no information about the reliability of some or all of its scores, those neglected scores should not be used until and unless their reliability is investigated and found to be adequate. "Lack of knowledge *about* measurement error does not remove error from any set of scores" (Feldt & Brennan, 1989, p. 105). Users need to know how much confidence they can place in the consistency of the scores.

Assessing the adequacy of reliability data provided in manuals of published tests is beyond the scope of this book; however, our web site at ablongman.com/hannadettmer provides information to assist persons interested in undertaking this task.

Reliability is a major practical concern in developing effective classroom tests. It also has practical importance in evaluating and using published measures. The topic has great high-road transfer potential to other fields because imperfect consistency of findings is common to the quantitative and qualitative methods in all fields. A universal need exists to enhance the reliability of data and judgments to the extent that (a) practical constraints enable and (b) the importance of the decisions to be made from the test scores will merit.

Reliability Versus Validity.   How do reliability and validity differ? On the one hand, recall that validity is the extent to which an instrument measures what (and only what) it is *being used to measure.* Thus, a test is *not* at all valid if it consistently measures the wrong thing (i.e., suffers from total construct irrelevance). Similarly, a test isn't optimally valid if it consistently assesses only a part of what it is supposed to assess (i.e., suffers from construct underrepresentation), such as a test that assesses only factual information when more complex mental processing is also targeted.

On the other hand, reliability is the *consistency* with which a device measures *whatever* it measures. Reliability is eroded *only* by *random* error. Systematic or consistent error (e.g., construct irrelevance or construct underrepresentation) does *not* reduce reliability (AERA, 1999); it *does* reduce validity.

Readers should take pains to use these technical terms in the ways they are defined in the discipline of educational and psychological measurement. Because this is more easily said than done, we shall further compare and contrast reliability and validity.

Let's approach the distinction between reliability and validity from another angle. Figure 14.1 shows the results of four peoples' archery tests. Student A consistently hits the bull's eye; this performance is consistently on target—both valid and reliable. Student B is just as consistent as Student A, but is consistently off-target; this performance is reliable but *not* valid. Student C is

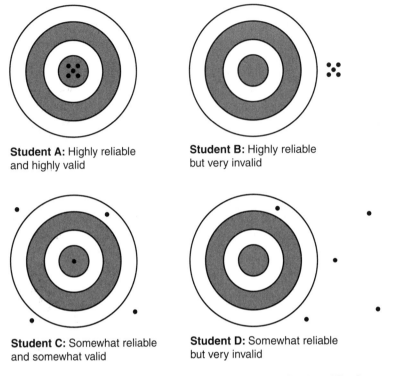

Student A: Highly reliable and highly valid

Student B: Highly reliable but very invalid

Student C: Somewhat reliable and somewhat valid

Student D: Somewhat reliable but very invalid

FIGURE 14.1   Reliability and Validity of Four Archery Students' Performance.

Source: Adapted from Linn and Gronlund (2000), p. 75.

much less consistent, yet the arrows center approximately on target; this performance might be said to be somewhat reliable and somewhat valid. Student D's consistency equals that of Student C, but is off-center as well; this performance is somewhat reliable and very *in*valid.

There can be no student whose performance is always on target yet inconsistent. *Validity cannot exist in the absence of reliability.* Therefore, reliability is an essential attribute of all assessments. Without some consistency of measurement, instruments have no value. A completely unreliable test would be one whose scores are entirely random; its use would be a total waste of time.

Consequently, reliability is said to be a necessary but not sufficient condition for validity. It would be more accurate to say that the limits of a test's reliability create limits on its potential validity. It is important to realize that consistency doesn't guarantee validity; consistency merely enables validity.

Connecting Reliability, Economy, Authenticity, and Validity.   In this section, we shall integrate the understanding of reliability with several other topics from past chapters that relate to validity. Thus, we now will take a tour through the validity landscape, which has components of reliability, economy, and authenticity.

Recall that authenticity (i.e., real-world relevance) is an essential attribute of any achievement measure. Without some realism (i.e., construct-relevant focus), instruments and procedures are useless. Realism (like reliability) also can be said to be a necessary but not sufficient condition for validity. Yet this fails to reveal that both realism and validity exist on continua; thus, it is more accurate to say that the limits of a test's relevance create limits on its potential validity. It is important to realize that authenticity doesn't guarantee validity; authenticity merely enables validity.

Let's now consider three examples that successively incorporate more and more of our past learning. To repeat, in this section we are not focusing exclusively on reliability; rather, we are reexamining its relationship to economy and relevance (as we did in Chapter 9) and seeing how it contributes to validity.

An Extreme, Yet Vivid, Example.   Suppose a vocabulary test were somehow believed to measure running speed. It may be very reliable as a measure of what it measures (i.e., its scores may be quite replicable or consistent), yet it would be wholly invalid as a measure of running speed because it is wholly construct irrelevant.

A More Realistic Example.   Suppose a poorly constructed history test contains many item clues. Test-wise students have an unfair advantage. Let's consider two things that this test measures:

- It taps with some *consistency* the construct-*relevant* domain of history. The consistency contributes to reliability. The relevance of what is consistently assessed contributes to validity.
- It taps with some consistency the construct-*ir*relevant domain of test-wiseness. The consistency of measuring *anything* contributes to reliability. The *ir*relevance of what is consistently assessed *detracts* from validity.

A CAPstone Example.   Suppose four teachers have each taught (a) precautions to avoid bites from poisonous snakes and (b) procedures to follow if bitten.

A maximally authentic test of the precautions might involve a walk in the woods secretly following individual pupils to observe their naturalistic avoidance behaviors. This wouldn't be at all practical and it wouldn't be very reliable because of variations in circumstances from one walk to another.

Even a modest simulation of procedures to follow if bitten would involve individual performance testing, and it, too, would suffer from grave content-sampling error because any simulated bite would involve a person of a given size being bitten in a particular body part by a given kind of snake of a certain size.

Economy dominated the thinking of Mrs. W, the first teacher. She decided to restrict assessment to free-standing objective test items that tap *knowledge about* the two topics. Her hastily assembled objective items contained many ambiguities and irrelevant clues. In using free-standing objective items that assessed only knowledge, she paid too great a price in authenticity. In using flawed items, she also lost reliability. All said, her economy cost far too much in authenticity and reliability.

Reliability weighed most heavily in the thinking of the second teacher, Ms. X. She decided to carefully and skillfully prepare a relatively long test consisting of free-standing objective items tapping *knowledge about* the two topics. By avoiding ambiguous items, Ms. X achieved good reliability. Moreover, she obtained better validity than did Mrs. W by reducing construct-irrelevant assessment of test-wiseness. However, Ms. X paid an unacceptable price in authenticity. (See Brennan, 2001.)

Authenticity dominated the thinking of Mr. Y, the third teacher. He decided to take walks in the woods with small groups of pupils and to use simulated first-aid testing for the emergency procedures. He exhausted himself and his resources securing data of very limited reliability. He paid too great a price in both economy and reliability for the authenticity.

The final teacher, Miss Z, wisely considered authenticity, reliability, and economy jointly; that is, she used the decision-making sieve. She decided to carefully and skillfully prepare a test containing several interpretive exercises having verbal and pictorial stimuli. In addition, she used some free-standing objective items to tap knowledge about the topics. She used objective questions to assess precautions and both essay and objective items to assess procedures to follow if bitten. Her interpretive exercises provided modest authenticity by use of paper-pencil simulations, acceptable reliability, and acceptable economy.

Let's now note that *validity is impacted by the interaction of authenticity, reliability, and economy.* (Indeed, validity subsumes the other topics.) This is illustrated by Miss Z's success. Her overall validity was relatively high for three reasons:

1. She achieved reasonable *authenticity.* Although realism certainly wasn't optimized (because interpretive exercises are only modest simulation of the real thing), her authenticity didn't cost so much that it ruined reliability and/or economy.

2. She obtained good *reliability.* Although reliability wasn't maximized (because a fixed amount of testing time can accommodate more free-standing objective items than items requiring time for stimuli, because essays sample less content than do objective items, and because the scoring of essays is not as consistent as that of objective items), her reliability didn't cost so much that it ruined authenticity or economy.

3. She achieved good *economy.* Although economy wasn't optimized (because interpretative exercises require more time to take and to develop than free-standing objective items and because essays require more time to take and to score than objective items), her economy avoided undesirable consequences of diverting resources from needs of authenticity and reliability.

Collectively, these features characterize a test that is about as valid as resources allowed. In other words, *validity is enhanced by the appropriate balance among authenticity, reliability, and economy.* This balance yields valid instruments and procedures; that is, measures that have the greatest potential to be of practical use, to have desirable consequences, and to lack undesirable consequences.

Many readers will have noticed with regret that Teachers X, Y, and Z all focused their assessments on students' maximum behavior. Only Teacher W's wholly impractical approach provided coverage of typical behavior. This is another example of the regrettable reality that assessment of typical performance sometimes has to be sacrificed in assessing individual students. As explained in Chapter 9, typical performance can, however, be creditably assessed for program assessment by use of anonymous surveys.

This completes our bird's-eye tour. We now return to a focused consideration of reliability.

Major Sources of Measurement Error

We will identify four common sources of random measurement error that erode the reliability of educational measures. These are: content-sampling error, occasion-sampling error, examiner error, and scorer error. Although other sources of error exist (Stanley, 1971), these four are the most significant for both teacher-made and published measures. They will be presented in a nontechnical manner.

Content-Sampling Error.   *A test is a sample of behavior.* Sampling is especially prominent in Context C. The plans used for developing tests are designed to help them appropriately sample their content domains.

However, even the best of samples can happen to hit on a disproportionate fraction of an examinee's strong or weak topics. A student can be lucky or unlucky in the luck of the draw of items that appear in a test—and pupils understand this at a young age. Witness common comments such as "If Mrs. Stone asks so and so, I'm dead" or "I hope the test has a big essay item on such and such."

Because of **content-sampling error,** some scores overrepresent examinee status whereas others underrepresent it. Such error is inevitable in Context C tests where the domains are too expansive to be tested in their entirety. Tests must sample, and whenever there is sampling, sampling error will occur. Content-sampling error is a fact of life.

Nonetheless, it is a contaminant. To the extent that scores are a function of which form of a test happens to be administered rather than a pure measure of examinee competence, scores won't perfectly represent examinee true status on the domain. Thus, content-sampling error limits the extent to which appropriate generalizations can be made from the content sampled to the domain of interest.

Minimizing Content-Sampling Error.   A straightforward way to reduce content-sampling error is to test more content. Obviously, longer tests can more adequately sample domains' content than shorter tests can.

It is equally obvious, however, that enhancement of reliability—that is, reduction of random error—should not be pursued with a singleness of purpose. Thus, balance is needed between the undesirable presence of content-sampling error and the undesirable expenditure of time for testing.

A Common Mistake.   People who lose sight of this unavoidable trade-off between economy and reliability are at risk of making serious errors. A common mistake along these lines is to seek a published test that will provide several reliable subscores in very little testing time. A reliable score can be secured only by investing adequate testing time. If one is only prepared to ask three or four questions per score, one must be prepared to live with scores that contain an enormous element of chance. In Context C, it would be more realistic to plan for 10, 20, or more items per useful score. The highly unreliable scores from 3-to-5-item subsets can do more harm than good if users don't realize that huge margins of error need to be provided with their interpretation.

Professional educators should be very skeptical of those who make claims that commercial instruments are conveniently brief *and* highly reliable. A given test can quite readily be *either* short *or* reliable, but not both. Beware of pies in the sky.

Classroom Implications.   Teachers who conscientiously implement the test-making procedures described in Part II of this book will, other things being equal, produce much more reliable (and valid) instruments than those who are careless.

Essay and other product tests and performance assessments suffer from more content-sampling error than objective tests because they can provide fewer content "chunks." In general, many small chunks of information provide a better basis for generalizing than do fewer large chunks. This is one of the reasons for the sieve's recommendation that teachers should ordinarily use objective items whenever they are construct relevant.

Occasion-Sampling Error.   "Luck of the draw" also occurs as to *when* one happens to be assessed. Everyone has good days and bad days. Behavior is influenced by such things as illness, fatigue, motivation, domestic stress, weather, and social factors. If other things are equal, tests administered on a person's good days are likely to overestimate status, whereas those hitting the bad days are prone to underestimate it.

Fortunately, among well-motivated students, the impact of **occasion-sampling error** is rarely great. However, among poorly motivated individuals, it can be significant.

One could argue that it isn't the fault of the test that student performance differs from one occasion to another. This is true, but immaterial. The point is that test scores are ordinarily used to *generalize about examinee status over a period of time.* To the extent that scores are impacted by when people happen to be assessed rather than representing a pure measure of their status, the scores cannot be trusted to signify status on the domain. Thus, occasion-sampling error limits the extent to which safe generalizations can be made from the particular occasion when the test is given to the period of time in question.

Minimizing Occasion-Sampling Error.   An obvious way to reduce occasion-sampling error is to test on more occasions. Suppose, for example, that a middle school social studies teacher has been giving four, 50-item objective tests per semester. The teacher could reduce occasion-sampling error by testing more often. If the teacher wanted to maintain the same amount of testing time (and content-sampling error), the same 200 items could be redistributed among, say, eight, 25-item quizzes during the semester.

Frankly, the gain in reliability from this reduction of occasion sampling error probably wouldn't compensate for the added trouble of testing more frequently. However, more frequent testing also tends to enhance learning (Bangert-Drowns, Kulik, & Kulik, 1986). The benefits derived from pacing student study and motivation may well justify more frequent testing, and the reduction on occasion sampling error might better be viewed as a desirable side effect.

Examiner Error.   Test scores should generalize across examiners; that is, assessments should reflect student status, not who happened to assess them. Therefore, any differences in scores that arise from differences in examiners is a source of measurement error. One meaning of **examiner error** that comes to mind involves examiner mistakes (e.g., errors in timing a test). Examiner error also includes other impacts on scores deriving from who administered the test. Examiners differ in how well they elicit maximal effort through reduction of test anxiety, advance "stage setting," and establishment of good rapport. Several kinds of examiner differences impact examinee performance (Kaplan & Saccuzzo, 2001).

Examiner error is not a very worrisome source of unreliability in typical group-administered instruments. It isn't, that is, when examiners prepare carefully and follow instructions conscientiously. Examiner error is, however, a major source of concern in individually administered aptitude and achievement tests such as those commonly administered by special education teachers and by school psychologists. It is also a source of great potential error in performance assessments such as athletic tryouts, drama auditions, and musical contests.

Minimizing Examiner Error.   *The fundamental way by which to minimize examiner error in published instruments is to follow the administration instructions to the letter* and to adhere to sound practices on issues that aren't addressed by the directions. Persons whose work requires use of individually administered tests, which are more vulnerable to examiner error, often take special courses devoted to their use.

Scorer Error.   Just as test results ought to generalize across (a) the particular form of the test that chances to be used, (b) the occasion on which it happens to be administered, and (c) the particular examiner who chances to administer it, they should also generalize across scorers. Scores should reveal examinee achievement, independent of who happened to assess the work.

For objective tests, **scorer error** is of minor concern. That's why such instruments are said to be objective—the scores are not sensitive to the scorer. However, scorer error is a major contributor to unreliability of essay, other product measures, and performance assessments. At times, scores can depend more on the quirks of the marker than on examinee performance. Recall the emphasis in Chapters 8 and 9 on the careful and thoughtful use of scoring rubrics to assess products and performances. As Congdom and McQueen (2000) observed, performance assessments may be enthusiastically espoused for their directness or authenticity; however, they need to be evaluated with the same validity and reliability criteria as other kinds of measures. Prominent among their sources of error are differences associated with raters. As we have seen, authenticity is not achieved without costs of reliability and/or economy.

Minimizing Scorer Error.   The more practical means of reducing errors of scoring classroom tests is to follow relevant recommendations from Part II of this book. An example would be having students *circle* T or F for true-false items rather than having them *write* T or F; this avoids errors in deciphering their marks (and saves time). Similarly, the recommended procedures of scoring essays were developed for the express purpose of minimizing scoring errors. Using rubrics for assessing products and performances helps greatly to reduce scorer error. Finally, if it is worth the sacrifice in economy, multiple scorers can be used.

Correlational and Quasi-Correlational Methods of Assessing Reliability

The consistency or reliability of a set of measures can be approached from two somewhat different viewpoints. One perspective is based on *inter*individual variability. In this approach, attention is directed at the consistency with which people maintain their *relative* positions in a group when a measure is repeated. The focus is on relative *consistency,* and results are expressed in correlation or quasi-correlation coefficients that have a possible range of values from 0.0 to 1.0. Such correlation coefficients are called **reliability coefficients.**

This interindividual approach is relatively technical and is beyond the scope of this book. However, if interested, you will find a discussion of it at <u>ablongman.com/hannadettmer</u>; this information would enable you to evaluate the information that authors of published tests are expected to provide regarding reliability of their products (AERA, 1999).

The Standard Error of Measurement: The Other Side of the Coin

Alternatively, reliability can be approached from the perspective of *intra*individual variability, or the *consistency among replications of measurement of the same person.* In this approach, attention is directed to measurement error expressed in the same units as scores (Stanley, 1971). This error-of-measurement perspective builds on the previous discussion of major sources of error in teacher-made and published tests.

To illustrate, suppose a person were repeatedly weighed many times on the same bathroom scale. This would yield a *distribution of scores for the one individual.* The standard deviation of this distribution of repeated estimates of the person's present status is called the *standard error of measurement (SEM). SEM*s are *measures of measurement error.*

*SEM*s report the extent to which scores are contaminated by random factors. Although we won't divert attention to its calculation, we will make good use of this statistic in the next chapter when we need to provide a margin for error for our interpretive statements.

Reliability of Mastery Tests.   Manuals of some poorly prepared mastery tests dismiss reliability as.irrelevant. It is true that correlational methods are typically inappropriate for mastery tests, but this in no way exempts their authors from reporting information about score consistency. Lack of knowledge about measurement error does not remove it from scores (Feldt & Brennan, 1989). *Test manuals should provide* SEM*s for the total score and each subscore that is reported* (AERA, 1999).

Because ignoring the topic is not a responsible option, what should the authors of mastery tests do? Several approaches are appropriate (Feldt & Brennan, 1989); we will mention only the simplest one. Namely, the easiest way to report the consistency of mastery test scores is based on *SEM*s. The suitability of the well-known *SEM* for mastery tests leads us to suggest that professionals should have zero tolerance for authors of published mastery tests who fail to report research concerning measurement error or measurement consistency. This applies to tests by whatever name (e.g., test, informal inventory, alternative assessment).

The Reliability of Difference Scores.   In many practical situations, test users wish to compare two or more scores. Some examples involve a person's *gain* over time. Others concern a *comparison* between two people. Still others compare a person's *relative status* on two attributes. For example:

- Helen's reading has improved this year.
- Helen reads better than Joe.
- Helen reads better than she spells.
- Helen reads better than her aptitude test scores would lead us to expect.

Regardless of the kind of comparison, all involve a *difference* between two scores.

Comparing two scores creates a double risk of measurement error because each score may err. If they happen to err in opposite directions, the difference between them is seriously distorted. To illustrate, consider a simple example.

Ruth is trying to improve her keyboarding speed. Last week she entered 24 words per minute on a five-minute timed test. This week she managed 27 words per minute on a parallel test. How much, if any, has she really improved? Measurement error can cause either score to overestimate or to underestimate her status. On either occasion, her performance may have been unusually good or unusually poor. The *double jeopardy of measurement error* renders conclusions more error prone than they would be if they were focused on either of the separate scores. Hence, we don't know how much, if any, she has really improved.

The relatively low reliability of difference scores has many important practical implications. One of the reasons that instructional objectives should be stated in terms of *terminal* student status rather than on improvement concerns the greater reliability of terminal-status assessments.

Another hazard involved in use of difference scores is found in such statements as "John is not achieving up to expectancy." Such statements regarding aptitude-achievement discrepancies are based on a comparison of two scores and, therefore, have lower reliability than either of the scores on which they are based. This creates a serious problem in identifying persons with learning disabilities.

One way to cope with this difficulty is to realize that tests can be properly used to generate hypotheses or to test hypotheses, but not for both at the same time. A teacher who notices that Hubert doesn't seem to work up to his apparent ability might refer him for testing. Now the school psychologist or the special education teacher has a hypothesis to investigate. If tests given to investigate this hypothesis reveal the aptitude score to be significantly higher than the achievement score, then a much better basis exists to consider Hubert to have a true discrepancy.

Still another practical implication of the relative unreliability of difference scores concerns profile analysis. When a test battery provides several scores or a test furnishes several subscores, interpretation can focus on the one-by-one interpretation of these scores or on comparisons among them. Making comparative statements among several scores may place the interpretation in jeopardy.

For example, if a profile contains scores A, B, C, D, E, and F, even the seemingly innocuous statement that Sue's strongest area is subtest C is tantamount to saying "C is greater than A," "C > B," "C > D," "C > E," and "C > F." Thus, *five* comparisons were implicit, each having double risk of measurement error. Unless Sue's obtained score on subtest C was much greater than *each* of the others, the statement that her strongest area *is* C is probably wrong.

Although C has the greatest probability of being the strongest area, there are five opportunities for it not to be. Even though it is the place to put your money if you have to bet, it usually isn't wise to give good odds. An everyday analogy may be helpful. A pregnancy's due date is the most likely delivery date, but the baby may be born on any of *many* other dates. Even though the due date is the most likely *single* date, fewer than 10% of babies arrive on it.

The inherently low reliability of interpreting profiles is a major reason why many test users would better interpret the scores in a test or battery one at a time without comparative statements or implications. Indeed, wherever practitioners can avoid the use of difference scores, they often would be well advised to do so (Cronbach, 1984; also see AERA, 1999).

CHAPTER RECAP

Practical features were the first characteristics of good measuring instruments to be considered. Although less important than the topics that follow, features such as time and cost, ease and convenience of use, speed and accuracy of scoring, and compatibility of time limits with school schedules all significantly impact the feasibility and costs of test use.

Interpretability is another important feature of effective measures. Unless there is a basis by which to interpret its scores, a measure is useless. Two roads to reporting are domain referencing and norm referencing. The nature of the subject matter and the purpose of the interpretation dictate the kind(s) of interpretation that should be given.

Norm-referenced interpretations can be based on national data, local data, gender-specific data, ethnic group data, and so on. Reference groups should be relevant to the purpose of the interpretation.

Publishers providing derived scores for tests are obliged to describe the reference groups on which these scores are based. This description should be detailed enough to allow prospective test users to (a) judge the relevance of the reference group(s) to their needs and (b) evaluate the adequacy with which the data were gathered.

The validity of a test use or of a procedure is the extent to which it (a) fully assesses the relevant construct in desired proportions and (b) does not assess irrelevant attributes. Validity can also be thought of as the extent to which tests facilitate decision making that has desirable consequences and lacks undesirable ones. In addressing consequences of test use, values inevitably enter into judgments concerning validity.

Some validity evidence is focused on test content and its match with instructional objectives. This is the kind of evidence that is typically most (but not exclusively) important for achievement tests. Criterion-based evidence is appropriate when one or more credible bases exist against which the utility of a test can be evaluated. A rich diversity of other sources of evidence can also be used to build a circumstantial case that a test measures what it is being used to measure and nothing else. Such cases are founded in logic and are built with data. Validity of instruments (such as tests) and of procedures (such as grading practices or making referrals) is a fabric woven from material developed in all previous parts of this book. This chapter's systematic treatment of validity has served as a capstone.

Reliability, like validity and interpretability, is an essential attribute of all measures. Reliability involves several kinds of consistency. The most important are consistency from one content sample to another, from one occasion to another, from one examiner to another, and from one scorer to another. Limitations of a test's reliability place limits on its possible validity. Likewise, limitations of a measure's authenticity or economy place limits on its possible validity. Unfortunately, efforts that enhance authenticity or economy are likely to erode reliability, and inversely. Thus, valid measures are built with relevance, reliability, and economy all in mind.

DERIVED SCORES AND THEIR INTERPRETATION

CHAPTER OVERVIEW

COMMON KINDS OF DERIVED SCORES

BEST USES OF VARIOUS KINDS OF DERIVED
   SCORES

HOW TO PROVIDE NORM-REFERENCED
INTERPRETATION OF SCORES OF
PUBLISHED INSTRUMENTS TO STUDENTS
AND PARENTS

KEY TERMS

rank	stanines
percentile rank (*PR*)	normal curve equivalent (*NCE*)
grade equivalent (*GE*)	standard error of measurement (*SEM*)
age equivalent	confidence band
standard score	percentile band
T-score	expectancy table
deviation *IQ* (*DIQ*)	

Chapters 4 and 12 explained that when the boundaries and difficulty of content domains are not explicit, raw and percent scores lack domain-referenced meaning because interpretation cannot be referenced to expansive domains. Interpretation of differentiating survey tests of expansive, unmasterable content is, therefore, referenced to the performance of other people. Thus, meaningful reporting for Context C achievement tests *must* be norm referenced, as must interpretations of other expansive constructs such as aptitude, interest, and adaptive behaviors.

Derived scores are essential to norm referencing. In order to achieve comparative, people-referenced interpretation, raw scores are transformed into derived scores, which have been developed by use of a reference group of other people whose test performance is known. As seen in Chapter 14, the reference group(s) used to interpret a test's scores should be well described and relevant to the purpose(s) of the interpretation.

Unfortunately, a perplexing variety of derived scores exists, and many educators are unclear about their relative merits. A goal of this chapter is to complete the elementary presentation of the major kinds of derived scores that was started in Chapters 4 and 11.

Although the professional consensus is that every teacher should be competent in reporting student performance on published tests (Sanders et al., 1990), many educators are unacquainted with principles of sound interpretation. Another major purpose of this chapter is to recommend appropriate uses of derived scores. This topic of interpretation is closely related to the content of the last chapter.

KINDS OF DERIVED SCORES AND THEIR FEATURES

As indicated in Chapter 4, scores can be classified as follows:

1. Raw and percent scores (used in making domain-referenced interpretations)
2. Derived scores (used in making norm-referenced interpretations)
   a. Simple ranks and percentile ranks
   b. Grade and age equivalents
   c. Standard scores

The vast majority of derived scores fit quite neatly into one of these three subdivisions. We shall examine them in turn.

Ranks

A simple **rank** indicates the standing of an individual in a group *counting from the top*. Thus, Hazel's rank of 3 in a race signifies that she was the third person to finish the race. Likewise, Mark's rank of 46 in his high school graduating class indicates that he was 46th from the top of his class. The ease with which ranks are understood explains their popularity.

Although conceptually simple, ranks have the awkward feature of requiring a second number. How good was it for Hazel to place third? It obviously depends on the number of people in the race. (Of course, it also depends on the nature of the group. That is why it was emphasized in Chapter 14 that reference groups must be not only relevant to the purpose of the test use, but also must be described in sufficient detail so that prospective users can evaluate their relevance.)

Likewise, Mark's class rank of 46 will indicate one thing if obtained in a class of 1,000 and a vastly different thing if attained in a class of only 46. Therefore, it is necessary to report the size of the group along with the rank (e.g., 3rd in 25 and 46th in 50). For this reason, simple ranks are uncommon in reporting test scores.

This inconvenience can be avoided if each group's size, and each person's rank within it, is altered to make all groups equivalent to 100. Thus, Hazel's 3rd in 25 can be viewed as equivalent to 12th in 100. (That is, one may multiply both the "numerator" and "denominator" by 4 in order to make the denominator 100 without changing the value of the fraction. It doesn't change the value of the fraction because $4/4 = 1$, and multiplying a number by 1 doesn't alter its size.) Likewise, Mark's 46th in 50 is the same as 92nd in 100 (i.e., $46/50 \times 2/2 = 92/100$). With the understanding that the rank is always based on a group size of 100, there is no need to report group size.

Recall from Chapter 11 that, as the name implies, a **percentile rank (*PR*)** indicates rank per 100, but reports the individual's rank *counting from the bottom* of the distribution. Thus, Hazel's rank of 12 in a group of 100 is equivalent to a *percentile rank* of 88. That is, she beat 88 out of every 100 people in the race. Likewise, Mark's simple rank of 46 in a group of 50 equates to a *PR* of 8; he outperformed only 8% (4 out of 50) of the people.

These examples are based on a kind of *PR* that is defined as the percent of the reference group excelled. As noted in Chapter 11, *PR*s can also be defined as the percent of the reference group excelled or equaled. Another widely used kind of *PR* is defined as the percent excelled plus one-half the percent equaled. Fortunately, the differences among them are usually minor in measures having many items.

It is important to remember that *PRs count from the bottom of distributions*—opposite from the familiar convention with simple ranks of counting from the top.

Major Strengths of *PRs*.   *PRs*, sometimes called *centiles*, are easily understood. Neither esoteric jargon, intimidating technical explanations, confusing figures of normal curves, nor anxiety-provoking mathematical symbols are needed for the meaningful interpretation of students' *PR* scores.

Another desirable feature of *PRs* is their widespread applicability. They do not suffer from traditions that restrict their use to certain kinds of instruments (e.g., as grade equivalents to achievement tests). Rather, *PRs* are widely employed to interpret scores of achievement tests, aptitude tests, interest inventories, and personality surveys.

Limitations of *PRs*.   *PRs*, nonetheless, have some minor, yet important, limitations. One potential problem is their appearance of great precision. On viewing the 99 entries in a *PR* table, a parent or student can reasonably, yet incorrectly, infer that the test is reliable enough to classify examinees this precisely. We'll see later how to avoid this problem.

Another limitation of *PRs* is their inequality of units. Like simple ranks, *PR* units tend to be small near the center of distributions and large near the extremes.

To make this intuitively obvious, imagine 100 children running a race. It is relatively easy to identify and rank order the first several and the last several as they complete the race. But think how hard it would probably be to identify the middle child who finishes among the great thundering stampede in the central part of the distribution.

For another example of unequal *PR* units, review the frequency distribution for the State Capitals Test in Table 11.1 on page 269. Notice how more people are clustered near the center than at the extremes. That is why in Table 11.3 on page 271 the corresponding *PRs* are more widely separated by single raw points near the center of the range than near its ends.

The normal curve will be introduced at this time because it further reveals the inequality of *PR* units. The normal distribution is the familiar bell-shaped, unimodal, symmetric distribution that occurs whenever a large number of independent events, such as test items,[1] collectively determine an outcome (e.g., a test score). Its formula and detailed explanation, which can be found in statistics texts, are not central to our purposes here.

Figure 15.1 reports how *PRs* relate to selected *z*-scores *in normal distributions.* (Readers who have forgotten what a *z*-score is are urged to review the topic in Chapter 11.) The area enclosed by the curve and the baseline represents 100% of the scores in a distribution. The vertical lines partition the total area into *SD* intervals. The percent of the total area enclosed by each section is shown. This reports the percentage of a normally distributed group that will have scores between successive whole *z*-score intervals.

Notice how two people who differ by, say, 1 *SD* are separated by a variable number of *PR* units, depending on their place in the distribution. For example, between *z*-scores of −3.0 and −2.0, there are fewer than 2 *PR* units, but the difference between *z*-scores of 0.0 and 1.0 is about 34 *PR* units.

---

[1]Technically, the items of a test ordinarily are not completely independent; that is, they are positively intercorrelated. This makes the distributions of test scores a bit flatter than would occur with truly independent events, such as flips of a coin.

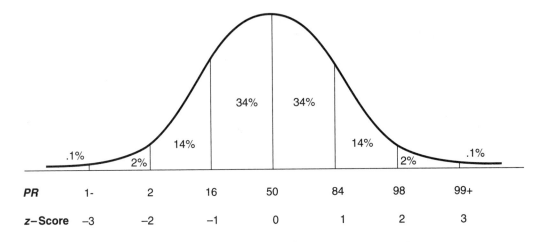

| PR | 1- | 2 | 16 | 50 | 84 | 98 | 99+ |
| z-Score | -3 | -2 | -1 | 0 | 1 | 2 | 3 |

FIGURE 15.1   **Corresponding Percentile Ranks and z-Scores in a Normal Distribution.**

This inequality of *PR* units can create misunderstandings among lay people. For example, if Jim's *PR*s in an achievement test battery's reading and science subtests are 11 and 1, respectively, the 10-point difference is revealed in Figure 15.1 to represent a big difference. However, if his *PR*s in the math and social studies subtests are 45 and 55, respectively, then that 10-point difference is seen in Figure 15.1 to represent only a small difference. We thus see that the importance of a *PR*-point difference depends upon its location in the distribution.

Because of their unequal units, *PR*s *are not suitable for calculation.*

Recommended Uses of *PR*s.   *Because of the ease with which students and parents can under-stand them,* PR*s are highly recommended for making interpretations.* Their only interpretive disadvantage is the precision implied by their fine units. A solution to this problem will be offered in the last major section of this chapter.

Grade and Age Equivalents

A contrast will be useful. *PR*s and standard scores are typically used to show a person's status in a group to which he or she belongs. In contrast, a *developmental score* indicates the group within which an examinee's performance would be at the median.[2] For example, if fifth-grader John takes a fifth-grade math test and earns the same raw score on it as the median eighth grader would obtain on it, then his grade equivalent is 8.

The school year is customarily divided into 10 intervals to enable decimalized reporting of **grade equivalents (*GE*s).** Thus, a *GE* of 1.0 is the level of performance exhibited by the typical be-

---

[2]A few tests have developmental scores defined in terms of means.

ginning first grader. A *GE* of 5.7 signifies median achievement among students who are in the seventh month of fifth grade. (A few tests omit the decimal and report *GE*s as two-digit numbers. Thus, 1.0 becomes 10 and 9.7 becomes 97.)

Similarly, an **age equivalent** indicates the age at which a given youngster's status would be at the median. For example, if four-year-old Lucy takes a listening vocabulary test and obtains the same raw score as typical five-year-olds receive, then her age equivalent is 5.

The calendar year is divided into 12 months. Thus, an age equivalent of 4–2 is the level of performance typical of children who are four years and two months old. An age equivalent of 8–11 signifies median status among children who are eight years and 11 months old. Notice that a dash— not a decimal point—is used in age-equivalent scores.

Certain derivatives of age equivalents were once widely used. The best known of these was the original kind of *IQ,* or "intelligence quotient." It was a quotient because it was found by dividing a child's mental age (i.e., the age equivalent obtained from an "intelligence" test) by her or his chronological age and multiplying the result by 100. This original kind of *IQ,* now called "ratio *IQ,*" has not been used by test publishers during the last 40 years.

Strength of Grade and Age Equivalents.   Responsible advocates of *GE*s defend them as measures of growth during elementary school. They believe *GE*s are useful indicators of pupil growth, but they also point out that *GE*s *should not be used to assess pupils' standing in their grades or their relative performance on different tests. PR*s should be used for these purposes (Hieronymus, Hoover, & Lindquist, 1986).

That was a short list of strengths. Highlighting the major limitations will require much more space!

Limitations of Grade and Age Equivalents.   Age and grade equivalents enjoy great popularity "because they seem so blessedly simple to understand" (Popham, 1990, p. 164). Yet this appearance is deceptive. "These scores are confusing and lend themselves to erroneous interpretations" (Lyman, 1998, p. 115). These problems lead to widespread misunderstanding, misinterpretation, and misuse. A few of the many shortcomings most relevant to classroom teachers are examined next.

A feature that contributes to age and grade equivalents' apparent simplicity is an *illusion* of being domain-referenced thresholds that everyone should meet. Although a spelling *GE* of 6.9 sounds to many people like a statement of what the examinee can or should do, it isn't. The *GE* indicates the norm-referenced information that the examinee performed as well on the test as the typical end-of-sixth-grade pupil performs on it. Nobody (except, perhaps a resident of the mythical Lake Wobegon) would suggest that everyone should be above the 50th percentile. "Yet, people talk continually as if all sixth graders should be reading at or above the sixth-grade equivalent" (Mehrens & Lehmann, 1991, p. 237).

Like *PR*s, grade and age equivalents lack equal units of measure. Figure 15.2 provides a generalized growth curve for school-aged people. A basic developmental trend is that growth slows as maturity is approached. By the time maturity is attained, growth stops. For example, a sizable difference exists between the spelling skills of first and second graders. There is much less difference between eleventh and twelfth-graders' spelling. Grade- and age-equivalent scores therefore have unequal units. This precludes their use for computational purposes.

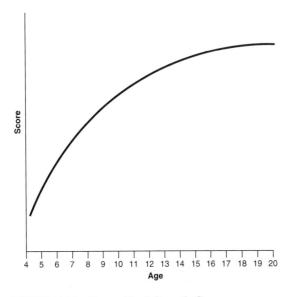

FIGURE 15.2   Generalized Growth Curve.

Another ramification of the unequal units concerns the impossibility of expressing the status of superior adults in age or grade equivalent units. Suppose a man is six feet two inches tall. How could you represent his stature as an age equivalent? That is, at what age does the average American male reach this height? Likewise, how could the mental age of the average reader of this book be expressed as an age equivalent? It cannot.

Another problem with *GE*s is school attrition. Sad to say, many youths drop out of high school. Therefore, the difference between the median scores obtained by eleventh- and twelfth-graders on a test may be more a function of attrition than of growth between the grades. Attrition is an even bigger factor in the college years.

A logical issue concerns the most relevant reference group for interpretive purposes. Suppose a boy aged 4–0 is measured for height and is tall for his age. How would his norm-referenced status best be reported? His age equivalent could be reported to be 5–3. This would report the group within which he would be at the median. It would provide a comparison with a group to which he does *not* belong. Isn't it preferable to report his status within a group to which he *does* belong (e.g., "compared with other age 4–0 males, he is taller than 90 out of every 100")?

Yet another difficulty with *GE*s is the frequency with which they are misunderstood by parents and students. Let's return to our opening example. Fifth-grader John took a fifth-grade math test and obtained the same raw score that the average beginning eighth grader receives; hence, his *GE* is 8.0. When his parents hear this, they are likely to think they have been told that their prodigy is doing eight-grade math work (and perhaps wonder why he has not been double promoted).

Consider more carefully what the interpretation actually stated: John performed as well on the *fifth-grade* math test as the average beginning eighth grader would *on a fifth-grade math test.*

He didn't take an eighth-grade test that would include content that fifth graders have not yet studied. Therefore, the test results report nothing about how well he handles eighth-grade work. However, the likely misinterpretation is not stupid. The problem is that *GEs veritably beg to be misinterpreted.*

Another limitation of age- and grade-equivalent scores is their unequal variability across different attributes. In general, the variability of *GEs* is less for some subjects, such as math, than it is for others, such as reading. Here is an example. Brice, who is in the middle of the eighth grade, took an achievement battery. His *GEs* for the major subscores were all 10.0. The typical teacher, parent, principal, or student would interpret this to mean that Brice performed uniformly well across the subject matter areas. Not so! The *PR* equivalents of these *GEs* may range from 75 or 80 in language and reading subtests to about 85 or 90 in math subtests. Thus, developmental scores are ill suited for profile interpretation.

Recommended Uses.   Age and grade equivalents are inadequate for calculation because of their unequal units. For a variety of reasons, they are also ill suited for the majority of the interpretative purposes to which they are put; they are widely misunderstood and misinterpreted. Cronbach (1984, p. 102) summed it up well by saying that "professional opinion is critical of grade conversions." Similarly Lyman (1998) offered as a "best conclusion: *Use another kind of score."*

Their *only* legitimate use is in the assessment of growth in elementary (and possibly middle) schoolchildren—and even this use is controversial. Many authorities (e.g., Cronbach, 1990) do not favor even this use, whereas others (e.g., Hoover, 1984) defend it.

Standard Scores

A **standard score** indicates an individual's deviancy from a group's mean expressed in standard deviation units. The kind of standard score introduced in Chapter 11 was the *z*-score, which is the prototype of all standard scores. Recall the formula:

$$z\text{-score} = \frac{x}{SD}$$

where *x* is the individual's deviation score expressed in terms of the raw score units and *SD* is the standard deviation, also expressed in terms of the raw score units. When the two units of measurement cancel out, the *z*-score is left free of any unit-of-measure artifact.

Because *z*-scores are accompanied with algebraic signs and are expressed in such large units that they usually are reported to one digit beyond the decimal point, they are inconvenient to use in hand calculations. Various transformations are used to create more convenient kinds of standard scores. Some of the more common ones will now be introduced.

Decimalized scores can be eliminated if *z*-scores are multiplied by a specified number. Common multiplicative constants are 10, 15, 16, and 100.

Negative *z*-scores can be eliminated if a specified number is added to each *z*-score. Common additive constants are 50, 100, and 500.

TABLE 15.1   Defining Constants for Selected Standard Scores

KIND OF STANDARD SCORE	M	SD
z-score	0	1
T-score	50	10
DIQ_{15}	100	15
DIQ_{16}	100	16
Stanine	5	2
CEEB	500	100
NCE	50	21.06

Table 15.1 provides the constants that are used to develop several of the common varieties of standard score.[3]

T-*Scores.*   A kind of standard score known as the ***T*-score** is used in many psychological tests and a few education ones (e.g., the PSAT, to be discussed in Chapter 16). T-scores are obtained by multiplying the z-score by 10 and then adding 50. The formula is expressed as T = 10z + 50. The second row of Table 15.1 provides information about T-scores; their SD of 10 is achieved by multiplying by 10, and their mean of 50 is achieved by adding 50.

A sense of how *T*-scores correspond to *PR*s can be obtained from Figure 15.3, which provides the corresponding values at selected points in a normal distribution. Figure 15.3 also reveals that *T*-scores and other varieties of standard scores are really just relabeled *z*-scores.

Deviation IQs.   Over half a century ago, authors of some then-advanced intelligence tests sought better derived scores for their tests than the old IQs (now called ratio IQs). To attain public acceptance of the newer scores, a system of standard scores was developed to mimic IQs. These standard scores were assigned a mean of 100 and a standard deviation of 15 or 16. The third and fourth rows of Table 15.1 provide the data for these scores.

Although they are true standard scores, they were called **deviation *IQ*s (*DIQ*s).** Their computational properties are far superior to those of old ratio *IQ*s, which have fallen into disuse. Figure 15.3 shows the relationship among *DIQ*s, *PR*s, *z*-scores, and *T*-scores.

---

[3]Technically, there are two major groups of standard scores—normalized and nonnormalized. The latter are described in this section by the constants presented in Table 15.1. The differences between normalized and nonnormalized standard scores involve technical issues to which practitioners need not attend. The two kinds of scores rarely differ significantly, and test users generally need not be aware of which kind is provided for a given test.

For those interested, normalized standard scores are obtained first by computing the *PR* corresponding with each raw score. Then each *PR* is converted into the *z*-score equivalent in a normal distribution. This *z*-score is then transformed into any of several other kinds of standard scores as explained in this section.

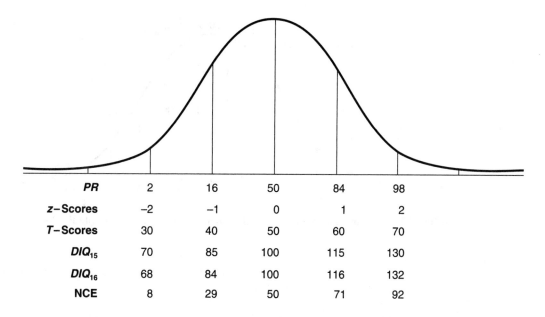

PR	2	16	50	84	98
z–Scores	-2	-1	0	1	2
T–Scores	30	40	50	60	70
DIQ_{15}	70	85	100	115	130
DIQ_{16}	68	84	100	116	132
NCE	8	29	50	71	92

FIGURE 15.3   Percentile Rank Equivalents of Selected Standard Scores in a Normal Distribution.

As will be mentioned in Chapter 16, newer aptitude tests and recent editions of most older ones have retained the kind of standard score known as *DIQ*s but have replaced their *name* with terms that more aptly describe the scores' meaning.

Stanines.   Another type of standard score has a *M* of 5 and a *SD* of 2, as shown in the fifth row of Table 15.1. Limited to nine intervals, these "standard nines" are called **stanines.** Figure 15.4 shows their relationship to *PR*s.

College Entrance Examination Board Scores.   The College Entrance Examination Board (CEEB) devised a novel kind of standard score for its college admissions *Scholastic Assessment Test* (SAT) (formerly known as the Scholastic Aptitude Test). The same system is used for the *Graduate Record Examination* (GRE), which is widely used for admission to graduate programs. These standard scores have a *M* of 500 and a *SD* of 100. (For interpretive purposes, the SAT and GRE soundly provide examinees with *PR*s.)

(In addition to their main use in predicting students' academic success, the SAT has been used to study trends in applicant test performance. By statistical linkage to groups as far back as 1941, the performance of examinees has, with much attendant publicity, been compared over the decades.)

Normal Curve Equivalents.   We should also mention the **normal curve equivalent (NCE),** a variety of standard score having a *M* = 50 and a *SD* = 21.06. Federal regulations require many schools

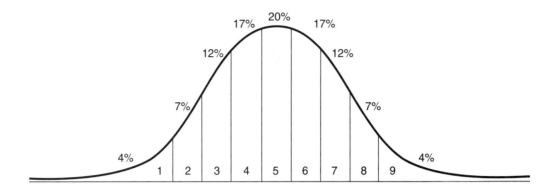

FIGURE 15.4   Relationship of Stanines to the Normal Curve and Percentile Ranks.

to use NCEs in reports about their federally funded remedial programs. Figure 15.3 also shows the relationship of NCEs to other kinds of scores.

Strengths of Standard Scores.   Standard scores have equal units and are therefore suitable for calculation and research purposes. With the exception of stanines, which have larger units and accompanying grouping error, one kind of standard score is about as good as another.

Limitations of Standard Scores.   An understanding of standard scores requires technical knowledge. Hence, they are generally unsuitable for interpretive purposes to lay people.

Two kinds of standard scores merit special caveats. First, *IQ*s and scores that simulate them "are especially open to misinterpretation" (Cronbach, 1990, p. 117). Although *DIQ*s have great *technical* merit over obsolete ratio *IQ*s, they are, nonetheless, ill-advised for interpretive purposes. *PR*s serve much better.

Second, stanines are sometimes used for interpretations because they don't overrepresent test precision. However, stanines suffer from grouping error (with an accompanying loss of reliability). Moreover, they are rather esoteric. To give them meaning, most people who interpret them to students or parents use a figure similar to Figure 15.4. Aside from the intimidating and needlessly distracting impact that a normal curve can have, it should be noted that stanines are *given meaning via definitions in terms of* PRs. It seems more sensible to simply use the *PR*s. The important goal of avoiding the impression that a test is more accurate than it really is is better met by use of confidence bands, a topic addressed in the next section.

Recommended Uses of Standard Scores.   Because of their equal units, standard scores are recommended for computational purposes.

Because of their technical nature, standard scores are not well suited for interpretive purposes. It is especially wise to avoid interpretive use of the kinds of standard scores that are misunderstood to signify that a test measures attributes that it doesn't, in fact, measure. Thus, *DIQ*s are particularly ill-advised for interpretive purposes.

THINKING CAP EXERCISE 15.1 ???

For items 1–3, select the kind of derived score that would best be used for the indicated test use.
  A. Percentile ranks
  B. Grade or age equivalents
  C. Standard scores

1. A teacher wants to calculate the mean class score on a published reading test from individual student scores.

2. A teacher wants to explain to a student how she scored on the published reading test.

3. A school psychologist wants to compare Fred's verbal aptitude test score with his silent-reading comprehension test score to determine if there is enough difference between the scores for him to qualify for a learning disabilities program.

For each of the following items, select the best option. Use Figure 15.3 as needed.

4. A *DIQ* of 100 is equivalent to a *z*-score of
  A. −2.
  B. −1.
  C. 0.
  D. 1.
  E. 2.

5. A *DIQ* of 70 is equivalent to a *PR* of about
  A. 1.
  B. 2.
  C. 50.
  D. 70.
  E. 98.

6. A *PR* of 98 is equivalent to a *DIQ* of approximately
  A. 2.
  B. 70.
  C. 98.
  D. 100.
  E. 130.

7. Which has the largest units?
  A. Stanines.
  B. *T*-scores.
  C. CEEB scores.
  D. *DIQ*s.

8. Scores of three children on a math test are given below. The same reference group was used to derive each kind of score. Which child performed the best?
  A. Adam had a *PR* of 30.
  B. Beth had a *T*-score of 30.
  C. Chad had a stanine of 8.

KEY TO THINKING CAP EXERCISE 15.1

ITEM	ANSWER	EXPLANATION
1.	C	Because standard scores have equal units of measure, they are suitable. (A teacher wishing to avoid them might consider use of the median rather than the mean. It could be obtained for *PR*s).
2.	A	Comparison with a pupil's grade-mates is best achieved by *PR*s.
3.	C	This numerical comparison requires a scale having equal units. The school psychologist would be acquainted with the technical features of the various kinds of standard scores.
4.	C	From Figure 15.3, it is seen that a *DIQ* of 100 is at the mean. The corresponding *z*-score is 0.
5.	B	Figure 15.3 shows that a DIQ_{15} of 70 and a DIQ_{16} of 68 equate to a *PR* of 2.
6.	E	Figure 15.3 shows that a *PR* of 98 is equivalent to a *z*-score of 2, a *T*-score of 70, or *DIQ*s of 130 or 132.
7.	A	Because stanines have only nine possible values, these nine intervals must cover the entire distribution. Hence, each unit is large.
8.	C	A *PR* of 30 is a little below average. A *T*-score of 30 is two full *SD*s below average. A stanine of 8 is between 1.25 and 1.75 *SD*s above average.

APPROPRIATE COMPUTATIONAL USES OF DERIVED SCORES

Recall from Chapter 11 that the computation of the mean and all statistics based on it require equal units of measure. We have seen that simple ranks and *PR*s lack equal units. Rank units tend to be smaller near the center of distributions than at the extremes. Therefore, simple ranks and *PR*s have limited utility for data analysis and summary. For example, the median is the most powerful measure of central tendency that can legitimately be used with *PR*s.

We have also seen that age- and grade-equivalent scores lack equal units of measure. Units tend to be smaller in size as maturity is approached, to have zero size after maturity is reached, and to have negative size as deterioration occurs. Therefore, developmental scores have little computational utility. For example, the median is the most powerful appropriate measure of central tendency for age- and grade-equivalent scores.

The various kinds of standard scores are blessed with equal units of measure.[4] This renders them suitable for the kinds of data manipulations educators often perform. Therefore, *standard scores are the preferred score to use when calculations are performed.*[5]

Of the various kinds of standard scores, two are notably less suitable for computation than others. One is stanines. The alleged advantage of stanines is that their broad units do not imply undue precision. The concomitant problem is that broad intervals create grouping errors. That is, they hide differences within each interval, and they exaggerate trivial differences between borderline cases of adjacent intervals.

The other kind of standard score that is less suitable than most for calculational purposes is one used to report subtests of certain aptitude tests. These standard scores have a *M* of 10 and a *SD* of 3. The small *SD* (making each unit large) renders them relatively inaccurate.

APPROPRIATE INTERPRETIVE USES OF DERIVED SCORES[6]

Those who interpret test scores have several simultaneous concerns. Brief mention will first be made of two. First, it is necessary for the recipient of the interpretation to understand clearly the content domain measured by the test. Even in norm-referenced interpretation, substantial information about test content is necessary for the scores to have meaning. The simple statement, "Your national *PR* of the math test was 73," is meager. Does the test focus on computation, concepts, problem solving, or some blend of these? At what educational level is the test targeted? Even large and expansive domains can and should be clarified to some extent (e.g., "As you know, the test assessed your ability to perform computational skills and to apply fifth-grade math to a wide variety of situations.")

[4]As noted in Chapter 11, raw scores often do not have perfectly equal units. Similarly, nonnormalized standard scores (being derived via linear transformations of raw scores) lack perfectly equal units of measure. However, unit inequality is minor and is wisely ignored by practitioners (Nunnally, 1978).

[5]Some authorities, therefore, urge the use of standard scores for combining components for grading purposes. Because most teachers prefer not to routinely convert their raw scores into standard scores, the approach presented in Chapter 12 avoided this use. This was achieved by attending very closely to variability by other means.

[6]Parts of this section are adapted from (Hanna) *Journal of Counseling and Development,* Volume 6, 1988, pages 477–483. © AACD. Used with permission. No further reproduction is authorized without written permission of the American Counseling Association.

Second, the reference group needs to be identified. Derived scores can be based on local, regional, or national groups. They can be gender specific or combined. They can be based on age-based peers or on grade-based peers. Combinations of these are suitable for some interpretive needs. The point is that any reference group used should be relevant to the purpose of the interpretation, and it should be identified (e.g., "Compared with other fourth graders in our school district . . . ," "In comparison with a national cross section of eighth-grade girls . . . ," or "Compared with a national sample of second-year, high school German students . . . .").

Following are interpretive suggestions that are central to this chapter on derived scores and their interpretation.

Replace Misleading Names with Descriptive Ones

The names given tests and constructs and the names and kinds of derived scores used can lead to misunderstandings. Following are some cautions concerning how certain terms often lead to serious misunderstandings regarding what a test measures or what its scores mean.

Names of Constructs and Tests.   The distinction between aptitude and achievement, to be discussed in Chapter 16, is less than clear to most lay people. Persons receiving interpretations should be helped to understand the nature of the test under discussion. The word "ability" is especially likely to blur distinctions, because, depending upon context, it can mean either aptitude or achievement. The word is often better avoided.

Similarly, students who have taken an interest inventory are apt to forget the nature of its items and think it is a measure of achievement or aptitude. The distinction may have to be pointed out more than once during an interpretation.

Perhaps the most commonly misunderstood construct name is "intelligence." To many people, this word stands for far more than *estimated present aptitude for school-type learning based on a sample of current behavior.* Yet that is what most so-called intelligence tests are designed to assess. The *Cognitive Abilities Test* and the *Otis-Lennon School Ability Test* exemplify contemporary tests that avoid altogether the oft-misunderstood word "intelligence."

Names of Derived Scores.   Certain derived scores have names that are often misunderstood. "IQ" tops the list. "The intelligence quotient (*IQ*) is one of the most misunderstood concepts in measurement" (Mehrens & Lehmann, 1991, p. 234). Vast numbers of lay people, forgetting that aptitude tests only *sample current behavior,* think of "*IQ*" as a genetically fixed attribute that is unaffected by environment. Moreover, contemporary tests' "*IQ*s" (i.e., *DIQ*s) are not quotients at all; rather, they are standard scores. Many of the better tests now use more descriptive terms such as "standard age score" or "school ability index" instead of the widely misunderstood *IQ*. We urge educators to avoid the terms "*IQ*" and "*DIQ*" for interpreting scores to parents or students. More descriptive terms that are more easily grasped should replace these obsolete and widely misunderstood terms.

Another term that is sometimes misunderstood is "percentile rank." Although *PR*s *are* the kind of derived score of preference for most *interpretive* purposes, they have some minor problems. For one thing, the term "percentile rank" seems to demand a grasp of the concept of percent of the reference group. For young children and older persons for whom math is only a bad memory, this term can be an affective and conceptual barrier to clear understanding. Fortunately, this problem is easily circumvented by avoiding the terms "percentile," "centile," and "percent." *PRs can be used without use of their name.* For instance, one might say, "Pedro ran the lap faster than 79 out of every 100 eight-year-old boys in the country," or "Igmar scored better on the reading test than 25 out of every 100 tenth graders in our school." By avoiding use of words such as "percent," the confusion is easily avoided.

Another problem is that the term "percentile" often causes lay people (including some well-educated ones) to confuse the idea of percent *of a reference group of other people* with the notion of percent *of test items.* The unfamiliar word "percentile" may be decoded erroneously as "percent," and people's prior associations in test interpretations with percent scores are retrieved with the consequence that thinking shifts to a percent score. Such a percent-of-raw-score interpretation would be suitable for a domain-referenced interpretation of Context A subject matter rather than for a people-referenced interpretation necessary of Context C material, as has been stressed repeatedly throughout the book.

Fortunately, this confusion is also easily forestalled by avoiding the word "percentile" with people who may not understand it. We reiterate: *Use the concept of* PR *without necessarily employing its troublesome name.* For example, the statement "Harry received a percentile score of 65 on a nationally normed seventh-grade math computation test" may elicit an anguished parental cry, "Heavens! That's barely passing!" The parent has apparently interpreted the statement to mean that Harry answered 65% of the items correctly. The misunderstanding could be corrected by explaining that percentile scores do not refer to percent of items answered correctly, but rather to *percent of other examinees that his performance equaled or surpassed.* It is better, however, to prevent the confusion in the first place by avoiding the word "percentile"; for example, "Harry's math computation score was equal to or better than 65 out of every 100 seventh graders in the country." If greater simplicity were sought, the "65 out of every 100" could be reduced to "13 out of every 20" or rounded to "about 2 out of 3."

Avoid Jargon

Those who interpret test scores need to communicate what scores mean as simply as possible without introducing complicated and confusing symbols or jargon. We need to go to pains not to overwhelm or confuse students or parents. *Our purpose is to facilitate understanding.*

It is helpful for those of us who interpret test scores to put ourselves in the shoes of the person who is receiving an interpretation. This can be achieved by moving outside one's own professional field. When, for example, we receive an X-ray interpretation from our dentist, we don't want to be confused by technical jargon; rather, we need the *meaning* of the findings as *simply and completely* as possible.

Here is a useful self-test for professionals: *If an expert cannot provide an interpretation in nontechnical language that typical lay people can understand, then there is reason to doubt how well the professional understands the material.* Thus, if your dentist cannot or will not explain the meaning of your X-rays in terms you understand—cost, inconvenience, discomfort, cosmetics, and durability of alternative treatments (or nontreatment)—then you may need a new dentist. If an attorney cannot explain the meaning of a rental agreement or a will in ways you can understand, then you have cause to wonder just how well the attorney understands the document beyond the ability to parrot jargon. And, if a teacher, counselor, or administrator cannot explain the meaning of a derived score from a published test in terms that typical parents and students can readily grasp, then the educator probably does not have an adequate command of the underlying concepts.

A central goal of test interpreters is thus to reveal the meaning of the test scores in ways that are meaningful to the person receiving the interpretation. Recipients vary in their background knowledge. Interpretations should, therefore, be varied to be appropriate to the particular audience.

Provide for a Margin of Error

An important goal of interpretation is to avoid *over*interpretation. Measurement error is ubiquitous, yet many people tend to take test scores far too seriously—forgetting that tests provide only imperfect, fallible measures. Test interpreters have the joint responsibilities of:

- Reporting as much as the test scores reveal
- Disclosing the limits of confidence that should be placed in this information

In other words, interpreters need to point out the implications of the score and to allow a margin of error in these interpretations.

This balancing act is best achieved by somewhat different means in interpretations that *describe* a person's current status rather than in ones that *predict* future performance.

Making Descriptive Interpretations.   As seen in Chapter 14, standard errors of measurement provide an excellent way to express the random measurement error as the amount of error to be expected in an individual's scores, with this error expressed in the test's score units. These features make it very useful in test interpretation. The most common measure of such error is the *standard error of measurement (SEM)*.

If a person were to be measured, say for height, with the same device, slight variation would occur among the several measures. If there were no measurement error, all the scores would be identical. To the extent that the repeated measures varied, error would be present. Again, the measure of this measurement error is called the *standard error of measure.*

A "true," or infallible, score is an abstraction resembling a Platonic ideal. All that any examinee ever has is an obtained score that is a mere estimate of the "true" score. To secure an interval within which the true score probably lies, a confidence band is constructed around the obtained score.[7] Confidence bands of various widths are usually based on how many *SEM*s are included on either side of the obtained score. The most common intervals are:

- The obtained score ± 1 *SEM*. This provides an interval within which the probability is .68 that the true score falls; these 68 chances out of 100 are often rounded to 2 out of 3 or expressed as "2 to 1 odds."
- The obtained score ± 2 *SEM*s. This yields a range within which the probability is .95 that the true score lies; this is often reduced to 19 chances out of 20.

OK, some readers are thinking, *SEM* is the flip side of the reliability coin, but why bother to look at both sides? Wouldn't one side be enough?

---

[7]This procedure reverses the theoretical, but wholly impractical, process conceptualized in which the confidence band is constructed around the true score.

Actually, the two approaches to the topic richly complement each other. Reliability coefficients provide a good way of comparing the consistency of different tests. However, they have little utility in interpreting scores to lay people because they are based on technical concepts and jargon.

*SEM*s, by contrast, have a major advantage in interpretations. They can be used to interpret scores to students and parents without resorting to esoteric ideas and language. This is possible because *SEM*s report error of measurement *in the same unit of measure that is used for the test scores themselves.*

The examples given earlier, weight and stature, were remote from educational applications. Similar examples for attributes that are not influenced by being measured could be based on oven temperature, and readings of light meters. However, in typical educational testing, students experience a practice effect, and, if retested, their scores tend to improve. Because the attribute being measured is influenced by the measurement process, it is not practical to estimate the *SEM* of educational measures by the method of repeated measurement. The examples were useful in revealing the meaning of *SEM,* but they don't show how to go about finding *SEM*s of educational measures. It is the responsibility of authors of published tests to supply *SEM* data in the test manuals (AERA, 1999).

We have now completed our digression into the meaning of *SEM*s and can return to the topic of making descriptive interpretations.

We have seen that out of every 100 people who obtain a given score, 68 will have a true status that is less than 1 *SEM* from the obtained score. Similarly, about 95% of people's true status on what a particular test assesses will lie within the range created by adding and subtracting 2 *SEM*s from their obtained scores.

Such ranges provide intervals within which the correct values probably lie. A **confidence band,** or confidence interval, is a range that probably contains the true status. An everyday example is provided by someone asking, "How old would you estimate Professor Brown to be?" A common answer might be, "Oh, I'd say about 43, give or take five years." Or, you are asked, "What is your status in spelling?" You might answer, "Probably between the 65th and 80th *PR*s of the adult population of college graduates."

In each case, a confidence band has been offered (although the likelihood of it containing the true status is unknown). Confidence intervals can be used either with raw scores (as in the first example) or derived scores (as in the second example). Confidence bands based on *SEM*s enable one to know the likelihood of the band containing the true status. Such confidence bands are used in a wide variety of situations to report simultaneously (a) what is known from a measurement and (b) the extent of uncertainty that accompanies this knowledge.

Reporting assessment results without an accompanying emphasis on measurement error often leads to naive misuse of those results. Providing only a specific *PR* implicitly (mis)represents the tests as being reliable enough to pinpoint a person's status. The problem, then, is that in trying to communicate what has been learned from a measure with a single number that represents the examinee's most likely status, an interpreter can easily imply much more precision of measurement than is actually present.

The remedy is to report scores in such a way that a lay person will be sure to understand the key point that *we do not know the examinee's exact status;* we only know how he or she scored on a particular occasion on a certain form of the test administered by a given examiner and scored by a particular scorer. (Notice how the last sentence covered the four major sources of unreliability treated in the last chapter.)

The goal and challenge is to openly report all that is known from a test about the person's true status without fostering overconfidence in an exact score. This is best achieved by reporting a range that probably contains the score the examinee would have received on a hypothetical, perfectly reliable form of the test. This emphasizes that no score is free of error, so it is best to think of a score not as a discrete number, but as a range of numbers, any one of which could represent the examinee's true status on an error-free test (Airasian, 2001).

Some published tests provide **percentile bands** for this purpose. *PR* intervals can be presented as numeric ranges, such as 55–79 or represented graphically in a variety of ways. When they are depicted with visual aids, it is usually beneficial to use a scale that adjusts for the unequal units of measure. Figure 15.5 shows a vertical bar graph used for showing a percentile band of 68–96 based on the obtained score plus and minus 1 *SEM;* thus, the odds are about 68 in 100 that the examinee's true state lies within this range.

FIGURE 15.5   Vertical Bar Graph of Percentile Band.

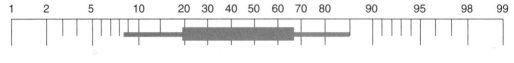

FIGURE 15.6   Two-Level Confidence Band.

Figure 15.6 displays a two-level confidence band. The heavy, dark segment (19–67) is based on an obtained score ±1 *SEM*. The chances are thus about 2 in 3 (i.e., 68 in 100) that the examinee's true level of functioning lies within this range. The light segment (8–85) is based on the obtained score ±2 *SEMs*. The odds are, therefore, about 19 in 20 (i.e., 95 in 100) that the person's true status lies within this broader interval.

Notice the trade-off. If a very precise statement is made (e.g., "Your true status is better than 43 out of every 100"), it has little chance of being true. If a somewhat less precise statement is ventured (e.g., "Out of every 100 people obtaining the same score as you, about two-thirds would get *PR*s between 19 and 67 on an error-free form of the test"), then better odds of being correct are obtained. In order to secure decent odds of being correct, the price was a somewhat vague statement. If still better odds are desired, further trade-off with vagueness must be made (e.g., "Out of every 100 students scoring like you, about 95 would receive *PR*s between 8 and 85 on a perfectly consistent form of the test").

Visual displays of percentile bands are especially helpful in interpreting multiscore batteries. This can be seen by a look ahead to Figure 16.1 on page 403. When the confidence intervals of two or more scores overlap, it is hazardous to try to identify a person's relative strength and weakness among the scores. Thus, in Figure 16.1, the person's true score in social studies might be higher than in reading. Similarly, we aren't certain that the person's true status in math is higher than in science.

Mention should be made of a public relations and rapport problem that sometimes attends use of confidence bands. Some test interpreters fear that reporting broad ranges of scores within which a person's real status probably lies is not specific enough to provide the examinee with needed information about her or his performance. To say that Maria's *PR* is somewhere between 50 and 78 is so vague that it appears to some people to constitute an admission of inadequacy of the test and/or its interpreter. On the contrary, it is a *disclosure* of the extent to which the particular test, like all measures, lacks total reliability. Qualified professionals honestly reveal the limitations of their knowledge. To obscure these limitations is to deceive and to misrepresent. *Competent test interpreters meaningfully disclose the fact that scores lack great precision.*

If Maria's parent is dismayed that the test is so inaccurate, then it should be explained that this and similar tests *are* imprecise and that it is, therefore, very important to *recognize* and allow for this reality. The greater the distress over the size of a confidence band, the greater the naivete about the reliability of the scores. The greater the outrage because of crudeness of measuring devices, the greater the need for the person to realize the extent of tests' crudeness of measurement.

Overinterpreting scores of commercially prepared instruments (i.e., failing to communicate their limitations) is the most common problem in explaining their meaning (Airasian, 2001). Similarly, many observation-based assessments that are not expressed numerically (e.g., teachers' estimation of student effort) also should be interpreted with a very healthy respect for imperfect reliability.

In helping lay persons to grasp measurement error, it is often helpful to provide examples of some kinds of measures or observations with which the person is familiar to illustrate the need to allow for a *margin of error.* The following example illustrates this.

Suppose Jane Quigley took a mechanics-of-expression test and earned a *PR* of 58 with respect to a representative national reference group of tenth graders. Suppose the *SEM* yields a band of 38–76. (Note that 38–76 is not exactly symmetrical around the score of 58 and recall that this is because the *PR* units near the center of the distribution are smaller.)

The following monologue explains how the interpretation of Jane's percentile band might be made with each of the aims discussed in this section in mind. As you read, specifically note:

- The domain description
- The description of the reference group
- The explanation of *PR*s
- The introduction of the notion of measurement error (in content sampling and occasion sampling) in terms that lay people can readily understand

> As you know, Mrs. Quigley, Jane took the *Mechanics of Expression Test* to give us an estimate of how well she manages such things as capitalization, punctuation, noun-verb agreement, and word choice (such as who vs. whom and me vs. myself). We interpret performance on this kind of subject matter by seeing how students compare with a national sample of other tenth graders.
>
> The way we show how a person's performance compares with that of others is to report a percentile rank, which is the percentage of students that was outperformed or equaled. For example, if we said Joe's percentile rank was 15, it would mean that his status on this particular sample of behavior was as good as or better than only 15 out of every 100. If we said that Al's percentile rank was 50, it would mean that his performance was average. In this way, we are able to show how a student's score on the test compares with the scores of a large group of grademates across the country.
>
> It is important to realize that Jane's performance on the particular form of the test that happened to be administered on this particular day doesn't provide the last word on her true command of mechanics of expression. It is always possible that the test may have caught her on an unusually bad (or good) day. Or, the questions in a certain form of the test could happen to hit on a disproportionate fraction of the things she knows best (or least). Achievement tests, like measures in every field, are not completely accurate. Wise use of any kind of measure makes allowance for error of measurement.
>
> Whenever we measure anything, we should think of a margin of error to allow for imperfect accuracy. For example, an oven thermometer will give slightly different readings depending on its location in an oven. The odometers of several cars making the same trip will show slightly different mileage readings. Several carpenters measuring a board are not likely to agree exactly on its length. Thus, error of measurement is present in all fields, and education is no exception.
>
> Now if we placed 100 different thermometers in various parts of an oven and read each, we could establish a range of scores within which most of the readings would lie. Similarly, if the odometer readings for a given trip were secured from many different cars, we could make a range of values—such as 341–348 miles—within which most of the distances would agree. If we ask many carpenters to measure the board, we could express its length as a range of scores within which some fraction, say, two-thirds, of the carpenters agreed.
>
> Jane's percentile band is 38–76. Thus, the percentage of tenth graders she excels or equals is probably between 38 and 76. We are, therefore, quite confident that her status is *not* in the bottom third or so of the representative national sample of tenth-grade students. We are also reasonably assured that her true achievement is not in the top fourth. Her mechanics of expression appears to be somewhere in the average range. If her status differs from the average, it is a little more likely to be slightly above average than below, but in any case, it is probably fairly close to average.

To ReCAP.   To summarize, percentile bands combine the utility of *PR*s with an emphasis that a score should not be considered precise. They also have the advantage over gross-unit scores, such as stanines, in that consecutive bands differ only slightly. This is possible because visual displays of percentile bands can be centered on actual obtained scores,[8] not on preestablished gross intervals (Lyman, 1998). Percentile bands, therefore, provide a superb way of communicating to students and parents both what scores reveal and the *limits* of what they reveal. They are recommended for use in interpreting examinee status.

Making Predictive Interpretations.   Clint Weber is a counselor whose duties include helping eighth graders decide whether to take a foreign language the following year. Clint uses eighth-grade English grades to predict students' grades in each first-year language course offered the following year. Let's use French to illustrate. How correlated are the two measures?

Being a research buff, he looks up the two grades for each of 150 recent students and computes the Pearson *r* between them, finding *r* to equal .49. Although this informs Clint's judgment about the utility of the English grades in predicting French grades, this predictive validity coefficient doesn't help students understand how well the predictor forecasts future achievement.

To help students and parents understand the meaning of the predictive measure, Clint wisely formats his research findings concerning the past experience of his sample of former students into an **expectancy table** (American Psychological Association, 1985; Cronbach, 1990). Table 15.2 shows the results.

TABLE 15.2   Expectancy Table

		No.	F	D	C	B	A
			PERCENT RECEIVING EACH ENGLISH GRADE WHO LATER RECEIVED EACH FRENCH GRADE				
	A	27	4%	11%	19%	30%	37%
Grade	B	38	3%	16%	26%	34%	21%
in	C	47	2%	30%	34%	21%	13%
English	D	33	27%	30%	27%	9%	6%
	F	5	60%	20%	20%	0%	0%
Total No.		150					

To Use Table for Predictions: Locate student's eighth-grade English grade at left. Then read across that row to find the percentage of students who received that English grade who later received each grade in French.

[8]By "centered," we mean graphically (on scales like those in Figures 15.5 and 15.6 that compensate for the unequal units of measures that *PR*s have. Thus, the obtained score is in the center of the band. It is not, however, in the numeric center of the ranks corresponding to the end points of the band.

Such a table enables a student or parent to understand two critical things about the prediction. First, expectancy tables show how valid the predictor was in predicting the criterion. Second, they reveal with equal clarity the extent to which predictions are imperfect. These two concerns, the amount of confidence to have in a prediction and the amount of margin to allow for error, are indispensable to informed use of data.

Suppose Samantha had a B in eighth-grade English, and Mr. Weber is explaining to her what this means in terms of her probable grades in French. He can use Table 15.2 to show her that out of every 100 students who received a B in eighth-grade English 3 failed French, 16 were awarded grades of D, 26 obtained grades of C, 34 received B grades, and 21 earned grades of A. Walking through a row of an expectancy table will do much to help Samantha understand both the amount of forecasting power the predictor has and the limits of this power.

THINKING CAP EXERCISE 15.2 ???

Following are questions about predictions in algebra. Use the expectancy table on pge 396 to answer these questions.

1. Chi received a prognosis test score of 67. What grade is he most likely to receive in algebra?

2. Out of every 100 students receiving a score of 32, how many fail algebra?

3. If Max receives a score of 95 on the prognosis test, are we *certain* that he will pass algebra?

KEY TO THINKING CAP EXERCISE 15.2

1. He is more apt to receive a C than any other grade. He should also understand that his chances of receiving a grade above C are much greater than those of receiving a grade below C.

2. 21

3. No. Of the 97 youngsters in the validation sample who scored at about this level, none received a grade of less than B, but it *is* possible. With a much larger sample, some probably would have. It would be best simply to indicate that fewer than 1% who scored as well as he earned a grade lower than B.

CHAPTER RECAP

Derived scores are necessary for norm-referenced interpretation; they are the means of reporting examinee status relative to other people. Hence, derived scores are always based on the performance of people in a reference group, and interpreters should ensure the relevance of the reference group for the interpretive purpose.

One way of categorizing derived scores is provided by the distinction between status scores and developmental scores. Percentile ranks are a kind of status score that indicates the percentage of a reference group (usually grade, age, or course peers) that an examinee equaled or excelled. *PR*s and percentile bands *are well suited for interpreting scores to students and parents. PR*s are poorly suited for computation because they lack equal units of measure.

TABLE 15.3   Expectancy Table Showing Percentages of Students in the Validity Sample Earning Each Final Grade in Algebra at Successive Intervals of the *Orleans-Hanna Algebra Prognosis Test Scores*

PROGNOSIS TEST SCORE		FINAL ALGEBRA SCORE				
Total Raw Score (0–98)	*Number of Students*	*Percentage Earning Each Grade*				
		F	*D*	*C*	*B*	*A*
95–98	97	0	0	0	3	97
90–94	447	0	0	2	19	79
85–89	516	0	1	7	35	57
80–84	527	1	1	12	42	44
75–79	443	3	4	25	49	20
70–74	513	4	5	25	43	23
65–69	443	4	7	41	34	14
60–64	326	4	15	37	35	10
55–59	288	13	12	36	31	8
50–54	242	12	17	44	20	7
45–49	220	7	31	38	20	4
40–44	176	14	28	31	24	2
35–39	111	15	32	37	9	6
30–34	98	21	23	27	24	4
20–29	104	23	28	36	8	6
0–19	35	51	14	31	3	0
Total *N* 4,586		5	9	24	32	29
Mean = 69.1 SD = 18.2						

Used by permission of Harcourt Educational Materials.

Standard scores are another group of status scores that indicate examinee deviancy from a group (usually grade, age, or course peer) mean in standard deviation units. Having equal units, *standard scores are generally the best-suited kind of derived scores for calculation.* Standard scores are poorly suited for making interpretations to lay people because they are based on technical concepts that hinder meaningful communication.

Developmental derived scores, unlike status scores, indicate the group within which the examinee would be typical. They are popular with many teachers and administrators, but they have horrendous limitations. *Grade- and age-equivalent scores should not be used to interpret a person's status, to analyze relative strengths and weaknesses, or to perform statistical calculations.* If they have any legitimate function, it is in the assessment of growth at the elementary school level.

Persons responsible for interpreting test scores to students and parents have a responsibility not only to report what the scores indicate, but also *to avoid overinterpretation by disclosing the extent to which the scores are unreliable or invalid.* In descriptive reports of an examinee's current status, percentile bands provide the best way to simultaneously accomplish these two important aims. In predictive interpretations, expectancy tables offer the best means of revealing the extent to which the test forecasts validly.

CHAPTER 16

PUBLISHED INSTRUMENTS

CHAPTER OVERVIEW

A PEEK AT THE HISTORY OF ASSESSMENT

SCHOOL USES OF PUBLISHED MEASURES

ACHIEVEMENT TESTS

APTITUDE TESTS
　What Aptitude Is
　What "Intelligence" *Isn't*

OTHER PUBLISHED INSTRUMENTS

HOW TO FIND AND EVALUATE PUBLISHED MEASURES

KEY TERMS

test battery
aptitude-achievement continuum

Tests in Print
Mental Measurements Yearbook (*MMY*)

In the last few chapters, we have considered issues that apply to the use of both teacher-made and published measures. We now apply that material to a consideration of some features of published instruments that are relevant to the work of classroom teachers. After providing a brief historical sketch of selected assessment measures, we consider uses of published instruments, clarify some of the constructs they assess, briefly examine samples of the variety of instruments, and close with some "how to" information on finding and evaluating published measures.

A FEW GLIMPSES OF ASSESSMENT HISTORY

Assessment and evaluation have been used for millennia. Let's imagine a prehistoric person facing the ultimate multiple-choice item when targeted as dinner by a ravenous, ferocious beast: "Do I— A, jump in creek; B, climb a tree; C, stand and fight; D, lie down and play dead; or E, run for my life? Which is the single *best* response?" We must assume that many of our ancestors performed well on these kinds of tests.

Advancing through time and many centuries of progress, we might note two explicit biblical examples of assessment in Judges. The consequence of failing one of those one-item tests (i.e., mispronouncing the word "shibboleth") was death!

Or, we could learn about the 2200 B.C. system in China for determining which citizens would obtain prestigious government positions. The rationale for the exams was that achievement in certain subjects (e.g., writing, arithmetic, and music) could be used to predict performance in a larger sphere of activities.

Examinations in the field of medicine were initiated during the tenth century A.D. in Baghdad. A few decades later, European universities began giving examinations in law. Jesuit teachers made systematic use of written classroom tests by 1500 A.D. We are left to wonder if all these various methods of purposeful testing were well aligned with the skills and competencies that were needed in those times.

Fast-forward to the twentieth century and its milestones in testing. In France, Alfred Binet was commissioned by the education ministry to develop a test for identifying learning needs of mentally deficient school-age children (Kaufman & Lichtenberger, 2002). The results were used to provide the children with educational programs better designed to enhance their learning. Interestingly, at the time Binet cautioned against perceiving test results as fixed for life (Good, 1974).

In the United States, the Binet scale was modified by Lewis Terman to become the Stanford-Binet Scale of Intelligence and was used to predict success in school and later life. By 1920, the United States Army was administering group tests to classify soldiers either for officer candidacy or for placement in the infantry.

Other countries put their school students through grueling examinations in order to chart their futures—the "eleven-plus" in Great Britain, the baccalauréat in France, the German test for admission to Gymnasien, the competitive exams in the Soviet Union, and the ongoing, rigorous tests given in Japanese schools.

The testing movement, with its published instruments, fixed procedures, and use of test results for a wide range of decision-making purposes, mushroomed during the twentieth century. In the first half of the century, published tests in a wide variety of subjects became available in the United States. In the second half, student rights and special needs became driving issues for legislation and practice. In the 1970s, federal legislation was enacted to guarantee due process procedures in the placement of students in special programs, to ensure nondiscriminatory testing, and to protect confidentiality of school records. Moreover, Public Law 94-142 focused on identifying children in need of special services, with assurance that needed services would be provided and directed by their individualized programs, and by mandating that formal assessment instruments and procedures would be used.

The 1980s brought a push for holding teachers and schools accountable for student learning. On the heels of those movements came increased public interest in standards, outcomes-based education, school improvement, teacher certification, quality-performance accreditation, and "authentic" assessment. In that context, Shepard (2000) suggested that "Teachers need help in fending off the distorting and demotivating effects of external assessments."

In the 1990s, the heat grew more intense for educators to provide state-mandated, high-stakes outcomes assessments. With the passage of the No Child Left Behind Act in 2001, the stakes for testing during the new millennium had become even higher; unfortunately, the NCLB legislation failed to allocate a level of funding needed to support the mandate.

In the midst of all of these issues, it is clear that educators need a keen understanding of assessment, and that they must wisely apply this understanding. However, as Bracey (2000, p. 7) succinctly observed, "Unfortunately, the increased use and reporting of tests has not always been accompanied by increased understanding of how tests can or ought to be used. Teachers need to know what the tests can and cannot say about children." Knowledge of assessment and evaluation can provide powerful tools for fruitful use of such things as accountability, outcomes-based learning, and quality performance that legislators, school boards, and other stakeholders (e.g., communities, families, students) seek. Wise use of published instruments is an important part of assessment for effective teaching.

USES OF PUBLISHED INSTRUMENTS FOR ASSESSMENT

Most published instruments are designed to assess open-ended domains of achievement (e.g., reading comprehension or biology) or other expansive, abstract constructs (e.g., academic aptitude, artistic interest, or self-concept). Therefore, most published devices are given norm-referenced interpretations. Herein is a fundamental advantage of published tests—they ordinarily supply reference-group data for groups larger than individual classes.

Another major virtue of published instruments is that most are developed by relatively specialized professionals. Therefore, they typically exhibit higher technical quality than teacher-made tests in such matters as freedom from item flaws, item differentiation, formatting, printing, and reliability.

The decisions that published measures are designed to inform are typically broad rather than detailed (e.g., "What level of reading would most benefit Tyrone?" rather than, "Does Tyrone know how to pronounce a particular diphthong?"). Like teacher-made measures, published instruments should be used only when they are likely to improve decision making. Some of the decisions facilitated by published tests are instructional in nature and are made by teachers, others are made by school administrators, and still others are made by individual students and their parents.

This final chapter presents general information about published achievement and aptitude tests and selected examples of other types of scales. The examples are designed to illustrate a variety of instrument features. In keeping with our primary focus on enhanced teaching through effective student assessment, we will not systematically name or describe specific tests.

ACHIEVEMENT TESTS

Published achievement test are, by and large, summative measures designed to assess broader segments of content than teacher-made unit tests. Of course, generalizations have exceptions. Some published achievement tests are designed to yield domain-referenced interpretations and are not accompanied by normative data. Some focus on separate objectives or small instructional segments rather than broad content areas. Nonetheless, these generalizations are ordinarily true.

Separate Tests.   On occasion, educators use specialized tests of particular subjects, such as biology, reading, or algebra. Reading is often singled out because of its enormous importance. Aside from reading, separate achievement tests have their greatest use at the secondary level in subjects not taken by all students, such as chemistry or French. Achievement in elective high school subjects cannot, of course, be surveyed by batteries designed for all students; special end-of-course tests are needed for use with students enrolled in the respective subjects. Interpretation of such test scores is best referenced to the performance of other students who have taken the respective courses. Most of these tests are published and normed separately. For example, a German test could not be normed using the same students as a trigonometry test because different students enroll in the courses. However, they could be referenced to students in the same schools.

Recency of any test merits attention for two reasons. First, course content changes over time. This is obviously true in subjects such as chemistry or recent history. It is even true in more stable content such as Latin or geometry because curricular emphases may change. Second, student achievement may change over time. Recency of a test's normative data is important because student achievement may be in a state of change. If reference group data are seriously aged, there is cause to wonder if contemporary students would perform the same as those used for the norm-referenced interpretation.

Informal reading inventories, unlike most published tests, are typically alleged to be domain referenced. They attempt to identify students' specific word-recognition and comprehension skills (Silvaroli, 1986). To be of practical use, diagnostic scores such as those obtained from domain-referenced reading inventories must be reasonably reliable. Recall that reliability data are just as necessary for domain-referenced interpretations as for norm-referenced ones. Unless reliability data are reported for all scores and subscores, it is not prudent to assume that all is well. Unfortunately, reliability and validity data for informal reading inventories are rare!

Commercially Prepared, Customized Tests. Several publishers market customized test-making services. These are organized to allow school districts to custom order their content-area tests. Typically, school personnel examine a list or catalog of instructional objectives and select those deemed relevant to the local curriculum. The publisher then prints a test consisting of about three items per objective, and the district may set a passing score for each (e.g., 2 out of 3). Student answer sheets are sometimes scored in terms of mastery of the separate objectives.

This service is attractive to districts having a mandate to engage in a variety of outcomes-based assessment and requires documentation of each student's mastery of each objective. Unfortunately, the method is often used indiscriminately rather than reserved for Context A for which it is suited. In Context C, there is little merit in having meaningless and arbitrary "thresholds" of "mastery." And in every context, there is little merit in using highly unreliable subscores.

We do believe, however, that there is merit in commercially marketed collections of test items from which a district might select those that help fulfill testing needs established by its two-dimensional tables of specifications. In these instances, there would be no need to engage in a meaningless ritual of matching each item to an explicit mastery objective and setting a mastery threshold for it.

Achievement Batteries. Most schools elect to test achievement with coordinated sets of tests, called **test batteries.** Achievement batteries are widely used prior to high school for the assessment of regular academic subjects. Their use at the high school level is limited to subjects that constitute the common core of the curriculum.

Achievement batteries offer significant advantages over separate, cafeteria-style collections of uncoordinated tests for several content areas. Content can be dovetailed so that it neither overlaps redundantly among tests nor gets lost between areas. For example, the topics of charts, tables, and graphs can fit in math, social studies, science, or study skills. Another advantage of batteries concerns intraindividual comparisons such as "Is Ramon better in reading than in math?" *The subtests have all been normed on the same reference group.* This simplifies the task of interpreting difference scores (although the endeavor is still hazardous).

Another reasonable question that parents, teachers, and students ask concerns year-to-year growth. A pupil might well ask, "Has my math improved much during the past year?" If each grade's math test is well targeted in difficulty for that grade, then a pupil may not take the same test in successive years. Rather, the student may have taken successive *levels* of the same test—tests articulated to be parallel except for differences in curricular emphases and for grade-to-grade changes of difficulty. Because various levels assess slightly different content domains, scores of different levels are not directly equivalent. Therefore, most batteries are accompanied by developmental scales that enable successive-year comparisons (this very technical topic was largely untreated in Chapter 15). Assessing growth is also complicated by the reduced reliability with which it is measured. All things considered, plotting growth is a tricky technical and problematic, yet important, enterprise.

This is as good a place as any to note that *raw* scores of alternate forms of the same test may *not* be assumed to be equivalent. Even if carefully based on the same specifications, parallel forms may differ slightly in difficulty and/or in variability. Only derived scores of alternate forms—not the raw scores—may safely be considered to be interchangeable.

Some achievement batteries provide a variety of interpretive information spanning norm-referencing and domain-referencing (or curriculum-referencing, as the latter is sometimes called). It might be noted—and lamented—that several batteries supply domain- or criterion-referenced interpretation quite indiscriminately, without regard to the meaningfulness of such referencing for the kind of subject matter tested. The scoring services that users can purchase may include mastery information for individual students concerning open-ended, unmasterable objectives. Such information, of course, lacks meaning because a student's raw or percentage score will depend on the difficulty of the items that *happen* to be sampled in the test. Fortunately, the availability of this questionable scoring service need not be a disadvantage to knowledgeable users. Educators who understand that Context C subject matter should be given only norm-referenced interpretations will know better than to purchase or use such scoring services.

However, a student's norm-referenced status on such objectives could be useful *if* it were sufficiently reliable; alas, decent reliability is not likely given the small number of test items that sample individual objectives.

Examples of achievement batteries are the Comprehensive Tests of Basic Skills (CTBS), Stanford Achievement Test Series, and the Iowa Tests of Basic Skills (ITBS). The ITBS is complemented by the high school achievement battery, Tests of Achievement and Proficiency (TAP). Both are companion tests to the aptitude battery, the Cognitive Abilities Test. Others are the Woodcock-Johnson Psychoeducational Battery-Revised (WJ–R), the Wide-Range Achievement Test–3 (WRAT–3), and the Peabody Picture Vocabulary Test–III (PPVT–III).

Recall the need in interpreting scores to allow for measurement error, especially if error has multiple opportunities to occur as it does in the several scores of a battery. It is extremely useful for achievement batteries to provide confidence bands that signal the need to allow for margins of error. A visual representation of percentile bands helps the interpreter steer clear of making big things out of relatively small differences. In this same vein, it is very helpful in interpretations to emphasize the outlying scores that deviate significantly *from the person's own mean*. Many students have uneven profiles worth noting. Many others do not.

Figure 16.1 illustrates a situation in which one would *not* want to make much of differences between pairs of subtest scores unless the confidence bands did *not* overlap. Thus for the student whose profile is displayed, we could say that the person seems better in reading than in science. However, we should *not* say that the achievement in social studies is higher than in language arts.

	NPR	1	5	10	20	30	40	50	60	70	80	90	95	99
Reading	94										▬▬▬▬▬▬		
Language Arts	81								▬▬▬▬▬▬▬				
Mathematics	65							▬▬▬▬▬▬					
Science	55						▬▬▬▬▬▬						
Social Studies	91									▬▬▬▬▬▬			

FIGURE 16.1   Hypothetical Profile of a Student's Percentile Bands on a Five-Subtest Achievement Battery.

THINKING CAP EXERCISE 16.1   **???**

Use Figure 16.1 to answer the following questions. Each confidence band is ±1 *SEM*. These exercises provide you with a review of important concepts from Chapters 14 and 15. Note the scale of *PR* at the top is laid out in a manner to reflect the unequal units of measure inherent in *PR*s.

1. The confidence bands for math and science overlap a great deal. What does this mean?

2. How might one describe the student's status in language arts in nontechnical language?

3. Between which two subtests does the student have the greatest likelihood of having a real difference in achievement?

4. Which subtest appears to be the *least* reliable? How can we tell?

5. The student's national percentile rank for language arts is 81, yet if we estimate the end points of that confidence band, they appear to be about 63 and 94. Now, 81 is *not* the mean of 63 and 94. What's wrong?

KEY TO THINKING CAP EXERCISE 16.1

1. Overlapping bands suggest that we should *not* assume that the difference in scores (*PR*s of 65 and 55 in this case) are large enough to justify saying with confidence that a real difference in true status exists.

2. Your score indicates that you are probably in about the top half of a national sample of other students in your grade in the kind of material that this subtest assessed. Yet, you are probably not in the top twentieth.

3. Reading and science. The scores for these were the outliers for this individual.

4. Reading confidence band is the longest. If it has the most error of measurement, it is the least reliable.

5. Nothing. The obtained *PR* is at the center of the *graphic* confidence band. However, because *PR* units are closer together near the center of a distribution than at the extremes, the *numerical* band is *not* centered at 81. Typically, percentile bands have more units on the side of the obtained score nearer the mean than on the other side of it.

ENCAPSULATION

SOME CLASSIFICATION CATEGORIES

To keep our learning "sorted out" in helpful ways, we might review some of the numerous ways in which we have classified measures of achievement in various places in this book. In general, these dimensions are independent of one another; thus, many a test could be categorized on most or all of the following dimensions:

- Summative–formative
- Cognitive–affective–psychomotor–social
- Verbal–quantitative–nonverbal
- Maximum performance–typical performance
- Mastery–differentiating
- Objective–subjective
- Group administered–individually administered
- Paper-pencil–product–performance
- Speed–power
- Published–teacher-made
- Standardized (e.g., administered under strictly supervised conditions)–nonstandardized (e.g., done out of class)

Attention now turns to the distinction between measures of achievement and measures of aptitude. Some, yet not all, of these same ways to classify achievement measures also relate to aptitude measures.

APTITUDE TESTS

This section and the next will focus on instruments that teachers do not ordinarily produce; that is, on devices that are available mainly from test publishers. There is, however, substantial similarity between classroom achievement tests and a wide variety of commercially marketed measures of other attributes. For example, the universal characteristics of good measures (reliability, validity, a basis for interpretation, and economy/practicality) all apply to aptitude tests, interest inventories, and other commercially produced tests as much as they do to published or teacher-made achievement tests. Moreover, the similarity between achievement and aptitude tests turns out to be much greater than their names may imply.

Most aptitude assessment involves prediction of one sort or another. Aptitude test interpretations are norm referenced because the instruments assess expansive constructs. Like other measures, aptitude tests lack perfect reliability; hence, in using them for decision making, allowance must always be made for measurement error.

This section provides general information about aptitude tests and the nature of "aptitude." In addition, features of aptitude measures will be highlighted.

The Aptitude-Achievement Continuum

If asked, "What is the difference between aptitude and achievement?" the proverbial person on the street might answer along the lines, "Achievement is what you have learned; aptitude is your ability or capacity to learn." Although this understanding is not entirely wrong, it is very deficient; psychologists have long understood that intelligence (i.e., general academic aptitude) tests do not provide simple and direct measures of potential (Stanovich, 1991). This section attempts to clarify what aptitude tests actually measure by two means. First, aptitude will be compared and contrasted with achievement. Second, attention will focus on what aptitude is *not*.

What Is Achievement?   Perhaps the clearest way to define achievement is in terms of the processes, methods, and operations by which it is measured. The way to be most explicit concerning "What is achievement in fifth-grade language arts?" is to agree on the way it is to be measured. Once the parties to the discussion can agree on a measure, they have an operational definition—achievement in fifth-grade language arts is that which is measured by the test. Such operational definitions nicely achieve their aim—clarity.

Although clear, an operational definition may be poor. Thus, if the test doesn't measure what educators agree constitutes fifth-grade language arts, the test isn't valid and the definition is poor. Yet this clarity provides a means to improve the definition and the impact of the resulting scores. *A test that is a valid measure of a construct* (i.e., a test that is reliable, is cost-effective, and that avoids both construct underrepresentation and construct irrelevance) *is a good operational definition of that construct.* (Of course, the clarity of single operational definitions of multifaceted constructs also highlights the shallowness of definitions based on single indicants. That was a basis for our advocacy of multiple, triangulated indicants for expansive domains by use of expansive, developmental Context C objectives.)

Much of this book has been devoted to making classroom achievement tests valid—that is, making teacher-made tests good operational definitions of the kinds of achievement that they value. Therefore, we want achievement tests to focus on important material, to tap complex mental processes, to assess transfer of learning, to be free of item flaws that enable content-ignorant persons to deduce keyed responses, to reflect the objectives of instruction, and so on.

Instructional sensitivity is the extent to which persons who have received instruction perform better on an achievement test than those who have not been instructed. Thus begins a part of the description of the **aptitude-achievement continuum** shown in Figure 16.2. At one end are Context A achievement measures that are extremely sensitive to instruction—mastery tests on which well-prepared students get perfect or near-perfect scores. Near this end of the continuum are other Context A achievement tests that require a little processing of material beyond what was specifically taught, for example, comprehending paraphrased material and making low-road transfer of training. Still further from the instructionally sensitive end are Context C achievement measures that require deeper thinking and high-road transfer of learning.

As mentioned in Chapter 7, there comes a point at which teachers should regard some problems as demanding too much high-road transfer and not enough of what was taught. Such items would not be considered to measure (enough) course achievement, rather, they would be measures of aptitude or problem solving.

Descriptive Characteristic	**The Aptitude-Achievement Continuum**			
	Achievement			Aptitude
Sensitivity to Instruction vs. Nonsensitivity to the Culture	Explicit (Context A) domains are very instructionally sensitive	Expansive (Context C) domains are only moderately instructionally sensitive	Content moderately sensitive to the general culture	Content not very sensitive to the general culture
Kind of Test/Thinking Demands	Mastery Context A tests requiring only rote knowledge Mastery Context A tests requiring some processing and low-road transfer	Differentiating Context C tests requiring deep thinking and high-road transfer	Differentiating tests on expansive, heterogeneous achievement, high-road transfer, and problem solving Differentiating tests requiring much novel problem solving that isn't tightly linked to particular subjects	Differentiating nonverbal tests requiring much novel problem solving
Domains Assessed	Achievement tests tightly focused on a small, explicit unit in one subject Achievement tests restricted to a single school subject		Aptitude tests content loosely reflects the general culture	Aptitude tests tap things relatively novel to the general culture
Purpose of Assessment	Used to assess past learning		Used to predict future learning	

FIGURE 16.2   Descriptive Features of the Aptitude-Achievement Continuum.

Achievement tests are reasonably focused. A math test is limited to math, a biology test to biology, and so on. As shown in Figure 16.2, this introduces another way in which the achievement end of the aptitude-achievement continuum is described.

What Is Aptitude?   One way to characterize aptitude or "intelligence" tests is that they move too far from the instructional-sensitivity end of the continuum to be legitimate measures of achievement *in a particular subject.* A second way of describing "intelligence" involves descriptions of intelligent behavior. Although no single definition has achieved universal acceptance, the flavor of the construct was captured long ago by Binet's description of intelligent behavior as the tendency to take and maintain direction; the ability to adapt; and the capacity to judge well, to reason well, and to comprehend well (Binet & Simon, 1916; Terman, 1916).

Still another way to think of aptitude tests concerns their function. The main legitimate uses to which general intelligence tests and narrower aptitude tests are put involve prediction of future success in more or less academic settings. Much misunderstanding and ill feeling concerning intelligence and IQ would be avoided if discussion were to shift away from an abstract psychological construct and come to focus on the *purposes of aptitude testing.* Such tests are used to predict. "Intelligence" testing is primarily a forecasting endeavor. This point is also made in Figure 16.2.

Yet another way to characterize aptitude assessments is that they are not ordinarily limited to particular content fields, but often span many fields and include out-of-school learning as well as school-type learning. Aptitude tests are thus *not* very sensitive to instruction in *any one* subject. Yet it is important to realize that most aptitude or so-called intelligence tests do measure broad-scope achievement that is impacted by the general intellectual, educational, and cultural environment.

Here are several examples of the kinds of questions that appear in major "intelligence" tests. They could be fashioned either as completion items for individual administration or as written multiple-choice items for group administration.

- At what temperature does water freeze?
- What country is also an entire continent?

- Who was Moses?
- President is to country as mayor is to _____.
- Jim and Bob Brown are brothers. What is the relationship between Jim's daughter and Bob's daughter?
- Who wrote *Tom Sawyer*?
- What is the name of your state's governor?
- What is photosynthesis?
- What is a baby deer called?
- What is the main source of income of most newspapers?
- What is an ideograph?
- In what century did most American homes get telephones?
- What number comes next in this series: 1, 2, 6, 15, 31?
- What purposes are served by a U.S. Census?

This is one kind of material measured in most so-called intelligence tests. Such questions obviously measure learning, much of which is school learning. Operationally, intelligence is what is measured by valid tests of the construct. If a test samples *acquired behaviors* that psychologists agree to label "intellectual," then the test provides a good operational definition of intelligence (Mehrens & Lehmann, 1991). The sample items listed thus help to convey what so-called intelligence is—*and what it is not.*

Some tests are near the middle of the continuum. A vocabulary test would be an ambiguous case in point.

What Intelligence *Isn't*.   Clearly, intelligence is not something you are born with. Nor is it capacity. Nor is it unchangeable. Nor is it neural tissue. Intelligence is (operationally) evidenced by present ability to handle the kinds of material assessed by leading intelligence tests. Because the words "intelligence" and "IQ" are so widely misunderstood to mean some of the things that intelligence is not, it is better, where possible, to avoid the terms altogether and to use others that better convey what is measured. Such terms as "academic aptitude," "cognitive abilities," "school ability," and "scholastic aptitude" serve quite well.

Scholars agree that it is not possible to assess genetic endowment or so-called innate potential. Rather, intellectual development involves an interaction of heredity and environment (including the prenatal environment). Their interactive contributions to performance on any achievement or aptitude test makes them inseparable. Attempting to divide their relative influence on a person's status is an exercise in futility (Kaufman & Kaufman, 1983).

Even if we could separate the impact of heredity and environment, this dichotomy would not equate to a distinction between things that are alterable and those that are fixed at conception. "Many inherited characteristics are changeable and conversely, many environmentally acquired characteristics are extremely resistant to change" (Angoff, 1988, p. 78).

It would be worthwhile to review Figure 16.2 at this time to verify that the aptitude end of the scale does not describe aptitude in any of the ways identified in this section as things that intelligence is not. Most of the problems in grasping what intelligence is concerns shedding misconceptions that so often clothe the construct.

Another important issue is the recurring distinction between maximum behavior (which tests assess) and typical behavior in everyday life. The latter is not typically assessed by so-called intelligence tests. In using such tests, it is important to keep in mind that intelligent behavior in everyday circumstances is a function of the *disposition* to act intelligently as well as a function of the ability to do so (Perkins, Tishman, Ritchhart, Donis, & Andrade, 2000).

Why Aptitude Tests Measure What They Measure.   Many people have wondered why intelligence tests are not constructed so as to avoid past achievement. They could be based on *completely* novel material. As shown in Figure 16.2, such tests lie at the aptitude end of the continuum. Note that to avoid all culturally relevant material the test content must avoid language and numbers. Indeed, even using paper and pencil or having a time limit assumes acculturation with regard to these cultural artifacts.

A test with completely novel material was a good idea that had to be tested to determine that it was no panacea to impacts of environmental inequities upon aptitude test scores. Such tests can be constructed, but they are not as effective as conventional aptitude tests in fulfilling their primary mission—academic prediction. Predictive measures tend to work best when they are intrinsically related to the thing being predicted (Anastasi & Urbina, 1997). Hence, if we want to predict school learning in the future, tests that assess past learning tend to do the job better than tests that assess something else that is less construct relevant.

Then why do we have aptitude tests at all? Why not base all predictions on measures of relevant past achievement? In point of fact, it is often possible to make better predictions based on past achievement than on aptitude measures. For example, college freshman grades are generally predicted slightly more validly from high school grades than from college admissions tests. Two good reasons answer the question "Why use aptitude tests?"

First, at times, no past achievement in the subject being predicted can be observed. If we need to predict how well students will do in first-year Arabic or computer programming, we cannot administer an achievement test because they have not yet studied the subject. Aptitude tests are valuable in providing predictions in settings where there is no past achievement to assess.

Second, even when there is achievement to be measured, better predictions can be made with a suitable weighted combination of predictors than with one alone. Thus, college freshman grades are predicted more validly by use of both high school grades and college admissions test scores than by either alone. Similarly, second-year Arabic could be forecasted more accurately by joint use of first-year grades and verbal aptitude measures than by grades alone.

We said earlier that aptitude tests that relate to past school learning tend to be superior for typical students over those that are not academic in flavor. Yet there is a place for tests that are less loaded with school learning than many aptitude tests are. And there is a very important place for tests that are not saturated with subcultural content. Culturally loaded tests are clearly not appropriate for examinees who do not have the common background of experience in the culture for which the test was developed. Nonverbal or "culture-fair" tests may be the only suitable measures for students who are not conversant with Standard American English or with the mainstream United States culture.

However, beware of so-called culture-free tests. Intelligence can't be measured directly like height or weight. Like other constructs, *intelligence can be assessed only indirectly* (preferably, with several well-triangulated indicants); *it must be inferred from indicants of intellectual behavior.* "'Culture-free' tests are culture free in name only—there are no tests that measure potential or aptitude directly" (Hopkins, 1998, p. 354). "All intelligence tests are inherently culturally loaded in varying degrees, reflecting their developers' experiences, knowledge, values, and conceptions of intelligence" (Valencia & Suzuki, 2001, p. 113).

It is clear, then, that we would not use a verbal, culturally loaded test with students unfamiliar with the language or general culture. (Sadly, this transparent truth was not obvious to some psychologists and politicians in the 1920s who based national immigration policy on results of tests administered to incoming immigrants at Ellis Island!)

Such a clear-cut answer cannot be given, however, about pupils who speak variant dialects of English or ones for whom English is not the first language or ones whose homes are culturally unusual. Is a culturally saturated test fair to them?

From one angle, of course not. Their cultural differences place them at a disadvantage.

From another angle, yes. Although circumstances beyond their control have placed such people at a cultural disadvantage, *the purpose of aptitude tests is to predict.* Such people's circumstances will usually also place them at a disadvantage in schools. The main job of aptitude tests is to forecast school success. Therefore, for a test to be able to do its predictive job, such people should be at an equal disadvantage on the aptitude test. One would not condemn the weather forecaster who usually correctly predicts lower temperatures for Minneapolis than for Miami. Nor would one condemn a physical exam whose results lead to predictions that students who are lame will not, on average, run as rapidly as those having no physical impairment.

For typical examinees who share reasonable amounts of the culture for which the test was developed, a culturally relevant test will predict academic success better than one that is less culturally relevant. Schools, after all, are culture saturated.

Like achievement tests, aptitude tests should be used only when they are likely to improve decision making. Some such decisions are instructional in nature and are made by teachers, some are administrative decisions, and others are made by individual students and their families.

Tests of General Academic Aptitude

Examples of general academic aptitude tests are the Otis-Lennon School Ability Test (OLSAT), Raven's Progressive Matrices, the Stanford-Binet Intelligence Scale Fifth Edition, the Kaufman Assessment Battery for Children (K–ABC), the Wechsler Preschool and Primary Scale of Intelligence (WPPSI–III), the Wechsler Intelligence Scale for Children (WISC–IV), and the Wechsler Adult Intelligence Scale (WAIS–III). The Stanford-Binet, K–ABC, and the Wechsler Scales are individually administered tests.

Tests of Specific Aptitudes

A number of special aptitude tests are available for school and college use. Some are designed to help institutions such as medical and law schools make wise selection decisions. Others are designed to help students make wise educational and occupational decisions (e.g., tests of musical aptitude, mechanical aptitude, algebra aptitude, artistic aptitude, and modern language aptitude).

Many special aptitude tests, such as those used to predict success in algebra or law school, are better described as tests with specialized purposes than as tests that measure unique aptitudes. However, the use of a specialized test does have advantages over a general aptitude test. These include customization to provide optimal content blend, face appeal or credibility to students and parents, and the likely inclusion in its manual of validity data that focus on its predictive validity for the specialized purpose. Furthermore, most such tests are accompanied by expectancy tables to aid in their meaningful interpretation.

Aptitude Batteries

Multiple aptitude batteries are based on the belief that so-called intelligence is multifaceted and that it is useful to assess various aptitudes separately. Such testing leads to an aptitude *profile*—an integrated presentation of several scores. Some such tests, being consistent with the belief in multiple aptitudes, do not provide a total score.

The idea of multiple aptitudes has been around for some time. Early research by Thurstone (e.g., 1938) led to a widely used test designed to assess seven "primary mental abilities." More recently Gardner (e.g., 1983, 1993) and others have repopularized the idea of a set of "intelligences" rather than one global "intelligence."

A key purpose of an aptitude profile is differential prediction. To illustrate, suppose a student is going to do better (or worse) next year in Spanish than in geometry. A single-score test could not possibly predict this difference. Multiple aptitude batteries might be able to. The extent to which they can correctly forecast such a difference is a manifestation of their *differential* validity. Unfortunately, a common feature of multiple-score aptitude batteries is their disappointing performance in this regard (Anastasi & Urbina, 1997).

Another major purpose of aptitude profiles involves educational and occupational counseling. In educational and vocational planning, it is useful to know a person's relative strengths and weaknesses.

Examples of aptitude batteries are the Cognitive Abilities Test, the Differential Aptitude Tests, the Armed Services Vocational Aptitude Battery, and the Woodcock-Johnson Psychoeducational Battery-Revised. The Woodcock Johnson Tests of Cognitive Abilities and Tests of Achievement (WJ III) battery is used extensively in special education to provide individual assessment enabling comparison of aptitude and achievement, and scores that have been derived from the same reference group. It is similar to the K–ABC in being an individually administered battery that accommodates comparison of comparable derived scores for aptitude and achievement.

College Admissions Tests

As students near the completion of high school, many consider applying to postsecondary educational institutions. At this point, college admissions testing becomes a central part of most high school testing programs. Stakes are high for examiners. College admission tests are controlled and managed very tightly by their publishers in order to ensure test security. A new edition is typically prepared for each of the several dates a test will be administered nationally. The tests are given only at designated, supervised testing centers. Test booklets are kept sealed until administration time, which takes place simultaneously in all testing centers. Following test administration, answer sheets are sent for centralized scoring.

SAT.   Prior to the 1920s, each college and university that wanted to use an admissions test had to develop, administer, and score its own. Students applying to several colleges would have to take several such tests. Then, a number of colleges cooperatively formed the College Entrance Examination Board, which published a common exam for use by all member institutions. This instrument, the Scholastic Aptitude Test (SAT) is now known as the Scholastic Assessment Test (SAT). It has undergone extensive research.

The Preliminary Scholastic Assessment Test (PSAT) is a shortened version of the SAT designed for use about a year before the SAT. It provides a basis to predict how well students will do on the SAT and thus enhances educational planning. It also provides experience with the test format, procedures, and item types. In addition, it is used to identify National Merit Scholarship Semifinalists.

The College Entrance Examination Board also publishes the Advanced Placement Program tests for students who take high school courses for college credit or advanced placement. Because the courses taken for advanced placement differ in content and quality, the tests provide a means of "authenticating" the courses.

Many efforts have been made to provide assistance to future examinees on the SAT to improve their scores. This can take the form of sound, balanced *instruction designed to raise examinee status on attributes* sampled by the test. Efforts also can take the form of *coaching designed to impact the scores without having comparable influence on the attribute being assessed.* Like teaching to the test, coaching is designed to cause test scores to *mis*represent the domains they sample, and thereby to overpredict examinee success in college. This *in*validates test use. Many studies have been conducted on the impact of coaching. A summary conclusion is that intensive drill on items similar to those of the SAT is not likely to produce much greater gains than those associated with a year of regular high school instruction (Anastasi & Urbina, 1997).

ACT.   The Enhanced American College Testing (ACT) Assessment consists of tests in English, mathematics, reading, and science reasoning, a student-profile section, and an interest inventory. The ACT's purposes are similar to those of the SAT. Both assess present readiness for college work, and both are best used along with high school grades in predicting college achievement.

They do, however, occupy somewhat different niches. Traditionally, institutions using the ACT have tended to be less selective in their admission practices than have those using the SAT. Also, although both are used nationally, the SAT is most used by colleges and universities in the Northeast, especially Ivy League ones, whereas use of the ACT is more typical in the Midwest.

OTHER PUBLISHED INSTRUMENTS

The achievement and aptitude tests just discussed are similar in being cognitive tests of maximum performance that tap thinking activities. Other parts of this book have discussed psychomotor tests of maximum performance that assess how well pupils can perform various acts, such as holding a pencil, playing a musical instrument, or dancing. In contrast to measures of maximum performance, most of the instruments considered in this section are affective measures of typical performance. In addition, published adaptive behavior scales will be examined briefly.

The affective domain encompasses values, feelings, attitudes, interests, motivation, self-control, and other noncognitive personality attributes. Affective and social measures typically assess expansive domains by use of either direct observation (which is expensive in time demands and relatively low in reliability) or self-report. Some assessment difficulties stem from lack of clarity concerning the meaning of abstract affective and social constructs.

Measures of typical performance seek some ideas as to what "examinees are really like or what they actually do, rather than what they are capable of doing" (Lyman, 1998, p. 20). This can be achieved in several ways:

- By *observing* people when they don't know they are being evaluated. This approach is often used to assess students for reporting or grading.
- By using *informants* (e.g., parents or teachers) who know the person being assessed very well.
- By eliciting honest, undistorted *self-reports.*

Much of the difficulty associated with measuring typical behavior arises from the fact that *most self-report affective and social measures are fakable.* When examinees falsify self-reports, the instruments tap *maximum behaviors,* not typical behaviors.

However, self-report works well in circumstances in which people *have no motive to fake* or mislead, as in counseling or program evaluation situations where grades are not at stake. Self-reports are widely used to assess occupational interests, attitudes, temperament, and self-concept.

Interest Inventories.   Educational and psychological measurement can contribute several things to the related tasks of choosing an occupation and planning the educational preparation for it. Achievement testing provides useful, objective data, and aptitude testing enhances prediction of how well the person would be able to perform in preparation for the given occupation. However, these aren't enough. One may have the aptitude to learn a job and to acquire necessary knowledge and skills to do it, yet be miserable in the work.

One of the difficulties in measuring occupational interest is the fact that examinees often have no prior experience with the occupation being considered. Interest inventories help people organize what they already know about themselves. They typically provide norm-referenced interpretation of responses to objective items. Many of the items concern common activities that secondary students understand from their personal experience.

In receiving and understanding the results of interest inventories, students need to understand what was measured—their self-reports of interests and preferences. It is common for them to jump track and think of the inventory as a test of maximum performance like an achievement test. A tell-tale student comment is, "How well did I do?" It is important to clarify that there are no good or bad areas of vocational interest, no right or wrong answers.

Students and parents often think interest scores tell what students *can* do best. They don't. The correlations between interest scores and corresponding abilities are close to zero. They are not good predictors of success in academic work or vocational training. They indicate what people would *enjoy* doing if they survive the training, not what they *can* do (Cronbach, 1990). Therefore it may be desirable to avoid the word "test" with such assessments, and describe them as inventories, scales, or surveys.

Some examples of interest inventories are the Kuder General Interest Survey, the Career Interest Inventory, the Self-Directed Search, and the Strong Interest Inventory.

The School Testing Program.   School administrators, and sometimes counselors, too, may have responsibility for the school-wide or district-wide use of published instruments. The process of planning a local testing program can yield benefits such as:

- Identifying evaluation needs of individuals and programs
- Prompting thoughtful review of school objectives
- Tracking characteristics of student subpopulations
- Highlighting ongoing efforts to improve the curriculum
- Providing articulation with state assessment programs
- Facilitating more effective interpretation and use of test results
- Enhancing chances of using instruments that will yield results that are comparable from year to year

A school testing program should not be imposed by administrative, board of education, or legislative fiat (Ebel & Frisbie, 1986). Most effective programs are planned by a committee or other cooperative structure. Participants should, at a minimum, include teachers, administrators, and guidance personnel because each has distinctive knowledge to contribute and because each group should feel ownership of the results. Lay persons such as parents or board members also may contribute constructively by bringing outside perspectives and enhancing the degree to which the plan will be acceptable to outside constituents.

The most important thing in selecting tests is to select those that improve decisionmaking. The committee should study the tests, manuals, and related materials, avoiding tests that have unclear or incomplete information.

A testing program entails expenses, and these costs must be budgeted.

Time of year (fall or spring) for testing merits careful attention. Each has advantages. Fall testing provides information to teachers that is helpful for diagnosing student needs. It also avoids tendencies to grade pupils and evaluate teachers with the results, and it discourages undesirable practices such as "teaching for the test." Spring testing is more amenable to evaluating the effectiveness of the school; however, it obtains information too late in the year for classroom planning and too late to correct learning deficiencies which it reveals.

Table 16-1 presents our views concerning the parts of minimum, medium, and comprehensive programs.

TABLE 16.1   Local District-Wide School Testing Programs

	EXAMPLE OF GRADE LEVELS AND TESTS IN VARIOUS LEVELS OF TESTING PROGRAMS		
	Minimal Program	*Medium Program*	*Comprehensive Program*
Achievement Battery	2, 4, 6, 8, 11	2, 4, 6, 8, 10, 12	1, 2, 3, 4, 5, 6, 7, 8, 10, 11, 12
Reading Test		1, 3	
School Aptitude	2, 4, 6	2, 4, 6, 10	1, 3, 5, 7, 10
Differential Aptitude	8, 11	8, 11	8, 11
Interest Survey	11	8, 11	8, 11
Adaptive Behavior			1, 4

Measures of Self-Concept.   Prior to the 1960s, many schools routinely screened for personal adjustment or self-concept in an effort to identify students in need of special attention. Then attitudes of conservative and liberal groups converged into concerns about invasion of student and family privacy and intrusiveness in general (Cronbach, 1990). The political climate now leads most schools to use measures of personal adjustment and self-concept only sparingly, and only after securing written consent from parents.

Measures of self-concept tend to be more intrusive and more threatening to both students and parents than interest inventories. They also are more vulnerable to distortion. Some responses to items are clearly more socially desirable than others, and in this culture there is a natural tendency to tilt responses in socially desirable directions. This not only includes intentional falsification, but also the general adaptive tendencies to present oneself in a favorable light. Thus, these scales are afflicted with more serious technical measurement problems than are achievement tests, aptitude tests, or even interest inventories.

Measures of self-concept include the Piers-Harris Self-Concept Scale (The Way I Feel About Myself), the Adjective Checklist, and the Tennessee Self-Concept Scale.

Measures of Adaptive Behavior.   Another important realm of behavior concerns self-help skills, how well students look after their own practical needs, and how dependable they are in taking responsibility for themselves in their daily routines. These domains encompass both maximum behaviors (e.g., knowing how to lock the house or take turns on the swing) and typical behaviors (e.g., remembering to lock the house or being willing to take turns).

Adaptive behavior scales use indirect assessment of certain important self-help motor activities, such as zipper use and teeth brushing, and mixed cognitive, psychomotor, and affective activities, such as street crossing. Typically, a standardized, structured interview is conducted with a parent or teacher of the child to obtain reports of the adaptive behaviors in which the individual does and does not engage.

Measures of adaptive behavior contribute to the comprehensive picture of the child's functioning. Many socialization behaviors are part of the school curriculum and are important to successful living. Systematic assessment of adaptive behaviors help balance schools' natural, yet undesirable, overemphasis on cognitive achievement.

Inadequacies in some everyday living behaviors (e.g., remembering one's keys and getting along with others at work or with one's parents, domestic partner, and children) cause people more trouble in life than inadequacies in academic skills such as spelling or computation. Schools would therefore better serve learners if they spent more energies in assessing and enhancing important adaptive behaviors and less in assessing the easier-to-measure, low-level cognitive outcomes of schooling (such as state capitals).

Yet the major uses of published adaptive behavior scales focus on persons who are thought to have various disabilities. Assessment of children with intellectual, emotional, or physical disabilities is both more common and more comprehensive as a result of the enactment in 1975 of P.L. 94-142 and later the IDEA 1997 legislation. Adaptive behavior scales include the Vineland Adaptive Behavior Scales, for which a Spanish-language version is available. This is especially important in helping make a distinction between clinical mental retardation and mere deficit in the language of the school that happens not to be the language of the home.

LOCATING AND EVALUATING PUBLISHED INSTRUMENTS

Finding published instruments from which to make informed selections requires certain specialized knowledge. This section describes the major sources of information about published measures and how they can be used to locate tests.

The subsequent task of evaluating available instruments in order to select the one that best meets one's needs requires a much more extensive professional knowledge base. That material has already been sketched in Chapter 14. Recall the characteristics of effective assessment instruments:

- Economic and practical considerations
- Validity
- A (domain-referenced and/or norm-referenced) basis for meaningful and relevant interpretations
- Reliability

We turn now to the task of finding the instruments and locating information with which to evaluate them. This discussion is applicable to all kinds of published instruments.

Analyzing the Need for Testing

Before embarking on a search for "the right" test, one needs to determine if a published instrument is needed at all. Recall from Chapter 1 that a test should not be used unless it is reasonable to expect it to help in decision making. As an example, the following list contains some of the reasons a school or district might consider using an achievement battery[1]:

- To provide parents with information concerning their child's achievement status
- To monitor student progress in basic skills
- To provide teachers with information that will help in establishing instructional groups for certain subjects (e.g., reading and math)
- To provide teachers with information useful in individualizing instruction
- To identify extremes of relative strengths and weaknesses in broad areas of achievement for any students exhibiting them
- To assess the extent to which each student is working up to her or his measured aptitude for schoolwork[2]
- To assess either intended or unintended strong and weak features of a school's curriculum in comparison with a national cross section of schools
- To assist in identifying students needing referral for assessment of the need for special services
- To provide information to various constituencies concerning student achievement

[1]Adapted from parts of Stanford Achievement Test Series Test Coordinators Handbook (The Psychological Corporation, 1990).

[2]Recall, however, that the assessment of aptitude-achievement discrepancies, although commonly attempted, is fraught with difficulties.

These and other reasons lead most schools to administer a published achievement battery or a comprehensive state assessment battery at least on alternate years between at least grades 3 and 8. Many schools test annually and some do so from grades K to 12.

Increasing numbers of states now mandate state assessments. This has caused some school districts to reduce their discretionary achievement testing in order to provide time to use required state tests.[3] In this section, however, we are addressing the selection of instruments where that professional decision may be made at the district level.

The first and most important steps in test selection are to consider why a test is needed, what type of information it is likely to yield, and how that information will be used (Mehrens & Lehmann, 1991). These considerations will go far to prevent the use of tests whose results fail to serve useful decision-making purposes.

Locating Available Tests

Having decided to select a test, a school or district next needs to locate those instruments from which the choice can be made. Two primary sources of information about available published instruments are publishers' catalogs and *Tests in Print.* These may be consulted in either order, depending on convenience.

Test Publishers' Catalogs.   Test publishers, like other merchants, promote their products. Their catalogs are the advertising medium most helpful to people in search of prospective instruments.

Although scores of test publishers exist (Plake & Impara, 2001), most instruments can be secured from a few publishers/distributors, for example, Harcourt Educational Measurement, McGraw-Hill, Riverside, and American Guidance Service. Some school districts maintain a collection of current catalogs. An exhaustive list of test publishers can be found in the current edition of *Tests in Print,* which is discussed in the next section.

Catalogs are, of course, good sources for learning about available tests. They are the best means of learning the current prices. They also provide excellent information about the types of derived scores supplied with an instrument and the amount of time it takes to administer it. Beyond that, one should remember that catalogs are designed to sell instruments. Hence, they are *not* good sources of information on such attributes as validity for various test uses, the excellence of the normative data, and the degree to which the product is reliable. Such information is not neatly summarized in catalogs. For such data, the test manual(s) must be consulted.

Tests in Print.   A particularly useful reference is a series that lists instruments that are commercially available. *Tests in Print V* (Murphy, Plake, Impara, & Spies, 2002) is the most recent edition at this writing. ***Tests in Print*** is revised at approximately three-year intervals. At times when its latest edition is recent, this is a singularly effective resource for learning of the existence of English language measures one might wish to consider. Between editions, it may need to be supplemented with current test catalogs.

---

[3]It isn't clear to us why assessment of achievement in subjects such as reading and math should be undertaken simultaneously state by state. Is reading different in some way between Colorado and Ohio? Is math in Alaska different from math in Florida? How many times does the wheel have to be invented? We believe the underlying reasons for state assessment to be much more political than educational!

The first two steps in the test-selection process have now been addressed. Figure 16.3 pictures these and the remaining steps. After analyzing the needs for an instrument and deciding that one is needed, one learns of the available options from which to choose. The next two steps—reading reviews about the tests under consideration and studying them and their manuals—can be undertaken in either order.

Test Reviews.   It is wise to get some expert opinion before making a final test-selection decision, and multiple expert opinions are better than only one. Such opinions are most readily available in the form of test reviews. Unless an instrument is very new, it is likely that reviews of it (or at least of an earlier edition) have been published.

Reviews ordinarily result from an editor inviting experts to review a particular instrument. Reviewers ordinarily try to provide an evenhanded evaluation of the major features of the instrument by use of recognized professional criteria, the latest summary of which is *Standards for Educational and Psychological Testing* (AERA, 1999).

Several professional journals publish test reviews. A reading journal may contain reviews of reading tests, a counseling journal may offer reviews of instruments relevant to counseling, and so on. Library databases and indices are the best way to locate journal-published reviews of a particular test.

The best single place to locate reviews or critiques of particular tests is in volumes of instrument reviews. By far the best known of these is a series, published since 1938 at irregular intervals, known as the ***Mental Measurements Yearbook (MMY).*** Founded and long edited by O. K. Buros, the "yearbooks" are now published or supplemented every year or two by the Buros Institute at the University of Nebraska. *The Fifteenth Mental Measurements Yearbook* (Plake, Impara, & Spies, 2003) is the most recent at this writing.

The *MMY*s aspire to identify all tests published worldwide in English. Those instruments supported by data concerning such issues as reliability, validity, and reference-group data are ordinarily reviewed independently by two reviewers. Instruments lacking all supporting data are listed

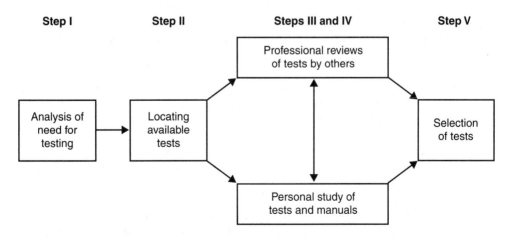

FIGURE 16.3   Flow Chart for Test Selection.

with an explanation that they were not reviewed because of lack of essential information. Likewise, instruments for which the publishers refuse to provide information are listed with that explanation of their not being reviewed.

Between publications, research libraries can access recent (yet-to-be-published on paper) reviews through SilverPlatter. The web site of the Buros Institute, http://www.unl.edu/buros/, is the best source of current information about *Tests in Print, MMY*s, and other products.

Although *MMY* reviews provide descriptive information for each instrument, the reviews *focus on critical evaluation* of the measure. Such volumes are housed in most large research libraries in the reference section (with encyclopedias, dictionaries, etc.) where they cannot be checked out.

A word might be imparted concerning the sophistication of persons who are invited to review tests in *MMY*s or journals. Their insightfulness and attentiveness to detail varies greatly. Most are highly competent professionals whose reviews share considerable consensus. However, a few are written by persons who are relatively unsophisticated in assessment. It is, therefore, wise to take the contents of a review as points to be given serious consideration, but not to blindly accept a reviewer's judgments.

A word about style may also be helpful. Reviewers usually try to be mannerly. Most are reluctant to say anything as strong as, "In the total absence of reliability data, this test should not be used for any applied use" or "In view of the confused and confusing discussion of validity, this test is not recommended for any foreseeable purpose." About the strongest negative condemnation that most reviews are willing to make is something along the lines, "The release of this instrument was seriously premature" or "This test can be recommended for research purposes only." Readers should understand that such statements are strong indications that avoidance is being advised.

At this point, it would be worth your while to read the most recent *MMY* reviews of two or three tests that are of interest to you. Compare and contrast the comments of different reviewers of the same test.

Figure 16.3 shows steps III and IV to be parallel, indicating that their order is variable. Persons considering tests may choose to obtain copies of the instruments and their supporting publications or to read the reviews first. The choice may well be based on convenience. Regardless of order, however, both steps are important. If the *MMY* lists a test for which no pertinent data are available or for which the publisher will not supply data, avoidance of the instrument would obviously be prudent. On occasion, however, a relatively new instrument may not be listed in the *MMY*. In that case, the next step becomes even more crucial.

Specimen Sets.   Just as a prospective house buyer should make a very careful inspection of the house, prospective test buyers should make a very detailed examination of the measure being considered. This is enabled by securing from the publisher or distributor an examination kit or a specimen set for the instrument. This should include:

- A copy of at least one form of the test (at the level(s) of interest if the instrument has multiple levels).
- A copy of each answer medium available.
- A manual containing administration and scoring information.
- Information concerning reference group sampling, reliability, and validity. This may be included in the above manual or contained in additional manual(s) or technical supplements.

Here is the place that your command of the material in Chapter 14 is applied to the assessment of published instruments. Issues of economy or practicality will have been addressed from information secured earlier from the test catalogs. Following are three paragraphs that review the essential characteristics of all measures.

To be useful, a test must be *interpretable*. Interpretability via domain referencing is best evaluated by examining the domain description in the manual, considering the domain specifications, and judging the match between the test content and the domain that should be incisively described. Interpretability via norm referencing is best judged by examining the manual's description of the kind(s) of reference group(s) provided, evaluation of the adequacy with which sampling was conducted, and judging the relevance of the reference group(s) for one's intended test use(s).

Validity is also an essential characteristic of effective measures. In the case of achievement tests, validity interest focuses primarily on test content; this is investigated by studying the rationale and methods of content selection described in the manual, examining the table of specifications in the manual, and especially, *scrutinizing the test, item by item.* In the case of predictive tests, interest focuses mainly on criterion-related, predictive validity evidence; data concerning this are most often available in the test manual or technical supplements. In the case of tests designed to assess other constructs, a variety of construct-related validity evidence will probably be most important. It is most commonly found in the technical manual or in research publications that are cited in the manual.

Finally, *reliability* is an essential feature of all effective measures. It is a fundamental obligation of authors and publishers to supply such information *for every score and subscore provided.* Test manuals and technical supplements are the primary source of information concerning reliability and standard errors of measurement. Regardless of whether the test is designed for norm- or domain-referenced interpretations, information about the consistency of all its scores is essential. Prudent prospective buyers will study such data carefully—or deplore its absence—before deciding for or against purchase.

Selection.   The final step in the instrument-selection process comes after reviewing the measure and its manual(s) and after studying the reasoned evaluations of others (if available). In most cases, those making the selection decision will experience some ambivalence. One competitor may be accompanied by the most reassuring reliability data, one may have the best construct representation, another may be the easiest to interpret, and yet another may be the least expensive. Final decisions are often prefaced with phrases like, "all things considered" and "on balance." Such phrases catch the spirit of what informed test selection involves—the balanced consideration of all the pertinent characteristics of effective measures.

CHAPTER RECAP

Standardized assessment instruments have been used for a variety of purposes over the millennia. However, recently developed measures usually have several features of interpretability, validity, reliability, and practicality that render them much more dependable and user-friendly than those of ancient times!

Published tests are often technically superior to teacher-made tests and are typically accompanied by reference-group data external to the particular class. In achievement tests, the trade-off is that published measures are not customized to the needs of the individual class. Achievement batteries offer the major additional advantage of enabling norm-referenced comparison of achievement among several content areas, between achievement in successive years, and, in some cases, between achievement and aptitude measures. These interpretations involve difference scores and each has its hazards; nevertheless, the importance of such comparisons prompts many users of achievement batteries to use them.

Aptitude tests differ from achievement tests more in degree than in kind. In contrast to achievement measures, aptitude tests are designed mainly for predictive use, have scores that are less sensitive to short-term instruction, and are usually broader in scope. Some provide only a global score, whereas others are designed to profile several different kinds of aptitude, and still others serve both purposes. Various aptitude tests differ in their aims. Some serve only narrow purposes (e.g., dental school admissions). Others are used to make many different kinds of academic predictions. Scores of most aptitude tests are interpreted with respect to age-based reference groups.

So-called intelligence tests and the IQ scores that have traditionally accompanied them have been misunderstood by large segments of the public to represent a much wider spectrum of valued attributes than such tests actually measure, to represent inborn capacity, and to represent something that is relatively unchangeable. Users of such tests need to take pains to ensure that people who receive the scores understand the falsity of each of these ideas. The communication is best achieved by avoiding the term "intelligence" and replacing it with more accurate descriptive terms such as "school abilities," "academic aptitude," and "cognitive abilities." Similarly, IQs are derived scores that are best avoided; percentile ranks serve much better for interpretation without misconceptions.

Commercially produced instruments vary greatly in quality. Professionals who use published measures should adopt a cautious attitude toward evaluating them. The merits of each measure should be thoughtfully considered in light of evidence that the authors and others have provided. Test users can obtain much help in evaluating tests by studying the criteria by which instruments are evaluated. The best compilation of professional opinion concerning bases for evaluating published instruments is *Standards for Educational and Psychological Testing* (AERA, 1999). Having decided to adopt a given test, one should maintain an evaluative mode in considering various interpretive aids, report forms, and scoring services that can be purchased for the test.

In addition to its surface content, this chapter has woven many key concepts from earlier parts of the book into a discussion of published measures. This was done both to enlighten discussion of commercially available instruments and to serve as an integrating review of relevant prior learning.

EPILOGUE

THE VALIDITY OF CLASSROOM ASSESSMENTS

In Chapter 1, the validity of the use of an instrument or a procedure was given a preliminary and jargon-free description of being the collective extent to which it:

- Assesses what it is supposed to assess
- Measures all that it is supposed to measure
- Assesses the subelements in the desired proportions
- Taps nothing besides what it is supposed to tap
- Has desirable consequences
- Is free from adverse consequences

Let's now engage in a brief unifying review of these six points with the aim of beholding, better understanding, and more fully appreciating how various topics throughout the book are woven together in order to achieve overall validity of classroom assessment.

Measuring the Intended Subject Matter and Mental Processes.   The answer to the question, "Does a test measure what it is supposed to measure?" is a central concern of validity. A math computation test used to assess spelling or math application clearly isn't valid for those purposes even though it might be a good measure of math computation. Similarly, a paper-pencil test isn't a valid way to find out if a person can ice-skate. Chapters 2 and 5 addressed planning assessments to tap the desired kinds of learning. Chapters 6 through 9 provided assistance in constructing and scoring objective tests, product measures, and performance tests in ways to ensure that they measure what they were intended to measure. This includes measuring achievement with appropriate realism or authenticity. Chapter 12 focused on marking and reporting practices that cause marks to reflect what they are meant to report. Finally, Chapter 16 addressed the selection of published achievement tests that assess the intended subject matter and mental processes.

Assessing All That One Intends to Assess.   As mentioned in Chapters 1 and 2, educators have long been aware that teacher-made and published assessments often neglect complex cognitive processes as well as affective, social, and psychomotor objectives. Chapter 5 urged planning to ensure that all intended kinds of learning were assessed, and Chapters 6 through 9 addressed how to measure varied kinds of learning.

Assessing the Components in the Desired Proportions.   Chapters 2 and 4 provided assistance in clearly identifying one's objectives for instruction and assessment. Chapters 5 through 10 focused on preestablishing and achieving desired weights among objectives and among subject matter topics.

From a different angle, Chapters 8 and 9 addressed the development of scoring rubrics that enable one to provide the desired relative weights to various elements of a product or performance.

Chapter 11 provided methods for ensuring planned proportionality among the components that contribute to grades. Chapters 11 and 15 noted that only certain kinds of derived scores reflect differences between successive points in uniform scales, thereby avoiding inadvertent disproportionality among scores. Finally, Chapter 16 addressed how published achievement, interest, and aptitude batteries can provide coverage to various subdomains without leaving holes of unassessed material and without wasteful overlap.

Measuring No Unintended Components.   Chapters 6 through 10 pointed out numerous ways in which objective tests, essays and other product measures, and performance assessments can avoid tapping such attributes as test wiseness, unintended emphasis on speed, or unintended emphasis on enabling abilities such as being able to read math application problems. Chapters 8 and 9 also focused on the use of rating rubrics to help teachers assess achievement without being unduly influenced by extraneous factors such as handwriting (in, say, a history test) or eloquence of expression or neatness (in, say, a biology test). In discussing assessment accommodation for persons with disabilities, Chapter 13 highlighted additional provisions that sometimes need to be made to prevent a test from tapping unintended and irrelevant capabilities, such as vision in an objective social studies test. Some aspects of test fairness discussed in Chapter 14 concern avoiding the measurement of irrelevant examinee characteristics. The need for reliable measures, emphasized in Chapter 14, argued for using assessments that aren't contaminated by random chance. Finally, item analysis, addressed in Chapter 10, also focuses on minimizing random measurement error.

Achieving Desirable Consequences from Assessments.   Chapter 1 launched the theme that classroom assessment practices influence what students try to learn, how much they study, and how they pace their study. This theme of "harness assessment power" has permeated the entire book. The benefits of harnessing test power were central in Chapters 2, 3, and 4 to the need to use a kind of instructional objective with each of three kinds of subject matter that is appropriate to the kind of learning and kind of transfer that is sought. Similarly, the consequences of decisions concerning how to have individual differences expressed, whether to use mastery or differentiating tests, what kinds of scores to use, and what kinds of interpretations to make were considered in Chapters 3 and 4.

Pursuit of desirable consequences was behind the strong recommendation in Chapter 5 that assessment be planned in conjunction with the planning of instruction in order to use assessment power to the best advantage. Consideration of consequences was also a key part of the rationale in Chapters 5 through 9 for providing appropriate assessment emphasis to both simple kinds of learning and to complex learning targets.

The importance of attending to consequences of assessment practices was especially emphasized in Chapters 2, 4, 5, 8, and 9, which, in numerous practical ways, urged educators to let students know what is expected of them so that they will know the criteria that will be used to assess them and therefore work on the outcomes that teachers deem important. At the same time, students gain proficiency in self-assessment.

Major emphasis was also given in Part II to the importance of achieving balance among authenticity (or realness to life), reliability (or consistency) of measurement, and economy of resources (e.g., testing time, scoring time, and expenditures). The flow chart shown in Chapter 9 is repeated here as Figure E.1, helps educators avoid the undesirable consequences of neglecting any of these three attributes while pursuing another with inappropriate exuberance.

FIGURE E.1   **Decision-Making Flow Chart.**

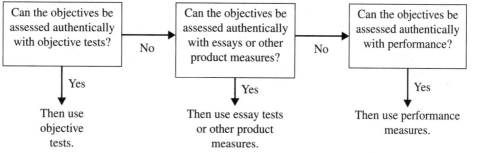

Caution 1. This flow chart is only applicable to the assessment of short-term objectives of maximum performance. It does not address objectives concerning typical performance or long-term objectives.

Caution 2. The issues leading to this flow chart are not the only issues that merit consideration. For example, the consequences of evaluation methods on student effort, balanced assessment, and logistic issues also merit consideration.

Chapter 12 addressed the purposes of marks and communication with parents and others in situations where transmittal of information leads to desirable consequences. In further pursuit of these favorable consequences of communication, Chapter 15 provided means of indicating both the extent and the limits of what we know from test scores.

In Chapter 14, the relative consequences of two kinds of referral errors—referring a student who turns out not to have the suspected condition and failing to refer a person who really does have the condition—led to the advice, "When in doubt, refer." Finally, the importance of anticipating and monitoring the consequences of classroom assessment was reviewed in Chapter 14.

Avoiding Undesirable Consequences from Assessment.   This aspect of validity is, of course, the inverse of the previous one. Along these lines, use of the flow chart in Figure E.1 yields balance among authenticity, reliability, and economy. This balance, pictured in Figure E.2, safeguards validity by preventing any of the three elements from being unacceptably low.

FIGURE E.2   **Maximizing Validity with Balance Among Authenticity, Reliability, and Economy.**

In addition, Chapters 3 and 4 were especially relevant to the avoidance of undesirable consequences that so often result when the eight aspects of context-adaptive planning for effective teaching are mismatched. Figure E.3, which is repeated from Chapter 4, reflects these interrelated concepts.

Concluding Statement.   These pieces converge into the "big picture"—a vision splendid—of teachers using valid classroom assessment practices to make major positive contributions to student learning.

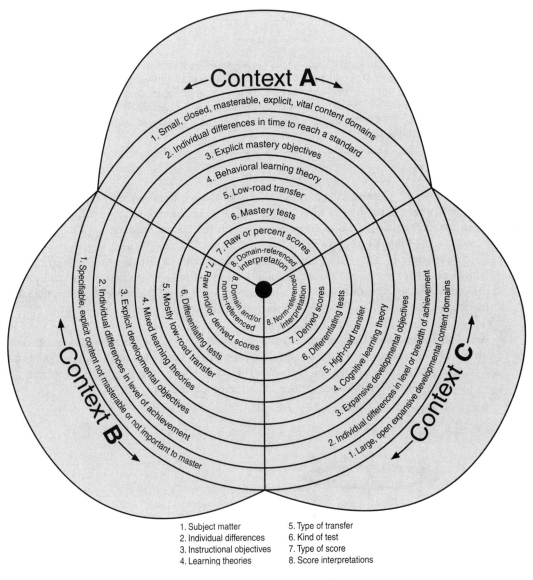

1. Subject matter
2. Individual differences
3. Instructional objectives
4. Learning theories
5. Type of transfer
6. Kind of test
7. Type of score
8. Score interpretations

FIGURE E.3   The CAP Perspective: Context-Adaptive Planning.

REFERENCES

Ahmann, S. J., & Glock, M. D. (1981). *Evaluating student progress: Principles of tests and measurements* (6th ed.). Boston: Allyn and Bacon.

Airasian, P. W. (2001). *Classroom assessment* (4th ed.). New York: McGraw-Hill.

American Educational Research Association, American Psychological Association, National Council on Measurement in Education. (1999). *Standards for educational and psychological testing* (3rd ed.). Washington, DC: Author.

American Psychological Association. (1985). *Standards for educational and psychological testing.* Washington, DC: Author.

Amrein, A. L., & Berliner, D. C. (2003). The effects of high-stakes testing on student motivation and learning. *Educational Leadership, 60*(5), 32–38.

Anastasi, A. (1958). Heredity, environment, and the question of "how"? *Psychological Review, 65,* 197–208.

Anastasi, A. (1976). *Psychological testing* (4th ed.). New York: Macmillan.

Anastasi, A., & Urbina, S. (1997). *Psychological testing* (7th ed.). Upper Saddle River, NJ: Prentice-Hall.

Anderson, L. W., & Krathwohl, D. R. (Eds.). (2001). *A taxonomy for learning, teaching, and assessing.* New York: Longman.

Angoff, W. H. (1988). The nature-nurture debate, aptitudes, and group differences. *American Psychologist, 43,* 713–720.

Arlin, M. (1984). Time, equality, and mastery learning. *Review of Educational Research, 54,* 65–86.

Arter, J. (1999). Teaching about performance assessment. *Educational Measurement: Issues and Practice, 18*(2), 30–44.

Arter, J., & McTighe, J. (2001). *Scoring rubrics in the classroom: Using performance criteria for assessing and improving student performance.* Thousand Oaks, CA: Corwin.

Babbie, E. (2001). *The practice of social research* (9th ed.). Belmont, CA: Wadsworth.

Bandura, A. (1977). *Social learning theory.* Englewood Cliffs, NJ: Prentice-Hall.

Bandura, A. (1986). *Social foundations of thought and action: A social cognitive theory.* Englewood Cliffs, NJ: Prentice-Hall.

Bangert-Downs, R. L., Kulik, J. A., & Kulik, C. C. (1986). *Effects of frequent classroom testing.* (ERIC Document Reproduction Service No. 274672).

Bayer, L. M., & Bayley, N. (1976). *Growth diagnosis* (2nd ed.). Chicago: University of Chicago Press.

Bigge, M. K., & Shermis, S. S. (1992). *Learning theories for teachers* (5th ed.). New York: Harper-Collins.

Binet, A., & Simon, T. (1916). *The development of intelligence in children.* Baltimore: Williams & Wilkins.

Bloom, B. S. (1976). *Human characteristics and school learning.* New York: McGraw-Hill.

Bloom, B. S., Engelhart, M. D., Furst, E. J., Hill, W. H., Krathwohl, D. R. (1956). *Taxonomy of educational objectives; Handbook 1: Cognitive domain.* New York: McKay.

Bogle, J. C. (1999). *Common sense on mutual funds: New imperatives for the intelligent investor.* New York: John Wiley & Sons.

Boyer, E. K. (1987). *College: The undergraduate experience in America.* New York: Harper & Row.

Bracey, G. W. (2000). *A short guide to standardized testing.* Bloomington, IN: Phi Delta Kappa Educational Foundation.

Bracey, G. W. (2002). The 12th Bracey report on the condition of public education. *Phi Delta Kappan, 83,* 135–150.

Brennan, R. L. (1998). Misconceptions at the intersection of measurement theory and practice. *Educational Measurement: Issues and Practices, 17*(1), 5–9.

Brennan, R. L. (2001). An essay on the history and future of reliability from the perspective of replications. *Journal of Educational Measurement, 38,* 295–317.

Brookhart, S. M. (2002). What will teachers know about assessment, and how will that improve instructions? In R. W. Lissitz & W. D. Schafer (Eds.), *Assessment in educational reform: Both means and ends.* Boston: Allyn and Bacon.

Brookhart, S. M. (2004). *Grading.* Upper Saddle River, NJ: Pearson.

Brownell, W. A. (1946). In N. F. Henry (Ed.). *The forty-fifth yearbook of the national society for the study of education, Part I: The measurement of understanding.* Chicago: University of Chicago Press.

Bruner, J. (1977). *The process of education.* Cambridge, MA: Harvard University Press.

Bryant, R., Dean, M., Elrod, G. F., & Blackbourn, J. M. (1999). Rural general education teachers' opinions of adaptations for inclusive classrooms: A renewed call for dual licensure. *Rural Special Education Quarterly, 18*(1), 5–11.

Bursuck, W., Polloway, E. A., Plante, L., Epstein, M. H., Jayanthi, M., & McConeghy, J. (1996). Report card grading and adaptations: A national survey of classroom practices. *Exceptional Children, 62*(4), 301–318.

Butler, F. M. (1997). A better way to grade special education students. *CEC Today,* 4(3), 14.

Canady, R. L., & Seyfarth, J. T. (1979). *How parent-teacher conferences build partnerships (Fastback #132).* Bloomington, IN: Phi Delta Kappa Educational Foundation.

Carr, J. F., & Harris, D. E. (2001). *Succeeding with standards: Linking curriculum, assessment, and action planning.* Alexandria, VA: Association for Supervision and Curriculum Development.

Chase, C. I. (1968). The impact of some obvious variables on essay-test scores. *Journal of Educational Measurement, 5,* 315–318.

Chase, C. I. (1979). Impact of achievement expectations and handwriting quality on scoring essay tests. *Journal of Educational Measurement, 16,* 39–42.

Chase, C. I. (1983). Essay test scoring: Interaction of relevant variables. *Journal of Educational Measurement, 23,* 33–41.

Cole, N. S., & Moss, P. A. (1989). Bias in test use. In R. L. Linn (Ed.), *Educational measurement* (3rd ed.). New York: Macmillan.

Congdon, P. J., & McQueen, J. (2000). The stability of rater severity in large-scale assessment programs. *Journal of Educational Measurement, 39,* 163–178.

Cook, W. W., & Clymer, T. (1962). Accelerating and retardation. In Henry, N. F. (Ed.), *Individualizing instruction: The sixty-first yearbook of the National Society for the Study of Education, Part 1.* Chicago: The National Society for the Study of Education.

Council for Exceptional Children Public Policy Unit. Council for Exceptional Children. (1997). Making assessments of diverse students meaningful. *CEC Today,* 4(4), 1, 9.

Cox, W. F. Jr., & Dunn, T. G. (1979). Mastery learning: A psychological trap? *Educational Psychologist, 14,* 24–29.

Cronbach, L. J. (1971). Comments on mastery learning and its implications for curriculum development. In W. W. Eisner (Ed.), *Confronting curriculum reform.* Boston: Little, Brown.

Cronbach, L. J. (1984). *Essentials of psychological testing* (4th ed.). New York: Harper & Row.

Cronbach, L. J. (1990). *Essentials of psychological testing* (5th ed.). New York: Harper Collins.

Cronbach, L. J., & Furby, L. (1971). How we should measure "change"—or should we? *Psychological Bulletin, 74,* 68–80.

Crooks, T. J. (1988). The impact of classroom evaluation practices on students. *Review of Educational Research, 58,* 438–481.

Cross, L. H., & Frary, R. B. (1999). Hodgepodge grading: Endorsed by students and teachers alike. *Applied measurement in education, 12*(1) 53–72.

Danielson, C. (1996). *Enhancing professional practice: A framework for teaching.* Alexandria, VA: Association for Supervision and Curriculum Development.

Darling-Hammond, L. (1993). Reframing the school reform agenda. *Phi Delta Kappan, 74,* 752–761.

Deci, E. L., Koestner, R., & Ryan, R. M. (2001). Extrinsic rewards and intrinsic motivation in education: Reconsidered once again. *Review of Educational Research, 71*(1), 1–27.

Dettmer, P. (1995). New blooms for established fields. Annual conference of the Kansas Association for Gifted, Talented, and Creative. Topeka, KS.

Dettmer, P. (1997, September). *New blooms for established fields.* Presented at the annual conference of the Kansas Association for Gifted, Talented, and Creative, Hutchinson, KS.

Dettmer, P., Thurston, L. P., & Dyck, N. (2002). *Consultation, collaboration, and teamwork for students with special needs* (4th ed.). Boston: Allyn and Bacon.

Dillman, D. A. (2000). *Mail and Internet surveys: The tailored design* (2nd ed.). New York: John Wiley & Sons.

Dodge, K. A., Putallaz, M., & Malone, D. (2002). Coming of age: The Department of Education. *Phi Delta Kappan, 83*(9), 674–676.

Dooley, D. (2001). *Social research methods* (4th ed.). Upper Saddle River, NJ: Prentice-Hall.

Dunbar, S. B., Koretz, D. M., & Hoover, H. D. (1991). Quality control in the development and use of performance assessments. *Applied Measurement in Education, 4*(4), 289–303.

Ebel, R. K., & Frisbie, D. A. (1986). *Essentials of educational measurement* (4th ed.). Englewood Cliffs, NJ: Prentice-Hall.

Elliott, J., Ysseldyke, J., Thurlow, M., & Erickson, R. (1998). What about assessment and accountability? Practical implications for educators. *Teaching Exceptional Children, 31*(1), 20–27.

Elliott, S. N., Kratochwill, T. R., & Schulte, A. G. (1998). The assessment accommodation checklist. *Teaching Exceptional Children, 31*(2), 10–14.

Ericksen, S. C. (1983). Private measures of good teaching. *Teaching of Psychology, 10,* 133–136.

Feldt, L. S., & Brennan, R. L. (1989). Reliability. In R. L. Linn (Ed.), *Educational measurement* (3rd ed.). New York: Macmillan.

Findley, W. G., & Scates, D. E. (1946). Principles applicable to the evaluation of understanding. In N. F. Henry (Ed.). *The forty-fifth yearbook of the national society for the study of education, Part I: The measurement of understanding.* Chicago: University of Chicago Press.

Fitzpatrick, R., & Morrison, E. J. (1971). Performance and product evaluation. In Thorndike, R. L. (Ed.). *Educational measurement* (2nd ed.). Washington, DC: American Council on Education.

Flaugher, R. L. (1978). The many definitions of test bias. *American Psychologist, 33,* 671–679.

Fleming, M., & Chambers, B. (1983). Teacher-made tests: Windows on the classroom. In W. E. Hathaway (Ed.), *Testing in the schools.* San Francisco: Jossey-Bass.

Forsyth, R. A. (1991). Do NAEP scales yield valid criterion-referenced interpretations? *Educational Measurement: Issues and Practices, 10,* 3–9, 16.

Frisbie, D. A. (1988). Reliability of scores from teacher-made tests. *Educational Measurement: Issues and Practice, 7,* 25–35.

Frisbie, D. A., & Becker, D. F. (1991). An analysis of textbook advice about true-false tests. *Applied Measurement in Education, 4,* 67–83.

Fuchs, L. S., Fuchs, D., Eaton, S. B., Hamlett, C., Binkley, E., & Crouch, R. (2000). Using objective data sources to enhance teacher judgments about test accommodations. *Exceptional Children, 67*(1), 67–81.

Gandal, M., & McGiffert, L. (2003). The power of testing. *Educational Leadership, 60*(5), 39–42.

Gardiner, S. (2001). Cybercheating: A new twist on an old problem. *Phi Delta Kappan, 83,* 172–174.

Gardner, H. (1983). *Frames of mind: The theory of multiple intelligences.* New York: Basic Books.

Gardner, H. (1993). *Multiple intelligences: The theory and practice.* New York: Basic Books.

Geisert, P. G., & Futrell, M. K. (1995). *Teachers, computers, and curriculum* (2nd ed.). Boston: Allyn and Bacon.

Gettinger, M. (1984). Individual differences in time needed for learning: A review of literature. *Educational Psychologist, 19,* 15–29.

Glaser, R. (1963). Instructional technology and the measurement of learning outcomes: Some questions. *American Psychologist, 18,* 519–521.

Glass, G. V., & Smith, M. L. (1978). The technology and politics of standards. *Journal Educational Technology, 18,* 12–18.

Glover, J. A. (1989). The testing phenomenon: Not gone but nearly forgotten. *Journal of Educational Psychology, 81,* 392–399.

Good, P. (Ed.). (1974). *Human behavior: The individual.* New York: Time-Life Books.

Goodall, J. (1999). *Reason for hope.* New York: Warner.

Gravetter, F. J., & Wallnau, L. B. (2000). *Statistics for the behavioral sciences* (5th ed.). Belmont, CA: Wadsworth.

Gronlund, N. E. (1970). *Stating behavioral objectives for classroom instruction.* New York: Macmillan.

Gronlund, N. E. (1985). *Stating objectives for classroom instruction* (3rd ed.). New York: Macmillan.

Gronlund, N. E. (2000). *How to write and use instructional objective* (6th ed.). Upper Saddle River, NJ: Merrill.

Gullickson, A. R. (1984). Teacher perspectives of their instruc-tional use of tests. *Journal of Educational Research, 77,* 244–248.

Guskey, T. R. (1997). *Implementing mastery learning* (2nd ed.). Belmont, CA: Wadsworth.

Guskey, T. R. (2002). Computerized grade books and the myth of objectivity. *Phi Delta Kappan, 83,* 775–780.

Gustafson, J., & Undbeim, J. O. (1996). Individual differences in cognitive functions. In D. C. Berliner & R. C. Calfee (Eds.), *Handbook of educational psychology.* New York: Macmillan Library Reference USA.

Haertel, E. (1986). *Choosing and using classroom tests: Teachers' perspectives on assessment.* Paper presented at the annual meeting of the American Educational Research Association, San Francisco, CA.

Haladyna, T. M. (1997). *Writing test items to evaluate higher-order thinking.* Boston: Allyn and Bacon.

Haladyna, T. M., & Downing, S. M. (1989a). A taxonomy of multiple-choice item-writing rules. *Applied Measurement in Education, 1,* 37–50.

Haladyna, T. M., & Downing, S. M. (1989b). The validity of a taxonomy of multiple-choice item-writing rules. *Applied Measurement in Education, 5,* 73–88.

Hales, L. W., & Tokar, E. (1975). The effect of the quality of preceding responses in the grades assigned to subsequent responses to an essay question. *Journal of Educational Measurement, 12,* 115–118.

Hanna, G. S. (1988). Using percentile bands for meaningful descriptive test score interpretations. *Journal of Counseling and Development, 6,* 477–483.

Hanna, G. S. (1989). To change answers or not to change answers: That is the question. *The Clearing House, 62,* 414–416.

Hanna, G. S., & Cashin, W. E. (1988). *Improving college grading.* IDEA Paper No. 19, Manhattan, KS: Kansas State University, Center for Faculty Evaluation and Development.

Harrow, A. J. (1972). *A taxonomy of the psychomotor domain: A guide for developing behavioral objectives.* New York: McKay.

Henry, N. F. (Ed.). (1946). *The forty-fifth yearbook of the national society for the study of education, Part I: The measurement of understanding.* Chicago: University of Chicago Press.

Herman, J., Aschbacher, P., & Winters, L. (1992). *A practical guide to alternative assessment.* Alexandria, VA: Association for Supervision and Curriculum Development.

Hieronymus, A. N., Hoover, H. D., & Lindquist, E. G. (1986). *ITBS preliminary teacher's manual.* Chicago: Riverside.

Hills, J. R. (1981). *Measurement and evaluation in the classroom* (2nd ed.). Columbus, OH: Merrill.

Hills, J. R. (1991). Apathy concerning grading and testing. *Phi Delta Kappan, 72,* 540–545.

Hively, W. (1974). Domain-referenced testing: Part one. *Educational Technology, 14,* 5–10.

Hoover, H. D. (1984). The most appropriate scores for measuring educational development in the elementary schools: GE's. *Educational Measurement: Issues and Practice, 3,* 8–14.

Hopkins, K. D. (1998). *Educational and psychological measurement and evaluation* (8th ed.). Boston: Allyn and Bacon.

Howell, K. W., & Nolet, V. (2000). *Curriculum-based evaluation: Teaching and decision making* (3rd ed.). Belmont, CA: Wadsworth.

Hughes, D. C., Keeling, R., & Tuck, B. F. (1980). *Journal of Educational Measurement, 17,* 131–135.

James, W. (1899). *Talks to teachers on psychology and to students on some of life's ideas.* New York: Holt.

Jeager, R. M. (1987). Two decades of revolution in educational measurement. *Educational Measurement: Issues and Practice, 6,* 6–14.

Johnson, D. W., & Johnson, R. T. (2002). *Meaningful assessment: A manageable and cooperative process.* Boston: Allyn and Bacon.

Johnson, E., Kimball, K., Brown, S. O., & Anderson, D. (2001). A statewide review of the use of accommodations in large-scale, high-stakes assessments. *Exceptional Children, 67*(2), 251–264.

Johnson, F. R. (1976). *The reliability and concurrent validity of multiple-choice tests derived by four distractors selection procedures.* Unpublished doctoral dissertation. Kansas State University.

Kampfer, S. H., Horvath, L. S., Kleinert, H. L., & Kearns, J. F. (2001). Teachers' perceptions of one state's alternate assessment: Implications for practice and preparation. *Exceptional Children, 67*(3), 361–374.

Kane, M. T. (2001). Current concerns in validity theory. *Journal of Educational Measurement, 38,* 319–342.

Kane, M., Crooks, T., & Cohen, A. (1999). Validating measures of performance. *Educational Measurement: Issues and Practices, 18*(2), 5–17.

Kaplan, R. M., & Saccuzzo, D. P. (2001). *Psychological testing: Principles, applications and issues* (6th ed.). Belmont, CA: Wadsworth.

Kaufman, A. S., & Kaufman, N. L. (1983). *Kaufman Assessment Battery for Children interpretive manual.* Circle Pines, MN: American Guidance Service.

Kaufman, A. S., & Lichtenberger, E. O. (2002). *Assessing adolescent and adult intelligence* (2nd ed.). Boston: Allyn and Bacon.

Kerlinger, F. N. (1986). *Foundations of behavioral research* (3rd ed.). New York: Holt, Rinehart & Winston.

Kirst, M. W. (1991). Interview on assessment issues with Lorrie Shepard. *Educational Research, 20,* 21–23, 27.

Kleinert, H., Green, P., Hurte, M., Clayton, J., & Oetinger, C. (2002). Creating and using meaningful alternate assessments. *Teaching Exceptional Children, 34*(4), 40–47.

Kleinert, H. L., Haig, J., Kearns, J. F., & Kennedy, S. (2000). Alternate assessments: Lessons learned and roads to be taken. *Exceptional Children, 67*(1), 51–66.

Kleinert, H., & Thurlow, M. (2001). An introduction to alternate assessment. In H. Kleinert & J. Kearns (Eds.), *Alternate assessment: Measuring outcomes and supports for students with disabilities* (pp. 1–15). Baltimore: Paul H. Brookes.

Krathwohl, D. R. (1998). *Methods of educational and social science research* (2nd ed.). New York: Longman.

Krathwohl, D. R., Bloom, B. S., & Masia, B. B. (1964). *Taxonomy of educational objectives; Handbook II: Affective domain.* New York: McKay.

Krathwohl, D. R., & Payne, D. A. (1971). Defining and assessing educational objectives. R. L. Thorndike (Ed.), *Educational measurement* (2nd ed.). Washington, DC: American Council on Education.

Kubiszyn, T., & Borich, G. (2003). *Educational testing and measurement: Classroom application and practice* (7th ed.). New York: John Wiley & Sons.

Lewis, A. C. (2002a). The will to leave no child behind? *Phi Delta Kappan, 83*(5), 343–344.

Lewis, A. C. (2002b). A horse called NCLB. *Phi Delta Kappan, 84*(3), 179–180.

Linn, R. L., & Gronlund, N. E. (1995). *Measurement and evaluation in teaching* (7th ed.). Englewood Cliffs, NJ: Merrill.

Linn, R. L., & Gronlund, N. E. (2000). *Measurement and assessment in teaching* (8th ed.). Englewood Cliffs, NJ: Merrill.

Loree, M. R. (1948). *A study of a technique for improving tests.* Unpublished doctoral dissertation, University of Chicago, Illinois.

Lyman, H. B. (1998). *Test scores and what they mean* (6th ed.). Boston: Allyn and Bacon.

Mackenzie, D. E. (1983). Research for school improvement: An appraisal of some recent trends. *Educational Research Journal, 29,* 182–198.

Madaus, G. F., & O'Dwyer, L. M. (1999). A short history of performance assessment: Lessons learned. *Phi Delta Kappan, 80,* 688–695.

Mager, R. F. (1962). *Preparing objectives for programed instruction.* San Francisco: Fearon.

Mager, R. F. (1997). *Preparing instructional objectives* (3rd ed.). Atlanta: The Center for Effective Performance.

Marby, L. (1999). Writing to the rubric: Lingering effects of traditional standardized testing on direct writing assessment. *Phi Delta Kappan, 80,* 673–679.

Marshall, J. C. (1967). Composition errors and essay examination grades reexamined. *American Educational Research Journal, 4,* 375–385.

Marshall, J. C., & Powers, J. M. (1969). Writing neatness, composition errors and essay grades. *Journal of Educational Measurement, 6,* 97–101.

Marso, R. N., & Pigge, F. L. (1993). Teachers' testing knowledge, skills, and practices. In S. L. Wise (Ed.), *Teacher training in measurement and assessment skills*. Lincoln, NE: Buros Institute of Mental Measurements.

Martinez, M. E. (1999). Cognition and the question of test item format. *Educational Psychologist, 34*, 207–21.

Marzano, R. J. (2000). *Transforming classroom grading*. Alexandria, VA: Association for Supervision and Curriculum Development.

Mayer, R. E., & Wittrock, M. C. (1996). Problem-solving transfer. In D. C. Berliner and R. C. Calfee (Eds.), *Handbook of educational psychology*. New York: Macmillan.

McCammon, R. W. (1970). *Human growth and development*. Springfield, IL: Thomas.

McGloughlin, J. A., & Lewis, R. B. (1994). *Assessing special students* (4th ed.). New York: Merrill.

McKeachie, W. J. (1986). *Teaching tips* (8th ed.). Lexington, MA: D. C. Heath.

McMillan, J. H. (2001). Secondary teachers' classroom assessment and grading practices. *Educational Measurement: Issues and Practices, 20*, 20–32.

McMillan, J. H. (2004). *Classroom assessment: Principles and practices for effective instruction* (3rd ed.). Boston: Allyn and Bacon.

Mehrens, W. A., & Lehmann, I. (1991). *Measurement and evaluation in education and psychology* (4th ed.). Fort Worth, TX: Holt, Rinehart & Winston.

Mehrens, W. A., Popham, W. J., & Ryan, J. M. (1998). How to prepare students for performance assessments. *Educational Measurement: Issues and Practices, 17*(1), 18–22.

Messick, S. (1989). Validity. In Linn, R. L. (Ed.), *Educational measurement* (3rd ed.). New York: Macmillan.

Millman, J. (1970). Reporting student progress: A case for a criterion-referenced marking system. *Phi Delta Kappan, 52*, 226-230.

Millman, J., & Green, J. (1989). The specification and development of tests of achievement and ability. In Linn, R. L. (Ed.), *Educational measurement* (3rd ed.). New York: Macmillan.

Mueller, D. J., & Wasser, V. (1977). Implications of changing answers on objective tests items. *Journal of Educational Measurement, 14*, 9–13.

Munk, D. D., & Bursuck, W. D. (1998). Can grades be helpful and fair? *Educational Leadership, 55*(4), 44–47.

Murphy, L. L., & Impara, J. C. (Eds.). (1999). *Tests in Print V*. Lincoln, NE: University of Nebraska at Lincoln.

Murphy, L. L., Plake, B. S., Impara, J. C., & Spies, R. A. (2002). *Tests in print VI*. Lincoln, NE: The Buros Institute, University of Nebraska-Lincoln.

National Council for Accreditation of Teacher Education. (2001). *Professional standards for the accreditation of schools, colleges, and departments of education*. Washington, DC: Author.

Nitko, A. J. (1980). Distinguishing the many varieties of criterion-referenced tests. *Review of Educational Research, 50*, 461–485.

Nitko, A. J. (1989). Designing tests that are integrated with instruction. In Linn, R. L. (Ed.), *Educational measurement* (3rd ed.). New York: Macmillan.

Nitko, A. J. (2001). *Educational assessment of students* (3rd ed.). Upper Saddle River, NJ: Merrill.

Nitko, A. J. (2004). *Educational assessment of students* (4th ed.). Upper Saddle River, NJ: Pearson.

Nunnally, J. C. (1978). *Psychometric theory* (2nd ed.). New York: McGraw-Hill.

Oosterhof, A. (2001). *Classroom applications of educational measurement* (3rd ed.). Upper Saddle River, NJ: Merrill.

Oosterhof, A. (2003). *Developing and using classroom assessments* (3rd ed.). Upper Saddle River, NJ: Merrill.

Oosterhof, A. C. (1987). Obtaining intended weights when combining students' scores. *Educational Measurement: Issues and Practice, 6*, 29–37.

Ormrod, J. E. (2000). *Human learning* (3rd ed.). Upper Saddle River, NJ: Merrill.

Paris, S. G., & Cunningham, A. E. (1996). Children becoming students. In Berliner, D. C., & Calfee, R. C. (Eds.). *Handbook of Educational Psychology*. New York: Macmillan.

Payne, D. A. (1992). *Measuring and evaluating educational outcomes*. New York: Macmillan.

Payne, D. A. (1997). *Applied educational assessment*. Belmont, CA: Wadsworth.

Perkins, D., Tishman, S., Ritchhart, R., Donis, K., & Andrade, A. (2000). Intelligence in the wild: A dispositional view of intellectual traits. *Educational Psychology Review, 12*, 269–293.

Perkins, D. N., & Salomon, G. (1988). Teaching for transfer. *Educational Leadership, 46*, 22–32.

Petersen, N. S., Kolen, M. J., & Hoover, H. D. (1989). Scaling, norming, and equating. In Linn, R. L. (Ed.). *Educational measurement* (3rd ed.). New York: Macmillan.

Phillips, J. L. (2000). *How to think about statistics* (6th ed.). New York: Freeman.

Pitoniak, M. J., & Royer, J. M. (2001). Testing accommodations for examinees with disabilities: A review of psychometric, legal, and social policy issues. *Review of Educational Research, 71*(1), 53–104.

Plake, B. S., & Impara, J. C. (Eds.). (2001). *The fourteenth mental measurements yearbook*. Lincoln, NE: University of Nebraska at Lincoln.

Plake, B. S., Impara, J. C., & Spies, R. A. (2003). *The fifteenth mental measurements yearbook*. Lincoln, NE: The Buros Institute, University of Nebraska-Lincoln.

Pomerance, H. H., & Krall, J. M. (1979). *Growth standards in children*. New York: Harper and Row.

Popham, W. J. (1990). *Modern educational measurement: A practitioner's perspective* (2nd ed.). Englewood Cliffs, NJ: Prentice-Hall.

Popham, W. J. (1994). The instructional consequences of criterion-referenced clarity. *Educational Measurement: Issues and Practice, 13,* 15–18.

Popham, W. J. (1999). Why standardized tests don't measure educational quality. *Educational Leadership, 56*(6), 8–15.

Popham, W. J. (2000). *Modern educational measurement: Practical guidelines for educational leaders* (3rd ed.). Boston: Allyn and Bacon.

Popham, W. J. (2002). *Classroom assessment: What teachers need to know* (3rd ed.). Boston: Allyn and Bacon.

Rich, D. (1998). What parents want from teachers. *Educational Leadership, 55*(8), 37–39.

Ricks, J. H. (1971). Local norms—when and why. *Test Service Bulletin No. 58.* San Antonio: Psychological Corporation.

Robinson, C. E., & Craver, J. M. (1989). Assessing and grading student achievement. Arlington, VA: Educational Research Service cited in Marzano, R. J. (2000). *Transforming classroom grading.* Alexandria, VA: Association for Supervision and Curriculum Development.

Rolheiser, C., Bower, B., & Stevahn, L. (2000). *The portfolio organizer: Succeeding with portfolios in your classroom.* Alexandria, VA: Association for Supervision and Curriculum Development.

Rose, L. C. (2003). Public education's Trojan horse? *Phi Delta Kappan, 85*(1), 2.

Rosenblum, S., Weiss, P. L., & Parush, S. (2003). Product and process evaluation of handwriting difficulties. *Educational Psychology Review, 15*(1), 41–81.

Sadler, D. R. (1983). Evaluation and the improvement of academic learning. *Journal of Higher Education, 54,* 60–79.

Salomon, G., & Perkins, D. M. (1989). Rocky roads to transfer: Rethinking mechanisms of a neglected phenomenon. *Educational Psychologist, 24,* 113–142.

Salvia, J., & Ysseldyke, J. E. (1991). *Assessment in special and remedial education* (5th ed.). Boston: Houghton Mifflin.

Sanders, J. R., Hills, J. R., Nitko, A. J., Merwin, J. C., Trice, C., Dianda, M., & Schneider, J. (1990). Standards for teacher competence in educational assessment of students. *Educational Measurement: Issues and Practices, 9,* 30–32.

Sanders, J. R., & Vogel, S. R. (1993). The development of standards for teacher competence in educational assessment of students. In S. L. Wise (Ed.), *Teacher training in measurement and assessment skills.* Lincoln, NE: Buros Institute of Mental Measurements.

Sattler, J. M. (1992). *Assessment of children* (3rd ed.). San Diego: J. M. Sattler.

Sax, G. (1997). *Principles of educational and psychological measurement and evaluation* (4th ed.). Belmont, CA: Wadsworth.

Schunk, D. H. (2000). *Learning theories: An educational perspective.* Upper Saddle River, NJ: Merrill.

Shepard, L. A. (1990). Inflated test score gains: Is the problem old norms or teaching the test? *Educational Measurement: Issues and Practice, 9,* 15–22.

Shepard, L. A. (1991). Psychometricians' beliefs about learning. *Educational Researcher, 20,* 2–16.

Shepard, L. A. (2000). The role of assessment in a learning culture. *Educational Researcher, 29*(7), 4–14.

Shepard, L. A., & Smith, M. L. (1990). Synthesis of research on grade retention. *Educational Leadership, 47,* 84–88.

Silvaroli, N. J. (1986). *Classroom Reading Inventory* (5th ed.). Dubuque, IA: William C. Brown.

Silverlake, A. C. (1999). *Comprehending test manuals: A guide and workbook.* Los Angeles: Pyrczak.

Simpson, E. J. (1972). *The psychomotor domain, vol. 3.* Washington, DC: Gryphon House.

Singer, P. (2000). *Writings on an ethical life.* New York: Harper Collins.

Slavin, R. E. (1987a). A theory of school and classroom organization. *Educational Psychologist, 22,* 89–108.

Slavin, R. E. (1987b). Mastery learning reconsidered. *Review of Educational Research, 57,* 157–213.

Slavin, R. E. (1989). PET and the pendulum: Faddism in educational and how to stop it. *Phi Delta Kappan, 70,* 753–758.

Spinelli, C. G. (2002). *Classroom assessment for students with special needs in inclusive settings.* Upper Saddle River, NJ: Merrill Prentice-Hall.

Stainback, W., Stainback, S., & Stefanich, G. (1996). Learning together in inclusive classrooms: What about the curriculum? *Teaching Exceptional Children, 28*(5), 14–19.

Stalnaker, J. M. (1951). The essay type of examination. In E. F. Lindquist (Ed.). *Educational measurement.* Washington, DC: American Council on Education.

Stanley, J. C. (1971). Reliability. In R. L. Thorndike (Ed.), *Educational measurement* (2nd ed.). Washington, DC: American Council on Education.

Stanovich, K. E. (1991). Discrepancy definitions of reading disability: Has intelligence led us astray? *Reading Research Quarterly, 26,* 7–29.

Starch, D., & Elliott, E. (1912). Reliability of grading high-school work in English. *School Review, 20,* 442–457.

Starch, D., & Elliott, E. (1913). Reliability of grading work in history. *School Review, 21,* 676–681.

Stiggins, R. J. (1987). Design and development of performance assessments. *Educational Measurement: Issues and Practice, 6,* 33–42.

Stiggins, R. J. (1991). Assessment literacy. *Phi Delta Kapan, 72,* 534–539.

Stiggins, R. J. (1993). Teacher training in assessment: Overcoming the neglect. In S. L. Wise (Ed.), *Teacher training in measurement and assessment skills.* Lincoln, NE: Buros Institute of Mental Measurements.

Stiggins, R. J. (1997). *Student-centered classroom assessment* (2nd ed.). Upper Saddle River, NJ: Merrill.

Stiggins, R. J. (1999). Evaluating classroom assessment training in teacher education programs. *Educational Measurement: Issues and Practices, 18*(1), 23–27.

Stiggins, R. J. (2001). *Student-involved classroom assessment* (3rd ed.). Upper Saddle River, NJ: Prentice Hall.

Stiggins, R. J. (2002). Assessment crisis: The absence of assessment FOR learning. *Phi Delta Kappan, 83,* 758–765.

Stiggins, R. J., & Bridgeford, N. J. (1985). The ecology of classroom assessment. *Journal of Educational Measurement, 22,* 271–286.

Stiggins, R. J., & Bridgeford, N. J. (1986). Student evaluation. In R. A. Berk (Ed.), *Performance assessment.* Baltimore: Johns Hopkins University Press.

Stiggins, R. J., & Conklin, N. F. (1992). *In teachers' hands: Investigating the practices of classroom assessment.* Albany, NY: State University of New York Press.

Stiggins, R. J., Conklin, N. F., & Bridgeford, N. J. (1986). Classroom assessment: A key to effective education. *Educational Measurement: Issues and Practice, 3,* 5–17.

Stiggins, R. J., Frisbie, D. A., & Griswold, P. A. (1989). Inside high school grading practices: Building a research agenda. *Educational Measurement: Issues and Practice, 8,* 5–14.

Stiggins, R. J., Rubel, E., & Quellmalz, E. (1986). *Measuring thinking skills in the classroom.* Washington, DC: National Education Association.

Swanson, D. B., Norman, G. R., & Linn, R. L. (1995). Performance-based assessment: Lessons from the health professions. *Educational researcher, 24*(5), 5–11, 35.

Terman, L. M. (1916). *The measurement of intelligence.* Washington, DC: National Education Association.

Terwilliger, J. S. (1971). *Assigning grades to students.* Glenview, IL: Scott, Foresman.

Terwilliger, J. S. (1989). Classroom standard setting and grading practices. *Educational Measurement: Issues and Practices, 8,* 15–19.

The Psychological Corporation. (1990). *Stanford Achievement Test Series test coordinators handbook.* San Antonio: Author.

Thorndike, E. L. (1910). Handwriting. *Teachers College Record, 11,* 83–175.

Thorndike, E. L. (1924). Mental discipline in high school studies. *Journal of Educational Psychology, 15,* 1–22, 83–98.

Thorndike, R. L. (1969). Helping teachers use tests. *NCME Measurement in Education, 1,* 1–4.

Thorndike, R. L. (1971). Editor's note. In R. L. Thorndike (Ed.), *Educational measurement* (2nd ed.). Washington, DC: American Council on Education.

Thorndike, R. L. (1982). *Applied psychometrics.* Boston: Houghton Mifflin.

Thorndike, R. L., & Hagen, E. P. (1977). *Measurement and evaluation in psychology and education* (4th ed.). New York: John Wiley & Sons.

Thorndike, R. M. (1997). *Measurement and evaluation in psychology and education* (6th ed.). New York: Prentice-Hall.

Thorndike, R. M., & Dinnel, D. L. (2001). *Basic statistics for the behavioral sciences.* Upper Saddle River, NJ: Merrill.

Thorndike, R. M., Cunningham, G. K., Thorndike, R. L., & Hagen, E. P. (1991). *Measurement and evaluation in psychology and education* (5th ed.). New York: Macmillan.

Thurlow, M., & Thompson, S. (2000, January). Diploma options and graduation policies for students with disabilities. *NCEO Policy Directions #10* (ERIC Document Reproduction Service No. ED434447).

Thurlow, M. L., Ysseldyke, J. E., & Reid, C. L. (1997). High school graduation requirements for students with disabilities. *Journal of Learning Disabilities, 30,* 608–616.

Thurstone, L. L. (1938). Primary mental abilities. *Psychometric Monographs,* No. 1.

Tindel, G. (2002). How will assessments accommodate students with disabilities? In R. W. Lissitz & W. D. Schafer (Eds.). *Assessment in educational reform: Both means and ends.* Boston: Allyn and Bacon.

Tinkelman, S. N. (1971). Planning the objective test. In Thorndike, R. L. (Ed.). *Educational measurement* (2nd ed.). Washington, DC: American Council on Education.

Tishman, S., Perkins, D. N., & Jay, E. (1995). *The thinking classroom: Learning and teaching in a culture of thinking.* Boston: Allyn and Bacon.

Tomlinson, C. A. (2000). Reconcilable differences? Standards-based teaching and differentiation. *Educational Leadership, 58*(1), 6–11.

Truog, A. L., & Friedman, S. J. (1996). *Evaluating high school teachers' written grading policies from a measurement perspective.* Paper presented at the annual meeting of the National Council on Measurement in Education. New York.

Tuckman, B. W. (1998). Using tests as an incentive to motivate procrastinators to study. *Journal of Experimental Education, 66*(2), 141–147.

Tyler, R. W. (1931). A generalized technique for constructing achievement tests. *Educational Research Bulletin, 10,* 199–208.

Valencia, R. R., Suzuki, L. A., & Salinas, M. F. (2001). *Intelligence testing and minority students: Foundations, performance factors, and assessment issues.* Thousand Oaks, CA: Sage.

Venn, J. (1994). *Assessment of students with special needs.* New York: Merrill.

Vispoel, W. P. (2000). Reviewing and changing answers on computerized fixed-item vocabulary tests. *Educational and Psychological Measurement, 60,* 371–384.

Ward, A. W., & Murray-Ward, M. (1999). *Assessment in the classroom.* Belmont, CA: Wadsworth.

Wesman, A. G. (1971). Writing the test item. In R. L. Thorndike (Ed.), *Educational measurement* (2nd ed.). Washington, DC: American Council on Education.

Wesson, C. L., & King, R. P. (1996). Portfolio assessment and special education students. *Exceptional Children, 28*(2), 44–48.

Whittaker, C. R., Salend, S. J., & Duhaney, D. (2001). Creating instructional rubrics for inclusive classrooms. *Teaching Exceptional Children, 24*(2), 8–12.

Wiggins, G. (1993). *Assessing student performance.* San Francisco: Jossey-Bass.

Wolf, J. S., & Stephens, T. M. (1989). Parent/teacher conferences: Finding common ground. *Educational Leadership,* 28–31.

Woolfolk, A. E. (2001). *Educational psychology* (8th ed.). Boston: Allyn and Bacon.

Yell, M. L. (1998). *The law and special education.* Upper Saddle River, NJ: Merrill.

Ysseldyke, J. E., & Algozzine, B. (1990). *Introduction to special education* (2nd ed.). Boston: Houghton Mifflin.

Name Index

Subject Index